TWO STAGE

Biblical Creation

Uniting Biblical Insights Uncovered by Ten Notable Creation Theories

THOMAS PATRICK ARNOLD

THOMAS ARNOLD PUBLISHING

Contents

Preface

The great question before us is this:

How did the Creator make the universe?

Many books have proposed creation theories—but other books support or modify *just one theory*. Their approach has resulted in every theory so far still having at least one major flawed claim.

Two Stage Biblical Creation considers
- Biblical claims of ten major and a dozen minor creation theories.
- Over one hundred Bible creation texts from Hebrew and Greek.
- Key insights from ancient to modern Biblical creationists.

Only after considering these is the two stage theory proposed.

This multiple theory approach has several great advantages:
- The reader becomes familiar with the creation theories.
- The reader will learn about the Bible's creation texts.
- The reader can evaluate the basis of each theory.
- The reader can evaluate the final theory, two stage Biblical creation, intelligently and Biblically.

May our Lord and Creator bless you as you read.

Acknowledgements

Many people helped me put together the puzzle of creation:

My honored father, Patrick Arnold, graduated from Stetson University in geology and from seminary in Bible. He taught young Cuban pastors who would go through very difficult times. He believed that geology and a literal interpretation of the Bible could fit together.

A. C. Fortosis at Ben Lippen urged me to think logically.

Robertson McQuilkin and Buck Hatch of Columbia Bible College introduced me to hermeneutics, principles of Bible interpretation.
Merrill C. Tenney at Wheaton College emphasized the Second Person, the Word, in the creation.

Henry Morris introduced me to Biblical creationism with his lectures as I was beginning to teach biology and Genesis. John Whitcomb, Duane Gish, and Ken Ham added their insights.

Bryce Augsburger taught me hermeneutics. His son Bryan has been my faithful pastor.

At Trinity Divinity School of Trinity International University:
- John and Paul Feinberg, my mentors at Trinity, pushed me to consider hermeneutics for interpreting the two Testaments.
- John Sailhamer, my Hebrew teacher, emphasized the narrative.
- Walter Kaiser urged me to seek the single meaning of each text.
- Douglas Moo encouraged me to see fullness of a single meaning.
- Donald Carson challenged me to examine the text thoroughly.
- Kevin Vanhoozer helped me consider the tools of language.
- Grant Osborne emphasized hermeneutics.
- Hugh Ross, a visiting speaker, presented his creation theory.

Michael Heiser, academic editor of Logos Bible software; Paul Wright, president of Jerusalem University College; and Rod Decker of Baptist Bible College have given me key Hebrew and Greek pointers.

My two eldest sons, David and Timothy, have given me much needed critiques. Timothy designed the diagrams.

Melissa Meyer kindly edited this book.

Matthew Kaufman designed the cover and flowed the text.

I am most thankful for my excellent wife.

Above all, I thank our Lord and Savior Messiah Jesus for His multiple and great mercies on me as I asked His enabling in this book.

Part I

The Universe

Chapter 0
Seeking the Origin of the Universe

What a Question!

What does the Creator say in the Bible that He did when He created the heavens and the earth?

What a Universe!

And what a universe it is! For millennia, no one had circled our blue, green, and white-cloud streaked planet. Then in 1519, Ferdinand Magellan, with five ships and about 260 men, sailed west from Spain to reach the Spice Islands of Indonesia. Three years later, Captain Juan Elcano, with one ship, the *Victoria,* and the remaining crew of 18, returned to Spain having circumnavigated planet Earth. Planet Earth is 40,030 kilometers (or 24,873 miles) around. That is a long way around. Yet the gas giant planet Jupiter could swallow 1,300 earths.

Planet Earth circles our local star that we call the sun. Our sun is an average star, yet it could contain one million earths within its roiling furnace. Earth is so far from the sun that we measure the distance with the speed of light. In a vacuum, light travels at 299,792,458 meters (about 186,282.4 miles per second or 7 times around the Earth every second), the "cosmic speed limit." Apparently nothing in the physical universe can travel faster than light. Yet at that immense speed, sunlight takes eight minutes to reach planet Earth. The sun is eight light-minutes away from Earth.

Stars are other great suns that are far more distant. Their distance is so great that we measure it in light-years. A light-year is the distance light travels in one year in a vacuum. This distance is 9.46 trillion kilometers (or 5.88 trillion miles). Light from Proxima Centauri, the *nearest* star besides our sun, takes 4.22 years to reach planet Earth. So that star is 4.22 light-years away, and its light is 4.22 years old when it reaches us.

On a dark night away from city lights, we can see the thin veil of our galaxy blush across the high sky. Ancients did not know what that veil was, so they called it the Milky Way. Today we know that it is our spiral galaxy seen edge on. It is made of several hundred billion suns, and at its core is an immense black hole that has gobbled up the mass of millions of suns. The spiral arms of the Milky Way stretch out to about 100,000 light-years across. Light takes 100,000 years to travel from one side of our galaxy to the other. Yet far beyond our own Milky Way are over a hundred billion more galaxies, clustered and grouped in orderly array.

Five Non-Biblical Claims vs. Five Biblical Claims about Universe

Many ancient myths concerning origins begin with chaos, which itself had no beginning. Also, ancients saw the stars as fixed in place and number (except for "wandering stars" we now know are planets, exploding stars we know as novas, and comets). Ancient Greeks—Hipparchus in 129 BC and Ptolemy of Alexandria, Egypt, in 150 A.D.—counted the visible stars. Ptolemy published a star catalogue called the *Mathematike Syntaxis* ("The Mathematical Arrangement"), or *Almagest*. He listed 1,022 stars visible at one time from Alexandria. This publication became the standard star catalogue used by Greeks, Arabs, and Europeans until the seventeenth century.[1]

Starting with Galileo and the telescope, astronomers realized that far more than 1,022 stars are visible at one time. Yet nineteenth century astronomers still thought that our galaxy contains all the stars that exist. True, these astronomers saw spiral clouds that they called spiral nebula. They debated whether these nebulae are just clouds in our galaxy or the wild idea that they are other galaxies far beyond our Milky Way. And most considered the stars static, fixed in place.

So the five early non-Biblical claims about the universe were:

1. The ancient past was chaos.
2. The chaos had no definite beginning.
3. The stars (other than "wandering stars") are fixed in place.
4. The stars are static, shining forever.
5. The number of stars is limited to at most a few thousand.

Edwin Hubble would answer the debate and solve the mystery. But long before Hubble and Einstein, the Bible declared five great announcements about *ha-shāmayim*, "the heavens," which by extension includes the entire universe. These are the Biblical claims:

1. God began the universe

The Bible declares that the heavens or universe is not eternal. "In the beginning God created the heavens and the earth" (Gen. 1:1, NASB). Nehemiah 9:6 declares that God created all things:

You alone are the LORD [Read God's name reverently, Exod. 20:7]
You have made the heavens,
Heaven of the heavens with all their *starry* host,
The earth and all that *is* on it,
The seas and all that *is* in them.
And You give life to them all,
And the hosts of heaven *are* worshiping You.[2]

God created all things in the beginning. God is eternal. The universe and time had a beginning—when God created them.

2. God has been stretching out the universe

Since God made the heavens, He has been stretching them out. David in Psalm 104:1–2 declared that God, beginning with light around Himself, has been stretching out the heavens, the universe, as a Bedouin stretches out the curtain of his tent in the desert:

Praise the LORD, O my soul!
The LORD my God,
    You are very great.
    You are clothed in splendor and majesty:
Wrapping Yourself with light as with a cloak,
Stretching out *the* heavens like a *tent* curtain.

Isaiah 42:5 declares these two great facts—God created and stretched out the universe. He did these before spreading out Earth's land and making people.

Thus says God, the LORD:
Who created the heavens,
  and stretched them out,
Who spread out the land,
  and its offspring,
Giving breath to people on it,
  and spirit to those walking on it.[3]

Isaiah reports in 40:21–22 that from the beginning before the founding of Earth, and even into Isaiah's time, God continues to stretch out the heavens "like a canopy" and "like a tent." When a dark Bedouin tent canopy is spread out, one can see light through tiny holes in the coarse goat hair fabric, like stars in the sky. These holes spread farther apart as the fabric is stretched taut by center poles and ropes to pegs in the desert sand. These poetic similes, from tent dwellers, describe God's literal work of spreading out the universe. This fact had been told "from the beginning."

> Do you not know?
> Have you not heard?
> Has it not been declared to you from the beginning?
> Have you not understood from the foundations of the earth?
> It is He who sits above the sphere of the earth,
>   And its inhabitants are like grasshoppers,
> Who stretches out the heavens like a canopy,
>   And spreads them out like a tent to inhabit.

Zechariah 12:1 names three steps in God's work—stretching out the universe, then founding planet Earth, and finally forming the spirit of humans within them:

> Thus says the LORD,
> Who stretched out the heavens,
> And founded the earth,
> And formed the spirit of man within him.

Eleven or twelve times the Bible declares that God has been stretching out or expanding the heavens, the universe.
- He created the heavens and stretched them out (Isa. 42:5).
- He wrapped Himself in light and stretched out the heavens (Ps. 104:2–3).
- He stretched out the heavens as He founded Earth (Isa. 51:13).
- He stretched out the heavens as He hung Earth on nothing (Job 26:7).
- He made Earth firm and stretched out the heavens (Jer. 10:12; 51:15).
- He darkened Earth and stretched out the heavens (Job 9:7–8).
- He stretched out the heavens as He spread the land (Isa. 44:24).
- He created man and stretched out the heavens (Isa. 45:12).
- He spoke to Isaiah as He stretched the heavens out (Isa. 40:22–26).

God has been continually stretching out the heavens since He created the universe.

3. God arranged the universe like an organized army

Ever since the Fall of man, powerful leaders have sent their young men to war. New soldiers were taught to form into a disciplined, organized arrangement for battle. That order for battle may have included one or more shield walls of many foot soldiers deep, bristling with spears. On the flanks were lines of horse-mounted cavalry and chariots. Archers and slingers took their assigned areas. Reserves were held back for emergencies. The commander was positioned on a high spot to see the battle and issue commands to ready signalers or messengers to send to unit commanders. The army was then said to be "in array," in a planned order.

As God completed the creation, the Narrator summed up all that He had done:

> Thus the heavens and the earth were completed in all their vast array (Gen. 2:1, NIV).

Isaiah said that God numbered the stars He created, so each appeared by number. Each has a name. The heavens were created with order:

> Lift your eyes to the heavens and look!
> Who created [*bārā'*] these?
> He brings out *the starry* host by number,
> He calls them each by name.
> Because of His great power and mighty strength,
> not one of them is missing (Isa. 40:26).

The Psalmist gives praise "To Him who made the heavens with skill" (Ps. 136:5). Almighty God making something with skill does not result in chaos. God created the heavens as an orderly universe.

4. The universe is running down, so will not continue forever

David, in Psalm 102:25–27, says the universe is running down:

> In the beginning you laid the foundations of the earth,
> and the heavens are the work of your hands.
> They will perish,

but you remain.
They will all wear out like a garment,
Like clothing you will change them and they will be discarded.
But you remain the same, and your years will never end.

God is eternal, but the universe is running down, wearing out.

5. God declares the number of stars so vast *we* cannot count them

God not only brings the stars out "by number," but He "calls them all by name" (Isa. 40:26, NASB). Psalm 147:4 says, "He counts the number of the stars; He gives names to all of them" (NASB).

God easily counts the stars, but God says that *we* humans cannot count the vast number of stars. God said to Abraham, "Look up at the heavens and count the stars—if indeed you can count them" (Gen. 15:5, NIV). The stars are too many for us to count.

Which Set of Five Claims Is Correct?

Are the five old, non-Biblical ideas correct?
(1) The ancient past was chaos.
(2) The chaos had no definite beginning.
(3) The stars (except "wandering stars") are immovable, fixed in place.
(4) The stars are eternally static, shining forever.
(5) The number of stars is limited, so we can count them (about 1,022).

Or are the five Biblical claims correct?
(1) The universe and all the stars in it had a beginning.
(2) The universe has been stretching out.
(3) The universe is in orderly array.
(4) The universe is subject to decay (entropy) so is running down.
(5) The universe has so many stars that we cannot count them.

The Great Discovery: Expanding Universe

Many people in 1676 thought light traveled instantaneously. Danish astronomer Ole Römer was timing the orbit of the moon Io around Jupiter. He discovered that as Earth moved farther from Jupiter, Io seemed to lag behind schedule, but when Earth approached Jupiter, Io's orbit time moved ahead of schedule. Römer realized that light was taking time to travel from Io to Earth. When Jupiter was distant, light took longer to reach Earth. He calculated the speed of light at 140,000 miles (225,000 km) per second.[4] This first estimate was slower than the actual speed of 186,282 miles (299,792 km) a second. Light has not been speeding up. Römer's measurements were less exact.[5]

In 1728, English astronomer James Bradley made a great advance in precision. He measured light at 185,000 miles (298,000 km) per second, only 1 percent slower than light's actual speed.

Albert Michelson measured light speed at 186,355 and then 186,285, both slightly faster estimates than today's measurement of 186,282.4 miles per second (299,792,458 meters per second).

In a famous experiment, Michelson measured the speed of light in the direction Earth was moving and across the direction Earth was moving, expecting one to be slower. But both were exactly the same. Light always travels at the same speed no matter how fast the source is moving. If someone throws a baseball at 60 mph forward from the bed of a pickup truck moving 60 mph, the ball would travel at 120 mph (.03 miles/sec.). But the light from the truck's headlights travels at the same 186,282.4 miles per second no matter how fast the truck moves. This strange result prompted Einstein toward his relativity theory.

Albert Einstein "Unpredicts" the Expanding Universe

In 1915, Albert Einstein developed his famous general theory of relativity. Einstein realized that his theory predicts that the universe is expanding (or contracting), but cannot be static. To an astronomer, an expanding universe would mean that the galaxies should be moving away from us and away from each other. An expanding universe would overturn the old idea that the stars and galaxies are static, unmoving.

But if the universe is expanding, we can envision the history of the universe in reverse, which means that the universe had a beginning at some point in the past.

A beginning of the universe was upsetting to Einstein because it suggested God created the universe. So Einstein added a "fudge factor" that he called the "cosmological constant" to make the universe stand still—theoretically. But the "cosmological constant" was pure invention. Einstein had no hard evidence, no astronomical observations, and no proof at all that the universe is static rather than expanding.

The Great Nebulae Debate

Five years later, two astronomers held a famous debate. Shapley argued two things: Our Milky Way galaxy is huge; and our galaxy is the entire universe, so spiral nebulae "clouds" are inside our galaxy. Curtis claimed the opposite: Our Milky Way galaxy is not huge, so nebulae are distant galaxies. Neither man could prove either claim.

The race was on for proof. Each debater would turn out to be half right—but which half?

Then Came Edwin Hubble

The man who would solve both mysteries was Edwin Hubble. The athletic Midwesterner earned a scholarship to Oxford. He served with distinction in WWI; then he went to Mount Wilson Observatory with its magnificent one-hundred-inch telescope, the world's largest. Edwin Hubble predicted that "spiral nebulae" are distant galaxies, like our own Milky Way galaxy.

Two discoveries would help Hubble answer the two questions: Is our galaxy big or small? And are nebulae just clouds in our galaxy or distant galaxies?

A "Standard Candle" Measures Distance in Space

During the early years of Mount Wilson Observatory, women were excluded, so Henrietta Leavitt made her discoveries by studying star photographs that men had taken. She discovered 2,400 variable, or pulsing, stars, including a special kind called Cepheid variable stars. Big Cepheids pulse slowly, but smaller Cepheids pulse rapidly. In fact, all Cepheid stars with the same pulse rate have the same average actual brightness. She had found a "standard candle."

How does a "standard candle" measure distance in black space? A candle ten feet away will appear four times brighter than an identical candle twenty feet away. Distance to nearby Cepheids up to one hundred light-years away can be calculated using trigonometry by slight differences in angle from the extreme sides of Earth's orbit. A Cepheid star of the same pulse rate but one-fourth the apparent brightness of one measured at one hundred light-years away is two hundred light-years away. Although very dim, a Cepheid that is one million light-years away will appear four times brighter than one that is two million light-years away. Henrietta Leavitt gave Hubble a tool to measure the distances to other galaxies.

The "Red Shift" Measures Speed Away in Space

The second great discovery was the "red shift," or Doppler Effect, of light from distant galaxies. When a train whistle or ambulance siren comes toward us, its sound is high pitched; but as it passes by, the sound becomes lower. The sound waves racing toward us were hitting our eardrums with greater frequency, so the pitch was high. As the whistle receded, the waves hit our eardrums less frequently, so the pitch became lower.

Light is seen in colors instead of pitch. When a light source is moving away rapidly, the wave frequency becomes lower, shifting toward low frequency red. An approaching light source shifts toward higher frequency blue. How far the frequency is shifted tells us how fast the object is moving away. Hubble had two new tools—Cepheid variable stars to measure distance and red shift to measure speed away from us.

Edwin Hubble Discovers Galaxies and the Expanding Universe

Year after year Hubble sat in the cold night air at the Observatory constantly adjusting the great telescope's aim like a patient hunter gathering in the dim, ancient light of a nearby galaxy onto his photographic plate.

In 1924, Hubble found Cepheids among the several hundred billion suns of our neighboring galaxy, Andromeda, and estimated its distance from our galaxy. It is over two million light-years away, so its light when it reaches us is two million years old. Hubble measured distances to farther galaxies. Spiral nebula are separate galaxies far beyond our own Milky Way and they are huge, 100,000 light-years across.

Five years later, the Observatory's night janitor, Milton Humason, started helping Edwin Hubble. They began to measure the amount of red-shift or blue-shift of galaxies. To their surprise, every galaxy (except Andromeda, the nearest) was red-shifted. In fact, the more distant a galaxy was measured from Earth, the greater its red-shift. This correspondence is called Hubble's constant. If the farther a galaxy is from Earth, the faster it is receding, then the universe has been and *is* expanding. Hubble demonstrated what Einstein predicted—that the universe is expanding.

Abbé Georges Lemaître: the Universe Had a Beginning

It took a Bible scholar/physicist to put it all together. Belgian Catholic Abbé Georges Lemaître ran the expansion backward. If the universe has been expanding, and we run the expansion backward, we come to "In the beginning." The universe and time had a beginning at a point in the past, and the universe has been expanding ever since.

In 1931, Einstein, Hubble, and Lemaître met. After the meeting, Einstein called his added cosmological constant the "greatest blunder of my life." Einstein had mathematically predicted what Hubble discovered and Lemaître fully grasped—that the universe had a beginning and has been expanding ever since.

Understanding the Beginning and Expansion of the Universe

If we know the speed and distance traveled, we know when a particular trip began. For example, if a car drives at fifty miles per hour and we know that the car has gone one hundred miles, then the trip began two hours earlier. The most distant objects seen in the universe (as of this writing) are about thirteen billion light-years away and are traveling near the speed of light. Unless there is another explanation, this light is thirteen billion years old, so one would conclude that the universe is over thirteen billion years old. The Bible does not confirm this age of the universe. Adam must be dated relatively recently by his descendants' genealogies. But how do we understand the beginning and age of the universe?

Did the Universe Have a Beginning, and Is It Really Expanding?

British atheist Fred Hoyle proposed that the universe had no beginning. He theorized (with no evidence or proof whatsoever) that the reason the universe has been expanding is that new matter is constantly forming new galaxies forever. He scoffed at the idea of a sudden beginning of the universe, mockingly calling that powerful event the "Big Bang." What an unsavory idea to an atheist, for a "Big Bang" would mean that the universe had a beginning, strongly suggesting a Creator. Besides, such a "Big Bang" should leave a low temperature cosmic background radiation all across the universe, but no one had found that background radiation. Atheist Fred Hoyle mocked the idea that the universe had a beginning that would suggest God created it.

Then at Bell Labs, Arno Penzias and Robert Wilson accidentally discovered the cosmic background radiation, the faint afterglow left by the beginning of the universe. The universe had a beginning!

Recently others have suggested that the universe expands, slows down, contracts, then starts all over in a never-ending cycle—anything to get away from the universe having a beginning, suggesting an eternal Creator. But this unending cyclical universe idea was quashed by Saul Perlmutter's discovery of type 1a supernovae explosions "on demand." All type 1a stars go supernova at the same size, providing a new massive "standard candle" for huge distances. Supernovae are so huge that they can be seen across the universe, giving us the age, not of a galaxy, but of the whole universe. Measurements of these huge supernovae strongly suggest that the universe's expansion seems to be speeding up, not slowing down. It will never "re-collapse."[6] The universe definitely had a beginning. Atheist Fred Hoyle was wrong.

The discovery of slight variations in the cosmic background radiation by the COBE satellite developed by George Smoot strongly confirmed that the universe had a beginning and was designed precisely for life on planet Earth, just as the Bible says. George Smoot said of the discovery, "It's like looking at God."[7]

Are the Number of Stars So Vast Humans Cannot Count Them?

How many stars are there? The question is not, Do we have big enough numbers? The question is, Can we count how many stars exist?

The answer is very simple. We do not even know how many stars are in our own galaxy (100,000,000,000 to 500,000,000,000). On top of that, we do not know how many galaxies are in the universe (over 100,000,000,000). And we have to multiply (not add) those numbers to even estimate the number of stars in the universe. The number of stars is staggering.

Is the Universe in an Orderly Arrangement?

The stars in the galaxies form spirals and other amazing shapes. They are in beautiful order.

Meanwhile, astronomers began mapping the universe. They discovered to their amazement that the galaxies are in orderly arrangements, with great empty areas between. The universe is not random, but amazingly orderly. The galaxies are arranged on the sides of great bubbles, with empty space between. One formation of galaxies is called the Great Wall. Our universe is definitely arranged with beautiful order.

Moreover, the physical constants of the universe and Earth are set to very narrow limits, the precise limits required for human life on Earth.[8]

Can the Bible Tell Us about the Origin of the Universe?

So which is right—the old mythological, early scientific, non-Biblical ideas that the stars are fixed in place for eternity and are easily counted? Or is the Bible right, declaring all along that the universe had a beginning, that its stars are running down, that its stars are beyond counting, that the universe is in orderly array, and that the heavens are expanding? The Bible is correct on all five.

How could the Bible's Author have known millennia before modern science about this beginning, order, and expansion of the universe? The only way that the Author of the Bible could have known these facts is if He was there at the creation. The God of the Bible is the Creator of the universe.

There are some questions about the origin of the universe that science cannot answer. These are the ultimate questions: What is the source of the universe? Was there a Creator? If so, who is the Creator? Was the universe planned? Does it have a purpose, and do we have a purpose in it? Only someone who was there can answer these questions.

The Great Questions

Life is too short for trivial questions. In our attempt to understand creation, we are answering *great* questions.

The First Great Question

The first great question is, What is the source of the universe?—specifically, Who is the Creator?

The Bible alone declares that the universe had a beginning and has been expanding ever since. Only the Creator of the universe could have known those facts long before modern science discovered them. The God of the Bible is the Creator of the universe. But Who is that Creator?

Solomon asked:
Who has gone up to heaven and come down?
Who has gathered up the wind in the hollow of his hands?
Who has wrapped up the waters in his cloak?
Who has established all the ends of the earth?
What is his name, and the name of his son?
Tell me if you know! (Prov. 30:4, NIV)

Hebrews 1:2 answers:
In these last days he has spoken to us by his Son,
      whom he appointed heir of all things, and
      through whom he made the universe (NIV).

God the Father through God the Son is the Creator of the universe.

John 1:1–3 and 14 declares:
In the beginning was the Word,
and the Word was with God,
and the Word was God.
He was with God in the beginning.

Through him all things were made;
without him nothing was made that has been made.
The Word became flesh and made his dwelling among us.
We have seen his glory, the glory of the One and Only,
who came from the Father, full of grace and truth (NIV).

God the Son, who was with God the Father in the beginning, is the Creator of all things. He is the eternal One. He is Messiah Jesus.

Not only is God the Father through God the Son the Creator, but the second verse of the Bible says the Spirit of God was hovering over the surface of the deep water. An Observer was present on the scene. To find answers to our ultimate questions about the origin of the universe, we can actually look within that Observer's communication—the Bible. The Bible is not just another religious book. The Bible contains proof that it is from the Creator. And within its words are the answers to all the great questions, including how the universe began.

Our Goal in this Book: To Answer the Second Great Question

Our ultimate goal in this book is to come a little closer to answering the *second* great question about creation: What does the Creator say in the Bible that He did when He created the heavens and the earth?

Questions Not Asked

Our question is *not* about:
- Ancient Near Eastern creation myths
- Creation versus evolution
- Science and the Bible
- Historical-critical, source, redaction, or other critical views
- Creation of life
- A mere summary of creation theories

Rather, we will seek to answer the second great question by carefully studying the most Biblically supported claims of the ten major creation theories and by comparing them to Hebrew and Greek Bible texts on creation. We will stand on the great shoulders of those notable creationists who have gone before us. Then we will analyze the main theories by four diagnostic questions. In the end, we will propose a unified eleventh creation theory that, God willing, may come closer within the hermeneutical spiral[9] to what God says in the Bible that did when He created the heavens and our planet Earth.

(I capitalize Earth, as I do Mars, when I use the term to mean Earth as a whole including both land and sea. Usually I will not capitalize the phrase "heavens and earth" and I will leave Scripture quotes as they are. Uncapitalized earth may indicate land or soil.)

The Problem

We have the creation account from the Creator. Now how do we interpret that creation account? Bible scholars have proposed ten major theories and over a dozen minor theories about how God created the universe. Why are there so many theories? Which is right? Even the age of the universe is viewed radically different: Is the universe 13.7 billion years old or 6,000 years old? And why has no creation theory prevailed widely among Bible-believing Christians?

Why No Creation Theory Has Prevailed

Members of a church that accepts Hugh Ross's progressive creationism day-age theory may think that view is universally accepted—until they visit a church that accepts the young earth scientific creationism theory developed by Henry Morris in the 1960s. Each viewpoint can prove at least one claim of the other side incorrect, so no theory is universally accepted across the spectrum of churches.

That there are so many theories, but none is universally accepted by the church as a whole, may tell us something. It may be telling us that none of the theories is quite right.

Why has no one studied all of the creation theories and gathered the Biblical claims into a unified creation theory? That would be honoring those great Bible creationists who have gone before us.

Instead, advocates of the various theories have busily attacked each other's ideas. Each theory has at least one claim that is open to attack because it lacks or goes against Biblical evidence. So the church as a whole has not accepted any one theory.

Read Other Creationists to Learn, Rather than to Attack

I began to read the various theories seeking to understand their claims rather than to criticize them. I discovered that every one of the ten theories holds part of the answer. How do I know that?

Before studying all the creation theories, I had studied in Hebrew and Greek the five major and over one hundred shorter Bible texts on creation and derived from them an understanding of creation. The major texts are Genesis 1 and 2, Job 26, Job 38, Psalm 104, and Proverbs 8. In this book, we will compare the claims of the ten theories to the Hebrew and Greek Bible texts on creation.

We are not alone in seeking the answer to this second great question. We can learn a great deal if we humble ourselves and seek wisdom first from the Bible itself and then second from the Biblical insights of those creationists who have gone before us.

This book begins with that study of these ten notable theories and their Biblical insights. After gathering their valuable insights, we will be ready for the next great step. Out of their Biblical insights we will form a unified creation theory within the hermeneutical spiral[10] that, God willing, may approach a more Biblical understanding of creation.

Summaries of Ten Major Creation Theories

Before listing the claims of the ten theories, forming an eleventh, and evaluating all eleven, here are summaries of the theories:

(1) *Pre-Creation Chaos Theory.* Before creation in Genesis 1, God and unformed "pre-creation chaos" both existed. No explanation is given for the origin of the pre-creation chaos. Waltke calls its preexistence a "mystery."[11] "Creation" in Genesis 1:1 was not God creating *ex nihilo* the heavens and the earth. Instead, in Genesis 1:2–31, God creatively entered the chaos and turned it into orderly cosmos.[12]

(2) *Title or Summary Theory.* Genesis 1:1 is not the declaration of God's initial *ex nihilo* creation of the heavens and earth but is a title or summary of Genesis 1:2–31. Genesis 1:1 titles or summarizes the eight command units of creation in 1:2–31.[13] Waltke's version of this theory integrates the pre-creation chaos theory (before Gen. 1:1) with the title or summary theory (Gen. 1:1) and the literary framework understanding of the eight commands and six days (Gen. 1:2–31).[14]

(3) *Literary Framework Theory.* The eight command units of Genesis 1 form a nonliteral and nonsequential literary framework, revealing real historical creation events in thematic rather than chronological order. Creation themes, not the "days," are important. The days are not in chronological order, particularly days one (light) and four (sun, moon, and stars), which were probably the same event. So the Genesis 1 framework probably indicates an old Earth, but chronology is not the point of Genesis 1.[15] The Bible does not date the universe.

(4) *Initial Chaos Theory.* Only God existed before He created all things in Genesis 1:1. God created *ex nihilo* the heavens and earth as chaos. God turned this chaos into the orderly cosmos in six days. The young earth scientific creationism variant claims the days were literal, normal days, but other variants may claim long day-age days. A minority traditional variation (the unified eleventh theory follows in this tradition) claims a no-chaos initial creation.

(5) *Young Earth Scientific Creationism Theory.* The Genesis 1:1 *ex nihilo* creation was *in* day one of six consecutive night-day days, because according to Exodus 20:11 all creation was "*in* six days." The two big claims are that the *ex nihilo* creation was *in* day one, and the days were ordinary days. God created "all space (heavens), all time (beginning), and all matter (earth),"[16] and all this was the "*ex nihilo* creation of the universe by God on the first day."[17] "God created the world, the universe, and everything in them in six ordinary, twenty-four hour days."[18] On day four God "placed these 'lights' [sun, moon, and galaxies of stars] . . . being made of the same 'earth' that had been created on Day One."[19] Since Adam is dated roughly 6,000 years ago,[20] the universe is a few days older. The flood formed most fossils.

(6) *Day-Age, Old Earth Progressive Creationism Theory.* In the beginning God created *ex nihilo* the universe (apparently by the big bang) and planet Earth. "In the beginning" in Hebrew consistently indicates an extensive beginning time period. By Genesis 1:2, planet Earth was uninhabitable, uninhabited, sea-covered, and dark (Job says by thick, dark cloud). Narrated from the Spirit's perspective location just above the water surface, God commanded light (we may infer diffuse sunlight penetrating the cloud layer) to Earth's surface, beginning day-age one. Because *yôm* elsewhere in the Bible may mean a time longer than a day and because Earth is almost certainly old, *yôm* in Genesis 1 must mean a geological day-age era. During

these eras, God made Earth habitable and progressively created life. In the fourth day-age, God caused the sky to clear, so the already created luminaries were in Earth's sky for the first time. The second revelation, the creation, dates the universe to 13.7 billion years.[21]

(7) *Theistic Big Bang and Relativistic Days Theory.* In the beginning God created the big bang, which produced light in the early expanding universe. The big bang's light began the first of six literal days of billions of years, forming the universe and Earth. "Evening" and "morning" were not the end of day-night days but a progression from disorder toward order. Relativity's time dilation allows 13.7 billion years to be six literal days on God's "eternal clock."[22]

Gerald Schroeder, an Israeli Hebrew speaker, is adamant that *yôm* does *not* mean day-ages in Genesis 1, but all six were twenty-four-hour days on God's clock. (Only God's clock counts because only God was there.)

(8) *Creation Revealed in Six Days Theory.* Mesopotamian tablets from the patriarch era recorded origins, family histories, and genealogies. Each tablet ends in a colophon with the title and author's name. The Genesis narratives, each ending in a *tôleddôt* with the author's name, follow the same pattern. Because Adam was not present at the creation until the very end, God gave the words of the six brief narratives of Genesis 1:1—2:4a, recounting six creation eras to Adam in six days. So the six days were not creation days but six days in which God revealed creation to Adam. This creation narrative and successive eyewitness narratives by Noah, Shem, Abraham, Isaac, Jacob, and Joseph, each (except Joseph's) end in a *tôleddôt* with the author's name. The narratives were recorded accurately on clay tablets and passed on to Moses, who edited them into the book of Genesis.[23]

(9) *Gap or Creation-Ruin-Restoration Theory.* In the beginning God created *ex nihilo* the heavens and the earth. Next, during a long gap of time at Genesis 1:2, God first created land and all kinds of life. But Lucifer fell into sin, resulting in animal death, disease, and destructive "natural" disasters—and fossils. Lucifer led pre-Adamites (pre–Homo sapiens hominids) into sin. God judged Earth by "Lucifer's flood," killing all life and forming more fossils (Isa. 14:12–15; Ezek. 28:12–17). So Earth *became* chaos. Then (leaving the fossils in place) in six day-night days of restoration, God reconstituted Earth and re-created entirely new life. (No life today descended from any ancient life.) God commanded light (we may infer sunlight penetrating the cloud layer) to Earth's surface, producing literal day

one. On the fourth day of His work, God commanded the already-created luminaries to be in the expanse of Earth's sky to separate day and night, apparently by breaking open the cloud layer.[24] Genealogies date Adam, not the universe. The universe was created in the beginning at an unstated time long before the six days.

(10) *Historical Land Creationism Theory.* Hebrew professor John Sailhamer explains that the Hebrew word "In the beginning" consistently means an extensive beginning time period. In that beginning time, God created the heavens and the earth. God also made land and a multiplicity of life during Genesis 1:1. The length of the beginning time period is unstated, so the universe may be "billions of years old."[25]

The "land/earth" from Genesis 1:2 onward in chapters 1—2 means Eden or the Promised Land. Life covered earth from its creation in 1:1, except for one place. According to Genesis 1:2, "the land"—that is, Eden— was an uninhabitable wilderness, empty of life. Then in six day-night days in the narrative of 1:2–31, God prepared the Garden of Eden (the future Promised Land), making it habitable for the first humans[26] and filling it with life. Thus, the recipients of Genesis (Israel at Mount Sinai) would know Who their God is—the Creator of all things—and the importance of the Land they were promised. That Land would be the place to reestablish a covenant relationship according to the Sinai Covenant with their Creator in the renewed Eden or Promised Land.

(11) *Two Stage Biblical Creation Theory.* The most Biblically supported insights of the ten theories may be combined into an eleventh theory. This eleventh unified creation theory does not seem to have any odd claims.

This two stage Biblical creation theory has two big claims: In the beginning God created the literal heavens and the literal Earth, but Earth was still unfinished—uninhabitable and uninhabited (*tōhû vᵃbōhû*), and darkened on its sea surface. So by eight command units and six literal work days, God finished planet Earth, culminating in literal Adam and Eve created in His own image.

Eleven Special Claims by the Eleven Main Theories

One way to remember a theory is to list its main, unique, or special claim. That a claim is unique does not necessarily make it incorrect. The real question is whether the claim is Biblical. Later we will compare claims to the Bible. Then we may draw nearer to how the Bible says God created the heavens and earth.

Special claims:

(1) *Pre-Creation Chaos Theory*: Chaos existed before creation.

(2) *Title or Summary Theory*: Genesis 1:1 does not declare the *ex nihilo* (out of nothing) creation of heavens and earth, but is a title or summary of chapter 1.

(3) *Literary Framework Theory*: The days were neither literal nor sequential.

(4) *Initial Chaos Theory*: In the beginning God created chaos or unformed matter.

(5) *Young Earth Scientific Creationism Theory*: God created the heavens (all space), earth (all matter of the universe), and beginning (all time) *in* day one.

(6) *Day-Age, Old Earth, Progressive Creationism Theory*: The six day-ages were six geologic eras.

(7) *Theistic Big Bang and Relativistic Days Theory*: By relativity, day one was billions of years, yet was a literal day on God's clock.

(8) *Creation Revealed in Six Days Theory*: God spoke the six brief narratives of Genesis 1 to Adam in six days.

(9) *Gap or Creation-Ruin-Restoration Theory*: In a time gap at Genesis 1:2, vast life flourished but was killed, forming fossils.

(10) *Historical Land Creationism Theory:* God created vast life on Earth in Genesis 1:1. Later God worked six days on Eden.

(11) *Two Stage Biblical Creation Theory:* "In the beginning God created the heavens and the earth." "For six days God worked on the heavens and the earth, the sea, and all that *is* in them."

Old, Young, or Undated Creation

Another way to view the theories is by classifying them into "Old Earth Creation" (OEC), "Young Earth Creation" (YEC), and "Undated Heavens and Earth Creation" (UEC). "Old or Young" indicates that some advocates claim an old universe, but others a young universe. "Undated" means the Bible does not indicate the date.

Biblical Age of the Universe		Old	Young	Undated
(1)	*Pre-Creation Chaos Theory*	✔		
(2)	*Title or Summary Theory*	*probably* ✔		
(3)	*Literary Framework Theory*	*probably* ✔		*and* ✔
(4)	*Initial Chaos Theory*	✔ *or*	✔	
(5)	*Young Earth Scientific Creationism*		✔	
(6)	*Day-Age, Old Earth Theory*	✔		
(7)	*Theistic Big Bang Theory*	✔		
(8)	*Creation Revealed in Six Days*	✔		
(9)	*Gap or Creation-Ruin-Restoration*	✔		*and* ✔
(10)	*Historical Land Creationism*	*probably* ✔		*and* ✔
(11)	*Two Stage Biblical Creation*			✔

"Old" (OEC) means far older than ~6,000 years. Many OEC advocates agree with the current scientific view that the age of the universe is about 13.7 billion years[27] and that Earth is about 4.5 billion years.[28] Some quotes from older OEC books will say about 15 billion years, but now science has refined the date.

"Young" (YEC) means that the universe is dated by Adam's descendants' genealogies to about 6,000 years old. Some would extend that age of the universe to a range of 6,000 to 10,000 years old.

"Undated" (UEC) means the Bible does not state or imply the creation date of the heavens and earth. Scientists may debate evidence of the age of Earth and the universe. God knows the exact date of "the beginning." But nowhere does the *Bible* tell *us* the date. Only the two stage eleventh theory is purely and very strongly committed to Biblically "undated."

Developing a Unified Theory in Chapter 11

One purpose of this book is to explore the ideas of the ten main creation theories. We need to listen to the ideas of other creationists. That will be our study in chapters 1–10.

The second purpose is to gather and organize all the Biblical insights from the Bible and from the other theories. In chapter 11 we will reap the benefits by putting together all the Biblical insights from the previous ten theories. There we will develop a unified creation theory.

After we have studied all eleven theories and added insights from over a dozen minor theories in chapter 12, in chapter 14 we will evaluate the theories by four pairs of diagnostic questions, laying aside theories that are inadequate. In the end, we may discover the most Biblically supported creation theory—one that approaches more closely to how God created the heavens and the earth.

Four Pairs of Diagnostic Questions

Question A: Long Days or Normal Days?

Does Genesis 1 indicate day-ages, framework, or revelatory days?
Or does Genesis 1 indicate six normal day-night days of God's work?

Question A asks the meaning of the Bible word *yôm*, or "day," in the context of Genesis 1. This is the big question for Hugh Ross's day-age theory. In his books *The Genesis Question* and *Creation and Time,* Ross says that the days were six long geological day-ages.[29] Question A is the key to the claim of "relativistic stretched time" days by the theistic big bang theory of Gerald Schroeder in *Genesis and the Big Bang.*[30] Question A is the key to evaluating the literary framework theory of Lee Irons and Meredith Kline, also advocated by Bruce Waltke. Finally, question A is at the heart of the six revelatory days theory of P. J. Wiseman's *Creation Revealed in Six Days.*[31] In contrast, several theories claim normal days.

Does Genesis 1 indicate the six days were long day-ages, framework days, or revelatory days? Or were they day-night cycle normal days of actual creation work?

Question B: Chaos or *Ex Nihilo* Creation?

In Genesis 1:1, did God create ex nihilo *the heavens and earth?*
Or did God creatively turn unformed chaos into cosmos?

Pre-creation chaos is central to Bruce Waltke's theory. He has combined three of these theories in his book *Creation and Chaos.*[32] The three theories are the pre-creation chaos theory before Genesis 1:1, the title or summary theory of Genesis 1:1, and the framework theory of the six days. These three are not necessarily linked, but Waltke has linked them logically. Also, the initial chaos theory and the young earth scientific creationism theory both claim initial chaotic unformed matter. Finally, the middle stage of the three stage creation-ruin-restoration or gap theory claims Earth became chaos. In contrast, several theories claim there was no chaos.

Question B does *not* ask which chaos theory is correct. Question B asks, Did chaos ever exist?

Question C: Creation Once or Twice?
Did God create the life kinds once—by eight commands and six days?
Or did He create life kinds twice—once long ago, then in the six days?

Two theories claim that life was created or introduced twice. The creation-ruin-restoration or gap theory by Pember and Custance claims two creations of life—one in a long time gap at Genesis 1:2 and a second recent creation of new life in the six days. Based on Hebrew grammar, Sailhamer explains that a time gap at Genesis 1:2 is not possible. But in *Genesis Unbound*,[33] he also claims two introductions of life—an ancient creation of life in Genesis 1:1 and a recent second creation or introduction of life into the Garden of Eden. Most theories say God made life once, by the eight command units and six days. Question C asks if there were two creations of life, or just one.

Question D: Creation in Day One or "In the beginning"?
Did God create the literal heavens and earth "in the beginning"?
Or did He create heavens as space and earth as pre-matter in day one?

Young earth scientific creationism defends six literal days (the previous issue) and that the initial creation was *in* day one. A number of theories believe in six literal days. Six literal days is *not* the unique claim of young earth scientific creationism. The unique claim of modern young earth scientific creationism is that the *ex nihilo* creation was *in* day one of the six days, based on Exodus 20:11. YEC assumes that "In the beginning" was instantaneous not only in its initiation but instantaneous or at the most a few hours in its total duration. So "in the beginning" was *in* day one. The YEC unique claim is that the *ex nihilo* creation was the first instant of day one, during which God created the heavens (all space), beginning (all time), and earth (all unformed matter) "throughout the darkness of space." All this was *in* day one.

In contrast, the two stage Biblical creation theory says, "In the beginning God created the heavens and the earth." The beginning was the beginning time during which God created *ex nihilo* (out of nothing) the literal heavens and the literal Earth *before* His command for light began day one on Earth. Question D asks, Did God create the heavens and earth *in day one* of the six days, or did God create the heavens and earth *"in the beginning"* before the six days?

Honoring Creationists before Us

In my analysis of each theory, I will emphasize the primary author of each view: Bruce Waltke (several views), Mark Rooker, Meredith Kline, George Pember, Henry Morris, Ken Ham, Hugh Ross, P. J. Wiseman, Gerald Schroeder, and John Sailhamer.

I honor these great creationists. These men had already uncovered all the claims of the eleventh unified theory, but none had put all the Biblically supported claims together into a single creation theory. They had already published their selection of these wonderful Biblical insights while I was still groping for understanding. The goal of this book is to gather together those Biblically supported claims into one unified theory.

Unfortunately, each also has a Biblically unsupported claim. I will point out their unsupported claims. When I do point out these claims not supported by the Bible, I do not intend any personal criticism of these great men. I have met and talked about creation with many of them and heard lectures by or studied under others, specifically Henry Morris, John Whitcomb, Hugh Ross, Ken Ham, Duane Gish, Carl Wieland, John Sailhamer, Bruce Waltke, William Dembski, and others. I consider these honorable Christian men. We all make mistakes, and part of writing for the public involves others critiquing our mistakes. I intend my critique to be gracious even when pointing out problems in the ten theories. I, too, will make errors. I am still learning. Hopefully others will be gracious in pointing out my errors. I point out the errors, not as an attack, but in order to sift out these unsupported claims so we will keep only Biblical claims.

I have found that every one of these great men has given us invaluable insights into what the Bible says God did when He created the heavens and the earth. In this book, I am gathering their Biblically supported claims together. So in the eleventh theory, to the degree that I am Biblical, I am also honoring the Bible insights they already had. By building on their insights, I pray that I may add to their great work by bringing us closer to understanding what God says that He did when He created the heavens and the earth.

Part II
The Creation Theories

Chapter 1

Theory 1
Pre-Creation Chaos Theory

Bruce Waltke, a renowned Hebrew scholar, is the author of the massive *Introduction to Biblical Hebrew Syntax*. He has given us many insights into the Hebrew Bible, particularly in the book of Proverbs. His knowledge of Ancient Near East (ANE) mythology is legendary. I heard him quote part of the ancient Babylonian creation myth, the *Enuma Elish*, as easily as we might quote Genesis 1:1.

Bruce Waltke is deservedly first of the ten because Waltke's insight into the other theories is key to the final analysis of the ten theories. We will also consider the brilliant clause study by Michael Heiser,[34] Academic Editor to Logos Bible Software, a program I use to great benefit.

In a nutshell, the pre-creation chaos theory says that God could not have created chaos *during* Genesis 1:1, as all the initial chaos theories claim (young earth scientific creationism and old earth creationism). The gap theory—that the world became chaos *after* Genesis 1:1—is not supported by Hebrew grammar. So chaos preexisted along with God *before* 1:1. Rather than creating out of nothing (*creatio ex nihilo*) in 1:1, God creatively transformed that preexisting chaos into the orderly heavens and earth during Genesis 1:2–31.

The idea of pre-creation chaos has a long history in ANE creation myths. The modern Christian pre-creation chaos theory may have begun with Hermann Gunkel's *Schöpfung und Chaos*. Gunkel claimed that in the Bible's version of the "creation myth," Yahweh replaced the other gods.[35] Since chaos was common in ANE myths, pre-creation chaos must be in the Bible also.

Waltke has introduced an evangelical version of this theory. He has integrated his immense learning in ANE mythology with his immense knowledge of Biblical Hebrew to form his pre-creation chaos theory.

Many of my readers may not realize that this pre-creation chaos theory, combined with the title theory and framework theory (in the next two chapters) is becoming the dominate theory in many evangelical and mainline seminaries.

The reason for this shift is that Waltke has shown that the initial chaos theory (which includes young earth scientific creationism and old earth creationism) and the gap theory each have a major flawed claim.

So far, no one has explained an adequate alternative theory that fits all the creation texts (our goal in this book). That leaves the pre-creation chaos theory holding the field by default. In addition, many Hebrew professors were trained by Bruce Waltke, so his theory is becoming dominant in many seminaries.

Preunderstandings of the Pre-Creation Chaos Theory

Many theories include one or more presuppositions, or preunderstandings. These are *not* part of the theory but are how the developer of the theory thinks. These preunderstandings may influence his study of the Bible's creation texts and his resulting claims. I will number these preunderstandings with zero and a capital letter.

(**1.0A**) *Logic rules*. Bruce Waltke respects logic. "Logic will not allow us to entertain the contradictory notions: God created the organized heavens and earth; the earth was unorganized."[36]

(**1.0B**) *Chaos ruled*. The great origin myths of the ancient near east rise out of a worldview of preexisting unorganized chaos. Waltke knows these myths well. Waltke says that striking parallels between the Bible and ANE pre-creation chaos myths, especially the *Enuma Elish*, confirm this worldview for the Bible as well.

Claims of the Pre-Creation Chaos Theory

(**1.1**) *"The heavens and the earth" meant the entire orderly universe, the cosmos.* The phrase אֵת הַשָּׁמַיִם וְאֵת הָאָרֶץ, *et ha-shāmayim v^{e}ēt hā 'āretz*, "the heavens and the earth," is "a merism," that is, "a Hebrew designation of the universe as a whole."[37] A merism is a figure of speech in which the whole is indicated by contrasting parts. This merism, "the heavens and the earth," means the entire organized universe.[38] The heaven was everything above the writer and readers; the earth was everything below. Hebrew has no single word for "universe," so "the heavens and the earth" meant all things, what we would call "the universe." The phrase "the heavens and the earth" also indicates an orderly universe.

Creation Merism: "The heavens and the earth" meant the entire orderly universe.

(1.2) **Tōhû vᵃbōhû** *in Genesis 1:2 meant disordered chaos.* To understand *tōhû vᵃbōhû*, we need to set aside a modern idea of chaos: "I did not clean up today, so the room is chaos." That is *not* the sense intended by chaos theories. The pre-creation chaos theory has a much more radical sense of chaos.

Genesis 1:2 begins, "Now the earth was *tōhû vᵃbōhû*." The words תֹהוּ וָבֹהוּ (*tōhû vᵃbōhû*) are the two Hebrew words translated in the KJV as "without form and void," or in the NIV as "formless and empty." Waltke interprets *tōhû vᵃbōhû* by his vast knowledge of ANE chaos myths. So he says that *tōhû vᵃbōhû* means disordered chaos — "unorganized,"[39] "uncreated or unformed,"[40] "a state of material prior to its creation," "a state of material devoid of order, or without being shaped or formed into something."[41]

(1.2a) *All was unformed, disordered chaos.* Genesis 1:2 says, "Now the earth was *tōhû vᵃbōhû*." Waltke explains that *tōhû vᵃbōhû* "is a rhyming expression that indicates a state of material prior to its creation." The description *tōhû vᵃbōhû* is "not in the sense that [pre-creation] material does not exist but rather in the sense that an orderly arrangement, a creating, a cosmos, has not as yet taken place."[42] Since "a creating" had not yet taken place, then everything was disordered.

(1.3) *An orderly God could not have created disorderly chaos.* Logically the "God of order and goodness" could not have created "disorder" of "unformed" material.

No mention is made anywhere in Scripture that God called the unformed, dark, and watery state of verse 3 into existence. . . . The deep and darkness in verse 2 are less than desirable and were not called into existence by the God of order and goodness. It . . . makes God the Creator of disorder, darkness, and deep, a situation not tolerated in the perfect cosmos and never said to have been called into existence by the Word of God.[43]

Order in 1:1 contradicts disorder in 1:2. The answer is that God could not and did not create "disorder, darkness, and deep." Therefore, the chaos described in Genesis 1:2 already existed *before* Genesis 1:1.

The two main alternative theories are the initial chaos theory (which includes both young earth scientific creationism and old earth creationism) and the gap theory. If these two theories are impossible, then the pre-creation chaos theory will be the last chaos theory standing, so must be the correct theory.

(**1.3a**) *The initial chaos creation theory—that God created the orderly cosmos* during *1:1 and that it was unformed disordered chaos in 1:2—is logically impossible.* "The initial chaos view . . . interprets Genesis 1:1 as a declaration that God created the original mass called heaven and earth out of nothing, and verse 2 as a clarification that when it came from the Creator's hand, the mass was unformed and unfilled."[44] The merism "the heavens and the earth" in 1:1 implies an orderly cosmos. But the initial chaos theory claims that God created the unformed, chaotic matter described in Genesis 1:2 *during* Genesis 1:1.

Waltke agrees that the phrase "the heavens and the earth" in 1:1 means the orderly cosmos. Then 1:2 declares this cosmos was disordered chaos (*tōhû v*ᵃ*bōhû*). He concludes that the sentences may make sense grammatically, but they are "impossible"[45] logically. Also, God could not have created disordered chaos. The initial chaos idea that God created unformed disordered chaotic matter *during* Genesis 1:1 is logically "impossble."

The Initial Chaos Theory: God created chaos during 1:1

God created orderly heavens and earth out of nothing during 1:1. The earth was unformed chaos in 1:2.

Waltke: The initial chaos theory is logically impossible.

(**1.3b**) *The "gap" of the gap theory—that Earth "became" chaos in 1:2—is not supported by the Hebrew grammar.* The gap theory claims God created land and all kinds of life in a gap of time in Genesis 1:2. Then Lucifer fell. Eventually, God judged Lucifer and his domain of Earth. So Earth "became" chaos *after* Genesis 1:1. Then God re-created in six days.

Bruce Waltke is a Hebrew scholar and responds that Genesis 1:2 should *not* be translated: "Now the earth <u>became</u> *tōhû v*ᵃ*bōhû*." The Hebrew grammar in 1:2 is a description, not an action. The standard translation is correct: "Now the earth was *tōhû v*ᵃ*bōhû*." "Was" denotes a description, not an action. The gap theory requires the action "became." The gap theory, that Earth become chaos *after* 1:1, is grammatically flawed.

"We conclude, then, that this popular [gap theory] interpretation of Genesis 1:1–2 is impossible on both philological and theological grounds."[46] The words, grammar, and theology eliminate the gap theory.

The Gap Theory: Earth "became" chaos *after* 1:1

God created orderly heavens and earth

out of nothing during 1:1.

The earth <u>became</u> *tōhû vᵃbōhû*, unformed chaos, in 1:2.

Waltke: "The descriptive verb 'was' does not mean the action "became."' The gap theory is grammatically impossible.

(1.4) *If* tōhû vᵃbōhû *means chaos, yet God could not have created chaos, then unformed chaos must have existed before creation.* Waltke says of the initial chaos theory, "Logic will not allow us to entertain the contradictory notions: God created the organized heavens and earth; the earth was unorganized."[47] Logic eliminates the initial chaos theory's belief that God created chaos *during* 1:1.

Waltke shows that grammar disproves the gap theory's notion that Earth "became" chaos *after* 1:1.

Therefore, "the chaos of verse 2 existed before the creation,"[48] as pre-creation chaos. Waltke concludes that the pre-creation chaos theory is the last chaos theory standing.

Waltke's Logical Alternative

If an *ex nihilo* creation of chaos during 1:1

is logically impossible,

and gap chaos after 1:1 is grammatically unworkable,

then pre-creation chaos must have

existed with God before 1:1.

(1.4a) *The chaos was before creation.* Parallels exist between ANE myths of preexisting chaos and the Bible's creation narrative. These parallels support pre-creation chaos in the Bible. God would not have created this chaos *during* Genesis 1:1. Grammar rules out chaos forming *after* 1:1. So the chaos must have been *before* creation in Genesis 1.

Waltke identifies his theory as "the pre-creation chaos theory of cosmogony, which holds that the chaos of verse 2 existed before the creation mentioned in the Bible."[49] Genesis 1:2 describes the *tōhû vᵃbōhû* "state of material prior to its creation."[50] "Creation" means changing the already existing pre-creation chaos into orderly cosmos in the six days of 1:3–31.

(**1.4b**) *Preexisting unformed chaos, darkness, and deep sea were not from God.* God could not have created the primordial deep and darkness because "a good God characterized by light could not, in consistency with His nature, create evil, disorder, and darkness."[51] "The deep and darkness in verse 2 are less than desirable and were not called into existence by the God of order and goodness."[52] So God did not create deep ocean water or darkness.

(**1.4c**) *The source of the chaos, dark, and deep is unknown.* Waltke asks, "But what about the uncreated or unformed state, the darkness and the deep of Genesis 1:2? Here a great mystery is encountered, for the Bible never says that God brought these into existence by His word."[53] Waltke answers that the source of chaos, darkness, and deep is unknown. Chaos is contrary to the nature of God. "The Book of Genesis does not inform us concerning the origin of that which is contrary to the nature of God. . . . But the truth is that the Book mocks us. The Bible provides no information regarding that which is dark and devoid of form."[54]

(**1.4d**) *God triumphed over the anti-creation chaos sea monster.* Bruce Waltke explains that there is a tight syntactical relationship between the Genesis creation narrative and parallel ANE creation myths, particularly the *Enuma Elish*. In the Sumerian Ninurta myth, in the Indian Vedas, and in the Akkadian *Enuma Elish* there is a "repressive" "anti-creation dragon monster" conquered by a god who turned chaos into order.[55] "With this background, it is now certain that Rahab or Leviathan [in the Bible] is an anti-creation dragon monster, for the Biblical texts imply the same three or four features found in these other mythical cosmogonies."[56] These features are (1) a chaos monster, (2) a god defeats the chaos monster, and (3) the god turns chaos into order. "The Rahab-Leviathan emblem is . . . the figure to describe God's creative activity in the pre-historic past" as "Yahweh's victory" over chaos "prior to creation."[57] By His triumph over chaos, God was "assuring man that it [the chaos monster] was under the dominion of the Spirit of God."[58] So God's triumph over Rahab (Isa. 51:9) and over Leviathan (Job 41:1) form the Biblical accounts of pre-creation chaos being transformed into orderly beautiful cosmos.

(1.5) *Chaos preexisted, so there was no* **ex nihilo** *creation in Genesis 1:1.* Waltke explains that *tōhû vᵃbōhû* in Genesis 1:2 means disordered chaos,[59] but God could not have created chaos, so logically there was no creation of the organized universe in Genesis 1:1. So God did *not* create *ex nihilo* ("out of nothing") "the heavens and the earth" in Genesis 1:1.

To put it another way, since unformed chaotic material already existed before Genesis 1:1, then 1:1 does *not* declare the *ex nihilo* creation of all things in the beginning. Both God and chaos predated Genesis 1.

The Waltke Exclusion Principle: "Logic will not allow us to entertain the contradictory notions: God created the organized heavens and earth; the earth was unorganized."[60] If there was preexisting chaos, there was no *ex nihilo* creation of the organized heavens and earth. The converse is also logically possible: If there was *ex nihilo* creation of the organized heavens and earth, then there was no unorganized chaos. Waltke claims chaos, and no *ex nihilo* creation.

> If all was pre-existing chaos,
> there was no *ex nihilo* creation.
>
> But the converse is also logically possible:
>
> If there was *ex nihilo* creation,
> there was no pre-existing chaos.

(1.6) *"Creation" meant transforming the preexisting disordered chaos into order in Genesis 1:2–31.* Waltke explains that since there was no *ex nihilo* ("out of nothing") creation in Genesis 1:1, the word "creation" meant God's six framework days conquering the chaos by turning it into an orderly cosmos. "The state of material prior to its creation [was] 'nothing' . . . in the sense that an orderly arrangement, a creation, a cosmos, has not as yet taken place."[61] Creation was transforming the preexisting chaotic material into an orderly state during the six literary units of Genesis 1. (The literary framework theory is in chapter 3.) Creation should be understood as "God steps creatively into the primordial abyss and darkness to transform it into a magnificent, ordered, balanced universe."[62]

> **Waltke:** Since chaos existed before creation,
> "creation" was transforming pre-creation chaos into cosmos.

(1.7) *Genesis 1:2 functions as a parenthesis setting up the first creative act, which was in 1:3.* Chaos preexisted before Genesis 1:1. So 1:1 is really out of the picture with no action of any kind. Genesis 1:2 does not relate back to 1:1 but only forward to 1:3. Genesis 1:2 is like a parenthesis, a setup of the chaotic situation that God would fix beginning in 1:3.[63]

Michael Heiser is a Hebrew scholar and academic editor of Logos Bible Software. He has analyzed Genesis 1:1–3 as clauses. "A clause is a string of words that presents a single thought." An "independent clause" is a complete thought independent of any other clause. Genesis 1:1 is a complete thought, so it is an independent clause. A "dependent clause" depends on another clause to be a fully complete thought. "Now the earth was uninhabitable" is not a complete thought, so it is a dependent clause. How we interpret Genesis 1:1–3 depends on "which clauses are independent clauses and which are not, and then which independent clauses are modified by which dependent clauses."[64] The following is my much-simplified version of his outstanding detailed analysis (Heiser would not set it up quite this way, so see his paper to view his arrangement):

Gap Theory

1:1	Independent Clause	"In the beginning God created . . . ."
1:2	Independent Clause	"Then the earth <u>became</u> *tōhû v^abōhû* . . . ."
1:3	Independent Clause	"Then God said, 'Let there be light.'"

Traditional Initial Creation Theory (YEC, OEC, 2SBC)

1:1	Independent Clause	"In the beginning God created . . . ."
1:2	Dependent on 1:1	"Now the earth was *tōhû v^abōhû* . . . ."
1:3	Independent Clause	"Then God said, 'Let there be light.'"

Pre-Creation Chaos Theory (Waltke)

1:1	Independent Title	"In the Beginning God Created . . . ."
1:2	Dependent on 1:3	("Now the earth was *tōhû v^abōhû* . . . .")
1:3	1st Independent Clause of the actual narrative	"Then God said, 'Let there be light.'"[65]

Waltke shows that the initial "and/now" (vav/waw disjunctive) prefixed noun ("the earth") of 1:2 makes 1:2a a dependent descriptive clause describing the condition of Earth. Genesis 1:2 continues with two more descriptive clauses in 1:2b and 1:2c. In other words, 1:2 describes the situation, so the 1:2 description relates to (modifies) another sentence, either 1:1 or 1:3.

The gap theory claims that 1:2 is an independent clause that declares an independent action: "And/then the earth <u>became</u> *tōhû vᵃbōhû*." Waltke demonstrated that "became" is an incorrect translation. Michael Heiser says the gap theory has "no grammatical or syntactical support." "It is also suspect for its poor word study analysis ["became" instead of "was"] and theological speculation" about Satan's fall and the resulting catastrophe, all in 1:2. Therefore, the gap theory is not a truly viable Biblical creation theory.

The remaining two theories correctly recognize that 1:2 is dependent. The question for these two remaining theories is whether 1:2 relates to 1:1 or only to 1:3.

The traditional initial creation theory says God created the heavens and earth in the beginning in 1:1. Genesis 1:2 is *not* a parenthesis. Genesis 1:2 relates to or modifies 1:1 by describing the unfinished *tōhû vᵃbōhû* condition of Earth that resulted from God's initial *ex nihilo* creation in 1:1. No doubt, 1:2 also supplies the setting for the creation events to come.

Waltke's view is the pre-creation chaos theory. Chaos preexisted, so nothing happened in Genesis 1:1. (1:1 is a title, as the next chapter will explain.) Genesis 1:2 is a parenthesis describing pre-creation chaos *only* as a setup for God's work in His first creative act. That first creative act is in Genesis 1:3, the creation of light. So 1:2 relates *only* to 1:3, not to the title in 1:1. Genesis 1:1 is structurally completely unrelated to 1:2.

(1.8) The eight command units of the six days all follow a similar pattern. Each of the eight command units "typically follows a pattern of *announcement, commandment, separation, report, naming, evaluation, and chronological framework*" (italics in original).[66]

In summary, Waltke's theory is this: *Tōhû vᵃbōhû* means unformed chaos. But God could not have created chaos. This is a dilemma: Since God could not have created chaos, then logically God did not create chaos *during* Genesis 1:1. The gap idea that Earth became chaos *after* Genesis 1:1 is not supported by the Hebrew grammar. The solution to the dilemma is that chaos was the state of material that existed *before* Genesis 1:1. If that is the case, then there was no initial *ex nihilo* creation by God in Genesis 1:1. So "created" meant turning preexisting chaos described in Genesis 1:2 into orderly cosmos in the six literary units of Genesis 1:3–31.

I will be evaluating all ten theories. I desire to do so in a gracious yet Scripturally discriminating spirit. Acts 17:11 commended the Bereans, "Now the Bereans were of more noble character than the Thessalonians, for they received the message with great eagerness and examined the Scriptures every day to see if what Paul said was true" (NIV). Not all claims are true. J. P. Moreland said, "Reality makes propositions true or false."[67] Reality is both (**1**) the Bible as true communication from the Creator including truth about the creation (Ps. 119:160; John 1:3, 14) and (**2**) the creation itself (Ps. 19:1–4; Rom. 1:19–20). I will especially focus on whether claims match the Bible. I ask my readers to be like the noble Bereans and evaluate their own favorite theories with me, by the Bible, in a cooperative enterprise. In evaluating other theories, I am *not* attacking the great and godly authors of these theories. We are all in a cooperative enterprise seeking the truth about creation, but seeking truth includes pointing out claims that lack Biblical support before gathering the great Biblical claims from these honored men into a single more Biblical creation theory.

In the response section, I will add **u-** before Biblically unsupported claims, **ps-** before partially supported, and **s-** before claims in which the *main idea* seems Biblically supported, although not necessarily all related details are.

Unsupported Claims of the Pre-Creation Chaos Theory

Respectfully, I submit that even Bruce Waltke makes mistakes. He made a key faulty assumption that has thrown his theory off target.

(**u-1.0B**) *Chaos ruled.* An all-pervasive powerful chaos is at the core of the ANE origin myths that Waltke knows so well. Out of this world-view, he assumes chaos. Therefore, he also assumes that one of the three major *chaos* theories must be the correct understanding of Biblical creation. He never even evaluates the no-chaos option. But does *tōhû v^abōhû* mean unformed chaos?

(**u-1.2**) **Tōhû v^abōhû** *in Genesis 1:2 meant disordered chaos.* Waltke claims that *tōhû v^abōhû,* understood by ANE chaos myths, meant unformed chaos, a pre-creation chaos that was "a state of material devoid of order, or without being shaped or formed into something."[68] Waltke argues primarily from ANE chaos myths, only touching briefly on Jeremiah 4:23–26 and Isaiah 34:11.[69] This is Waltke's underlying fundamental claim.

Everything else in his pre-creation chaos theory is built on this claim based largely on ANE mythology.

Contra Waltke, the Bible's two other uses of *tōhû* and *bōhû* together do not mean chaos in the sense of "nothing or an unformed state." These two are Isaiah 34:11 and Jeremiah 4:23.

Isaiah 34:11 predicts the conquest of Edom. The land of Edom would be left *tōhû* and *bōhû*. Edom would be devastated by conquest. All that would remain would be bare rock and sand. I have been in much of Edom (in today's Kingdom of Jordan). Without people to collect water and ingeniously tease life from the rock and sand, Edom becomes an uninhabitable wilderness of stone and sand, empty of life. But even after conquest, Edom was not in "a state of material devoid of order, or without being shaped or formed into something."[70]

Jeremiah 4:23 purposefully pictures the conquered land of Judah becoming as desolate as Earth was before the six days. But Jeremiah was still in Judah after it was conquered. So the land of Judah was not in "a state of material devoid of order."[71] Most of the people were carried off into captivity. The conquering Babylonian army devastated the cities—burning, looting, and breaking down walls. The cities were left in ruins and empty of inhabitants. The farmland reverted to wilderness because it, too, was largely uninhabited.

That is the meaning of *tōhû vᵃbōhû*. *Tōhû* means uninhabitable wilderness. *Bōhû* means empty, particularly empty of life, like Judah or Edom after conquest. Moses daily saw this kind of land in the wilderness of Sinai. The difference was that Earth was uninhabitable because it was covered by water and thick darkness.

Neither *tōhû* nor *bōhû* means chaos—"nothing or an unformed state," "a state of material devoid of order." The land of Judah was devastated, not in "a state of material devoid of order." I have seen a deserted village like this in the Middle East—the fields reverted to wild rocky land and the houses caved in, leaving the land uninhabitable.

Earth was simply in its first stage, a complete planet but still uninhabitable, just as Venus and Mars are today. But we do not consider Venus or Mars to be "unformed chaos" simply because they are uninhabitable.

There was no chaos, so there is no reasonable objection to the orderly heavens and unfinished Earth being created by God *ex nihilo* during Genesis 1:1. Waltke's supposed dilemma has a solution: there was no chaos. Chaos is an ANE myth idea, not a Bible teaching. The phrase *tōhû vᵃbōhû* in Genesis 1:2 means Earth was "uninhabitable and uninhabited," not "chaos." God did not create chaos. In Genesis 1:1, God created the orderly heavens and unfinished Earth.

(u-1.2a) *All was unformed, disordered chaos.* Sometimes Waltke says Earth was chaos, but he also indicates that *everything* was chaos.

Contrary to everything being *tōhû v*ᵃ*bōhû,* much less everything being chaos, Genesis 1:2 says, "And the earth was *tōhû v*ᵃ*bōhû.*" Only planet Earth was declared unfinished. Finishing Earth would be God's purpose for His upcoming six days of work.

(u-1.4) *If* **tōhû v**ᵃ**bōhû** *means chaos, yet God could not have created chaos, then unformed chaos must have existed before creation.* Waltke claims, "Logic will not allow us to entertain the contradictory notions: God created the organized heavens and earth; the earth was unorganized."[72] So Waltke claims that unformed chaos existed before creation.

(u-1.4a) *The chaos was before creation.* Parallel ANE myths tell of preexisting chaos. Since the Bible's creation narratives have similar features, these parallels support pre-creation chaos in the Bible.

In response, *tōhû v*ᵃ*bōhû* in Genesis 1:2 does not mean chaos. If there was no chaos, then there is no hindrance to the plain reading of Genesis 1:1, that God created the heavens and earth in the beginning. There was no unformed chaotic matter before creation. John Calvin has already answered Waltke:

> He moreover teaches by the word 'created,' that what before did not exist was now made; for he has not used the term יצר (*yatsar*), which signifies to frame or form, but ברא, (*bara*), which signifies to create. Therefore his meaning is, that the world was made out of nothing. Hence the folly of those is refuted who imagine that unformed matter existed from eternity. . . . This indeed was formerly a common fable among the heathens [ANE mythology].[73]

(u-1.4b) *Preexisting unformed chaos, darkness, and deep sea were not from God.* Waltke says God could not have created "disorder, darkness, and deep," a situation not tolerated in the perfect cosmos and never said to have been called into existence by the Word of God.[74]

Waltke confuses the metaphor of dark, picturing evil, with the physical absence of light photons. He interprets darkness in Genesis 1:2–5 as if it were a metaphor picturing moral evil. Since God does not create moral evil, Waltke claims God did not create darkness. So he claims that the darkness preexisted.

In response, Waltke's claim fails if "darkness" in Genesis 1:4–5 simply means the absence of light photons. Moreover, Job 38:9 says God made darkness. Also Isaiah 45:7 says, "I form the light, and create darkness" (KJV). Waltke's claim that God did not make darkness is incorrect. God does not create moral evil, but He does make both light and absence of light, or darkness.

Waltke also claims God could not have created the deep sea.

In response, Revelation 10:6 says God created "the sea and the things in it." Psalm 95:5 states, "The sea is His, for it was He who made it" (NASB).

Last, Waltke claims God could not have made disorder or unformed chaos.

In response, as previously shown, God did not create chaos because there was no chaos. Unfinished is not the same as chaos. Earth was simply unfinished. This chaos claim underlies Waltke's entire pre-creation chaos theory and his title theory, and the claim fails.

(**u-1.4c**) *The source of the chaos, dark, and deep is unknown.* Waltke asks, "But what about the uncreated or unformed state, the darkness and the deep of Genesis 1:2? Here a great mystery is encountered, for the Bible never says that God brought these into existence by His word."[75] Waltke claims, "The Book of Genesis does not inform us concerning the origin of that which is contrary to the nature of God," but "mocks us," providing "no information."[76]

Contrary to Waltke, the Bible does *not* mock us. Genesis 1:1 answers clearly: "In the beginning God created the heavens and the earth," a merism meaning *everything*. John 1:3 explains, "*All things* were made by him [the Word]; and without him was not any thing made that was made" (KJV). Hebrews 1:2 speaks of the "Son, whom he [the Father] appointed heir of *all things*, and through whom he made *the universe*" (NIV, emphasis added). The Father through the Word created *all things*. God created the whole universe, including both day and night; including the deep sea. There is no problem about God and chaos, for there was no chaos.

(**u-1.4d**) *God triumphed over the anti-creation chaos sea monster.* Bruce Waltke finds chaos in Rahab and Leviathan. "The Rahab-Leviathan emblem is . . . the figure to describe God's creative activity in the pre-historic past" as "Yahweh's victory" over chaos "prior to creation."[77]

I respond that Rahab and Leviathan are *not* explicitly related by the Bible to a pre-creation situation. Even in Job 9:13, Rahab cowers *after* the creation of the constellations of the heavens. In Job 26:12, Rahab was a storm, perhaps in the third creation day as God gathered the seas, *after* the creation of the moon and light to Earth. Isaiah 51:9 is about a monster, but is otherwise unclear. Rahab may simply mean a monstrous storm or great stormy sea creature. Rahab as pre-creation chaos seems a rather uncertain interpretation, certainly not a strong enough basis for a major doctrine of creation.

God spoke of Leviathan as a real and dreaded sea creature that Job knew about (Job 41). Also, it was a figurative symbol of Satan (Isa. 27:1). Either way, Leviathan was not pre-creation chaos.

Contra Waltke, many verses explicitly say that God did create the heavens and earth: Genesis 1:1, 2:4a; Psalm 33:6, 90:2; Isaiah 42:5, 45:18; John 1:3; Ephesians 3:9; Colossians 1:16; Hebrews 1:2, 11:3; Revelation 4:11, 10:6, and 14:7. With no explicit Bible evidence for pre-creation chaos, but overwhelming Bible evidence that God in the beginning created the heavens and earth, we can conclude, "In the beginning God [actually] created the heavens and the earth."

(u-1.5) *Chaos preexisted; so there was no* **ex nihilo** *creation in Genesis 1:1.* Waltke claims that *tōhû v^{a}bōhû* meant the world was unformed chaos. But God could not have created unformed chaos, darkness, or deep ocean water. Therefore, God did not *bārā'*, create, the world out of nothing, so the chaos must have preexisted. There was either chaos or *ex nihilo* creation, but not both.

Waltke is correct that there was either chaos or *ex nihilo* creation, but not both. If there was chaos, logically there could not have been *ex nihilo* creation. He says there was chaos, so there was no *ex nihilo* creation. He does not add the converse, but following his logic, the converse is the other alternative. If there was *ex nihilo* creation, there was no chaos. I am suggesting this latter alternative.

Contra Waltke, the text evidence of Genesis 1:1–3 and later Scripture supports *ex nihilo* creation in 1:1. The verb בָּרָא, *bārā',* is "emphasizing the initiation of the object" or "initiating something new."[78] God did not just transform pre-creation chaos into order. He created *ex nihilo* "something new," namely, the heavens and the earth. Nowhere else in the Genesis 1 narrative is *bārā'* used again of either the heavens or the earth. Since *bārā'* was used in 1:1, but not of the heavens and earth later in chapter 1, then 1:1 cannot be a summary of the creation of the heavens and earth later in the chapter. God actually created as described by, "In the beginning God created the heavens and the earth." Genesis 1:1 is mirrored by the final summary sentence in this narrative, Genesis 2:4a: "This is the account of the heavens and the earth when they were created [*bārā'*]." Together 1:1 and 2:4a form an inclusio surrounding the creation narrative. Both 1:1 and 2:4a refer to the same "the heavens and the earth." Both use *bārā'*, create, emphasizing the initiation of something new. God actually created the heavens and the earth as something new, *ex nihilo*, in 1:1, and then completed His work on Earth in 1:3–31. The Latin words *ex nihilo* are not in Genesis 1:1, but the concept of "out of nothing" is implied in 1:1. God created all things *ex nihilo*, out of nothing, in the beginning.

Strongly contra Waltke, John 1:1–3 declares that everything was created by God the Father through the Son. John 1:1 intentionally mirrors Genesis 1:1: "In the beginning was the Word." Then John 1:3 declares, "πάντα δι' αὐτοῦ ἐγένετο," "All things were made through him, and without him was not any thing made that was made" (ESV). Hebrews 1:2 says, "In these last days he has spoken to us by his Son, whom he appointed heir of all things, and through whom he made the universe" (NIV). There was no preexisting chaos. "All things were made through him." The Father through the Son created all things, so before God created all things, nothing but God existed. Therefore, the creation was *creatio ex nihilo*.

Contra Waltke, Hebrews 11:3 says, "By faith we understand that the universe was formed at God's command, so that what is seen was not made out of what was visible" (NIV). God did create *ex nihilo*.

The pre-creation chaos theory fails to meet the burden of proof. God did create all things in the beginning and He did so *ex nihilo*. For an excellent technical defense of creation *ex nihilo*, I recommend *Creation out of Nothing* by Paul Copan and William Lane Craig.

A great mist of pre-creation chaos could blind one to the theological ramifications of eliminating *ex nihilo* creation. If autonomous chaos, uncreated by God, coexisted with God, then God is not the sovereign sole creator of all things, as the Bible claims from Genesis 1:1 through Revelation 14:7. Waltke's claim of no *ex nihilo* creation, if it were true, would present a serious *theological* problem. But Waltke's claim of no *ex nihilo* creation is incorrect.

(u-1.6) *"Creation" meant transforming the preexisting disordered chaos into order in Genesis 1:2–31.* By "creation," Waltke does not mean an initial *ex nihilo* creation by God. Instead, to him "creation" meant the six days conquering the preexisting chaos monster by turning it into an orderly cosmos.

In response, Hebrews 11:3 declares that "the universe was formed at God's command, so that what is seen was not made out of what was visible" (NIV). God did not simply rearrange preexisting autonomous chaos into order. God the Father through God the Son created the universe out of nothing by His invisible, powerful Word (Ps. 33:6; Heb. 11:3).

(u-1.7) Genesis 1:2 functions as a parenthesis setting up the first creative act, which was in 1:3. In Waltke's theory, chaos preexisted before Genesis 1:1. So 1:1 has no action or event. Genesis 1:2 does not relate back to 1:1 but only forward to 1:3. Genesis 1:2 is like a parenthesis, a setup of the chaotic situation that God would fix, beginning with His first creative act—the Genesis 1:3 command for light.

In response, now we may answer the question posed by Michael Heiser. (I am not claiming that Michael Heiser will agree with my conclusions.) The key to choosing between the two remaining theories is by answering, What does 1:2 modify—1:1 or 1:3?

If God created the heavens and earth *ex nihilo* in the beginning in 1:1, and then 1:2 describes the unfinished *tōhû v^a bōhû* condition of Earth that was the result of God's creation in 1:1, then the traditional initial *ex nihilo* creation theory is correct. (Genesis 1:2 is then said to modify 1:1.) No doubt, 1:2 describing unfinished Earth also sets the stage for the eight commands finishing Earth.

Waltke's view is the pre-creation chaos theory. Chaos preexisted, so nothing happened in Genesis 1:1. (1:1 is only a title.) Genesis 1:2 is a parenthesis describing pre-creation chaos *only* as a setup for God's work in His first creative act. That first creative act was in Genesis 1:3, the creation of light. Genesis 1:1 is solely a title, so is structurally unrelated to 1:2. Genesis 1:2 can *only* relate to or modify 1:3.

These are the two options Michael Heiser lists as viable. So which clause does Genesis 1:2 modify—1:1 as the initial creation theory claims (also setting the stage for 1:3–31), or *only* 1:3 as Waltke's pre-creation chaos theory claims?

In response contra Waltke, Genesis 1:2 describes Earth resulting from its creation in the beginning in Genesis 1:1. Genesis 1:2 contains three descriptive (*vav/waw* disjunctive) clauses that describe the conditions of Earth resulting from its creation in 1:1. Genesis 1:1 ends with "God created the heavens and the earth." Then Genesis 1:2 begins with "Now the earth was [*in this condition*]," speaking of the same Earth. In fact, the last word of 1:1, *ha'āretz* ("the earth"), is the same word as the first word in 1:2, *v^e-hā'āretz* ("Now the earth"). Earth was created in 1:1. Then it was described in Genesis 1:2.

No doubt, 1:2 also supplies the background for the narrative of 1:3–31.[79] But structurally it modifies 1:1.

In claim **u-1.5**, the evidence for *ex nihilo* creation proved strong. God created the heavens and earth in 1:1. Then 1:2 describes the unfinished *tōhû vᵃbōhû* condition of Earth that was the result of God's creation in 1:1. Therefore, the evidence supports the initial creation theory.

However, we have one more factor. The Waltke Exclusion Principle says, "Logic will not allow us to entertain the contradictory notions: God created the organized heavens and earth; the earth was unorganized."[80] If there was preexisting chaos, there was no *ex nihilo* creation of the organized heavens and earth. The converse is also logically possible: If there was *ex nihilo* creation of the organized heavens and earth, then there was no unorganized chaos. Either there was chaos and no *ex nihilo* creation of the organized heavens and earth. Or there was *ex nihilo* creation of the organized heavens and earth and no preexisting chaos. Waltke claims chaos and no *ex nihilo* creation of the organized heavens and earth. There cannot be both.

In response, in claim **u-1.4**, the evidence against chaos also proves strong. The initial creation theory is usually listed as the "initial *chaos* creation theory," because the majority of initial creation advocates claim chaos. But the Waltke Exclusion Principle opposes this creation of chaos view. The minority view, however, is the initial *no-chaos* creation theory. So we can now approach the Heiser question with an initial *ex nihilo* no-chaos creation option.

Contra the chaos view, day and night in 1:3 requires an already-rotating planet Earth from 1:1. Genesis 1:3 began the first alternating daytime and nighttime. The only command in 1:3–5 was the command for light. Genesis 1:2 is a description, not an action, so rotating Earth could not have been created in 1:2. Unless God created the Earth as a (rotating) planet back during 1:1, as 1:1 actually explicitly states, there would have been no day and night in 1:3. Day and night do not occur in unformed amorphous chaos. Day and night occur only on a rotating planet. So God did *not* create *chaos*, nor did chaos preexist. God actually created planet Earth during Genesis 1:1 as 1:1 states. Then 1:2 describes Earth's unfinished condition resulting from its creation in 1:1.

Job 26:8–9 and 38:9 say Earth was covered by thick dark cloud, blocking out even the light of the full moon. That is why Earth's sea surface was dark in Genesis 1:2b. At God's command, light penetrated the cloud to Earth's sea for the first time. Because Earth was rotating, there was day and night. Earth was not chaos; Earth was a rotating planet.

If rotating Earth in 1:2 is the result of its creation in 1:1, then the initial creation theory is supported by the text. This conclusion is not harmed if 1:2 also secondarily sets up the conditions for 1:3–31. Once it is established that Earth in 1:2 is the result of its creation in 1:1, which the text evidence affirms, then the initial creation theory (without chaos) is also established.

For Waltke's view to be the case, 1:2 can modify *only* 1:3. In Waltke's theory, the only relationship possible between 1:1 and 1:2 would be one way — for the 1:1 title to summarize 1:2. But 1:1 does not summarize 1:2 at all.

The Heiser clause analysis method, even in my simplified use, does seem to give a decision between the two theories. That decision favors the initial creation theory — as long as the erroneous idea that *tōhû v^abōhû* means chaos is excluded. (If chaos were included, then I would have to agree that both theories might be about equally problematic, although both are better than the gap theory.) We will carry this initial *no-chaos* creation theory into the unified theory in chapter 11.

The Genesis 1:2 Earth was the result of its creation in 1:1. The precreation chaos premise is incorrect. The initial creation theory (but not the initial *chaos* creation version) is supported by the Bible text. "In the beginning God [actually] created the heavens and the earth. Now the earth was uninhabitable and uninhabited, and darkness was on the surface of the deep *ocean*. And the Spirit of God was hovering over the surface of the waters." End of the first paragraph. Genesis 1:2 relates to 1:1.

Waltke's pre-creation chaos and title premises are incorrect. These were thrown off target by his assumption that *tōhû v^abōhû* means chaos. Contra Waltke, I affirm *ex nihilo* creation, but not chaos.

On the other hand, Bruce Waltke has much to offer. He pointed out the grammatical error in the gap theory. He also showed that the initial chaos theory has a basic logical problem. The Waltke Exclusion Principle is of great value. These insights by Waltke are keys to the analysis of the other theories in preparation for our unified creation theory.

Partially Supported Claims of the Pre-Creation Chaos Theory

(**ps-1.0A**) *Logic rules.* Bruce Waltke claims, "Logic will not allow us to entertain the contradictory notions: God created the organized heavens and earth; the earth was unorganized."[81]

Yes, God built the logic of non-contradiction into the universe. But if our imperfect logic attempts to overrule an explicit Bible text such as, "In the beginning God created the heavens and the earth," we err in our Biblical interpretation or *our use* of the logic God built into the universe. Waltke erred in interpreting *tōhû v^abōhû* as chaos. Waltke dismissed the *ex nihilo* creation because God would not create chaos.

But if there was no chaos, then logically there is no more hindrance to God creating *ex nihilo* the heavens and earth in 1:1.

(ps-1.3) *An orderly God could not have created disorderly chaos.* Waltke claims that logically the "God of order and goodness" could not create "disorder" of "unformed" earth, the deep, and darkness.

I respond that if *tōhû vᵃbōhû* does not mean chaos, then there is no conflict. God could and did create the orderly heavens and earth, just as Genesis 1:1 says. God did create the deep ocean and the cloud cover darkening it (Job 38:8–9). Earth was simply unfinished in 1:2.

Supported Claims of Pre-Creation Chaos Theory

(s-1.1) "The heavens and the earth" means the entire orderly universe, the cosmos. Waltke claims the "the heavens and the earth" in Genesis 1:1 is a merism meaning the entire organized universe, the cosmos.[82]

Most Bible commentators agree that "the heavens and the earth" is "an expression of totality,"[83] the whole universe. Cassuto says that since "earth is to be understood here [as] everything under the heavens including the sea," together the two terms—"the heavens and the earth"—constituted everything created. "In fact, Wisdom of Solomon uses the Greek words ὁ κόσμος, the cosmos, to refer to Genesis 1:1."[84] "The heavens and the earth" in Genesis 1:1 means the entire created universe, the organized cosmos. Waltke has ably proven this claim.

(s-1.3a) The initial chaos theory—that God created the orderly cosmos during 1:1 and that it was disordered chaos in 1:2—is logically impossible. The initial creation chaos theory says God created chaos or unformed matter during Genesis 1:1. Waltke responds that "the heavens and the earth" imply an orderly cosmos. Order in Genesis 1:1 would contradict chaos in Genesis 1:2. "Logic will not allow us to entertain the contradictory notions: God created the organized heavens and earth; the earth was unorganized."[85] The initial chaos theory is logically impossible.

I agree with Waltke that the chaos idea in the initial chaos theory—that Genesis 1:1 means God created the orderly heavens and the earth, but it was unformed disordered chaos in 1:2—is illogical. Even more, it is unbiblical, because *tōhû vᵃbōhû* does not mean chaos.

The Waltke Exclusion Principle is correct: If there was chaos, there was no *ex nihilo* creation of the organized heavens and earth. But it is the converse that is the case: If there was *ex nihilo* creation of the organized heavens and earth, then there was no preexisting unorganized chaos. The Bible teaches *ex nihilo* creation; so there was no chaos.

(s-1.3b) The "gap" in the gap theory—Earth "became" chaos in 1:2—is not supported by the Hebrew grammar. The gap theory says Earth "became" chaos at Lucifer's fall. Waltke responds that Genesis 1:2 should *not* be translated, "Now the earth <u>became</u> *tōhû vᵃbōhû*," as claimed by gap theory adherents. (1:2a is correctly translated, "And/Now the earth <u>was</u> *tōhû vᵃbōhû*.") Waltke's Hebrew arguments show that the middle stage of the gap theory—the gap—is not supported by Hebrew grammar. Most modern scholars agree with him.

The two alternative theories have fatal flaws.

The initial chaos theory errs in claiming order in 1:1,
but chaos in 1:2.

The gap theory errs in claiming earth
became chaos in 1:2.

(s-1.8) The eight command units of the six days all follow a similar pattern. Each of the eight command units "typically follows a pattern." This insight is very helpful for our unified theory.

Bruce Waltke has given us an outstanding analysis of the problems in the initial chaos creation theory and the gap theory. His Exclusion Principle is profound. Unfortunately, he took the chaos option. He claimed that because the initial chaos theory (that God created chaos *during* Genesis 1:1) and the gap theory (that Earth became chaos *after* Genesis 1:1) are impossible, his pre-creation chaos theory (that chaos existed *before* Genesis 1:1) is the only remaining option.

I respond that if *tōhû vᵃbōhû* means "uninhabitable and uninhabited," rather than "chaos," then all three theories are incorrect. There was no chaos *during* 1:1—the initial chaos theory. There was no chaos *after* 1:1—the gap theory. And there was no chaos *before* Genesis 1:1—Waltke's pre-creation chaos theory.

Contra Waltke, God created the orderly heavens and earth in 1:1. Earth in 1:2 was quite acceptable as planets go, as good if not better than Venus or Mars. Earth was no more chaos than Mars is today. But Earth was still uninhabitable. It was an ocean-covered, thick-cloud-darkened planet. By His eight command units and six days, God did this transformation of Earth by the eight command units that follow the pattern that Waltke explained.

Contra Waltke, Earth in 1:2 was quite acceptable as planets go, as good if not better than Venus or Mars.

Instead of believing in pre-creation chaos, instead of denying *ex nihilo* creation, instead of seeing Genesis 1:1 as a title empty of any act by God, I urge followers of Waltke to believe that "In the beginning God [actually] created the heavens and the earth."

Summary of the Pre-Creation Chaos Theory

Waltke says it all began with God and chaos. Everything was chaos. God would never have created chaos. So He did not create chaos *during* Genesis 1:1. The Hebrew grammar shows that Earth did not become chaos in 1:2 *after* Genesis 1:1. Therefore, chaos must have existed with God *before* Genesis 1:1 as pre-creation chaos. Since chaos existed *before* Genesis 1:1, then Genesis 1:1 could not have been creation out of nothing (*creatio ex nihilo*). Instead of *ex nihilo* creation, chaos existed with God before Genesis 1:1, then God creatively transformed that chaos into cosmos in the six framework days.

Conclusions about the Pre-Creation Chaos Theory

Waltke has great Biblical insights, but he overlooked the option that chaos never existed. If there was no chaos because *tōhû vᵃbōhû* does not mean chaos, then Waltke's own theory, that chaos existed with God *before* Genesis 1:1, is also incorrect. Otherwise, he has greatly contributed to our understanding of creation.

Bruce Waltke effectively refutes a key idea in the initial chaos theory and its modern offshoot, young earth scientific creationism—the idea that God created unformed disordered chaotic material *during* Genesis 1:1. Because of Waltke's critique, the initial chaos theory and young earth scientific creationism have not been fully accepted by many Hebrew scholars.

Waltke also convincingly demonstrated that the "gap" in the gap theory—that Earth became chaos *after* Genesis 1:1 in a time gap at 1:2—is grammatically unworkable. As a result, the gap theory has gone out of favor. We can carry these insights over into the unified theory.

Bruce Waltke rightly explains that "the heavens and the earth" is a merism that means the entire created universe. This understanding of "the heavens and the earth" will be helpful for our unified theory.

If you are finding this book helpful, tell others. Biblical creation is important. Fill out a request to your public library or college library to buy this book. Include the ISBN number from the front pages and add the web site, thomasarnoldpublishing.com. I would appreciate any web site or magazine reviews that you may write, because as a self-publisher, I will not have the advertising of a large publishing company. I will be glad to receive copies of reviews and suggestions to TAP, P.O. Box 805, Arlington Heights, IL 60006-0805. Together, let us improve our understanding of the Bible's teaching about the creation.

1. Pre Creation Chaos Theory

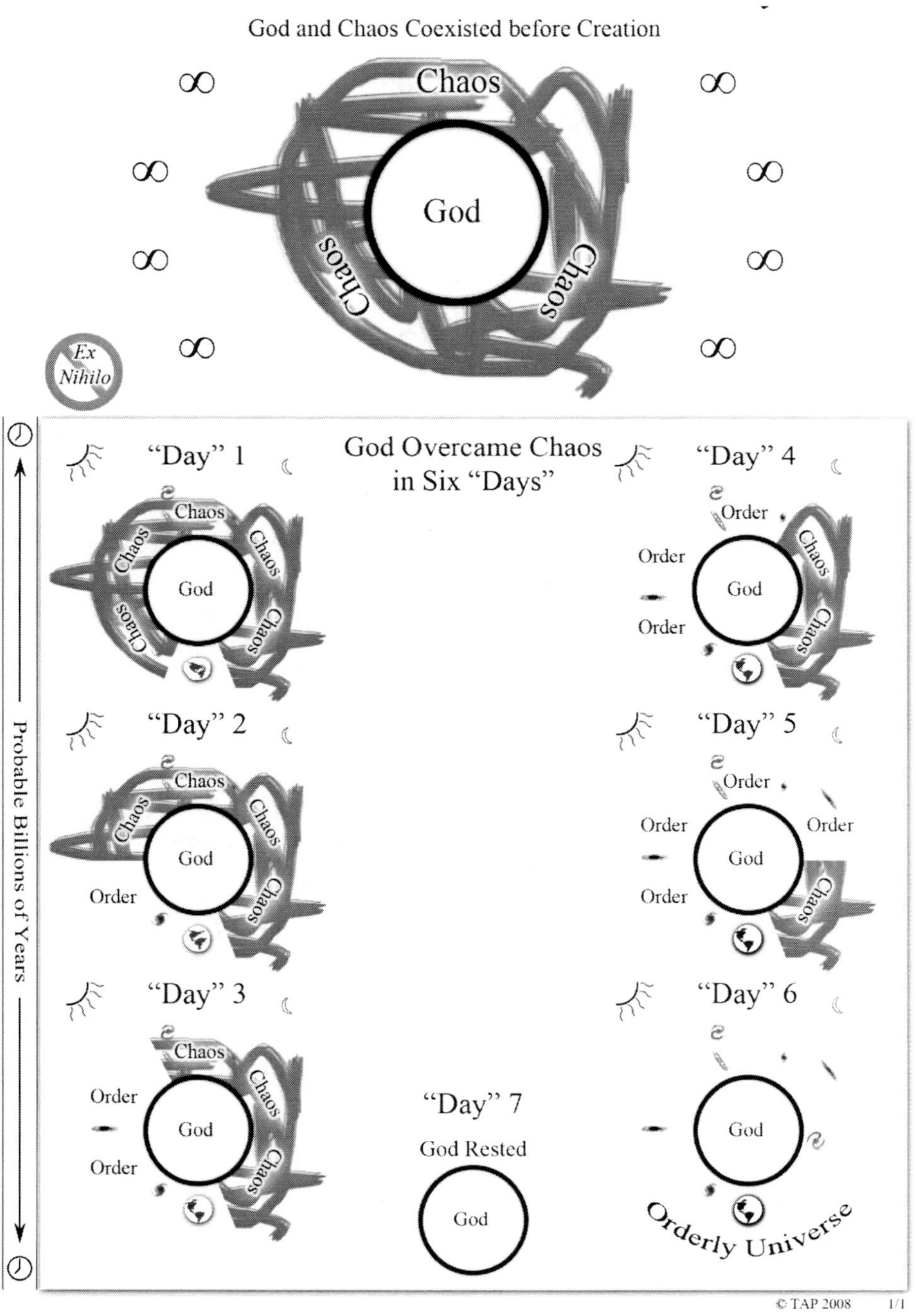

1. Claims of the Pre-Creation Chaos Theory

(Biblically supported claims in non-italics **bold,** unsupported in *italics*)

(1.0A) Logic rules.

(1.0B) Chaos ruled.

(1.1) "The heavens and earth" meant the entire orderly universe.

 (1.2) Tōhû vᵃbōhû in Genesis 1:2 meant disordered chaos.

  (1.2a) All was unformed disordered chaos.

(1.3) An orderly God could not create chaos.

   (1.3a) The initial chaos theory is logically impossible.

   (1.3b) The "gap" is grammatically unworkable.

(1.4) Unformed chaos must have preexisted before creation.

  (1.4a) The chaos was before creation.

  (1.4b) Preexisting unformed chaos, dark, and deep sea were not from God.

  (1.4c) The source of the chaos, deep, and dark is unknown.

  (1.4d) God triumphed over the anti-creation chaos sea monster.

(1.5) Chaos preexisted, so there was no ex nihilo creation in Genesis 1:1.

(1.6) "Creation" meant transforming preexisting chaos into order in Gen. 1:2–31.

(1.7) Gen. 1:2 functions as a parenthesis, modifying 1:3, God's first creation act.

(1.8) The eight commands of the six days follow a similar pattern.

Major Supported Claims from the Creation Theories

The Correct Translation of Genesis 1:1: "In the beginning God created the heavens and the earth." It is *incorrect* to translate 1:1 as "When God began to create."

The Waltke Merism: "The heavens and the earth" meant the entire orderly universe.

The Waltke Exclusion Principle: "Logic will not allow us to entertain the contradictory notions: God created the organized heavens and earth; the earth was unorganized."[86] If there was preexisting chaos, there was no *ex nihilo* creation of the organized heavens and earth. The converse is also logically possible: If there was *ex nihilo* creation of the organized heavens and earth, then there was no preexisting unorganized chaos. (Waltke concludes there was chaos, so there was no *ex nihilo* creation, but the converse equally flows from his logic.)

The Heiser Clause Analysis: Begin analyzing creation by determining which clauses (especially in Gen. 1:1–3) are independent clauses and which are dependent clauses, and then which independent clauses are modified by which dependent clauses, and so how they fit together.

Chapter 2

Theory 2
Title or Summary Theory

Genesis 1:1—title or creation?

The title theory is advocated most ably by Bruce Waltke. His pre-creation chaos theory covers the time *before* Genesis 1:1; his title theory is about Genesis 1:1 itself.

In a nutshell, the title theory says that the creation of the heavens and the earth could not have been in Genesis 1:1 because God could not have created the chaos described in 1:2. Nor did earth become chaos after 1:1. So Genesis 1:1 was not an action but is a title or summary of the creation events in 1:2–31. As a title, nothing happened in Genesis 1:1. The chaos of 1:2 already preexisted.

Waltke connects the pre-creation chaos theory and the title theory. But the connection between the two theories is not necessary. Don Batten of young earth scientific creationism also seems to holds a form of the title/summary theory, but Batten does *not* hold the pre-creation chaos theory. Batten explains, "Since Genesis 1:1 says God created everything, we see that it summarizes the whole creation process, the rest of the chapter providing the details. In other words, Genesis 1:1 does not describe a primal creation in the distant past, but the whole creation in six days. . . . Genesis 1:1 is the summary of the whole creation process."[87] Waltke, apparently Batten, and others claim that Genesis 1:1 is a title or summary of the rest of chapter 1.

Previous Claims from the Pre-Creation Chaos Theory

Waltke's version of the title or summary theory is built on the seven main claims of his pre-creation chaos theory. These claims are listed in the previous chapter. The pre-creation theory says that chaos existed along with God *before* Genesis 1:1. Because chaos preexisted, God did *not* create the heavens and earth out of nothing in 1:1. Creation was transforming that preexisting chaos into the orderly heavens and earth during Genesis 1:3–31.

Three Claims of the Title or Summary Theory

(2.1) Genesis 1:1 is correctly translated, *"In the beginning God created . . . ,"* not *"When God began to create. . . ."* Waltke explains that Genesis 1:1 in Hebrew is an independent clause (see Heiser in 1.6a) and ,תְּיאשִׁר, *b^{e}rē'shît* ("in the beginning"), is absolute in its sense. So Genesis 1:1 should be translated in the traditional way: "In the beginning God created the heavens and the earth." "All ancient versions (LXX, Vulgate, Aquila, Theodotion, Symmachus, Targum Onkelos)" translate this traditional way.[88] Waltke adds, "Moses could not have used any other construction to denote the first word as in the absolute state [the normal traditional translation of Genesis 1:1], but he could have opted for a different construction to indicate clearly the construct state."[89] The traditional translation of 1:1 is correct.

Some have objected to the standard translation because the first word, *b^{e}rē'shît*, has no "the," no definite article indicating "The" beginning. Heiser responds, "Grammatical work in the Hebrew text has shown, though, that time words do not need the article to be definite."[90]

Simply put, Genesis 1:1 should continue to be translated, "In the beginning God created the heavens and the earth." Genesis 1:1 should not be translated, "When God began to create heaven and earth—the earth being unformed. . . ."[91] The vast number of conservative scholars and translations agree. The difference may seem unimportant, but it actually influences how we view God and His sovereignty over the creation.

Traditional Translation: Waltke affirms the traditional translation of 1:1: "In the beginning God created the heavens and the earth."

(2.2) *Genesis 1:1 is a title because God could not have created the tōhû v^{a}bōhû chaos of 1:2.* All was chaos, but God does not create chaos. So 1:1 was not the creation of chaos but is a title or summary of the rest of chapter 1.

(2.2a) *Genesis 1:1 is a title because logic rules out "God created the orderly cosmos; it was chaos."* "Logic will not allow us to entertain the contradictory notions: God created the organized heavens and earth; the earth was unorganized."[92] The world was unorganized chaos. The chaos had to have been pre-creation chaos. So 1:1 is the title to the six days of transforming pre-creation chaos into orderly cosmos.

(2.2b) *Genesis 1:1 is a title because there was no creation in 1:1.* God does not create chaos. So Genesis 1:1 was not the *ex nihilo* creation of anything. Genesis 1:1 is a title because there was no creation in 1:1.

> **Waltke:** Chaos existed. God does not create chaos.
> So 1:1 was not creation of chaos, but a title to 1:2–31.

(2.2c) *Genesis 1:1 is a title because 1:1 summarizes 1:2–31.* Waltke calls his theory "The View that Verse 1 Is a Summary Statement." "Verse 1 is a summary statement, or formal introduction, which is epexegeted in the rest of the narrative. It appears to this author [Waltke himself] that this is the only viewpoint that completely satisfies the demands of Hebrew grammar."[93] Genesis 1:1 summarizes Genesis 1:2–31. So Genesis 1:1 is a title or summary, not the creation.

(2.2d) *Genesis 1:1 is a title because titles are independent.* Titles stand alone. If Genesis 1:2 ("Now the earth was *tōhû v^abōhû*") relates only to 1:3 ("And God said, 'Let there be light'") rather than back to 1:1, then 1:1 stands alone. So 1:1 is a title.[94]

(2.2e) *Genesis 1:1 is a title like 2:4a, because the verses following each title (1:2–3 and 2:4b–7) are parallel in form.* Genesis 2:4a is a title. Genesis 1:1 and 2:4a are each followed by a set of similar clauses in 1:2–3 and 2:4b–7 respectively. Genesis 2:4a is the title, heading, or summary to the Adam narrative in 2:4b—4:26. So Genesis 1:1 must be the title, heading, or summary to the creation narrative in 1:2—2:3.[95]

(2.3) ***God sovereignly created by eight command units with a common pattern.*** "The essence of the creative process is the *will* of God expressed through His *word*. A basic pattern runs through each creative act. Westermann analyzed that common pattern as follows:[96]

Announcement: And God said . . .
Command: let there be . . . let it be gathered . . . let it bring forth . . .
Report: And it was so.
Evaluation: And God saw that it was good.
Temporal framework: And there was evening, and there was
    morning, the . . . day.

This same pattern runs through the two triads of days and eight acts. "The number of creative acts also increases within each triad: from a single creative act (days 1 and 4) to one creative act with two aspects (days 2 and 5) to two separate creative acts (days 3 and 6)."[97]

Unsupported Problematic Claims of the Title or Summary Theory

(u-2.2) *Genesis 1:1 is a title because God could not have created the* tōhû vᵃbōhû *chaos of 1:2.* Waltke says that all was chaos, but God does not create chaos. So 1:1 was not the creation of chaos but is a title or summary of the rest of the chapter.

What Waltke is claiming is that Genesis 1:1 is a title *instead of being the actual creation*. He is claiming nothing happened in 1:1. There was no *ex nihilo* creation. Chaos preexisted. Genesis 1:1 is merely, only, solely a title to 1:2–31.

(u-2.2a) *Genesis 1:1 is a title because "God created the orderly cosmos; it was chaos" is contradictory.* Waltke says, "Logic will not allow us to entertain the contradictory notions:

God created the organized heavens and earth;

the earth was unorganized."

One of the two halves of the sentence must be false. Waltke assumes the first half is false, and the second half true. He says the world was chaos. So Genesis 1:1 was not the creation, but was merely a title or summary of the six days of 1:3–31.

In response, the first half of the sentence, "God created the orderly cosmos," matches 1:1 and many other Bible texts claiming God created all things (John 1:3; Col. 1:16; Eph. 3:9; Rev. 4:11). So, contra Waltke, the first half is affirmed—"God created the organized heavens and earth."

Waltke's second clause, "it was chaos," is the one that is incorrect. George H. Pember responds that the translation of *tōhû vᵃbōhû* as "without form and void" "is not the sense of the Hebrew, but a glaring illustration of the influence of the chaos-legend."[98] Pember correctly translates *tōhû* as "desolation" and *bōhû* as "'that which is empty,' probably with reference to the absence of all life."[99]

Hebrew professor John Sailhamer responds, "Were it not for the Greek notion of 'primeval chaos,' the phrase never would have been translated that way ["without form and void"]. The sense of the Hebrew phrase suggests something quite different, a sense some early translators identified quite clearly." The meaning is "uninhabitable" and "wilderness" "that had not yet become inhabitable for human beings."[100] Jeremiah 4:23–26 uses the two terms with the sense of "deserted and uninhabited."[101] *Tōhû vᵃbōhû* meant Earth was uninhabitable and uninhabited, *not* unformed chaos.

Pember and Sailhamer are correct. The phrase *tōhû v^aḇōhû* does not mean chaos. If *tōhû v^aḇōhû* does not mean chaos, Waltke's carefully constructed precreation chaos and title premise implodes.

(u-2.2b) *Genesis 1:1 is a title because there was no creation in 1:1.* Waltke claims that God did not create chaos, so Genesis 1:1 is not the *ex nihilo* creation of anything. Waltke rejects an *ex nihilo* creation in Genesis 1:1.

In response, I call the apostle Paul as witness for creation *ex nihilo*:

> Yet for us there is *but* one God, the Father, from whom are all things, and we *exist* for Him; and one Lord, Jesus Christ, by whom are all things, and we *exist* through Him (1 Cor. 8:6, NASB).

> For by Him [God the Son] all things were created, *both* in the heavens and on earth, visible and invisible, whether thrones or dominions or rulers or authorities—all things have been created by Him and for Him (Col. 1:16, NASB).

> God who created all things (Eph. 3:9b, NASB)

Since all things were created by God, then before He created them, only God existed. Since only God existed, God created all things out of nothing. God the Father through God the Son created all things *ex nihilo* in the beginning, in agreement with Genesis 1:1. Genesis 1:1 is more than a mere title; Genesis 1:1 is the declaration of the actual *ex nihilo* creation in the beginning.

(u-2.2c) *Genesis 1:1 is a title because 1:1 summarizes 1:2–31.* Waltke says Genesis 1:1 is a title or summary of the six "days." Genesis 1:1 summarizes 1:2–31.[102]

In response, Genesis 1:1 does not really summarize the six days. Genesis 1:1 is about God creating (*bārā'*) the heavens and earth in the beginning. There is no command in Genesis 1:2–31 creating (*bārā'*) the heavens or planet Earth. Nowhere after 1:1 is Earth created. Even the command on the fourth day of God's work on the heavens was not a creation command but a purpose clause: "Let lights be in the expanse of the sky to separate."[103] After "and it was so" is the report that God made the lights be in the sky to serve their purpose. So Genesis 1:2–31 also includes no command creating the heavens. God had already created the heavens and earth in 1:1. The only *bārā'* commands in 1:2–31 were when God created, not heavens and earth, but sea and flying life and human life. Genesis 1:1 does not summarize verses 2–31. Genesis 1:1 was the initial *ex nihilo* creation of the orderly heavens and unfinished earth.

Genesis 2:1 *does* summarize 1:3–31: "Thus the heavens and the earth were completed, and all their hosts" (NASB). The verb *vay^ekuliû*, "completed" in the qal means "bring a process to completion."[104] In Genesis 1:3–31 God completed the heavens and earth and all their hosts. In contrast, *bārā'* in 1:1 has the sense of creating something new. *Bārā'* was the *ex nihilo* initiation of the heavens and earth in the beginning before the completing work in 1:3–31. The verb *vay^ekuliû*, "completed," is not in 1:1. The completion of the six days' work on the sky/heavens and Earth (1:3–31) is summarized by Genesis 2:1, not 1:1.

(u-2.2d) *Genesis 1:1 is a title because titles are independent.* Titles stand alone. If Genesis 1:2 ("Now the earth was *tōhû v^abōhû*") relates only to 1:3 ("And God said, 'Let there be light'") rather than to 1:1, then 1:1 stands alone. Therefore, 1:1 is a title.

In response, Genesis 1:1 ends with "the earth." Then 1:2 begins with "Now the earth was . . . ," so 1:2 *does* modify 1:1. Genesis 1:2 describes the conditions of planet Earth that had been created in 1:1. However, titles are not modified. Therefore, Genesis 1:1 is not a title.

Partially Supported Claim of the Title or Summary Theory

(ps-2.2e) *Genesis 1:1 is a title like 2:4a, because the verses following each title (1:2–3 and 2:4–7) are parallel in form.* Genesis 2:4a is a title. Genesis 1:1 and 2:4a are each followed by a set of structurally similar clauses in 1:2–3 and 2:4b–7 respectively. Genesis 2:4a is the title of 2:4b—4:26. So Genesis 1:1 is the title of 1:2—2:3.[105]

In response, Rooker says, "The correspondence between 1:1–3 and 2:4—7 is indeed similar, it is not exact."[106] Let us agree that the clauses *after* 1:1 and 2:4a are rather similar in form. This similarity is to be expected because the Adam narrative in 2:4b—5:1a would naturally follow somewhat the same form as the Holy Spirit's narrative of the creation in 1:1—2:4a.

Waltke claims that because 2:4a is a title, 1:1 must be a title or summary as well. However, there are two problems with this claim.

First, 2:4a does not summarize 2:4b—4:26 *after* it. Waltke says 1:1 summarizes 1:2–31, as 2:4a summarizes 2:4b—4:26. Genesis 2:4a says, "These *are* the generations of the heavens and the earth when they were created." Genesis 2:4a is the concluding title or summary of the narrative *before* it—the creation of the heavens and Earth in 1:1—2:3. In fact, 2:4a at the end forms an inclusio: with 1:1 at the beginning. "In the beginning God created the heavens and the earth" begins the inclusio; then 2:4a is the ending title of the inclusio, "These *are* the generations of the heavens and the earth when they were created." P. J. Wiseman has demonstrated that each *tôlᵉdôt* (generations) title (colophon) in Genesis is at the *end* of its respective narrative (except for a *tôlᵉdôt* beginning a genealogy), like a closing signature at the end of a letter.[107] Genesis 2:4a is not the title of the Adam narrative *after* it in 2:4b—4:26 as Waltke claims. Genesis 2:4a is the closing title of the creation narrative of 1:1—2:3 *preceding* it. So Genesis 2:4a, not 1:1, is the title, like a letter signature in the normal ancient near east style, closing the creation narrative.

Second, grammatically 1:1 is not a title, but 2:4a is. Genesis 1:1 and 2:4a are *not* parallel. The Genesis 2:4a *tôlᵉdôt* (generations) phrase really is the title phrase. It has no verb. It is the concluding title phrase, ending the creation narrative in the common ANE style. The following is true to the Hebrew but not a good English translation: "These *the* generations [*tôlᵉdôt*] of the heavens and of the earth." This title formula phrase is repeated nearly a dozen times at the end of the succeeding Genesis narratives (or at the beginning of genealogies). The next two are: "This *the* book of the generations of Adam" (5:1) and "These *the* generations of Noah" (6:9). Sailhamer explains, "In Hebrew, titles consist of simple phrases."[108] In contrast, Genesis 1:1 is a complete independent sentence with a time-frame (In the beginning), subject (God), verb (created), and object (the heavens and the earth). Unlike 2:4a, Genesis 1:1 is not a title phrase. Genesis 1:1 is a full sentence declaring the actual *ex nihilo* creation of the heavens and the earth.

On this claim, we may conclude that 2:4a really is an ending title, but 1:1 is not. Genesis 1:1 was the actual *ex nihilo* creation.

(ps-2.3) What 1:1 summarizes is the eight commad units with a common pattern. "A basic pattern runs through each creative act."

Waltke is correct about eight command units, but incorrect that 1:1 summarizes them. 1:1 was the initial *ex nihilo* creation. 1:3-31 was God's work on earth.

Supported Claims of the Title or Summary Theory

(s-2.1) Genesis 1:1 is correctly translated, "In the beginning God created . . . ," not "When God began to create. . . ." Waltke is correct in his stand defending the traditional translation of Genesis 1:1. The first verse is an independent clause and the first word, *bᵉrē'shît* ("in the beginning"), is absolute in its sense.

Waltke stood against the attempt to retranslate Genesis 1:1 as "When God began to create" as in the JPS 1985 Tanakh (and NRSV). Waltke affirmed, "Genesis 1:1 should be translated in the traditional way: 'In the beginning God created the heavens and the earth.'" This correct translation agrees with all ancient translations, the majority of Hebrew scholars, and the overwhelming majority of modern translations.[109] This translation of the cornerstone creation verse is foundational to our unified theory. For this contribution, thank you, Dr. Bruce Waltke.

Summary of the Title Theory

The title or summary theory is built on the claims of Waltke's pre-creation chaos theory that unformed chaos existed with God before Genesis 1:1. Waltke adds three more claims in the title theory.

He previously claimed that *tōhû v^abōhû* in 1:2 means chaos, but God could not have created chaos. So now he claims that 1:1 is only a title rather than the creation of that chaos. Genesis 1:1 is a title or summary of God's creative acts in the six days when God transformed the ancient pre-creation chaos into an orderly world. Since 1:1 is a title, there was no action, no *ex nihilo* creation, in 1:1.

Waltke opposes the improper translation, "When God began to create." He stands firm that Genesis 1:1 is correctly translated, "In the beginning God created the heavens and the earth." He also recognizes that God created by eight command units.

Conclusions about the Title Theory

Waltke errs in his claim that *tōhû v^abōhû* in Genesis 1:2 means chaos. So he is off target in the resulting claims—that there was no *ex nihilo* creation in 1:1, so 1:1 is merely a title with no creation act. Contra Waltke, Genesis 1:1 declares the actual *ex nihilo* creation of the heavens and the earth.

Waltke affirms that Genesis 1 is composed of eight command units. He also affirms the traditional translation of 1:1. This correct translation will be foundational to our unified theory.

2. Title or Summary Theory

Eternity
Chaos
Chaos
God
Chaos
Chaos
Eternity
Eternity
Ex Nihilo

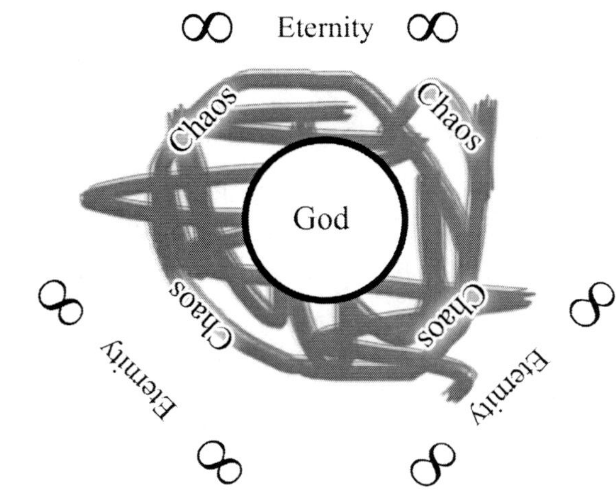

Genesis 1:1 is only a title summarizing Creation

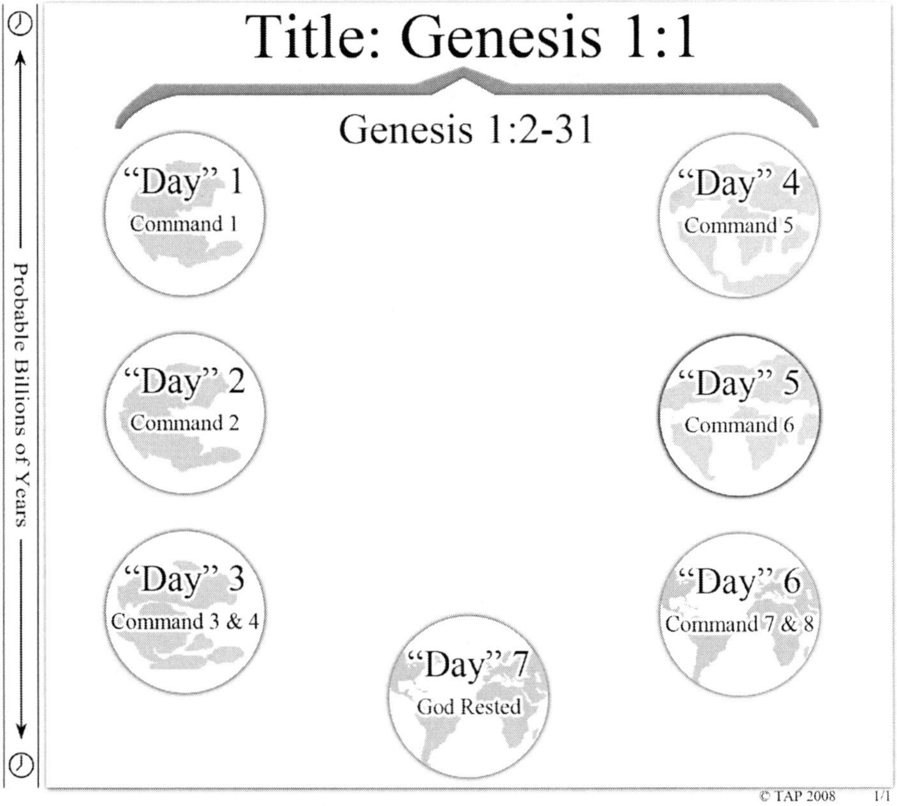

Title: Genesis 1:1
Genesis 1:2-31
"Day" 1
Command 1
"Day" 4
Command 5
"Day" 2
Command 2
"Day" 5
Command 6
"Day" 3
Command 3 & 4
"Day" 6
Command 7 & 8
"Day" 7
God Rested
Probable Billions of Years
© TAP 2008 1/1

2. Claims of the Title or Summary Theory
(Biblically supported claims in non-italics **bold,** unsupported in *italics*)

(2.1) Genesis 1:1 is, *"In the beginning God created . . . ."*
(2.2) 1:1 is a title because God could not have created the tōhû vᵃbōhû *chaos of 1:2.*
   (2.2a) 1:1 is a title - "God created the cosmos; it was chaos" is contradictory.
   (2.2b) 1:1 is a title - God does not create chaos, so no ex nihilo *creation in 1:1.*
   (2.2c) 1:1 is a title - Genesis 1:1 summarizes 1:2–31.
   (2.2d) 1:1 is a title - Genesis 1:2 modifies 1:3, not the title in 1:1.
   (2.2e) 1:1 is a title - Genesis 1:1 is a title because it matches the 2:4a title.
(2.3) What 1:1 summarizes is eight command units with a common pattern.

Major Supported Claims from the Creation Theories

The Correct Translation of Genesis 1:1: Waltke affirms the traditional translation of Genesis 1:1: "In the beginning God created the heavens and the earth." It is *incorrect* to translate 1:1 as "When God began to create."

The Waltke Merism: "The heavens and the earth" meant the entire orderly universe.

The Waltke Exclusion Principle: "Logic will not allow us to entertain the contradictory notions: God created the organized heavens and earth; the earth was unorganized."[110] If there was preexisting chaos, there was no *ex nihilo* creation of the organized heavens and earth. The converse is also logically possible: If there was *ex nihilo* creation of the organized heavens and earth, then there was no preexisting unorganized chaos.

The Heiser Clause Analysis: Begin analyzing creation by determining which clauses (especially in Gen. 1:1–3) are independent clauses and which are dependent clauses, and then which independent clauses are modified by which dependent clauses, and so how they fit together.

Chapter 3

Theory 3
Literary Framework Theory

God often used means: No rain, no plants; rain, then plants (Gen. 2:5–6).

Meredith Kline and Lee Irons have served as ministers of the Orthodox Presbyterian Church. Kline was a professor at Westminster Theological Seminary and wrote the insightful article "Because It Had Not Rained."

Kline and Irons together wrote the article "The Framework View" in *The Genesis Debate*. These two men are following earlier ideas of Henri Blocher, author of *In the Beginning: The Opening Chapters of Geneis*.

The two big claims of the framework view are "nonliteral interpretation of the days and a nonsequential ordering of the creative events."[111] By "nonsequential," Kline and Irons mean that day four apparently occurred at the same time as day one. By "nonliteral," they mean that the days were "days" in a heavenly sense (what they call "upper-register") but were not necessarily literal day-night days on Earth (what they call "lower-register"). "Framework" means that the first three days were parallel with the last three days and that all culminated in the Sabbath. Kline and Irons consider this theological culmination in the Sabbath important. Literal days and sequential chronology are not important.

Framework says the days were *not* literal days
and *not* in order.

But they were in a framework of two triads,
ended by the Sabbath.

In a nutshell, the framework theory claims the days were *not* literal days and the days were *not* in order. But they were in a framework of two triads culminating in the Sabbath.

Waltke also accepts this framework theory of the six days. His order is pre-creation chaos before Genesis 1:1, then 1:1 as a title, and finally a literary framework of the six days and Sabbath in 1:2—2:4.

Preunderstandings of the Framework Theory

(3.0A) *Presuppositionally, Scripture has priority over science.* Kline believes that "Scripture has hermeneutical and presuppositional priority over our fallible study of general revelation."[112]

(3.0B) *Presuppositionally, Scripture will not contradict itself.* "The analogy of Scripture" requires us "to adopt an interpretation of Genesis 1:1—2:3 that does not conflict with Genesis 2:5–6."[113]

(3.0C) *Presuppositionally, Scripture's covenantal purpose, not sequential chronology, is important.* Kline stresses that Genesis 1 addresses "theological and literary concerns."[114] He continues, "While Scripture inerrantly reports historical and chronological information, it always does so with a covenantal and redemptive historical purpose."[115]

Kline's fellow Westminster professor Daniel McCartney says, "The most important thing is to have the correct goal in interpretation."[116] That goal is the covenant theology message of redemption in Christ.[117] Kline says, "The real theological message [of Genesis 1:1—2:3] has been drowned out by its alleged sequential and chronological message."[118] The "covenantal and redemptive historical purpose"[119] of Genesis 1, not chronology of events or the length of the six days, is important.

Claims of the Framework Theory

(3.1) *Genesis 1 is not chronologically sequential.* Kline says the Genesis 1 "account has been shaped, not by a concern to satisfy our curiosity regarding sequence or chronology, but by predominately theological and literary concerns."[120] Henri Blocher said that the Genesis 1 text "is not to be taken literally. The author's intention is not to supply us with a chronology of origins. . . . He wishes to bring out certain themes and provide a theology of the Sabbath."[121] Kline "regards the seven-day scheme as a figurative framework."[122] The first five of the seven days were not necessarily in chronologically sequential order. Days one and four apparently were the same "day."

(3.1a) *The Bible is silent about the age of Earth.* "We must speak where the Bible speaks, and be silent where the Bible is silent." "The inspired text, rightly interpreted, is simply silent with regard to the age of the earth and universe." Most framework advocates claim old earth creation, but this is not part of the theory.[123]

(3.1b) *Genesis 1 has eight command units.* "There are a total of *eight* distinct creative works distributed over *six* days. The last day within each triad (i.e., Days 3 and 6) contains *two* creative acts."[124]

(3.1c) *Genesis 1 is in topical, not sequential chronological, order.* Kline says that Genesis 1:1—2:4a "functions as a literary structure in which the creative works of God have been narrated in a topical order." "They are narrated in a nonsequential order within the literary structure or framework of a seven-day week."[125] So Genesis 1 is *not* in sequential chronological order.

(3.1d) *Day one and day four were simultaneous.* Kline explains, "The creation of the luminaries, and in particular the solar system, on Day 4 actually coincides with the creation of daylight on Day 1. Thus the text is narrated in a topical rather than a purely sequential order."[126] "Day 4 is an example of temporal recapitulation: the narrator returns to events that he had previously reported but now retells in greater detail."[127] Days 1 and 4 are the reason for the claim that the days were not in chronological order. Days 1 and 4 needed to be the same event because the sun was the means God used for day and night to rotating Earth. Therefore, days 1 and 4 were the same event.

(3.1e) *Some events, such as the Sabbath, are in sequential chronological order.* "We cannot conclude that *nothing* in the text has been arranged sequentially. The Sabbath of the seventh day, for example, must follow the previous six days of creation, and man is created last due to his position of delegated dominion over all creation."[128]

(3.2) **The days in Genesis 1 were not literal.** Kline's second overarching claim is, "The total picture of God's completing His creative work in a week of days is not to be taken literally."[129]

(3.2a) *The Bible gives symbolic meaning to some numbers.* The symbolic use of seven in the Bible "is highly significant for our interpretation of the 'week' of creation."[130] Since seven has symbolic significance, the seven days need not be taken literally.

> A framework "day" could have been billions of years, millions of years, or even twenty-four earth hours.

(3.2b) *The "days" were metaphorical.* "The days are part of an extended chronological metaphor. In all metaphors, words are employed to make a comparison between a literal referent and a metaphorical referent. . . . Thus the word yôm in Genesis 1 denotes an ordinary, lower-register, solar day. Yet it is being used metaphorically to describe an upper-register unit of time that is not defined by the Earth's rotation with respect to the sun."[131] The metaphorical meaning of "day" is 'heavenly" ("upper register"), so the days could have been billions of years, millions of years, or even twenty-four earth hours.

Three Arguments Supporting the Two Claims

Kline's two overarching claims are "a nonliteral interpretation of the days and a nonsequential ordering of the creative events."[132] He offers three arguments supporting these two claims:

(**3.3**) *The six "days" are a literary framework in two triads.* Kline's first argument for the two overarching claims listed above is that Genesis 1 forms a two-triad framework:

Creation kingdoms		Creature kings	
Day 1	Light	Day 4	Luminaries
Day 2	Sky	Day 5	Sea creatures
	Seas[133]		Winged creatures
Day 3	Dry land	Day 6	Land animals
	Vegetation		Man

The Creator King	
Day 7	Sabbath

This framework scheme emphasizes the covenantal relationship of the kings to the kingdoms and the ultimate covenantal rule of the Creator King.

(**3.3a**) *The initial creation in Genesis 1:1 took place before the six days.* "Proverbs 8:22–31 defines 'the beginning' of Genesis 1:1 as the time prior to the progressive fashioning of the world described in the subsequent six days of creation."

According to Proverbs 8:22–24,

The LORD possessed me [Wisdom] at the beginning [*rē'shît*]. . . .
When there were no depths [plural of "deep" in Gen. 1:2] (NASB).

The beginning was before God made the *t^ehôm* (deep ocean), which was present in Genesis 1:2. After God made the *t^ehôm* (deep ocean) described in Genesis 1:2, the six days began in 1:3 with light starting day one. So the beginning period was before the six days.

> Proverbs 8:22–30 provides an inspired commentary on Genesis 1:1. . . . According to that inspired commentary, "in the beginning" cannot be a general time-reference to the entire six-day creation period, for Wisdom explicitly placed the events of the six days *after* "the beginning."[134]

The Kline Order: Proverbs 8:22–31 says that "the beginning," when God created Earth (Gen. 1:1), was "when there were no depths." Ocean depths existed by 1:2, so "In the beginning" was before 1:2 and before the six days. The Genesis 1 and Proverbs 8 order is this: Heavens, Earth, deep ocean, and then six days.

(3.3b) *The young earth scientific creationism claim that the beginning was in day one is incorrect.* Young earth scientific creationism claims that the beginning creation of Genesis 1:1 was *in* the six days. Kline responds that a beginning creation "*in* the six days" violates Proverbs 8. Solomon says that the beginning (Prov. 8:22) was when there was no deep ocean (Prov. 8:24), yet there was a deep ocean by the time of the description of dark Earth in Genesis 1:2. So the beginning was in 1:1 before 1:2. Day one began with God's command for light in Genesis 1:3, corresponding to Proverbs 8:27b. Day one ended with evening (Gen. 1:5), which began nighttime, and morning, which ended nighttime. Since day one began with daylight and ended with nighttime and the dawn of morning, day one could not have also contained the dark time of 1:2 or it would have been nighttime-daytime-nighttime, more than one day. Day one was after the beginning of Genesis 1:1 and after God formed the dark cloud-covered ocean present in 1:2. Kline has shown that the YEC claim that the beginning was in day one is proven incorrect by Proverbs 8:22–31.

(3.3c) *The framework emphasizes the Sabbath.* Blocher says, "He [Moses] wishes to bring out certain themes and provide a theology of the Sabbath."[135] The theological culmination of the creation is the Sabbath.

(3.4) *The Kline Claim: When the Bible does not indicate a miracle, Genesis 2:5–6 shows God probably used ordinary means in the creation era, just as today.* Kline's second argument for his two claims is fully explained in his article "Because It Had Not Rained." The question is "whether the *modus operandi* of divine providence was the same during the creation era as that of ordinary providence now." The answer is in Genesis 2:5. "Verse 5 itself describes a time when the earth was without vegetation." Then 2:5c gives the "explanation—a perfectly natural explanation . . . for the absence of vegetation at that time: 'for the LORD God had not caused it to rain upon the earth.'"[136] "The works of creation were interlaced with the work of providence." In other words, God did *both* miracles *and* works of normal cause-and-effect means during the creation tim.

The Kline Claim: When the Bible does not indicate a miracle, Genesis 2:5–6 (no rain, no plants; rain, then plants sprouted) shows God probably used ordinary means in the creation era, just as today.

Genesis 2:5 refers back to the time before God made plants sprout. After God gathered the waters into seas and caused the land to appear (Gen. 1:9), the land was *dry* ground (*yabāshâh*). So before God made land plants sprout, there was need for rain clouds and then rain upon the land. Genesis 2:5 explains that no vegetation had sprouted *because* there was no rain. The noun *ᵉd* should be translated "rain-cloud."[137] Kline translates Genesis 2:5–6:

> Now no shrub of the field was yet in the earth, and no plant of the field had yet sprouted for the LORD God had not yet caused it to rain upon the earth (and there was no man to cultivate the ground). So a rain-cloud began to arise from the earth and watered the whole surface of the ground.[138]

Job explains the water cycle, "For He draws up the drops of water, They distill rain from the rain-cloud" (Job 36:27, NASB, except *ᵉd* translated "rain-cloud," not "mist"). Solomon adds, "All streams flow into the sea, yet the sea is never full. To the place the streams come from, there they return again" (Eccles. 1:7, NIV). The Bible explains the water cycle that consists of clouds rising from the sea, rain falling onto the land causing plants to grow, and the water returning in streams to the sea, where the cycle is repeated. This is the normal providential means God uses to cause plants to grow.

No plants grew on the dry land *until* God made rain fall, then just as now. In Genesis 1:11, God commanded plants to sprout, yet Genesis 2:5–6 adds that He used ordinary non-miraculous means—water.[139] Along with creation miracles, God also used ordinary means that "any reader would recognize as normal in the natural world of his day."[140]

That God used means in no way reduces His sovereignty. He designed and implemented the means.

The Kline Claim says that when the Bible does not indicate a miracle, Genesis 2:5–6 (no rain, no plants; rain, then plants sprouted) shows God apparently used ordinary means in the creation era, just as today.

(**3.4a**) *Since God used ordinary means, the light on day one must have been sunlight.* Kline says the idea that God created the sun on day four after light on day one "must be incorrect. For such an interpretation would require the day/night cycle to be sustained by a supernatural providence for three days until an ordinary providential means (our current solar system) was established."[141]

> If the Creator was concerned to establish a natural watering system prior to creating vegetation to avoid relying unnecessarily upon extraordinary providence in His maintenance of vegetation, would we not be imputing the divine procedure with inconsistency if we suggested that the Creator was not similarly concerned to avoid unnecessarily relying upon extraordinary providence in His maintenance of daylight and the division between day and night?[142]

Proverbs 8 indicates the heavens were in place before the light to Earth's surface, so God used normal means for the light on day one. Proverbs 8:27 says God set the heavens in place. Next Solomon says God marked a horizon circle on the surface of the deep ocean. A horizon is formed by light. So God put the heavens, which were understood as luminaries in the sky, in place as the source of light to Earth.

Simply stated, God normally uses ordinary means. The light on day one was diffuse sunlight penetrating Earth's thick dark cloud cover for the first time.

(**3.4b**) *Young earth creationism undervalues Genesis 2:5–6 that shows God used cause-and-effect means in the third day.* Young earth creationism claims God made dry land out of a watery matrix, followed by plants and trees with miraculous appearance of age, all in the third day. Kline responds by referring to Genesis 2:5: "Now no shrub of the field was yet in the earth, and no plant of the field had yet sprouted, for the LORD God had not sent rain upon the earth." Genesis 1:9 indicates that the land that rose was *yabāshâh*, dry ground. Then Genesis 2:6 says God sent water by the normal means of rain clouds. The implication is that after the ground was watered, then the plants grew. God used normal means to start the plants sprouting from the dry ground—water. "It becomes evident, then, that the 24-hour [all by miracles] view cannot be correct."[143]

Duncan defends the YEC views by responding, "But the question before us presents no real problem, especially if we assume the miraculous."[144]

Kline responds in turn that Genesis 2:5 shows we are unjustified to "assume the miraculous," because in 2:5 God used normal means—water—to cause plants to sprout. God used *both* miracles *and* ordinary providential means in the creation time.

(3.4c) *God used the ordinary means of meat to feed carnivores before the Fall.* Romans 5:12–21 says, "Though one man sin entered into the world, and death through sin, and so death spread to all men because all sinned." The world (*kosmos*) that death entered was the world of men, just as in John 3:16, "For God so loved the world," means the world of humans. Romans 5:12–14 is not about animal death. Genesis 1:29–30 does not say animals ate only plants, just that God gave them *every* green plant to eat, whereas God gave Adam and Eve every seed and fruit-bearing plant to eat. And if the Millennium described in Isaiah 11:6–9 and 65:25 (wolf and lamb together, lion eating straw) is cited, Isaiah 65:20 indicates humans will die, so it would seem animals will die also. So the YEC claim that lions certainly ate straw in Eden seems unsupported by the Bible.

Psalm 104:19–28, about the creation, says that the lions seek their food from God. And 1 Timothy 5:1–4 says do not forbid eating meat. Carnivorism is not evil, so animal death before sin is allowed. Therefore, the Earth and life on it may be older.[145]

(3.5) *The word "day" is heavenly "upper register" language rather than "lower register," so the Genesis 1 days were not literal Earth days.* Kline's third argument for his two claims is "the created cosmos comprises an upper and a lower register, that is, the invisible and the visible dimensions." "The days of Genesis belong to the upper register."[146] "Upper register" means the invisible heavenly realm, and "lower register" means the visible earth and universe. "The days and the evenings and mornings are . . . lower-register language being used metaphorically in descriptions of the upper register."[147] A day "is not literal,"[148] not a twenty-four-hour day-night earth day.

Metaphorical earth days represent God's days. The six days were "nonliteral and nonsequential."[149]

Unsupported Problematic Claims of the Framework Theory

(u-3.0C) *Presuppositionally, Scripture's covenantal purpose, not sequential chronology, is important.* Kline claims, "While Scripture inerrantly reports historical and chronological information it always does so with a covenantal and redemptive historical purpose."[150] The "covenantal" purpose, rather than chronology, is vital.

In response, we recognize that the Bible has theological purposes. Theology is the study of God and His acts. But the Bible tells us about God largely by His acts in history. Kline's claim is the either/or fallacy—either theological purpose or chronological history. But the Bible has both theology *and* chronological history. In fact, the Bible teaches much of its theology *through* chronological history such as the chronologically sequential account of our Lord's preexistence, miraculous conception, humble birth, sinless life, substitutionary death, burial, resurrection, appearances, ascension, and future return. Only rarely (for teaching purposes) are events out of chronological order in the Bible, and none of those are numbered.

(u-3.1) *Genesis 1 is not chronologically sequential.* Kline's first overarching claim of the framework hypothesis is the "nonsequential nature of the narrative."[151] Kline claims that the "account has been shaped, not by a concern to satisfy our curiosity regarding sequence or chronology, but by predominately theological and literary concerns."[152] "The creation of the luminaries, and in particular the solar system, on Day 4 actually coincides with the creation of daylight on Day 1. Thus the text is narrated in a topical rather than a purely seuential order."[153]

I respond that Genesis 1:3–31 was written with each action in each verse beginning with a *waw/vav* consecutive, which is the Hebrew way of saying these events were one after the other, in order.

Technical note – *Waw/vav* Consecutive (conversive, conservative)
(Seminary spelling is *waw*; modern Hebrew pronunciation is *vav*)
- Historical narrative is indicated by a series of *vav* consecutives.
- Each consecutive event begins with a *vav* prefixed initial verb.
- If the first verb is perfect without a *vav*, the following verbs are imperfects (converted to function as additional perfects).
- Example of consecutive successive actions in Genesis 1:
  o 1:1 first act is perfect *bārā'*, "created," without *waw/vav*.
  o 1:3a next act, *vav* prefixed imperfect, *vayomer*, "and said."
  o 1:3b next act, *vav* prefixed imperfect, *vayᵉhi*, "and was."
  o 1:4a next act, *vav* prefixed imperfect, *vayarᵉ*, "and saw," etc.
All acts/events were consecutively one after another, in order.

Contra Kline, the *waw/vav* consecutive clauses show that the six days, and even the events within the six days, were in chronologically consecutive order. The events occurred in the order in which they are listed.

I further respond that if days one and four were the same day, then there were *not six days*. Without six days, Kline's goal—a theological interpretation of six work days followed by a seventh Sabbath rest day—makes no sense.

Finally, how can numbered days in the Bible not be in order?

(u-3.2 & 3.5) ***The Genesis 1 days were not literal earth days but were heavenly "upper register" language.*** Kline's second overarching claim of the framework hypothesis is "the nonliteral . . . nature of the narrative."[154] Kline claims, "The total picture of God's completing His creative work in a week of days is not to be taken literally."[155] "The word *yôm* in Genesis 1 . . . is being used metaphorically to describe an upper-register unit of time that is not defined by the earth's rotation with respect to the sun."[156]

I respond that Genesis 1:3–31 was written with *vav* consecutives indicating historical narrative format. Narrative is not metaphorical (although *later*, a type or allusion can be drawn from the literal events). Therefore, a sequence of numbered days with daylight, evening, night, and morning in a narrative should be understood as normal days.

Kline agrees the light was sunlight. Day one began with literal sunlight, so it was a literal day. It also had an evening beginning a nighttime that ended in the sunlight dawn of morning. It was numbered "day one." That defines a normal day. Kline emphasizes the seventh day as a literal day of rest. If Kline takes the seventh day of rest literally, then he should also take God's six work days literally, or there is no basis for the seventh day of rest.

Although Kline's two overarching claims are unfounded, several of his supporting arguments offer valuable insights into Genesis 1 and 2.

Partially Supported Claim of the Framework Theory

(ps-3.3) *The six "days" are a literary framework in two triads.* Kline helpfully shows the parallelism in the two triads of days. He correctly recognizes that the initial creation was before the six days, so I am adding that initial creation to his diagram:

Kingdom creation			
Genesis 1:1 *ex nihilo* creation			

Creation kingdoms		Creature kings	
Day 1	Light	Day 4	Luminaries
Day 2	Seas[157]	Day 5	Sea creatures
	Skies		Winged creatures
Day 3	Dry land	Day 6	Land animals
	Vegetation		Man

The Creator King	
Day 7	Sabbath

I added his idea of the initial creation before the six days. This arrangement yields a 1-3-3-1 structure—or, if we view the structure by kingdoms, as a 1-5-5-1 structure. These have a total of 7 days or 12 units. In any case, the structure becomes symmetrical.

However, other people have seen this same order, but have not concluded that it proves a nonsequential and nonliteral framework. If anything, this diagram implies orderly chronological progression. The *ex nihilo* creation had to have been first. The light on day one would be needed for life, even though it was at first diffused by overcast cloud cover. Skies were needed before flying creatures, seas were needed before sea creatures, and dry land with vegetation was needed before land animals and man. Finally, the seventh day of rest makes sense as the final day. So we may agree with the diagram, but contra Kline, the diagram fits a sequential chronology quite nicely.

(ps-3.3c) *The framework emphasizes the Sabbath.* "He [Moses] wishes to bring out certain themes and provide a theology of the Sabbath."[158] The theological culmination of the creation is the Sabbath.

There is no doubt that Moses brings out the latent example of the Sabbath. But that was several thousand years after Adam. In its original setting, the point was not the Sabbath, but God as the one and only Creator, Who created the heavens and the earth, the successive "generations of the heavens and the earth," and finally created Adam and Eve, who could know and glorify Him. The Sabbath is so secondary that the word is not even used in anywhere in Genesis. The theological emphasis of creation is God as Creator and His relationship to man, whom God created in His own image.

Largely Supported Claims of the Framework Theory

(s-3.0A & 3.0B) Scripture has priority and is noncontradictory. Kline believes "Scripture has hermeneutical and presuppositional priority over our fallible study of general revelation."[159] Also, Scripture is noncontradictory. "The analogy of Scripture" requires us "to adopt an interpretation of Genesis 1:1—2:3 that does not conflict with Genesis 2:5–6."[160]

I agree with the priority and internal consistency of the Bible. This view is supported, not only presuppositionally, but also by strong evidence.

(s-3.1a) The Bible is silent about the age of Earth. "We must speak where the Bible speaks, and be silent where the Bible is silent. . . . The inspired text, rightly interpreted, is simply silent with regard to the age of the earth and universe."[161]

Kline is correct that the Bible does not tell us the age of either the universe or our Earth. Adam's genealogies tell us only *Adam's* approximate age. Kline leans toward an older universe but claims an *undated* earth creation.

(s-3.1b) Genesis 1 has eight command units. "There are a total of *eight* distinct creative works distributed over *six* days. The last day within each triad (i.e., Days 3 and 6) contains *two* creative acts."[162]

Kline is correct that Genesis 1 has eight distinct command units, two with the last day of each triad of days. We can accept this insight without accepting his nonsequential, nonliteral interpretation.

(s-3.3a & 3.3b) The initial creation in Genesis 1:1 took place before the six days; the YEC claim of creation in day one violates Proverbs 8. "Proverbs 8:22–31 defines 'the beginning' of Genesis 1:1 as the time prior to the progressive fashioning of the world described in the subsequent six days of creation." According to Proverbs 8:22–24, "The

Lᴏʀᴅ possessed me [personified Wisdom] at the beginning. . . . When there were no depths" (NASB).[163]

Kline is correct. The beginning included the time when there were no "depths," so was *before* the "deep" ocean in Genesis 1:2. The "deep" was dark in 1:2. Day one began in Genesis 1:3 by light to that deep dark ocean—day one ending in evening beginning the nighttime, and morning ending the nighttime. So the beginning was before day one, not *in* day one as YEC claims.

(s-3.4) *The Kline Claim: When the Bible does not indicate a miracle, Genesis 2:5–6 shows God probably used ordinary means in the creation era, just as today.* Kline recognizes that God used ordinary providence along with creation miracles during the six days. Kline explains, "Moses demonstrates the tightness of the causal connection (no rain; therefore, no vegetation) in this context."[164] He concludes that we should *presume* that if an event in Genesis 1 or 2 may be interpreted as God using a normal cause-and-effect process, we should interpret the event that way, rather than as a miracle.

I agree that God used both miracles and cause-and-effect means. I would add that it is proper objective hermeneutics to look for *text evidence* identifying which is which.

(s-3.4a) Since God used ordinary means, the light on day one must have been sunlight. If God used rain to grow plants by command three, why not the sun to give light by command one?[165]

The Kline Claim is correct that the Genesis 2:5 principle of ordinary means (rain then plants) implies ordinary means elsewhere in chapter 1, such as sunlight in Genesis 1:3. The Bible text does not indicate that the light God commanded on day one was from an artificial source or that it was temporary light for just three days. That light caused day and night, and the Bible indicates that until the Lord becomes our everlasting light in the future, daylight is from the sun (Isa. 60:19). The assumption, unless the text indicates otherwise, should be the normal means. The norm for daylight is sunlight.

Hugh Ross provides the Biblical explanation for days one and four. (We will study his ideas in detail in chapter 6.) Ross says that God created the sun as part of the heavens in Genesis 1:1. But by the time of 1:2, Earth's deep ocean surface was dark. Job 26:8–9 and 38:9 explain that God covered Earth with thick dark cloud, which blocked out the light of the luminaries. From the Spirit's perspective just above the dark water, at God's command there was light, corresponding to Job 26:10 when God marked out a horizon on the surface of the deep. Sunlight penetrating the thinning cloud of the rotating planet began day-night cycle one on Earth. I have driven my car on foggy mornings along the seacoast. The fog was so thick that I could hardly see the taillights of the car in front of me. But it was daylight in the thick white shimmering fog. That is what day one must have been like. On the second work day the cloud rose from the sea. Job 26:13 describes how God caused the overcast sky to clear. Clear sky on the fourth day allowed the luminaries that had been created in Genesis 1:1 to be in the sky to separate and rule day and night. Therefore, Kline's idea that day one and day four coincide is unnecessary and, in fact, detracts from the sequential clearing of the sky through the first four work days. God used the normal means of sunlight and cloud cover.

If the sunlight was literal, then the days were literal, contra Kline's claim of nonliteral days. Also, if the sunlight penetrated the cloud cover on day one, and on the fourth day the sky cleared so the luminaries separated and ruled day and night, then the days make perfect sense in their stated order. Since the light was sunlight, and Earth's sky progressively cleared, there is no need for the claim that day one and day four were the same day. Kline's claim that the light was sunlight is correct.

(s-3.4b) Young earth creationism undervalues Genesis 2:5–6 that shows God used cause-and-effect means in the third day. Young earth creationism claims that on day three God raised dry land from the water, and then from this land plants miraculously appeared instantaneously or miraculously grew very rapidly.

Kline responds that this young earth creationism claim undervalues Genesis 2:5. God used rain to cause the plants to sprout.

Young earth creationists Duncan and Hall respond, "If the events described were supernatural, then obviously, the text does not refer to the natural process of growth."[166]

Kline says the point of Genesis 2:5 is that there was no vegetation *because* God had not sent rain on the land. After God caused rain, He caused the ground to produce vegetation. Rain followed by plant growth indicates "the natural process of growth." YEC makes an unwarranted assumption of miracles where the Bible does not indicate miracles.

I would respond that the Kline Claim honors the Bible text by recognizing both miracles and means as the text indicates. I would emphasize, and Kline would no doubt agree, that God is sovereign over all events, whether miracles or "natural" means.

<h2 style="text-align:center">Summary of the Framework Theory</h2>

Kline makes five claims. His two overarching claims are "a nonliteral interpretation of the days and a nonsequential ordering of the creative events."[167] Then he backs those two claims with three important lines of evidence.

Before the two overarching claims about the days, Kline says that the very first event of creation was the *ex nihilo* creation of the heavens and the earth in the beginning before the six days. The last event was the Sabbath. Kline says that between the *ex nihilo* creation and the Sabbath, the six "days" of Genesis 1 are nonsequential and nonliteral. Nonsequential and nonliteral interpretation of the six days are the two overarching claims of the framework theory.

There are three evidences for these two overarching claims. First, the six days are in a symmetrical literary framework of two triads of days. So days one and four are really the same day.

Second, Genesis 2:5–6 demonstrates that when a miracle is not indicated, God probably used ordinary providential cause-and-effect means. Genesis 2:5 explains: no rain, no plants; rain, then plants. Light without the sun does not fit the Genesis 2:5 principle. The reasonable source of the diffuse light in Genesis 1:3 was the sun.

Third, since Earth may be older, the "days" were metaphorical "lower register" days describing "upper register" heavenly realities. So the "days" were not literal days on Earth. They may have been billions of years, millions of years, or even twenty-four hours in the lower earth register of time.

Conclusions about the Framework Theory

Kline claimed nonsequential days. I responded that if days one and four are the same day, then there were not six work days, the very point of his six work days and one Sabbath day argument. Six normal days would support the Sabbath much better than nonsequential days.

Kline also claimed nonliteral days. I responded that a numbered day with daylight, evening, nighttime, and morning in historical narrative means a normal day.

Kline has given us several helpful insights into the Bible's creation texts. Although the two overarching claims have fallen short, several of his lines of evidence are highly insightful. He points out that Proverbs 8:22–31 says "the beginning" when God created Earth (Gen. 1:1) was "when there were no depths." There were dark ocean depths by the time of Genesis 1:2, so "In the beginning" was before 1:2 and so was *before* the six days of 1:3–31. God created the heavens and earth before the six days. That means the Bible is silent about Earth's age. The order of creation events was heavens, Earth, deep ocean, and then the six days.

Another outstanding contribution is the Kline Claim: When the Bible does not indicate a miracle, Genesis 2:5–6 (no rain, no plants; rain, then plants sprouted) shows God probably used ordinary means in the creation era, just as today. Therefore, the light on day one was normal sunlight from the sun created in Genesis 1:1.

These insights seem to fit the Bible's creation texts. We can carry these very helpful insights over into the unified theory.

3. Literary Framework Theory

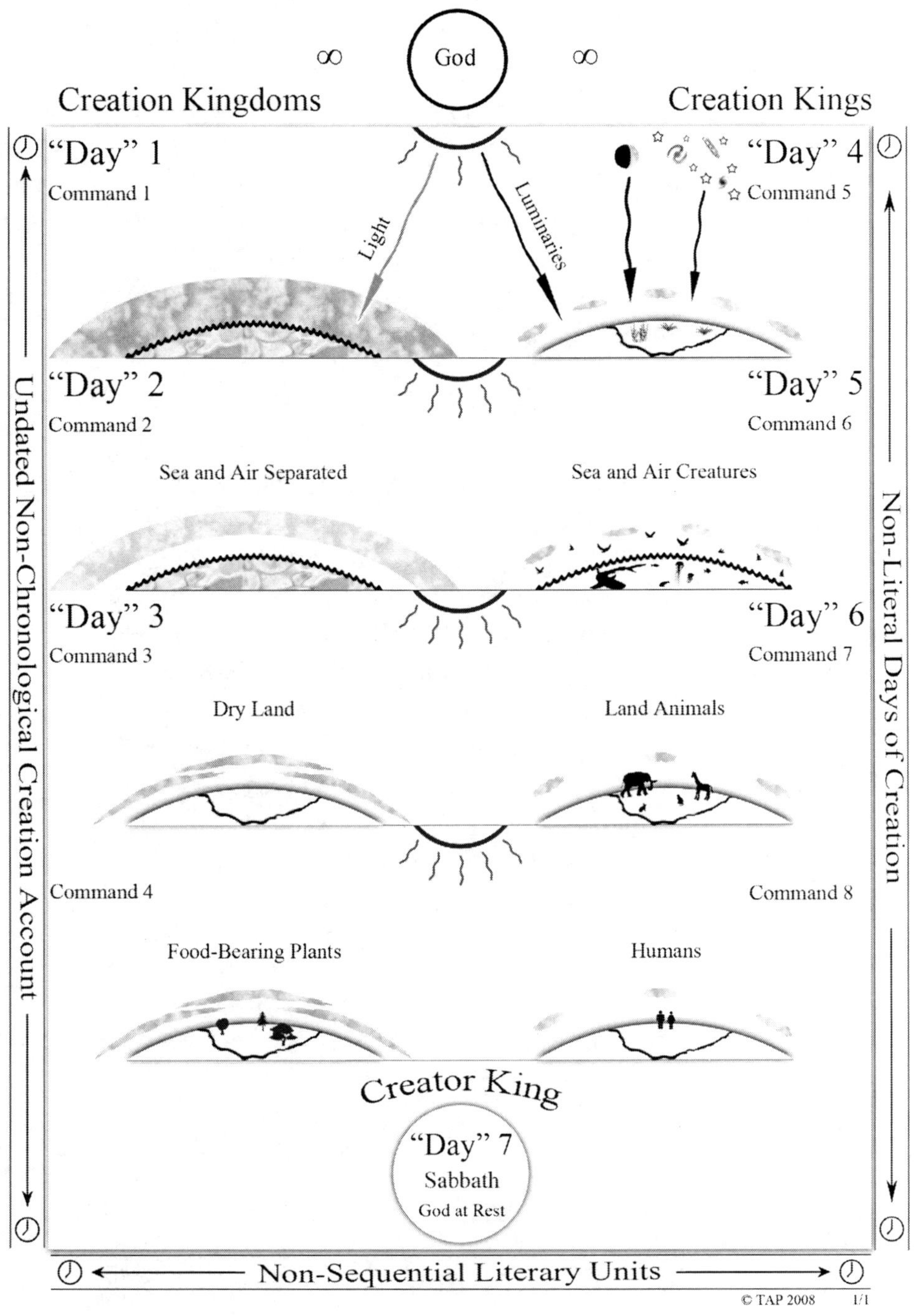

3. Claims of the Literary Framework Theory
(Biblically supported claims in non-italics **bold,** unsupported in *italics*)

(3.0A) Presuppositionally, **Scripture has priority over science.**

(3.0B) Presuppositionally, **Scripture will not contradict itself.**

(3.0C) Presuppositionally, covenantal purpose *trumps chronology.*

(3.1) Genesis 1 is not chronologically sequential.

> **(3.1a) The Bible is silent about the age of Earth.**

> **(3.1b) Genesis 1 has eight command units.**

> *(3.1c) Genesis 1 is in topical order, not in sequential chronological order.*

> *(3.1d) Day one and day four were simultaneous.*

> **(3.1e) The Sabbath is in sequential chronological order.**

(3.2) The days in Genesis 1 were not literal.

> (3.2a) The Bible gives symbolic meaning to some numbers.

> *(3.2b) The "days" were metaphorical.*

(3.3) The six "days" are a literary framework **in two triads.**

> **(3.3a) The initial creation in Genesis 1:1 was before six days.**

> **(3.3b) YEC claim—beginning was in day one—is incorrect.**

> (3.3c) The framework emphasizes the Sabbath.

(3.4) The Kline claim: God used both miracles and means.

> **(3.4a) The light on day one must have been sunlight.**

> **(3.4b) YEC undervalues God using means in creation.**

> (3.4c) God used the ordinary means of meat to feed carnivores before the Fall.

(3.5) The "days" are upper register heavenly days, not lower register literal days.

Major Supported Claims from the Creation Theories

The Correct Translation of Genesis 1:1: "In the beginning God created the heavens and the earth." It is *incorrect* to translate 1:1 as "When God began to create."

The Waltke Merism: "The heavens and the earth" meant the entire orderly universe.

The Waltke Exclusion Principle: If there was preexisting chaos, there was no *ex nihilo* creation of the organized heavens and earth. The converse is also logically possible: If there was *ex nihilo* creation of the organized heavens and earth, then there was no unorganized chaos.

The Heiser Clause Analysis: Begin analyzing creation by determining which clauses (especially in Gen. 1:1–3) are independent clauses and which are dependent clauses, and then which independent clauses are modified by which dependent clauses, and so how they fit together.

The Kline Order: Proverbs 8:22–31 says that "the beginning," when God created Earth (Gen. 1:1), was "when there were no depths." Ocean depths existed by 1:2, so "In the beginning" was before 1:2 and before the six days. Creation order: Heavens, Earth, sea, then six days.

The Kline Claim: When the Bible does not indicate a miracle, Genesis 2:5–6 (no rain, no plants; rain, then plants sprouted) shows God probably used ordinary means in the creation era, just as today.

A Generational Genesis: The worldview of Genesis was generations. The six begetting (literal) days of Genesis 1 introduced the most ancient generations of all—"the generations of the heavens and the earth."[168]

Chapter 4

Theory 4
Initial Chaos Theory

In the beginning eternal God created everything out of nothing.

Mark Rooker explains the initial chaos creation theory with its five positive and two negative claims.[169] The five positive claims are: Genesis 1:1 was the initial creation by God. Creation was *ex nihilo,* out of nothing. *Tōhû vᵃbōhû* in Genesis 1:2 meant chaos, unformed matter, or desolate Earth. Earth's *tōhû vᵃbōhû* condition was how God created it in 1:1. Then God transformed the chaos or desolation into our orderly planet in six days.

In a nutshell, the initial chaos theory says that in the beginning God created the heavens and the earth out of nothing. But the world God created in 1:1 was chaotic or desolate. So God transformed it into the orderly cosmos in six days.

The initial chaos theory is an umbrella theory including both old earth creationism and young earth creationism. It is an umbrella theory also having versions claiming three levels of chaos. One version holds a strong view of chaos—in Genesis 1:1 God created the universe as chaos.

A second version of the initial chaos theory is modern young earth scientific creationism (chapter 5). The YEC version claims that in Genesis 1:1 God created unformed matter *in* day one of the six days. This YEC version holds a medium view of chaos—*tōhû vᵃbōhû* applied to the universe, which was unformed matter, but perhaps not quite utter chaos. We will study these two views of initial chaos first.

A third version is the traditional initial (not-really-chaos) creation theory. This traditional view, held by Rooker, claims that the initial *ex nihilo* creation of the heavens and desolate empty Earth "could merely refer to the *first stage* of creation" (emphasis Rooker's).[170] This third version holds a mild sense of chaos (not even really chaos). The desolation applied only to Earth. Then Earth was completed in the six days. Some advocates of this third version accept that the initial creation took place in the beginning before the six days. (The unified theory in chapter 11 picks up this idea of two stages of creation—an initial creation of the heavens and desolate lifeless Earth, then the six days' work on Earth. The unified theory is even further from chaos, holding a no-chaos view with a lifeless unfinished Earth.) Rooker's third version of the initial (not-really-chaos) creation theory seems to have been the view of Calvin and Luther.[171] At the end of this chapter, we will review Rooker's mild view.

The initial chaos creation theory also has two negative claims: First, *tōhû v*ᵃ*bōhû* was not a condition *before* Genesis 1:1 as claimed by the pre-creation chaos theory (theory 1). Second, *tōhû v*ᵃ*bōhû* was not a change *after* Genesis 1:1 as claimed by the gap theory (theory 9).

The idea of the negative claims is that if chaos can be disproved *before* Genesis 1:1 and *after* Genesis 1:1, then chaos must have been the condition *during* Genesis 1:1. All versions of the initial chaos theory claim that God created—whether chaos, unformed matter, or an unfinished empty-of-life Earth—*during* Genesis 1:1 in an initial *ex nihilo* creation. First, we will consider the strong and medium (YEC) versions of the initial chaos theory. Rooker explains both these stronger versions and his preferred milder version. So I will quote him here, but reserve his own version to the end of the chapter.

Preunderstanding of the Initial Chaos Theory

(4.0A) *Chaos is assumed.* The initial chaos theory assumes chaos. And since there was chaos, the three chaos theories can be compared—the pre-creation chaos theory, the initial chaos theory, and the gap theory. The question asked is *when* chaos took place—before Genesis 1:1 (pre-creation chaos theory), during 1:1 (initial chaos theory), or after 1:1 (gap theory).[172]

Claims of Strong and Medium Versions of Initial Chaos Theory

(4.1) *God created all unformed matter* **during** *the Genesis 1:1 initial creation.* God created everything *during* the initial creation in Genesis 1:1. Then verse 2 provides "a description of this original creation."[173] The *tōhû vᵃbōhû* world described in 1:2 was what God created *during* Genesis 1:1.

(4.2) *The initial creation was* **ex nihilo,** *out of nothing.* All versions of the initial chaos theory strongly affirm *ex nihilo* ("out of nothing") creation. "The key difference between pagan cosmogonies and Genesis 1 is *creatio ex nihilo* and the absence of preexisting matter."[174] All versions of the initial chaos creation theory reject preexisting matter and strongly affirm *ex nihilo* creation.

The Rooker Reaffirmation: "The key difference between pagan cosmogonies and Genesis 1 is *creatio ex nihilo* and the absence of preexisting matter."

(4.3) Tōhû vᵃbōhû meant chaos or chaotic unformed matter. The strong version says *tōhû vᵃbōhû*, or "without form and void," in Genesis 1:2 meant chaos. The medium version says the phrase meant unformed matter.[175]

(4.4) *So tōhû vᵃbōhû in Genesis 1:2 described the condition of the chaotic initial creation that came about* during *(not before or after) Genesis 1:1.* The phrase *tōhû vᵃbōhû* in Genesis 1:2 provides a "description of this original creation mentioned in verse 1." Simply stated, God created chaos or unformed matter *during* Genesis 1:1.

(4.5) *God transformed the chaos or unorganized matter into the organized cosmos in six days.* The initial disorder was transformed into order in the six days.

The next two claims are the negative claims. The initial chaos creation theory denies that *tōhû vᵃbōhû* was the condition *before* Genesis 1:1 (the pre-creation chaos theory) or a change from order to chaos *after* Genesis 1:1 (the gap theory).

(4.6) *Four major claims of Waltke's pre-creation chaos theory err.* Rooker explains that four major claims of Waltke's precreation chaos and title theory are incorrect:

First, Waltke's pre-creation chaos theory claims Genesis 1:1 is only a title or summary statement.

Rooker responds that if 1:1 were a title or summary statement, then 1:2 would start the narrative. But 1:2 begins with "and." "No historical narrative begins with 'and' (vs. 2)."[176] Genesis 1:1 is not a title but was the actual *ex nihilo* creation. Then 1:2 describes the Earth that had been created in 1:1.

Second, Waltke's pre-creation chaos theory claims that *bārā'* in Genesis 1:1 was not *ex nihilo* creation (creation "out of nothing").

Rooker responds that God is the acting subject of *bārā'*, "create." "The primary emphasis of the word is on the novelty of the created object," so "the word [*bārā'*] lends itself well to the concept of creation *ex nihilo*." Genesis 1:1 does not even hint at any preexisting material. Rooker points out that the famous Rabbi Nahmanides wrote, "We have in our holy language no other term for the bringing forth of something out of nothing but *bara*."[177] Together the two words *bᵉrē'shît* ("in the beginning") with *bārā'* ("create") indicate that in the beginning God created that which was new.

This creation *ex nihilo* is explicitly stated in Hebrews 11:3.

Third, Waltke's pre-creation chaos theory claims that Genesis 1:2 describes something bad—orderless chaos and darkness. God could not have created something bad—orderless chaos or darkness. So orderless chaos and darkness preexisted.

Rooker responds that the "the phrase תֹהוּ וָבֹהוּ [*tōhû vᵃbōhû*] need not be understood as an orderless chaos as Waltke claims, but that the earth was not yet ready to be inhabited by mankind."[178] As for darkness, God named the light "day," but He equally named the darkness "night." He treated the two equally. The darkness was not evil. Rooker continues, "Isaiah 45:7 states God created the darkness." Waltke confuses physical darkness with its symbolic connotation of evil. God actually created the unfinished dark Earth in 1:1.[179]

Fourth, Waltke's pre-creation chaos theory claims that the Israelite view of creation was different from ANE cosmogonies, yet both according to Waltke began with pre-creation chaos.

Rooker responds that one of the profound differences between Genesis 1:1 and pagan cosmologies is the very thing Waltke denies—the *ex nihilo* creation—creation out of nothing. The Bible does not say God made everything out of pre-creation chaos as Waltke claims. The Bible says God created all things. Since He created all things, there was no uncreated pre-creation material. Therefore, He created all things *ex nihilo,* out of nothing (Gen. 1:1; Heb. 11:3).

Rooker concludes that these four claims of Waltke's pre-creation chaos theory err. Pre-creation chaos did not exist together with God. Eternal God existed alone before He created all things out of nothing in Genesis 1:1. The pre-creation chaos theory is incorrect.

(4.7) *The gap in the gap theory conflicts with Hebrew grammar.* Among conservative Christians in the first three quarters of the twentieth century, the gap theory was the main competitor to the initial chaos creation theory and its modern offshoot, young earth scientific creationism.

Pember's gap theory (chapter 9) states, "Genesis 1:1 refers to the original creation of the universe, and sometime after this original creation Satan rebelled against God and was cast from heaven to the earth. As a result of Satan's making his habitation on the earth, the earth was judged. God's original creation was then placed under judgment, and the result of this judgment is the state described in Genesis 1:2: Earth was 'formless and void'[180]".(תֹּהוּ וָבֹהוּ Earth "became" chaos *after* Genesis 1:1. Then God re-created Earth in the six days, but He left in Earth's rocks the fossils from the judgment.

Rooker, like Waltke, responds that there was no time gap or events at Genesis 1:2 as the gap theory claims. The "and" beginning 1:2 is a *vav/waw* disjunctive that tells us that 1:2 is a description of Earth after its creation, not an action or event in which Earth "became" chaos. This grammar shows that Earth did not *become* chaos as the gap theory claims. All Genesis 1:2 does is describe Earth's condition after its creation in 1:1. Rooker says, "The gap theory should no longer be considered a viable option in explaining the meaning of Genesis 1:1–3. The view is grammatically suspect, and Scripture is silent on the idea that Earth was judged when Satan fell. Waltke's critique of the gap theory is devastating. . . . Scripture nowhere states that God judged the world when Saan fell."[181]

God did not simply fix pre-creation chaos that already existed from *before* Genesis 1:1 (pre-creation chaos theory). God did not *re*-create from gap chaos *after* Genesis 1:1 (gap theory). So the initial chaos creation theory must be the last chaos theory standing. Therefore, Rooker concludes that the initial chaos theory must be correct—that God created chaos or unformed matter *during* Genesis 1:1.

The two alternative theories have fatal flaws.

The pre-creation chaos theory errs in
claiming no *bārā'* creation in 1:1.

The gap theory errs in claiming earth became chaos in 1:2.

Unsupported Assumption and Claim of Initial Chaos Creation

Before we evaluate the claims of the initial chaos creation theory, a very interesting situation arises from comparing Waltke's defense with Rooker's defense. Both men compare three chaos theories to see which is the last chaos theory standing. They compare pre-creation chaos *before* Genesis 1:1, initial chaos *during* Genesis 1:1, and the gap theory that Earth became chaos *after* Genesis 1:1.

Waltke shows that the initial chaos theory and the gap theory are both incorrect. Rooker in turn shows that Waltke's pre-creation chaos theory and the gap theory are both incorrect. Also, Waltke and Kline show that the young earth scientific creationism theory (in the next chapter) has a fundamental error. This suggests that none of the theories so far has put together all the right components in a way that agrees with the Bible's creation data.

That will be our goal in chapter 11. But we have six more major theories to examine first. Back to the initial chaos creation theory:

(u-4.0A) *Chaos is assumed.* The strong and medium versions of the initial chaos creation theory especially assume chaos.

In response to these stronger chaos versions, Rooker himself recognizes that *tōhû vᵃbōhû* does not really mean chaos. The two other uses of *tōhû* and *bōhû* in the Bible do not mean chaos. Isaiah prophesied the conquest of Edom (Isa. 34:11), and Jeremiah sorrowfully predicted the conquest of Judah (Jer. 4:23). Both lands would become *tōhû* and *bōhû*. They were conquered, but they did not become orderless chaos. Rooker says that *tōhû* and *bōhû* means "a desert-like place" and "empty."[182] Earth was desolate and empty of life. Genesis 1:2 does *not* say Earth was chaos, and certainly does not say the universe was chaos.

I would go even further from chaos than Rooker. God did not ever create any chaos. Chaos implies lack of control. God is sovereign over all things "according to His purpose who works all things after the counsel of His will" (Eph. 1:11, NASB). God created the orderly heavens. Earth was still unfinished in 1:2, but it was precisely right for that stage in God's plans. There was no chaos.

(u-4.3) Tōhû vᵃbōhû *meant chaos or unformed matter.* The strong view of chaos claims *tōhû vᵃbōhû* meant chaos or chaotic unformed matter.

In response, *tōhû vᵃbōhû* does not mean chaos. In Deuteronomy 32:10, Moses used *tōhû* as a "howling wilderness." *Tōhû* may be understood as an uninhabitable desolation and *bōhû* as emptiness, particularly empty of life like the rocky wilderness of Edom. Edom after its conquest became *tōhû vᵃbōhû*. I crossed part of Edom by camel. It takes great human ingenuity to gather water for life in the Edom desert of stone and sand. Even today, only a few amazingly desert-skilled Bedouin live there. Once Edom was conquered and the humans gone, Edom became empty of life. In Genesis 1:2, the *tōhû vᵃbōhû* Earth was a very seriously uninhabitable planet, but Earth was not orderless chaos.

Major Hebrew scholars including Bruce Waltke, Gordon Wenham, and Brevard Childs explain that the merism "heavens and earth" indicates order.[183] Nehemiah 9:6 speaks of God making the heavens in orderly array, like a host of soldiers: "You have made the heavens, The heaven of heavens with all their host" (NASB). A host referred to an army of soldiers in orderly array before a battle, not in chaos. The psalmist gives praise "To Him who made the heavens with skill" (Ps. 136:5, NASB). God the Creator making something with skill does not produce chaos.

Perhaps most telling of all is Paul's explanation: "Since the creation of the world His invisible attributes, His eternal power and divine nature, have been clearly seen, being understood through what has been made" (Rom. 1:19–20, NASB). God has continually revealed His invisible attributes through what He made "since the creation of the world." The creation *from its inception* has been a continual revelation of God's attributes. So if God created the world in the beginning as chaos, then His invisible attribute would be chaos. That is obviously false. God created the heavens in orderly array according to His purpose and plan from the beginning. He revealed His invisible attributes of orderliness and purpose. Even Earth was not created as chaos, but rather unfinished until God finished it by the progressive stages of His work in the six days. An invisible characteristic of God is that He often does His work in purposefully planned stages. We speak of the "progress of redemption." The Bible progressively reveals the promise after the Fall, the sacrificial system, Christ's death and resurrection, and the consummation when sin will be done away with. God often does His plan in stages. God created Earth in an unfinished condition as a first stage of His work. There was no chaos.

Partially Supported Claims of the Initial Chaos Theory

(ps-4.1) *God created all unformed matter* during *the initial creation in Genesis 1:1.* The initial chaos theory claims that verse 2 describes the results of the initial creation.[184] Genesis 1:1 was the initial *ex nihilo* creation of chaos or unformed matter in space.

The Bible affirms that Genesis 1:1 was the initial creation. Up to that point, the initial chaos creation theory is correct. The problem is the claim that what He created was chaos. God did not create chaos because *tōhû vᵃbōhû* does not mean chaos.

(ps-4.5) *God transformed the chaos or chaotic matter into the organized cosmos in six days.* The initial chaos creation theory claims God transformed the chaotic unformed matter into order during the six days of Genesis 1:3–31.

Most creationists agree that God worked six days. However, if *tōhû vᵃbōhû* does not mean chaos, then transforming chaos into cosmos is an overstatement. Also Genesis 1:2 says, "Now the earth was *tōhû vᵃbōhû*," so all that needed transforming was unfinished Earth. What God transformed in six days was not a chaotic universe but rather the unfinished Earth.

Supported Claims of the Initial Chaos Theory

(s-4.2) The initial creation was *ex nihilo*, out of nothing. All versions of the initial chaos theory claim an *ex nihilo* creation.

Rooker is correct; God created all things. Therefore *ex nihilo* creation is implied or affirmed in Genesis 1:1, 2:4a; Psalm 33:6; Isaiah 42:5, 45:18; John 1:3; Ephesians 3:9; Colossians 1:16; Hebrews 1:2, 11:3; Revelation 4:11, 10:6, and 14:7.

(s-4.4) *Tōhû vᵃbōhû* in Genesis 1:2 described the condition of the initial creation that came about during (not before or after) Genesis 1:1. The initial chaos view understands that the phrase *tōhû vᵃbōhû* in Genesis 1:2 provides a "description of this original creation mentioned in verse 1."

Rooker is correct. The *tōhû vᵃbōhû* condition of Earth in Genesis 1:2 resulted from the creation in 1:1.

(s-4.6) Four major claims of Waltke's pre-creation chaos theory err. Mark Rooker identifies four problematic claims of the pre-creation chaos theory (chaos *before* Gen. 1:1): (1) Genesis 1:1 was only a summary statement; (2) *bārā'* in Genesis 1:1 was *not* creation out of nothing; (3) Genesis 1:2 describes something bad, implying it was not created by God but preexisted; and (4) the Israelite view of creation was different from ANE cosmogonies, yet both supposedly began the same way—with chaos.[185]

Rooker's critique of Waltke's pre-creation chaos theory is outstanding. Waltke is incorrect. Rooker is correct that God created *ex nihilo* the heavens and the earth in the beginning.

(s-4.7) The gap in the gap theory conflicts with Hebrew grammar. After the initial creation, the gap theory claims a first creation during Genesis 1:2 of land, plants, animals, and pre-Adamite proto-humans. Then they claim the fall of Lucifer into sin, Lucifer leading the "pre-Adamites" into sin, and finally God's judgment of Earth and the destruction of all life, all in Genesis 1:2.

Mark Rooker, Weston Fields, and others have shown that this "gap" in the gap theory is incorrect.[186] The gap theory translates the verb in Genesis 1:2 as "became," describing an action or event. "And earth <u>became</u> *tōhû vᵃbōhû*." This translation is not supported by Hebrew grammar. The verb is correctly translated "was."

Rooker responds that all the supposed events in 1:2 are based on silence. Neither the gap nor the judgment are in Genesis 1:2. (Lucifer's fall and his judgment by God are in the Bible, but not during Genesis 1:2.) Neither the Hebrew grammar nor the actual words of Genesis 1:2 support the gap. There was no gap. The only *re*-creation is future—the new heavens and new earth.[187]

Claims of an Initial Mild Chaos Creation
(Leaning toward Two-Stage?)

Mark Rooker titles his theory "The Initial Chaos Theory,"[188] yet, based on his Bible study, his personal conclusions are much milder than the strong chaos position. Also, he seems to lean toward a proto two-stage creation position.

I have not added a response section to Rooker but have inserted occasional responses at the end of some of his initial mild chaos creation claims. I am numbering his view **4M** for **m**ild chaos or **M**ark Rooker.

(4M.1) *God created the universe* during *the Genesis 1:1 initial creation.* Rooker says, "Proponents of the initial chaos theory maintain that Genesis 1:1 refers to the original creation."[189] The heavens and the unfinished Earth did not come into existence before or after Genesis 1:1, but *during* Genesis 1:1.

(4M.2) *The initial creation was* **ex nihilo***, out of nothing.* Rooker emphasizes, "The key difference between pagan cosmogonies and Genesis 1 is *creatio ex nihilo* and the absence of preexisting matter."[190]

(4M.2a) *The initial creation in Genesis 1:1 was a first stage of creation.* Rooker says, "The phrase ['the heavens and the earth'] could merely refer to a *first stage* of creation" (emphasis his). He continues, "This idea that Genesis 1:1 refers to the first stage in God's creative activity might be supported by the context, which clearly reveals that God intended to create the universe in progressive stages."[191]

(4M.2b) *That first stage was either in day one or in the beginning before the six days.* Although he does not emphasize the point, Rooker says, "The heavens and the earth were created on the first day of God's creative activity."[192] However, he quotes Tsumura, who sees the initial creation as a first stage resulting in the description in 1:2 of "earth's unlivable and empty condition before these six days."[193]

(4M.3) **Tōhû vᵃbōhû** *meant "desolate and empty,"* **not chaos.** Rooker explains, "Making the earth habitable for man is the purpose of the account [of the six days] by improving on the earth's initial status as desolate and empty." Tsumura says *tōhû vᵃbōhû* meant "uninhabitable" or "a desert-like place" and "empty."[194] Rooker himself provides the excellent translation, "desolate and empty."[195]

(4M.4) **Tōhû vᵃbōhû in *Genesis 1:2 described the condition of the desolate Earth that came about during (not before or after) Genesis 1:1.*** The phrase *tōhû vᵃbōhû* in Genesis 1:2 provides a "description of this original creation mentioned in verse 1." God created the heavens and desolate empty Earth *during* Genesis 1:1.

(4M.4a) *Only planet Earth is described in Genesis 1:2 as "desolate and empty."* Rooker quotes Tsumura, "The author in v. 2 focuses not on the 'heaven' but on the 'earth' . . . as 'still' not being the earth which they all are familiar with."[196] "This [two triads of days forming and filling the desolate and empty earth] supports the claim that תֹהוּ וָבֹהוּ [tōhû vābōhû] is restricted to the earth's unlivable and empty condition before these six days."[197]

Rooker also quotes Cassuto, who explains, "The construction וְהָאָרֶץ הָיְתָה תֹהוּ וָבֹהוּ wᵉhāʾāreṣ hāᵊytāʰ ṭōhû wāḇōhû ["and the earth was *tōhû vᵃbōhû*"] proves . . . that *v.* 2 begins a new subject."[198] That new subject of 1:2 is "Now the earth." Genesis 1:2 clearly specifies that Earth, not the heavens and earth, was *tōhû vᵃbōhû.* So Genesis 1:2 changes the focus to Earth. God's six work days would transform Earth into our familiar planet fit for humans.

Rooker correctly recognizes that Genesis 1:2 applied *tōhû vᵃbōhû* only to Earth. John Calvin also applies these words to our world, apparently meaning Earth: "Undoubtedly Moses placed them [the two words *tōhû vᵃbōhû*] both in opposition to all those created objects which pertain to the form, the ornament and the perfection of the world."[199] Our world, not the universe, was *tōhû vᵃbōhû.*

I, too, agree that the grammar of Genesis 1:2 indicates that *tōhû vᵃbōhû* described the condition of Earth as it was by the end of 1:1.

(4M.5) ***God transformed the "desolate and empty" Earth in six days into our present Earth fit for humans.*** God used "progressive stages"[200] in the creation. "Genesis 1:2 states the condition of earth as it was when it was first created until God began to form it into the present world."[201] "He did not leave the earth in the initial state." This "state He then transformed (vv. 3–31) to make the earth into a place that could be inhabited by man."[202] In the six days, "God converted the uninhabitable land into a land fit for man."[203] Although he does not say it explicitly, Rooker may imply that the six days may have formed a second stage of God's creation work.

(4M.6) ***Four major claims of Waltke's pre-creation chaos theory err.*** The pre-creation chaos theory errs in its four claims.[204]

Rooker demonstrates that the pre-creation chaos theory is incorrect. Genesis 1:1 was the *ex nihilo* creation. At the end of the Genesis 1:1 time, Earth was simply desolate and empty of life.

(**4M.7**) *The gap in the gap theory "conflicts with Hebrew grammar."* Rooker is correct that the Hebrew Bible does not support the gap in the gap theory.

Mark Rooker holds a mild form of the initial chaos creation theory and seems to lean toward a proto two-stage creation. Perhaps being Biblical simply leads toward two-stage creation.

Summary of the Initial Chaos Creation Theory

In Genesis 1:1, in the beginning God created everything from nothing. God created *ex nihilo* a chaotic desolate world. Genesis 1:2 describes the *tōhû vᵃbōhû* condition of the world as it was formed *during* Genesis 1:1. In Genesis 1:3–31, God transformed that initial chaotic condition into the organized world in the six days.

The initial creation theory denies that *tōhû vᵃbōhû* was the condition *before* Genesis 1:1 (the pre-creation chaos theory) or *after* Genesis 1:1 (the gap theory). Instead, God produced the condition described in Genesis 1:2 *during* the Genesis 1:1 creation.

Conclusions about the Initial Chaos Creation Theory

I responded that if we remove the idea of chaos from this theory, we have begun to gather an outline that will go into our unified creation theory. The unified two stage Biblical creation theory (chapter 11) recognizes that God created *ex nihilo* the heavens and the earth in the beginning. *Tōhû vᵃbōhû* describes Earth as desolate and empty of life. Genesis 1:2b indicates that Earth was also dark and sea covered. 2SBC agrees that God worked six days making Earth lighted, habitable, with land, and inhabited.

4. Initial Chaos Creation Theory

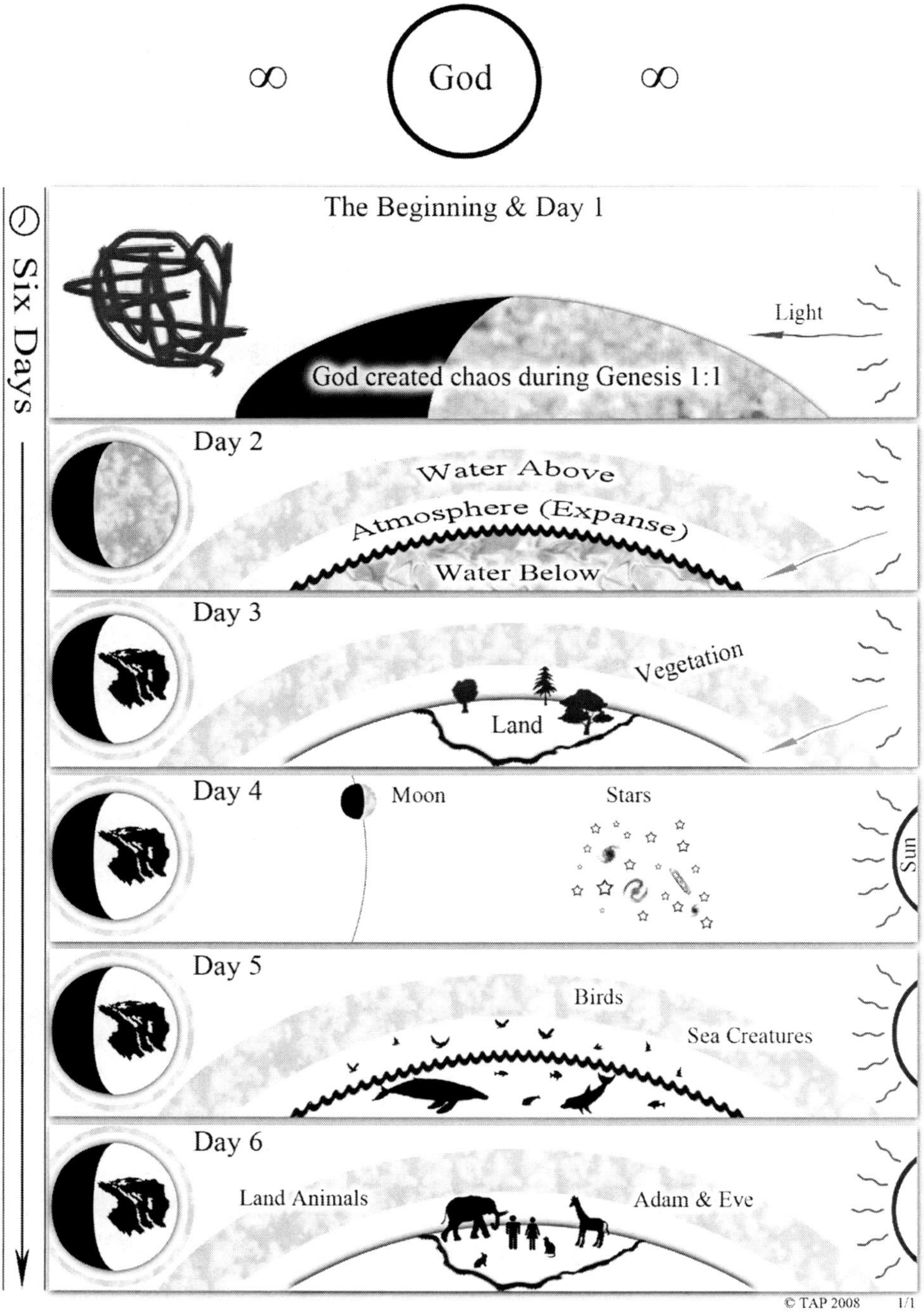

4. Claims of the Initial Chaos Creation Theory
(Biblically supported claims in non-italics **bold,** unsupported in *italics*)

Initial Strong Chaos Creation Version
(4.1) God created all *unformed chaotic* **matter during Genesis 1:1.**

(4.2) The initial creation was *ex nihilo,* **out of nothing.**

(4.3) Tōhû v^abōhû meant chaos or unformed matter throughout dark space.

(4.4) The *tōhû v^abōhû* **condition came about during Genesis 1:1.**

(4.5) God transformed *the chaos* **into organized cosmos in six days.**

(4.6) Four big claims of Waltke's pre-creation chaos theory err.

(4.7) The gap in the gap theory conflicts with Hebrew grammar.

Mark Rooker's Initial Mild Chaos Creation Version
(4M.1) God created the universe during the Genesis 1:1 creation.

(4M.2) The initial creation was *ex nihilo,* **out of nothing.**

(4M.2a) The initial creation in 1:1 was a first stage of creation.

(4M.2b) That first stage was *either in day one or* **in the beginning.**

(4M.3) *Tōhû v^abōhû* **meant "desolate and empty," not chaos.**

(4M.4) The *tōhû v^abōhû* **condition came about during 1:1.**

(4M.4a) In 1:2, only planet Earth was "desolate and empty."

(4M.5) God transformed "desolate and empty" Earth in six days.

(4M.6) Four big claims of Waltke's pre-creation chaos theory err.

(4M.7) The gap in the gap theory conflicts with Hebrew grammar.

<h2 style="text-align:center">Major Supported Claims from the Creation Theories</h2>

The Correct Translation of Genesis 1:1: Waltke affirms the traditional translation of Genesis 1:1: "In the beginning God created the heavens and the earth." It is *incorrect* to translate 1:1 as "When God began to create."

Waltke Merism: "The heavens and the earth" meant the entire orderly universe.

The Waltke Exclusion Principle: If there was preexisting chaos, there was no *ex nihilo* creation of the organized heavens and earth. The converse is also logically possible: If there was *ex nihilo* creation of the organized heavens and earth, then there was no unorganized chaos.

The Kline Order: Proverbs 8:22–31 says that "the beginning," when God created Earth (Gen. 1:1), was "when there were no depths." Ocean depths existed by 1:2, so "In the beginning" was before 1:2 and before the six days. Creation order: Heavens, Earth, sea, then six days.

The Kline Claim: When the Bible does not indicate a miracle, Genesis 2:5–6 (no rain, no plants; rain, then plants sprouted) shows God probably used ordinary means in the creation era, just as today.

A Generational Genesis: The worldview of Genesis was generations. The six begetting (literal) days of Genesis 1 introduced the most ancient generations of all—"the generations of the heavens and the earth."

The Rooker Reaffirmation: "The key difference between pagan cosmogonies and Genesis 1 is *creatio ex nihilo* and the absence of preexisting matter."[205]

Chapter 5

Theory 5
Young Earth Scientific Creationism Theory

"Thousands, not millions!" YEC

The young earth scientific creationism theory has ten main claims, like a mighty bridge built on ten supporting pier columns, spanning the troubled waters of chance-driven macroevolution. Nine of the supporting pier columns are concrete and steel sunk deep into the bedrock of God's Word. But one lacks Biblical support. The advocates of this theory desire to be Biblical. In honor of that desire, I will explain why one YEC main claim lacks Biblical support. It is the missing bridge column. This one main claim is Biblically unsupported, not just in my opinion, but in the studies of other Bible scholars. This one support column needs to be replaced by a solid column that is Biblically sound. In this chapter, we will identify this one Biblically unsupported claim. I will seek to correct it in the unified theory. Apart from this unsupported main claim and its many subclaim props, the young earth scientific creationism theory has made many major contributions to creation studies. Nine of its ten main claims are sound contributions that I will include in the unified theory.

In a nutshell, the unique claim of young earth creationism is that *in day one* God created the heavens as space, and earth as unformed matter. Based on Exodus 20:11, all creation was *"in* six days." Because Adam is dated about 6,000 years ago, and the heavens and earth were created a few days earlier *in* the six days, the universe is also about 6,000 years old.

In 1961, Henry M. Morris, a professor of hydrologic (fluids) engineering, and John C. Whitcomb, a professor of Old Testament, published *The Genesis Flood,* launching the modern young earth scientific creationism movement.[206] I have met and discussed creation cordially with both men, and I honor them as pioneers in creation theory. Above all others, Henry Morris, by his lectures and books, has been foundational in my thinking on creation. I explained my theory in its early form to John Whitcomb, and although he did not express full agreement with my one major change from the YEC theory, he was quite supportive. I deeply respect these founders. In pointing out their Biblically unsupported claim, with its consequent subclaims, I am honoring the Bible they honor and respectfully building on their work.

This modern young earth scientific creationism movement has two big claims, like the two central piers of the great bridge. First, the six days were literal normal days. A number of the other theories also affirm six normal days. Six normal day-night days has an old and honorable heritage in the church and before that in Jewish tradition. Six literal days is important, but it is *not unique* to modern young earth scientific creationism.

Second, the unique claim of modern young earth scientific creationism is that the initial *ex nihilo* creation was *in* day one, based on "For *in* six days . . ." of Exodus 20:11: "For *in* six days the LORD made heaven and earth, the sea, and all that in them *is*, and rested the seventh day" (KJV).

The title of this theory is "young earth scientific creationism." However, not only is *Earth* about 6,000 years old, but also the *universe* is about 6,000 years old. A more accurate title of this group would be "The Creation of Heavens and Earth *in* Day One So 6,000-Year-Old-Universe Theory." But that title is too long.

Some advocates of this theory claim that creation was at 4004 BC, but Henry Morris and others claim a 6,000- to 10,000-year-old universe. Ken Ham and his Answers in Genesis organization claim "about 6,000 years ago." For convenience, I will use "about 6,000 years ago" for all of modern young earth creationism.

Young earth creation has several variations. The older traditional six-literal-days theory says that God created the heavens and earth in the beginning (*before* the six days), followed by six literal days' work on earth about 6,000 to at the most 10,000 years ago. This older two stage six-literal-days theory is a precursor of two stage Biblical creation (chapter 11). The older two stage creation is largely overlooked today.

This chapter is about the modern *one* stage young earth scientific creationism, which has dominated young earth creationism since 1961. So I will use the abbreviation YEC for this dominant modern variation. This widespread, well-publicized, modern YEC is a *one* stage creation—just the six days. I will emphasize Henry Morris's explanation of this modern variation along with quotes from Ken Ham.

There is also a sizable young earth *non*scientific creationism group that emphasizes creation miracles. I will review the nonscientific version at the end of this chapter.

Modern YEC has a major rival—old earth creation (OEC), which claims that the universe is 13.7 billion years old (older versions estimated 15 billion years). Hence the YEC slogan, "Thousands, not millions," meaning life is thousands, not millions, of years old. The new slogan is "Thousands, not billions," meaning the universe is thousands, not billions, of years old.

Earlier, the gap theory was also a major rival, but the three stage gap theory has been dying because the second stage, the "gap," is not supported by Scripture.

In the dispute between the remaining two dominant theories, YEC and OEC, the far less publicized middle alternative has been overlooked. That middle alternative is the older two stage six-literal-days creation theory. This two stage theory supports an undated earth creation (UEC), followed by six literal days. We will consider this two stage six-literal-days theory in chapter 11.

YEC is a major view with many claims, many advocates, and several variations. It is a big theory. So be prepared for a big chapter.

Even in a long chapter, I cannot list all the ideas of the many somewhat varied YEC subgroups—Creation Research Society, Answers in Genesis (AiG), Creation Ministries International, etc. A YEC subgroup may not agree with every detail of the preunderstandings and claims I list, especially since these subgroups disagree among themselves on some subclaims. To represent the multiple subgroups, I have attempted to select claims published either by the founders (Morris and Whitcomb) or by at least two YEC subgroups or authors. So to YEC advocates reading this chapter, please understand that you may not agree with all claims listed here, because I am trying to broadly summarize many YEC subgroups.

The great bridge of YEC is attached to the two shores by two abutments—YEC's two big assumptions, or preunderstandings. One abutment anchors the bridge to solid rock. The solid rock is "The Bible is inerrant." Preunderstandings 5.0A–5.0C are based on this affirmation. The final preunderstanding, 5.0D, is linked to the one problematic main claim.

Preunderstandings of Young Earth Scientific Creationism

(5.0A) *The Bible is inerrant; so interpret Genesis as literal history.* Begin with the "complete divine inspiration and perspicuity of Scripture,"[207] including the inerrancy of the autographs. Henry Morris under "Principles of Interpretation" affirms, "The writers of the New Testament, and Jesus Christ Himself, accepted the Genesis record as literal history." Therefore, interpret Genesis as "literal history."

(5.0B) *The Bible is inerrant, so has priority over science.* The Bible is inerrant, but science is not. So the Bible has priority. Since the Bible text is inerrant, creation study starts with the Bible's meaning. Many YEC leaders are scientists, so YEC is not saying science is unimportant, but that the Bible has priority over science. The YEC stand is this: recognize the independence and priority of the Bible. After studying the Bible and then science, attempt to correlate the two—but always recognize that the Bible has priority.

(5.0C) *The Bible inerrantly reveals what God did; science may tell us how He did it and provide evidence that He did it.* Henry Morris made a breakthrough in modern creation studies by seeking scientific means to explain the flood. That is why this view calls itself "*Scientific* Creationism."[208] Also, the creation provides evidence that God designed and created Earth and the universe.

Before Drs. Whitcomb and Morris, someone raised the question, "Why are there millions of saltwater seashells fossilized within the stone of high mountains?" Fossilized seashells can even be found in yellow rock layers near the top of Mount Everest. In the past, some Christians answered that God created the fossils there.[209] Others attributed the shells to the flood, but with no explanation of how they were fossilized *within* the rock rather than left lying on the surface. Then came a related question: "Why are there over a dozen different distinct rock layers in the Grand Canyon?" Until Whitcomb and Morris's seminal book, *The Genesis Flood,* many Christians assumed that God *created* the rock layers in place with their fossils.

Drs. Whitcomb and Morris popularized the approach: the Bible tells what happened; then science may tell how He brought it about. Unlike most other creation theories, the young earth scientific creationism theory includes the flood as an integral part of their *creation* theory. Earth is about 6,000 years old, yet the geology looks older. The answer is that the Biblical flood was the means that produced those geological features. Science may tell us how it happened. Whitcomb and Morris proposed a method for those trillions of seashells becoming fossilized in the stone and for the many thick rock layers exposed by the water-caused cut in the earth that we call the "Grand Canyon." That method was the hydrologically violent Genesis flood. The flood resulted in massive layered deposits of sediment containing dead animals and plants that became fossils. Morris was ideal for this idea as a hydrologist—a scientist who studies the effects of the movement of water.

But when it comes to seeking the means for the events of the six days, YEC splits into two subgroups. Henry Morris affirms that God used *both* means and miracles. But Duncan and Hall see only miracles. The latter view is at the end of this chapter under young earth *non*scientific creationism.

Young earth *scientific* creationism takes the approach that the Bible inerrantly reveals what God did; accurate evidence from science may uncover the means and provide evidence for what He did. This was a major breakthrough by Henry Morris in modern creation studies.

(**5.0D**) *"In the beginning" means the instantaneous start of all time.* "In the beginning" was "all time (beginning)."[210] Both Henry Morris and Ken Ham indicate that the meaning of "In the beginning" was the instantaneous start of all time.[211]

Claims of Young Earth Scientific Creationism

(**5.1**) *God created all things—time, space, and matter-energy—out of nothing* (**ex nihilo**). YEC founder Henry Morris declares:

> The very first verse is the one upon which all the others depend. "In the beginning God created the heavens and the earth" (Gen. 1:1). This simple declarative statement can only have come by divine revelation. Its scope is comprehensively universal, embracing all space (heaven), all time (beginning), and all matter (earth) in our space/time/matter cosmos. It is the first and only statement of real creation in all the cosmogonies of all the nations of past or present. All other creation myths begin with the universe already in existence, in watery chaos or in some other primordial form. Evidently man, with unaided reason, cannot conceive of true creation; he must begin with *something*. But Genesis 1:1 speaks of creation *ex nihilo*; only God could originate such a concept, and only an infinite, omnipotent God could create the universe.[212]

Eternal God created all things—time, space, and matter-energy—*ex nihilo*, out of nothing. This *ex nihilo* creation fits with God being uniquely the eternal Creator of all things.

(**5.1a**) *Some YEC advocates are turning away from* ex nihilo *creation in 1:1 to the title theory.* Recently some young earth advocates have been turning away from *ex nihilo* creation in Genesis 1:1. They have begun to claim that Genesis 1:1 was a title or summary of the six days rather than the actual *ex nihilo* creation by God. Since 1:1 was a title, there was no event in Genesis 1:1, so no *ex nihilo* creation in 1:1. The six days were all that ever happened in creation.[213] So far, this is a minority view in YEC.

In contrast, Henry Morris says, "Neither can verse 1 as a whole be considered a title or summary of the events described in the succeeding verses of the chapter." Morris explains that Genesis 2:1, not 1:1, is the six days' summary: "Thus the heavens and the earth were finished, and all the host of them." [214] Morris affirms that Genesis 1:1 was the actual act of "the primeval creation of the universe itself."[215]

(5.2) *Each numbered* **yôm** *in Genesis 1 was a literal, normal day, totaling six literal days.* Young earth scientific creationists consistently have defended the six days as literal normal days. This six normal days affirmation is one of the two central claims of YEC. Although several other theories also claim normal days, YEC advocates have especially vigorously defended six literal days.[216]

Next is the distinctive claim of modern young earth scientific creationism: Based on *"in* six days" of Exodus 20:11, the Genesis 1:1 *ex nihilo* creation took place *in day one.*

(5.3) *In day one God created heavens (space), Earth (matter), and beginning (time)—based on Exodus 20:11—"For* **in** *six days."* Henry Morris says, "The tremendous events of creation week . . . began with the *ex nihilo* creation of the universe by God on the first day."[217] "The primal creation of the heavens and the earth in the beginning was the first act of the first day of the six days, calling into existence the basic elements of the space-mass-time continuum which constitutes the physical universe."[218] The current YEC leader, Ken Ham, agrees: "God . . . made time (beginning), space (heaven), and matter (earth). This was the beginning of our universe, all part of the first day in time."[219] The foundation of modern young earth scientific creationism is that the initial *ex nihilo* creation was *in day one* of the six days based on Exodus 20:11: "For *in* six days. . . ."

Ken Ham quotes Exodus 20:11, explaining, "Now, when the Creator God spoke as recorded in Exodus 20:1, what did He (Jesus) say? As we read on, we find this statement: *For in six days the* LORD *made the heavens and the earth, the sea, and all that is in them, and rested the seventh day.* . . . Yes, Jesus did explicitly say He created in six days"[220] (italics his).

"For *in* six days" (Exod. 20:11) is the foundation of modern young earth scientific creationism. Subclaims 3a through 3z are supports for *ex nihilo* creation *in* day one based on all creation *"in* six days" (Exod. 20:11).

(5.3a) Bārā' *and* 'āsâh *are interchangeable in Genesis 1 and Exodus 20:11.* Don Batten explains, "'make' [Heb. *'āsâh*] and 'create' (Heb. *bara*) are used interchangeably in Genesis 1."[221] Ken Ham says,

The fact is that the words *bārā'* and *'āsâh* are often used interchangeably in the Old Testament; indeed, in some places they are used in synonymous parallelism (e.g., Genesis 1:26–27; Exodus 34:10; Isaiah 41:20; 43:7). Applying this conclusion to Exodus 20:11 (cf. 31:17) as well as Nehemiah 9:6, we see that Scripture teaches that God created the universe (everything) in six days, as outlined in Genesis 1.[222]

"The words *bārā'* and *'āsâh* are often used interchangeably," so *'āsâh* means "created" in Exodus 20:11 in the identical sense that *bārā'* means "created" in Genesis 1:1. "Applying this conclusion to Exodus 20:11 . . . , we see that Scripture teaches that God created the universe (everything) in six days, as outlined in Genesis 1."[223] So Exodus 20:11 means, "For *in* six days the LORD *created* [*'āsâh*] heaven and earth, the sea, and all that in them *is*" (KJV, except "created" substituted for "made").

Since *'asâh* and *bārā* "are interchangeable in Genesis 1," *'āsâh* in Genesis 1:16 also means "create." Genesis 1:16 means, "And God *created* [*'āsâh*] two great lights; the greater light to rule the day, and the lesser light to rule the night: *he created* the stars also" (KJV, except "created" substituted for "made"). So "Scripture teaches that God created the universe (everything) in six days" as Genesis 1 and Exodus 20:11, "*in* six days," say.

(5.3b) *God "from the beginning made them male and female," so the beginning of time and the universe was recent.* In Matthew 19:4, Jesus said that God "from the beginning made them male and female" (NASB), so do not divorce. An "Answers in Genesis" article says, "Jesus goes back to the beginning of time." The related diagram is titled, "Jesus and the age of the universe." "Jesus is saying that Adam and Eve were at the beginning of creation." "He [Jesus] is talking about the whole creation from Jesus' day back to the very first moment of creation, just as Paul is referring to the whole creation during all of history in Romans 1:18–20 and Romans 8:19–23. In other words, Jesus is saying that Adam and Eve were created at the beginning of history."[224]

Adam's genealogies date him about 6,000 years ago, and he and Eve were created at "the beginning of time," so the universe is about 6,000 years old. This conclusion agrees with "*in* six days" (Exod. 20:11).

(5.3c) *God created four things in day one: space (heavens), matter (earth), time (beginning), and light.* Henry Morris says that in day one, God created "all space (heaven), all time (beginning), and all matter (earth)."[225] Ken Ham agrees, saying that God "made time (beginning), space (heaven), and matter (earth). This was the beginning of our universe, all part of the first day in time." He continues, "God gives us a summary of what happened on each of the six days of Creation. Day 1: time, space, Earth, light."[226] This four-item creation in day one supports *ex nihilo* creation of everything "*in six days*" (Exod. 20:11). This initial creation of space, Earth, time, and light all occurred *in* day one, based on "*in six days*" (Exod. 20:11).

(5.3d) *"Heavens" meant "all space" without luminaries.* "In Genesis 1:1, the term [heavens] refers to the component of space in the space-mass-time universe."[227] "The essential meaning of the word [heavens] corresponds to our modern term *space*."[228]

(5.3e) *"Earth" meant "all matter" in the universe.* "The term 'earth' refers to the component of matter in the universe."[229]

(5.3f) *All this matter ("earth") in the universe was unformed prematter in day one.* Genesis 1:2 declares that "earth" was *tōhû vᵃbōhû.* Since "earth" was "all matter"[230] in the universe (5.3e), then all matter in the universe was *tōhû vᵃbōhû,* or "without form, and void" (KJV). All matter in the universe was "totally without structure."[231] "'Earth' was only some kind of amorphous prematter."[232] "Earth had been created in a formless watery dispersion"[233] throughout space.

From a tiny part of this prematter of "earth," God would make our planet on day three. Then out of the great mass of "earth" that was spread out in space, He would make the sun, moon, and galaxies of stars on day four.

(5.3g) *"In the beginning" was the time component of the space-mass-time universe.* Henry Morris begins his commentary on Genesis with five headings in this order: "God," "Created," "Heaven," "Earth," and "In the beginning." "In the beginning" means God created time. So God created three things in day one—heaven, earth, and time,[234] and then also light.

Henry Morris concludes his commentary on 1:1, "Thus, Genesis 1:1 can legitimately and incisively be paraphrased as follows:

> The transcendent, omnipotent Godhead called into existence the space-mass-time universe.[235]

"Not only does the first verse of the Bible speak of the creation of space and matter, but it also notes the beginning of time."[236] "In the beginning" was the creation of the *time* component of "the space-mass-time universe."

(5.3h) *This creation of time was at the beginning of day one.* In the first instant of day one God created the beginning of "all time (beginning)."[237]

(5.3i) *Day one began time in the entire universe.* Day one began time in the entire universe. "God . . . made time (beginning), space (heaven), and matter (earth). This was the beginning of our universe, all part of the first day in time."[238] Day one began time in the entire universe.

(**5.3j**) *The dark evening of Genesis 1:2 began the first night, followed by the morning in 1:3 as the evening and morning of day one.* Recently a number of YEC advocates have said that the dark of Genesis 1:2 began day one with nighttime. So day one was a night-day cycle day beginning with evening followed by morning. "The text clearly suggests that Day 1 began with 'In the beginning' and following that first evening of darkness (v.2) was the first morning, when God said, 'Let there be light' (v.3)."[239] Evening and morning in Genesis 1:5 were the evening of Genesis 1:2 and the morning of Genesis 1:3. Each of the six days was the "cycle of evening, night, morning, and daytime."[240] This fits Genesis 1:1–2 into day one, in keeping with "*in* six days" of Exodus 20:11.

On the other hand, Henry Morris and some other older YEC advocates do *not* accept this night-day subclaim.

(**5.3k**) *The deep was mixed with "earth" as a "watery matrix."* "Initially . . . the earth had no form; and similarly, this state must apply to the waters also. The picture presented is one of all the basic elements sustained in a pervasive watery matrix throughout the darkness of space."[241] "God put His big hands into that developing liquid-like 'earth' and spread it out all over the cosmos."[242] A relatively tiny water-earth blob would become planet Earth on day three.

(**5.3l**) *Darkness "upon the face of the deep" was darkness throughout space.* The deep extended throughout space, so "darkness on the face of the deep" was darkness throughout space. The entire physical universe had "no light."[243] "The picture presented is one of all the basic elements . . . throughout the darkness of space."[244]

(**5.3m**) *The light on day one began three-day temporary light.* God shone temporary light on "earth." This temporary light may have turned on and off every twelve hours as it shone onto the prematter of earth throughout space. Or this temporary light shone directionally onto the one relatively small rotating blob that would become Earth. Either way, there was no sun in days one through three. "God shined some temporary light on the initial earthen substance until He made the sun on Day 4."[245]

(**5.3n**) *The light was created in transit as if from sun, moon, and stars that had not yet been made.* "Light was coming during the day as though from the sun and during the night as though from the moon and stars, even though they had not yet been made. . . . It therefore did not take a billion years for the light from a star which is a billion light-years distance to reach the earth after the star was created. The light-trail from the star was created in transit, as it were, all the way from the star to earth, three days before the star was created."[246]

All light, including from galaxies billions of light-years away, is at most about 6,000 years old—because the universe was created only a few days before Adam, who is dated to about 6,000 years ago. This is because everything was created "*in* six days" (Exod. 20:11).

A number of non-miraculous proposals also have been suggested—relativity, light slowing, time zones in space, etc. But other YEC scientists say that none of the proposals to date has compelling evidence.[247] The most viable option remains the original proposal by Morris. He said that light was created miraculously in transit, as if from luminaries that had not yet been created.

(**5.3o**) *The light of day one energized the entire universe.* Henry Morris says, "The physical universe, though created, was as yet neither formed nor *energized*" (emphasis his). "The force of gravity was not yet functioning."[248] The light on day one was "activating and energizing the newly created physical universe,"[249] "setting the electromagnetic forces into operation."[250] "So the nuclear forces maintaining the integrity of matter were activated by the Father . . . , the gravitational forces were activated by the Spirit . . . , and the electromagnetic forces were activated by the Word when He called light into existence out of the darkness."[251]

(**5.3p**) *In day two, God made the* rāqîa', *the* "*expanse*" *of the atmosphere, below a vast vapor canopy that would be the source of the rain for the flood.* Morris says that God's work on day two was "making the firmament (that is, the atmosphere) to form the great hydrosphere of the earth, dividing into two great water masses, one above and one below the atmosphere."[252] "The upper waters would provide a sort of protective canopy."[253] This "antediluvian water canopy," he says, "was analogous to the cloud cover around the planet Venus"[254] as "a marvelous sustainer of vigorous life conditions on earth." Although debated by some YEC advocates, the idea is that this canopy would have protected Adam's race from harmful radiation (thus their longer lives) until the water fell as the rain for Noah's flood.[255]

(**5.3q**) *In day three, solid planet Earth precipitated out, forming crust with dry land and seas; God made trees with appearance of age.* "The planet was not formed until day 3. . . . Prior to that 'earth' was only some kind of amorphous prematter . . . ready to be made into the planet and other celestials."[256] Within a relatively tiny local blob of amorphous watery matrix, "tremendous chemical reactions got under way, as dissolved elements precipitated and combined with others to form the vast complex of minerals and rocks making up solid earth—its crust, its mantle and its core." But there were "many substances still in solution."[257] "Great earth movements also got under way. . . . Finally, surfaces of solid earth appeared above the waters [as] rising continents. Great subterranean water chambers" formed.[258] These huge subterranean water chambers contained the water that would become the fountains of the deep for the future Noahic flood.

Later in day three, God made "full grown plants" (that either were created fully grown or grew very rapidly) with "appearance of age"[259] on the dry land.

(**5.3r**) *In day four, God created the sun, moon, and galaxies from "earth."* "It is clear from Genesis 1 that the sun was not created until the fourth day. . . . The sun was created to rule the day that already existed. . . . God deliberately left the creation of the sun until the fourth day . . . because He knew cultures would try to worship the sun."[260] That same day, God "placed these 'lights' [sun, moon, and stars] throughout the infinite space of heaven that had been created on Day One, these also being made of the same 'earth' that had been created on Day One."[261]

(**5.3s**) *In days five and six God made sea, air, and land life and created Adam and Eve.* "God proceeded to make animal life for the atmosphere and hydrosphere on the fifth day, and then animal life for the lithosphere and biosphere on the sixth day."[262] God created man with "an *eternal* spirit, possessed of esthetic, moral, [and] spiritual attributes." Moreover, "man was made in God's image."[263]

(**5.3t**) *Rain did not fall until the flood.* Morris states, "There was no rainfall on the earth" until the flood. That was because of the great water vapor canopy. "The original hydrologic cycle was thus drastically different."[264] The vapor canopy contained the water for the massive rain of the flood. The flood produced almost all of Earth's geology. Flood geology formed essentially all the earth's sedimentary rock layers within the one flood year.

(**5.3u**) *All was perfect on the sixth day—without disease, physical calamities, or death.* Henry Morris explains,

Everything in the universe . . . was still at this time exceedingly good, in God's own omniscient judgment. There could have been nothing that was *not* good in all creation: no struggle for existence, no disease, no pollution, no physical calamities (earthquakes, floods, etc.), no imbalance or lack of harmony, no disorder, no sin and, above all *no death!* Even Satan was still good at this point; his rebellion and fall must have come later[265] (emphasis his).

Ken Ham recognizes that Romans 5:12–21 and 1 Corinthians 15:21–22 explicitly say only *human* death came by Adam's sin. But he says that the Bible's overall implications indicate that animal death also came by Adam's sin.[266] Originally, "everything was perfect."[267]

(**5.3v**) *Originally, there were no predators.* "There was no death and struggle in the animal kingdom."[268] "As far as carnivorous animals are concerned, their desire for meat must also have been a later development, either at the time of the Curse or after the Flood."[269] Instead of meat, God gave them "every green plant for food" (Gen. 1:30).

(**5.3w**) *Satan did not fall until after day six.* YEC says, "Even Satan was still good at this point [the sixth day]; his rebellion and fall must have come later."[270]

(**5.3x**) *No death before Adam's Fall meant no fossils before Adam's Fall.* Had Adam not sinned, animals would have had eternal physical life. Adam's sin caused all death of *nephesh* ("soulish") animals. "Fossils, of course, speak of death—often of violent and sudden death, . . . disease and injuries. . . . The fossil record now found in the sedimentary rocks of the earth's crust could only have been formed sometime *after* man sinned . . . The cataclysmic events of the great Flood in the days of Noah are quite sufficient to account for all the phenomena of the sedimentary rocks and the fossil record."[271]

(**5.3y**) *Genealogies date Adam about 6,000 years ago, so the universe can be dated to about 6,000 years old.*[272] "As far as the creation of the universe is concerned, this took place five days earlier than the creation of man."[273] Adam is dated to about 6,000 years ago by his descendants' genealogies. Therefore, the universe is about 6,000 years old because the universe was created "*in* six days," only a few days before Adam.

Answers magazine (AiG) states, "The key to correct dates is the infallible Word of God."[274] "Some galaxies are so far away that it is thought to take billions of years for their light to get to earth. Yet the Bible indicates that the entire universe is only thousands of years old."[275] The light from distant galaxies millions of light-years away is "thousands, not millions," of years old based on Adam's genealogies. Adam's genealogies date everything, because Exodus 20:11 says the universe was created only a few days before Adam, all "*in* six days."

(**5.3z**) *God created the universe with "appearance of age."* Since the *ex nihilo* creation was *in* day one, the universe is only about 6,000 years old. Yet the universe appears much older. Morris concludes, "The whole universe had an 'appearance of age' right from the start."[276]

A more drastic "appearance of age" theory is the "omphalos hypothesis," named after the creationist book *Omphalos* by Philip Gosse.[277] Gosse argued that God created everything with appearance of age, including Adam and Eve with belly buttons (omphalos) and fabricated fossils created inside rocks.

Whitcomb and Morris in *The Genesis Flood* reacted against this view. They presented the case that a very active Noahic flood laid down sediment with dead plants and animals that formed fossils.[278]

Wherever possible, Morris has avoided appearance of age, but the apparent age in the universe has proven much more difficult than fossils in Earth's sedimentary rock layers. Morris states:

> There is no reason why God could not, if he had so willed, [have] created "pulses" in the [light] trails. . . . When such pulses reached the earth they would then be interpreted as, say novas, when they were in reality merely created bursts of energy in the light trails connected with various stars. Though the reason for God doing such a thing is not yet clear.[279]
> The light-trail from the star was created in transit, as it were, all the way from the star to the earth, three days before the star was created.[280]

Morris concludes that events beyond about 6,000 light-years away are just light pulses.

However, following Henry Morris's example of means for the flood, a few young earth scientific creationists have suggested means to avoid deceptive appearance of age of a 6,000-year-old universe. Barry Setterfield suggested that the speed of light has slowed down greatly. Jason Lisle proposes that objects are in different time zones.[281]

D. Russell Humphreys in *Starlight and Time* tentatively suggests that the universe may appear to be about 13.7 billion years old, yet actually is only 6,000 years old, the difference explained by relativity.[282] Humphreys in his video, *Starlight and Time*, explains the reason for his proposal: "Even if my particular theory should eventually turn out to be wrong, I know that there is a correct creation model of the cosmos, because observation and Scripture both confirm that God made the universe very recently. 'For *in* six days God made the heavens and the earth'" (Exod. 20:11).[283]

But other young earth creationists have responded, "There is currently no wholly satisfactory solution that is accepted by the majority of creation scientists."[284]

Perhaps the most representative YEC position on this age of starlight issue remains Henry Morris's original suggestion: "The light-trail from the star was created in transit, as it were, all the way from the star to the earth, three days before the star was created."[285]

The above 3a–3z are all subclaims of claim 3, that the initial *ex nihilo* creation was *in* day one, based on Exodus 20:11 — "For *in* six days." I repeat that not all variations of YEC will hold all the views listed, but I have tried to be representative of YEC in general. Now let us return to the remaining main claims of the YEC theory.

(5.4) *God apparently gave the Genesis 1:1—2:4a account to Adam.* Morris explains that because no human was at the actual creation, God spoke the Genesis 1:1—2:4a creation narrative to Adam. "He revealed it verbally to Adam. . . . It was vital that Adam and Eve, along with their descendants, should know about their own origin as well as that of their earthly 'dominion,' if they were to be responsible stewards thereof."[286] Later *tôlᵉdôt* narratives, or generational accounts, are followed by the writer's name. But the creation narrative (Gen. 1:1—2:4a) was from God, so no human author was listed.

The next *tôlᵉdôt,* Genesis 2:4b—5:1a, was "originally by Adam himself" "and represents his own perspective on the creation and the first events of human history."[287] That account begins in Genesis 2:4b and concludes with Adam's name as the author in Genesis 5:1a. Adam's account was an *eyewitness* narrative[288] of his own life and the generations after him during his lifetime. He recounted the events in the Garden and the Fall, and then successive generations of his descendants *within his lifetime* that he would have known—Cain, Abel, Seth, and Enosh.

The New Testament says all five books of the Pentateuch, or Torah (Genesis—Deuteronomy), were from Moses. Morris explains that New Testament quotes from Exodus through Deuteronomy are attributed to Moses but that quotes from Genesis are not. That is because Moses was "compiler and editor" rather than author of Genesis. The Genesis events took place before Moses lived. Henry Morris says that Moses "took actual written records of the past, collected them, and brought them together into a final form, again as guided by the Holy Spirit."[289] So Moses "served mainly as compiler and editor of the material in the Book of Genesis."[290] He compiled Genesis from the accounts by Adam, Noah, Shem, Ham, Japheth, Terah, Abraham, Isaac, Jacob, Esau, Judah, and Joseph, who "recorded on tables of stone or clay, in common with the practice of early times, handed down from father to son finally coming into the possession of Moses."[291]

(5.5) *Adam's sin resulted in death.* The Biblical event was this: God told Adam, "But from the tree of the knowledge of good and evil you shall not eat, for in the day that you eat from it you shall surely die." Adam was not deceived (1 Tim. 2:14), but deliberately chose to eat the forbidden fruit of the tree of the knowledge of good and evil. So God pronounced the curse, "For you are dust, and to dust you shall return." Henry Morris says, "The sin of Adam, rebelling against the word of God, brought death. . . . If sin and death are not real, then salvation and eternal life are not real."[292] Adam's sin and the resulting death for each individual member of the human race is real.

(5.5a) *All humans have descended from Adam, so all humans have a fallen nature and are subject to spiritual and physical death.* Henry Morris says, "In the face of such clear-cut passages as Romans 5:12–21 and 1 Corinthians 15:21–22, few who accept the Bible as the Word of God will deny that Adam's sin and fall introduced *spiritual* and *physical* death into the human race"[293] (emphasis his). All humans have descended from Adam. So all humans are born with a sin nature so are spiritually dead until born again, and are subject to physical death.

(5.5b) *All humans have descended from Adam, so all humans are related to Christ, who can be our Kinsman-Redeemer.* All humans are also related through Adam and Eve to Jesus, so humans can be saved by Jesus as our Kinsman-Redeemer. "The gospel makes sense only on the basis that all humans alive, and all who have ever lived are descendants of the first man, Adam. Only descendants of Adam can be saved, because Isaiah spoke of the coming Messiah as literally the Kinsman-Redeemer, that is one who is related by blood to those He redeems (Isa. 59:20)."[294]

Humans die because of Adam's sin. But what about animals?

(5.5c) *As created, all* nephesh *(soulish) animals had eternal physical life; Adam's sin resulted in all* nephesh *animal death.* Henry Morris is a little cautious about animal death from Adam's sin: "Although the sentence of death was specifically pronounced only on man and on the serpent used by Satan as the vehicle of temptation, the most obvious implication is that this curse on the master of creation [Adam] extended likewise to his dominion [the animals]."[295]

In *The Genesis Flood,* Morris quotes from 1 Corinthians 15:21, "By *man* came death," and from Romans 5:12, "By *one man*, sin entered into the world, and death by sin"[296] (KJV, emphasis his). "Therefore, we feel compelled to date all of the rock strata which contain fossils of once living creatures as subsequent to Adam's fall."[297]

This claim of no animal death before Adam has been attacked with the counterclaim that even if there was no carnivorism, elephants still would have stepped on insects, earthworms, mice, etc., and blue whales with wide open mouths would have swallowed squid, fish, diving sea birds, and baby sea turtles, along with the plant plankton.

YEC responds that only *nephesh* animal death counts as Biblical death. YEC explains, "*Nephesh* conveys the basic idea of a 'breathing creature'. Perhaps *nephesh* refers to a certain level of consciousness."[298] Air-breathing animals include amphibians, reptiles, birds, and mammals. Fish death, squid death, and earthworm death do not count. And either all mice escaped elephants' feet and all baby sea turtles escaped blue whales because mice and turtles are *nephesh* life (breathing animals), or mice and turtles did not reach the "level of consciousness" required. There was no death of *nephesh* animals before Adam sinned.

Ken Ham says,

Originally, when everything was perfect, there were no meat eaters. Adam and Eve weren't frightened of any of the animals, they all lived in perfect harmony. There was no death, disease, suffering or bloodshed in the world. By the way, when plants are eaten, they don't "die" in the sense that animals do today. In the Hebrew language, animals and humans have a special life principle called a *nephesh*. Plants do not have this, because they are VERY different from animals—plants were given for food. There was no death of animals or humans in the original Creation. As God said, it was *very good* (emphasis his).[299]

(5.5d) *Animals did not die before Adam's sin, just as they will not die in the future restoration.* "The world will one day be restored (Acts 3:21) to a state in which, once again, there will be no such death and violence in the animal kingdom. . . . Lambs, wolves, leopards, kids, bears and calves will all dwell together peacefully. Lions will once again be plant eaters."[300] The future Millennium is described as a time when "the wolf and the lamb shall graze together, and the lion shall eat straw like the ox" (Isa. 65:25, NASB). The Edenic condition before Adam sinned will be largely restored in the Millennium.

(5.5e) *All animals were vegetarians before Adam's sin.* In the future Millennium "the lion shall eat straw like the ox" (Isa. 65:25b). Therefore, back in Eden, lions ate straw before Adam sinned. In fact, all animals ate only vegetation before Adam sinned. Genesis 1:30 says that God gave animals "every green plant for food."

(5.5f) *To question animals' eternal physical life before Adam sinned resulting in the curse is to undermine the atonement.* Animals' death instead of animals' eternal physical life before Adam's sin and the resulting curse undermines the atonement. Death before Adam's sin means the curse was before Adam's sin. Then how can the Second Adam (Messiah Jesus) make atonement for the First Adam's Fall, if the curse for the Fall was before he fell?

AiG submits that the question of the earth's age is vital because it involves the accuracy of the Genesis record, and more importantly, the Bible's atonement message itself. You see, if a person accepts the belief that the earth is millions of years old, then it follows that the Curse must have occurred *before* Adam appeared. In this scenario, then, there would be the remains of dead things before the Fall of Adam—and diseases like cancer. In this way, the atonement message is undermined.[301]

(5.6) *Noah's flood was real, violent, and worldwide.* There was a real, violent, worldwide flood; a real Noah; and a real ark on which eight people survived.[302] This flood occurred about 2300 BC[303] or 2500 BC,[304] or possibly as early as 3000 BC.[305] The flood produced most of Earth's geology.

(5.6a) *Exodus 20:11 teaches a young Earth; the Noahic flood explains why this young Earth appears older.* Morris and Whitcomb in *The Genesis Flood* practiced the method that the Bible reveals what happened, then science may discover how He brought it about.[306] Unlike most creation theories, the young earth scientific creationism theory includes the flood as an integral part of its theory. Exodus 20:11 combined with Adam's genealogies tells us Earth is only about 6,000 years old. The Bible reveals there was a flood. Earth's geology may look older, but those geological features were caused by the flood. The flood made Earth appear ancient while actually being only about 6,000 years old.

(5.6b) *The flood formed most geologic features and fossils.* Whitcomb and Morris explain that during the violent flood "creatures of the sea bottoms would universally be overwhelmed," forming the lowest fossil layers, followed by deposited layers of sediment with fish, and then the upper geologic layers, "entombing animals or reptiles, together with great rafts of vegetation . . . on top of other deposits."[307] Because all animal death originated from Adam's sin, animals died only after Adam's Fall. Therefore, most fossils as well as oil and coal deposits are by the flood and subsequent pressure of sediment.

John Baumgartner added the idea of rapid post-flood plate tectonic movement. Collision of Earth's surface plates forced some of the fossil-bearing layers from the flood to rise. As the plates collided, they formed mountain ranges. All this occurred in the few thousand years since the flood.[308]

This flood model by Whitcomb and Morris may explain how the many thick rock layers were laid down around the world. Then the Grand Canyon was cut by massive runoff from the North American continent at the end of the flood. Baumgartner's addition explains how those millions of seashells became fossilized in the stone of most mountain ranges, including near the top of Mount Everest.

A variety of possible means for the flood have been suggested: water vapor canopy,[309] watery comet,[310] hydroplate tectonics,[311] Black Sea flood,[312] a meteor hitting the Indian Ocean forming Burckle's undersea crater around 4,800 to 5,000 years ago,[313] and deep ocean methane hydrate release of methane gas producing fountains from the deep and tsunamis.[314] This discussion of means God may have used is healthy. By being open to various proposed means, the actual means God used may be discovered.

Four Denials by Young Earth Scientific Creationism

(5.7) *YEC denies chance-driven naturalistic molecules-to-man macroevolution.* God created life by His commands out of materials He had created.[315] Chance-driven evolution cannot be the source of life.

Morris says, "The real issue is whether evolution can explain the *increase of genetic information content—*enough changes to turn microbes into men, *not* simple change through time" (emphasis his). Scientific creationists deny sufficient chance-driven mutations producing "*increase of genetic information content*" resulting in macroevolution of "microbes into men."[316]

(5.7a) YEC *accepts rapid* micro*evolution from about 5,000*[317] *"kinds" on the ark to the modern 25,000 air-breathing land species.* YEC affirms microevolution speciation (*micro*evolution from one "kind" to several species), from a limited number of "kinds" Adam named and that were on the ark (estimates vary from 2,500 to 15,000), to the many modern species. But this speciation is mainly by redistribution of already created genetic information.

All genetic codes for later species were already in the gene pool of each "kind." "The biblical creation/Fall/Flood/migration model would also predict *rapid* formation of new varieties and even species. This is because all the modern varieties of land vertebrates must have descended from comparatively few animals that disembarked from the ark only around 4,500 years ago."[318] "But no reputable creationist denies speciation—in fact, it is an important part of creationist biology."[319] By rapid speciation, the 2,500 to 15,000 kinds on the ark became the modern 25,000 air-breathing land and flying species.

(5.8) *YEC denies the entire gap theory.* Many Hebrew scholars from many theories have recognized the fatal grammatical error in the gap, the second stage of the gap theory.[320] YEC advocates seem to oppose the entire gap theory. The refutation of the gap theory will be covered in chapter 9.

(5.9) *YEC denies the pre-creation chaos theory, and the majority denies the title/summary theory.* Henry Morris says that Genesis 1:1 reports the actual "primeval creation of the universe itself."[321] The pre-creation chaos theory errs.

Contra Waltke's title theory, Morris says, "Neither can verse 1 as a whole be considered a title or summary of the events described in the succeeding verses of the chapter." Genesis 2:1, rather than 1:1, is the summary of chapter 1: "Thus the heavens and the earth were finished, and all the host of them."[322] The title theory errs.

Morris points out that one of Waltke's reasons for the title and pre-creation chaos theory is the claim that God could not have created darkness. But that claim is incorrect. "The idea that God, being Light could not create a world of darkness is invalid. God Himself said: 'I form the light, and create darkness . . .' (Isaiah 45:7)."[323] Waltke's pre-creation chaos and title theories err.

(5.10) *YEC denies all non-day-night "days" theories.* YEC advocates explain that *yôm,* "day," with consecutive numbers and evening and morning, is always a literal normal day. Therefore, all nonliteral "days" of all kinds err. The six days were normal days.

"Thousands, not millions," of years has been the slogan of YEC. This slogan is based on the second word, "*in,*" of "For *in* six days" of Exodus 20:11. If everything was created "*in* six days," then everything can be dated by Adam's genealogies plus a few days. So the universe is thousands, not billions, of years old, specifically about 6,000 to at the most 10,000 years old. The foundation of this theory's unique third claim—*ex nihilo* creation *in* day one—is the second English word of "For *in* six days" of Exodus 20:11, the word "*in.*"

One Unsupported Pre-understanding and One Major Unsupported Claim of Young Earth Scientific Creationism

Young earth scientific creationism has made major contributions to creationism. Henry Morris, especially, is right on target with most of his main claims. I owe him the greatest debt of gratitude. He has been foundational to my study of creation. I have profited from John Whitcomb, Duane Gish, Carl Wieland, Ken Ham, and Jonathan Sarfati as well. Many other YEC writers have been of great benefit to me. So it is out of great respect that I point out that YEC has made an error on one of its ten main claims. Nine of the ten main claims appear to be Biblically supported.

My goal is to gather those Biblical claims. Significantly, only the two stage Biblical creation theory agrees with all nine Biblically supported YEC main claims. These nine claims form the backbone of the second stage of the two stage Biblical creation theory (chapter 11). Thank you, Dr. Henry Morris and many others in YEC.

Examining the one problematic claim will be big, but it is the unique core claim of the YEC theory. YEC also has one pre-understanding related to the same claim. With respect, and honoring the Bible these creationists honor, it is only right to explain from the Bible why this one main claim and one related pre-understanding are Biblically unsupported. Here is the pre-understanding:

(u-5.0D) *"In the beginning" means the instantaneous start of all time*. YEC takes "In the beginning" as the instantaneous start of "all time."[324] "In the beginning" began the *time* component of "the space-mass-time universe."[325]

Most creationists would agree that "the beginning of time" is a true implication of "In the beginning." And most creationists agree that the beginning of time started instantaneously. But "the beginning of time" is only an implication of *bᵉrē'shît*, not its meaning.

In response, *bᵉrē'shît* ("in the beginning") or the unprefixed *rē'shît* ("first, beginning, best, chief, firstfruits") when used of time or events (rather than of a first or best object) consistently means an extensive beginning time period. Certainly it started instantaneously. But *bᵉrē'shît* does not mean either an instant or "all time."

After Genesis 1:1, the next use of *rē'shît*[326] is in Genesis 10:10—"The beginning [*rē'shît*] of his [Nimrod's] kingdom was Babel and Erech and Accad and Calneh, in the land of Shinar" (NASB). Later Nimrod had other cities, but these were his first four. It would have taken time for Nimrod to develop a kingdom of four cities in that initially sparsely populated world after the flood. A four-city kingdom was not accomplished instantaneously or in one day.

When Jacob blessed his twelve sons, he began, "Reuben, you are my firstborn; My might and the beginning [*rē'shît*] of my strength" (Gen. 49:3, NASB). This use of *rē'shît* is more in the sense of chief or first strong son, not so much a time sense. Nonetheless, Jacob was not speaking of the "instant" of Reuben's birth, but of the years in which Reuben became his first mighty warrior-son. Reuben and his next brother killed all the men of a city whose prince had violated their sister (Gen. 34). Reuben was that mighty warrior son for many years.

Rē'shît is also used repeatedly of firstfruits of the harvest. Again, it is not really used in a time sense. However, firstfruits need most of the growing season to develop. To the Israelite farmer, the firstfruits do not grow instantaneously, but take many months. Grape vines, fig trees, olive trees, and date palms take years before their firstfruits grow. There are no instant firstfruits in an agricultural society.

Moses promised "a land for which the Lord your God cares; the eyes of the Lord your God are always on it, from the beginning [*rē'shît*] even to the end of the year" (Deut. 11:12, NASB). The sense is not that God cares the first instant and the last instant of the year. The sense here is that God cares all year, from the first half all the way through the second half of the year, inclusively, with no break. In Hebrew, the *rē'shît* was the beginning part of the year, not the first instant of the year.

The next clear time-use of *rē'shît* is in Job 8:7. Bildad said to Job, "Your beginnings [*rē'shît*] will seem humble, so prosperous will your future be" (NIV). The book ends, "The Lord blessed the latter *days* of Job more than his beginning [*rē'shît*]." Then the list of Job's renewed possessions were doubled (Job 42:12, NASB). Job's *rē'shît,* or beginning, spanned his entire life up to his disasters. Before his misfortunes, Job sat as an honored elder in the city (Job 29:7–11). He also had twelve adult children, suggesting he was at least half a century in age. After his testing (still in the time of long lives), he lived 140 years. The symmetry of the book (12 children before and 12 children after, as well as double livestock after) suggests that perhaps either 70 or 140 years passed before his testing. So Job's *rē'shît,* his beginning, was at least 50, probably 70, or even 140 years, with an ending period of another 140 years.

David speaks of the *rē'shît* of wisdom: "The fear of the Lord is the beginning [*rē'shît*] of wisdom" (Ps. 111:10, NASB). Solomon in Proverbs says the same: "The fear of the Lord is the beginning [*rē'shît*] of knowledge" (Prov. 1:7, NASB); and "The beginning [*rē'shît*] of wisdom *is*: Acquire wisdom; And with all your acquiring, get understanding" (Prov. 4:7, NASB). Although *rē'shît* here does not emphasize a time sense, acquiring wisdom is *not* instantaneous; it takes many years.

God spoke of possessing wisdom at the beginning:

> The LORD possessed me [wisdom]
> at the beginning [*rē'shît*] of His way,
> from before [*m'pad'mê*] His works of old;
> from everlasting [*m'olam*] I was established,
> from the beginning [*m'rosh* from *rē'shît*],
> from the earliest times [*m'qedem*] of the Earth"
> (Prov. 8:22, 23 [cf. 8:12], my translation).

These phrases, although not fully synonymous, are examples of closely related Hebrew parallelism. All five phrases describe the long past when God possessed wisdom. It is not possible that the *rē'shît* phrases mean "for an instant" while the other three indicate a long period of time. All indicate a long period of time, even into eternity past—"from everlasting" [*m'olam*], "from *the* beginning" [*m'rosh*], and "from *the* earliest times" [*m'qedem*] of Earth. So "beginning," even though not fully synonymous with "everlasting," certainly would not indicate an instant or a day.

B'rē'shît ("in the beginning") is used four more times after Genesis 1:1, all in Jeremiah. Only one verse reveals the actual time, so the other three, which are very similar, may be judged by that one. "Now in the same year, in the beginning [*b'rē'shît*] of the reign of Zedekiah king of Judah, in the fourth year, in the fifth month" (Jer. 28:1, NASB). The *b'rē'shît* of King Zedekiah's reign included four years and five months of his eleven-year reign. The "beginning" of these kings was not an instant but the beginning portion of their reigns.

God said of Israel, "I saw your forefathers as the earliest fruit on the fig tree in its first [*B'rē'shîtâ*] season" (Hos. 9:10, NASB). Today we live in an instant gratification society, so we see the firstfruits of a new crop as if appearing instantly in a supermarket. It is improper to import this instant gratification idea back into *B'rē'shîtâ* instead of recognizing its actual context in the ancient farming society. Most Israelites were farmers. Farmers know that the firstfruits season was *never* an instant. It takes a farmer many years of work for a fig tree to reach its first bearing season. In the same way, Israel's "forefathers" were not instantaneous but lived and grew in faith in God through centuries.

B^erē'shît in Genesis 1:1 indicates an extensive beginning period of time, not an instant or a few hours. I invite readers to check all references using *rē'shît*. Some do not indicate time but rather objects, such as the first, best, or chief nation; firstfruits; or firstborn: Genesis 1:1; 10:10; 49:3; Exodus 23:19; 34:26; Leviticus 2:12; 23:10; Numbers 15:20; 18:12; 24:20; Deuteronomy 11:12; 18:4; 21:17; 26:2, 10; 33:21; 1 Samuel 2:29; 15:21; 2 Chronicles 31:5; Nehemiah 10:38; 12:44; Job 8:7; 40:19; 42:12; Psalm 78:51; 105:36; 111:10; Proverbs 1:7; 3:9; 4:7; 8:22; 17:14; Ecclesiastes 7:8; Isaiah 46:10; Jeremiah 2:3; 26:1; 27:1; 28:1; 49:34–35; Ezekiel 20:40; 44:30; 48:14; Daniel 11:41; Hosea 9:10; Amos 6:1, 6; Micah 1:13.

"Beginning" in *English* is what confuses, because our English word "beginning" may indicate a beginning instant. It appears that YEC assumes the idea of an instant from the *English* word. So YEC claims that "In the beginning" means "all time" with its instant start, but it means neither an instant nor all time. In contrast, in Hebrew, *b^erē'shît* or *rē'shît*, when used of time, consistently indicate an extensive beginning time period, commonly measured in years.

We may conclude that "*b^erē'shît*," when indicating time rather than objects, indicates at least beginning months, usually years. *B^erē'shît*, when about time, never means either an instant or "all time." Since "the heavens and the earth" last far longer than human kings or fig trees, we may conclude that in Genesis 1:1 "In the beginning" may have been a very long beginning indeed.

Next is the key claim, the one unique claim of the young earth scientific creationism theory—*ex nihilo* creation *in* day one. This key claim is based on the second word, "*in*," of "For *in* six days" beginning Exodus 20:11. If all things were created "*in* six days," then everything can be dated by Adam's genealogies plus a few days. So that second word of Exodus 20:11 is the source of the 6,000-year-old universe claim. It is all based on the second word of "For *in* six days" of Exodus 20:11—"*in*."

(u-5.3) *In day one God created heavens (space), Earth (matter), and time (beginning)—based on Exodus 20:11—"For in six days."* The one unique and distinctive main claim of modern young earth scientific creationism is that the Genesis 1:1 *ex nihilo* creation took place *in* day one. Henry Morris says, "The tremendous events of creation week . . . began with the *ex nihilo* creation of the universe by God on the first day."[327] Ken Ham agrees: "God . . . made time (beginning), space (heaven), and matter (earth). This was the beginning of our universe, all part of the first day in time"[328]

The source of this claim, that the *ex nihilo* creation was in the six days, is Exodus 20:11. Ken Ham states, "Now, when the Creator God spoke as recorded in Exodus 20:1, what did He (Jesus) say? As we read on, we find this statement: *For in six days the LORD made the heavens and the earth, the sea, and all that is in them, and rested the seventh day. . . .* Yes, Jesus did explicitly say He created in six days"[329] (italics his). So the unique claim of YEC is God created everything *in* six days, based on the second English word of Exodus 20:11, "For *in* six days"—the word "*in.*"

In response, there is no "*in*" in the inspired Hebrew of Exodus 20:11.

Ken Ham emphasizes that the Fourth Commandment, Exodus 20:8–11 and 31:17, was "written by the finger of God" (Exod. 31:18). This is what God actually wrote (read Hebrew from right to left):

כִּי שֵׁשֶׁת־יָמִים עָשָׂה יְהוָה אֶת־הַשָּׁמַיִם וְאֶת־הָאָרֶץ אֶת־הַיָּם וְאֶת־כָּל־אֲשֶׁר־בָּם

them-in that all and sea the earth the and heavens the Yahweh *'āsâh* days six For

What was "written by the finger of God" was כִּי שֵׁשֶׁת־יָמִים, "for six days," not "for in six days." God did not write "in" on the tablets of stone of the Law that He gave to Moses.

What does the italics (used by the KJV) of "*in*" indicate? "For *in* six days the LORD made heaven and earth, the sea, and all that in them *is.*" Italics by the KJV indicates that the word is not in the inspired Hebrew. There is no "*in*" in the inspired Hebrew text of the Fourth Commandment in Exodus 20:11.

Contra Ken Ham, Jesus did *not* say He created in six days. The only way to make that claim is to rank the English above the Hebrew.

The only other "For six" verse followed by a time word is 1 Kings 11:16: "For six months did Joab remain there with all Israel" (KJV). The Hebrew כִּי שֵׁשֶׁת, "for six," in 1 Kings 11:16 is identical to Exodus 20:11. But no version translates 1 Kings 11:16, "For *in* six months did Joab remain there with all Israel." The KJV translates 1 Kings 11:16, "<u>For six</u> months did Joab remain there with all Israel." The NKJV says, "<u>Because for six</u> months Joab remained there with all Israel." No translation of 1 Kings 11:16 includes "in."

Adding "*in*" to Exodus 20:11 began with the Hellenistic Alexandrian Septuagint (LXX) translation, ἐν γὰρ ἓξ ἡμέραις ἐποίησεν, "for in six days made." But the LXX is not inspired. The Alexandrian Jews added the word ἐν, "*in.*"

The Latin Vulgate is a better rendering: "*sex enim diebus fecit,*" "For six days made," or "Indeed, for six days made." Unfortunately, most English versions went back to using "for in." But Young's Literal Translation correctly says, "for six days hath Jehovah made." Long before I saw this absence of "*in*," Wiseman and Northrup pointed out that "*in*" is absent from the Hebrew. Northrup translated well, "Because six days the Eternal Lord worked upon the heaven and the earth, the sea and all that is in them."[330] Wiseman agrees: "In the Hebrew version we find that the word 'in' does not appear."[331]

Can the Hebrew add an "in" to "six"? Easily. Job 5:19 says, "He shall deliver you *in six* troubles, Yes, *in seven* no evil shall touch you" (NKJV). Both six and seven have the b^e, "in," prefix. But God did not write the b^e, "*in*," prefix in 20:11a on the Tablets of the Law, nor did Moses write it in Exodus 31:17.

We must remember that only the Hebrew original (not our many translations) was inspired by God. And in the case of the Ten Commandments, the Bible says, "He [Yahweh] gave Moses the two tablets of the testimony, tablets of stone, written by the finger of God" (Exod. 31:18). with His finger beginning Exodus 20:11 was כִּי שֵׁשֶׁת־יָמִים, "For six days."

Moreover, the שֵׁשֶׁת־יָמִים, "six days" in Exodus 20:11 is parallel to 20:9, and Exodus 31:17 is parallel to 31:15:

20:9　Six days you shall labor and do all your work (NASB).

20:11　For six days the LORD worked on the heavens and the earth (my translation from the Hebrew).

31:15　For six days work may be done (NASB).

31:17　For six days the LORD worked on the heavens and the earth (my translation from the Hebrew).

Exodus 20:11 (or 31:17) says nothing about "*in*" the six days. The Fourth Commandment says man should work six days and rest the seventh *because* God worked six days and rested the seventh.[332] The entire basis of YEC's third claim does not exist. Claim three is the missing bridge support. What is missing is the "*in*" of Exodus 20:11. Exodus 20:11a has no "*in*."

The Fourth Commandment is *not*:
Work six days, but keep the Sabbath (seventh) holy by not working, for *in* six days God created . . . but rested the seventh day.
The Fourth Commandment is:
Work six days, but keep the Sabbath (seventh) holy by not working, because six days God worked . . . but rested the seventh day.

In Exodus 20:11, "for" has the sense of "because." So Exodus 20:9–11 may be translated, "Six days you shall labor and do all your work. But the seventh day *is a* Sabbath to the LORD your God. On it you shall not do any work . . . <u>because</u> for six days the LORD worked on the heavens and the earth, the sea, and all that *is* in them, and rested on the seventh day." *"In"* is not in the first phrase in the inspired Hebrew written by God Himself.

A foundational misinterpretation can have a damaging trickle-down effect on subsequent related interpretations. This foundational misinterpretation based on a nonexistent *"in"* has resulted in an entire series (5.3a–5.3z) of attempted supports for *ex nihilo* creation *in* day one about 6,000 years ago. Most of these attempted supports also err.

Lest all this seem very negative, claim three is only one of ten main claims of YEC. The other nine main claims seem Biblically supported, so they will be a great asset to our unified theory. But before we can gather those great Biblical claims, we must separate out the one Biblically unsupported claim and its many subclaims. Now back to the subclaims of this errant main claim three.

(u-5.3a) Bārā' *and* 'āsâh *are interchangeable in Genesis 1 and Exodus 20:11.* Don Batten explains, "'make' [Heb. *'āsâh*] and 'create' (Heb. *bara*) are used interchangeably in Genesis 1."[333] Ken Ham says,

> The fact is that the words *bārā'* and *'āsâh* are often used interchangeably in the Old Testament; indeed, in some places they are used in synonymous parallelism (e.g., Genesis 1:26–27; Exodus 34:10; Isaiah 41:20; 43:7). Applying this conclusion to Exodus 20:11 (cf. 31:17) as well as Nehemiah 9:6, we see that Scripture teaches that God created the universe (everything) in six days, as outlined in Genesis 1.[334]

The point of this claim is so YEC can say Exodus 20:11 means "For *in* six days the LORD *created* [*'āsâh*] heaven and earth, the sea, and all that in them *is*, and rested the seventh day" (KJV, except *"created"* substituted for "made"). So YEC claims that *āsâh* ("do, make") in Exodus 20:11 really means "created" in the same sense as *bārā'* ("create") in Genesis 1:1. So God created everything in six days. Ken Ham, referring to 20:11 says, "Yes, Jesus did explicitly say He created in six days."[335]

Respectfully, I will respond by answering two big questions:
First, what do *bārā'* ("create") and *'āsâh* ("do, make") mean?
Second, are *bārā'* and *'āsâh* interchangeable in Genesis 1 and in the verses listed by Ken Ham?

What do bārā' *("create") and* 'āsâh *("do, make") mean?*

The meaning of *āsâh* ("do, make") is the key for understanding Exodus 20:11. Don Batten claims, "'Make' ['*āsâh*] and 'create' (Heb. *bara*) are used interchangeably in Genesis 1."[336] Ken Ham indicates they are interchangeable in Exodus 20:11. So YEC claims that *āsâh* ("do, make") in Exodus 20:11 really means "created." Ken Ham says, "Jesus did explicitly say He created in six days."[337] Therefore, the universe is about 6,000 years old.

Words have both a basic meaning and a semantic range, the full range of related meanings extending out from that basic meaning.

'Asâh: *'Asâh* has the basic meaning of "do, make."[338] But it has a wide variety of related meanings. For *'āsâh* Gesenius lists "(1) to labor, to work about anything (2); To make, to produce by labour."[339] Strong's lists, "1) to do, fashion, accomplish, make 1a) (Qal) 1a1) to do, work, make, produce."[340] Harris lists, "do, fashion, accomplish." "When used in the sense of 'make' the emphasis is on the fashioning of the object."[341] VanGemeren lists "prepare, set up, create, deal, effect, bring about, obtain, complete, execute, to commit (s.t.), perform work, service; deal with, act, inflect, serve."[342] The last list of related meanings of *'āsâh* includes a weak sense of "create" out of materials. But *'āsâh* especially has the sense of "work," "do work," "to labor," "to produce by labour," "perform work."

The idea is "doing work" on already created materials. Which sense is in Exodus 20:11 — "create" or "do work"? The intended sense is determined by the context.

Walter Kaiser says, "Context is king." The context of *'āsâh* in Exodus 20:11 is the entire Fourth Commandment of 20:8–11. The Fourth Commandment is God's command to work six days, but not work the seventh day.

'Asâh in 20:11 is a greater to lesser parallel with 20:9–10.

20:9 "six days shall you labor and do [*āsâh*] all your work."
20:10 "But the seventh day . . . you shall not do ['*āsâh*] any work"
20:11 "*Because* for six days God '*āsâh*. . . ."

Exodus 20:11 is the grounds and warrant (logical justifying reason and connection of the reason to the claim) for not working on the Sabbath, "*Because* for six days God '*āsâh*. . . ."

One of the most commonly listed meanings of *'āsâh* is various forms of "do work" (see **'Asâh** in previous paragraph). In the context of Exodus 20:8–11 of working six days but not working the seventh, "do work" is the meaning of *'āsâh* intended in verse 11. "*Because* for six days the LORD worked on/did work on the heavens/sky and the earth, the sea, and all that *is* in them, and rested on the seventh day." This meaning of *'āsâh* as "do work" is confirmed by the antonym "rested" at the end of 20:11.

Bārā': In contrast, *bārā'* has the basic meaning in the qal (the Hebrew form in Genesis 1:1) of "create." In the qal, *bārā'* ("create") always has God as the acting subject. The semantic range of *bārā'* is much narrower than *'āsâh*. VanGemeren lists "create, separate."[343] Strong's lists "create, shape, form." Brown, Driver, and Briggs list "shape, create."[344] Benner says the ancient sense was "fill,"[345] so to create by filling when there had been nothing there.

Harris-Archer-Waltke explain another important nuance of *bārā'*: "The root *bārā'* has the basic meaning 'to create.' It differs from *yasar* 'to fashion' in that the latter primarily emphasizes the shaping of an object while *bārā'* emphasizes the initiation of the object." Harris continues, "The root *bārā'* denotes the concept of 'initiating something new.'" "The word also possesses the meaning of 'bringing into existence' in a number of passages."[346] In the context of Genesis 1:1, *bārā'* means "create," in the sense of God "bringing into existence" or "initiating something new."

We may divide the *bārā'* sense of "create" into two subsenses:

First, *bārā'* has the strong sense of creating "something new,"[347] "initiating something new," "bringing [it] into existence."[348] Since אֵת הַשָּׁמַיִם וְאֵת הָאָרֶץ *et ha-shāmayim v*ᵉ*ēt hā 'āretz* ("the heavens and the earth") is a merism meaning "everything," then God created everything brand new when He brought everything into existence in Genesis 1:1. *Bārā'* in Genesis 1:1 fits with God creating everything new or *ex nihilo,* out of nothing. Although *ex nihilo* is not explicitly in the meaning of *bārā',* this first sense fits *ex nihilo* creation stated explicitly in Hebrews 11:3. *Bārā'* is the only Hebrew word with this strong sense that God created something new. Since the range of meaning of the word *'āsâh* does not include this special strong sense of creating something new, *'āsâh* could not have been used interchangeably with *bārā'* in Genesis 1:1. The Holy Spirit chose *bārā',* not *'āsâh,* for Genesis 1:1.

Bārā' has the second sense of "create or make out of materials." Even in this second sense, *bārā'* has the added nuance of something new. There may be a little overlap between this second sense of *bārā'* and *'āsâh,* "make." God made (*'āsâh*) man in His image, his body out of previously created dust (Gen. 2:7). Yet Adam as a body-soul human was something new, so Genesis 1:27 three times uses the word *bārā',* emphasizing this new and unique object of creation—the first body-soul man. Both words were needed to express these two aspects of the creation of man. They are not interchangeable.

Both *bārā'* and *'āsâh* are also needed to summarize all God did. *Bārā'* has the nuance of creating something new, whereas *'āsâh* emphasizes God doing the work making items out of already created materials. Genesis 2:2–3 uses both words. *Asâh* is used twice in 2:2 of "all the work which He did [*'āsâh*]." The sense is "to do work." Then 2:3 summarizes what the work of God was: first *bārā'*, creating new (the *ex nihilo* creation); followed by *'āsâh,* doing the work to form the various items from the created matter. Neither word alone is sufficient because they are not interchangeable. Both words with their different nuances were chosen by the Spirit to summarize all of God's work.

However, the very specific sense of the initial *ex nihilo* creation of Genesis 1:1 fits *bārā'*, "create," alone. The Jewish scholar Rabbi Nahmanides wrote, "We have in our holy language no other term for the bringing forth of something out of nothing but *bara*."[349] (No one is claiming he was a Christian, but he did have insights into Hebrew, if one leaves out his Kabbalist ideas.)

We may diagram the possible slight overlap of the two words:

Bārā'	Possible slight overlap	*'Asâh*
create (new), separate	form/make from materials	do, make, work, accomplish, produce, fashion, act, effect[350]

Bārā' in Gen. 1:1		*'Asâh* in Exod. 20:11
create (new)		do work

So *bārā'*, with the meaning "create," alone fits the initial *ex nihilo* creation of Genesis 1:1. In contrast, *'asâh*, with the meaning "do work," fits Exodus 20:11 in the Fourth Commandment.

Asâh and *bārā'* are *not* interchangeable and there is no "*in*" within Exodus 20:11a. We should understand Exodus 20:8–11 as saying that man is to work six days and rest the seventh, "*Because* for six days the LORD worked on the heavens/sky and the earth, the sea, and all that *is* in them, and rested on the seventh day."

Are bārā' *and* 'āsâh *interchangeable in Genesis 1 and Ham's verse list?*

We will examine verses in Genesis 1 because YEC claims *bārā'* and *'asâh* are interchangeable in Genesis 1. Then we will examine all the verses Ken Ham lists.

Genesis 1:1. "In the beginning God created [*bārā'*] the heavens and the earth." Batten says, "'make' and 'create' (Heb. *bara*) are used interchangeably in Genesis 1."[351]

In response to YEC, God chose the word *bārā'*, "create," not *'āsâh,* "do, make," in Genesis 1. By choosing *bārā',* God "emphasizes the initiation of the object," "creation by divine fiat," "initiating something new," and "bringing into existence"[352] of "the heaven and the earth," the entire universe. *Bārā',* "create," is in the qal perfect, which indicates completed action. Completed action suggests that stage one, the initial *ex nihilo* creation of the heavens and earth, was finished during the beginning time. Even Earth as a rough planet was completed to the precise measurements God intended (Job 38:4, 5). The Genesis 1:1 initial *ex nihilo* creation, bringing into existence something new, fits *bārā',* "create," not *'āsâh,* "do, make." They are not interchangeable in Genesis 1:1.

Genesis 1:11. "Then God said, 'Let the earth sprout vegetation, plants yielding seed, and fruit trees o bearing [*'āsâh*][353] fruit'" (NASB). Batten says that "'make' and 'create' (Heb. *bara*) are used interchangeably in Genesis 1."[354]

In response, plants actually "make" [*'āsâh*] fruit by the normal process under God's normal providence. *Bārā'* would be the wrong word for fruit trees making fruit in 1:11. *Bārā'* (create) and *'āsâh* (do, make) are not interchangeable in Genesis 1:11.

Genesis 1:14–16. This is God's fourth day command: "Then God said, 'Let there be lights in the expanse of the heavens to separate the day from the night, and let them be for signs, and for seasons, and for days and years'" (NASB).

YEC claims, "It is clear from Genesis 1 that the sun was not created until the fourth day."[355]

In response, Genesis 1:14–15 contains the actual commands for the fourth day of God's work. Neither verse uses either *bārā'* or *'āsâh,* so nothing was "created" or "made" on the fourth day. Young's Literal Translation expresses the sense of the command, "And God saith, 'Let luminaries be in the expanse of the heavens, to make a separation between the day and the night'" (1:14a, YLT). The NIV says, "in the expanse of the sky." God commanded the luminaries, which had been created as part of the heavens in Genesis 1:1, now to "be" in the expanse of Earth's sky to carry out their functions to Earth. For the first time, the luminaries would be lights in the sky from the perspective of the divine Narrator, the Spirit of God, located just over the waters. At the end of Genesis 1:15 God said, "And it was so," meaning the fourth day's work was done as commanded.

Here is the command and the report (Hebrew ← right to left): 1:14 Command:

וְהָיוּ לִמְאוֹרֹת֙   וְהָיוּ לְאֹתֹת֙   לְהַבְדִּ֗יל   יְהִ֤י

for-lights and-let-be...for-signs and-let-be...to-separate...let-be

1:16 Report: לְמֶמְשֶׁלֶת   וַיַּעַשׂ

for rule/governing...And-made

The triple command is not a creation command. Genesis 1:14 is a jussive (mild command form) *purpose* clause.[356] In 1:14, God commanded the luminaries to be in the expanse of the sky *to carry out the purpose* of separating day and night, *to carry out the purpose* of being (time marking) signs, and *to carry out the purpose* of being lights.

The report in Genesis 1:16–18 declares that God acted to make the luminaries do as commanded. In Genesis 1:16, 'āsâh has the sense of "to act with effect"[357] or "bring about"[358] the intended result. "And God <u>made</u> ['āsâh] the two great lights, the greater light <u>to govern</u> the day, and the lesser light <u>to govern</u> the night" (Gen. 1:16, NASB). God made the lights govern, rather than God created the lights. In 1:16, God acted with the effect of making the luminaries separate day and night (as commanded), by the greater light governing the day and the lesser light and stars governing the night. In 1:17–18 God set the (already created in 1:1) luminaries in the expanse of the sky (in the perspective of the Narrator, through the first openings in the cloud layer) for the result that they would give light on Earth, govern day and night, and separate light from darkness.

The command in 1:14–15 declared the triple *purpose* (none of which was a creation purpose), and the report in 1:16–18 states God *acted with the effect* of making the luminaries carry out that triple purpose (none of which was a creation act). Since the triple command was not a creation command, neither were the reported actions in 1:16–18.[359] So 'āsâh in the report could not mean the creation of the luminaries, as if interchangeable with *bārā'*, because the triple command was not a creation command. *Bārā'* and *'āsâh* are not interchangeable in Genesis 1.

Next is the list of all verses in which, according to Ken Ham, *'āsâh* and *bārā'* are "used with synonymous parallelism." Synonymous parallelism is a technical term that means the two key words are identical in meaning in two parallel clauses.

Genesis 1:26, 27. "Then God said, 'Let Us make [*'āsâh*] man in Our image, according to Our likeness; and let them rule over the fish of the sea and over the birds of the sky and over the cattle and over all the earth, and over every creeping thing that creeps on the earth.' And God created [*bārā'*] man in His own image, in the image of God He created [*bārā'*] him; male and female He created [*bārā'*] them" (NASB).

In response, God stated His intent: "Let us *'āsâh,* "make," man in Our image." Then He speaks His further intent that mankind should rule the physical world of animal life as God rules the whole universe. With this emphasis on the physical in verse 26, *'āsâh* may emphasize more "fashioning of the object."[360] God would fashion physical man from dust, according to Genesis 2:7, using the verb *yatsar,* "form, fashion."

Then Genesis 1:27 was the actual act when God "created" man in His image and likeness. Verse 27 says three times that God *bārā',* "created," man in His image—both male and female. This triple emphasis indicates that the body-soul or body-soul-spirit human was something new, "created" in the image of God. The two verbs have some parallelism, but *'āsâh* emphasizes "making," while *bārā'* emphasizes "creating something new." This great text would be incomplete without *both* significantly different words. The parallelism is not fully synonymous; it is synthetic, the second verb going beyond the first. It would be improper to substitute *'āsâh* for the three *bārā'* verbs.

Exodus 20:11 and 31:17. As already explained, the context of Exodus 20:11 (and 31:17) is, "'Remember the sabbath day, to keep it holy. Six days you shall labor and do all your work, but the seventh day is a sabbath of the LORD your God; *in it* you shall not do any work'" (Exodus 20:8–10, NASB). Next, verse 11 gives Jesus' warrant and grounds for the Sabbath: "*Because* for six days the LORD worked on the heavens/sky and the earth, the sea, and all that *is* in them, and rested on the seventh day" (my translation from the Hebrew).

In this context of working six days but not working the Sabbath, the sense of *'āsâh* is "perform work."[361] The Israelites should work six days and rest the seventh because God worked six days and rested the seventh. The meaning of *'āsâh* in Exodus 20:11 is "do work." And there is no "*in*." For six days God worked on the heavens/sky, land, and sea to make them lighted, habitable, and full of life.

Nowhere in the six days was our planet *bārā'*, "created." The creation of "the heavens and the earth" had already been done "in the beginning" before the six days. Genesis 1:1 is about the initial *ex nihilo* creation of planet Earth, but Exodus 20:11 is about God's six days of continued work on the already created planet. So the two verses are not about the same events. *Bārā'* in Genesis 1:1 is not interchangeable with *'āsâh* in Exodus 20:11 as YEC advocate Ken Ham claims.

Exodus 34:10. This is next verse in which, according to Ken Ham, *'āsâh* and *bārā'* "are used in synonymous parallelism":

> Then God said, "Behold, I am going to make a covenant. Before all your people I will perform [*'āsâh*] miracles which have not been produced [*bārā'*] in all the earth" (NASB).

Ham claims that the two verbs have "synonymous parallelism," the same meaning.

In response, actually each term has its classic meaning. *'Asâh* here means "do or perform" miracles, but *bārā'* means "initiating something new"[362] that had never before been produced in all the Earth. The two verbs are *not* synonymously parallel and *not* interchangeable.

Isaiah 41:20. This verse uses both *'āsâh* and *bārā'*.

> That they may see and recognize,
> And consider and gain insight as well,
> That the hand of the Lord has done [*'āsâh*] this,
> And the Holy One of Israel has created [*bārā'*] it" (NASB).

Ken Ham says that this verse, too, is "synonymous parallelism."

In response, the clauses are parallel, but the context shows that the parallelism is synthetic, in which the second line adds to the first, rather than synonymous, in which meanings are identical.

The words "done [*'āsâh*] this" in 41:20 refer back to 41:18–19 about God's future end-times restoration of the land of Israel.

I will put the cedar in the wilderness,
The acacia, and the myrtle, and the olive tree;
I will place the juniper in the desert,
Together with the box tree and the cypress (Isa. 41:19, NASB).

In contrast, the words "And the Holy One of Israel has created [*bārā'*] it" refer to the amazing promises by "the Holy One of Israel," Who is the Redeemer of Israel.

"Do not fear, you worm Jacob, you men of Israel;
I will help you," declares the LORD,
"and your Redeemer is <u>the Holy One of Israel</u>" (Isa. 41:14).

Here is the classic meaning of *bārā'*: The Redeemer will create something new—a redeemed Israel. Restoration work of growing trees is not synonymous with creating new spiritual life by *redeeming* the up-till-then largely unbelieving Chosen People. The two verbs are very definitely *not* synonymously parallel. They do not mean the same thing.

<u>*Isaiah 43:7.*</u> This verse uses four verbs.

Everyone who is called [*qārā'*] by My name,
And whom I have created [*bārā'*] for My glory,
Whom I have formed [*yātsar*],
even whom I have made [*'āsâh*] (NASB).

YEC claims that *bārā'* ("create") and *'āsâh* ("do, make") have synonymous parallelism, the same meaning—in order that *'âsâh* in Exodus 20:11 can mean that God "created" everything *in* the six days.

The four verbs in Isaiah 43:7 have poetic parallelism. But is the parallelism synonymous, and therefore each phrase means the same thing, or synthetic, so each phrase adds more meaning?

The context is bringing back God's Chosen People to the land of Israel. The verse describes Israel with four phrases and four verbs:

"called [*qārā'*] by My name,"
"created [*bārā'*] for My glory,"
"formed" [*yātsar*] by God, and
"made" [*'āsâh*] by God.

The form is synthetic parallelism, not synonymous parallelism. "Called by My name" is not synonymous with "created for My glory," which is not synonymous with "formed" and "made" by God. If this were synonymous parallelism, all four phrases would have had the same meaning. They do not. Only the last two phrases may be synonymous — "formed" [*yātsar*] by God, and "made" [*'āsâh*] by God. "Formed," *yātsar*, means fashioned from materials. *Asâh* means made from materials. But neither means "created [*bārā'*] for My glory."

Nehemiah 9:6. Ken Ham claims that Nehemiah 9:6 "teaches that God created the universe (everything) in six days, as outlined in Genesis 1."[363] Let us see what this verse says about "six days."

> Thou alone art the LORD.
> Thou hast made [*'āsâh*] the heavens,
> The heaven of heavens with all their host,
> The earth and all that is on it,
> The seas and all that is in them.
> Thou dost give life to all of them,
> And the heavenly host bows down before Thee.

Nehemiah 9:6 does not say "that God created the universe (everything) in six days" as Ken Ham claims. In fact, this verse says nothing about "in six days." It would seem that Ken Ham must assume "(everything) in six days" so much that he reads it into Nehemiah. Nehemiah 9:6 only summarizes that God alone made everything so all the heavenly hosts rightly bow before Him.

The YEC claim "that God created the universe (everything) in six days, as outlined in Genesis 1"[364] lacks any evidence from the very Bible texts listed to support the claim.

I conclude with respectful but firm dissent that the YEC claim is incorrect that *bārā'* ("create") and *'āsâh* ("do, make") are "interchangeable" and "synonymous" in meaning in Genesis 1 and Exodus 20:11. YEC is proven completely incorrect in its most basic claim, that Exodus 20:11 says that the initial creation took place "*in* six days." There is no "*in*" within 20:11a. YEC is incorrect that "The primal creation of the heavens and the earth in the beginning was the first act of the first day of the six days."[365] Instead of creation *in* the first day, Genesis 1:1 literally says, "In the beginning God created the heavens and the earth."

(u-5.3b) *God "from the beginning made them male and female," so the beginning of time and the universe was recent.* YEC says that Jesus' statement (Matt. 19:4; Mark 10:6) against divorce proves a young universe.

"He who created *them* from the beginning made them male and female" (Matt. 19:4, NASB).

"But from the beginning of creation, *God* made them male and female" (Mark 10:6, NASB).

In a YEC article, Mortenson, with Answers in Genesis, says, "Jesus goes back to the beginning of time." The related diagram is titled, "Jesus and the age of the universe."[366] "He [Jesus] is talking about the whole creation from Jesus' day back to the very first moment of creation, just as Paul is referring to the whole creation during all of history in Romans 1:18–20 and Romans 8:19–23."[367]

YEC defines two of Jesus' words:
1. "beginning" = "beginning of time," "very first moment of creation"
2. "creation" = "the whole creation (universe) during all of history"

YEC also uses "*at* the beginning of creation God made them male and female" (NIV), rather than "*from* the beginning" as in the NASB. The Greek word ἀπό (*apo*) really does mean "from," not "at."
Summary of YEC claim 5.3b:
• Jesus, by "beginning," meant "the very first moment of creation."
• Jesus said God made male and female *at* the beginning of creation.
• Therefore, Adam's beginning 6,000 years ago dates the beginning of "the whole creation [the universe] during all of history."

1. YEC definition of Jesus' word "beginning"
According to this YEC definition, the word "beginning" in Jesus' statements referred to "the beginning of time."[368] This reflects one of the English language senses of "beginning" as instantaneous or nearly so. "From the beginning" indicates "the very first moment of creation." YEC cannot allow the "beginning" to be even six days long because its unique main claim is that "In the beginning" was *in* day one. "The primal creation of the heavens and the earth in the beginning was the first act of the first day of the six days."[369] So the "beginning" must have been "the very first moment of creation."

Response to the YEC definition of Jesus' word "beginning"

Jesus was Hebrew. He was speaking to fellow Jews with a Hebrew mind-set. He likely spoke in Aramaic Hebrew, which may explain the two versions of His statement when translated into Greek by Matthew and Mark. His intended meaning of "beginning" would have been the Hebrew sense of *rē'shît* as the beginning time period.

"In the beginning" is a technical term for the time of Genesis 1:1. But Jesus used a different phrase: "from the beginning, male and female." By adding "male and female," He included not only the initial *ex nihilo* creation initiating time, but also the six days in the Hebrew sense of an extended beginning time period.

Two stage creation consistently understands "beginning" as a beginning time period of unstated length. So the Hebrew word *bᵉrē'shît* indicates the beginning time period of Genesis 1:1; and this Greek word, κτίσεως, in the context of human creation, includes the beginning time period of both Genesis 1:1 *plus* the six days.

Within this extended beginning time period that included both the initial creation and the six days, there were three *"bārā'"* creation acts. These were the creation of the heavens and the earth, the creation of breathing (*nephesh*) sea creatures, and the creation of male and female. All three use the word *bārā'*, "create." In fact, the creation of male and female uses *bārā'* three times. So which *bārā'* act did Jesus emphasize in His explanation against divorce—the universe (YEC choice), breathing sea creatures, or male and female (Adam and Eve)?

In order to answer which Jesus emphasized, we will consider the two versions of Jesus' statement (read Greek left to right):

ὁ   κτίσας ἀπ᾽ ἀρχῆς ἄρσεν καὶ θῆλυ ἐποίησεν αὐτούς
The creating from beginning male and female He made them

He who created *them* from the beginning made them male and female (Matt. 19:4, NASB).

ἀπὸ δὲ ἀρχῆς   κτίσεως ἄρσεν καὶ θῆλυ ἐποίησεν αὐτούς· [370]
But from beginning of creation male and female, He made them.

But from the beginning of creation, *God* made them male and female. (Mark 10:6, NASB).

So which *bārā'* act did Jesus emphasize as He spoke against divorce—the creation of the universe (as YEC claims), the creation of *nephesh* sea animals, or the creation of male and female (Adam and Eve)?

Jesus answers. What Matthew and Mark record is a word-for-word quote from Genesis 1:27 in the Greek Septuagint: "ἄρσεν καὶ θῆλυ ἐποίησεν αὐτούς" ("He made them male and female"). Jesus did not quote from the creation of *nephesh* sea animals in Genesis 1:20 or from the creation of the universe in Genesis 1:1. He quoted Genesis 1:27 of the creation of male and female, Adam and Eve.

Jesus said that God made male and female "from the beginning." YEC understands "beginning" as "the very first moment of creation." However, male and female were not created in "the very first moment of creation," but in the sixth day. This is a contradiction in the YEC claim. YEC cannot change its understanding of "beginning" from "the very first moment of creation" to a longer period of time including the six days because that would nullify its third main claim that "In the beginning" was *in* day one.

In the three-point summary of this YEC claim, the first line misses the Hebrew understanding of "beginning." Misunderstanding "beginning" results in the contradiction of creation of male and female both *at* "the very first moment of creation,"[371] yet in the sixth day:

- Jesus, by "beginning," meant "the *very first moment of creation*."
- Jesus said God made male and female *at* the beginning of creation.
- Therefore, Adam's beginning 6,000 years ago dates the beginning of "the whole creation (the universe) during all of history."

In response, the Bible says God created male and female in the sixth day (Gen. 1:27–31), *not* at "the very first moment of creation." This YEC claim is impossible and self-contradictory.

Jesus used "beginning" in the Hebrew sense as the beginning time period, in this case extended to include the six days with the creation of male and female in the sixth day. Two stage Biblical creation (2SBC) understands "beginning" in the Hebrew sense as a beginning time period of unstated length, in this case extending to include the six days. Then there is no contradiction.

Jesus said, "From the beginning." By "beginning" He meant the Genesis 1 creation time period. From then on, "from" indicates the 4,000-plus years to Jesus or the 6,000-plus years *since* the beginning time period. The 6,000-plus years *since* the creation are not part of the beginning time, but are the years *after* the beginning. *From* that beginning creation time when God made male and female, people are not to divorce.

Two stage Biblical creation summary of Jesus' statements:
• "Beginning" meant the beginning time period including the six days.
• Jesus said God made male and female during that beginning time.
• Therefore, from Adam and Eve onward, do not divorce.

Jesus said nothing in these verses about the beginning of the universe. Jesus said that God created a male and female pair during the beginning, to be understood in the Hebrew sense as the beginning creation time period. So from the beginning onward, do not divorce.

2. YEC definition of Jesus' word "creation"

Mortenson says, "He [Jesus] is talking about *the whole creation* from Jesus' day back to the very first moment of creation, just as Paul is referring to *the whole creation during all of history* in Romans 1:18–20 and Romans 8:19–23."[372] The related diagram is titled, "Jesus and the age of *the universe*"[373] (italics added).

Response to YEC definition of Jesus' word "creation"

Danker's *Greek-English Lexicon* lists two meanings for "κτίσις," "creation"—"**1. the act of creation;**" "**2. the result of a creative act, *that which is created.***"[374] Strong's agrees. Bauer agrees.

In both Matthew and Mark, Jesus quoted from Genesis 1:27: "He made them male and female." Genesis 1:27 is "**the act of creation.**" Jesus was emphasizing the creation of male and female, namely, of Adam and Eve. Jesus was not talking about "all of history," as Mortenson says. Jesus' whole point was that during the beginning, which was the time of the acts of creation, God made the male and female pair in the last creation act. So from that creation of Adam and Eve onward, people are not to divorce.

Mortenson claims that by "creation" Jesus meant "the whole creation during all of history," which is the second meaning of creation, "*that which is created.*" The YEC idea is that in comparison to "all of history," the six days were relatively minor. So YEC can say Adam and Eve were created *essentially at* the beginning of creation. So the creation can be dated by Adam's genealogy to 6,000 years ago. Here is how Mortenson tries to soften the YEC contradiction:

Jesus goes back to the beginning of time. Jesus spoke these words about 4000 years after the beginning. If we equate those 4000 years with a 24-hour day, then Jesus was speaking at 24:00 and the creation of Adam and Eve on the sixth literal day of history would be equivalent to 00:00:00:35 (half a second after the beginning), in the non-technical language of Jesus here is the beginning of time. So, Jesus is indeed saying that Adam and Eve were at the beginning of creation.[375]

Mortenson says, "Adam and Eve were at the beginning of creation." He uses the word "creation" as *that which is created,* the product — the universe in all of history for the 4,000-plus years until Jesus (or 6,000-plus years until our day). He is saying the creation *is* the 4,000 years. And for the Greek word ἀπὸ, he uses the interpretive translation "at," "at the beginning of creation." Adam and Eve were *at* the beginning of all of the history of the universe. So the universe can be dated by Adam's genealogy.

In response, as already shown, Jesus quoted Genesis 1:27: "He made them male and female." This was a past **"act of creation."** Jesus was countering the pro-divorce Pharisees. He said that *from* [ἀπὸ] the beginning time period [ἀρχῆς] — namely, from the time of the acts of creation [κτίσεως] — God made male and female. So *from* the time of that first example onward, do not divorce.

The next few paragraphs are a little technical: Mark 10:6 includes the phrase κτίσεως, "of creation." Κτίσεως is genitive. It is either partitive genitive (part of the whole) or the fairly common genitive of apposition (beginning, that is, of the creation).

YEC chooses the partitive genitive. YEC claims "beginning" was the first instant (part) of the whole creation (the universe) in all of history.[376] So Adam *at* the beginning dates the universe to 6,000 years.

In response, Jesus quotes Genesis 1:27, which shows that He meant the act of the creation of Adam and Eve. That act was the *last* act of the creation time. God created Adam and Eve as the *last* event, not the first moment, of creation. The partitive genitive that YEC chooses produces a contradiction. Adam and Eve could not have been created both at the "very first moment of creation"[377] and at the end of the creation in the sixth day.

The alternative is that κτίσεως is genitive of apposition. In apposition, the head noun ("beginning") states a larger category, and the genitive ("creation") names the specific example. So ἀρχῆς (beginning) is modified by κτίσεως (of creation). In the phrase, "the land of Egypt" (Acts 7:40), "land" is the larger category, and "of Egypt" is the specific land. In the phrase, "the beginning of creation," "beginning" is the larger category, and "of creation" modifies "beginning" by specifying *which* "beginning," namely the creation beginning in Genesis 1 (not some other beginning like the beginning of the Law or beginning of Israel). Jesus speaks of "the beginning," namely "creation," when God made male and female.

Jesus' words fit perfectly with "creation" as genitive of apposition—from the beginning, that is, the time of the creation acts. "But from the beginning *time period, which was the time* of the creation *acts*, He made them male and female." "Creation" clarifies which "beginning." That is why Matthew can leave out "of creation," because Mark's inclusion "of creation" is simply clarifying. Jesus said that from the beginning, understood in the Hebrew sense as a time period, specifically the time of the creation acts of Genesis 1, God made male and female (Gen. 1:27). So *from* then on, do not divorce.

In summary, Jesus used the word "beginning" in the Hebrew sense of *rē'shît* indicating an extensive beginning time period, in this case extended to include the six days when God made male and female. Jesus used "creation" as God's acts of creation in Genesis 1 in that beginning time period. God created Adam and Eve in the sixth day, at the *end* of the extended beginning creation time period. The Bible does not say how much time passed during Genesis 1:1 before the six days. Therefore, the creation of the heavens and earth in the 1:1 time at the *start* of the beginning time period before the six days cannot be dated by Adam's date at the *end* of the six days. The universe remains undated by the Bible.

Mark 10:6	**YEC**	**2SBC**
Beginning	English sense: very first instant	Hebrew sense: beginning time period
Creation	Product—the universe in its 6,000-year history	Acts—creation acts of Gen. 1 ending in Adam and Eve
Genitive: of creation	Partitive—beginning was first instant of the creation (universe) in all history	Apposition—beginning time period, which was time of the creation acts
Age of universe	Adam made at beginning of 6,000-year creation, so the universe is dated by Adam to 6,000 years old	Universe created in 1:1 before six days, Adam was created sixth day; universe undated by Adam
Adam	Adam made in the sixth day at the end of creation; and at the beginning, which was first instant of all history—contradiction	God made Adam and Eve in the beginning creation time ending in sixth day, so from then on do not divorce—harmony

God created the heavens and the earth *ex nihilo* in the
beginning, an unstated amount of time before the six days
and Adam at the end of creation. The age of the universe
cannot be dated by Adam.

(**u-5.3c**) *God created four things* in *day one—space (heaven), matter (earth), time (beginning), and light.* Ken Ham claims, "God . . . tells us in this first verse that He made time (beginning), space (heaven), and matter (earth). This was the beginning of our universe, all part of the first day in time."[378] Ken Ham assumes the creation of space (heaven) and all pre-matter (earth) was *in* "the first day in time," based on the "*in*" of Exodus 20:11.

In response, as already pointed out, there is no "*in*" in Exodus 20:11. Therefore, there is no basis for forcing Genesis 1:1 into day one. Genesis 1:1 does not say the creation of the heavens and earth was in day one.

What did God command in day one? "Let there be light."

When did day one begin? With light. Each of the eight commands and six days began with "And God said, 'Let there be . . . ,'" so day one began with God's command "And God said, 'Let there be light.'" That command for light was the *only* command in day one. Light began day. Evening beginning nighttime, and morning ending nighttime, concluded day one.

The Bible, God's Word, identifies the time of when "God created the heavens and the earth" as "In the beginning" (Gen. 1:1), not as in "the first day in time."

The fundamental issue in all this is Biblical authority. On YEC claim three, if young earth scientific creationism continues to proclaim "*in six days,*" thus continuing to add an "in" that is not there, that act will constitute a violation of Biblical authority.

(**u-5.3d**) *"Heavens" meant "all space" without luminaries.* YEC claims, "In Genesis 1:1, the term [heaven] refers to the component of space in the space-mass-time universe."[379] God created "all space (heaven)."[380]

In response, Moses gave his meaning of *ha-shāmayim,* "heavens," in Deuteronomy 4:19—"the sun and the moon and the stars" in the sky (NASB). Moses saw "the sun and the moon and the stars" in the sky daily and nightly.

YEC improperly redefines the ancient Hebrew term *ha-shāmayim* ("heaven, heavens, sky") as the modern concept of "space" meaning "outer space." But "outer space" is not the meaning of *ha-shāmayim.* This is an example of the semantic anachronism fallacy—forcing a modern meaning into the ancient text.[381] Moses could not possibly have meant the modern concept of "outer space" by the ancient Hebrew term *ha-shāmayim*.

(u-5.3e) *"Earth" meant "all matter" in the universe.* YEC claims, "The term 'earth' refers to the component of matter in the universe."[382] God created "all matter (earth)."[383]

This is another semantic anachronism fallacy. By the term "earth," Moses could not have meant "all matter" of the universe. Earth was what was under Moses' feet.

Subclaims 5.3d–5.3e are an attempt to support the claim that "God . . . tells us in this first verse that He made time (beginning), space (heaven), and matter (earth). This was the beginning of our universe, all part of the first day in time."[384] Contra this YEC claim, I propose that we should believe Genesis 1:1 literally: "In the beginning [not in day one] God created the heavens [not just space] and the earth [not unformed matter]."

(u-5.3f) *All this matter ("earth") in the universe was unformed pre-matter in day one.* YEC claims, "The term 'earth' refers to the component of matter in the universe."[385] "'Earth' [all matter] was only some kind of amorphous prematter."[386]

In response, Genesis 1:2 changes the subject from "the heavens and the earth" in 1:1 to only "Now the earth" in 1:2. What was described as *tōhû v*ᵃ*bōhû* was only planet Earth. The earth was what was under Moses' feet, although our planet was still unfinished in 1:2. The Bible never describes Earth as "unformed, amorphous prematter" throughout space. By declaring only Earth unfinished, Genesis 1:2 implies that the heavens were essentially finished. The heavens in Genesis 1:1 fit Moses' understanding as the sky with "the sun and the moon and the stars" (Deut. 4:19). God created the heavens in Genesis 1:1 as "the sun and the moon and the stars," not as "space," nor earth as "amorphous prematter." God created the earth as what was under Moses' feet, although our planet was still unfinished in 1:2.

(u-5.3g & u-5.3h) *"In the beginning" was the creation of the time component of the space-mass-time universe.* Henry Morris says, "Genesis 1:1 can legitimately and incisively be paraphrased as follows:

> The transcendent, omnipotent Godhead called into existence the space-mass-time universe.[387]

"Not only does the first verse of the Bible speak of the creation of space and matter, but it also notes the beginning of time."[388] Morris is claiming that Genesis 1:1 declares the creation of "space," "matter," and "time." "In the beginning" was the creation of the *time* component of "the space-mass-time universe."

In response, "In the beginning" certainly included the start of time. And time started instantaneously. But the start of time was only an aspect of "In the beginning," not its meaning. "Beginning" does not mean either "instant" or "time" in Hebrew or English. The reason Henry Morris leaves out "In the beginning" in the above paraphrase is Exodus 20:11. Because of the mistranslation of Exodus 20:11 by the addition of "*in*"—that God created everything "*in* six days"—Morris assumed that the initial creation was *in* day one, not "in the beginning" before day one. So he concluded that "in the beginning" only means the creation of time. He concluded that "In the beginning" identifies *what* was created—time. So he leaves "In the beginning" out of his paraphrase.

Actually, "In the beginning" answers the question *When?* It tells us the time period *when* "God created the heavens and the earth." *Bᵉrē'shît*, "In the beginning," was normally measured in years. *Bᵉrē'shît* certainly includes the instantaneous start of time, but its *meaning* is the entire beginning time period *when* God created the heavens and earth, not just *what* was created, time.

Genesis 1:1 declares more than the creation of "space," "pre-matter," and "time." Genesis 1:1 declares that in the beginning (understood in the Hebrew sense as in the beginning time period) God created the actual literal heavens (not just "space") and the literal Earth, our unfinished planet (not just raw unformed pre-matter).

(**u-5.3i**) *Day one began time in the entire universe.* YEC claims that God created everything "*in* six days," so day one on Earth was the beginning of time throughout the universe. "God . . . made time (beginning)." "This was the beginning of our universe, all part of the first day in time."[389]

In response, God literally "created the heavens and the earth" "in the beginning," before day one began later on rotating Earth with "And God said, 'Let there be light'" (Gen. 1:3). Therefore, day one on Earth was an unstated amount of time after the beginning when God created the heavens and the earth.

Day one was the start of *daylight-nighttime measured days* on *Earth's* rotating surface. Day one on rotating Earth says nothing about time passage in the heavens that had been created back "In the beginning."

(**u-5.3j**) *The dark evening of Genesis 1:2 began the first night, followed by the morning in 1:3 as the evening and morning of day one.* Henry Morris, who founded YEC, affirmed day-night days.

Opposed to Dr. Morris recently in the premier YEC *Technical Journal*, Frank DeRemer claims, "The text clearly suggests that Day 1 began with 'In the beginning' and following that first evening of darkness (v. 2) was the first morning, when God said, 'Let there be light' (v. 3)."[390] DeRemer claims each of the six days was the "cycle of evening, night, morning, and daytime."[391] The dark of Genesis 1:2 was the night half of day one. YEC advocate Jason Lisle agrees: "A day was an evening and a morning."[392] In order to support the third main YEC claim (which says Gen. 1:1–2 were in day one), day one had to have begun with evening in the darkness of Genesis 1:2 as the first half of day one. Then morning began with the light of 1:3 as the daytime second half of day one.

Contra DeRemer, Henry Morris correctly claimed "a cyclical succession of days and nights—periods of light and periods of darkness," "a cyclical light-dark arrangement."[393] The Morris view is Biblically supported. The DeRemer view has fatal Biblical problems.

First, the Hebrew grammar of Genesis 1:2 indicates 1:2 was a description. Verse 2 was not a time period. DeRemer claims Genesis 1:2 was "the first evening of darkness (v. 2)." The claim that Genesis 1:2 was a time period (the first evening) is the very same fatal error as in the gap theory. The gap theory also incorrectly claims Genesis 1:2 was a time period—the gap. If the gap theory is wrong, so is DeRemer's claim.

If YEC were to claim that Genesis 1:1 (instead of 1:2) was the time period of evening beginning the twelve hours of darkness of nighttime, then they are accepting the meaning of *bᵉrē'shît*, "in the beginning," as a beginning time period as used in the Hebrew Bible. But in the Bible, *bᵉrē'shît* was measured normally in years, never in hours. A beginning measured in years would no longer fit into day one, the problematic third YEC claim. Also, contra YEC, the heavens of 1:1 were never declared dark; only the surface of the deep ocean in the 1:2 description of Earth was declared dark. The whole third main claim of YEC is impossible to put together with the Bible.

Second, God began each of the eight commands and six days with the same words: "And God said, 'Let there be . . .'" All eight commands and six days follow this same pattern. Day one began with God's command in Genesis 1:3: "And God said, 'Let there be light.'"

Third, grammatically, evening and morning were the *last* two consecutive events in day one, not the first two as DeRemer claims. Each of the events in day one is prefixed with *vav/waw* consecutives "And . . ." (except the phrase "and the darkness He called night"), indicating that the events were in sequential order. Day one began with God's command for light to begin the daylight part of the day. After God commanded the light, saw that it was good, separated the light from the darkness, and named the light "day" and darkness "night," then the last events were evening beginning nighttime, then the morning dawn ending nighttime. All six days were normal, full day-night days.

The grammar proves with certainty that day one *ended* in evening, (night) and morning, a full nighttime. If DeRemer's previous night in 1:2 were added to day one, then day one would have had two nights, as a night-day-night, more than a day. DeRemer errs.

Numbers 9:15–21, also written by Moses, contains an example of a day. It consisted of daytime followed by evening then morning.

> Now on the day that the tabernacle was erected, the cloud covered the tabernacle, the tent of the testimony, and in the evening it was like the appearance of fire over the tabernacle, until morning. So it was continuously; the cloud would cover it *by day*, and the appearance of fire by night (9:15–16, NASB).

The daytime was followed by nighttime. "Evening . . . until morning" delineates only the nighttime when there was fire, not nighttime and then daytime as a night-day of twenty-four hours. All six days were full day-night days.

Long after the creation, when Israel was established under the Law, the Jewish holy days of Passover, Sabbath, and festivals began at evening (Exod. 12:6, 18; Deut. 16:4). But God's seventh day in Genesis 1 was *not* called a "Sabbath." Much later, in Exodus 20, God's seventh day of rest was used as an illustration for Israel. But an illustration works only forward, never back in time. God's seventh day of rest can be imported forward as an illustration for the Israelite Sabbath, but the Sabbath beginning at evening cannot be imported back into God's seventh day. So it would be incorrect to import the later Jewish holy days' evening-nighttime-daylight order back into any of the seven days of Genesis 1:3—2:4a.

After the daylight, there came the evening, night, and first crack of dawn of morning ended the night, completing the sixth work day. Then the original seventh rest day began with daylight, and necessarily ended with nighttime because it was "the seventh day," a full day. All seven were full day-night days.

Henry Morris is correct that there was "a cyclical succession of days and nights—periods of light and periods of darkness," "a cyclical light-dark arrangement."[394]

DeRemer understands the crucial importance to YEC of his night-day subclaim. For the YEC's third claim (that Genesis 1:1–2 was in day one) to stand, "that first evening of darkness (v. 2)" *had* to have begun day one. But as shown here, DeRemer is without question incorrect. Contra DeRemer, day one began with daylight to Earth's surface at "And God said, 'Let there be light.'" Day one ended as the divine Narrator's side of Earth rotated into evening dusk, night, and morning dawn, completing day one. "And there was evening and there was morning, day one." YEC's novel third claim that Genesis 1:2 was *in* day one is impossible.

The dark of Gen. 1:2 could not have been the evening of day one because 1:2 was not a time period.

And if 1:2 were a time period, adding the dark of 1:2 to day one would have made a night-day-night, more than one day.

(u-5.3k) *The deep was mixed with earth as a "watery matrix."* YEC claims that the deep was "a pervasive watery matrix throughout the darkness of space."[395]

In response, the *tᵉhôm,* "deep ocean," was not something in space. *Tᵉhôm* is associated with the word *māyim,* "waters," as the Spirit was hovering above the surface of Earth's deep ocean water. During the second command unit, God would separate the deep ocean waters below from the foggy water in the air, apparently by causing the fog to rise from the ocean. In the third command unit, land would appear out of the deep ocean water. The flood narrative speaks of that same ocean when "all the fountains of the great deep [*tᵉhôm*] burst open" (Gen. 7:11). The *tᵉhôm,* or "deep," was Earth's early deep ocean, not water "throughout . . . space."

(u-5.3l) *Darkness "upon the face of the deep" was darkness throughout space.* YEC says, "The picture presented is one of all the basic elements . . . throughout the darkness of space."[396]

In response, the deep was Earth's early ocean (Gen. 7:11; 8:2). Genesis 1:2 begins, "Now the earth was *tōhû vᵃbōhû,* and darkness was over the surface of the deep." So the darkness of 1:2 was on the surface of the deep ocean that covered Earth, *not* "throughout the darkness of space." Since God had created the heavens in Genesis 1:1 and Moses understood the heavens as "the sun and the moon and the stars" (Deut. 4:19), not as "space," then the heavens were not dark. Only the surface of Earth was declared dark in Genesis 1:2. We find the reason for the dark in Job 38:9: "I made a cloud its [the sea] garment, And thick darkness its swaddling band."

Only Earth's deep sea's surface was declared dark by Genesis 1:2, and it was darkened by thick dark cloud cover.

(u-5.3m) *The light on day one began three-day temporary light.* YEC claims, "God shined some temporary light on the initial earthen substance until He made the sun on Day 4."[397] "Light was coming during the day as though from the sun."[398]

This claim of temporary light for three days is necessary to prop up the creation-in-day-one third main claim. YEC claims that "the heavens" in Genesis 1:1 was only "space." So YEC claims that on day four the sun was either created *ex nihilo* or made from part of "earth."

In response, Genesis 1:1 declares God created the heavens in the beginning. Moses understood the heavens as the sky with "the sun and the moon and the stars" (Deut. 4:19).[399] The light was sunlight that at God's command penetrated Earth's dark cloud cover to the water-covered surface (Job 38:9) for the first time on day one. The Bible nowhere indicates the light of day one was temporary light. Nor does the Bible declare an end to temporary light. Both temporary light and its termination are simply assumed by YEC, but the Bible says nothing about either one.

(u-5.3n) *The light was created in transit as if from sun, moon, and stars that had not yet been made.* Morris claims, "Light was coming during the day as though from the sun and during the night as though from the moon and stars, even though they had not yet been made."[400] "It therefore did not take a billion years for the light from a star which is a billion light-years distance to reach the earth after the star was created. The light-trail from the star was created in transit, as it were, all the way from the star to earth, three days before the star was created."[401]

For its third claim (that the entire creation was *in* the six days 6,000 years ago) to stand, YEC has to claim that all light is 6,000 years old or less. YEC claims that supernova explosions and spinning galaxies are merely light-trails created in transit.[402] These events *never actually happened.*

In response, the problem with this claim is not whether God can make supernova explosions appear that never happened. The problem is that supernovae that we see, but never actually happened, are deceptive. Is God deceptive in the creation? Psalm 19:1 says, "The heavens declare the glory of God" (NIV). God's glory is not deceptive. This is a major YEC problem. This problem ceases if, instead of claiming that God created everything *in* the six days, we believe "In the beginning God created the heavens and the earth." The "beginning" was a time period, undated in length. The heavens (sun, moon, and stars) are however old they are. So if we accept Genesis 1:1 literally, then the light from stars is however old it is. Both the stars and light are real and reveal the glory of God.

(u-5.3o) *The light of day one energized the entire universe.* Henry Morris claims the light on day one was "setting the electromagnetic forces into operation," thus "energizing the physical cosmos."[403] "So the nuclear forces maintaining the integrity of matter were activated by the Father . . . , the gravitational forces were activated by the Spirit . . . , and the electromagnetic forces were activated by the Word when He called light into existence out of the darkness."[404]

I respond that this claim of specific Trinitarian work-division derived from modern physics is *not* in the Bible. It imports YEC ideas of physics into Moses' ancient text. It is an interpretive invention. Contra this YEC claim, the Bible says, "All things were made through Him," the Word, God the Son (John 1:3, KJV). This YEC claim of Trinitarian division of labor is contrary to the Bible and pure invention.

I also respond that Genesis 1:2 says that only *Earth's* sea surface was dark. The light God commanded was *not* "energizing the physical cosmos." That first daylight was sunlight penetrating the overcast cloud to Earth's surface and the Spirit's location, because only light to a rotating planet makes day and night. God had already created the sun, moon, and stars as an essential part of the heavens in 1:1. Therefore, day one was sunlight at God's command penetrating to Earth's rotating sea surface.

(u-5.3q) *In day three, solid planet Earth precipitated out, forming crust with dry land and seas; God made trees with appearance of age.* YEC claims that on day three, out of the "watery matrix," "dissolved elements precipitated and combined with others to form the vast complex of minerals and rocks making up solid earth — its crust, its mantle and its core."[405]

In response, I wish to say respectfully that this claim is not in the Bible. It also does not make physical sense. The claim that Earth's super-heated magma mantle and even hotter iron-nickel core was dissolved in water and precipitated out does not make sense.

Instead, Genesis 1:1 says God created Earth during the beginning. The Bible does not date "In the beginning," so our planet is however old it is. An undated Earth allows God to have used whatever processes He chose to make planet Earth into its present form, and to do so during however long He took. By the time of Genesis 1:2, planet Earth was covered with cloud-darkened ocean. By the time of Genesis 1:3, planet Earth was also necessarily rotating for day and night. Earth was a planet God formed during the beginning time period of Genesis 1:1 when God literally "created the heavens and the earth."

This YEC claim that our planet was formed on day three confuses the two senses of *'erets*, "earth"—land appearing apparently by rising out of the sea in the third work day, and the whole planet Earth created in 1:1. In day three God made the first *yabāshâh*, dry ground, appear from the ocean water. "And God said, 'Let the water under the sky be gathered to one place, and let dry ground appear'" (NIV). The same command cannot mean both the formation of the planet and the rise of the first granite continental land mass. Genesis 1:9 was God's command for the appearance (to the Spirit) of the first continental land as it rose out of the gathered waters. This first land appeared above the ocean surface on the already rotating planet Earth that God had created back in 1:1. YEC erroneously conflates the two senses of *'erets*.

Contra YEC, we should take Genesis 1:1 literally. God created planet Earth (unfinished) during the beginning in 1:1. The whole Earth was water-covered by the time of 1:2. Then in Genesis 1:9 God commanded the gathering of the water and the appearance from out of the water of dry ground, apparently the first continental land.

I need to clarify an issue. I am not saying Moses would have fully understood our Earth as a spherical planet rotating on its axis in the way we understand today. But he certainly did distinguish between the local sense of earth as land rising from the sea, and the sense of the whole Earth including sea and land below his feet in contrast to the heavens of sun, moon, and stars above. And beyond Moses, God, who gave the original account, and the Spirit, who inspired Moses, certainly understood and ensured that the account is accurate.

(u-5.3r) *In day four, God created the sun, moon, and galaxies from "earth."* YEC makes the claim, "It is clear from Genesis 1 that the sun was not created until the fourth day." "The sun was created to rule the day that already existed." "God deliberately left the creation of the sun until the fourth day."[406] So some YEC advocates seem to be claiming a second *ex nihilo* creation—the sun, moon, and stars on the fourth day. In contrast, Henry Morris claims that on the fourth day God "placed these 'lights' [sun, moon, and stars] throughout the infinite space of heaven that had been created on Day One, these also being made of the same 'earth' that had been created on Day One."[407]

In response to a second *ex nihilo* creation, God literally created *ex nihilo* "the heavens" "in the beginning." Moses understood "the heavens" to be the sky with "the sun and the moon and the stars" (Deut. 4:19). Therefore, God had already created these luminaries in the beginning time before the fourth day. *Bārā'*, "create," is not even in the fourth day.

In response to Henry Morris, making a hundred billion galaxies out of "earth" on the fourth day does not fit the Hebrew understanding of Earth. Earth was what was under Moses' feet. The Bible says nothing about all the stars being made of "earth." Besides, spectral analyses of stars indicate that they are primarily hydrogen and helium, not the heavier elements implied by the word *ha'āretz* ("earth").

The Hebrew explanation for why the fourth day was not a creation command is back in u-5.3a under Genesis 1:14–16.

In summary of my response, by His fourth day of work, God made the luminaries govern day and night, be time markers, and be lights in the sky through the first openings in the cloud layer above the Narrator (Job 26:13a). Neither *bārā'*, "create," nor even *'asâh*, "do, make," are in the commands of the fourth day (Gen. 1:14–15). *Asâh* is in the report, but as a purpose clause, "made . . . to govern," that God made the luminaries fulfill their purpose of governing day and night. The report was not as a creation command. God did not *bārā'*, create, the luminaries on the fourth day. He had already created the heavens, which Moses understood as "the sun and the moon and the stars" (Deut. 4:19) in the sky, back during the time of Genesis 1:1.

(u-5.3t) *Rain did not fall until the flood.* YEC claims, "The original hydrologic cycle was thus drastically different." "There was no rainfall on the earth" until the flood because of "the great vapor canopy."[408] In order to claim a 6,000-year-old Earth, YEC needs this vast vapor canopy claim. It ensures a massive source of enough rain, combined with fountains of the deep, to cause the water to rise over all the mountains (Gen. 7:20), and to make all the sedimentary geological layers of Earth's surface by the flood.

Kline answered this claim with the counter claim that Genesis 2:5–6 explains that there were no land plants because God had not sent rain—the ordinary means causing land plants to grow. Then on the third day of His work, God sent water by rain clouds (explained in Gen. 2:6), which made plants to grow. Genesis 2:5–6 indicates plants did not grow until provided with water.[409] Mark Futato explains that the water that made the plants grow on the third day was rain.[410]

(u-5.3u & 5.3x) *Everything was perfect on the sixth day. So before the sixth day there was no disease, physical calamities, predators, death, or fossils. Even Satan was good on the sixth day.* YEC claims that all was "perfect" before Adam's Fall, there was "no struggle for existence, no disease, no pollution, no physical calamities (earthquakes, floods, etc.), no imbalance or lack of harmony, no disorder, no sin and, above all *no death!* Even Satan was still good at this point."[411] "The fossil record now found in the sedimentary rocks of the earth's crust could only have been formed sometime *after* man sinned."[412] "Originally, when everything was perfect, there were no meat eaters."[413] YEC says, "everything was perfect."

In contrast, old earth creationism (OEC) claims that animal death is not morally evil. Animal death may not be emotionally pleasant, but the fox eating the mouse or grouse (breathing *nephesh* examples of mammals and birds) is not a moral evil. This allows animal death before Adam's sin. Romans 5:12 says that Adam's sin resulted in *human* death. OEC claims most fossils are ancient, from long before Adam. OEC says these fossils were the result of normal animal life cycles that God built into His very good creation.

To state the issue positively, YEC claims that animals had eternal physical life had Adam not sinned. (YEC usually expresses this in the negative as "no death.") OEC claims God created animals with their normal life cycles, and Lucifer's fall and Adam's Fall added moral evil.

In response to both YEC and OEC, I suggest that the Bible does not explicitly say whether animals had eternal physical life had Adam not sinned. Animals that God created now have normal life cycles, so the burden of proof is on YEC to demonstrate from the Bible that animals were created with eternal physical life until Adam sinned, and that the curse declares the beginning of all animal death. A definitive proof that Adam's sin caused animal death cannot be based on Romans 8:19–24, because that text does not mention Adam, the Fall, the curse, or animal death (see chapter 13).

The Bible explicitly says two things related to this subject: First, all that God made was "very good" on the sixth day. But this issue is not as simple as YEC suggests with its claim that all was "perfect" until Adam sinned. I will discuss the options on this issue in 11.11a.

Second, there was no *human* death before Adam's sin. A careful examination of Romans 5:9–21 and 1 Corinthians 15:22–23 shows that Paul was speaking of *human* death, *human* reconciliation to God by Christ's full atonement for our justification, and finally, *human* resurrection.

The YEC claim that animals certainly had eternal physical life before Adam sinned is more than the Bible says. Ross points out that Paul did *not* explicitly say anything about animal death in these texts. The curse in Genesis 3 affects animals negatively, but does *not* condemn animals to death (other than the serpent/Satan) as one would expect if animals had eternal physical life before Adam's sin.

Kaiser says that God Himself made "garments of skin for Adam and his wife," implying that God killed animals, yet God does only good. So he argues that since God killed animals and God is perfectly good, we cannot exclude normal animal life and death from the time when "God saw all that He had made, and behold, it was very good."[414] So the YEC claim that animals had eternal physical life had Adam not sinned seems based on less than clear implications.

I suggest that the Bible does not explicitly say whether animals had eternal physical life or normal life cycles before Adam's sin. A rigid YEC claim that there certainly was no higher animal death before Adam's sin seems more than the Bible explicitly says.

(u-5.3y) *Genealogies date Adam about 6,000 years ago, so the universe can be dated to about 6,000 years old.* YEC claims, "As far as the creation of the universe is concerned, this took place five days earlier than the creation of man."[415] YEC repeats the mantra, "Thousands, not billions."[416]

I respond that this YEC phrase does not say *what* is thousands, not billions, of years old. We need to thoughtfully ask ourselves, Who or what does the Bible say is thousands of years old? The Bible roughly dates *Adam* by his genealogy to thousands of years. But if we take Genesis 1:1 literally, the creation of the universe did not occur in day one, but "in the beginning." If we understand the normal use of "in the beginning" as an extensive beginning time period, then time unmeasured by the Bible passed before God commanded light to Earth to begin day one. So the universe is however old it is, not however old Adam would be.

(u-5.3z) *God created the universe with "appearance of age."* Henry Morris claims, "The whole universe had an 'appearance of age' right from the start."[417]

One problem with "appearance of age" is "last thursdayism." The idea of last thursdayism is that if God created everything by miracles with appearance of age, then He could have created everything last Thursday, implanting in all of us memories of events before last Thursday. Creation 6,000 years ago and creation last Thursday are equally unfalsifiable because both involve miraculous appearance of age. Last thursdayism is a refutation that takes this appearance of age claim to its extreme (*reductio ad absurdum*) to show its error.

A greater problem with appearance of age of the universe is deception. Carl Wieland, although he is a YEC advocate, recognizes the problem:

A common response from believers is to say that God could have created the light 'on the way'. But light from distant stars also carries information—galaxies rotating, stars exploding. So if that information never left the star, but was created 'en route', this means that in a 6,000-year-old universe, anything we see beyond 6,000 light-years away would be a phony light show. . . . The events would never have taken place in the actual stars themselves. In other words, it would involve a God of truth creating a completely unnecessary false history. It is really not far removed from the embarrassing suggestion around Darwin's time that God created the fossils in the rocks.[418]

Wieland is right. The Bible says, "God is not a man, that He should lie" (Num. 23:19, KJV). God wrote the Ninth Commandment: "Thou shalt not bear false witness" (Exod. 20:16, KJV). Surely He keeps His own Commandment. God does not lie nor deceive. He did not create the universe to be a false witness.

YEC affirms means for the flood, *avoiding false appearance of fossils' age.* But for the six days, many YEC advocates assume miracles not stated in the Bible, so they *claim an appearance of age for the universe.* A number of YEC advocates recognize the inconsistency.

God created the universe as evidence about Himself (Rom. 1:20). Much of that evidence is in the heavens: "The heavens declare the glory of God; the skies proclaim the work of his hands" (Psalm 19:1, NIV). Is the work of His hands a phony light show?

Paul in Romans 1:18–20 (NASB) explains,

For the wrath of God is revealed from heaven against all ungodliness and unrighteousness of men, who suppress the truth in unrighteousness, because that which is known about God is evident within them; for God made it evident to them. For since the creation of the world His invisible attributes, His eternal power and divine nature, have been clearly seen, being understood through what has been made, so that they are without excuse.

In Romans 1:18–20, Paul makes seven claims:

1. **God does not suppress the truth; man does.** A false appearance of age would mean God is suppressing the truth. But God does not do that.
2. **Suppression of truth is "unrighteous."** Certainly God is not unrighteous.
3. **God Himself made these general revelation truths "evident" to humans.** A false appearance of age hides truth rather than makes truth evident. And it is God, not "nature," who reveals truth by the creation.

4. **This revelation began with the created cosmos/universe** (noun κτίσεως from *ktisis*) (κόσμος, *cosmos*). From the cosmos that He created, God reveals truth about Himself. He did not make the created cosmos to reveal false appearance of age.

5. **What God has revealed from the creation are "His invisible attributes, His eternal power and divine nature."** He does not reveal that He is deceptive.

6. **God's divine nature is *clearly seen,* not concealed, by what He has made.** Deceptive appearance of age does not clearly reveal. And He makes that truth evident, clear, and understandable.

7. **This revelation is so clear that "they are without excuse."** God will reveal His wrath based on the clarity of having already revealed His divinity by the creation, but humans rejected that clear revelation. The damage to the universe by the fall is insufficient to deceive, because humans are still "without excuse."

If the heavens are deceptive by false appearance of age, then God is revealing the invisible attribute that He is a deceiver.

If the heavens are deceptive by a false appearance of age, then the heavens are not a clear revelation of truth, but a concealment of truth.

If the heavens are deceptive by false appearance of age, then humans do have an excuse.

But God did not create the universe or Earth with deceiving appearance of age. God does not deceive. The Bible never says that God created the heavens and Earth with appearance of age.

A creation theory that does not allow the character
and glory of God to be clearly revealed in the creation
is a defective theory.

This deceptive appearance of age and other problems of claim three disappear if, instead of claiming that *in* day one God created space and unformed watery matrix about 6,000 years ago, we believe literally that "In the beginning God created the heavens and the earth."

The solution is simple. If the universe was created "In the beginning," then the Bible allows the universe to be however old it is. The Bible does not date the universe and Earth because Genesis 1:1–3 shows that the initial creation was an unstated amount of time before day one. All this indicates a Biblically undated creation of the heavens and earth (UEC).

The character of God is of utmost importance. Deceptive appearance of age of the universe makes God appear to be a deceiver.[419] The question is not, *Can* God make something appear to have age? He can and occasionally has. Appearance of age is no problem theologically, ethically, or apologetically (the reasoned defense of the Christian faith). The real question is, Did God create the universe with appearance of age that is *deceptive*? That is a huge problem theologically, ethically, and apologetically!

Let me illustrate the difference. When I was in Israel on an archeological dig, we had to turn in all significant finds to the Israeli Antiquities Authority representative. So later at the *souk* (Arab open-air market), for five shekels I bought a replica clay oil lamp similar to one our team dug up. It appeared to be two or three thousand years old but was advertised as a replica. The appearance of age was not deceptive because everyone knew it was a replica. Neither the law of God nor of Israel was broken. But someone else tried to sell to us for five hundred shekels "the real thing" that had been "dug out of the ground." I had been told to beware of uncertified "authentic, antique, ancient" artifacts that were actually manufactured by expert antiquing artisans in the next Arab village by one of the seller's many uncles or cousins. Then it may have been "aged" a year or so in the ground before being "dug up" and sent to the *souk*. The second oil lamp also had appearance of age, but *it was deceptive,* so it was illegal under the laws of the Israeli Antiquities Authority and the law of God.

When Jesus multiplied bread or turned water into wine, no one who witnessed these miracles and ate and drank would have thought the bread or wine was counterfeit or deceptive, even though each appeared to have greater age than it did.[420]

In contrast, everything in the universe beyond 6,000 light-years (99+% of the universe is beyond 6,000 light-years) either is actually older than 6,000 years (most much older) or falsely appears much older, *deceiving* scientists and laypeople alike; or else an explanation has not yet been understood.

Why would distant galaxies be deceiving if the universe is actually only about 6,000 years old as YEC claims? The reason is that God built into the creation itself three or four overlapping measurement tools to discover the distance to and apparently the age of even distant galaxies. Unless these measuring tools are drastically flawed, which I agree is possible but honestly very unlikely, it appears that we can gain an approximate knowledge of the distance, size, and age of the galaxies and of the entire universe. Why did God allow us to discover these distance-measuring means that He built into the galaxies? To deceive us? Or so we can learn the apparent actual age and the immense size of the universe—to His glory? Romans 1:18–20 and Psalm 19:1 indicate the latter.

I want to emphasize this. The important point is *not* how old science says the universe is. Science can be wrong. Any one of the three or four measuring tools could have been miscalibrated or misunderstood. And the Bible does not date the universe. So I am *not* giving my affirmation to any particular age. The important point is that God Himself built into the universe objects and means that can serve as measuring tools—parallax, Cepheid variable stars, type 1a supernova explosions, and red shift. These objects apparently give us the ability to measure at least roughly the size and age of the universe. And God placed our solar system in just the right place in our galaxy so we have a clear view of the universe, which would not be the case in the galactic center or in a dust cloud.[421] That size and age, even if our measurements err significantly, would seem to contradict a 6,000-year-old universe. And God does not tell us in the Bible the date of the creation of the universe. Therefore, those who would date the universe (rather than just Adam) by Adam's genealogy at about 6,000 years old do so *on their own authority*, not on Biblical authority.

Equally, scientists who are Christians may tentatively propose an age of the universe from science (the estimate has been reduced from the earlier estimate of about 15 billion years old to the current estimate of 13.7 billion years old), but they should *not even imply that their claim of billions of years is based on Biblical authority*. Their claim of 13.7 billion years is based on their authority as scientists. The Bible does not date the universe (UEC).

My two points are: (a) The Bible deliberately does not date the universe. (b) God Himself has built into the universe objects that can serve as measuring tools that apparently indicate the universe is not 6,000 years old. To claim that God by the Bible dated the universe to about 6,000 years old would seem to make God either self-contradictory (His Word vs. His creation) or deceptive. But God is neither. And the Bible does *not* give us that date of 6,000 years old for the universe.

For those without a science background, I will explain more precisely what we alluded to in the early chapters. The speed of light in a vacuum is a physical constant (shorthand c) and the "cosmic speed limit." In metric measurement, c is 299,792,458 meters per second, or 1,079,252,848.8 kilometers per hour. In miles, the speed of light is approximately 186,282 miles per second, or 670,616,629 miles per hour. Even at that great speed, light from our sun takes eight minutes to reach us, so solar astronomers see sunspots or solar flares eight minutes after they happen. Light from the nearest star, Proxima Centauri, left that star 4.22 years ago because it took

4.22 years for that light to reach us; therefore, that star is said to be 4.22 light-years away from us. Astronomers call this "look-back time" because they are actually seeing 4.22 years into the past.

Light from the nearest full-size galaxy, the great Andromeda galaxy, apparently took 2.2 million years to reach us, because Andromeda is 2.2 million light-years away. Someone might say that is just an assumption. But that charge is incorrect. There is great evidence that the stars in Andromeda are the same as those in our Galaxy; so star size, number, and distance apart tell us a rough distance. And our universe contains over a hundred billion galaxies averaging a hundred billion suns each. The most distant objects our telescopes can detect apparently are over 12 billion light-years away, so the light that reaches us apparently left over 12 billion years ago. Scientists estimate that our universe is about 13.7 billion years old, which agrees with these most distant objects.

These distances are not guesses. The measurement of the distance to stars up to one hundred light-years away is by simple trigonometry from Earth at the extreme opposite sides of Earth's orbit, half a year apart. From these opposite sides, nearby stars appear to shift very slightly in their positions against distant stars. By measuring this shift and knowing the diameter of Earth's orbit, astronomers can easily calculate the change in angle and thereby the distance to the star.

Overlapping this method is the measurement of star distance by Cepheid variable stars. These stars oscillate in brightness with a regular rhythm. This time period of oscillation directly corresponds to the absolute brightness of the star. Brighter stars have longer oscillation periods. The ratio of apparent brightness to the oscillation period has been measured for nearby stars of known distance from us, giving us a standard for more distant Cepheid variables. Using this method, in 1912 American astronomer Henrietta Leavitt calculated the distance to globular clusters hundreds of thousands of light-years away. Then Edwin Hubble first measured the huge distance to the Andromeda galaxy, which we now have measured more precisely to 2.2 million light-years away.

Overlapping this measurement method are two methods for measuring even greater distances. Type 1a supernovae always explode with the same brightness. So their distance can be measured by the ratio of apparent brightness to absolute brightness to determine their distance from Earth.

Red shift also strongly correlates to distance from Earth. Undoubtedly, minor errors may be made. But even with the most conservative measurements, the universe is older than 6,000 years.

Why would God build into the universe these overlapping "yardsticks" unless He wanted us to learn the stars' true distance and age?

What about Earth's age? Strangely twisted rocks I have seen at Pemaquid Point lighthouse in Maine apparently are the same type as those on Norway's coast. Scientists have discovered that the rock layers all up and down the Atlantic East Coast of the Americas match with the rock layers on the opposite side of the Atlantic on the West Coast of Europe and Africa. Apparently, the two sides really were joined. The mid-ocean ridge is real, and the continental tectonic plates are spreading several centimeters a year. Even at 3 cm. a year, the spread would be less than a kilometer (far less than a mile) after 6,000 years. Planet Earth, too, appears significantly older than 6,000 years.

I am *not affirming* these ages or claiming the dating methods are infallible—either the 6,000 years that YEC claims, or the 13.7 billion years for the universe or 4.5 billion years for Earth that OEC and science claim. Instead, I am claiming that there is no explicit statement *in the Bible* declaring the age of the universe or Earth. So I am claiming that the Bible does not state or imply exactly when the creation of the universe and Earth occurred (UEC).

Many scientists are deeply interested in those ages, and they have come to their conclusions from evidence. Either these scientists are approximately right, or they have been deceived, or a compelling explanation has not yet surfaced. Young earth scientific creationism advocates have suggested various possibilities to show how the universe could actually be 6,000 years old, but none has been compelling or widely accepted among even young earth advocates.

D. Russell Humphreys has written a book and produced a video, both titled *Starlight and Time*.[422] Humphreys is seeking means for an apparently ancient universe that is 6,000 years old. His theory claims that the universe may have objects 12 billion light-years away, yet be only 6,000-year-old based on the theory of relativity. His claim may go back to the claim of Israeli cosmologist Moshe Carmeli, likely a progenitor of Schroeder's theory too. (We will consider Schroeder's theory in chapter 7.) Humphreys and Schroeder are theologically different, but seem to be seeking the same relativity solution to a 6,000 year old universe that each of their religious backgrounds claims.

But there are serious problems with Humphreys' theory. Humphreys is "not formally trained in general relativity or cosmology theory."[423] Samuel R. Conner and Hugh Ross, who do have expertise in cosmology and theoretical physics, report, "Feedback [to *Starlight and Time*] has been forthcoming, and, to our knowledge, it has been uniformly critical of the theory."[424] Even other YEC advocates have shown that Humphreys' theory is faulty.[425]

I would ask, Doesn't it take huge mass such as a black hole or immense velocity approaching the speed of light to change time passage significantly? Does Earth and its vicinity really have the immense mass or velocity to warp 13.7 billion years into six days? It is Earth, not some distant part of the universe, that has to fit into 6,000 years. And if such mass or velocity involved Earth, would Earth and life come out of the process intact?

So why does Humphreys make this claim? He answers in his video *Starlight and Time*:

Even if my particular theory should eventually turn out to be wrong, I know that there is a correct creation model of the cosmos, because observation and Scripture both confirm that God made the universe very recently. "For *in* six days God made the heavens and the earth" (Exodus 20:11).[426]

Humphreys assumes there must be a young earth solution because of "*in*" in Exodus 20:11a. But there is no "*in*" in Exodus 20:11a. I am saddened that a good Christian man such as Humphreys should spend a major part of his life trying to defend a theory based on a nonexistent "*in*." YEC has built a whole edifice on "*in* six days," but the edifice, the third claim, is a foundationless bridge section. I have written this book partly to prevent such disillusioning assumptions by well-meaning fellow Christians.

As already mentioned, Australian Barry Setterfield claimed that early measurements of light's speed were *faster* than today's measurements, indicating that light has been slowing down. He claimed light traveled so fast in the universe after its creation about 6,000 years ago that the light from distant galaxies 10–12 billion light-years away is only 6,000 years old.

In response, the earliest measurements of light were *slower,* not faster, than today's measurements. Danish astronomer Ole Römer first measured the speed of light. He calculated the speed of light at 140,000 miles (225,000 km) per second.[427] This first estimate was *slower* than the actual speed of 186,282 miles (299,792 km) a second. Light did not speed up; the earliest measurements were not very accurate. It appears that Setterfield *selected* measurements that were faster, but left out ones that were slower. However good his intentions may have been, using selective evidence is wrong.

Moreover, a change in the speed of light (c) would cause basic changes in physics, because fundamental processes are dependent on the constant c, such as $E=mc^2$. Evidence for such change in the speed of light is lacking. Also, since we have developed accurate measurement instruments, light speed has remained constant.

Criticism of Setterfield's proposal has come from other young earth creationists. Donald DeYoung asks, "Why did the value of c seem to settle down to its present constant value, just when we started to measure it accurately? We cannot see any change in c occurring today. This is a suspicious coincidence!"[428]

YEC leaders conclude, "There is currently no wholly satisfactory solution that is accepted by the majority of creation scientists."[429]

A young earth creationist might reply that there is no deception because the Bible says the universe is 6,000 years old. But that claim is simply incorrect. The Genesis genealogies roughly date Adam, not the universe. Exodus 20:11 does not require the creation of the universe *in* the six days, nor do Mark 10:6 or Matthew 19:4. Therefore, young earth scientific creationists may claim that creation took place 6,000 years ago, but they make that claim *on their own authority,* because the Bible makes no such claim.

We have found that there is no *"in"* in Exodus 20:11a; that $b^e r\bar{e}'sh\hat{i}t$ ("In the beginning") and $r\bar{e}'sh\hat{i}t$ consistently indicate a major time period (not an instant or hours; see my response to presupposition u-5.0D); and that all six days began with "And God said," so day one began with daylight in 1:3, after "In the beginning." These are facts that can be checked, not opinions. Combined, these facts make the novel YEC claim—that the *ex nihilo* creation of Genesis 1:1 was *in* day one—impossible.

Let us suppose that Humphreys or Setterfield turns out to be correct, that the universe actually is only about 6,000 years old and relativity (or something else) explains the apparent age of the distant galaxies. That still does *not change the Biblical data* that there is no *"in"* in Exodus 20:11, that $b^e r\bar{e}'sh\hat{i}t$ indicates a major time period, that day one started in 1:3, and that God created the universe "In the beginning" before day one. If Humphreys is right, then "In the beginning" was only some months or years before day one. Biblically, YEC's claim three is still just as impossible.

Whether the Genesis 1:1 *ex nihilo* creation "In the beginning" was only years before day one on Earth, thousands of years before day one, or billions of years before day one, the Bible does not say. But the Bible itself demonstrates that "In the beginning" was certainly *before* day one.

(u-5.5c) *As created, all* nephesh *animals had eternal physical life; Adam's sin resulted in all* nephesh *animal death.* Ken Ham says, "When

God had finished creating, everything was perfect and beautiful." "There was no death of animals or humans in the original creation."[430] In *The Genesis Flood* Morris quotes part of each verse: "Paul says: 'By *man* came death' (1 Corinthians 15:21) and in another place, 'By *one man*, sin entered into the world, and death by sin' (Romans 5:12)"[431] (emphasis his).

YEC normally makes this claim negatively, that there was "no death" before Adam's sin. However, I have stated the YEC claim positively so the contrast with the competing claim will be clear:

YEC: As created, animals had eternal physical life before Adam sinned. OEC (and possibly UEC): As created, animals had normal life cycles, because nowhere does the Bible say that was changed by Adam's sin.

In my response, I want to make it clear that I agree with YEC main claim 5.5, that there was no *human* death until Adam sinned. Henry Morris says, "In the face of such clear-cut passages as Romans 5:12–21 and 1 Corinthians 15:21–22, few who accept the Bible as the Word of God will deny that Adam's sin and fall introduced *spiritual* and *physical death into the human race*"[432] (emphasis his). I strongly agree.

I strongly agree that "if sin and death are not real, then salvation and eternal life are not real."[433] "The reason we need Christ as Savior is that in Adam (as well as in our own actions) we have sinned against our Maker."[434]

Let me also make it clear that I am not claiming *either* animal death before sin (OEC), or *no* animal death before sin (YEC). I am analyzing whether the YEC claim—as created, all *nephesh* animals had eternal physical life—is explicitly supported by the Bible or is more than the Bible actually says.

I respond that in *The Genesis Flood* Morris quotes only part of each verse: "Paul says: 'By *man* came death' (1 Corinthians 15:21) and in another place, 'By *one man*, sin entered into the world, and death by sin' (Romans 5:12)."[435] "For as in Adam all die" is often added. Based on these partial quotes, if I understand the claim correctly, YEC sees Paul's logic as this:

* All die because Adam sinned.
* Animals are part of the "all die."
* Therefore, all animal death is from Adam's sin, and conversely, before Adam sinned, there was no animal death.

Henry Morris concluded, "Therefore, we feel compelled to date all of the rock strata which contain fossils of once living creatures as subsequent to Adam's fall."[436]

In response, here are the whole Bible quotes:

Therefore, just as through one man sin entered into the world,
     and death through sin, [and through the sin the death, YLT]
and so death spread to all <u>men</u>, because all sinned (Rom. 5:12, NASB).

For since by a man *came* death,
by a man also *came* the resurrection of the dead.
For as in Adam all die,
so also in Christ all shall be made alive (1 Cor. 15:21–22, NASB).

Paul qualified "all" as "all men." (*Anthrōpos* = humans, not just male humans.) All humans were in Adam as our head and ancestor; all believing humans are "in Christ." So Paul's logic was actually this:

In Adam by his sin (confirmed by "all sinned") all men die.
In Jesus by His atonement all believing men are justified to life.

Paul's logic did *not* include animals:

Animals were not "in Adam," nor are animals "in Christ."
If all animals died in Adam,
     will all animals be resurrected in Christ? No.
So "all" means all humans.

The Greek of Romans 5:12 says "the sin" and "the death." Although not intended for normal reading, Young's Literal Translation makes this clear: "And through the sin the death." "The sin" is identified in 5:14 as "the offense of Adam." "The death" is specific. It is not death in general, death of everything including animals, or a general principle of death. "The death" is specifically the death that "spread to all men," as explained in Romans 5:12. Paul's object of "the death" is "men," not animals, just as Paul's object of "the resurrection" is all humans in Christ, not animals.

There is no doubt that animals were harmed by the Fall (Gen. 3:14). Sin harms others, as well as the creation. But harm is not the question. The question is, Did Paul say that Adam's sin began animal death? Paul does not mention animal death in Romans 5. YEC has not proven the claim that Adam's sin caused all animal death.

God's judgment in Genesis 3:14–19 says nothing about animal death, aside from the serpent/Satan. God pronounced the judgment of death on Satan embodied in the serpent. He pronounced the judgment of death on Adam, and so on Adam's race. The only higher living category God did not curse with death was animals—the very thing YEC claims was cursed with death.

Inside the Garden was the "tree of life" (Gen. 3:22) available for Adam to eat had he remained in the Garden. Adam and Eve were excluded from the Garden by Cherubim, "lest he stretch out his hand, and take also from the tree of life, and eat, and live forever." Apparently, Adam and Eve needed to eat from "the tree of life" to have had eternal physical life even if they had not fallen. But Adam and Eve did not eat from that "tree of life" to "live forever." If Adam and Eve did not have eternal physical life unless they ate of the "tree of life," it seems unlikely that animals inherently had eternal physical life.

The Bible nowhere makes an explicit statement like, "Through Adam's sin all animals die," or "And God cursed animals with death because Adam sinned," or "No animals died before Adam sinned." YEC claims more than the Bible says.

(u-5.5d) *Animals did not die before Adam's sin, just as they will not die in the future restoration.* YEC says, "The world will one day be restored (Acts 3:21) to a state in which, once again, there will be no such death and violence in the animal kingdom." "Lambs, wolves, leopards, kids, bears and calves will all dwell together peacefully. Lions will once again be plant eaters."[437] "The wolf and the lamb will graze together, and the lion will eat straw like the ox" (Isa. 65:25, NASB). In the future there will be a "restoration of all things" (Acts 3:21), so the Eden condition will be restored. Therefore, in Eden, lions ate straw before Adam sinned.

In response, although Isaiah does not always separate the Millennium from the eternal New Heavens and New Earth, the verse, "The wolf and the lamb will graze together, and the lion will eat straw like the ox" (Isa. 11:7, 65:25) is widely recognized as a Millennium prediction.

Contra YEC, there will be human death, so presumably animal death in the Millennium. "For the youth will die at the age of one hundred and the one who does not reach the age of one hundred shall be *thought* accursed" (Isa. 65:20). If YEC wants to add lions eating straw (65:25) to the original creation, then YEC would have to add human death (65:20) to the original creation also, which is clearly incorrect.

In the Millennium, "the wolf also shall dwell with the lamb." The wolf will not kill and eat the lamb. Apparently, there will be no animal carnivorism in the Millennium, but there will be death by old age (Isa. 65:20, NASB). Acts 3:21 speaks of "restoration." Many aspects of the Garden of Eden condition will be restored in the Millennium, but the two are not identical.

Did animals die before Adam sinned? Later, in 11.11a, there will be a full discussion of the options.

(**u-5.5e**) *All animals were vegetarians before Adam's sin.* YEC claims animals ate only vegetation before Adam's sin. YEC bases this claim on Genesis 1:30 that God gave to animals "every green plant for food."

In response, Genesis 1:29 and 1:30 form a contrast. God gave humans seeds and fruit to eat. In contrast, God gave animals "every green plant" to eat. These verses do not claim animals ate *only* green plants. Did blue whales with their great open mouths sieving out sea life eat only green plants (phytoplankton) but never baby turtles or a seabird diving among the small fish? Genesis 1:29–30 is silent about that. These verses simply say that in contrast to man eating just from seed plants and fruit trees, God gave animals "every green plant." Genesis 1:29–30 does not say God said animals ate *only* green plants. God was speaking to Adam, not to animals. God was telling Adam not to try to eat green oak leaves, green pine needles, or green fern fronds just because some animals do. The Bible does not say all animals ate *only* green plants.

(**u-5.5f**) *To question animals' eternal physical life before Adam sinned, resulting in the curse, is to undermine the atonement.* AiG claims that animal death before Adam's Fall meant the curse would have had to have been before Adam's Fall, thus undermining the atonement.

AiG submits that the question of the earth's age is vital because it involves the accuracy of the Genesis record, and more importantly, the Bible's atonement message itself. You see, if a person accepts the belief that the earth is millions of years old, then it follows that the Curse must have occurred *before* Adam appeared. In this scenario, then, there would be the remains of dead things before the Fall of Adam — and diseases like cancer. In this way, the atonement message is undermined.[438]

In response, this claim from AiG has one crucial unproven assumption, that if animals died before Adam's sin then "it follows that the Curse must have occurred *before* Adam appeared." The assumption is that the curse began animal death.

God cursed the serpent "more than" all livestock and wild animals.
God cursed the serpent with death.
YEC concludes, God cursed all livestock/wild animals with death.

Both premises are true. Genesis 3:14 and 15 (NIV) say: "So the LORD God said to the serpent, 'Because you have done this, Cursed are you above all the livestock and all the wild animals.' "He will crush your [the serpent's] head."

But the argument is invalid. The serpent was cursed "above" (NIV), or "more than" (NASB), "all the livestock and all the wild animals." Only the serpent, and ultimately Satan, was explicitly cursed with death.

Animals were cursed *less* than the serpent. So we cannot conclude that the curse on other animals was also death. Animals were harmed by the Fall and curse, but the curse does not say how. Animal death was *not* explicitly in the curse.

The YEC argument is unproven. Animal death is not linked explicitly by the Bible to Adam's sin and the curse, as YEC claims. If animal death is not linked to the curse, then animal death is not linked to the atonement.

Yes, animals were involved in the temporary offerings for sin in the Old Testament. But Hebrews 10:4 says, "For it is impossible that the blood of bulls and of goats should take away sins" (KJV). Animal death has never been the basis for permanent atonement.

What is critical for the atonement is that Adam's sin and the curse resulted in all *human* death. There was no human death before Adam sinned. And all humans are descended from Adam. Then the Lord Jesus as the God-man and our kinsman-redeemer (our relative through the seed of the woman) made atonement. Because we were all descended from Adam, we can all be saved by the second Adam, the Lord Jesus. Thus, the analogy in Romans 5:12–15 is upheld:

Sin entered the world through one man [Adam],
and death through sin, and so death spread to all men (5:12, NASB).
The gift . . . came by the grace of the one man, Jesus Christ (5:15, NIV).

The critical issue for the atonement is that there is *no human death* before Adam's sin, because all humans inherited from Adam both his sin nature and death. Animal death is not the issue.

It seems to me that in the attempt to uphold *"in* six days," YEC has tried to link the claim of animals' eternal physical life before the Fall to the precious truth of the atonement. This attempted link is more than the Bible says. This unproven link is an invalid and inappropriate appeal that the Bible itself does not make.

We may conclude that a claim of eternal physical life for animals had Adam not sinned is more than the Bible explicitly states.

In summary, we found that there is no *"in"* within Exodus 20:11a. The Fourth Commandment says we are to keep the Sabbath holy by working six days but not working the seventh—because God worked six days, then rested the seventh. Exodus 20:11 does not say God created everything *in* six days. Claim three, that God created everything in day one, is based on the *"in"* that is absent from *"in* six days" (Exod. 20:11). Jesus' statement against divorce is about the creation of male and female, not about the universe. Because creation was not *"in"* day one but actually "in the beginning," an unstated amount of time before day one, the creation of the universe cannot be dated by the creation of Adam. A 6,000-year-old universe with deceiving appearance of age, all based on *"in* six days," is a serious theological problem. The Bible does not support claim three. Claim three—that God created time, space, and unformed matter *in day one*—is in opposition to "In the beginning God created the heavens and the earth."

A foundational misinterpretation can have a damaging trickle-down effect on subsequent related interpretations.

Going back to the bridge illustration, YEC's third claim is the missing support column. Its many subclaims are attempts to patch a column that is not there. No subclaim actually supports main claim three. Most of these subclaims themselves err.

The solution is to turn from YEC's problematic claim three paradigm that *in* day one God created space and unformed earth-water matrix throughout the darkness of space.[439] It takes humility to change one's ideas. The solution is to humble ourselves and believe, "In the [literal] beginning God [literally] created the [literal] heavens and the [literal] earth."

Partially Supported Claims of YEC

(ps-5.3p) *In day two, God made the* rāqîa', *the "expanse" of the atmosphere, below a vast vapor canopy that would be the source of the rain for the flood.* Henry Morris explains that the *rāqîa'* was the expanse, or atmosphere, that was between the sea waters below and vast vapor canopy above. The canopy provided water for the flood.

I respond that Henry Morris is correct up to the point of the water vapor canopy. His vapor canopy idea has a major problem. For just three thousand feet of floodwater from rain (less than a kilometer, far less than one mile deep), water vapor in Earth's atmosphere before the flood would have caused about the same atmospheric pressure as that on Venus. Such pressure would have been about ninety times the present air pressure on Earth, totally unlivable for any higher life. If there was a vapor canopy, it had far less water.

(ps-5.6a & b) *Exodus 20:11 teaches a young earth; the Noahic flood explains why this young earth appears older. The flood formed most geologic features and fossils.* The Bible says there was a flood. Young earth creation science explains how the flood could make Earth appear ancient, while actually being only about 6,000 years old.

I support the open discussion of a variety of possible means that may have caused the flood. I agree that if a miracle is not indicated in the text,[440] we may seek by science the means God used. That God used means to bring about the flood in no way diminishes His sovereign control over the events.

The problem with this claim is that it forces science into a 6,000-year-old Earth presupposition that the Bible itself does not claim.

So I would affirm that the flood was real and took place roughly 5,000 years ago. But we need to drop the claim that Earth is certainly about 6,000 years old—because that claim is more than the Bible says. A 6,000-year-old Earth forces almost all geology into the flood. An error in Earth's age could in turn force a misinterpretation of what the Bible says actually happened in the flood.

Largely Supported Preunderstandings and Claims of YEC

In my evaluation of the ten main claims of YEC, only the third main claim is fundamentally incorrect. Otherwise, YEC has many valuable contributions to our understanding of creation.

(s-5.0A) The Bible is inerrant; so interpret Genesis as literal history. YEC believes in "complete divine inspiration and perspicuity of Scripture."[441] As Henry Morris says, "The writers of the New Testament, and Jesus Christ Himself, accepted the Genesis record as literal history."

Henry Morris is correct. I agree with these great statements. Jesus accepted Genesis as history, so I certainly do as well. That includes Genesis 1.

(s-5.0B) The Bible is inerrant, so has priority over science. YEC affirms that the Bible text is inerrant, but science is not, so science must not skew the Bible's meaning.

I agree. As I study creation events, my Hebrew and Greek Bible has priority. Once I understand the texts to the best of my ability, I compare them with related Bible texts and consider the Bible studies of others. After correlating the Bible data, I have found that the Bible claims do seem to match the most strongly affirmed conclusions from science. This is the correct order—Bible exegesis first, and then consider science. If the two correlate, fine. If not, then we need to study both more carefully rather than skew either to match the other.

YEC says, "A truly Biblical approach [understood as the young earth 6,000-year-old-universe theory] will eventually correlate all the factual data of science."[442] Most creationists of the other theories would agree that accurately understood Bible data and accurately understood creation data will correlate. But the "correlate" statement of YEC is largely one way; the YEC theory as "a truly Biblical approach" will "correlate all the factual data of science."[443] It seems YEC might view scientific data (or Biblical data raised by another theory) that does not correlate with their theory as necessarily *non*-factual. Otherwise, I agree with this great claim.

(s-5.0C) The Bible inerrantly reveals what God did; science may tell us how He did it and provide evidence that God did it. Henry Morris pioneered this approach by his groundbreaking study of the flood. Seeking scientific means of how God did His creation work and evidence for what He did was a breakthrough in creation studies.

I agree that the Bible inerrantly reveals what God did. Accurate evidence from science may reveal the means God used.

YEC enthusiastically seeks means for the flood. God used normal (although unusual) means of rain and fountains of the deep to produce the flood. YEC seeks out these means.

But YEC seems half-hearted when seeking means for events in the six days. For example, YEC claims miraculous creation of mature plants (or miraculously rapid growth) during the third day producing trees with "appearance of age."

Kline responds that Genesis 2:5 says plants had not yet sprouted because God had not yet sent rain. Then God sent water. God used the means of water to grow plants. God used normal means as well as miracles not only in the flood but also during the creation.

Both the flood and the six days' events were equally acts of God. Both came from the word of God—the six days by God's eight command units, and the flood by God's word: "I will send rain on the earth for forty days and forty nights" (Gen. 7:4, NASB). YEC sees the forty-day rainfall as unusual but brought about by means at the command of God. Why not see the watered ground sprouting plants in the third day (Gen. 2:5–6 with 1:11–12) occurring by normal means of water, soil, and sunlight at God's command?

Concerning Biblical inerrancy, I must add that the fundamental issue in all this is inerrant Biblical authority. On YEC claim three, if young earth scientific creationism continues to proclaim *"in six days"* based on an "in" that is not there, that act will constitute a violation of inerrant Biblical authority. And then their theory will not match the creation either, and will become a point of ridicule by the secular world against Christianity.

(s-5.1) God created all things—time, space, and matter-energy— out of nothing, *ex nihilo*. Henry Morris correctly says, "Genesis 1:1 speaks of creation *ex nihilo*; only God could originate such a concept, and only an infinite, omnipotent God could create the universe."[444]

Henry Morris is correct that God created all things *ex nihilo,* out of nothing. Hebrews 11:3 and Colossians 1:16–17 confirm this claim. I honor Henry Morris for his courageous stand for *ex nihilo* creation.

(s-5.2) Each numbered *yôm* in Genesis 1 was a normal day, totaling six normal days. YEC has mounted a linguistically rigorous defense of six normal day-night days.[445]

I find that the actual Hebrew texts support this claim. Later, with one of the four diagnostic questions, we will consider normal days versus day-ages. Then I will give this controversy a more thorough Biblical examination.

(s-5.3s) In days five and six God made sea, air, and land life and created Adam and Eve. Morris says, "God proceeded to make animal life for the atmosphere and hydrosphere on the fifth day, and then animal life for the lithosphere and biosphere on the sixth day."[446] Finally, "man was made in God's image."[447]

This claim seems in agreement with the Bible text.

(s-5.4) God apparently gave the Genesis 1:1—2:4a creation account to Adam. Henry Morris says, "He [God] revealed it [the Gen. 1:1—2:4a creation narrative] verbally to Adam."[448] The second *tôlᵉdôt,* or generational account, of Genesis 2:4b—5:1a was "originally by Adam himself" "and represents his own perspective on the creation and the first events of human history."[449] Adam's account was an *eyewitness* narrative,[450] recording events only during his lifetime. He concludes with his name in 5:1a: "This *is* the book of the generations of Adam."

Morris explains that Moses *compiled* Genesis from the accounts composed by Adam, Noah, Shem, Abraham, etc., who "recorded on tables of stone or clay, in common with the practice of early times, and then handed down from father to son, finally coming into the possession of Moses." Moses edited them into "the Book of Genesis as we have received it."[451]

I will be so bold as to say that the evidence from the *tôlᵉdôts* in Genesis itself, archeology, ANE culture, and linguistics confirms this claim by Morris and Wiseman.

(s-5.5) Adam's sin resulted in death. God told Adam, "But from the tree of the knowledge of good and evil you shall not eat, for in the day that you eat from it you shall surely die." Adam ate, so God pronounced the curse: "For you are dust, and to dust you shall return." Adam died and returned to dust just as God said he would.

I strongly agree with Henry Morris: "The reason we need Christ as Savior is that in Adam (as well as in our own actions) we have sinned against our Maker."[452] God the Son made full atonement for our sin, paying the full just penalty for all our evil thoughts, words, and acts, to reconcile us to Himself. Today, Adam's body is dust; but the Lord Jesus physically rose from the dead, so today Jesus in His glorified physical body sits at the right hand of God the Father in glory. Today, Jesus offers His payment-in-full for all who will believe in and receive Him.

(s-5.5a) All humans have descended from Adam, so all humans have a fallen nature and are subject to death. Henry Morris says, "In the face of such clear-cut passages as Romans 5:12–21 and 1 Corinthians 15:21–22, few who accept the Bible as the Word of God will deny that Adam's sin and fall introduced *spiritual* and *physical* death into the human race"[453] (emphasis his). All humans have descended from Adam. So all humans were born with a sin nature, are dead spiritually, and will die physically.

I agree.

(s-5.5b) All humans have descended from Adam, so all humans are related to Christ, who can be our Kinsman-Redeemer. YEC advocate Jonathan Sarfati correctly says,

The gospel makes sense only on the basis that all humans alive, and all who ever lived, are descendants of the first man, Adam. Only descendants of Adam can be saved, because Isaiah spoke of the coming Messiah as literally the "Kinsman-Redeemer," that is, one who is related by blood to those he redeems (Isa. 59:20).[454]

I agree. Isaiah 54:8 says, "'With everlasting lovingkindness I will have compassion on you,' says the LORD your Redeemer" (NASB).

(s-5.6) Noah's flood was real, violent, and worldwide. In *The Genesis Flood* Morris and Whitcomb argue for a hydrologically violent flood, a real Noah, and a real ark on which eight people survived.[455]

We need not agree with all the details of the various YEC flood proposals to agree in general that there was a violent worldwide flood.

Young earth scientific creationism also states four denials:

(s-5.7) YEC denies chance-driven naturalistic molecules-to-man macroevolution. Young earth scientific creationism vigorously denies chance-driven macroevolution. YEC advocates have attacked evolution publicly and persistently.[456]

I agree that the Bible does not allow chance-driven anything (Eph. 1:11). Evolution is a directionless chance-driven theory. Its fundamental principles are incorrect and diametrically opposed to the fact that "all things were created through Him [God the Son] and for Him" (Col. 2:16, NKJV). "Through Him" is not chance driven, and "for Him" is not directionless.

(s-5.8) YEC denies the entire gap theory. YEC has shown the fatal grammatical error of the gap in the gap theory.[457]

I strongly agree that the gap theory's middle of three stages—the gap—is incorrect. Bruce Waltke agrees. Most scholars agree.

However, young earth scientific creationists overreact by throwing out the entire gap theory as if nothing these Bible-believing creationists ever said was correct. Actually, only the gap, or second stage, has been proven grammatically incorrect. Perhaps YEC has opposed the gap theory so strongly because gap advocates have critiqued the problematic third YEC claim long before I did.

YEC tends to attack other theories using guilt by association. YEC incorrectly associates Gorman Gray's theory (minor theory twelve in chapter 12) with the gap theory. As Christians, they should refrain from this nonconstructive tactic, and instead debate the *Biblical issues* between their theory and other theories.

(s-5.9) YEC denies the pre-creation chaos theory, and the majority denies the title/summary theory. Morris correctly says, "Neither can verse 1 as a whole be considered a title or summary of the events described in the succeeding verses of the chapter." Genesis 2:1 is the six days' summary: "Thus the heavens and the earth were finished, and all the host of them."[458] Genesis 1:1 was the actual act of "the primeval creation of the universe itself."[459]

These words by Henry Morris should be a warning to YEC advocates who would abandon *ex nihilo* creation and instead claim the title theory. Recently, some young earth advocates have turned away from *ex nihilo* creation in Genesis 1:1 to the title theory (see u-5.1a).[460]

These YEC advocates who are abandoning *ex nihilo* creation in order to support claim three should heed Morris's words. They are paying a terrible price for their error. They are losing the fundamental doctrine that in the beginning God created the heavens and the earth out of nothing.

Morris is correct that the pre-creation chaos theory and the title or summary theory err. The Jewish people and the church both have supported *ex nihilo* creation. The grammar supports *ex nihilo* creation. *Bārā'* supports *ex nihilo* creation. The "and" beginning Genesis 1:2 supports *ex nihilo* creation. And the rest of the Bible supports *ex nihilo* creation (Heb. 11:3; Col. 1:16–17). The pre-creation chaos theory and title theory err.

"In the beginning God created the heavens and the earth" is the record of the actual *ex nihilo* creation.

(s-5.10) YEC denies all non-day-night "days" theories. YEC explains that each *yôm,* "day," with a consecutive number and evening and morning, was a normal daylight-evening-nighttime-morning cycle day (although recently some claim a night-day day).

I agree with six normal day-night days. I will discuss day-age versus normal day arguments in one of the diagnostic questions.

I agree with Henry Morris and YEC on nine of ten main claims. I regret that YEC made that one error concerning Exodus 20:11, an error that has harmed their otherwise outstanding theory. YEC has given us nine solid claims to use in building the unified Biblical creation theory. Thank you, Dr. Henry Morris!

I said at the beginning of this chapter that one main claim errs. That one missing pier of the great bridge needs replacing. That missing pier, that errant claim, is, "*In* day one God created space and unformed earth-water matrix throughout the darkness of space,"[461] based on an "*in*" that is not in Exodus 20:11. The steel and concrete Biblical replacement pier that we need to believe is, "In the [literal] beginning God [literally] created the [literal] heavens and the [literal] earth."

YEC Nonscientific Twenty-four-hour Days Variant

I wish to acknowledge briefly a YEC variant by J. Ligon Duncan III and David W. Hall. They present a young earth twenty-four-hour days creation theory that is *not* scientific creationism. The major difference from the previous YEC *scientific* creationism variant is this: YEC *scientific* creationism claims that God used means, discoverable by science, as well as miracles. The YEC *non*scientific variant rejects means and claims essentially only miracles.

Presuppositions of YEC Nonscientific Variant

(5B.00) *The Bible inerrantly tells what God did; natural revelation, proclaimed by science, not only lacks such authority, but is identified with "every man a liar."* Duncan and Hall declare, "The evangelical tradition has not assigned the same epistemological authority to natural revelation as to special revelation rightly interpreted. When forced to choose between conflicting sources of authority we join the chorus begun by the apostle Paul, 'Let God be true, and every man a liar' (Rom. 3:4)."[462]

(5B.0) *Not only the initial creation, but all six-day events were unmediated, instantaneous, miraculous acts.*[463] God used "unmediated creation,"[464] which was completed "instantly and without assistance from other forces."[465] God carried out the six days' events by miracles, not by processes or "mediated" "creation that depends on normal providence and secondary agents."[466] For example, the creation of sun, moon, and stars on day four "was a miracle in a week saturated with the miraculous."[467]

God *created* "light," "expanse and the seas," "land masses and vegetation," "celestial bodies," and "land animals."[468] All these items were created entirely miraculously—instantly or nearly so.

Claims of YEC Nonscientific Variant

The first several claims are the same as in the previous variant.

(5B.1) *God created everything* **ex nihilo** *in the initial creation.* Duncan and Hall explain, "He made everything. But the text also hints at the manner or method of this work: creation *ex nihilo*—out of nothing."[469]

(5B.2) *Each numbered* **yôm** *(day) in Genesis 1 was a normal, natural, twenty-four-hour day based on Genesis 1 and Exodus 20:11.* "Compelling exegetical evidence," say Duncan and Hall, "for reading the creation days as anything other than normal days is lacking."[470] Exodus 20:11 affirms that the six days were natural days.[471] The days were "'natural days,' a term that meant 24-hour days."[472]

(5B.3) *Exodus 20:11 indicates all creation came about in the six twenty-four-hour days.* Duncan and Hall emphasize that Exodus 20:11

indicates six natural twenty-four-hour days. They hold the same YEC claim that God created the universe *ex nihilo* "*in* six days," rather than before the six days. "At no time does the Pentateuch even hint at anything other than creation in six 24-hour days."[473]

(**5B.3a**) *The six days were night-day cycle days beginning with evening and ending in morning.* According to Duncan and Hall, each day began with an evening of twelve hours of darkness (night), followed by a morning of twelve hours of light (day).[474] This night-day cycle included the night of Genesis 1:2 and then the morning of "Let there be light." A "day" in Genesis 1 meant an *evening-morning* twenty-four-hour day.

(**5B.4**) ***Earth was formless and empty, so God would shape the formlessness and fill the emptiness in the six days.*** "Nothing existed prior to God's speaking (Heb. 11:3)."[475] "God shaped His creation from formlessness into order and filled it from emptiness into fullness."[476]

(**5B.4a**) *In those six twenty-four-hour days, God spoke "eight simple commands."*[477] Duncan and Hall explain, "By eight simple commands, God spoke the world into reality."[478] These commands filled a six-part formula: "(1) introductory word ('Then God said'); (2) creative word ('let there be'); (3) fulfillment word ('and it was so'); (4) lordship word ('God called'); (5) commending word ('it was good,' beginning on Day 3); (6) concluding word ('and there was evening . . .')."[479] For a comparison of parts, see Waltke (1.8).

(**5B.4b**) *God created the sun, moon, and stars instantly on the fourth day.* "Before the fourth day, God, the Creator, may have employed nonsolar sources of light before creating the sun."[480] "God is so independent of creation that He did not hesitate to create those grand luminaries until the halfway point in His work."[481] Donald DeYoung usually takes a *scientific* creationism view, but on this claim he seems to agree with Duncan and Hall. DeYoung says, "All the many stars appeared suddenly and supernaturally in space."[482] How could Adam have seen distant stars immediately? "The light," DeYoung explains, "was created together with the stars and instantly spread out across space."[483]

(**5B.4c**) *God created man after God's kind.* God made the plants and animals "after their kind," but He says that He created man "in Our image." Duncan and Hall clarify, "Moses is telling us that man is of the genus of God."[484]

(**5B.5**) *The Bible does not date the universe.* Duncan and Hall say, "We take no position on the age of the universe precisely because that question is not directly addressed by the canon."[485] Reynolds agrees: "On the question of the earth's age, the evidence is much less clear [than the reality of Noah and a real flood]. . . . The Bible no place states an age for the cosmos." Even the church fathers "were not united in the way they understood divine revelation on this point."[486] When the beginning occurred, the Bible does not say.

(5B.6) *All God created was good; Adam's Fall is entirely responsible for all evil.* Duncan and Hall say, "God's world was originally good and, therefore, different from the corrupted world in which we now live. . . . Man's sin is entirely responsible for corrupting original creation. God's character (justice and mercy) is revealed as He responds to the three 'low points' of primeval history—the Fall, the flood and Babel."[487]

Unsupported Claims of the YEC Nonscientific Variant

(u-5B.00) *The Bible inerrantly tells us what God did; natural revelation, proclaimed by science, not only lacks such authority, but is identified with "every man a liar."* Duncan and Hall say, "The evangelical tradition has not assigned the same epistemological authority to natural revelation as to special revelation rightly interpreted. When forced to choose between conflicting sources of authority we join the chorus begun by the apostle Paul, 'Let God be true, and every man a liar' (Rom. 3:4)."[488]

Duncan and Hall argue improperly by mixing issues. Most evangelicals, including myself, would agree with their first sentence—that the Bible "rightly interpreted" has greater authority than the natural revelation of the created universe.

The second sentence appears to make the following equations:

"Conflicting sources of authority"	=	"special revelation rightly interpreted" and "natural revelation"
"God be true"	=	"special revelation"
"every man a liar"	=	"natural revelation"

In response, if this is their intent, this is not proper theology. "Natural revelation" is not man's lies. Natural revelation is what is revealed by the physical creation from God. The Bible says, "The heavens declare the glory of God" (Ps. 19:1, KJV). In their quote, Duncan and Hall reveal their bias against natural revelation.

Hugh Ross has pointed out that both special revelation (the Bible) and natural revelation (the creation) are from God. Therefore, both necessarily reveal truth. I would add a caveat, that the Fall has harmed human perception of the created universe because humans suppress the truth by unrighteousness. And the Fall has added evil elements. Nevertheless, Romans 1:20 says that the invisible attributes of God can still be clearly seen in the created universe. The faulty view of creation is in us as we suppress the truth. Contra Duncan and Hall, the heavens still declare the glory of God, even after the Fall. The heavens are not out of focus. We have a sin astigmatism.

The actual comparison is *special revelation* in *words* from God compared to *natural revelation* in *materials* from God. The Bible is in words, so actually states truth propositions. Also, Jesus said, "Heaven and earth will pass away, but my words will never pass away" (Matt. 24:35, NIV). So Scripture does have priority, but both reveal truth.

Duncan and Hall conclude, "We side with what the Scriptures teach about the days of creation."[489] All ten theories intend to side with Scripture. If these two men mean that their interpretation equals Scripture, then they are claiming inerrancy for their interpretation. Hopefully, they do not actually mean that. God's Word alone is inerrant.

(**u-5B.0**) *All creation events were unmediated, instantaneous, miraculous acts.* Duncan and Hall claim that the creation was completed "instantly and without assistance from other forces."[490] God did not employ "normal providence and secondary agents."[491] "It was a miracle in a week saturated with the miraculous."[492]

Duncan and Hall repeatedly use the term "created," that God created — "light," "expanse and the seas," "land masses and vegetation," "celestial bodies," and "land animals"[493] — where the English translation does not use the word "created," because the Hebrew Bible does not use the term *bārā'*. This reflects their presuppositional belief that all these items were created miraculously — instantly or nearly so.

In response, Duncan and Hall mix three different claims — (1) that God performed miracles in creation, (2) that He was not assisted, and (3) that God did not use "normal providence and secondary agents."[494] By "normal providence and secondary agents," they mean that God did not use means and materials by His normal laws.

In response, I agree that (1) God performed miracles — certainly including the initial *ex nihilo* creation and the creation of body-soul man. I also agree that (2) God was not dependent on some other sentient agent to help create.

But the text itself does not declare that (3) God never used means or processes on substances that He had already created. Duncan and Hall, in their ardor to defend miracles, deny that God carried out any providentially mediated processes during the six days.

Concerning all the events that took place in the sixth day, Duncan and Hall say this is "no real problem especially if we *assume the miraculous*" (emphasis added). I would ask, Does the Bible declare that Adam naming the animals was a miracle?

Duncan and Hall seem to see only two options: to assume the "miraculous or impose a contradiction on Scripture."[495] This suggests an either/or fallacy. Unless everything in Genesis 1 was a miracle, does Scripture become contradictory? Duncan and Hall seem to have swung the pendulum too far toward miracles.

Duncan and Hall accuse Ross and Archer of claiming only natural processes.[496] However, in fairness to Ross and Archer, that is an incorrect accusation. Ross certainly believes that the initial creation of the universe, the creation of life, and the creation of Adam and Eve involved God's miraculous work. Ross states, "They [YEC] have been battling their ally: scientific advance on virtually all fronts, which increasingly support a theistic, interventionist [that is, miraculous] view of life's origin and development."[497]

Schroeder raises the question of whether God was consistently "choosing at will to violate the laws of nature." Although Schroeder's theology may be problematic, he has a corner of the Duncan and Hall problem. Since God created the universe and its laws, among other reasons to reveal his character (Rom. 1:19–20), it would seem that He would normally work within those laws, exceptions being for very good reasons.

I must wonder why Duncan and Hall add to their defense of normal days this unnecessary problematic claim that essentially *every* event in Genesis 1 was a miracle without means. All they had to do was show the Hebrew evidence for normal natural day-night days.

(u-5B.3) *Exodus 20:11 indicates all creation came about in the six twenty-four-hour days.* Duncan and Hall say, "Scripture attests to divine creation out of nothing by God's word in the space of six normal days."[498]

In response, the Genesis 1 text affirms six normal days, but neither Genesis 1 nor Exodus 20:11 in the inspired Hebrew says that all creation was "*in*" the six days. The Hebrew evidence supports the *ex nihilo* creation of Genesis 1:1 before day one began in 1:3.

(u-5B.3a) *The six days were night-day cycle days beginning with evening and ending in morning.* Duncan and Hall claim that each day began with an evening of twelve hours of darkness followed by a morning of twelve hours of light.[499] A "day" in Genesis 1 meant an *evening-morning* twenty-four-hour day.

In response, evening and morning is a merism for nighttime, as clearly shown in Numbers 9:15. Contra Duncan and Hall, nowhere does the Bible say that evening and morning is a full day. Evening and morning were the beginning and end of nighttime.

Day one, like all the days, began with, "And God said, Let there be," beginning with light in Genesis 1:3. "And" is a *vav/waw* consecutive indicating that Genesis 1:3 came after the previous event—the initial *ex nihilo* creation in Genesis 1:1. The *vav/waw* consecutives continue through day one—"And God saw the light," "and God separated," "And God called/named," then finally "And there was evening and there was morning, day one." *Vav/waw* consecutives indicate consecutive events one after the next, in order. The Hebrew grammar certainly demonstrates that evening beginning nighttime followed by morning ending nighttime were at the end of each of the six days. The night-day claim is provably incorrect.

(u-5B.4b) *God created the sun, moon, and stars instantly on the fourth day.* Duncan and Hall claim, "Before the fourth day, God, the Creator, may have employed nonsolar sources of light before creating the sun."[500] DeYoung says, "All the many stars appeared suddenly and supernaturally in space."[501]

This instantaneous creation of the universe 6,000 years ago comes out of Duncan and Hall's presuppositional commitment to *only* the miraculous in the six days.

In response, Genesis 1:1 says God created the heavens—understood by Moses as the sky with sun, moon, and stars—"in the beginning," not on day four. Moreover, Genesis 1:14–19 does not say God "created" the sun on day four. Duncan and Hall claim more than the Bible claims.

Partially Supported Claims of YEC Nonscientific Variant

(ps-5B.4) *Earth was formless and empty, so God would shape the formlessness and fill the emptiness in the six days.* Duncan and Hall say, "God shaped His creation from formlessness into order and filled it from emptiness into fullness."[502]

In response, "formless" is not a good translation of *tōhû*. A more accurate translation is "uninhabitable desolation." "Emptiness" in the sense of no life or uninhabited is a reasonable translation of *bōhû*. So a more accurate statement would be, "Earth was uninhabitable and empty of life, so God would make Earth habitable and full of life in the six days."

(ps-5B.4c) *God created man after God's kind.* Duncan and Hall say, "Moses is telling us that man is of the genus of God."[503]

This is a great insight—if it is not pushed too far. God made our human race in His image. I would add a word of caution: There are two senses in which "the genus of God" can be taken. The incorrect sense would be that we become divinity. I am sure Duncan and Hall would agree that is false. The correct sense is that we truly were made in the image of God, with a human spirit that can relate to Him. This is truly an amazing understanding of what God has done. We can know God because we are, in a limited sense, of the same kind as He is.

(ps-5B.6) *All God created was good; Adam's Fall is entirely responsible for all evil.* Duncan and Hall say, "God's world was originally good. . . . Man's sin is entirely responsible for corrupting original creation."[504]

In brief response, Adam did not do the tempting. Satan, too, must bear some responsibility for evil on Earth. On the other hand, I agree that the Bible clearly assigns Adam, as the head of humanity, 100 percent blame for humanity's original fall into sin (Rom. 5:12).

Supported Claims of YEC Nonscientific Variant

(s-5B.1) God created everything *ex nihilo* **in the initial creation.** Duncan and Hall say that God created the universe "*ex nihilo*—out of nothing."[505]

Hebrews 11:3 and Colossians 1:16 and 17 affirm this claim.

(s-5B.2) Each numbered *yôm* **(day) in Genesis 1 was a normal, natural, twenty-four-hour day based on Genesis 1 and Exodus 20:11.** "Compelling exegetical evidence," claim Duncan and Hall, "for reading the creation days as anything other than normal days is lacking."[506]

Their claim is Biblically well supported.[507] I prefer the phrase "day-night days" because day and night are in the Bible, but "twenty-four-hours" is not the way the Bible says it.[508] However, they are correct that "exegetical evidence" does not support days as geological eras.

(s-5B.4a) In those six twenty-four-hour days, God spoke "eight simple commands."[509] Duncan and Hall explain, "By eight simple commands, God spoke the world into reality."[510]

This insight, that Genesis 1 contains eight command units with the six days, is very helpful.

(s-5B.5) The Bible does not date the universe. Duncan and Hall say, "We take no position on the age of the universe precisely because that question is not directly addressed by the canon."[511]

They are correct. The Bible does not date the universe.

I conclude that Duncan and Hall have offered some Biblically supported insights. However, they also propose more miracles than the Bible indicates. That overstatement of miracles is based on an *"in"* that actually is not in Exodus 20:11. Based on *"in* six days," they claim that everything, including the initial creation, was *in* the six days. Added miracles are needed to fit everything into six days. I suggest that there is no need to "defend" God by claiming more miracles than the Bible does. That overstatement of miracles not in the Bible is remedied by turning from *"in* six days" to "In the [literal] beginning God [literally] created the [literal] heavens and the [literal] earth."

Interestingly, Duncan and Hall have made a vital first step in what I conclude is the right direction by holding to a Biblically undated creation.

My Suggestion

There really is *no* "in" in Exodus 20:11a. Jesus' statement against divorce really does *not* say anything about the age of the universe. *Bᵉrē'shît* in Genesis 1:1 really *does* mean a beginning time period.

I suggest that YEC at least allow that God created the heavens and the earth in the beginning time period before the six literal days. After all, the title is young earth creation, not young universe creation. YEC can legitimately say the Bible does not date the universe. This is a much more Biblical position. It will end the problem of appearance of age of the universe, because the universe is however old it is.

I suggest that YEC defend no time passage between the six literal days. At the same time, I suggest OEC accept six literal days instead of six long day-ages. Then OEC can defend time passage between the six literal days for an old earth creation. As a result, the discussion between YEC and OEC can become much more Biblical on both sides.

Summary of Young Earth Creationism

Young earth scientific creationism begins with Exodus 20:11. Everything was created *"in* six days" because *'āsâh* (being interchangeable with *bārā'*) meant "created" and *"in"* is emphasized. Therefore, God created everything within the six days. So the *ex nihilo* creation of Genesis 1:1 was in day one. The six days were consecutive twenty-four-hour days, taking place about 6,000 years ago. In day one God created the beginning as time, the heavens as space, and earth as unformed watery matter throughout dark space. God also created temporary light for the first three days.

On day two God formed a water canopy above Earth. On day three God precipitated out of the watery matrix a solid Earth and land. On day four, about 6,000 years ago, God created the galaxies of the universe from the rest of the unformed Earth. On day five God created all aquatic and flying life. On day six God created all land animal life; created Adam, who named all the land animal kinds; and made Eve from Adam. Everything had "appearance of age," or there is an explanation still unproven for why the universe appears older than 6,000 years. The genealogies of Adam date the universe, which is only a few days older than Adam, at "thousands, not billions," of years old.

Almost all fossils were deposited by the Noahic flood, which rose to cover all "high mountains" (which may have been only low hills then). Since the flood, there has been vast mountain building of new high ranges. Also since the flood, there has been major microevolution from the limited "kinds" of land animals and birds that Adam named and that were on the ark into several times that number of species today.

Young earth *non*scientific creationism differs in three claims: It distains natural revelation. It claims all acts in the six days were miracles. It explains that the Bible does not date the universe.

Conclusions about Young Earth Creationism

Young earth creationism has ten main claims. Its third main claim is that the *ex nihilo* creation of Genesis 1:1 was *in* day one, a few days before Adam. That unique third claim has no Biblical support. But the other nine main claims are Biblically supported and are ready to move on into the unified theory.

The 6,000-year-old universe third claim is not in the Bible. But if my understanding that the universe is undated by the Bible is correct, then the heavens and the earth could be only years older than the six days. Although there is no Bible evidence for a 6,000-year-old universe, YEC may still claim a 6,000-year-old date for the universe from science. If a YEC 6,000-year-old-universe claim based on science is correct, there should be massive and daily increasing evidence from science that the universe is 6,000 years old, but no verifiable evidence that the universe is older. But the Bible does not date the universe or support the YEC third claim. So if evidence pours in for an older universe and Earth, Christianity should abandon the 6,000 year old universe claim that is based on the incorrect TEC third main claim that the 1:1 creation was in day one. However, we should keep the other nine main claims.

Most certainly, YEC should abandon the "*in*" that is absent from Exodus 20:11a, and discard the consequent third main claim that the heavens and earth were created *in* day one. I urge YEC supporters to give up "*in* six days" and instead accept "In the [literal] beginning God [literally] created the [literal] heavens and the [literal] earth."

The fundamental issue in all this is Biblical authority. If young earth scientific creationism continues to proclaim all creation "*in* six days," thus continuing to add an "in" that is not there and that was never "written by the finger of God," that act will constitute a violation of Biblical authority, a violation of the Word of God.

On the other hand, Henry Morris and other YEC advocates have contributed greatly to creation science and to Biblical creation studies. They have given us the nine sound main claims that we will carry over into the unified theory. I honor them and thank them for those wonderful Biblically-sound contributions.

5. Young Earth Scientific Creationism Theory

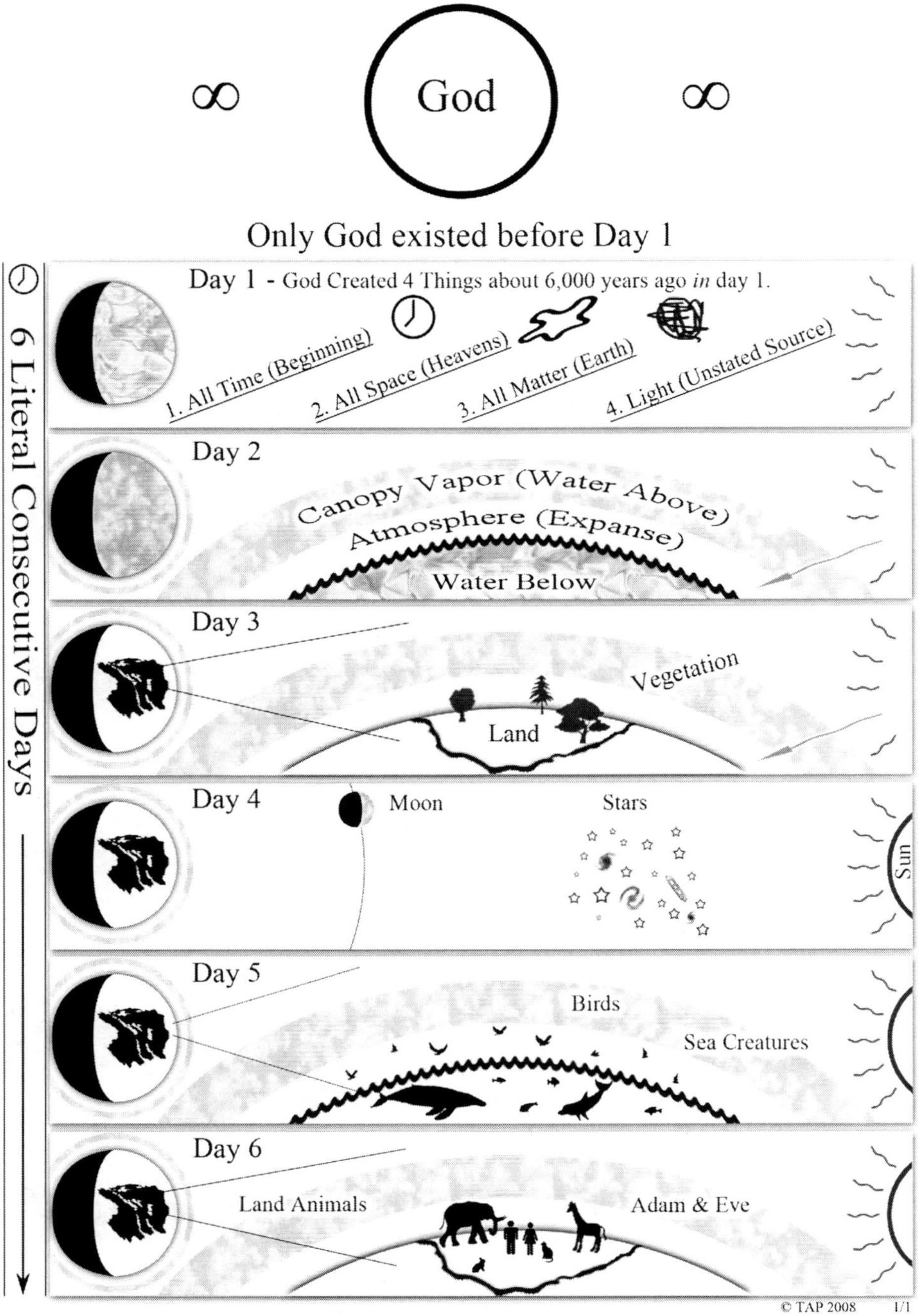

Only God existed before Day 1

<u>5a. Claims of Young Earth Scientific Creationism</u>

(Biblically supported claims in non-italics **bold,** unsupported in *italics*)

(5.0A) Bible is inerrant; so interpret Genesis as literal history.

(5.0B) The Bible is inerrant, so has priority over science.

(5.0C) Bible inerrantly reveals what God did; science tells how.

(5.0D) "In the beginning" means the instantaneous start of all time.

(5.1) God created time, space, and matter-energy out of nothing.

(5.1a) Some YEC advocates discard ex nihilo *creation in 1:1 for the title theory.*

(5.2) Each numbered *yôm* in Genesis 1 was a literal, *normal day.*

(5.3) In day one God created heavens (space), earth (matter), and time (beginning).

   (5.3a) Bārā' and 'āsâh are interchangeable in Genesis 1 and Exodus 20:11.

   (5.3b) Jesus' statement against divorce means that Adam dates the universe.

   (5.3c) Day one—space (heavens), matter (earth), time (beginning), and light.

   (5.3d) "Heavens" meant "all space" without luminaries.

   (5.3e) "Earth" meant "all matter" in the universe.

   (5.3f) All this matter, "earth," in the universe was unformed prematter.

   (5.3g) "In the beginning" was the time part of the space-mass-time universe.

   (5.3h) This creation of time was at the beginning of day one.

   (5.3i) Day one began time in the entire universe.

   (5.3j) The dark evening of 1:2 began night, followed by the morning of 1:3.

   (5.3k) The deep was mixed with "earth" as a "watery matrix."

   (5.3l) Darkness "upon the face of the deep" was darkness throughout space.

   (5.3m) The light on day one began three-day temporary light.

   (5.3n) Light was created in transit as if from sun, moon, and stars not yet made.

   (5.3o) The light of day one energized the entire universe.

   (5.3p) Day two—God made the open air atmosphere; below a vast vapor canopy.

   (5.3q) Day three—solid planet Earth precipitated out; land; trees with age.

   (5.3r) In day four God created the sun, moon, and galaxies from "earth."

(5.3s) Days five & six—sea, air, and land life; Adam and Eve.

   (5.3t) Rain did not fall until the flood.

   (5.3u–5.3x) All was perfect—no predators, disease or death.

   (5.3y) Genealogies date Adam 6,000 years ago, so universe is 6,000 years old.

   (5.3z) God created the universe with "appearance of age."

(5.4) God apparently gave the Genesis 1:1—2:4a account to Adam.

(5.5) Adam's sin resulted in death.

   (5.5a) All humans have descended from Adam, so all are fallen.

   (5.5b) In Adam all are related to Jesus as Kinsman-Redeemer.

   (5.5c) Eternal physical life of "nephesh" animals was ended by Adam's sin.

   (5.5d) Animals will not die in the future restoration, so did not die before sin.

(5.5e) All animals were vegetarians before Adam's sin.

(5.5f) To question animals' eternal life before sin undermines the atonement.

(5.6) Noah's flood was real, violent, and worldwide.

(5.6a) Exodus 20:11 teaches a young earth; Noah's flood explains how.

(5.6b) The flood formed *most* geologic features and fossils.

(5.7) YEC denies chance-driven molecules-to-man evolution.

(5.7a) YEC accepts microevolution from 5,000 "kinds" on ark.

(5.8) YEC denies the entire gap theory.

(5.9) YEC denies the pre-creation chaos and title/summary theory.

(5.10) YEC denies all non-day-night "days" theories.

<u>5B. Claims of Young Earth Non-scientific Creationism</u>

(Biblically supported claims non-italics **bold,** unsupported in *italics*)

(5B.00) **The Bible is inerrant;** natural revelation is *"every man a liar."*

(5B.0) All six-day events were unmediated, instantaneous, miraculous acts.

(5B.1) God created everything *ex nihilo* in the initial creation.

(5B.2) Each numbered *yôm* was a twenty-four-hour **day.**

(5B.3) *Exodus 20:11 says all creation came about in the six twenty-four-hour days.*

(5B.3a) The days were night-day, beginning with evening, ending in morning.

(5B.4) Earth was *formless* and empty; God formed and filled it in six days.

(5B.4a) God spoke "eight simple commands."

(5B.4b) God created the sun, moon, and stars instantly on the fourth day.

(5B.4c) God created man after God's kind.

(5B.5)The Bible does not date the universe.

(5B.6) All God created was good; Adam's Fall is responsible for *all* evil.

Major Supported Claims from the Creation Theories

The Correct Translation of Genesis 1:1: Waltke affirms the traditional translation of Genesis 1:1: "In the beginning God created the heavens and the earth." It is *incorrect* to translate 1:1 as "When God began to create."

Waltke Merism: "The heavens and the earth" meant the entire orderly universe. Also, evening and morning meant the entire nighttime.

The Waltke Exclusion Principle: If there was preexisting chaos, there was no *ex nihilo* creation of the organized heavens and earth. The converse is also logically possible: If there was *ex nihilo* creation of the organized heavens and earth, then there was no unorganized chaos.

The Kline Order: Proverbs 8:22–31 says "the beginning," when God created Earth (Gen. 1:1), was "when there were no depths." There were ocean depths by 1:2, so "In the beginning" was before 1:2 and the six days of 1:3–31. Creation order: Heavens, Earth, sea, six days.

The Kline Claim: When the Bible does not indicate a miracle, Genesis 2:5–6 (no rain, no plants; rain, then plants sprouted) shows God probably used ordinary means in the creation era, just as today.

A Generational Genesis: The worldview of Genesis was generations. The six begetting (literal) days of Genesis 1 introduced the most ancient generations of all—"the generations of the heavens and the earth."

The Rooker Reaffirmation: "The key difference between pagan cosmogonies and Genesis 1 is *creatio ex nihilo* and the absence of preexisting matter."

The Morris Maxim: In historical narrative, a numbered "day" was a day.

The Morris Method: The Bible reveals what God did; science may uncover how He did it.

The Morris One Fall Explanation: The creation was perfect. Man and animals were created about 6,000 years ago with eternal physical life. There was "no disorder, no sin and, above all, *no death!* Even Satan was still good at this point."[512] His first effect on Earth was the temptation. (There were two falls, but Lucifer's fall had no effect on Earth until his temptation of Eve, resulting in Adam and Eve's Fall.) Adam's Fall resulted in a "cosmic catastrophe" including all human and animal death and subsequent moral and natural evil.

Chapter 6

Theory 6
Day-Age, Old Earth,
Progressive Creationism Theory

See the story from the author's perspective.

Old earth creationism is an umbrella theory that includes the day-age theory of the days. Old earth creationism includes both theistic evolutionism and progressive creationism. I am limiting this chapter to the day-age progressive creationism version of old earth creationism. The day-age idea is that each "day" was a geologic age on Earth during which God made Earth habitable and made life. Progressive creationism is the idea that God intervened with creation acts during the long history of life. Modern advocates include Gleason Archer, Bernard Ramm, Robert Newman, and Hugh Ross. Gleason Archer is a renowned Hebrew scholar. Hugh Ross is an extraordinary gracious Christian astronomer and active apologist for Christianity. Ross is a prolific author on the subject, so I will list his ideas.

In a nutshell, the day-age theory says that in the beginning God created the heavens and the earth. But early Earth was uninhabitable and cloud-darkened. So in six long day-ages God made Earth lighted, habitable, and inhabited.

As an astronomer, Hugh Ross began to consider the biggest questions of all. He recorded his spiritual pilgrimage as he thought about the universe and asked the question, "Who did all this?" He found the answer in a Gideon Bible. He realized that the creation events recorded in the Bible "perfectly matched the established record of nature." After eighteen months of reading the Bible and not finding "a single provable error or contradiction," he realized, "its perfection could come only from the Creator Himself." He testifies,

I saw that my only rational option was to trust in the Bible's Inspirer to at least the same degree as I relied on the laws of physics. I realized, too, what a self-sufficient young man I had been. After a long evening of studying the salvation passages in the New Testament, I humbled myself before God, asking Him to forgive me of my self-exaltation and all the offenses resulting from it, . . . and received Christ as my Lord and Savior.[513]

Thus, Hugh Ross became a Christian. Breakthroughs in science consistently "made the case for Christianity stronger."[514] As he studied science and the Bible, he built an evidence-based case for Biblical creation. He has written many books on day-age, old earth creationism. Ross has been an effective witness to fellow scientists.

I have met and respect Hugh Ross as a scientist and Christian. He is to be honored as a truth seeker who has made great contributions to creation science. Among the greatest are his insights into how the universe was "tuned" precisely for human life.

That I do not agree with him on one main claim does not lessen my honor to this remarkable Christian astronomer and great apologist.

Four Key Preunderstandings

(6.0A) *The Bible is intentionally testable and provable, so untestable theories about the physical universe fail to measure up to Biblical standards.* Archer and Ross say, "Christianity's uniqueness resides not only in its gospel message, but also in its testability. Paul exhorts Christ's followers to 'test everything.'" Theories about the created universe based on *only* miracles and appearance of age are inherently untestable. Untestable creation theories do not measure up to the Biblical standard of "test everything" (1 Thess. 5:21).

(6.0B) *Correctly interpreted, both God's verbal revelation (the Bible) and physical revelation (the universe) will be in accord.* Hugh Ross believes in evidence. There is overwhelming evidence that the Bible's claims are true. The evidence from both the Bible and the creation should be examined to discover truth.

Archer and Ross quote the *Proceedings of the International Council of Biblical Inerrancy,* Summit II (1982) Article 20: "The Bible speaks truth when it touches matters pertaining to nature." "We further affirm that in some cases extrabiblical data have value for clarifying what Scripture teaches, and for prompting correction of faulty interpretations. WE DENY that extrabiblical views ever disprove the teaching of Scripture or hold priority over it."[515]

The Bible came from the Creator. Only the Creator could have stated, long before modern science, the many Bible claims that match modern discoveries of astronomy, astrophysics, cosmology, etc.

The universe came from the Creator because (a) it could not have started itself, (b) it has been precisely tuned for human life, and (c) it matches the claims by the Creator revealed in the Bible.

Evidence tells us that the Bible is true. Evidence from the creation matches the claims of the Bible. That match demonstrates that both the Bible and creation are from the God of the Bible. So both the Bible, rightly interpreted, and creation, rightly understood, will agree. Ross holds these conclusions evidentially.[516]

Since the evidence for the God of the Bible is 99+% provably certain, it is only reasonable to exercise faith for the last less then 1% that is beyond evidential proof. Ross has done just that, and he urges other scientists, and nonscientists, to do the same.

(6.0C) *The Bible and creation indicate God did miracles judiciously.* On the one hand, "An observed attribute of the Creator . . . is His economy of miracles—only what's needed to accomplish His purpose."[517] On the other hand, God certainly did miracles. The Reasons to Believe model affirms "the necessity of at least some interventionist miracles to explain the origin of humanity."[518] The other great miracle was the initial creation. And God did miracles at other events, but only as needed. Normally God works by the laws He designed into the universe so precisely in the beginning.

(6.0D) *The Bible tells us accurately what God did; science may tell us how He did it.* Hugh Ross may not realize it, but he is following the method pioneered by Henry Morris: the Bible tells us what God did, then science may tell us how He did it. Morris, a hydrology (water movement) engineer, practiced this method for the flood. Ross, an astronomer, practices this method on the origin of the universe.

The Bible reveals what God did.

Science may reveal how He did it.

Bible Interpretation Practice

I will list hermeneutical (Bible interpretation) practices as **H**.

(6.H1) *Interpret the Bible from the perspective of the Author.* Interpret the Bible from its original perspective. Ross says, "Begin by establishing [not assuming] the point of view."[519] Interpret "from the vantage point of an observer," "describing details as they would have appeared from that perspective."[50]

Interpret Genesis 1
from the perspective of the Divine Observer.

Claims of Day-Age, Old Earth, Progressive Creationism

(6.1) *Two Bible creation claims, beginning and stretching out of the universe, match two main claims discovered by science.* Hugh Ross says scientific evidence that the universe had a beginning and has been stretching out is very strong and growing continually stronger. Genesis 1:1 is the Biblical explanation of the cause of the beginning of the universe.[521] Ross sees that beginning as best described by the big bang. It is not that the Bible describes the big bang in modern scientific language. Rather, the Bible's two-part claim that God "created the heavens and stretched them out" (Isaiah 42:5) matches the two main claims of the big bang—beginning and expansion. The big bang theory has no explanation for the very first instant, but the Bible does: "In the beginning God created the heavens and the earth."

(6.1a) *The universe had a beginning—the big bang.* Hugh Ross explains that there are two options open to science: an unlimited infinite eternal steady-state universe, which may not require a Creator; or a universe in which the "matter and energy are finite in extent and in time,"[522] which would require a beginning of the universe. Matter and energy are "finite in extent and in time," so the universe had a beginning. A universe with a beginning needs an eternal Creator. The big bang theory has convinced most scientists that the universe had a beginning. Now Hugh Ross urges them to take the next step and believe in the Creator, who long ago revealed these two facts, the beginning and expansion of the universe, in the Bible.

Ross concludes about Einstein and Hubble, "All these scientists, however, were upstaged at least 2,500 years earlier by Job, Moses, David, Isaiah, Jeremiah, and other Biblical authors. The Bible's prophets and apostles stated explicitly and repeatedly the two most fundamental properties of the big bang, a transcendent cosmic beginning a finite time period ago and a universe undergoing general, continual expansion. In Isaiah 42:5 both properties were declared: 'This is what the Lord says—He who created the heavens and stretched them out.'"[523]

(6.1b) *The beginning of the universe indicates a transcendent personal Beginner.* Ross says, "The big bang theory points to a supernatural beginning and a purposeful (hence personal), transcendent (beyond the boundaries of space, time, matter, and energy) Beginner."[524]

Scientists do not know the big bang's cause. Ross says God is that Cause,[525] in agreement with Genesis 1:1.

(6.1c) *The universe has been expanding since God created it.* Before Lemaître and Hubble, the common idea was that the universe is eternal and static, neither expanding nor contracting.

Lemaître's insight from Einstein's equations matched Hubble's discovery that the universe is expanding. The galaxies are getting farther apart, and the space between them is expanding.

Ross points out that long before the big bang theory, God declared that the universe had a beginning and has been stretching out or expanding. Eleven Bible texts say that God has been stretching out the heavens. Isaiah 51:13 speaks of "the LORD your Maker, Who stretched out the heavens and laid the foundations of the earth" (NASB). These eleven texts' descriptions range in time from immediately after the initial creation through the time of Isaiah. So God has been continually stretching out the heavens since creation and throughout Biblical history.

Science had discovered evidence for the expanding universe. Cosmic background radiation left from the big bang expansion was discovered Arno Penzias and Bob Wilson. George Smoot's COBE satellite mapped the slight differences in that background radiation that account for the galaxies, confirmed more precisely by the WMAP satellite. This evidence for the beginning and expansion of the universe, suggesting a Creator, was not lost on Smoot. Seeing this evidence he said, "It's like looking at God."[526]

Since the universe is expanding, then the universe must have had a beginning from which it expanded outward.

> The Bible alone declares that the universe had a beginning and has been stretching out. Only the Creator could have known these facts long before modern science. The God of the Bible is the Creator.

(6.1d) *The precisely right conditions of the resulting universe, Earth, and life attest to the Creator revealed in the Bible.* The origin of the universe, the fine-tuning of the universe for life, the precise conditions on planet Earth for life, and the improbability of life by chance all give overwhelming evidence for a Divine Designer—the God of the Bible.[527] God created the universe precisely for life, especially for human life.

The fine-tuning of the universe is far too precise
to be by chance.

(6.2) *Each* **yôm** *apparently refers to an era of millions or billions of years.* Hugh Ross's book, *Creation and Time*, mixes two kinds of claims: claims that each *yôm*, "day," apparently was a long era, with claims that the universe is old. These two groups of claims are not the same, so I have separated them. (Several theories claim normal days, yet allow the universe to be Biblically undated or to be older.)

(6.2a) Yôm *referred to God's days.* Hugh Ross says, "Old earth creationists find many scriptural reasons, apart from science, for interpreting the creation days as long time periods." Psalm 90:4 refers to "the length of God's days": "For a thousand years in your sight are like a day that has just gone by, or like a watch [four hours] in the night" (NIV). Psalm 90:4 explains that God is not time-bound, so Ross says that the six creation days may "refer to something like millions of years" because "God's days are not our days."[528]

(6.2b) Yôm *has a semantic range including time periods longer than a day, allowing billion-year day-ages.* Ross gives examples of the semantic range of *yôm* being used for longer time periods.[529] These examples need not be listed because it is widely agreed that the semantic range of *yôm* includes times longer than a day.

(6.2c) Erev *and* bōqer, *"evening and morning," may be metaphorical.* Ross says that "evening" may have had "possible metaphoric usage."[530] A metaphorical day may represent a long era.

(6.2d) *The ordinal number series may allow a longer time.* Ross appeals to the ordinal numbers of the second through sixth days. Ross says, "Young-earth creationists have argued for twenty-four-hour days on the basis that *yôm* when attached to an ordinal (second, third, fourth, etc.) always refers to a twenty-four hour period." Ross turns to Hosea 6:2. Hosea prophesies that "after *two* days he [God] will revive us [Israel]; on the third day he will restore us" (NIV). Third is ordinal. Ross continues, "For centuries Bible commentators have noted that the 'days' in this passage (where the ordinal is used) refer to a year, years, a thousand years, or maybe more."[531]

(6.2e) *The grammar of the* yôm *sentences is unusual.* Hugh Ross says that the phrase "And was evening and was morning day X" "is clearly a departure from simple and ordinary expression." "It does suggest that 'day' here is to be taken in some unusual manner."[532]

(6.2f) *Chronological Bible statements are intended to be verifiable, but the six days are too short to verify their order unless they are day-ages.* Ross says, "For the creation days, long periods . . . are verifiable and useful for validating the supernatural accuracy of the writer's statements. But if all creation were completed in six 24–hour days, the most sophisticated measuring techniques . . . would be totally incapable of discerning the sequence of events. Thus, a major use of the [Bible] chronology [as evidence for accuracy] would be thwarted."

(6.2g) *The events of the sixth* yôm *were too many and too long to have been finished in twelve hours.* Ross lists all the events of day six: God created the three big classes of land mammals. God created Adam. Then God engaged Adam in "lengthy conversation," instructing "in their responsibilities in managing the plants, animals and resources of the earth."[533] Then Adam named thousands of the kinds of birds and land animals. This naming alone would seem to have taken longer than there was daylight. Ross says that all these events would fit better in a longer period of time, suggesting that six consecutive twenty-four-hour days may not be correct.

(6.2h) *The seventh* yôm *had no stated ending.* Ross says, "After the creation of Adam and Eve, however, God ceased from His work of creating new life-forms (the seventh day). Now His rest, or 'cessation,' continues to this day."[534] The seventh day has no ending evening and morning. "This distinct change in form for the seventh day strongly suggests that this day has (or had) not yet ended." If the seventh day was longer, then so must have been the previous six days.

(6.2i) Yôm *in Genesis 2:4b lasted longer than twenty-four hours.* Genesis 2:4b says, "In the day the LORD made the heavens and the earth."[535] Therefore, Ross concludes, "day" has a semantic range longer than twenty-four hours.

(6.2j) *A Sabbath week may be much longer than seven days.* A Sabbath week may refer to seven days, seven years, or even longer. For example, the seventieth week of Daniel (Dan. 9:25–27) apparently refers to seven years, commonly known as the Tribulation.

(6.2k) *The Bible says the heavens and earth are old, so the days must have been long.* Ross points out that Habakkuk 3:6 and 2 Peter 3:5 say the heavens and earth are old. If the heavens and earth are old, then the days must have been long.

(6.3) *The Bible and science indicate an old universe and Earth.* Ross says that the order of events in Genesis 1 matches the discoveries by science, but only if we recognize an older creation. Given an older creation, this match is a powerful apologetic for the truth of Genesis 1 and the fact that the God of the Bible is the Creator.

(6.3a) *Earth's ancient age illustrates God's eternality.* God's eternality is compared (as greater to lesser) to the "mountains" and the "foundations" of Earth (Ps. 90:2–6; Prov. 8:22–31).[536] If David wrote when Earth was only 3,000 years old, only three lifetimes of men like Methuselah, such a short time is hardly a good illustration of God's eternality.

(6.3b) *The Bible explicitly states that Earth is ancient.* Ross explains, "Habakkuk 3:6 directly declares that the mountains are 'ancient' and the hills are 'age-old.' In 2 Peter, the heavens (the stars and the universe) are said to have existed 'long ago.'"[537] Ross says that "age-old" strongly indicates an age older than four thousand years at the time of Habakkuk, only four lifetimes of Adam.

(6.3c) *The Bible says the stars are countless, which indicates the universe is ancient.* Beginning with Abraham (Gen. 15:5; 22:17), the Bible indicates that the stars are countless, their number parallel to the grains of sand of the seashores. "Hebrew (and Greek) numbering systems," says Ross, "included numbers up to the billions." "Countless" meant more than 100 billion stars. If the universe has at least 100 billion stars, and knowing the average density of stars, that works out to "no less than 56,000 light years." "Since no material in our universe moves more rapidly than the velocity of light, and since the velocity of light must remain constant for life to exist, we can conclude that the biblically stated *minimum* age of the universe is 56,000 years."[538] A 3,000-year-old universe at the time of writing does *not* fit "countless" stars.

Astronomers estimate that the universe has about 100,000,000,000,000,000,000,000 (one hundred sextillion) stars, and astronomers are able to see objects over 12 billion light-years away. So it is reasonable to conclude that the universe is about 13.7 billion years old which astronomers estimate.[539] This size and approximate number of stars certainly fits the Bible term "countless."

(6.3d) *Genesis 1 was the "generations of the heavens and the earth."* Genesis is divided by *tôlᵉdôt,* or generations statements. "In Genesis 2:4 the plural form, *generations*, is used, indicating that multiple generations have passed."[540] Genesis 2:4a ends the creation narrative with, "These *are* the generations of the heavens and of the earth when they were created" (KJV). One patriarch generation could be a hundred years before the birth of the succeeding son. The generations of "the heavens and the earth" would seem at least many years, rather than 144 hours. And if one combines this concept of generations of the heavens and the earth with the previous antiquity statements, then the generations of the heavens and earth may have been very long indeed.

(6.4) *Theology suggests an older universe, Earth, and life.* Ross explains that there is also a "theological basis"[541] for an old Earth and universe.

(6.4a) *God does not deceive in either the Bible or the creation.* "Whatever objects of His creation we subject to scientific analysis will reveal their true age—provided the analysis is theoretically valid, correctly applied, and accurately interpreted."[542] There is great evidence that the universe is billions of light-years in radius. The constant of the speed of light is not changing. If it did change, that would disrupt all of physics and life. The universe is billions of light-years across. Even at the immense speed of 186,282 miles per second, light from the most distant objects takes 12 billion years to reach us. So these objects are at least 12 billion years old. The conclusion is that the universe is about 13.7 billion years old. Also, both the Bible and science claim that the universe had a beginning. If we run the expansion of the universe backward, we come to a beginning about 13.7 billion years ago. "The abundant and consistent evidence from astronomy, physics, geology, and paleontology must be taken seriously."[543] Theologians generally agree that the Bible and the creation, when correctly understood, must be in accord because both are from God. Most theologians would also agree that God does not deceive either by his work or by His Word.

Since God does not deceive, and since numerous independent indicators from the created universe show an age of at least billions of years, these indicators tell the truth.

(6.4b) *By Adam's sin "death spread to all men," not to all animals.* If there was no animal death before Adam's sin, all other arguments about an older earth with life are irrelevant. Romans 5:12 states, "Therefore, just as through one man sin entered into the world, and death through sin, and so death spread to all men, because all sinned" (NASB). Ross makes a four-part claim.

First, "The death Adam experienced is carefully qualified in the text as being visited on 'all men'—not on plants and animals, just on human beings (Romans 5:12, 18–19)."[544] 1 Corinthians 15:21–22 states, "For since by a man *came* death, by a man also *came* the resurrection of the dead. For as in Adam all die, so also in Christ all shall be made alive" (NASB).

The parallelism between "in Adam all die" and "in Christ all shall be made alive" is precise. Since only human beings are "made alive" in Christ, then only human beings are subject to "in Adam all die."[545] Adam's sin resulted in human death. The curse for Adam's sin does not declare animal death. The claim by YEC that Adam's sin started animal death is an assumption that is more than the Bible says. On the basis of both Romans 5 and 1 Corinthians 15, "no reason is found to deny physical death for nonhuman life previous to Adam's sin."[546]

Second, Ross says that immediate death "through the sin" was spiritual death; physical death came later as the result of spiritual death. "When Adam sinned, he instantly 'died' just as God said he would ('In the day that you eat of it, you shall surely die'—Genesis 2:17, NJKV)."[547]

Third, Ross says that even YEC's problematic and unproven argument that all animals were vegetarians before Adam's Fall would not have stopped animal death. Before Adam's sin, large animals such as elephants would have stepped on small mammals.[548]

Fourth, Ross argues that God saw all He had made was "very good"; yet if animal death is not evil, then animal death could have been included in the "very good" world. Walter Kaiser asks, Who but God killed the animals for skins to cover Adam and Eve? And who but God is good?

By animal death, God made skin coverings for Adam and Eve.
God never does evil, not even for good ends.
Therefore, animal death is not inherently morally evil.

Someone might respond to Ross that God killed the animals *after* Adam sinned for the good purpose of covering their nakedness, picturing Jesus' death covering sin. But God does not do evil for a good purpose. Animal death is not inherently morally evil. If animal death is not evil, then there could have been animal death in the world when God saw all that He had made was "very good."

"Herbivores need carnivores. Unlike human hunters, other carnivores focus their hunting energies on the sick, the injured, the unwary, or the weak for their food supply. By removing these individuals from herbivore flocks or herds, carnivores alleviate herbivore suffering and prevent herbivore populations from becoming dangerously diseased and genetically weakened. They also stop herbivores from exhausting their food resources and starving to death."[549] Even parasites perform this last duty.

Also, Ross argues that the "very good" earth was not a "perfect" earth. For example, God could have eliminated hurricanes, but hurricanes provide much of the source of rainfall on land and enrich the continental shelf for the fishing industry.[550]

(6.4c) *Creation has been subject to the "bondage of decay" (entropy) since its beginning.* Hugh Ross quotes Romans 8:20–22 in the NIV:

> For the creation was subjected to frustration, not by its own choice, but by the will of the one who subjected it, in hope that the creation itself will be liberated from its bondage to decay and brought into the glorious freedom of the children of God. We know that the whole creation has been groaning as in the pains of childbirth right up to the present time.

Ross then explains that some creationists, I presume he means some young earth creationists, "assume that the law of entropy, which describes the decreasing order in the universe, did not take effect until Adam and Eve sinned."

Ross responds that without entropy, "work (at least in the universe God designed) would be impossible."[551] Using up useful energy made work possible. Adam was to "work" in the Garden. Entropy was in effect from the creation. But this also meant the universe has been "running down" (increasing in entropy) since the creation, before Adam's Fall. "Romans 8 explicitly indicates only when the bondage to decay will end. It says little about when if first began."[552]

(6.4d) *Standard theology recognizes two falls: the fall of angels and the Fall of man.* This claim is not from Hugh Ross, but from distinguished professor of Old Testament and president of Gordon-Conwell Theological Seminary Dr. Walter Kaiser. Walter Kaiser joined Hugh Ross (OEC) in "The Great Debate" opposite Ken Ham (YEC).[553] Moderator John Ankerberg referred to Romans 5:12—"Therefore, just as through one man sin entered into the world, and death through sin, and so death spread to all men, because all sinned." Old earth creationist Hugh Ross has written that this verse only says Adam's Fall resulted in *human* death. Young earth creationist Ken Ham agreed that Romans 5:12 only indicates that Adam's sin explicitly resulted in *human* death. Nevertheless, according to Ken Ham, Adam's sin resulted in animal death as well. Walter Kaiser responded that standard theology has always held that there were two falls, the angelic fall led by Lucifer, and the Fall of man by Adam's sin. The serpent, which Revelation 12:9 and 20:2 identify as the devil, was already fallen and present on earth before human sin. Therefore, any evil aspects of animal death may have been the result of Lucifer's fall long before Adam sinned. Everything God did was "good" and "very good." But between God's good acts, fallen Lucifer may have caused any evil aspects of disease and destruction we find in the fossil record. Ross certainly agrees that animal death is not inherently evil, but whether he agrees that before Adam's fall, Lucifer may have adding evil between God's good acts, Ross does not say clearly.

(6.4e) *Pain is necessary and only increased after the Fall.* "In Genesis 3:16, God says to Eve, 'I will greatly increase [or multiply] your pains in childbearing.' He does not say 'introduce.'" Increase implies that there was some pain even before the Fall.[554] Some pain is a necessary warning, but pain of childbirth would be *increased* after the Fall. Adam's sin did not introduce entropy/decay, pain, or animal death. Adam's sin introduced immediate *human* spiritual death, with *human* physical death certainly following. His sin increased *human* birth pain and *human* farming woes.

(6.4f) *An older universe and Earth do not require chance-caused evolution.* There was no chance-caused naturalistic macroevolution. "Do long creation days and an old earth and universe really make room for naturalistic evolution? The answer is a resounding no."[555] God, not chance, is the source of all life. Ross's chemistry partner, Fazale Rana, states, "The process of chemical evolution seemed unconvincing."[556]

(6.4g) *Four and a half billion years' preparation were needed for Earth to be ready for God's final creation—humans in His image.* A full explanation of this claim is in *Origins of Life*. "Human beings reap the benefit of nearly 4 billion years' worth of biodeposits."[557]

(6.5) *The six day-epochs were in sequential order.* "The six epochs revealed in Genesis 1 occurred in the order revealed."[558] An evidence for the six days being in sequential chronological order is all the chronological terms in Genesis 1. "Nowhere else in the Bible do we find such a density of chronological terms."[559]

Also, God's six work days were followed by a rest day, matching Exodus 20:8–11. God worked six days followed by the seventh rest day, so Israel was to work six days followed by the Sabbath—always in that order in the Hebrew Bible.[560]

Ross also says that the order of events in Genesis 1 precisely matches scientific discoveries about the history of Earth. But these scientific discoveries also indicate a long history of Earth, a history that could not fit into six sequential day-night days 6,000 years ago. So science is giving great evidence for the exact sequence of the days found in the Bible, but only if we recognize that the universe and planet Earth are old.

All this indicates that the six days were in sequential order. The framework theory's claim of nonsequential days errs. The six days were in the sequential order stated by the Bible.

(6.6) *God worked six days on Earth's sky, sea, and land rather than on the universe.* Genesis 1:2 changes the focus from "the heavens and the earth" to "the earth."

(6.6a) *Genesis 1:2 shifts focus from the universe to Earth.* Ross says, "As the text transitions from verse 1 to verse 2, the focus shifts from the cosmos to the early earth."[561] The rest of Genesis 1 will focus on planet Earth. Genesis 1:2 begins, "And the <u>earth</u> was *tōhû vᵃbōhû*," not "the heavens and earth were *tōhû vᵃbōhû*."

(6.6b) *The reference frame for the six days was the perspective of the stated Observer.* Ross says, "The reference frame also shifts. Genesis 1:2 says that the Spirit of God hovered above the primordial Earth's surface. This clue means that the subsequent description of early Earth (and the stages of its transformation) comes from the vantage point of an observer just above the surface of the waters, looking up at the sky and across the horizon, describing details as they would have appeared from that perspective."[562] Ross follows the scientific advice given by Galileo: "Begin by establishing [not assuming] the point of view."[563] "But with the point of view on the surface of the earth, looking up at the atmosphere of the earth, we recognize that God's miracles are taking place in the atmosphere of the earth, not beyond it in the galaxy and the solar system."[564]

(6.6c) *Tōhû vᵃbōhû meant Earth was unfit for life and empty of life.* After Genesis 1:2, these two terms are used together only in Isaiah 34:11 and Jeremiah 4:23. Both describe the land (*'eretz*) after its conquest. The conquered land was made "empty of human life and unfit for life." Together in Genesis 1:2 *tōhû vᵃbōhû* meant planet Earth was "unfit for life" and "empty of life,"[565] indicating the "desolate condition of early Earth." Ross says, "In fact scientists refer to this period of Earth's history (from 4.5 to about 3.9 billion years ago) as the Hadean Era, after Hades (Greek for hell)." This *tōhû vᵃbōhû*, "uninhabitable and uninhabited," era continued "beyond the 3.9-billion-year mark, even into the era after Earth had cooled sufficiently for oceans to form."[566] So *tōhû vᵃbōhû* applied specifically to planet Earth and indicated that our planet was still "empty of life and unfit for life." These two conditions would be remedied during the six day-ages.

(6.6d) *Darkness at the location of the Observer was caused by Earth's early opaque atmosphere.* Ross says, "When the planets were forming, opaque (or nearly opaque) atmospheres shrouded them."[567] This corresponds to Genesis 1:2b: "And darkness was over the surface of the deep" (NASB).

(**6.6e**) *God made Earth's core, mantle, and crust before the ocean.* Ross quotes Psalm 104:5–6 (NIV):

> He [God] set the earth on its foundations;
>   it [foundation] can never be moved.
> You [God] covered it [earth] with the deep as with a garment;
>   the waters stood above the mountains.

"This text implies that God established the planet's core, mantle, and crust before cloaking Earth in oceans."[568] Then the text "describes primordial Earth's surface covered entirely with water."

(**6.6f**) *Early Earth was ocean covered, just as Genesis 1:2 states.* "An observer would also note that Earth's entire surface was submerged below oceans. The biblical text implies that initially no permanent landmasses were present." Psalm 104:5–6 and Job 38:4–11 describe early earth's world-covering ocean.[569]

(**6.6g**) *God may have made primitive sea life early.* Ross adds, "Scientific evidence for ocean life predating land life poses no threat either. The Spirit of God 'brooded' over the face of the waters (Genesis 1:2), possibly creating life in the oceans before the events of the six creation days begin."[570] Ross explains that the third day mentions only land plants, not sea plant life, implying that sea plants may have been created earlier.

(**6.7**) *The events of the six days from the Bible and the creation agree—if Earth is older.* Ross affirms that the six days, like all Bible data, agree with the creation.

(**6.7a**) *In day-era one, light broke through to Earth's surface.* "Light was not created on the first creation day. On that day the light already created 'in the beginning' suddenly broke through to the earth's surface. This breakthrough required the transformation of the atmosphere (plus the interplanetary medium) from opaque to translucent."[571] "Job 38:8–9 [NIV] affirms that Earth's primordial waters were enshrouded by an opaque cloud cover":[572]

> Who shut up the sea behind doors [birth motif]
>   when it burst forth from the womb,
> when I made the clouds its garment
>   and wrapped it in thick darkness?

"During creation day one, light visibly broke though to earth's surface for the first time."[573] Day one began with sunlight breaking through the thick, dark cloud layer to the divine Observer for the first time.

(6.7b) *In the second day-era, water vapor rose from the sea surface, beginning a stable water cycle.* "Formation of water vapor in the troposphere under conditions that establish a stable water cycle" occurred in the second day-era.[574]

(6.7c) *In the third day-era, God formed continental land and land plants.* "Formation of continental land masses together with ocean basins" and the "production of plants on the continental land masses" occurred in the third day-era.[575]

(6.7d) *In the fourth day-era, God caused the sun, moon, and stars, which He had created "in the beginning," to be in the sky for the first time.* Ross explains, "The heavens and earth (*shamayim erets*) of verse 1 includes the entire physical universe of galaxies, stars, planets, etc." But "earth's primordial atmosphere" was only translucent, not transparent, until the fourth day. God made the sun, moon, and stars "distinguishable on that [fourth] day."[576] The Holy Spirit was located just above the sea surface under the overcast sky. In this day-era occurred the "transformation of the atmosphere from a translucent condition to one that is at least occasionally transparent."[577] The luminaries were in the sky for the first time from the perspective of the Holy Spirit, the divine Observer.

(6.7e) *In the fifth day-era, God created sea mammals and birds.* The fifth day-era involved "creation by God's fiat miracles of sea mammals and birds."[578]

(6.7f) *In the sixth day-era, God made three orders of modern land mammals.* God created three orders of land mammals. All three were *nephesh* animals (1:24), "soulish creatures that can relate to humans; creatures with qualities of mind, will, and emotion."[579] God made *remes,* which were not creeping insects (because insects are not *nephesh,* or soulish animals), but were modern "short legged land mammals such as rodents and hares." Also, God made *ᶜhāyâh ha'āretz,* the modern "long-legged quadruped usually described as wild," and *bᵉhēmâh,* the modern "long-legged quadruped that is easy to tame." "The fossil record confirms that such land mammals do not show up until after the initial appearance of birds and sea mammals."[580] These modern land mammals were made to be "capable of interacting with the future human race."[581]

(6.7g) *Also in the sixth day-era, God created humans uniquely possessing body, soul, and spirit.* The sixth day-era culminated in the "creation by God's fiat miracle of the human species." "The Bible clearly denies that any of these [human] species descended from lower forms of life. Human beings are distinct from all other animals, including the bipedal primates that preceded them, in that humans alone possess body, soul, and spirit."[582] God created "Adam and Eve as historical individuals." Humans are "qualitatively different from animals, including the great apes and hominids." "Only people bear the image of God."[583] Ross would date Adam and Eve substantially earlier than YEC would.[584]

(**6.7h**) *The seventh day-era of God's rest did not end in one day.* Ross says, "Information about the seventh day is given in Psalm 95 and Hebrews 4. In these passages we learn that God's day of rest continues." "We gather that the seventh day of Genesis 1 and 2 represents a minimum of several thousand years and a maximum that is open ended (but finite). It seems reasonable to conclude then, given the parallelism of the Genesis creation account, that the first six days may also have been long time periods."[585]

(**6.7i**) *God ceased creating new life kinds during this present seventh day-era.* "After the sixth creation day, God ceased to introduce new life forms on the earth." Hebrews 4 says that God is now at rest.

Hugh Ross offers a negative subclaim:

(**6.7j**) *YEC claims unreasonably rapid microevolution during this present seventh day-era.* There are about 25,000 higher air-breathing land-dwelling species on Earth today that YEC would accept as descendants from animals on the ark.[586] YEC claims the present 25,000 higher land species developed by microevolution after the flood. YEC does not include insects as kinds on the ark, but says they survived on floating vegetation. Young earth scientific creationism estimates that 2,500 to 8,000, possibly even 15,000, kinds or proto-species[587] were named by Adam and were on the ark. For ease of argument, let us round off the YEC claim to about 5,000 Ark animals.

Contra YEC, Ross replies that God ceased creating new life kinds in His present rest. "On this point, most interpreters agree [that God is now at rest]. However, the young-earth creationists' understanding of the Fall and the Flood requires that a huge number of new species of animal life appear on the earth in just a few thousand years."[588]

An increase from about 5,000 kinds to 25,000 species in 5,000 years is more than microevolution. That would seem to be hyper-micro evolution. Ross reprimands YEC for claiming this hyper-microevolution in God's seventh day of rest. Such rapid microevolution is far beyond what "the most optimistic Darwinist has ever dared to suggest. They [YEC] do so despite overwhelming physical evidence that denies the possibility of such rapid change."

YEC counters by denying that the microevolution added new genes, but that the new species merely diversified from the original gene pool by gene segregation. Each reproducing pair off the ark, such as the dog kind, had within its gene pool the present variations—wolves, coyotes, foxes, greyhounds, and dingoes. YEC says that this could have happened quite rapidly.

Ross replies, "If naturalistic evolutionary processes actually did proceed with such speed, they would, of course, be observable in real time in our time." [589] But such hyper-microevolution has not been observed in the history of science.

(6.8) *The agreement of the Bible, accurately interpreted, with the creation, accurately understood, gives evidence that the God of the Bible is the Creator of the universe.* Hugh Ross explains:

> Obviously, no author writing more than 3,400 years ago, as Moses did, could have so accurately described and sequenced these events, plus the initial condition, without divine assistance. And if God could guide the words of Moses to scientific and historical precision in this most complex report of divine activity, we have reason to believe we can trust Him to communicate with perfection through all the other Bible writers as well.[590]

Ross concludes, "We have potent evidence for a personal Creator, specifically for the God of the Bible."[591] "The evidence for a universe designed, initiated, shaped, and sustained exactly as the Bible describes, by God, continues to mount."[592]

One Major Problem Claim of Progressive Creationism

Have you ever walked through a a maze? There is an end point, but only one correct path leads all the way to that end. Hugh Ross knows the correct end point. The end point is that the Bible and general revelation from the creation agree, because both are from the Creator. Each of the creationists has explored part of the maze. I respectfully suggest that none including Dr. Ross, has gotten the entire path to the endpoint entirely correct. Most of what Hugh Ross has explored has been the right path. But I suggest that the day-age idea is an incorrect bypath. Hugh Ross seems to assume that this day-age idea is the only path to the end point of agreement of the Bible and the creation. But if there is anything this book shows, it is that at least a dozen paths have been tried. By gathering what others have learned, we may be able to put together the whole path that will reach the Biblical end point—a unified theory in which the Bible and general revelation agree about the creation.

(u-6.2) *Each* **yôm** *apparently refers to an era of millions or billions of years.* To his credit, Hugh Ross is not adamantly dogmatic on this point. He says, "The first six days *may* also have been long time periods"[593] (emphasis added).

(u-6.2a) Yôm *referred to God's days.* Hugh Ross says, "Old earth creationists find many scriptural reasons, apart from science, for interpreting the creation days as long time periods." Psalm 90:4 refers to the length of God's days: "For a thousand years in your sight are like a day that has just gone by, or like a watch [four hours] in the night" (NIV). So the six creation days may "refer to something like millions of years" because "God's days are not our days."[594]

In response, in Psalm 90, Moses was praising the everlasting God, not speaking of creation days on Earth. Moses used a "like" comparison to explain what is difficult for us to understand, that God is not time-bound. Moses did not say earth days were a thousand years, certainly not billions of years. In essence, Ross is arguing that God has long days, so the creation days were long eras on Earth. But Moses is saying that God does not have days *at all*. God is not time-bound by days. The context of Psalm 90:4 compares God's eternality to human mortality. The earlier context in Psalm 90:2 reads,

> Before the mountains were born,
> Or Thou didst give birth to the earth and the world,
> Even from everlasting to everlasting,
> Thou art God.

God is eternal. Psalm 90:4 is *not about creation days* on Earth. Even the one reference to Earth is not to the six days, but to *before* the mountains and even before the world.

In 2 Peter 3:8, the Apostle quotes Psalm 90:4. Peter is explaining that God is patience in judgment. God does not desire any to perish.

So Psalm 90:4 is about God's eternality, and 2 Peter 3 is about God's patience in judgment. Neither is about creation days on Earth.

In contrast to God's eternal existence, Genesis 1 defines the days by daytime and night, and evening and morning, indicating *normal earth days*. The diffuse sunlight caused day at the Spirit's location on rotating Earth.

The first earth day ended as the Spirit's location rotated into evening, night, and morning. Genesis 1 is about six *earth days*. Psalm 90:4 is about God's eternality. Psalm 90:4 and Genesis 1 are not even about the same subject.

(u-6.2b) Yôm *has a semantic range including time periods longer than a day, allowing billion-year day-ages.* Ross gives many examples of the semantic range of *yôm* ("day") being used for longer time periods.[595]

I respond that it is widely recognized that the semantic range of *yôm* includes times longer than a day. But the particular meaning is the author's use of the word in the sentence in context.

Two sentences illustrate:

"New York Yankee baseball player Babe Ruth sometimes broke his bat when he tried to hit a home run."

"In upstate New York, Yankee cave explorer Lester Howe discovered Howe Caverns, home of the cave bat, and he would run tours because his Caverns were a hit with tourists, until he went broke in the Depression."

The words "bat," "run," "hit," "broke," and even "Yankee" all have different meanings in these two sentences. The semantic range of "bat" includes the small flying mammal, a baseball bat, a cricket bat, a brick bat, and a cotton bat for quilting. The specific meaning of a word is understood by its context. The two meanings of "bat" in the above sentences cannot be switched just because both are in the semantic range of "bat." Nor does the word have both meanings in one sentence. Can you picture the Babe swinging a little gray mammal, or wooden baseball bats flying out of the Howe Caverns at dusk?

Yôm is used with the light of day and dark of night, evening and morning, and the number one, all on planet Earth. How could the context more clearly indicate one normal earth day?

(u-6.2c) Erev *and* bōqer, *"evening and morning," may be metaphorical.* Hugh Ross claims that "evening" may occasionally have had a "possible metaphoric usage."[596]

In response, Genesis 1 has no metaphors; it is written in Hebrew historical narrative form. All six verses with *erev* ("evening") and *bōqer* ("morning") refer to the normal evening and morning of a regular daylight-evening-nighttime-morning day. The metaphorical use of "evening," as in "the evening of one's life," is an English use, not a Hebrew Bible use. This evidence goes *against* Ross's claim of day-eras.

(**u-6.2e**) *The grammar of the* yôm *sentences is unusual.* Hugh Ross claims that the phrase "And was evening and was morning day X" "is clearly a departure from simple and ordinary expression." "It does suggest that 'day' here is to be taken in some unusual manner."[597]

In response, the phrase is a Hebrew colloquial merism for night-time. Evening began the nighttime, and about twelve hours later morning dawn ended the nighttime. The phrase delimits the night (Exod. 16:8) ending that first day-night day, just as "morning unto the evening" delimits daytime (Exod. 18:13). The phrase is odd in English, but may not be odd in Hebrew (Exod. 27:21).

(**u-6.2h**) *The seventh* yôm *had no stated ending.* Ross says, "The seventh day strongly suggests that this day has (or had) not yet ended."[598] He claims that if the seventh day were longer, then so were the previous six.

In response, the six days did have a day-night cycle with evening and morning, even if a day-night cycle of the seventh day is not stated. And the sixth day is unique—*ha-shishî,* "the sixth." None of the previous five days included the word "the." "*The* sixth" indicated that the series was complete. The seventh day, the rest day, was differentiated from the six. So even if the seventh were longer (which I believe it was *not,* based on Exodus 20:11), that length has little effect on the previous six.

(**u-6.2i**) Yôm *in Genesis 2:4b lasted longer than twenty-four hours.* Ross states that Genesis 2:4b begins, "In the day the Lord made the heavens and the earth." Therefore, "day" referred to the beginning time period or to all six creation days, or to both. So "day" in Genesis 2:4 was "a period longer than twenty four hours."[599]

In response, the Hebrew word is more than *yôm,* "day." It is *b^{e}yôm,* "in the day," a colloquial figure of speech meaning "when."[600] We use the phrase in English in a similar way. "In the day of George Washington . . ." does not mean George Washington lived only one day. Nor does it mean that a "day" is sixty-eight years long because that is how long Washington lived. The phrase means, "When George Washington was living. . . ." So *b^{e}yôm,* "in the day," in a sense may indicate more then twenty-four hours: but with the added *b^e*, this construct, *b^{e}yôm,* really no longer functions as a time unit, like an hour, day, or week. *B^{e}yôm* functions as a preposition, beginning a prepositional clause.[601] So how *b^{e}yôm* is used in Genesis 2:4 does not tell us how long the time units of day one (Gen. 1:5) or any of the other six day were.

Also, Genesis 2:4b begins a new narrative, the narrative of Adam. What Adam was saying was, "When [*b^{e}yôm*] the Lord God made the earth and the heavens . . . " NIV). Apparently, God told Adam about the work

He had done and Adam reported that to us in Genesis 2:4b–7. God had explained to Adam that the land once had no shrubs, so God sent water, and the shrubs and trees grew. In Genesis 2:4b, *b*ᵉ*yôm* meant "when," referring back to the time of the new bare land before plants sprouted in the third work day.

Contra Ross, we may conclude that *yôm* in Genesis 1:5, "And there was evening and there was morning, day one," was a normal, daylight-evening-nighttime-morning day. Day one began in 1:3 with light. The light was separated from the darkness. God called the light "day" and darkness He called "night." The day ended in evening and the night in morning. Day one was a normal day-night cycle day. And day one set the meaning for the following five days.

Hugh Ross is a sincere seeker of Bible truth. But his arguments that *yôm* meant a geologic long day-age of billions of years do not stand up under a close examination of the Bible texts he cites.

On the other hand, his arguments that the unverse and Earth are older are much stronger. He seems to assume that the two claims are the same and prove the same point, but they are not the same.

Partially Supported Claims of Progressive Creationism

(ps-6.0B) *Correctly interpreted, both God's verbal revelation (the Bible) and physical revelation (the universe) will be in accord.* Hugh Ross is correct that both the creation and the Bible are from God, both reveal truth, and both correctly interpreted will agree. Psalm 19:1–4 and Romans 1:20 say that the creation reveals the invisible about God: "For since the creation of the world God's invisible qualities—his eternal power and divine nature—have been clearly seen, being understood from what has been made (Rom. 1:20, NIV).

The only reason I put this under "partially supported," rather than fully "supported," is that in his early writings, Hugh Ross may have erred a little in treating the Bible and the creation as if they were identical and equal sources of data, both simply needing interpreting. I applaud his soon-after recognition of the priority of Scripture.

Hugh Ross made a good move in correcting that early tendency. The Bible and the creation are like gold and oranges, not the same kind of thing. The Bible contains inspired, inerrant words, pure gold that we may interpret. God intends His people to understand those words, although sometimes with much study.

The creation is more like an orange—hard to peel without distorting and damaging the good fruit inside. Science has many steps to follow; many human hands and minds take on these steps; these minds are fallen and may contain prejudice; and the process can distort or even damage the truth about the actual creation that science seeks. Science has developed safeguards, but still may err. Moreover, an orange may have faults because, as part of the fallen world, it has been harmed. Scientists are interpreting the fallen world. They wrongly blame God rather than the real culprits (fallen angels, Adam, and us) for its faults. But even those faults only degrade some of the data science discovers, especially about the biological world. The creation, especially the heavens, still reveals the invisible things of God (Rom. 1:20; Ps. 19:1).

Finally, God's Word is uniquely exalted even above His creation work. "Heaven and earth will pass away, but my words will never pass away" (Matt. 24:35, NIV).

Hugh Ross made a wise move to a balanced recognition of the priority of Scripture, yet also that the creation is from God. The Scripture itself indicates that the creation is an important source of truth that should not be overlooked (Ps. 19:1–4; Rom. 1:19–20). Ross correctly points out that especially young earth *non*scientific creationism, is seriously out of balance. That group errs by rejecting legitimate truth from the creation.

Technical Note – Special and General Revelation:
- God's Word and God's work in the creation both reveal truth.
- Both must be interpreted.
- God's Word, the Bible, is special revelation.
  - God's Word was given by inspiration of the Holy Spirit.
  - God's Word alone is inerrant in the autographs (originals).
  - The Bible is in sentences in context—verbal concepts.
  - Our practice of hermeneutics has biases yet self-correction within the hermeneutical spiral in the Biblical community.
  - God's Word is eternal and has priority.
- God's work in creation is general revelation.
  - General revelation is limited in what it reveals.
  - God's work in creation is matter-energy things.
  - Things are many steps (liable to error) from verbal concepts.

(ps-6.1 & 6.1a–6.1c) *Two Bible creation claims, the beginning and stretching out of the universe, match two main science claims.* Ross quotes Isaiah 42:5. God "created the heavens and stretched them out." Ross says this verse matches the two main claims of the big bang—that the universe had a beginning and that it is stretching out.

In response, on the one hand, the Bible does not explicitly affirm the modern "standard model" of the big bang. On the other hand, the Bible certainly does teach that time and the universe had a beginning. The Bible also teaches that God has been stretching out of the heavens ever since creation. These two Bible claims seem to correspond to what science has discovered about the universe. This correspondence is logical evidence that the God of the Bible is our Creator. Ross has a convincing insight. Thank you, Dr. Ross!

I list this claim as "partially supported" for a reason. I suggest caution in relating modern scientific concepts ("big bang") to the ancient Bible text. The two scientific discoveries seem to *agree with, correspond to,* or, to use Ross's words, be *"functionally equivalent"* to the two Bible claims.[602] I am not affirming the big bang, because that is a modern concept. I do affirm the beginning and expansion of the heavens—because these are Bible claims. This expansion suggests an older universe.

(ps-6.2d) *The ordinal number series may allow a longer time.* Ross says the ordinal numbers in Genesis 1 may allow a longer time. For example, "Hosea 6:2 prophesies that 'after two days he [God] will revive us [Israel]; on the third [ordinal number] day he will restore us.'" "For centuries," he continues, "Bible commentators have noted that the 'days' in this passage (where the ordinal is used) refer to a year, years, a thousand years, or maybe more."[603]

In response, Ross should have said "*some* commentators" suggest that Hosea may have prophesied about longer times. In contrast, commentator Leon Wood writes, "The reference to 'two days' and 'the third day' means only that the restoration mentioned in v.1 will come surely and quickly."[604] Commentator David Hubbard says the reference is to a short affliction after which God graciously brings relatively quick recovery.[605] Commentator Douglas Steward says literal days in Hosea 6:2 cannot be ruled out.[606] Even if Hosea spoke of a longer time, prophecy sometimes uses "day" differently than historical narrative. Genesis 1 is historical narrative.

All six uses of *yôm ehād,* "day one," in *non*prophetic Bible literature are of a day-night cycle day. The Morris maxim seems sustained: "In historical narrative, a numbered 'day' was a day." And day one as a normal day set the meaning for the next five days as normal days. So we may say with conviction that Hosea 6:2 does not prove billion-year days in Genesis 1. Billion-year days are unsupported.

However, the ordinal numbers may allow, but do not prove, an older Earth. We will examine this change from cardinal day one to the ordinal series of second day, third day, fourth day, fifth day, and the sixth day in theory fourteen.

(**ps-6.2f**) *Chronological Bible statements are intended to be verifiable, but six days are too short a time to verify their order unless they are day-ages.* Ross says, "For the creation days, long periods . . . are verifiable and useful for validating the supernatural accuracy of the writer's statements. But if all creation were completed in six 24-hour days, the most sophisticated measuring techniques . . . would be totally incapable of discerning the sequence of events. Thus, a major use of the [Bible] chronology [as evidence for accuracy] would be thwarted."

This argument may support either long day-ages or the Payne proposition of possible time between the six stated day-night days. But it does not prove either.

(**ps-6.2g**) *The events of the sixth* yôm *were too many and too long to have been finished in twelve hours.* Ross says that all these events would fit better in a longer period of time.

YEC advocate Kulikovsky responds that it was "a task which could easily have been achieved in a few hours." Kulikovsky says Adam named only about "2,500 proto-species."[607]

Ross realizes that the problem with this YEC response is that either there were more than 2,500 kinds (taking more time to name than was available in one day), or that YEC is supporting massive microevolution from "2,500 proto-species" to the present 25,000 species of higher land animals and birds. Such rapid massive microevolution is far beyond the rate of species formation observed.

In response, I would say that Ross's argument suggests that all the events of Genesis 1:24—2:25 would have been quite difficult to fit into roughly twelve hours of daylight. I agree it would have been difficult, but neither side has definitively proven its claim of long days or normal days by arguing how long these tasks took.

This Ross argument could actually favor the Payne proposition of time passage between the six literal days, so many of the events listed were between the fifth and sixth days. (I want to make it very clear that I am not affirming Payne, because the Bible neither explicitly affirms nor explicitly denies his idea of time passage between the six literal days.)

(**ps-6.2h – 6.2k**) *Examples of* yôm *being longer than a day suggests that the six days were longer than twenty-four hours.* Ross points out that

Habakkuk 3:6 and 2 Peter 3:5 say the heavens and Earth are old. If the heavens and Earth are old, then the days must have been long.

In response, the two claims are not the same, so an older Earth does not prove long days. Several theories suggest Earth is either undated or older, but do not claim long day-ages.

(ps-6.3) *The Bible and science indicate an old universe and Earth.* Hugh Ross argues for an older universe and Earth.

Two questions remain: If older, how old? And does an older earth require long days? Ross assumes that if Earth is older, then the days were day-ages. But an older Earth does not require long day-ages.

Ross says that science answers the first question of how old. I emphasize that the Bible does not, because Bible statements about "ancient mountains" or "age old hills" do not say *how* old.

(ps-6.3a) *Earth's ancient age illustrates God's eternality.* Ross says that God's eternality is compared (as greater compared to lesser) to the "mountains" and the "foundations" of the Earth (Ps. 90:2–6; Prov. 8:22–31).[608] So, he says, Earth must be very old.

In response, yes, God is certainly more ancient than the mountains. That comparison of God to the mountains suggests that the mountains are quite old. But it says nothing about the length of the six days—especially since Earth, with its mountains, was created in the beginning time before the six days. So earth may be older.

(ps-6.3b) *The Bible explicitly states that Earth is ancient.* Ross explains, "Habakkuk 3:6 directly declares that the mountains are 'ancient' and the hills are 'age-old.' In 2 Peter 3:5, the heavens (the stars and universe) are said to have existed 'long ago.'"[609]

In response, Habakkuk 3:6 was not talking about creation but destruction—even the ancient mountains crumble before the coming of the awesome God! Still Habakkuk does say the mountains are ancient. Peter says, "The heavens were of old." These verses do suggest an older heavens and earth. But they do not say *how ancient.* A Biblically undated earth creation would seem to fit better than a claim of old earth creation.

(ps-6.3c) *The Bible says the stars are countless, which indicates the universe is ancient.* Ross explains that God indicated to Abraham that the stars are "countless," parallel in number to the grains of sand on the seashores (Gen. 22:17). "Countless" stars would not fit with a 3,000-year-old universe at the time of Abraham. Any event beyond 3,000 light-years away would not have been real. The light seen from beyond 3,000 light-years would have been just a light beam that did not represent actual 3,000-plus-year-old events. Either those light beams were deceiving, or else God's statement that the stars are countless is not true.

In response, this is a significant argument for an older universe (but says nothing about long days). Still the Bible does not state a specific age of the heavens. General revelation in the creation, studied by science, may provide an approximate creation date. What I am claiming is that the *Bible* does not provide us a date of creation.

(ps-6.3d) *Genesis 1 was the "generations of the heavens and the earth."* Ross correctly says that Genesis is divided by *tôl^edôt*, or generations statements. "In Genesis 2:4 the plural form, *generations*, is used, indicating that multiple generations have passed."[610] All other examples of a generation in Genesis were of many years, so plural generations of the heavens and earth must have been a long time indeed. The time length of 144 hours does not seem to fit "generations of the heavens and the earth."

This argument has a minor weakness. Ross emphasizes the plural of *tôl^edôt* as if the singular were used elsewhere in the Bible, but all the examples of *tôl^edôt* in the Hebrew Bible are plural. Nevertheless, the word is plural.

In response, the creation account (Gen. 1:1 — 2:3) ends with "These are the generations of the heavens and the earth" (Gen. 1:4a). This generations statement is about the heavens and earth—God's work in the beginning and in the six days. Ross is correct that "the generations of the heavens and the earth" does not seem to fit well into the 144 hours of the YEC model. On the other hand, surely each "generation" began on the day of God's fiat command resulting in the items being (in a non-procreational way) "begotten" from the materials of the sky, sea, and earth. So Hugh Ross makes a key contribution with this claim. This claim does not prove day-ages, but it does suggest an older heavens and earth.

(ps-6.4) *Theology suggests long day-ages and an older universe, Earth, and life.* Hugh Ross says there is, in addition to science, a "theological basis"[611] for long day-ages and an old Earth and universe.

Again, he assumes that arguments for an old Earth are automatically also arguments for long day-ages. But that is incorrect.

(ps-6.4b) *By Adam's sin "death spread to all men," not to all animals.* Ross claims animal death before Adam's sin. If there was no animal death before Adam's sin; all other arguments about an older Earth with older life are irrelevant.

To analyze Ross's claim more precisely, we will divide it into four parts: First, Ross claims, "The death Adam experienced is carefully qualified in the text as being visited on 'all men'—not on plants and animals, just on human beings (Romans 5:12, 18–19)."[612]

I respond that Ross is correct that Romans 5 does only indicate that Adam's sin resulted in *human* death—physical and spiritual. Romans 5:18 implies that the kind of being that brought death is the same kind that is made righteous. The kind of being was human, not animal. Verse 12 says, "Therefore, just as through one man sin entered into the world, and death through sin, and so death spread to all men, because all sinned" (NASB). Paul only explicitly claims *human* death because of human sin. The converse, the "gift of righteousness", is also to humans. Ross is correct.

Second, Ross says that immediate death "through the sin" was spiritual death; physical death came later as the result of spiritual death.[613]

I respond that Adam died not only spiritually, but his physical death began and was ensured the day he sinned. In his earliest books, Ross under-emphasized the physical death,[614] but to his credit, he corrected that and recognizes the importance of physical death.[615]

Third, Ross says that even if all animals before the Fall were herbivores, that condition would not have eliminated death of, for example, small mammals crushed under elephants' feet.[616]

In response, Ross may be correct because nothing is said explicitly in the Bible about protecting animals from natural physical death before the Fall. The "tree of life" apparently was intended to give eternal physical life, implying that even Adam and Eve needed to eat of it to have eternal physical life. But nothing is said about animals eating of it. Did animals have eternal physical life before the Fall, as YEC claims? The Bible does not explicitly say so.

Fourth, Ross argues that God saw all that He had made was "very good," yet if animal death is not evil, then animal death was not excluded. Walter Kaiser asks, Who but God killed the animals for skins to cover Adam and Eve?

> God by animal death made skin coverings for Adam and Eve.
> God does not do evil, not even for good ends.
> Therefore, animal death is not inherently morally evil.

If animal death is not evil, then there could have been animal death even when God saw that all He had made was "very good."[617]

I respond that we may not like animal death, but the question is whether animal death is morally evil. A possible answer may be seen in other examples. Israelites were instructed to offer animal sacrifices, not just for sin, but simply as "fellowship offerings" or "freewill offerings" (Lev. 22:21). Also, although it was only in a dream, God said, "Arise, Peter, kill and eat." Peter did not respond that it was evil to kill and eat an animal. He was dismayed only because some of the animals were "unclean" (Acts 10:9–16). So Kaiser may be correct that animal death, even if unpleasant, is not morally evil.

How shall we respond to this overall claim about animal death before the Fall? YEC incorrectly often makes an emotional appeal about how terrible animal death is. YEC tends to ask questions like, "How could Eden have been made on top of bones of millions of dead animals?" I respond that the question must be answered, not by emotions, but by the Bible. Biblically, there is a vast chasm between animals and Adam's race, which was created in the image of God.

I respond further that, in my opinion, Ross has shown that YEC has not proven its case. But I have not seen a sufficient positive Biblical case from Ross that there definitely was animal death before the Fall.

In summary, Hebrew scholar Walter Kaiser argues that God killed animals, so animal death is not a moral evil. Animal death (other than the serpent/Satan) is not mentioned in the Fall. If that is so, then animal death was probably not a consequence of the Fall, so pre-Fall animal death could have been part of normal animal life cycles.

Although I am not affirming this argument, Ross missed an argument for time passage before the Fall that would suggest a problem in the YEC no-animal-death claim. Ross could have added Adam's apparent exploration of the Garden, which seems to have been before the Fall. Apparently, Adam explored the four rivers, especially the first two. That exploration could have taken years. If Genesis 2:4b—5:1a is Adam's narrative, then it was Adam who reported the Pishon "winds through the entire land of Havilah, where there is gold, . . . aromatic resin, and onyx." Adam reported all this before the Fall because he was an *eyewitness* to what he said, reporting it in Genesis 2 before the Fall in Genesis 3. If Adam took years before the Fall to explore Eden, then small animals such as mice might have overpopulated Earth if there were no predators eating the excess.

YEC has responded that the time before the Fall would seem to have been less than a month because Eve did not become pregnant before the Fall.

The problem with this YEC response is that "less than a month" is *not* stated in the Bible, but the description from the exploration of the rivers *is* in Adam's narrative in the Bible. So, while neither argument is definitive, the YEC argument is much weaker.

(ps-6.4c) *Creation has been subject to the "bondage of decay" (entropy) since its beginning.* Ross quotes Romans 8:20–22: "For the creation was subjected to frustration, not by its own choice, but by the will of the one who subjected it, in hope that the creation itself will be liberated from its bondage to decay." Ross says this "bondage of decay" indicates entropy, which operated from the beginning of creation, not just since Adam's Fall. Without entropy, "work (at least in the universe God designed) would be impossible."[618]

Ross seems to be correct that the universe has been "running down" ever since God created it. I would add that God did not intend *this* heavens and earth to be eternal. He had already planned an eternal "new heavens and a new earth" (Isa. 65:17) and "new Jerusalem" (Rev. 21:1). He made His plans *before the Fall* because "He chose us in Him before the foundation of the world" (Eph. 1:4) to be redeemed and to be its inhabitants. Therefore, entropy seems to be within His decreed plan. Whether animal death was a part of entropy seems less certain.

(ps-6.4e) *An older universe and Earth do not require chance-caused evolution.* Ross clearly does not believe in chance-caused naturalistic macroevolution of molecules to man that would circumvent God as Designer and Creator.

Ross is correct that belief in an older Earth does not require chance-driven naturalistic macroevolution. The Bible teaches that nothing happens by chance (Eph. 1:11). The age of Earth remains an open question.

(ps-6.4f) *Four and a half billion years' preparation were needed for Earth to be ready for God's final creation—humans in His image.* "Human beings reap the benefit of nearly 4 billion years' worth of biodeposits."[619]

Ross has made a scientific case that needs to be answered by YEC scientists. But this is not a Biblical claim, so I have no Biblical response.

(ps-6.5) **The six day-epochs were in sequential order.** Ross and Archer claim that the days "are sequential; that is, that the six epochs revealed in Genesis 1 occurred in the order revealed."[620] The nonsequential claim of the framework theory is wrong.

Ross and Archer are correct that the days were in order, even though days were not day-ages. Sequential days are demonstrated by the Hebrew *waw/vav* consecutives.

(ps-6.7) **The events of the six days from the Bible and the creation agree—if Earth is older.** Ross claims that the events of the six days from the Bible and from science correspond far too precisely for Genesis 1 to have been merely myth—but only if we understand the events as happening over long eras.

We may disagree with his claim that the days were long "day-ages" yet agree that the events of the six days match the real creation. As for Earth being older, the Payne proposition would be an alternative.

(ps-6.7a) *In day-era one, light broke through to Earth's surface.* Ross explains, "Light was not created on the first creation day. On that day the light already created 'in the beginning' suddenly broke through to the earth's surface. This breakthrough required the transformation of the atmosphere (plus the interplanetary medium) from opaque to translucent."[621] "Job 38:8–9 affirms that Earth's primordial waters were enshrouded by an opaque cloud cover. . . . During creation day one, light visibly broke though to earth's surface for the first time."[622]

Ross's case for sunlight beginning day one is sound. Actually, his argument supports normal days. Sunlight to Earth's rotating surface for the first time began day one on Earth. God Himself divided the first day into "day" and "night." The daylight ended in evening, and the night ended in morning (Gen. 1:5). The Observer/Narrator's location on Earth rotated from sunlight into darkness and to the edge of sunlight, again making one day, not one billion years. Ross is correct about sunlight, but the evidence actually opposes six long day-ages. The evidence supports six normal days.

(ps-6.7b) *In the second day-era, water vapor rose from the sea surface, beginning a stable water cycle.* Ross explains, "Formation of water vapor in the troposphere under conditions that establish a stable water cycle" occurred in the second day-era.[623]

Ross's idea of how God did the work of the second day seems probable. But God could have caused this event to have begun in a single day.

(ps-6.7c) *In the third day-era, God formed continental land and land plants.* Ross continues, "Formation of continental land masses together with ocean basins" and the "production of plants on the continental land masses" occurred in the third day-era.[624] The rise of continental land, after which God commanded the earth to sprout seed-bearing and fruit-bearing trees, would have taken far longer than a single day unless the miraculous is invoked. Therefore, Ross sees only two alternatives: (a) Miracles produced continental land with trees having appearance of age, as claimed by YEC. (b) Or the days were long day-ages during the development of an old earth (OEC). Ross opts for long days and an old Earth. However, there are several other options, including (c) the Payne proposition. But all three options have weaknesses.

The YEC option of six consecutive normal days introduces the tension of miracles where the Bible does not indicate miracles.

In His third work day, God commanded the sprouting of plants. God did not use the verb *bārā'* in the perfect, which could have indicated miraculous creation of mature trees completed within that day. The third day's command was:

Then God said, "Let the earth sprout (*dāshā*) vegetation, plants yielding seed, *and* fruit trees bearing fruit after their kind, with seed in them, on the earth"; and it was so (Gen. 1:11, NASB).

The word *dāshā* ("sprout") is a hiphil imperfect Hebrew verb. Hiphil indicates causing an event. God caused the earth to sprout plants. The word "sprout" (*dāshā*) indicates the beginning of growth. Genesis 2:4–5 indicates there was no vegetation until God sent water to the dry ground. Water was the means by which God caused the earth to sprout plants. Water and earth in sunlight indicate the normal process of sprouting. The kinds of plants are indicated by the participles—plants bearing seed and trees making fruit. "And it was so" indicates that these kinds of plants sprouted that very day, just as God commanded.

There is no doubt that God can create fully grown trees with fruit. However, Genesis 1:11 uses the word "sprout," indicating the beginning of growth, not its completion. This conclusion represents a problem in the young earth creationism theory.

Ross says such miraculous appearance of age of the plant life is not indicated by the Bible. So he opts for long day-ages of millions or billions of years that fit an old Earth. However, as already pointed out in my response in u-6.2, a numbered *yôm* with daylight, evening, night, and morning, all within historical narrative, really does not indicate millions of years of a long geologic era.

The third option is the Payne proposition. This theory (theory fourteen in chapter 12) says that to claim that time absolutely could not have passed between God's six work days is making too dogmatic a claim on too inconclusive evidence. The cardinal day one indicated literal day one, but the ordinals, second through sixth, may allow time passage between the six days. The six days were important to the narrative because of the work God did within those six literal days. There are eight command units but only six days, suggesting two command units were between the numbered days. Time between the days would have allowed a separation of the third and fourth command units related to the third day and the seventh and eight command units related to the sixth day. The third command for the gathering of the waters and the appearance of continental land could have been between God's second and third work days. Then by His fourth command, God caused the earth to sprout seed-bearing plants and fruit-bearing trees. That sprouting was within the literal third day-night day of God's work because 1:11 ends with "and it was so." Finally, the maturing of the seed-bearing plants and fruit-bearing trees could have occurred during time between the third and fourth work days. The seventh command for the three orders of animals could have been between the fifth and sixth work days. Time between the six normal work days allows both normal days and an undated Earth and life. However, there is a problem.

In my judgment, unless there is an additional basis beyond the ordinal numbers for time between the days, the Payne proposition seems inadequate. If there is an additional basis, it would have to be in the Genesis 1—2 text itself. Such a basis would have to have been immediately recognizable by the Genesis era generations who heard Adam's account. Ordinal numbers alone form an inadequate basis for the Payne proposition. I repeat my consistent response that the Payne proposition is neither explicitly affirmed nor explicitly denied by the Bible.

So there are tensions in all three options. Nevertheless, I respond to Hugh Ross that normal days are far more strongly indicated by each numbered *yôm* with daytime, evening, and morning than Ross's claim that each *yôm* meant a long geologic day-age era.

(**ps-6.7d**) *In the fourth day-era, God caused the sun, moon, and stars that He had created in the beginning to be in the sky for the first time.* Ross says that the heavens and earth of verse 1 included the "entire physical universe of galaxies, stars, planets, etc." But Earth's primordial atmosphere was translucent, not transparent, until the fourth day.[625] The Holy Spirit was located just above the planet surface under the overcast sky. In this day-era was the "transformation of the atmosphere from a translucent condition to one that is at least occasionally transparent."[626] As a result, luminaries were in the sky for the first time from the perspective of the Holy Spirit, the divine Observer.

In response, Ross brilliantly recognizes the effect of the breaking cloud cover described in Job 26 and 38. (I prefer the term "be," in the sky, rather than Ross's words "distinguishable" or "visible," because "be" corresponds to the Hebrew.) Ross established the concept of the Observer. God caused the luminaries to "be" in Earth's sky for the first time in the perspective of the Observer.

But also in response, Ross's understanding of the cloud cover breaking does not really require billion-year day-ages. The sky could have cleared for the first time in a single day over the location of the divine

Narrator. We all have seen gray overcast skies lasting for days, then, *in a single day*, clear blue appears between white puffy clouds with the sun shining through by day and the moon and stars by night. Contra Ross, the first clear sky was in a particular day, and that day was the fourth day of God's work—a normal day.

(**ps-6.7e**) *In the fifth day-era, God created sea mammals and birds.* Ross says that the fifth day-era involved "creation by God's fiat miracles of sea mammals and birds."[627]

I respond by asking, Since God created the first *nephesh* sea creatures and flyers (birds and bats) by fiat miracles, why couldn't He have made the first great breathing sea creatures and the first birds on the same day, a single day sovereignly chosen by God as the fifth day?

(**ps-6.7f**) *In the sixth day-era, God made three orders of modern land mammals.* Ross says that all three orders were *nephesh* (1:24), "soulish creatures that can relate to humans; creatures with qualities of mind, will, and emotion."[628] God made *remes,* which were not creeping insects (insects were not *nephesh,* or soulish animals) but were "short legged land mammals such as rodents and hares." Also, God made the *ᶜhayāh hā'āretz,* "long-legged quadruped usually described as wild" and the *bᵉhēmâh,* the "long-legged quadruped that is easy to tame." "The fossil record confirms that such land mammals do not show up until after the initial appearance of birds and sea mammals."[629]

In response, Ross's definitions may be a little narrow, particularly *bᵉhēmâh.* But I agree that these three orders of land animals were made by God, not by chance-driven macroevolution.

(**ps-6.7g**) *Also in the sixth day-era, God created humans uniquely possessing body, soul, and spirit.* Ross explains that the sixth day-era culminated in the "creation by God's fiat miracle of the human species." "The Bible clearly denies that any of these [human] species descended from lower forms of life. Human beings are distinct from all other animals, including the bipedal primates that preceded them, in that humans alone possess body, soul, and spirit."[630]

I appreciate Ross's commitment to the uniqueness of body-soul-spirit humans,[631] even though I respectfully disagree with day-eras.

(**ps-6.7h**) *The seventh day-era of God's rest did not end in one day.* Ross explains, "Information about the seventh day is given in Psalm 95 and Hebrews 4. In these passages we learn that God's day of rest continues."

I respond that Ross himself recognizes that the light of day one was sunlight. All six days were sunlight measured. If the days were defined by sunlight and night, they were normal days. If the six days were normal sun-measured days, than the seventh day when God rested was a normal sun-measured day. If not, how could the seventh day be an example for Israel to rest each sun-measured seventh day after working six days (Exod. 20:11)? That God also set aside the seventh year (Exod. 23:11) does not make the seven days into either years or geological eras.

Psalm 95:11 and Hebrews 4:3 say we can enter God's rest, implying that God continues resting after His designated seventh rest day. But God's seventh day and His continued rest are *not* one and the same. God rested a normal seventh day *and* God continues even now resting from creation. The two are related but not identical.

Hebrews 4 alludes to Israel failing to enter God's rest when they first came to the Promised Land. Even if Israel had entered God's rest in the Promised Land at their first approach, they still would have had to work six days and rest the seventh—because the seventh day and the general rest in God's Promised Land, though related, were not identical. So God's seventh day rest and His continued rest from creating, though related, are not identical.

Finally, even if God's seventh day were longer because it does not end with evening and morning, that still does not prove the six were longer. The six previous days *did* have that ending time marker—the normal ending of a day, evening beginning the nighttime, and morning ending the nighttime.

So Ross's argument, based on God's continued rest, does not prove that the six days were geological eras.

(**ps-6.7j**) *YEC claims unreasonably rapid microevolution during this present seventh day-era.* Ross says YEC claims unreasonably rapid microevolution from as few as 2,500 kinds or proto-species[632] that were on the ark to 25,000 present higher land and flying animal species in the past 5,000 years. Ross says this rapid speciation is far beyond what "the most optimistic Darwinist has ever dared to suggest."[633] Instead, Ross says that today God is resting from making new animal kinds.

YEC in turn claims that each pair of animals leaving the ark contained rich genetic variation. From the four chromosome sets of each animal pair, many species developed. Even though these diverging species do not interbreed now, their ancestors did in the past. This is *gene segregation.* Gene segregation diminishes diversity in each resulting animal. Because most of the diversity has been bred out, a Great Dane dog or a red fox (varieties of two species from one kind) have much less genetic diversity than the original wild dog kind.

YEC would agree that this rapid speciation is far beyond what "the most optimistic Darwinist has ever dared to suggest" because Darwinian evolution is based on *new genes* by *gene mutation,* and that would take millions of years. Gene mutation increases gene diversity. The slow Darwinian evolution model claiming millions of years is not the same thing as relatively rapid gene segregation over 5,000 years. This is why the two theories can claim different time scales. Whether correct or incorrect, YEC does have an answer to Ross's critique.

On the one hand, Ross seems to be correct that God is resting from making new animal kinds with significantly different genomes. In my opinion, neither YEC nor OEC has proven the other position impossible.

Largely Supported Claims of Progressive Creationism

Hugh Ross, apart from long days and related subclaims, has added greatly to our understanding of creation.

(s-6.0A) The Bible is intentionally testable and provable, so untestable theories about the physical universe fail to measure up to Biblical standards. Archer and Ross claim, "Christianity's uniqueness resides not only in its gospel message, but also in its testability. Paul exhorts Christ's followers to 'test everything.'" Theories about the created universe based on *only* untestable miracles and appearance of age are inherently untestable. (Ross is not claiming there were no miracles, but that God does testable works along with miracles.) Untestable creation theories do not measure up to the Biblical standard of "test everything" (1 Thess. 5:21).

In response, Ross attempts to follow Paul's command to "test everything," seeking truth. Neither Paul nor Ross are replacing faith with "test everything." Ross is simply saying that faith is based on sound evidence. As our understanding of the universe has progressed, we are able to test more and more. So each new generation has more evidence that the God of the Bible is our Creator.

Ross is saying that Duncan and Hall's YEC theory is untestable because it is based entirely on miracles and appearance of age, whereas the Bible's message about creation is actually quite testable. Therefore, the Duncan and Hall YEC theory does not measure up to the Biblical standard given by Paul.

One small caveat: "Test everything" in 1 Thessalonians 5:21 is actually about testing for good as opposed to evil. But the principle of testing for truth seems established elsewhere in the Bible. Paul commended the Bereans for examining the Scriptures to see if what he (Paul) said was true to Scripture. Ross has been criticized because this verse is about holding to "the good"; but isn't truth about the universe declaring the glory of God actually good?

(s-6.0C) The Bible and creation indicate God did miracles judiciously. Ross says that God did miracles, but judiciously, as needed. Normally God works by the laws He designed so precisely into the universe in the beginning.

In response, we may generally agree that God did both miracles and worked by His precisely designed laws.

(s-6.0D) The Bible tells us accurately what God did; science may tell us how He did it. Hugh Ross, just as Henry Morris before him, is seeking to answer from science how God did what He said He did.

However, Ross and young earth advocates differ some on the role of science in Bible interpretation. YEC starts with the Bible and tends to use science to attempt to prove a YEC interpretation of the Bible's creation events. YEC may risk fudging science to conform to the YEC interpretation of the Bible. Ross (OEC) emphasizes science and finds the results of science in the Bible. Perhaps Ross may risk fudging his interpretation of the Bible toward current science.

Both sides attempt to be Biblical, but both sides could be reminded to let the Bible speak in its own language, in its own time, with its own genre, all by its own authors. Then we may understand how the Bible's unchanging message corresponds to modern discoveries by science. I think Ross (and Morris before him) tries to do this.

(s-6.H1) Interpret the Bible from the perspective of the author. Interpret "from the vantage point of an observer," "describing details as they would have appeared from that perspective."[634]

Interpreting from the perspective of the author is a key insight into how to interpret Genesis 1. Take, for example, the creation of the heavens in 1:1. The Holy Spirit's perspective location *under* the cloud layer explains the darkness in Genesis 1:2, the diffuse sunlight breaking through the thinning cloud layer in 1:3, and the luminaries in the sky through clear openings in the clouds in 1:14.

(s-6.4a) God does not deceive in either the Bible or the creation. One of Hugh Ross's most fundamental claims is this: "Whatever objects of His creation we subject to scientific analysis will reveal their true age — provided the analysis is theoretically valid, correctly applied, and accurately interpreted." He continues, "The abundant and consistent evidence from astronomy, physics, geology, and paleontology must be taken seriously."[635] God does not deceive.

I agree that God our Creator is truthful, so we can take seriously the evidence from the creation. Ross is correct that God will not deceive by the creation—because God does not deceive.

Based on the claim that the Creator does not deceive, Ross argues from the creation for an older universe.

> God does not deceive by the universe that He has created.
> The evidence is overwhelming that the universe is older.
> Therefore, the universe actually is older.

I respond that the *Bible* does not give an age of the universe. Recognizing that the Bible does *not* date the universe frees the Christian to examine general revelation in the created universe for the actual age of the universe—whether young or old.

(s-6.4d) Pain is necessary and only increased after the Fall. Ross says, "In Genesis 3:16, God says to Eve, 'I will greatly increase [or multiply] your pains in childbearing.' He does not say 'introduce.'" Ross explains that "increase" implies that "there would have been some pain" even before the Fall.[636] Some pain is a necessary warning, but pain of childbirth would be *increased* after the Fall.

I respond that Ross is correct that *rābāh* really does mean increase or multiply, not introduce. The Fall certainly greatly increased birth pain. Would Adam before the Fall have experienced the warning of pain if he stubbed his toe on a rock and so learned not to harm himself? The curse says nothing about a change in this regard, so he probably would have experienced the benefit of warning pain. The YEC idea of a no-pain Earth seems contra Genesis 3:16.

(s-6.6) God worked six days on Earth's sky, sea, and land rather than on the universe. Ross explains that Genesis 1:2 changes the focus from "the heavens and the earth" to "the earth."

(6a) *Genesis 1:2 shifts focus from the universe to the Earth.* Hugh Ross says, "As the text transitions from verse 1 to verse 2, the focus shifts from the cosmos to the early earth."[637] The rest of Genesis 1 will focus on planet Earth. Genesis 1:2 begins, "And the earth was *tōhû v^abōhû*," not "the heavens and earth were *tōhû v^abōhû*."

Ross is correct. Genesis 1:2 does shift the focus of the creation work to the Earth.

(s-6.6b) The reference frame for the six days was the perspective of the stated Observer. Ross explains, "The reference frame also shifts. Genesis 1:2 says that the Spirit of God hovered above the primordial

Earth's surface. This clue means that the subsequent description of early Earth (and the stages of its transformation) comes from the vantage point of an observer just above the surface of the waters, looking up at the sky and across the horizon, describing details as they would have appeared from that perspective."[638] "Looking up at the atmosphere of the earth, we recognize that God's miracles are taking place in the atmosphere of the earth, not beyond it in the galaxy and the solar system."[639]

Ross has greatly helped us with this very important insight. All six days should be interpreted from the perspective of the Divine Observer just above Earth's surface. The light on day one was diffuse sunlight to rotating Earth, resulting in day and night. The expanse between the waters on the second work day was the open atmosphere around the Spirit with sea water below and cloud water above. On the third work day, land rose as the water gathered into seas within the view of the Spirit. On the fourth day, God commanded the luminaries to be in the sky, separating day and night above the Divine Observer. And on the fifth and sixth work days, the Spirit saw the creation of great breathing sea creations, birds, and then land animals and man.

(s-6.6c) *Tōhû v^abōhû* **meant Earth was unfit for life and empty of life.** Ross understands the meaning of *tōhû v^abōhû* as "empty of life and unfit for life."

Ross is correct, except his two phrases should be reversed. *Tōhû* means "unfit for life" or uninhabitable. *Bōhû* means "empty of life," as uninhabited as Edom after its conquest. God would change these conditions in His six-day work by making Earth both habitable and inhabited.

(s-6.6d) Darkness at the location of the Observer was caused by Earth's early opaque atmosphere. Ross says, "When the planets were forming, opaque (or nearly opaque) atmospheres shrouded them."[640] This corresponds to Genesis 1:2b: "And darkness was over the surface of the deep" (NASB).

Ross is correct. Genesis 1:2b is elaborated by Job 38:4–7, which describes how God laid Earth's foundations while the morning stars sang together (because the stars had already been created in the beginning). Together, Job 26:8 and 38:9 describe how God caused the birth of the ocean and then wrapped the ocean in clouds. The clouds were so thick that they obscured even the light of the full moon until God commanded light to the sunlit side of Earth beginning day one, forming a horizon circle on the surface of the ocean:

He stretches out the north over empty space,
And hangs the earth on nothing.
He wraps up the waters in His clouds.
He obscures the face of the full moon,
And spreads His cloud over it.
He has inscribed a circle on the surface of the waters,
At the boundary of light and darkness (Job 26:8–10, NASB).

In Job 26:10 that first boundary of the light (day) and darkness (night) on the surface of the waters was day one. In Job 38:8–9, God uses the metaphor of swaddling clothes of cloud wrapping the newborn sea. Job 38:8–9 says:

Or *who* enclosed the sea with doors [birth motif],
When, bursting forth, it went out from the womb;
When I made a cloud its garment,
And thick darkness its swaddling band (NASB).

In Genesis 1:2, Earth's sea surface was dark because it was wrapped in thick dark clouds. Then 38:10 describes the third day when the sea was finally limited (by land). This is a Biblically supported insight by Ross.

(s-6.6e) God made Earth's core, mantle, and crust before the ocean. Ross explains that Psalm 104:5 gives the order that "God established the planet's core, mantle, and crust before cloaking Earth in oceans." Then Psalm 104:6 "describes primordial Earth's surface as covered entirely with water."[641]

He [God] set the earth on its foundations;
  it [foundation] can never be moved.
You [God] covered it [earth] with the deep as with a garment;
  the waters stood above the mountains (NIV).

I suggest a little caution equating "foundations" with "the planet's core," but Ross is probably correct that earth's "foundations" are its interior. Verse 6a says, "it can never be moved." The surface of the Earth does move (erosion, crust plate movement, or Mount St. Helens), which is what verse 8 seems to be saying: "The mountains rose; the valleys sank down." But Earth's molten iron-nickel core remains in place.

Ross is also correct that Psalm 104 indicates God cloaked Earth with its dark fog-bound ocean *after* forming Earth's solid mass. This sequence of events would confirm that "In the beginning" was a time period during which God created the heavens and then formed the Earth in successive steps.

(s-6.6f) Early Earth was ocean covered, just as Genesis 1:2 states. "An observer would also note that Earth's entire surface was submerged below oceans. The biblical text implies that initially no permanent land-masses were present."[642]

Ross seems right. Job 38:4 and 7–9 with Psalm 104:6b describe the sequence:

Where were you when I laid the earth's foundation? . . .
while the morning stars sang together
and all the angels shouted for joy?
Who shut up the sea behind doors [birth motif]
when it burst forth from the womb,
when I made the clouds its garment
and wrapped it in thick darkness [Job 38:4, 7–9, NIV].

He sets the earth on its foundations; (same as Job 38:4)
It can never be moved.
You covered it with the deep as with a garment;
the waters stood above the mountains (Ps. 104:5–6, NIV).

The order seems to be this:
1. Stars (already in place)
2. Earth's foundation, presumably Earth's core (+ mantle, crust)
3. Sea
4. Cloud enveloped the sea
5. Sea above the mountains (1. to 5. = the conditions of Gen. 1:2)
6. Six days
7. Seventh day of rest

Steps 1 to 5 resulted in the deep-ocean-covered cloud-darkened planet Earth in the condition that is described in Genesis 1:2.

(s-6.7i) God ceased creating new life kinds during this present seventh day-era. Hugh Ross explains that God ceased creation work (but continues preserving work) on the seventh day. According to Hebrews 4:4, "His [God's] work has been finished since the creation of the world" (NIV).

Ross is correct. The named classes of plants and animals will reproduce "according to their kinds."

(s-6.8) The agreement of the Bible, accurately interpreted, with the creation, accurately understood, gives evidence that the God of the Bible is the Creator of the universe. Ross says, "We have potent evidence for a personal Creator, specifically for the God of the Bible."[643] He concludes, "The evidence for a universe designed, initiated, shaped, and sustained exactly as the Bible describes, by God, continues to mount."[644]

Ross is absolutely correct that the Bible has very detailed and persuasive evidence that the God of the Bible is the Designer and Creator of all things.

Even though we peacefully disagree on long day-ages and related claims, thank you, Dr. Ross, for your very helpful insights and your defense of the God of the Bible from both the Bible and science.

My Suggestion

The six days really were six normal day-night days. Yet Hugh Ross has produced major arguments that the universe is not young.

I suggest that he and other OEC advocates at least allow the possibility that after God created the heavens and the earth in the beginning time period, there really were six literal days of God's work. With a beginning time period of unstated length, OEC can legitimately claim that Biblically, the universe is however old it is.

I suggest OEC at least allow, as an option, six literal days with the claim of time passage between the days, instead of six long day-ages. Then OEC can defend time passage between the six literal days for an older Earth, in addition to an older universe based on 1:1 as a time period.

At the same time, I suggest that YEC allow an undated universe created in Genesis 1:1 before the six days, and defend no time passage between the six literal days. As a result, the discussion between OEC and YEC can become much more Biblical on both sides.

Summary of the Day-Age and Progressive Creation Theory

The Bible tells us accurately what God did; science tells us how He did it. Science also gives us ever increasing evidence that the universe was designed precisely for human life by the God of the Bible.

The Bible and science agree on the two main claims of the big bang theory: beginning and expansion. The big bang's beginning indicates a transcendent personal Beginner/Creator. The precisely tuned conditions of the resulting universe, Earth, and life demonstrate that the Creator is real.

The creation events revealed by the Bible and by science match so precisely that the Bible can only be from the Creator Himself.

Because *yôm* has a semantic range including times longer than a day, *yôm* in Genesis 1 meant long day-age eras. From science, we know that Earth and life are older, so each *yôm* ("day") must have referred to an era of millions or billions of years.

Vast evidence from independent sciences all strongly indicates that the universe and Earth are old. Since God does not deceive either in the Bible or in the creation, the universe must be much older than 6,000 years. Moreover, the Bible says that Earth is ancient.

After God created the heavens and Earth, then covered Earth with sea and thick dark cloud, Earth was declared *tōhû vᵃbōhû,* or unfit for life and empty of life.

Located just above the waters, the Observer, the Holy Spirit, had a perspective location from which He reported the six days' work on Earth's sky, sea, and land (rather than work on the universe) as God made Earth fit for life and filled with life.

On day-era one, sunlight broke through the thick cloud to the Observer's location just above rotating Earth's ocean surface. On the second day-era, water vapor rose from the sea surface, beginning the hydrological cycle and an open atmosphere between the cloud above and sea below. In the third day-era, God formed continents and land plants. In the fourth day-era, God caused the sun, moon, and stars that had been created "in the beginning" to be in the sky to divide day and night and carry out their other time-marking functions. In the fifth day-era, God progressively created sea mammals and birds. In the sixth day-age era God progressively made three orders of modern land mammals. Also in the sixth day-age era God created Adam, who named the kinds of animals, and God made Eve. God created both humans uniquely with spirit, in His image, in contrast to hominids.

The events of the sixth day could not have fit reasonably into one day, demonstrating that the days were long day-age eras.

Ross says animal death occurred before Adam sinned. Romans 5:12 says Adam's sin began human death (not animal death). Nothing in the curse says animals (other than the serpent/Satan) would begin to die for the first time. Humans will die in the Millennium, so animals presumably will also, and presumably did die in the pre-Fall world as well. Kaiser says God killed animals, so animal death, though unpleasant to us, is not morally evil. Since animal death is not morally evil, animal death could have preceded the curse.

God ceased creating new life kinds during this present seventh day of His rest. And today we do not see new higher life kinds.

The Bible, when accurately interpreted, and science, when accurately describing the same creation events, agree. This agreement gives evidence that the God of the Bible is the Creator.

Conclusions about the Day-Age and Progressive Creation Theory

Hugh Ross has given us many Biblical insights. His understanding of science related to the Bible is greatly beneficial.

I really find only one major claim in Ross's theory that does not seem to be supported by the Bible. Referring back to my maze illustration, Hugh Ross knows the *correct end point*. The end point is that the Bible and creation match because both are from the Creator. Hugh Ross says that the Bible does *not* declare and the creation does *not* match a 6,000-year-old universe based on "*in* six days" and so creation in day one. A 6,000-year-old universe based on "*in* six days" is an incorrect bypath. The other path he sees is day-ages. Most of his work has been correct, but I conclude that the final bypath of day-ages is not the correct way. So I will take all the Biblically supported claims he and others have made and try to lay out a more Biblical path to that Biblical end. Hugh Ross has contributed much to that path. He is a wonderful Christian writer and great pioneer in Biblical creation, especially as it relates to astronomy and astrophysics.

6a. Day-Age, Old Earth, Progressive Creationism Theory

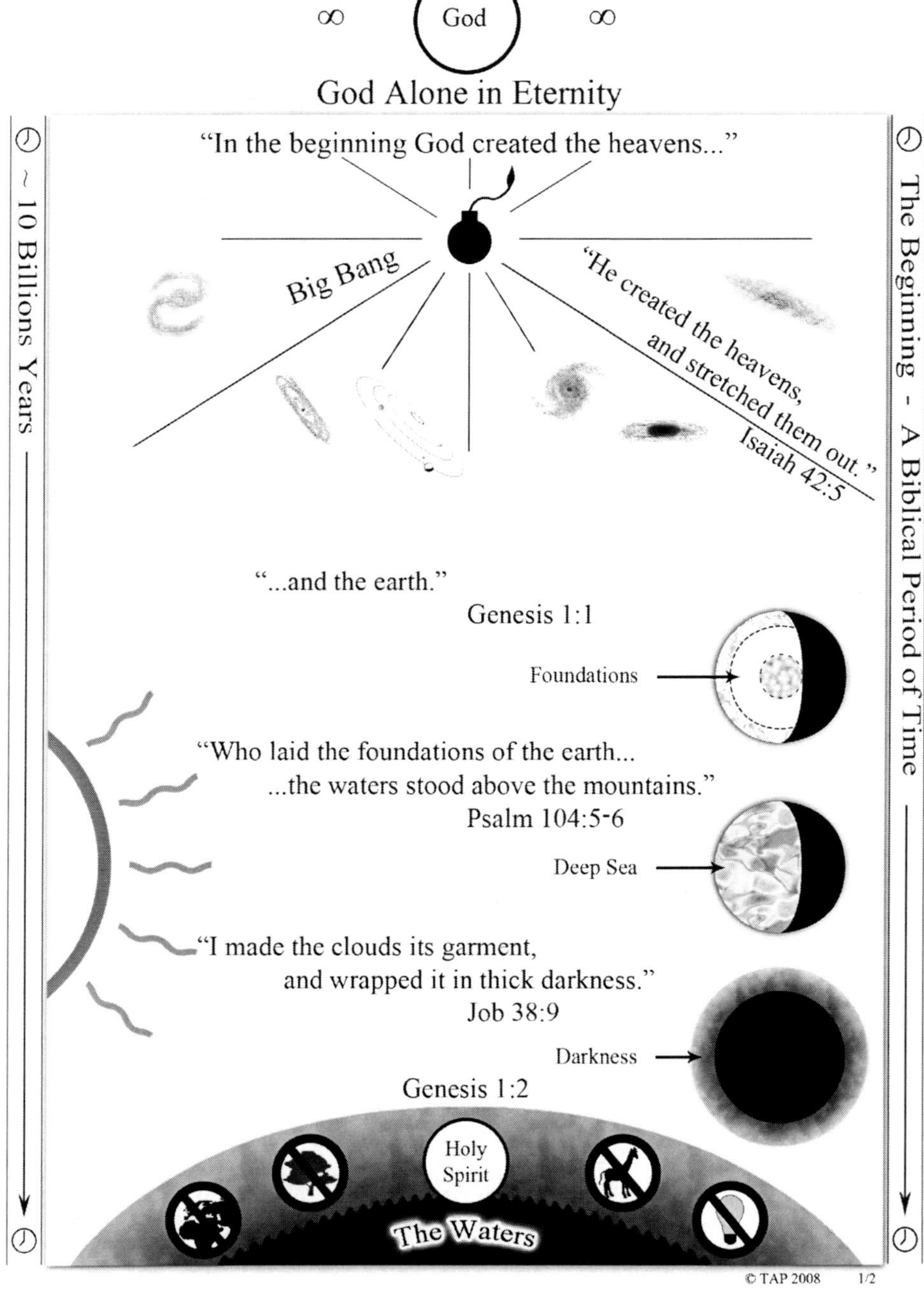

6b. Day-Age, Old Earth, Progressive Creationism Theory

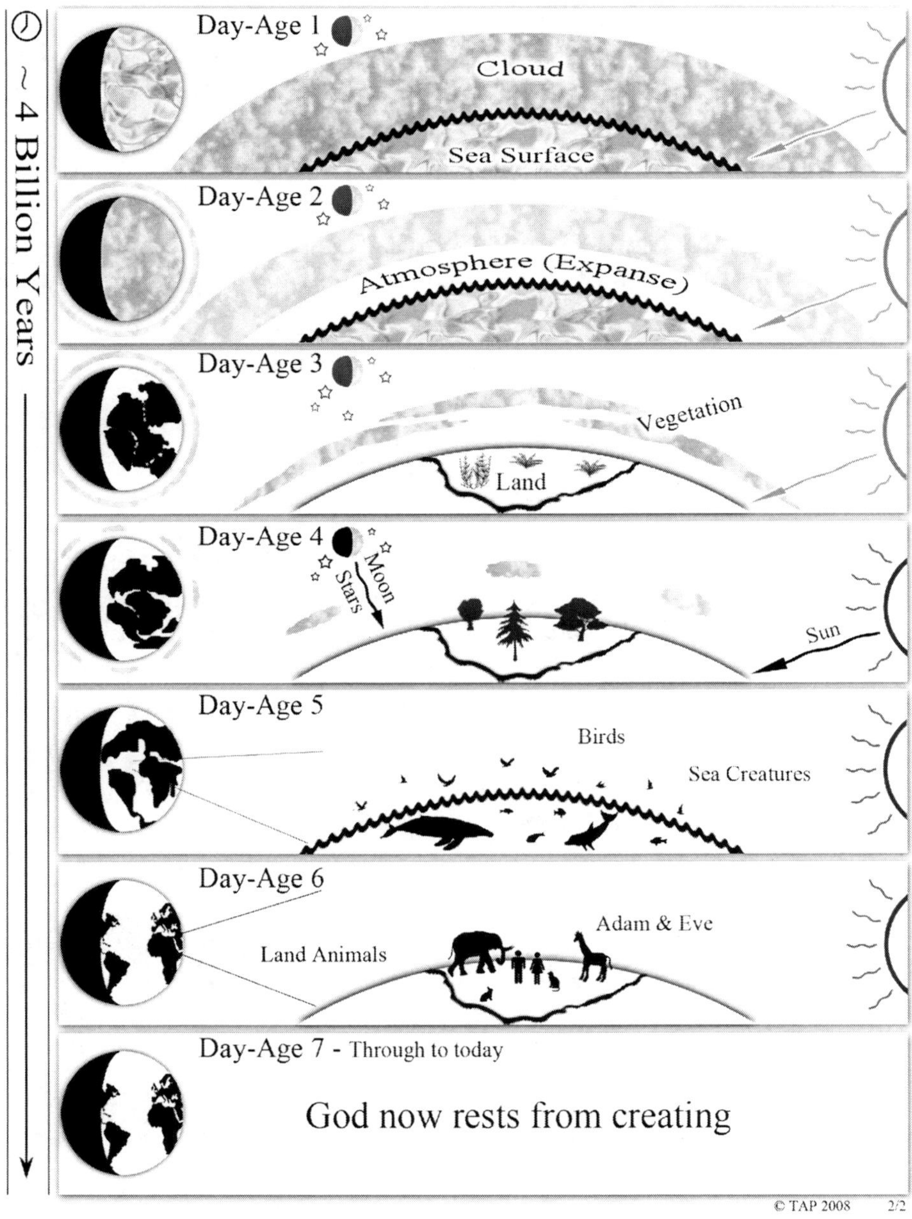

6. Claims of Day-Age, Old Earth, Progressive Creationism
(Biblically supported claims in non-italics **bold,** unsupported in *italics*)

(6.0A) Bible is testable; untestable theories fail the Biblical standard.

(6.0B) Correctly interpreted, the Bible and creation are in accord.

(6.0C) The Bible and creation indicate God did miracles judiciously.

(6.0D) The Bible reveals what God did; science may discover how.

(6.H1) Interpret the Bible from the perspective of the author.

(6.1) A beginning and the heavens stretching out match science.

    (6.1a) The universe had a beginning—the big bang.

    (6.1b) Universe began, so has transcendent personal Beginner.

    (6.1c) The universe has been expanding since God created it.

    (6.1d) Precisely right conditions of universe testify to Creator.

(6.2) *Each* yôm *apparently refers to an era of millions or billions of years.*

    (6.2a) Yôm *referred to God's days.*

    (6.2b) *Yôm* has a semantic range including longer time periods.

    (6.2c) *"Evening and morning," may be metaphorical.*

    (6.2d) The ordinal number series may refer to a longer time period.

    (6.2e) The grammar of the *yôm* ("day") sentences is unusual.

    (6.2f) Chronological Bible statements verifiable *only with day-ages.*

    (6.2g) *The events of the sixth yôm were too many and too long for twelve hours.*

    (6.2h) Seventh *yôm* had no stated ending, *so previous days were long.*

    (6.2i) Yôm *in Genesis 2:4b lasted longer than twenty-four hours.*

    (6.2j) A Sabbath week may be much longer than seven days.

    (6.2k) Bible says heavens and Earth are ancient, *so days were long.*

(6.3) Bible and science both indicate that the universe is old.

    (6.3a) Earth's ancient age illustrates God's eternality.

    (6.3b) The Bible explicitly states that Earth is ancient.

    (6.3c) Bible says stars are countless, so universe is big and ancient.

    (6.3d) Genesis 1 was "generations of the heavens and Earth."

(6.4) Theology suggests old universe, Earth, and life.

    (6.4a) God does not deceive in either the Bible or the creation.

    (6.4b) By Adam's sin "death spread to all men," not all animals.

    (6.4c) Creation is subject to "bondage of decay" since beginning.

    (6.4d) Kaiser: Standard theology recognizes two falls.

    (6.4e) Pain is necessary and only increased after the Fall.

    (6.4f) Old Earth does not require chance-caused evolution.

    (6.4g) *4 billion years* were needed to prepare Earth for humans.

(6.5) The six day-*epochs* were in sequential order.

(6.6) God worked six days on Earth rather than on the universe.

(6.6a) Genesis 1:2 shifts focus from the universe to the Earth.

(6.6b) Perspective of six days was that of the Observer.

(6.6c) *Tōhû vᵃbōhû* meant Earth was unfit for life, empty of life.

(6.6d) Darkness caused by Earth's early opaque atmosphere.

(6.6e) God made Earth's core, mantle, and crust before ocean.

(6.6f) Early Earth was ocean covered, as Genesis 1:2 states.

(6.6g) God may have made primitive sea life early.

(6.7) Six days from the Bible and creation agree—if Earth is older.

(6.7a) In day-*era* one, light broke through to Earth's surface.

(6.7b) In second day-*era*, water vapor rose from the sea surface.

(6.7c) In third day-*era*, continental land sprouted land plants.

(6.7d) In the fourth day-*era*, sun, moon, and stars "be" in sky.

(6.7e) In the fifth day-*era*, God created sea mammals and birds.

(6.7f) In the sixth day-*era*, God made modern **land mammals.**

(6.7g) Also God created humans uniquely body-soul-spirit.

(6.7h) The seventh day-*era* of God's rest did not end in one day.

(6.7i) God ceased creating new life kinds during present *day-era.*

(6.7j) YEC wrongly claims hyper-microevolution.

(6.8) Agreement of Bible and creation is evidence for God of Bible.

Major Supported Claims from the Creation Theories

The Correct Translation of Genesis 1:1: Waltke affirms the traditional translation of Genesis 1:1: "In the beginning God created the heavens and the earth." It is *incorrect* to translate 1:1 as "When God began to create."

Waltke Merism: "The heavens and the earth" meant the entire orderly universe. Also, evening and morning meant the entire nighttime.

The Waltke Exclusion Principle: If there was preexisting chaos, there was no *ex nihilo* creation of the organized heavens and earth. The converse is also logically possible: If there was *ex nihilo* creation of the organized heavens and earth, then there was no unorganized chaos.

The Kline Order: Proverbs 8:22–31 says "the beginning," when God created Earth (Gen. 1:1), was "when there were no depths." There were ocean depths by 1:2, so "In the beginning" was before 1:2 and before the six days. Creation order: Heavens, Earth, sea, six days.

The Kline Claim: When the Bible does not indicate a miracle, Genesis 2:5–6 (no rain, no plants; rain, then plants sprouted) shows God probably used ordinary means in the creation era, just as today. **Ross Addition:** "An observed attribute of the Creator . . . is His economy of miracles—only what's needed to accomplish His purpose."[645]

The Kline Undated Universe: "We must speak where the Bible speaks, and be silent where the Bible is silent. . . . The inspired text, rightly interpreted, is simply silent with regard to the age of the earth and universe."

A Generational Genesis: The worldview of Genesis was generations. The six begetting (literal) days of Genesis 1 introduced the most ancient generations of all—"the generations of the heavens and the earth."

The Rooker Reaffirmation: "The key difference between pagan cosmogonies and Genesis 1 is *creatio ex nihilo* and the absence of preexisting matter."

The Morris Maxim: In historical narrative, a numbered "day" was a day.

The Morris and Ross Method: The Bible reveals what God did; science may uncover how He did it.

The Morris One Fall Explanation: The creation was perfect. Man and animals were created about 6,000 years ago with eternal physical life. There was "no disorder, no sin and, above all, *no death!* Even Satan was still good at this point."[646] His first effect on Earth was the temptation. (There were two falls, but Lucifer's fall had no effect on Earth until his temptation of Eve, resulting in Adam and Eve's Fall.) Adam's Fall resulted in a "cosmic catastrophe" including all human and animal death and subsequent moral and natural evil.

The Kaiser Two Falls Explanation: Standard theology identifies two falls: the angelic fall led by Lucifer, and later the human Fall by Adam. God's concluding "very good" evaluation was about His work on Earth, not about angels such as Lucifer who had been created and likely fell early. Animal death is *not* inherently evil. God Himself killed an animal to cover human nakedness. Any pre-Fall evil aspects of animal disease and death could only have been initiated by fallen Lucifer (Ezek. 28:16–18; Heb. 2:14). Yet by the sixth day, God worked even those together for good or eliminated them until Adam's Fall. Adam was the original cause of human death (Rom. 5:12) and farming woes (Gen. 3:17–19), but Scripture does not say he caused animal death. So animal death may have preceded Adam's Fall. Animal life cycles fit the present noneternal world God created, anticipating human resurrection and the New Creation (Rom. 8:20).

The Ross Resolution: God does not deceive either by His Word or by His creation work. Correctly interpreted, both God's verbal revelation (the Bible) and physical revelation (the created universe) will be in accord.

The Observer's Perspective: Ross says interpret the Genesis 1 creation narrative from the perspective of the Observer/Narrator, the Spirit, hovering just above the surface of the water-covered Earth.

The Ross Apologetic: The Bible alone declares that the universe had a beginning and has been stretching out. Only the Creator could have known these facts long before modern science. The God of the Bible is the Creator, and the Bible is His accurate message to us.

The Ross Fine-Tuning Evidence: The fine-tuning of the universe and Earth for humans is evidence of the Designer, not chance.

It would be very difficult to explain why
the universe should have begun in just this way,
except as a act of a God
who intended to create beings like us.

Stephen Hawking

Chapter 7

Theory 7
Theistic Big Bang
and Relativistic Days Theory

*One man's journey
from the destruction of the atomic bomb,
to the Creator of the universe.*

Genesis and the Big Bang records physicist Gerald Schroeder's scientific and spiritual journey from MIT to Jerusalem. His journey took him from work on the atomic bomb and the big bang to the Hebrew Talmud. He sees in both cosmology and Genesis a development of the universe in stages from the big bang to humans, who can absorb "the amazing concept of ethical monotheism."[647] As a Hebrew speaker, he has key insights into the creation from the Hebrew Torah. As a physicist, he also suggests scientific ideas about creation.

Preunderstandings of Schroeder's Theistic Big Bang Theory

Key to Schroeder's creation ideas is his interpretation methods.

(7.0A) *Both literal and kabbalah interpretative meanings of the Bible, as well as science, reveal truth.* Gerald Schroeder comes from two traditions: first from science, and second from the Talmud combined with kabbalah.[648] The kabbalah tradition holds the interpretative idea that "a single biblical passage [may] have many meanings."[649] So "the entire Torah as a poem" and "the meaning of poems go well beyond the literal text." There are "*both* literal and interpretive [kabbalah] meanings."[650]

Claims of Schroeder's Theistic Big Bang Theory

In *Genesis and the Big Bang* Schroeder works *backward* in time through Israeli history and archeology, to Adam, through the six days, and finally back to the beginning. Readers who are used to the Genesis 1 order of starting at the beginning, followed by day one, day two, etc., will need to *reverse that order* to follow this theory from the present *back* to the big bang.

(7.1) *Since Adam, the Bible uses a normal human time scale, shown accurate by archeology.* Schroeder grew up in New York. Today he lives in Jerusalem. As an Israeli, he can see all around him that archeology confirms the accuracy of the Bible's chronology. For example, the archeology of Hazor fits the Biblical chronology.[651] Another example is, "Genesis attributes the start of sophisticated forging of copper and brass to Tuval-Caine, the son of Lemech (Gen. 4:22). This was some seven hundred years after Adam, or about five thousand years ago." This Bible reference to brass correlates with "the start of the Bronze Age at five thousand years before the present."[652] Archeology confirms the accuracy of the Bible's chronology. So since Adam, "the Bible adopts this Earthly [time] perspective."[653]

(7.2) *Before Adam, there were six literal days of relativistic "stretched time" on God's clock, while billions of years to us.* Schroeder says, "The period extending from 'the beginning' to Adam [involved] stretched time. This is the heart of the matter." "How are we to stretch six days to encompass 15 billion years? [He would now accept the more accurate 13.7 billion years, but this quote is from his first book when the estimate was "about 15 billion years."] Or the reverse, how do we squeeze 15 billion years into six days?"[654] "The suggestion is not as absurd as it may at first appear. In the Psalms of David we read, 'A thousand years in Your eyes are as a day that passes' (Ps. 90:4)." "Deep within Psalm 90, there is the truth of a physical reality: the six days of Genesis actually did contain the billions of years of the cosmos even while the days remained twenty-four-hour days."[655]

"This verse in Psalms is reminiscent of the dilation of time dealt with in Einstein's revolutionary thought experiments." "A billion years . . . can indeed pass for days." "Einstein's theory is no longer a theory."[656] "The difference in perceived time is called relativistic time dilation, the dilation that makes the first six days of Genesis reassuringly compatible with the 15 billion years of cosmology."[657] Einstein discovered that "the rate at which time passes is not the same at all places."[658] It is "*impossible* for a common [time] reference frame to have existed between the Creator and each part of the mix of matter" because "time differs from place to place."[659] "Until Adam appeared on day six, God alone was watching the clock. And that is the key."[660]

"In the first six days of our universe's existence, the Eternal clock saw 144 hours pass." The Bible "is truly referring to six 24-hour days."[661] "From a biblical perspective the six days of Genesis include the fifteen billion years we earthbound mortals estimate to be the span of time since the beginning of time, just as a watch in the night might include a thousand years [Ps. 90:4]."[662] So the "six days in God's space-time reference frame and 15 billion years in ours" are one and the same.[663]

(7.2a) *Scientific evidence really does indicate that the universe is about fifteen billion years old.* Schroeder emphasizes that the universe really is about fifteen billion years old in our earth time. Red shift of light from distant objects is only one of several ways to tell the age of the universe. Light travels about three hundred million meters per second in a vacuum. Red shift of light from distant stars is relative to distance, giving an approximate distance to the farthest visible objects of over twelve billion light-years away. So that light took over twelve billion years to reach Earth. "The implication is that our universe is expanding and has been expanding for some fifteen billion years."[664] So our universe is billions of years old in human time.

(7.2b) *Each yôm was a twenty-four-hour day, not a day-age.* As a Hebrew speaker, Schroeder explains that the six days of Genesis 1 were "truly referring to six 24-hour days."[665]

Schroeder disagrees with advocates of six long day-age epochs. He explains, "The approach that 'the six days were really six epochs' [geological periods of time] has scant biblical basis." "Modern students of the Bible might prefer that the days of Genesis be epochs. That would accommodate the findings of cosmology and paleontology in a cursory reading of Genesis."[666]

(7.2c) *The six days (fifteen billion years) were "days" of the universe.* Schroeder says, "The Bible describes the day-by-day development of our universe in the six days following the creation."[667] Genesis 1 is about the "development *of our universe* in the six days." "Day" one and most of the second "day" passed before Earth existed, so those "days" totaled billions of years of changes in the universe. Only the last four or five "days" resulted in changes on Earth.

The changes needed after the formation of hydrogen and helium in the big bang required all six days (fifteen billion years) to make the present universe and planet suitable for life on Earth.[668]

(7.2d) *Each day going back in time was progressively longer.* Schroeder says that the sixth day lasted about "¼ billion years" and that each previous day doubled in length. So the fifth day lasted about "½ billion years," the fourth day about "1 billion years," the third day about "2 billion years," the second day about "4 billion years," and day one about "8 billion years"—all by time dilation.[669]

(7.3) *The six days go back in time from Adam to the big bang.* Schroeder sees the six days going back to the big bang as the history of the universe on God's "eternal clock."[670]

(7.3a) *In the sixth day, God separated Adam and Eve with spiritual image from non-image-bearing Cro-Magnon.* I have tried to piece together from several of Schroeder's books a narrative of the Adam and Eve story. If I understand him correctly, the narrative would be something like this: God had planted a Garden in Eden. God had guided approximately "one million point mutations" in previous hominids toward the "goal" of Cro-Magnon.[671] Outside the Garden were the intelligent *Homo sapiens* animals, Cro-Magnon. Medieval Rabbi Moses Maimonides explained, "In the time of Adam . . . there co-existed animals that appeared as humans in shape and also in intelligence but *lacked the 'image'* that makes man uniquely different from other animals, being as the 'image' of God."[672] Cro-Magnons were not image-bearers, but they were the *Homo sapiens* ancestors of Adam and Eve. Making mankind would be in two steps.

First, God *'āsâh*, "made," man physically (Gen. 1:26). "The making of mankind related to the body of Adam."[673] About 4000 BCE two chosen Cro-Magnons, a baby boy and a baby girl, were born of Cro-Magnon parents. They had the exact genome God intended. They grew up in the Cro-Magnon family life, language, and skills. They had no false appearance of age because they each had a normal conception, birth, and childhood in their Cro-Magnon family. "Making [as opposed to creating] requires raw materials." "The Hebrew word *adam* has its root in the Hebrew *adamah*, meaning soil." God wants us to know that the materials from which Adam's Cro-Magnon body was made were the materials of dust or soil, absorbed as food grown from the *adamah*, the dust or soil of the earth. Animals were from the same *adamah*, or soil (Gen. 2:19). The two young Cro-Magnon's bodies were made, but they had not yet been created as "mankind." That would be next in Genesis 1:27.

Second, God did His *bārā'*, creating, work resulting in true body-soul mankind (Gen. 1:27). Choosing these two chosen Cro-Magnons', God created the first two persons of mankind in His image, both male and female (Gen. 1:27). He created each of them to be "a *neshama*—a being possessing the spiritual soul of humanity (Gen. 2:7)."[674] God did this by breathing the *neshama* into Adam.

Genesis 2:7 has a subtlety lost in the English. It is usually translated as: ". . . and [God] breathed into his nostrils the *neshama* of life and the *adam* became a living soul" (Gen. 2:7). The Hebrew text actually states: ". . . and the *adam* became *to* a living soul."[675]

The *lamedh* ("to, toward") prefixing "living soul" indicates that the already living Adam was transformed into a living soul kind of person. Schroeder says he was "transformed into *another* man."[676] Only Adam and Eve uniquely were newly created body-soul humans. They alone received the image that bore a "nonphysical resemblance" to the Creator. So what God created *de novo* on the sixth day was the soul-body Adam and Eve. They alone reached the "desired goal of a sentient, intelligent being able to absorb within it the amazing concept of ethical monotheism."[677] They were now in the image of their Creator, so they could relate to Him. "The root of the Hebrew word 'image' . . . is 'shadow.'"[678] Adam became a "shadow" representative of God on Earth, to rule over the Earth and all its living creatures. Both Adam and Eve were now in the image of God, but God had not yet brought the two of them together. God saw all that He had done—and all that He had done and made was "very good." Genesis 1:31 was the end of the sixth day.

In Genesis 2, God put Adam in the Garden to work it. God said it was not good for man to be alone. Adam named the land animals and birds, but found no helper. So God caused Adam to sleep. God woke Adam and introduced Eve to Adam. Then Adam declared the wedding union:

This one at last
Is bone of my bones
And flesh of my flesh.
This one shall be called Woman,
For from man was she taken" (Gen. 2:23, JPS Tanakh, 1985).

In this statement, Adam declared Eve uniquely of his new race—body-soul mankind.[679]

God gave Adam and Eve choice. Just as light has particle-wave duality and quantum unpredictability, so under His rule, God also made for humans "a world in which there is space for free will."[680] In the Garden were two trees representing life and death.[681] Eve and then Adam chose the tree of death. They did not eat of the tree of life, so they did not become physically immortal. Earlier God had removed Adam and Eve from non-image-bearing Cro-Magnon by putting the two into the Garden. Now after the Fall, Adam and Eve were forced from the Garden back to where Cro-Magnons lived.

Lingering Cro-Magnons explain Genesis 6:1–4 of mixed marriage with non-image-bearers, resulting in Nephilim. "The word Nephilim comes from the Hebrew root for fallen or inferior."[682] Cro-Magnon and the mixed race died out (presumably at the flood, although Schroeder does not believe the flood covered all mountains or the New World, but was primarily in the Tigris-Euphrates valley bounded on three sides by mountain ranges[683]). If all living humans are descended from Adam and Eve, this recent ancestry explains "the surprising genetic similarity among all humans."[684]

This scenario answers a number of difficulties. The 30,000-year-old cave paintings were by non-image-bearing Cro-Magnon. Human agriculture predated Adam, but the appearance of writing came shortly after Adam became a *nephesh* human. This is because simple agriculture was a non-image-bearing intelligent animal activity, but writing came from the new body-soul human.[685] Because they were born physically to Cro-Magnon parents, Adam and Eve did not have a problem of false "appearance of age." Genesis 1 and 2 do not conflict because 1:31 ends day six, when God breathed into the two the *neshama*, so they both became true humans in God's image. But they were not together.

Then Genesis 2 is about Adam *after* day six. Genesis 2:4–9 was Adam's explanation of his environment, and 2:10–15 was his exploration and discoveries about the Garden along its river systems. So there is no conflict between the sixth day of chapter 1 and the time after the sixth day in chapter 2. Adam had plenty of time to explore the rivers and discover the riches of the Garden. He had more than enough time to name the animals. The presence and need for "the tree of life also in the midst of the garden" (Gen. 2:9, JPS, 1917) even before their fateful decision indicates that their bodies were mortal to begin with. They had outstanding yet normal Cro-Magnon bodies, and also were uniquely in God's image.

(7.3b) *Land animals appeared in the quarter billion years of the sixth day.* "The Bible records that animal life appeared in the waters on day five and on the dry land on day six."[686] The sixth day included the "mammalian era in which we live," the K-T extinction of the dinosaurs,[687] and, before that, the age of the dinosaurs. The boundary between the sixth and fifth days was the Permian-Triassic mass extinction about a quarter billion years ago.

Each mass extinction provided new niches that were filled with new forms of life. The causes and timing of extinctions and changes in the DNA codes seem to have happened too "just right" to have been caused by pure chance. Logically, the Deity of the Hebrew Bible guided the extinction events and DNA changes to the present life forms.[688]

(**7.3c**) *Sea animals appeared in the half billion years of the fifth day.*
Schroeder explains that *taninim gedolim*, great sea creatures in Genesis
1:21, means the great *taneen* (singular). When Moses' rod turned into a
snake, it was called a *nahash*, a snake, and it was also called a *taneen*.
Taneen was the class of animal that snakes are in, the class reptiles.[689] So
Genesis 1:21 should be translated, "And God created big reptiles. . . ." A
major event in this era was the appearance of reptiles. These eventually
developed into great sea reptiles such as the long necked plesiosaurs, powerful jawed pliosaurs, and giant dinosaurs.

Before the reptiles, earlier in day five was the Cambrian explosion
in the ocean of all the major phyla of life. All these were sea life, in keeping
with the fifth day.

(**7.3d**) *Cloud had blocked out luminaries (but not diffuse sunlight)
until the fourth day.* Schroeder explains,

Resolution of the conflict is found in the use of the word *luminaries*
rather than *light* in Genesis 1:14. Prior to the appearance of abundant
plant life, the Earth's atmosphere was probably clouded with vapors
of the primeval atmosphere. This would be in accord with information
relayed from Soviet and U.S. spacecraft investigating the cloudy atmosphere of Venus. There was light on the third day, in the sense that the
atmospheric vapors transmitted radiant energy. The atmosphere, however, was translucent, not transparent. Therefore, individual luminaries
were not distinguishable. It was this diffuse light that provided energy
for the initial plant life.[690]

"The early plant life actually helped clear the atmosphere through
the process of photosynthesis."[691] Photosynthesis from plants made in the
third day produced oxygen. Oxygen cleared the atmosphere for the first
time. On the fourth day, the luminaries began to be in Earth's cleared sky
separating and ruling day and night.

(**7.3e**) *In the two billion years of the third day, sea, land, and plant
life formed.* Schroeder says that by the end of this day, land plants were
developing. This growth was enabled by the formation of land earlier in
this third day. But before plants could live on land, an ozone layer had to
have been formed to protect land life from deadly ultraviolet radiation.
Although Moses did not mention early ocean plant life, ancient ocean simple plant life—protected by water from deadly ultraviolet rays—produced
the first oxygen, resulting in the ozone layer protecting and enabling land

plant life. Ocean plant life was made possible by the forming of the oceans at the beginning of this third day.

(7.3f) *Supernovae in the four billion years of the second day made heavy elements for forming Earth.* Schroeder explains that the materials for early Earth and its earliest dense dark atmosphere were forming by the end of the second day. The early universe was made almost entirely of light elements (hydrogen and helium). The atmosphere required medium elements (oxygen and nitrogen); and the planet needed heavier elements (silicon, iron, etc.). The universe needed eight to twelve billion years of supernovae in days one and two to make the medium elements oxygen and nitrogen for our atmosphere, carbon as the ideal element for life, and the heavier elements for planet Earth.

(7.3g) *Evening and morning was the progression from chaos to cosmos.* Schroeder says that the words, "And there was evening and there was morning" marked the change from disorder to order in the very early universe.[692]

(7.3h) *After the inflation, light formed at God's first command in the eight billion years of day one.* Schroeder says Genesis 1:1 began with God creating the big bang. Genesis 1:1 also included the time period before light formed. "When the temperature [of the inflating big bang] fell below 3000° K, a critical event occurred: Light separated from matter and emerged from the darkness of the universe." This event corresponds with, "And God said, 'Let there be light.'"[693] Day one began with the formation of light after the big bang.

(7.3i) *Day one in Hebrew was cardinal, but the second through sixth days are ordinals.* Schroeder, perhaps with justifiable pride, points out that the Jewish Publications Society (JPS) translation of 1917 is one of the few English versions that correctly translates the phrase as "day one" instead of "first day."[694] (Young's Literal Translation also translates *yôm ehād* as "day one.") Cardinal one, ordinals two through seven, and "the" prefixing "the sixth day" are important contributions from the Hebrew made by Schroeder.

Payne (theory 14, chapter 12) will suggest these ordinals may allow time passage between the days. Jerry Schroeder and I discussed this by e-mail. He said that in themselves, the Hebrew ordinal numbers "contain no explicit implication of the time passage. That does not mean that it could not be so," but that would either be interpretive or there would have to be additional reason(s) in the text to make it so.[695]

(**7.3j**) *After the big bang, the universe inflated as the "wind of God" in Genesis 1:2c.* Schroeder says the *rûah 'elōhîm* was the "wind of God," the inflationary stage of the hyper-expanding universe just after the big bang.[696]

(**7.3k**) *Darkness of 1:2b was the initial big bang inflation.* Schroeder says the "darkness on the face of the deep" was a onetime inflationary epoch before light began.[697] "At the creation, we are told, the universe was dark."[698]

(**7.3***l*) *Tōhû v^aḇōhû of Genesis 1:2a describes the initial state of the universe.* Schroeder says that *tōhû v^aḇōhû* describes the chaotic building blocks just after the big bang before the basic subatomic particles were organized into hydrogen and helium.[699]

(**7.3m**) *The Bible says the universe had a beginning and is expanding, matching the beginning and expansion that science discovered.* The Hebrew Bible tells us in Genesis 1:1 that the heavens and earth were created at a definite beginning. He explains that science has discovered the same.

The Hebrew Bible also tells us that the universe is expanding. These Hebrew Bible texts originated over two thousand years ago, long before Edwin Hubble discovered the expansion of the universe in 1929. The discovery by Arno Penzias and Robert Wilson at Bell Labs in 1964 of the cosmic background radiation in all directions left over from the big bang further confirms this beginning and expansion of the universe.[700] Moreover, "only 10 to 20 percent of the matter required to cause the eventual contraction of the universe exists. What this means is . . . there was only one big bang." The universe will *not* contract into a "big crunch" only to explode again and again forever. Since the universe had only one beginning, it had "a Beginner."[701] That Beginner is the God of the Hebrew Bible. Both the Bible and science agree on the beginning and expansion of the universe.

(**7.3n**) *The heavens and earth were created out of nothing, in the* ex nihilo *creation act of Genesis 1:1.* "The creation of the heavens and the earth from absolute nothing is at the root of biblical faith."

(**7.3o**) *Only the Hebrew word* bārā' *fits the initial creation.* Schroeder explains that *bārā'*, "create," is the only Hebrew word that can specifically indicate "creation of something from nothing."[702] The God of the Hebrew Bible created the heavens and the earth out of nothing.

Schroeder, as a Hebrew speaker, would not agree with the young earth scientific creationism claim that the Hebrew words *bārā'* ("create") and *'āsâh* ("do, make") are interchangeable in Genesis 1 and in Exodus 20:11, so the universe is only 6,000 years old.[703]

Bārā', "create," is the only Hebrew word
that can specifically indicate
creation of something from nothing.

(7.3p) *The "beginning" started time and matter at the big bang.* "Time truly takes hold when matter forms." "That transition from energy to stable matter occurred 0.00001 seconds after the big bang." Radiant energy such as light "does not experience the flow of time." "Time, as we experience it, is totally related to the material world."[704] The words "In the beginning" of Genesis 1:1 require that time had a beginning.

Light illustrates the timelessness of God. At the speed of light, time ceases. God's Hebrew four letter name (in English, "I AM") indicates He is timeless, so all is present to Him.[705] He created time for us.

(7.4) *The universe fine-tuned for life and life itself show evidence of design.* Life on Earth, particularly human life, is the result of design by a Designer. Within that design, microevolution is real. But undirected macroevolution from chemicals to man is contradicted by the evidence.

Microevolution is real. Schroeder quotes Darwin, "There is grandeur in this view of life, with its several powers, having been originally breathed by the Creator into a few forms or one." Schroeder says the fossil evidence agrees with "development of classes of life," micro-evolution in a large sense.

But macroevolutionary gradualism from chemicals to all the phyla of the Cambrian is contrary to the fossil record. "The Burgess Shale fossils [showing a sudden explosion of all major phyla of life in the cambrian] contradicted, even confounded, this gradualism." "It is inter-phylum development that has been proven to be a fantasy."[706] These major categories of life seem beyond what evolution is capable of crossing.

The magnificent Natural History Museum in London devotes an entire wing to demonstrating the fact of evolution. They show how pink daisies can evolve into blue daisies, how gray moths change into black moths, how over a mere few thousand years, a wide variety of cichlid fish species evolved in Lake Victoria. It is all impressive. Impressive until you walk out and reflect upon that which they were able to document. Daisies remained daisies, moths remained moths, and cichlid fish remained cichlid fish. These changes are referred to as micro-evolution. In this exhibit, the museum's staff did not demonstrate a single unequivocal case in which life underwent a major gradual morphological change.[707]

Undirected macroevolution advocates hide the fact that they lack unequivocal proof of *macro*evolution, undirected molecules to man. They *assume* that because we are here, undirected naturalistic macroevolution must have happened. But such chance origin is contradicted by great evidence that the universe and life were *designed.*

(7.4a) *The universe was designed specifically for human life.* The universe and its laws were designed precisely for life, specifically for human life. The "flow of life [has been] channeled by laws." "These constraints are not by chance,"[708] but by design. Schroeder says,

> Professor Weinberg is an avowed skeptic but even he agrees . . . , "Life as we know it would be impossible if any one of several physical quantities had slightly different values. . . . One constant does seem to require incredibly fine tuning." This constant has to do with the energy of the big bang. Weinberg qualifies the turning as one part in 10^{120}. Scientific notation is an understatement and so I will expand that exponential into decimal notation. If the energy of the big bang were different by one part out of 100000000000000000000000000000000000000 0000000000000000000000000000000000000000000000000000000000 00000000000000000000000000000 there would be no life anywhere in our universe. The universe is tuned for life from its inception. Genesis agrees: when life first appears on the third day, the word creation does not appear. We are merely told "The earth brought forth" life.[709]

How could it be more obvious that our universe is fine-tuned for life? Our universe contains other fine-tuned constants that must be and are precisely right for any life, particularly for human life. Examples are the nuclear stability temperature shortly after the big bang;[710] the T-Tauri phase of stars and the resulting gasses such as oxygen and nitrogen for our atmosphere;[711] the strength of electromagnetic force; the strength of the strong nuclear force; strength of the weak nuclear force; the strength of gravity; the mass and energy of the big bang; the rate of expansion of the universe, and much more. "By chance? Not if our understanding of the laws of nature is even approximately correct." "Lottery upon lottery, and all winners."[712] The universe was designed for life on Earth, specifically for human life. Design indicates a Designer. We are not just an outrageously lucky, lucky, lucky, lucky accident! We have a Designer.

"By chance?
Not if our understanding of the laws of nature
is even approximately correct."

(7.4b) *Planet Earth was designed precisely for human life.* The physical constants of planet Earth were precisely tuned for life. These constants include the distance of Earth from the sun and the near circularity of Earth's orbit, resulting in a moderate temperature range on Earth.[713] In our atmosphere, these fine-tuned constants include the oxygen-nitrogen ratio of our atmosphere[714] and the protection of life in the sea until the ozone layer in the atmosphere was built up against deadly UV radiation on land also.[715] On Earth itself, these precise factors for human life include the level of internal radioactivity in Earth, the crust cooling sufficiently for human life, yet the iron core remaining molten to produce the "magnetic umbrella" protection against deadly cosmic radiation,[716] our just-right moon, and out-gassing of water from volcanoes and from comets contributing to our oceans.[717] Our planet was tuned far too precisely for human life to be by chance.

(7.4c) *Life begun by chance is contradicted by overwhelming evidence.* "There is now overwhelmingly strong evidence, both statistically and paleontologically, that life could *not* have been started on Earth by a series of random chemical reactions. Today's best mathematical estimates state that there simply was not enough time for random reactions to get life going as fast as the fossil record shows that it did."[718]

Schroeder explains that Earth's crust cooled "some 4.5 billion years ago," and the first sedimentary rock formed only "3.8 billion years ago." But, he continues, the "earliest evidence of life is dated less than 500 million years" later. "To reach the probable condition that a single protein might have developed by chance, we would need 10^{110} trials to have been completed each second since the start of time! To carry out these concurrent trials, the feed stock of the reactions would require 10^{90} grams of carbon. But the entire mass of the Earth (all elements combined) is only 6×10^{27} grams. In fact 10^{90} grams exceeds by many billion times the estimated mass of the entire universe."[719] And life requires a large number of specific proteins at the same time. Moreover, the time available is not "since the beginning of time" but only "500 million years." Schroeder concludes, "It is statistically . . . essentially impossible that random events produced this life in such a relatively short time."[720] Life was designed and created by a Designer.

The fine-tuning of the universe and Earth for humans is evidence of the Designer, not chance.

(7.4d) *Darwinian gradualism and the fossil record of abrupt species do not match.* "Ironically, it is the fossil record itself that is gradually dispelling the argument by chance."[721] The fossil record shows abrupt changes in species, not gradual continual transitions. "The statement Darwin repeats several times in *Origin of Species, 'natura non facit saltum'* — that nature does not make jumps — is simply false. Transitional forms are totally absent from the fossil record at the basic level of phylum and rare if present at all in class."[722] "A life form appears. There may be changes within the form, but its basic structure remains until it disappears and a new, different structure arises in its place, *suddenly.*"[723] Schroeder then quotes punctuated equilibrium advocate Niles Eldredge: "The fossil record we were told to find for the past 120 years [since Darwin] does not exist."[724] Life was guided and transformed by "a divinely inspired teleology, or purposeful goal."[725] Naturalistic evolution claims life developed gradually and has no goal, but the fossil evidence shows otherwise.

(7.4e) *Precisely designed laws indicate a Designer, and give the universe significance.* Schroeder says that British big-bang physicist Roger Penrose "finds the laws of nature tuned for life. This balance of nature's laws is so precise and so unlikely to have occurred by chance that he avers an intelligent 'Creator' must have chosen them."[726] Moreover, the laws are built into the universe, and since the universe has a beginning, so do the laws. Recognizing that the universe was designed also imparts great purpose to the universe. From the design in the universe, we can recognize the Designer.

In contrast, "Weinberg is saddened by the fact that, although the laws of nature show 'incredible fine tuning,' from all of his research into the substance and mechanics of the early universe, he finds the universe to be pointless, that life is only 'a little above the level of farce.'" A chance universe without a Designer is truly pointless. Without the Designer, life is meaningless and has no exit except extinction.

But the evidence is vast for the beginning and incredible fine tuning of the laws of the universe. There really is a Fine Tuner, a Designer, a Creator — the God of the Hebrew Bible.

(7.4f) *Behind all is the God of the Hebrew Bible.* Schroeder believes the precisely designed laws of the universe, the development of life, and the human race were designed by an "infinitely powerful Creator." That

Creator is the "biblical God." The God of the Bible set the laws in motion, but He does not need to exercise intimate detailed constant oversight.[727] But this is more than Deism. God intervenes as He deems fit, for example by the flood because of human wickedness, in the exodus, and in the giving of the Torah.

(7.4g) *The Bible, when carefully studied, agrees with creation.* "With a superficial reading of Genesis [even in Hebrew], and certainly with a superficial reading of the text in translation, we haven't a prayer of understanding the details."[728] However, by studying the Hebrew text thoroughly, that text will reveal the Creator's message about creation. Then science will come to agree with a correct understanding of the Bible. "Science, through its progressively improved understanding of the world, has come to agree with theology."[729]

Unsupported Claims of the Theistic Big Bang Theory

I respect Gerald Schroeder as an insightful searcher for the truth about creation and the God of the Hebrew Bible. His spiritual pilgrimage so far has been from being an "adversary" of any Creator to an active proponent of the God found in the Hebrew Bible as the Creator. Many of us have experienced that spiritual pilgrimage. And I count it the greatest possible privilege that I have recognized the Messiah of Israel as my eternal Creator and Savior.

I agree with most of Gerald Schroeder's claims. While I disagree on certain claims, I do so respectfully.

(u-7.0A) *Both literal and kabbalah interpretive meanings of the Bible, as well as science, reveal truth.* Sometimes Schroeder interprets the Bible normally and has very helpful insights. At other times he brings kabbalah interpretative meanings into the Bible.

In response, literal interpretation and kabbalah interpretive methods are opposites. Literal interpretation is reproducible by others studying the language of the text. Kabbalah is not reproducible because it brings outside ideas from "received hidden wisdom"[730] into the text.

A crucial test of good Bible study practice is reproducibility. Can others using the same Bible study tools see the same meaning in the text, even if they may not agree completely with the conclusions? As a scientist, Schroeder would use the principle of reproducibility in his experiments—Can others duplicate the results using the same materials and procedures? With some of his claims he uses the reproducible method of studying the Hebrew words and grammar in context, a method we normally use to read texts, whether a science article or the Bible. Using this normal literal method, he has valuable insights from the Hebrew. He also has helpful insights relating science to the Bible, such as the improbability of chance being the cause of the universe and life.

So it seems odd that on other claims he uses the *un*reproducible "many meanings" "beyond the literal text" kabbalah interpretation. As a scientist, Schroeder knows that good research is reproducible. But kabbalah interpretation allows nonliteral, multiple meanings from outside the Bible text, so is not reproducible. This double standard of interpretation results in problematic ideas mixed with Biblically supported ideas about creation. I would be grateful if in the future he would benefit us with reproducible interpretation from the Hebrew text.

(u-7.2) ***Before Adam, there were six literal days of relativistic "stretched time" on God's clock, while billions of years to us.*** This is Schroeder's unique claim. "The period extending from 'the beginning' to Adam [involved] stretched time." "Deep within Psalm 90," he claims, "there is the truth of a physical reality: the six days of Genesis actually did contain the billions of years of the cosmos even while the days remained twenty-four-hour days."[731] "The difference in perceived time is called relativistic time dilation, the dilation that makes the first six days of Genesis reassuringly compatible with the 15 billion years of cosmology."[732]

In response to the Bible side of his claim, in Psalm 90:4 Moses spoke of God's eternality compared to earth days. The context of Psalm 90:4 is God's personal eternality *before* the creation, not billion-year stretched earth days *during* the creation. "Before the mountains were born, Or Thou didst give birth to the earth and the world, Even from everlasting to everlasting, Thou art God" (Ps. 90:2). "For a thousand years in Thy sight Are like yesterday" illustrates that God is everlasting. The subject of Psalm 90 is God, not creation days.

No doubt Schroeder would say, "But God was the only Observer. So we have to measure by God's time." I would agree, but I would respectfully point out that the Observer was the Spirit of God just above the sea. (I would understand רוּחַ אֱלֹהִים [*rûah 'elōhîm*] in 1:2 as the Spirit of God, not wind.) And the Spirit of God experienced Earth's rotation in and out of sunlight during day-night days, not stretched "days" of billions of years.

Schroeder might respond in turn that there was no "space-time reference frame"[733] for the six pre-Adam days. I would point out that the Bible does give a definite "space-time reference frame" for the six days in Genesis 1:2: "Now the earth was תֹהוּ וָבֹהוּ (*tōhû v^ebōhû*), . . . and the Spirit of God hovered over the face of the waters" (JPS). So the six days were measured by day and night *on Earth*, and even more specifically from the Divine Narrator's location just above Earth's dark sea. So when sunlight first broke through to the Spirit of God's location on the rotating Earth, day one began. The reference frame for the six days was the *location of the Spirit of God* just above Earth's surface. The measurement of time was by the rotation of Earth in sunlight. The first daylight ended as the Spirit of God's location rotated into the dusk of evening, followed by nighttime, ending as the Spirit of God's location rotated into the dawn of daybreak. Day one was a normal earth day. Relativity would have had minimal effect on that Earth's surface reference frame. Schroeder has overlooked the stated "space-time reference frame,"[734] the Spirit of God's location just over the surface of the Earth. The Bible data is against Schroeder's claim.

Concerning the science side of his claim, Schroeder says that it is "*impossible* for a common [time] reference frame to have existed between the Creator and each part of the mix of matter" because "time differs from place to place."[735]

His claim is true but irrelevant because there *was* a specific reference point, the Spirit's location. Relativity somewhere else out in the universe has little or no effect on the one reference point of the Spirit's location on Earth. The Spirit's location rotated into or out of the sunlight, producing normal day-night days on Earth's surface.

Schroeder himself recognizes that "huge changes in gravity (G) and velocity (V) are required to produce easily measurable change in the flow of time."[736] *Very* huge changes in gravity and velocity had to have occurred to fit fifteen billion years into six days as "stretched" time.

Astronomers tell us that planet Earth formed in an outer spiral arm of our Milky Way galaxy. In this location, our planet has had fairly constant velocity and normal gravity. Relativistic time stretching is tiny on Earth, not nearly enough to transform fifteen billion years into six days. If I am correct, and I believe I am, then the physics of Schroeder's claim does not prove the immense time stretching he claims. The physics data is also against Schroeder's claim.

(u-7.2a) *Scientific evidence really does indicate that the universe is about fifteen billion years old.* Schroeder says that the universe is about fifteen billion years old based on scientific evidence.

My response is that the *Bible* does not date the universe. Therefore, the Bible data supports an *undated* universe and Earth creation. The universe is however old it is, but the *Bible* does not say how old that is.

(u-7.2c) *The six days (fifteen billion years) were "days" of the universe.* Schroeder claims, "The Bible describes the day-by-day development of our *universe* in the six days following the creation"[737] (emphasis added). "Day" one and most of the second "day" passed before Earth existed. Over nine billion years of those first two "days" were only about changes in the universe.

In response we may ask, How could the first nine billion years of days one and two be about normal days when according to Schroeder there was no planet Earth yet? Genesis 1:2 describes conditions on *Earth* before day one began: "Now the earth . . ." (NIV). *Earth* was a dark, uninhabitable, and uninhabited planet. The changes God brought about in the six days made *Earth* lighted, habitable, and inhabited. The six days were not about the universe. The universe had already been created back during Genesis 1:1. Day one begins in Genesis 1:3. The six days were about Earth. That is why they are called "days."

(**u-7.2d**) *Each day going back in time was progressively longer.* Schroeder claims that the sixth day was both a literal twenty-four-hour day "from the Bible's perspective," but was "¼ billion years" "from earth's perspective,"; the fifth day was "½ billion years," the fourth "1 billion years," the third "2 billion years," the second "4 billion years," and day one about "8 billion years"—all because of time dilation.[738] So from the Bible's perspective, each day was twenty-four hours, but by time dilation from Earth's perspective, each "day" was millions or billions of years.

I appreciate Schroeder's desire to be faithful to the meaning of *yôm* as a normal day-night cycle day. But his claim seems overreaching to assign Bible days the very specific lengths from an earth perspective of "¼ billion years," "½ billion years," etc. Its is a nice pattern, but where is the Bible basis for it? Moreover, his whole idea of literal days stretched to billions of years seems beyond any meaning Moses could have intended.

(**u-7.3**) ***The six days go back in time from Adam to the big bang.*** Schroeder applies days one and two to the universe (not to Earth) going back to the big bang. "During the development of the universe and prior to the appearance of mankind, God had not yet established a close association with the Earth. For the first one or two days of the six days of Genesis, the Earth didn't even exist!"[739]

In response, Genesis 1:1 declares that God created the Earth in the beginning. Genesis 1:2 does *not* say the heavens and the earth were *tōhû vᵃbōhû*. Genesis 1:2 declares that Earth was *tōhû vᵃbōhû* and its deep sea surface dark. Then when God commanded light, He separated the light from the darkness and called the light "day" and the darkness "night." Day and night are on a rotating planet, not in space. Both Henry Morris and I strongly contend that day and night require a rotating planet. Morris says,

"Light rays were impinging on the earth as it rotated on its axis during the first three days."[740] Day one was *not* the light of the big bang at the beginning of the universe as Schroeder claims. If so, where was day and night? Day one was the first light through Earth's dark cloud to the divine Narrator just above Earth's deep ocean.

(u-7.3a) *In the sixth day, God separated Adam with spiritual image from Cro-Magnon.* Schroeder claims that Adam and Eve were from Cro-Magnon. They were born into a family in the normal manner. They grew up as non-image-bearing *Homo sapiens.* Then God created His image in both. Finally, God brought them together in the Garden.

This claim about Cro-Magnon is not in the Bible.

(u-7.3b & u-7.3c) *Land animals appeared in the quarter billion years of the sixth day, and sea animals in the half billion years of the fifth day.* Schroeder says, "The Bible records that animal life appeared in the waters on day five and on the dry land on day six."[741]

The Bible says nothing about the sixth day lasting a quarter billion years or the fifth day half a billion years "from Earth's perspective."[742]

(u-7.3e) *In the two billion years of the third day, sea, land, and plant life formed.* Schroeder claims land plants, land, ozone, oxygen, ocean plant life, and oceans were formed in the two billion years of the third day.

God surely formed all these, but the Bible does not say in "two billion years." Schroeder is claiming more than the Bible says.

(u-7.3f) *Supernovae in the four billion years of the second day made heavy elements for forming Earth.* Schroeder says that medium elements for the atmosphere and heavier elements for the planet came from supernovae in the eight to twelve billion of years of the first few days.

Again, God may have used supernovae, but supernovae and four billion years is more than the Bible reveals.

(u-7.3g) *Evening and morning was the progression from chaos to cosmos.* Schroeder claims that the words, "And there was evening and there was morning" marked the change from disorder to order.

We may respond that day one included daytime ending with evening, and nighttime ending with morning—both parts of a numbered day. These are time words indicating a day. This claim of no literal evenings or mornings as part of the six days does not seem to fit Schroeder's claim of six literal days. In addition, the phrase *tōhû vᵃbōhû* does not mean chaos. And finally, even if *tōhû vᵃbōhû* did mean chaos, *tōhû vᵃbōhû* is not linked with evening and morning. Evening and morning were the beginning and end of nighttime, not the beginning and end of chaos.

Contra Schroeder, evening and morning
were the beginning and end of nighttime,
not the beginning and end of chaos.

(**u-7.3h**) *After the inflation, light formed as God's first command in the eight billion years of day one.* Schroeder says, "When the temperature [of the inflating big bang] fell below 3000° K, a critical event occurred: Light separated from matter and emerged from the darkness of the universe." He says this was the light of Genesis 1:3.

Again, I would respond that Genesis 1:2 changes the subject to planet Earth. The light on day one was light to the darkened Earth, resulting in day and night, requiring a rotating planet—planet Earth. The light on day one was not light at the beginning of the big bang. An expanding sphere of light after a big bang could not have had day and night. Schroeder's claim says more than the Bible says.

(**u-7.3j, 7.3k, 7.3*l*, 7.3p**) *After the big bang, the universe inflated as the "wind of God," darkness on the face of the deep" was the initial black hole, and* tōhû vᵃbōhû *describes the initial state of the universe.* Schroeder equates the *rûah 'elōhîm* ("Spirit of God")[743] with the inflationary stage of the universe, darkness as the initial "super black hole," and *tōhû vᵃbōhû* as the building blocks of hydrogen.[744]

This is kabbalah type interpretation, adding outside ideas to the Bible. How could Moses possibly have meant the "inflationary stage of the universe" by *rûah 'elōhîm,* "super black hole" by darkness, or the "building blocks" of hydrogen by *tōhû vᵃbōhû*?

I respond very respectfully, because Dr. Schroeder is an American-Israeli, to be honored. I also respect his Hebrew ability.

Partially Supported Claim of Theistic Big Bang

(**ps-7.3p**) *The "beginning" started time and matter at the big bang.* Schroeder says, "Time truly takes hold when matter forms" "0.00001 seconds after the big bang."[745]

To claim the big bang is to claim more than the Bible explicitly says. But *bᵉrē'shît* ("in the beginning") does include the beginning of time.

Largely Supported Claims of the Theistic Big Bang Theory

I am not saying that I agree with everything about these claims; rather, overall, these claims seem supported by the Bible.

(s-7.1) Since Adam, the Bible uses a normal human time scale, shown accurate by archeology.

The evidence supports Schroeder's claim. Gerald Schroeder lives in Israel where archeological finds are top news. I participated in such an archeological dig (Tiberius) and saw our finds published in Israel. Almost every month of the digging season (the spring, the beginning of the dry season before it is too hot) a new find confirms the Biblical data. Outsiders may scoff and call Bible history a myth, but I personally did not meet scoffers who actually dug.

(s-7.2b) Each *yôm* was a twenty-four-hour day, not a day-age. The Hebrew, Schroeder claims, indicates that the six days were "truly referring to six 24-hour days."[746] Schroeder disagrees with Ross and other long day-age advocates. Schroeder explains, "The approach that 'the six days were really six epochs' has scant biblical basis."

As I understand, Ross did not truly read Hebrew when he made his day-age claim. So Schroeder—who lives in Israel, speaks Hebrew, studies Genesis in Hebrew, and is familiar with Ross's work—weighs in heavily against Ross's long day-age claim.

While disagreeing with Schroeder's idea of stretched time, we may appreciate his analysis of *yôm* in Genesis 1 as a normal "day."

(s-7.3d) Cloud had blocked out luminaries (but not diffuse sunlight) until the fourth day. Schroeder explains, "Earth's atmosphere was probably clouded with vapors of the primeval atmosphere. . . . The atmosphere, however, was translucent, not transparent. Therefore, individual luminaries were not distinguishable. . . . The early plant life actually helped clear the atmosphere through the process of photosynthesis."[747] On the fourth day, the luminaries, which had been in space long before, began to be in Earth's sky, separating and ruling day and night.

We may accept Schroeder's explanation that on the fourth day the sky cleared, becoming at least partially transparent. I would not use the word "distinguishable" but rather that God commanded the luminaries to "be" in the sky "to separate" day and night and "be" signs for seasons, days, and years.

(s-7.3i) Day one in Hebrew was cardinal, but the second through sixth days were ordinals. Schroeder as a Hebrew speaker was quick to recognize this distinction.

Schroeder is correct in this claim. It can be checked easily in the Hebrew text.

(s-7.3m) The Bible says the universe had a beginning and is expanding, matching the beginning and expansion science discovered. The Hebrew Bible, explains Schroeder, tells us that the heavens and earth were created at a definite beginning. And the universe is expanding. These two claims were in the Bible over two thousand years before Edwin Hubble discovered the expansion of the universe in 1929.[748]

Schroeder is correct that the Bible's two claims—the heavens and the earth had a beginning and the heavens have been expanding—match the two claims that science discovered: the beginning and expansion of the universe. These two claims are very strong evidence that the Bible (but no other religious book) is from the Creator.

(s-7.3n) The heavens and earth were created from nothing in the *ex nihilo* creation act of Genesis 1:1. Schroeder says, "The creation of the heavens and the earth from absolute nothing is at the root of biblical faith."

Schroeder is correct. God is uniquely different from everything else. He is the eternal Creator. All else is created.

(s-7.3o) Only the Hebrew word *bārā'* fits the initial creation. Schroeder explains that *bārā'*, "create," is the only Hebrew word that can specifically indicate "creation of something from nothing."[749] Schroeder, as a Hebrew speaker, would not agree with the YEC claim that the Hebrew words *bārā'* ("create") and *'āsâh* ("do, make") are interchangeable in Genesis 1:1.[750]

Most Hebrew scholars, including in the other creation theories, agree with Schroeder that *bārā'* alone fits the idea of creation out of nothing. The novel YEC claim that *bārā'* and *'āsâh* are interchangeable is incorrect. The YEC idea is interpretive in an effort to claim that *'āsâh* in Exodus 20:11 means the same as *bārā'* in Genesis 1:1, so God created the universe "*in* six days" 6,000 years ago. Schroeder is correct about the Hebrew; YEC is incorrect.

(s-7.4) The universe fine-tuned for life and life itself show evidence of design. Schroeder says that life on Earth, particularly human life, is the result of design by our Creator. Schroeder gives much specific scientific evidence for the fine-tuning of the universe, planet Earth, and life.

Major and growing evidence strongly supports Schroeder's claim.

(s-7.4b) Planet Earth was designed precisely for human life. The physical constants of planet Earth were precisely tuned for life.

Schroeder is basing his claim on very well-supported evidence.

(s-7.4c) Life begun by chance is contradicted by overwhelming evidence. "There is now overwhelmingly strong evidence, both statistically and paleontologically, that life could *not* have been started on Earth by a series of random chemical reactions."[751]

Schroeder has the evidence to back his claim. Life was designed and created by the eternal Designer.

(s-7.4d) Darwinian gradualism and the fossil record of abrupt species do not match. Schroeder says, "Ironically, it is the fossil record itself that is gradually dispelling the argument by chance."[752]

From the fossil collecting that I have personally done and the far more detailed studies of others who are experts, I would conclude that Schroeder is right.

(s-7.4e) Laws are not eternal but were precisely designed. Schroeder explains that the "natural" laws are built into the universe. Since the universe has a beginning, so the laws also had a beginning.

Schroeder has the physics background to back up his claim. Both the universe and its laws were designed and created by God.

(s-7.4f) Behind all is the God of the Hebrew Bible. Schroeder believes the precisely designed laws of the universe, the development of life, and the human race were designed by an "infinitely powerful Creator," whom he correctly takes as the "biblical God."[753]

I agree. Schroeder has added to our evidence that the Biblical God is our Creator.

(s-7.4g) The Bible, when carefully studied, agrees with creation. Schroeder contends, "With a superficial reading of Genesis [even in Hebrew], and certainly with a superficial reading of the text in translation, we haven't a prayer of understanding the details."[754]

I might not put it quite that way, but we do need to study the Hebrew Bible very carefully to understand creation. And we certainly do need to pray, asking in Messiah's name for the Spirit of God to enable us to understand this difficult Bible subject.

In conclusion, I appreciate that Schroeder is on a spiritual journey from disbelief in a Creator to belief about the Creator revealed in the Bible. As a Hebrew speaker, he has some very helpful insights into the Hebrew text. But I am concerned about his kabbalah-type interpretations and some of his conclusions that I suspect are guided more by his science than by the Bible. To me, there is no greater privilege than to know the Messiah of Israel, and I hope this for Dr. Schroeder.

Summary of the Theistic Big Bang and Relativistic Days Theory

From the present back to Adam, the Bible has used a normal human time scale, shown to be accurate by archeology. But before Adam were six days of "stretched time" by relativity's time dilation. The word *yôm* does not mean day-ages. So the six days were each twenty-four-hour days on God's clock, while billions of years in the universe and on Earth. All six days' work (13.7 billion years) on a big universe were needed for human life on Earth.

On the sixth day, God separated Adam and Eve from Cro-Magnon by creating in them His spiritual image. In the quarter billion years of the sixth day and half billion years of the fifth day, God made land and sea animals. Darwinian macroevolution by chance alone is statistically impossible, and the fossil record of abrupt species does not match evolutionary gradualism. Life originated from the God of the Hebrew Bible.

Earth's clouded atmosphere blocked out the luminaries in Earth's sky until the fourth day, but not diffuse sunlight. In the two billion years of the third day, God made plant life, which produced oxygen that would clear the atmosphere on the fourth day. In the four billion years of the second day, medium and heavy elements formed by supernovae would be needed to make Earth and its atmosphere. Light formed in the very early universe beginning the eight billion years of day one. Time itself began with matter forming shortly after the big bang. Before the big bang, the God of the Hebrew Bible alone existed.

7. Theistic Big Bang and Relativistic Days Theory

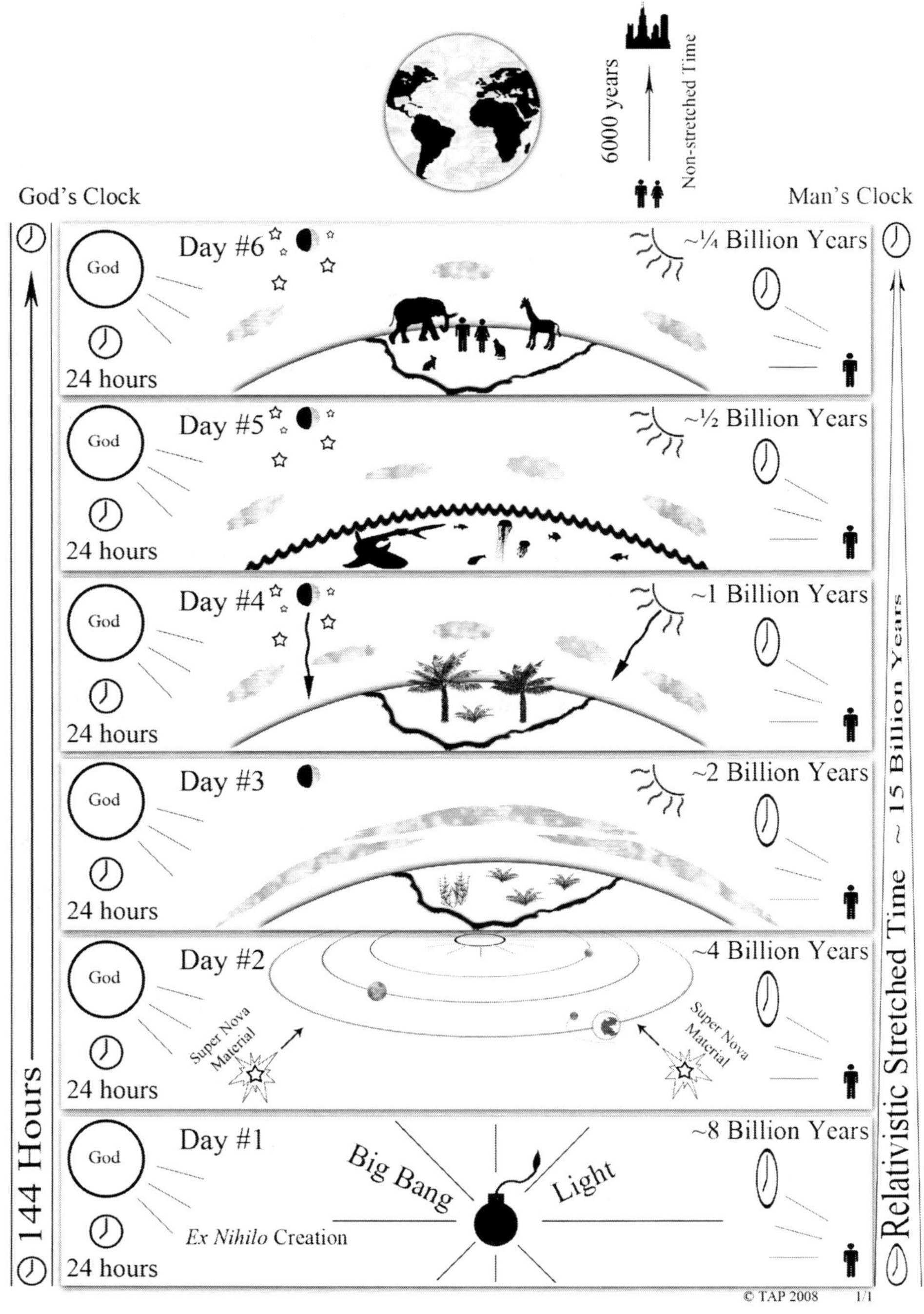

7. Claims of the Theistic Big Bang and Relativistic Days Theory
(Biblically supported claims in non-italics **bold,** unsupported in *italics*)

(7.0A) *Both* **literal** *and kabbalah interpretive meanings of Bible* **reveal truth.**

(7.1) Since Adam, the Bible uses normal human time.

(7.2) *Before Adam, there were six literal days of billions of years of relativistic time.*

(7.2a) Science indicates the universe is about fifteen billion years old.

(7.2b) Each yôm was a twenty-four-hour day, not a day-age.

(7.2c) *The six days (fifteen billion years) were "days" of the universe.*

(7.2d) *Each day going back in time was progressively longer.*

(7.3) *The six days go back in time from Adam to the big bang.*

(7.3a) *In the sixth day, God separated Adam from Cro-Magnon.*

(7.3b) *Land animals appeared in the quarter billion years of the sixth day.*

(7.3c) *Sea animals appeared in the half billion years of the fifth day.*

(7.3d) Cloud had blocked out luminaries until fourth day.

(7.3e) *In the two billion years of the third day plant life formed.*

(7.3f) *Supernovae in the four billion years of second day made heavy elements.*

(7.3g) *Evening and morning was the progression from chaos to cosmos.*

(7.3h) *After the inflation, light formed as God's first command in day one.*

(7.3i) Day one was cardinal, but second–sixth are ordinals.

(7.3j) *After the big bang, the universe inflated as "wind of God" in Gen. 1:2c.*

(7.3k) *Darkness of 1:2b was the initial big bang inflation.*

(7.3l) *Tōhû v^abōhû of Genesis 1:2a describe the initial state of the universe.*

(7.3m) Universe beginning and expanding matches science.

(7.3n) Heavens and earth were created from nothing in 1:1

(7.3o) Only the Hebrew word bārā' fits the initial creation.

(7.3p) "Beginning" started time and matter at the big bang.

(7.4) The universe and life show evidence of design.

(7.4a) The universe was designed specifically for human life.

(7.4b) Planet Earth was designed precisely for human life.

(7.4c) Life begun by chance is contradicted by great evidence.

(7.4d) Darwinian gradualism and fossil record do not match.

(7.4e) Laws are not eternal but were precisely designed.

(7.4f) Behind all is the God of the Hebrew Bible.

(7.4g) The Bible, when carefully studied, and creation agree.

Major Supported Claims from the Creation Theories

The Correct Translation of Genesis 1:1: Waltke affirms the traditional translation of Genesis 1:1: "In the beginning God created the heavens and the earth." It is *incorrect* to translate 1:1 as "When God began to create."

Waltke Merism: "The heavens and the earth" meant the entire orderly universe. Also, evening and morning meant the entire nighttime.

The Waltke Exclusion Principle: If there was preexisting chaos, there was no *ex nihilo* creation of the organized heavens and earth. The converse is also logically possible: If there was *ex nihilo* creation of the organized heavens and earth, then there was no unorganized chaos.

The Kline Order: Proverbs 8:22–31 says "the beginning," when God created Earth (Gen. 1:1), was "when there were no depths." There were ocean depths by 1:2, so "In the beginning" was before 1:2 and before the six days. Creation order: heavens, earth, sea, six days.

The Kline Claim: When the Bible does not indicate a miracle, Genesis 2:5–6 (no rain, no plants; rain, then plants sprouted) shows God probably used ordinary means in the creation era, just as today. **Ross Addition:** "An observed attribute of the Creator . . . is His economy of miracles—only what's needed to accomplish His purpose."

The Kline Undated Universe: "We must speak where the Bible speaks, and be silent where the Bible is silent. . . . The inspired text, rightly interpreted, is simply silent with regard to the age of the earth and universe."

A Generational Genesis: The worldview of Genesis was generations. The six begetting (literal) days of Genesis 1 introduced the most ancient generations of all—"the generations of the heavens and the earth" (Gen 2:4a).

The Rooker Reaffirmation: "The key difference between pagan cosmogonies and Genesis 1 is *creatio ex nihilo* and the absence of preexisting matter."

The Morris Maxim: In historical narrative, a numbered "day" was a day.

The Morris and Ross Method: The Bible reveals what God did; science may uncover how He did it.

The Morris One Fall Explanation: The creation was perfect. Man and animals were created about 6,000 years ago with eternal physical life. There was "no disorder, no sin and, above all, *no death!* Even Satan was still good at this point."[755] His first effect on Earth was the temptation. (There were two falls, but Lucifer's fall had no effect on Earth until his temptation of Eve, resulting in Adam and Eve's Fall.) Adam's Fall resulted in a "cosmic catastrophe" including all human and animal death and subsequent moral and natural evil.

The Kaiser Two Falls Explanation: Standard theology identifies two falls: the angelic fall led by Lucifer, and later the human Fall by Adam. God's concluding "very good" evaluation was about His work on Earth, not about angels such as Lucifer, who had been created and likely fell earlier. Animal death is *not* inherently evil. God Himself killed an animal to cover human nakedness. Any pre-Fall evil aspects of animal disease and death could only have been initiated by fallen Lucifer (Ezek. 28:16–18; Heb. 2:14). Yet by the sixth day, God worked even those together for good or eliminated them until Adam's Fall. Adam was the original cause of human death (Rom. 5:12) and farming woes (Gen. 3:17–19), but Scripture does not say he caused animal death. So animal death may have preceded Adam's Fall. Animal life cycles fit the present noneternal world God created, anticipating human resurrection and the New Creation (Rom. 8:20).

The Ross Resolution: God does not deceive either by His Word or by His creation work. Correctly interpreted, both God's verbal revelation (the Bible) and physical revelation (the created universe) will be in accord.

The Observer's Perspective: Ross says interpret the Genesis 1 creation narrative from the perspective of the Observer/Narrator, the Spirit, hovering just above the surface of the water-covered Earth.

The Ross Apologetic: The Bible alone declares that the universe had a beginning and has been stretching out. Only the Creator could have known these facts long before modern science. The God of the Bible is the Creator, and the Bible is His accurate message to us.

The Ross-Schroeder Fine-Tuning Evidence: The fine-tuning of the universe and Earth for humans is evidence of the Designer, not chance.

Chapter 8

Theory 8
Creation Revealed in Six Days Theory

Genesis is from eyewitness tablets edited into Scripture by Moses.

British Air Commodore P. J. Wiseman (1888–1948), during a tour of duty in Mesopotamia, became interested in Mesopotamian archaeology. As a serious part-time archeologist, he collected or discovered many tablets, including four tablets of the "Babylonian Chronicle"[756] that fixed the date of the fall of Jerusalem.[757] From his Babylonian tablet collection, Wiseman realized that the format of the ANE tablets closely matched the תּוֹלְדֹת (*tôlᵉdôt*, "descendants, generations" indicating generational annals or genealogical records) units of the book of Genesis. He published his ideas about his discoveries in *New Discoveries in Babylonia about Genesis* and his theory on creation revealed in Genesis 1 in *Creation Revealed in Six Days*. These studies were edited by his son, Donald J. Wiseman, professor of Assyriology at the University of London and coauthor of *Ancient Records and the Structure of Genesis.*

The creation revealed in six days theory is sometimes grouped with the vision theory, the view that God revealed the creation to Moses through six visions in six days, each ending in evening, night, and morning.[758] However, Wiseman disagrees with grouping his theory with the six visions theory because he explains that the revelation in six days was given *verbally in words,* not visually in visions. The very words of Genesis 1 came from God. And God spoke these words to Adam, not to Moses.

In a nutshell, the creation revealed theory says that God spoke to Adam in six days, communicating six brief creation narratives summarizing the long eras of creation. Adam passed down the creation narrative along with his own eyewitness narrative. These narratives were recorded on tablets, which Moses edited into the book of Genesis.

God spoke the creation narrative to Adam.

Wiseman says that God spoke in six days to reveal to Adam the creation events. Each day God revealed a creation event to Adam. That day's revealing ended in evening (when presumably Adam slept) and morning (when Adam arose to hear the next episode). Wiseman believes that the words God spoke to Adam were then recorded on a clay tablet (or tablets), as was common in the Ancient Near East, and passed down. Moses received the creation tablet, along with the succeeding tablets from Adam through Joseph and edited them into the book of Genesis. Moses added very little other than updating earlier place-names such as "Bela (that is, Zoar)." These updated place-names are common in the book of Genesis, but rare in the rest of the Pentateuch. For example, Moses simply used the current name, Zoar, in Deuteronomy 34:3.

Wiseman says God spoke the creation narrative to Adam. In addition, the six days were only the six days when God spoke rather than when God created. These two ideas are his creation revealed in six days theory. Then the creation narrative, Adam's narrative, Noah's narrative, through Joseph's narrative were transmitted by clay tablets down to Moses, who recorded them in Genesis. This is called the "Wiseman Tablet Theory," as opposed to the JEPD documentary hypothesis. The following are Wiseman's claims.

Claims of Creation Revealed in Six Days Theory

(8.1) *Genesis 1:1—2:4a is from an ancient source.* P. J. Wiseman and his son, D. J. Wiseman, give evidences demonstrating that Genesis 1:1—2:4a (and all of Genesis) is from an *ancient* source, much older than Moses. Genesis is composed of generational units ending with *tôlᵉdôt* colophons that are similar to other ancient near eastern (ANE) tablets ending with colophons. Additional evidences for an ancient origin of Genesis are Babylonian words in the earlier accounts and Egyptian words in the Joseph account. Genesis also has lost cities and place-names (often much older than Moses) that were only recently discovered by archeology, and pre-Mosaic cultural details in the Bible's record of the patriarchal era that fit the older ancient near eastern culture.[759]

Wiseman, based on this evidence, opposes the JEPD documentary hypothesis of *relatively recent* sources of Genesis. Without hard archeological or ancient Bible manuscript evidence, the JEPD theory claims that multiple manuscripts were patchworked together by late Israelite scribes. These included a J document supposedly composed about 950 BC, an E document about 850 BC., a D document between 650 and 621 BC, and a P document between 500 and 400 BC.[760] The JEPD documentary hypothesis claims that redactors stitched these relatively recent documents together into the five books of the Pentateuch. The documentary hypothesis claims the redactors did this a millennium or more after the events, if the events even happened. The documentary hypothesis also claims that the Genesis "creation myth" was borrowed from the "Babylonian Genesis" (*Enuma Elish*, Tablet VI, lines 1–38) and other ANE mythic sources. Moses wrote none of the "Five Books of Moses"

Wiseman disagrees. He says Moses compiled Genesis from ancient eyewitness reports on tablets predating the *Enuma Elish* mythical account. Wiseman reasons that Genesis 1:1—2:4a has an "absence of mythical or legendary matter that characterizes all other accounts of Creation." So Moses edited the Bible book of Genesis from a dozen or so eyewitness tablets that he had received. Then Moses was the eyewitness author of the events in Exodus through Deuteronomy.

Genesis is from about a dozen eyewitness
tablets edited by Moses.

(8.1a) *Isaiah 40:21 and tradition imply that God gave Adam the creation narrative.* Wiseman says Genesis 1:1—2:4a was originally God's words to Adam, later transcribed from clay tablets by Moses into the book of Genesis.

Isaiah 40:21 (NASB) asks about the creation, "Has it not been declared to you from the beginning [*mē-rōsh,* same root word as in Genesis 1:1]?" Isaiah affirms that the origin narrative, how God created and then stretched out the heavens (40:22, 26), had been declared from the very beginning. Implied is that God declared the creation narrative to Adam.

Jewish tradition says that God gave Adam, and later also Enoch, the exact words of the creation narrative.[761] Wiseman agrees. Genesis 1:1—2:4a was from God to Adam.

(8.1b) *Genesis 1:1—2:4a is pre-Israelite.* Wiseman says, "All the references in this first chapter are universal in their application and unlimited in their scope." There is "no mention of any particular tribe or nation or country, or any merely local ideas or customs." "There is no mention [in Genesis 1:1—2:4a] of any event subsequent to the creation of humans."[762] Moreover, "No Israelite of a later generation would have used the plurals 'us' and 'our' of God in verse 26." Also, "The term 'Sabbath' is not used. It is simply 'the seventh day.'"[763] Therefore, Genesis 1:1—2:4a was from an ancient pre-Israel source.

(8.2) *The Genesis narratives (beginning with the creation account) were probably transmitted on eleven tablets, each ending with* *a tôledôt colophon, collated by Moses.* Wiseman found ANE clay tablets ending with a "colophon phrase." "A colophon is a note added at the end of an account giving particulars of the title, date, [and] name of writer or owner." "The Oxford English Dictionary defines it as 'the inscription or device, *formerly placed at the end of a book or manuscript,* and containing the title, the scribe's or printer's name, date and place of printing, etc.'"[764] (emphasis Wiseman's).

Most scholars have recognized that these "*toledoth* phrases" must be important, but they have been misled by assuming incorrectly that these are the introduction to the text that follows. (Several modern translations have even garbled these phrases.) This has led to serious questions, because in several cases they don't seem to fit. For example, Genesis 37:2 begins, "These are the generations of Jacob. . . . " But from that spot on, the text describes Joseph and his brothers, and almost nothing about Jacob, who was the central character in the previous section.[765]

"The text just before the phrase 'These are the generations of . . .' [*Eleh tôledôt*] contained information about events that the man named in that phrase would have known about."[766] Wiseman says that the person named in the *tôledôt* clause "would have been the logical one to write . . . the text preceding that phrase." In the Mesopotamian style, the writer listed his name at the end of his narrative in a *tôledôt* as the colophon. Only in the Egyptian-style narrative of Joseph is there no *tôledôt* at the end.

Common subjects in ANE tablets were origin accounts, family histories, and genealogies. They ended with a colophon, similar to the *tôledôt* units of Genesis.[767] A *tôledôt* was a "history, properly of families." The first *tôledôt* was the history of the "origin of the heaven and earth."[768]

Wiseman says the narrative of each of the eleven tablets was "by an actual eye-witness to the events descried therein."[769]

The author's name is at the end of his
eyewitness family account.

The first two narratives predated the flood. Wiseman suggests that the creation and Adam's account may have been written by Adam, perhaps late in his lifetime, and the tablets taken onto the ark by Noah. Noah also wrote his account on a tablet. Shem would have preserved these tablets and added a tablet of his own, as well as kept records of the genealogical descendants of Shem, Ham, and Japheth during their lifetimes. These highly valued family history tablets would have been passed down to Abraham, and finally through Israel to Moses.

Oral traditions of the creation by other descendants of Noah were garbled and passed down as ANE myths. Examples are the Babylonian *Enuma Elish* about creation or the Gilgamesh Epic about the flood.[770]

The final narrative in the Bible, the Joseph narrative, does not end in a *tôl*e*dôt* because Joseph was not from Mesopotamia, where tablets ended in a colophon, but from Egypt. So Joseph used the Egyptian style, likely on a papyrus scroll. The Joseph narrative contains numerous evidences of its Egyptian origin.[771] It seems reasonable that such a high official of Egypt, who recorded his grain records, would have recorded his personal history.

All this suggests that Genesis was transcribed from eleven Mesopotamian tablets each ending with the *tôl*e*dôt* of the author, plus the final Egyptian-style Joseph narrative, likely on papyrus.

Documents of family origins were highly valued in ANE cultures. It is reasonable that Moses received, collated, and edited these tablets into Genesis. The fourteenth century BC Akkadian cuneiform Tel el-Amarna tablets,[772] found in Egypt, were Egypt's correspondence with Mesopotamia and Canaan.[773] These tablets indicated that learned Egyptians of Moses' time were able to read cuneiform. "Moses was educated in all the learning of the Egyptians" (Acts 17:22). If the tablets were in cuneiform, Moses could have learned to read such cuneiform while in Egypt and expanded his cuneiform ability during his forty years in Midian. The tablets Moses received may have been in archaic Hebrew, which does seem to have been in existence before Moses. Either way, the well educated Moses could have transcribed these eyewitness narratives into the Hebrew text of the book of Genesis. Moses' sources were eleven eyewitness tablets each ending in a *tôl*e*dôt* in the Mesopotamian colophon style, although the Joseph eyewitness narrative may have been on papyrus.

(**8.2a**) *Genesis was written as generational family histories, so Genesis 1:1—2:4a should be understood as the origin history of the generations of the heavens and the earth.* "The master key . . . of the book of Genesis is to be found in the phrase, 'These are the generations of.'" The narratives of Genesis are "begettings or genealogical histories."[774] Each *tôl*e*dôt* ["generations"] concluded a "family history." "The word [*tôl*e*dôt*] is used to describe history, usually family history *in its origin*. The equivalent phrase in English is, 'These are the historical origins of'" (emphasis his).[775] Genesis 1 is the historical origins of the heavens and earth in the narrative that God spoke to Adam. The creation narrative ends with the *tôl*e*dôt* title,

"These are the generations of the heavens and the earth when they were created." Therefore Genesis 1:1—2:4a should be interpreted as the history of the most ancient generations of all, the heavens and the earth.

(8.3) *Genesis 1 has a structure of two parallel parts, ending in the first colophon or* **tôlᵉdôt.** Wiseman says that Genesis 1 has a structure in which "the six days fall into two clearly parallel parts." The third day has two "And God said" commands. The sixth day also has two "And God said" commands with two additional "And God said" instructions for a total of eight commands or ten "And God said" statements.[776] "The key to the arrangement may be seen in the words 'without form and void' (verse 2). In the first three days we are told of the *formation* of the heavens and earth, and in the second three days of the furnishing of the void."[777] The account ends in the colophon or *tôlᵉdôt*, "These *are* the generations of the heavens and of the earth when they were created" (Gen. 2:4a, KJV).

(8.4) *The six days were normal days, but they were not creation days.* Wiseman says, "I suggest that every time the days are mentioned in both these passages [Genesis 1 and Exodus 20:9–11] they are intended to be taken literally as ordinary days."[778]

Wiseman qualifies this affirmation that the days were ordinary days with his idea that it is an "incorrect assumption that what God did on the six days was to CREATE all life and man"[779] (emphasis his).

To affirm his theory, Wiseman shows how each of the other major creation theories has a claim that is not supported by the Bible. The assumption is that by proving each of them has an unsupported claim, his theory will be the last theory standing, so must be right.

(8.4a) *The day-age theory fails to prove that a day with daytime, evening, and morning was a geologic era.* Wiseman says, "The geologic 'day' theory [or day-age theory] does not deal with the six 'evening and morning'" terms. "Was each of them an indefinitely long night in which there was no light? Was the geologic night as long or almost as long as the geologic 'day?'"[780]

Wiseman responds that the geologic long "day" interpretation is simply wrong because it does not fit the day, evening, night, and morning arrangement of the six days.

(8.4b) *The gap theory, with a first creation of life and its destruction, is an argument from silence.* Wiseman continues, "The second theory—that of six days *re*-creation—puts forward the idea that there has been two quite distinct creations and that these were separated by an unknown period lasting possibly millions of years." "The second verse is said to leave room

All three major theories have fatally flawed claims:
Gap – Bible is silent on a first creation, destruction, and re-creation.
OEC – Billion-year day-ages do not fit morning and evening.
YEC – No "in" in Exod. 20:11a, so creation was not in day one.

Therefore, there must be a different solution to what God did (*'āsâh*) during the six days.

(8.5) *Genesis 1:1—2:4a was not the creation in six days but revelation in six days about the ancient creation.* Wiseman says, "Because the six days have been misunderstood as though they were periods occupied by God in His creative acts, instead of the time occupied by Him in revealing what He had created in the infinite past, the first page of the Bible has fallen into not a little reproach, and has become a stumbling-block to many."[791]

(8.5a) *In Exodus 20:11, '*āsâh *means God "shewed" creation in six days.* Wiseman turns to four King James texts that translate *asah* as "shewed" (an older English term for "showed"):

Genesis 19:19—"which thou hast shewed."
24:14—"thou hast shewed kindness."
32:10—"the truth, which thou hast shewed unto thy servant."
Judges 6:17—"then shew me a sign that thou talkest with me."[792]

"If the Fourth Commandment had been similarly translated it would have read, 'For in six days the LORD shewed the heavens and the earth and all that in them is and rested on the seventh day.'"[793]

(8.5b) *In the six days all God did was talk to Adam about creation.* Wiseman asks, "What did God do in the presence of man for six days? . . . God was saying something about creation. Each of those six days commences with 'God said', and it is a record of what God *said to man* as stated in verse 28, 'And God said unto them.'"[794] Genesis 1 "is His revelation to men about His creative acts in time past." "It is a narrative of what 'God said' to man, *there is no suggestion that the acts or processes of God had occupied those six days*"[795] (emphasis Wiseman's).

God spoke to Adam the six brief narratives of Genesis 1 during six days. God did no creation work in the six days.

(8.5c) *On the seventh day, God ceased "shewing" creation.* Wiseman says, "The word translated rested, like the same word in Genesis 2:3, simply means ceased, or desisted. It does not necessarily mean the rest of relaxation; for this, quite a different Hebrew word is used."[796] God ceased "shewing" creation on the seventh day.

(8.5d) *On the seventh day, Adam rested from God's six days "shewing" creation.* Wiseman asks, "What did God do on those six days? And why did He cease on the seventh? . . . *Our Lord Himself ANSWERED IT. He declared that 'the Sabbath was made for man'* (Mark 2:27)" (emphasis Wiseman's).[797] After the six days of revealing creation, God gave Adam a day to rest from the revealing.

Wiseman's unique claim is that the six days were days when God *revealed* the creation account; then *Adam* rested on the seventh.

Unsupported Claims of the Creation Revealed in Six Days Theory

(u-8.5) *Genesis 1:1—2:4a was not the creation in six days but revelation in six days about the ancient creation.* Wiseman has one major odd claim: "The six days have been misunderstood as though they were periods occupied by God in His creative acts, instead of the time occupied by Him in revealing what He had created in the infinite past."[798]

The Bible text does *not* support this novel idea. Each of the eight command units begins with the mild command form ("jussive in form and meaning"[799]), "And God said, 'Let there be. . . .'" This is not simple narrative. In the fifth day, immediately after the command, "And God said, 'Let the water teem . . .'" is "So God created" (*bārā'*). God actually created the sea creatures. No other major theory agrees that the days were not creation days in at least some sense. Wiseman's claim that the days were only six days of revelation is incorrect.

(u-8.5a – 8.5d) *In the six days all God did was "shew" creation to Adam. On the seventh day, He ceased showing, so Adam rested.* Wiseman uses four brief phrases out of context.

Genesis 19:19—"which thou hast shewed."
24:14—"thou hast shewed kindness."
32:10—"the truth, which thou hast shewed unto thy servant."
Judges 6:17—"then shew me a sign that thou talkest with me."[800]

In these verses, the KJV translates *'āsâh* as "shewed."[801] Longer quotes make it clear that *'āsâh* means "showed" mercy in the sense of "did" an act of mercy or "do" a sign. None means God *revealed* a narrative:

Genesis 19:19—"Thou hast magnified thy mercy, which thou hast shewed unto me in saving my life." (The angels did an act of mercy to Lot. "Showed" meant *doing* the act of mercy, not revealing a narrative.)

Genesis 24:14—"Thereby shall I know that thou hast shewed kindness unto my master." (God *did* an act of kindness to Abraham by directing his servant to the right wife for Isaac.)

Genesis 32:10—"I am not worthy of the least of all the mercies, and of all the truth, which thou hast shewed unto thy servant." (God *did* acts of mercy to His servant Jacob.)

Judges 6:17—"If now I have found grace in thy sight, then shew me a sign that thou talkest with me." (Gideon asked God to *do* a sign, not reveal a narrative.)

Wiseman claims all God did in the six days was *reveal* the six parts of the creation narrative to Adam. All God did was talk to Adam.

In none of the four verses does "shewed" from 'āsâh mean "revealed" a narrative account. In all four, the meaning of 'āsâh is a nuance of the basic meaning of "do" or "did."

Wiseman claims, "Each of those six days commences with 'God said', and it is a record of what God *said to man* as stated in verse 28, 'And God said unto them'"[802] (Gen. 1:28).

In response, this claim is incorrect. Verse 28 really was God instructing Adam and Eve. In contrast, seven of the eight previous "And God said" commands came before Adam and Eve were even created, and the eighth was their creation. God actually commanded the events making Earth lighted, habitable, and inhabited.

Finally, Genesis 2:3 clearly opposes Wiseman's creation revealed in six days view: "He [God] rested from all His work which God had created [bārā'] and made ['āsâh]" (NASB). God rested from creating; Adam did not rest from revealing. Exodus 20:11 is the warrant and grounds that after God worked six days, He rested the seventh, as an example that Israel should work six days and rest the seventh. Wiseman's theory would have God working six days revealing, then Adam resting one day from listening. In that form, the example in Exodus 20:11 would make no sense. Besides, Exodus 20:11 says God rested, not Adam rested.

Wiseman's claim that all God did in the six days was reveal the creation account is incorrect.

Partially Supported Claim of the Creation Revealed in Six Days

(ps-8.4) The six days were normal days, *but they were not creation days.* Wiseman claims the six days were days of revelation.

Later in this study at the four diagnostic questions, I will give evidence from the text for the first half of Wiseman's claim. If we consider just the Genesis text (rather than evidence for an older Earth), the six days were normal days.

But the Bible text does not agree that God did no creation work in the six days.

Supported Claims from the Creation Revealed in Six Days Theory

(s-8.1) Genesis 1:1—2:4a is from an ancient source. Wiseman gives evidence that Genesis 1:1—2:4a came from ancient eyewitness accounts passed down to Moses, who wrote these texts as the book of Genesis.

Wiseman's claim is confirmed by evidence from the Bible and from ancient tablets that he found.

(s-8.1a) Isaiah 40:21 and tradition imply that God gave Adam the creation narrative. Wiseman says God spoke Genesis 1:1—2:4a to Adam, who wrote the account on a tablet(s). Later, Moses transcribed the words of God into the beginning of the book of Genesis. Isaiah 40:21 says, "Has it not been declared to you from the beginning?" This verse is in the context of creation.

I find his case compelling that Genesis 1:1—2:4a was spoken by God to Adam. Wiseman adds that Adam wrote the account on a tablet(s). I suggest, more likely, the first two narratives were passed down orally to Noah. Noah (or Shem) likely recorded them on tablets before the end of his life 350 years after the flood. One reason I suggest Noah (or possibly Shem) wrote the account is that written tablets have been discovered overlapping the end of the lifetime of Noah. Regardless of who first wrote it on a tablet, the internal Bible evidence is that Adam knew the Genesis 1:1—2:4a narrative, because he began his 2:4b—5:1a narrative in a parallel manner.

(s-8.1b) Genesis 1:1—2:4a is pre-Israelite. Wiseman gives evidences that Genesis 1:1—2:4a was pre-Israelite. For example, "No Israelite of a later generation would have used the plurals 'us' and 'our' of God in verse 26."

Wiseman's evidence is compelling. Scribes in Israel were careful to the point of obsession about how they wrote of God. A supposed ninth century BC writer or fifth century BC redactor (as claimed by the JEPD documentary hypothesis) would not have used the first person plural of God, "Let us make man in our image, in our likeness."

(s-8.2) The Genesis narratives (beginning with the creation account) were probably transmitted on eleven tablets, each ending with a *tôlᵉdôt* colophon, collated by Moses. Wiseman found ANE clay tablets each ending with a "colophon phrase" of the title and writer's name. The colophon of the ANE tablets are very similar to the eleven *tôlᵉdôt* phrases ending the units of Genesis. This suggests Genesis was passed down on eleven tablets to Moses.

His claim has good support. If Genesis is true, but was not dictated to Moses by God, then it must have been from eyewitnesses. Genesis is from about a dozen eyewitness written accounts.

(s-8.2a) Genesis was written as generational family histories, so 1:1—2:4a should be understood as the origin history of the generations of the heavens and the earth. The master key . . . of the book of Genesis is to be found in the phrase, "These are the generations of.'" Genesis 1:1—2:4a should be interpreted as the origin account of the generations of the heavens and the earth.

I respond that Wiseman is correct. The worldview of Genesis was generations. Later, in Exodus, Moses emphasized the workweek. But a workweek hardly fit the worldview of the original hearer of Adam's narrative and the time of the patriarchs in Genesis. The worldview of the patriarchs was that of nomadic shepherds. Nomadic shepherds cared for their sheep every day. Time passed for the shepherd in generations of sheep, and for the family in generations of their children and grandchildren. The next generation had the highest priority. The worldview of the ancient world of Genesis was successive generations, as is very clearly emphasized in the detailed genealogies throughout Genesis. Genesis had a generational worldview, not a workweek worldview. From the beginning of Adam's narrative in 2:4b through the end of Joseph's narrative, neither a Sabbath nor a workweek is mentioned. It is not that a week was unknown, because a wedding week was mentioned in Genesis 29. Exodus began emphasizing the workweek worldview. Genesis 1:1—2:4a should be interpreted as the generations of the heavens and the earth.

Rather than Wiseman's six days when God *told* Adam about the generations of the heavens and the earth, the six days *were* the six days in which God commanded the begetting of light, atmosphere, plants, sun-marked days, sea and air life, and man. Genesis 1:1—2:4a is the history of the actual origin of the six generations of the heavens and the earth.

(s-8.3) Genesis 1 has a structure of two parallel parts, ending in the first colophon or *tôlᵉdôt*. Wiseman says that in Genesis 1, "the six days fall into two clearly parallel parts."

This arrangement of Genesis 1 is widely recognized.

(s-8.4a) The day-age theory fails to prove that a day with daylight, evening, and morning was a geologic age. Wiseman explains that the days were literal days, not day-ages.

He is correct that the "geologic-day theory" does not fit the evening and morning statements of the six days.

(s-8.4b) The gap theory, with a first creation of life and its destruction, is an argument from silence. Wiseman points out that Genesis 1:2 says nothing about a first creation of life and its destruction. And the six days say nothing about a *re*-creation.

Wiseman is correct that the Bible is silent on a first creation of life, its ruin in a gap at Genesis 1:2, and the six days as a *re*-creation.

(s-8.4c) The young earth creation theory's claim that the initial ex nihilo creation was in the six days based on *"in"* in Exodus 20:11 fails because there is no *"in."* Wiseman explains that the modern young earth scientific creationism theory is built on a misinterpretation of Exodus 20:11. Within the Fourth Commandment, Exodus 20:11 declares that the work God did took six days—as the warrant and grounds for man's six work days followed by the Sabbath. Exodus 20:11 does not declare that God created the heavens and earth *in* six days.

Wiseman is correct. There is no *"in"* in the Hebrew of Exodus 20:11, and *'āsâh* in 20:11 does not mean "created."

P. J. Wiseman insightfully gives evidence that the creation narrative is ancient. He explains that God spoke the words to Adam. But Wiseman's claim that all God did in the six days was reveal the six-part narrative to Adam is incorrect.

Summary of the Creation Revealed in Six Days Theory

Mesopotamians commonly recorded origins, genealogies, and family history narratives on clay tablets, each ending in a colophon with the title and author's name. Genesis 1:1—2:4a ends in a *tôlᵉdôt* of a very similar style. Given the accuracy and universality of the creation narrative and the fact that God alone was there, the only plausible source of Genesis 1:1—2:4a was that God revealed the creation narrative, apparently to Adam. Isaiah 40:21 implies that God did exactly that. The *tôlᵉdôt* in 2:4a ending the Genesis 1:1—2:4a narrative is a claim of an eyewitness origin account of the generations of the heavens and earth created by God.

Then Wiseman makes the odd claim that the six days were not days of actual creation events, but six days during which all God did was reveal the six parts of the creation narrative to Adam. This claim is not supported by the commands in the narrative of Genesis 1.

In his "tablet theory," Wiseman says the Genesis creation narrative was passed down on a tablet(s) ending in the *tôl^edôt* of the heavens and the earth. Adam added his narrative, ending in his own *tôl^edôt* in 5:1a. Almost a dozen successive eyewitness tablets, each (except the Joseph narrative) ending with a *tôl^edôt*, were passed down. Moses transcribed these tablets, with minor editing, into Genesis.

Conclusions about the Creation Revealed in Six Days Theory

Wiseman has offered us several key insights. Genesis was composed of ancient eyewitness reports. Each ended with the author's name. Moses received these reports on tablets and edited them into the book of Genesis.

On the other hand, Wiseman had the novel idea that the six days were days when God *told* Adam about the generations of the heavens and the earth. Instead, the six days *were* the six literal days of God's fiat commands making earth lighted, habitable, and inhabited.

We may reject Wiseman's claim that all God did in the six days was talk to Adam about creation. Yet his explanation of the eyewitness source tablets, which Moses later edited into Genesis, seems well supported.

8. Creation Revealed in Six Days Theory

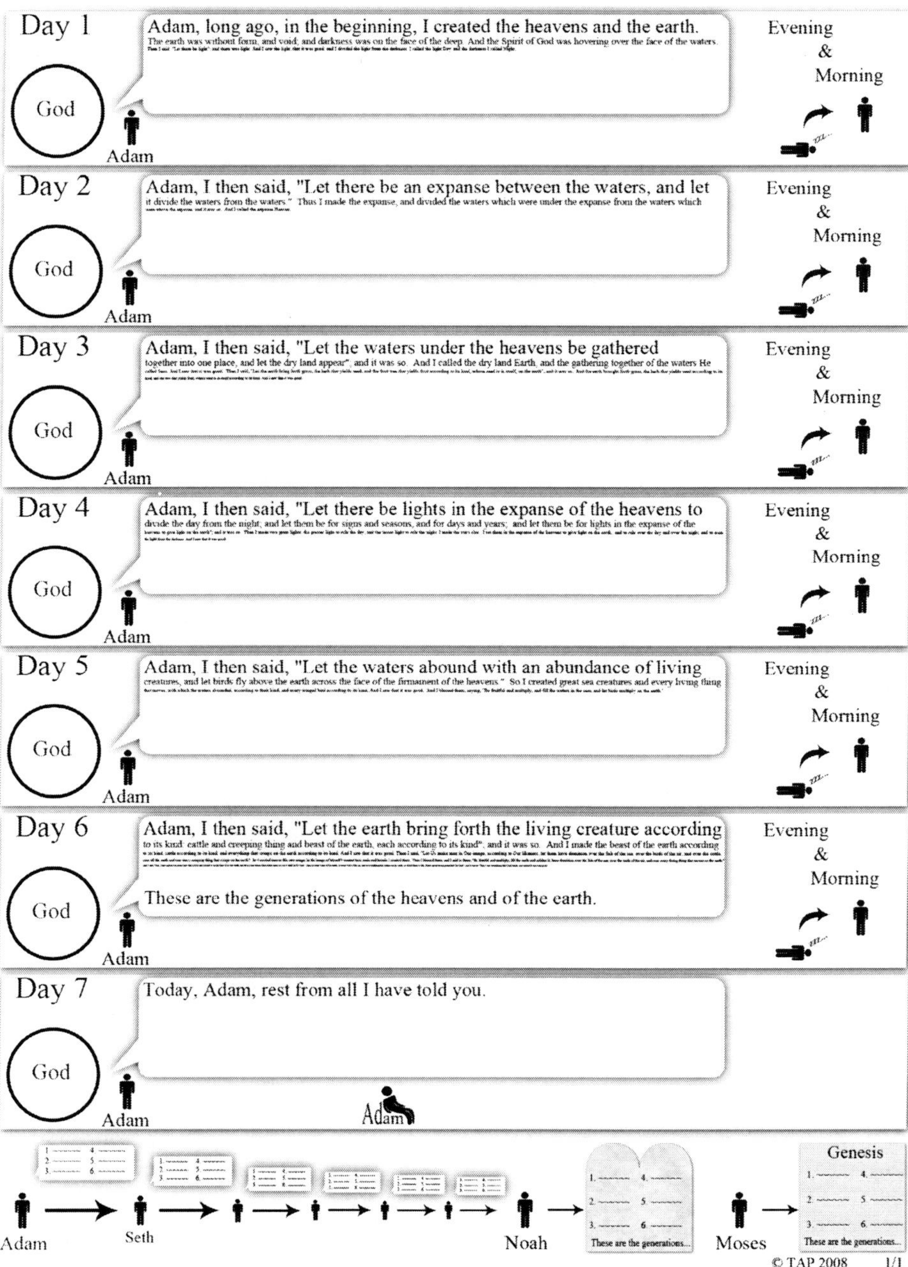

8. Claims of the Creation Revealed in Six Days Theory
(Biblically supported claims in non-italics **bold,** unsupported in *italics*)

(8.1) Genesis 1:1—2:4a is from an ancient source.

    (1a) Isaiah 40:21 implies God gave Adam the narrative.

(8.2) Genesis accounts were passed down to Moses on tablets.

(8.2a) Genesis 1 was generations of the heavens and the earth.

(8.3) Genesis 1 has two parallel parts, ending in the first *tôlᵉdôt*.

(8.4) The six days were normal days, *but they were not creation days.*

    (8.4a) Day-age theory fails to prove days were geologic eras.

    (8.4b) The gap with a first creation of life argues from silence.

    (8.4c) Young earth creation fails—no "*in*" in Exodus 20:11a.

(8.5) *Genesis 1:1—2:4a was not creation in six days but revelation in six days.*

    (8.5a) *In Exodus 20:11, 'āsâh means God "shewed" creation in six days.*

    (8.5b) *In the six days all God did was talk to Adam about creation.*

    (8.5c) *On the seventh day, God ceased "shewing" creation.*

    (8.5d) *On the seventh day, Adam rested from God's six days "shewing" creation.*

Major Supported Claims from the Creation Theories

The Correct Translation of Genesis 1:1: Waltke affirms the traditional translation of Genesis 1:1: "In the beginning God created the heavens and the earth." It is *incorrect* to translate 1:1 as "When God began to create."

Waltke Merism: "The heavens and the earth" meant the entire orderly universe. Also, evening and morning meant the entire nighttime.

The Waltke Exclusion Principle: If there was preexisting chaos, there was no *ex nihilo* creation of the organized heavens and earth. The converse is also logically possible: If there was *ex nihilo* creation of the organized heavens and earth, then there was no unorganized chaos.

The Kline Order: Proverbs 8:22–31 says "the beginning," when God created Earth (Gen. 1:1), was "when there were no depths." There were ocean depths by 1:2, so "In the beginning" was before 1:2 and before the six days. Creation order: heavens, earth, sea, six days.

The Kline Claim: When the Bible does not indicate a miracle, Genesis 2:5–6 (no rain, no plants; rain, then plants sprouted) shows God probably used ordinary means in the creation era, just as today. **Ross Addition:** "An observed attribute of the Creator . . . is His economy of miracles—only what's needed to accomplish His purpose."

The Kline Undated Universe: "We must speak where the Bible speaks, and be silent where the Bible is silent. . . . The inspired text, rightly interpreted, is simply silent with regard to the age of the earth and universe."

A Generational Genesis: The worldview of Genesis was generations. The six begetting (literal) days of Genesis 1 introduced the most ancient generations of all—"the generations of the heavens and the earth."

The Rooker Reaffirmation: "The key difference between pagan cosmogonies and Genesis 1 is *creatio ex nihilo* and the absence of preexisting matter."

The Morris Maxim: In historical narrative, a numbered "day" was a day.

The Morris and Ross Method: The Bible reveals what God did; science may uncover how He did it.

The Morris One Fall Explanation: The creation was perfect. Man and animals were created about 6,000 years ago with eternal physical life. There was "no disorder, no ^Isin and, above all, *no ^Ideath!* Even Satan was still good at this point."[803] His first effect on Earth was the temptation. (There were two falls, but Lucifer's fall had no effect on Earth until his temptation of Eve, resulting in Adam and Eve's Fall.) Adam's Fall resulted in a "cosmic catastrophe" including all human and animal death and subsequent moral and natural evil.

The Kaiser Two Falls Explanation: Standard theology identifies two falls: the angelic fall led by Lucifer, and later the human Fall by Adam. God's concluding "very good" evaluation was about His work on Earth, not about angels such as Lucifer, who had been created and likely fell earlier. Animal death is *not* inherently evil. God Himself killed an animal to cover human nakedness. Any pre-Fall evil aspects of animal disease and death could only have been initiated by fallen Lucifer (Ezek. 28:16–18; Heb. 2:14). Yet by the sixth day, God worked even those together for good or eliminated them until Adam's Fall. Adam was the original cause of human death (Rom. 5:12) and farming woes (Gen. 3:17–19), but Scripture does not say he caused animal death. So animal death may have preceded Adam's Fall. Animal life cycles fit the present noneternal world God created, anticipating human resurrection and the New Creation (Rom. 8:20).

The Ross Resolution: God does not deceive either by His Word or by His creation work. Correctly interpreted, both God's verbal revelation (the Bible) and physical revelation (the created universe) will be in accord.

The Observer's Perspective: Ross says interpret the Genesis 1 creation narrative from the perspective of the Observer/Narrator, the Spirit, hovering just above the surface of the water-covered Earth.

The Ross Apologetic: The Bible alone declares that the universe had a beginning and has been stretching out. Only the Creator could have known these facts long before modern science. The God of the Bible is the Creator, and the Bible is His accurate message to us.

The Ross-Schroeder Fine-Tuning Evidence: The ^Ifine-tuning of the universe and Earth for humans is evidence of the Designer, not chance.

The Wiseman Tablet Theory: The Genesis narratives were eyewitness reports recorded on tablets received by Moses. The name of each author was at the *end* of his narrative.

The Wiseman-Gray 20:11 Recognition: Exodus 20:11a has no "in," allowing the natural grammatical reading of Genesis 1:1 as the initial creation of the actual heavens and planet Earth "in the beginning" before the six days.

Chapter 9

Theory 9
Gap or Creation-Ruin-Restoration Theory

Distinguish trash from treasure.

Have you ever seen pictures of miners panning for gold during the gold rush? If they could tell garbage from gold, trash from treasure, they might strike it rich!

With the gap theory, we must be like miners panning for gold. Hebrew scholars have realized that the *gap* in the gap theory is incorrect. But then young earth scientific creationism advocates threw out the whole gap theory as *all* wrong. But *all* wrong is not what the Hebrew scholars said. There is garbage, the "gap," and yet, as in all the theories, if we take the time to sift the elements of the gap theory, we will find among the garbage gold nuggets of Bible truth.

A Brief History of the Gap or Creation-Ruin-Restoration Theory

Thomas Chalmers (1780–1847), a brilliant mathematician and caring pastor, first presented the creation-ruin-restoration or gap theory in lectures in Scotland. Chalmer's idea was carried on by William Buckland, who championed a geological view known as Neptunism, which claimed a catastrophic Lucifer's flood ended ancient life in a time gap at Genesis 1:2. Scottish geologist Hugh Miller published Chalmer's theory in *The Testimony of the Rocks*.[804]

At the end of the nineteenth century, George H. Pember contributed *Earth's Earliest Ages,* which is still in print.[805] Most recently, Arthur Custance, in *Without Form and Void,* defended the gap theory's claim that Genesis 1:2 should be translated, "And the earth had become without form and void."[806] Merrill Unger realized the grammar of verse 2 does not allow a time gap at Genesis 1:2, but he did not form a widely accepted substitute theory.[807]

When Bruce Waltke conclusively showed that a gap in 1:2 and the translation "had become" (in place of "was") are incorrect grammatically, the theory began to die. The gap is incorrect, but before and after the gap are nuggets of Biblical insight.

In a nutshell, the gap theory says that in the beginning God created the heavens and the earth. In a long time gap at Genesis 1:2, He created vast ancient life on earth. Earth was under Lucifer's rule, but Lucifer fell, resulting in death, diseases, and disasters. After untold millions of years of patience, God finally judged Earth with "Lucifer's flood," which destroyed all that ancient life, turning much of it into fossils. So Earth *became* chaotic, ocean-covered, and dark. Leaving the fossil record in place, in six literal days God restored Earth and re-created life on Earth.

Three Stages of the Gap or Creation-Ruin-Restoration Theory

Stage one: Gap theory advocate Custance recognizes stages in the creation. "The *first* stage of God's creative activity" was the initial creation in Genesis 1:1. Buckland said, "The first verse of Genesis seems explicitly to assert the creation of the Universe, the heavens, including the sidereal systems [of stars] and the earth, more especially our own planet."[808]

Stage two: "Millions and millions of years may have occupied the indefinite interval, between the beginning in which God created the heavens and the earth and the . . . commencement of the first day." Custance explains that this second stage was a first creation of life, but then the fall of Lucifer resulted in animal death, diseases, and disasters. Led by Lucifer, the pre-Adamites (pre-Adam men such as Neanderthal) fell too. After untold millions of years, God judged Earth. By this "Lucifer's flood" judgment, all life was destroyed. All that was left was the "chaos which resulted from some catastrophic event marring what had formerly been an orderly and beautiful world."[809] "Verse 2 described a ruin and not a first stage in the creative process."[810] Buckland says the result "may be geologically considered as designating the wreck and ruins of a former world."[811] So Earth "became" "formless and void." Earth was covered with water and its sea surface was darkened by cloud as recorded in Genesis 1:2. Yet the fossil record remained.

The third stage was the recent six literal, normal days of restoration. God reconstituted Earth and re-created new life, unrelated to the gap life. The ancient fossil record from Lucifer's flood remained.

These are the gap theory's preunderstandings and claims:

Preunderstandings of the Three Stage Gap Theory

(9.0A) Tōhû vᵃbōhû *in Genesis 1:2 means "chaos."* Most gap theory advocates assume *tōhû vᵃbōhû* in Genesis 1:2 means chaos. Unger titles his section "Order Out of Chaos." Custance repeatedly speaks of chaos resulting from a "catastrophic event marring what had formerly been an orderly and beautiful world."[812] Both Unger and Custance assume chaos.

(9.0B) *God could not have created chaos (the initial chaos theory), so Earth became chaos (the gap theory).* Since *tōhû vᵃbōhû* means chaos, then a chaos option must be true. Merrill Unger explains:

> If Genesis 1:1 refers to the original creation of the universe out of nothing, Genesis 1:2 must either be construed to be the original chaotic state in which the earth was created [initial chaos theory] or to be the result of a subsequent judgment [gap theory]. But the first interpretation [initial chaos theory that God created chaos] is contradicted by both Scripture and theology.[813]

Custance agrees:

> Essentially, there are two possible interpretations of Gen. 1:2. Either it is a chaos which marks the *first* stage of God's creative activity [the initial chaos theory that God created chaos in 1:1], or it is a chaos which resulted from some catastrophic event marring what had formerly been an orderly and beautiful world [the gap theory].[814]

Therefore, the starting point of the creation-ruin-restoration or gap theory is the assumption that the only Biblical option is that Earth "became" chaos.

The Main Alternative Theory Has a Fatal Flaw:
The initial creation theory (including young earth creationism) claims God created chaos or unformed chaotic matter.

But God is a God of order, so He does not create chaos.

(9.0C) *Study Scripture and creation independently; both, correctly interpreted, ultimately will agree.* Custance says:

> If we are once sure what a particular passage is saying, we should not allow science to determine for us—and I am speaking as a scientist—what we may believe in Scripture; nor are we to allow a clear statement of Scripture to determine what the scientist may observe in his laboratory. Demonstrable fact in the one cannot ultimately conflict with demonstrable fact in the other, though

interpretations often do. Where a conflict of evidence seems to exist, we must search for some means of reconciliation: failing this, we need not abandon either piece of evidence if we are reasonably sure of both, but only wait for further light.[815]

Claims of the Three Stage Gap Theory

Creation was in three stages. *Stage one*: God created the heavens and earth during the beginning time period in 1:1. *Stage two*: In a time gap at Genesis 1:2, God made a first creation of land, plants, animals, and pre-Adamites under the headship of Lucifer. But Lucifer fell into sin. After millions of years of patience, God judged Lucifer and the Earth, killing all life. *Stage three*: In six literal normal days, God restored Earth, re-created all life, and created man.

(9.1) *Stage one was God's* **ex nihilo** *creation of the organized heavens and earth in the beginning time period of Genesis 1:1, before the six days.* Gap theory advocates take Genesis 1:1 literally: "In the beginning God created the heavens and the earth." God created the literal heavens and literal earth, and He did so before the six literal days.

(9.1a) *The "beginning" was the beginning time period before day one.* The creation of the heavens and earth was a "period anterior to the first day."[816] The beginning was not an instant but rather a time period of "some unstated amount."[817]

(9.1b) *God created the heavens and the earth before the six days. So the young earth creation claim that 1:1 took place in the six days about 6,000 years ago is incorrect.* Gap theory advocate Pember says, "We are told that in the beginning God created the heavens and the earth; but the Scriptures never affirm that He did this in the six days."[818] "The work of the six days . . . began in verse 3."[819] Custance cites Thomas Aquinas (1226–1274): "*Sedmelior videtur dicendum quod creatio fuerit aute omnem diem.*"[820] ("It seems better to maintain that creation was prior to any day.") Aquinas agrees with this first claim, but he was *not* a gap theory advocate.

John Harris in *The Pre-Adamite Earth,* explained:

Now, that the originating act, described in the first verse, was not meant to be included in the account of the six Adamic days, is evident from the following considerations: first, the creation of the second, third, fourth, fifth and sixth days begins with the formula, "And God said." It is only natural, therefore, to conclude that the creation of the first day begins with the third verse where the said formula first occurs, "And God said, 'let there be light.'" But if so, it follows that the act described in the first verse, and the state of the earth spoken of in the second verse, must both have belonged to a period anterior to the first day.[821]

One may wonder if YEC's adamant opposition to the entire gap theory may be because gap theory advocates pointed out the error of YEC's third claim long before I did.

(9.1c) *The beginning was a period of time of unstated length before the six days, so the beginning is undated by the Bible.* "The work of the six days . . . began in verse 3,"[822] but the initial creation took place in 1:1, an "unstated amount" of time before the six days; therefore, "the writings of Moses do not fix the antiquity of the globe."[823]

The previous quote by Thomas Aquinas shows that he and other earlier theologians "would not have agreed with Ussher that Creation occurred 4000 BC," says Custance. He continues, "They might very probably have assented to his chronology as applied to the creation of *Adam* but they would have set the creation of the Universe (the heavens and the earth) further back in time by some unstated amount. Genesis 1.2 does NOT represent the condition of things immediately after the initial creation . . . but some time later"[824] (emphasis his). The creation of the heavens and earth occurred "some unstated amount" of time before the six days, so that initial creation of the heavens and earth in Genesis 1:1 is undated by the Bible.

(9.1d) *The original "bārā'" creation out of nothing was different from six-day primarily "'āsâh" fashioning work. So the young earth creationism claim that the terms are used interchangeably in Genesis 1 is incorrect.* Buckland said, "By the *bārā'* creation in Genesis 1:1 we understand that . . . the Universe is not eternal and self-existent, but was originally created by the power of the Almighty."[825]

Buckland said, "The work of those [six] days was . . . quite a different thing from the original creation."[826] "*Asah* is generally used in connection with them [the work of the six days]." "Now *asah* signifies to make, fashion, or prepare out of existing material; as for instance, to build a ship, erect a house, or prepare a meal."[827]

Pember explains that there were two additional *bārā'* ("create") acts in the six days. "God is said to have created the inhabitants of the waters and the fowls of heaven." By this *bārā'* ("created") act, God gave the first animals a "life force." "Just in the same way man is said to have been created, though in the second chapter we are expressly told that his body was formed from dust" (Gen. 1:27; 2:7).[828] Adam's spirit was *bārā'*, created, out of nothing. But the verb in 2:7, *yatzar,* which means "to shape," indicates that God shaped Adam's body from already existing materials. God *bārā'* ("created") the heavens and earth, the soulish aspect of animals, and the soul/spirit of man out of nothing. God also worked to shape already created materials, described by *'āsâh* ("do, make") and *yātsar.* The young earth scientific creationism claim that *bārā'* ("create") and *'āsâh* ("do, make") are used interchangeably in the creation is incorrect.

(9.1e) *God created the orderly literal heavens and earth in 1:1; so the YEC claim that God created only their raw materials errs.* Pember explains, "God, then, in the beginning created the heaven and the earth, not merely the materials out of which they were afterwards formed. . . . The heavens mentioned in the first verse of Genesis is the starry heaven, not the firmament [atmosphere] immediately surrounding the earth."[829] God created the orderly starry heavens and earth, not chaotic raw materials, by His *ex nihilo* work described by the verb *bārā'* ("create") in Genesis 1:1. YEC is incorrect in its claim that only the raw material, "earth," was created in 1:1. YEC is also incorrect that planet Earth was made in day three, and the luminaries in day four from the raw material "earth."

If we take Genesis 1:1 literally,
then God literally created the literal heavens
and literal (unfinished) earth in the literal beginning
before the six literal days.

(9.1f) *Only Earth was described in 1:2 as* tōhû vᵃbōhû; *so the YEC claim that the universe was chaos is incorrect.* Pember explains that Genesis 1:2 changes the subject from "the heavens and earth" to the condition of "the earth." *Tōhû vᵃbōhû,* meaning "desolate" and "empty," described Earth. So God's work in the six days "did not affect the sidereal heaven, but only the earth and its immediate surroundings."[830] The initial chaos and young earth theories' claim that the universe was *tōhû vᵃbōhû* is completely incorrect. Genesis 1:2 explicitly says, "And the earth was *tōhû vᵃbōhû.*"

(9.1g) *Genesis 1:2 shows that 1:1 is not a mere title or summary; 1:1 was the actual creation, so the title/summary theory errs.* Pember explains, "If it [1:1] were a mere summary, the second verse would be the actual commencement of the history and certainly would not begin with a copulative." But Genesis 1:2 does begin with the copulative *vav/waw* disjunctive "and." Because "Now the earth" describes Earth's *tōhû vᵃbōhû* condition in 1:2, Earth had to have been created in 1:1 to have been *tōhû v^ʾbōhû* in 1:2.

The Bible contains summary verses. Genesis 2:4a and Genesis 5:1a complete and summarize the creation and Adam narratives. In both cases, "the next sentence begins without a copulative," but rather with *b^ʿyôm,* "when," followed by the action verb.[831] Genesis 1:1 does not match these summaries in 2:4a or 5:1a. Nor does Genesis 1:2 match 2:4b or 5:1b. The grammatical evidence is against 1:1 being a title or summary and the first act occurring in 1:2. God's first act was the *ex nihilo* creation in Genesis 1:1. So 1:1 is *not* a title.

Gap theory advocates have shown that the initial chaos theory, and title theory err. So they conclude the gap theory is the last theory standing.

(9.2) *Stage two was a long time gap at Genesis 1:2 when God first created life; Lucifer's fall resulted in animal death; and finally God judged Earth, so it became chaos.* Stage two in this three stage gap theory was a very long time gap (millions of years) at Genesis 1:2 during which God first created life. That life flourished. But Lucifer fell into evil. The fall of Satan is described in Isaiah 14:12–17. The gap theory places his fall at Genesis 1:2. Lucifer's fall resulted in animal death, diseases, and destructive "natural" disasters. After much patience, God finally judged Lucifer, the Earth, and its inhabitants, destroying all life. Many of the dead plants and animals formed fossils. So Earth "became" *tōhû v^ʾbōhû,* but the old fossil record remained.

(9.2a) *The verb "was" in Genesis 1:2 should be translated "became": "And the earth became* tōhû v^ʾbōhû.*"* Pember claims, "The verb translated 'was' is occasionally used with a simple accusative in the sense of 'to be made' or 'became.'"[832] Gap theory advocates cite several examples of the verb *hāy^ʿtā^h* from *hāyâh,* "to be," being translated as "became." Custance points to Genesis 3:20 in the NIV, which translates *hāy^ʿtā^h* as "would become": "Adam named his wife Eve, because she would become [*hāy^ʿtā^h* from *hāyâ^h*] the mother of all the living." Pember tells us that Lot's wife "became [*t^ʿhî* from *hāyâ^h*] a pillar of salt" (Gen. 19:26, NIV). Then he says, "We may therefore adopt it [the "became" meaning from Gen. 19:26] and render [Gen. 1:2], 'And the earth became desolate and void; and darkness was upon the face of the deep.'"[833] Arthur Custance goes to great lengths in his book *Without Form and Void: A Study of the Meaning of Genesis 1:2* to attempt to establish that *hāy^ʿtā^h* in Genesis 1:2 may mean "had become" in some contexts.

Also, both Pember and Custance point out that Isaiah 45:18 says, "God did not create the earth a *tohu*."[834] God did not create Earth desolate. "We see, then, that God created the heavens and earth perfect and beautiful in their beginning, and that at some subsequent period, how remote we cannot tell, the earth had passed into a state of utter desolation, and was void of all life. . . . Not merely had its fruitful places become a wilderness, and all its cities been broken down, but the very light of its sun had been withdrawn. . . . The ruined planet, covered above its very mountain tops with the black floods of destruction, was rolling though space in a horror of great darkness."[835]

(9.2b) *The gap occurred in or around Genesis 1:2, but gap theory advocates disagree precisely when.* Pember seems to claim a gap of time *during* Genesis 1:2. Many gap theory advocates and the popular Scofield Bible claim a time gap at the *beginning* of 1:2 with judgment described in 1:2. Unger argues for a gap *before* Genesis 1:1, so 1:1 describes the re-creation.

(9.2c) *Lucifer was head of Earth's ancient pre-Adamites and animal life in the time gap.* Pember claims, "But who were these ancient possessors of the lands? . . . It is our own great enemy, the Prince of this World and of the Power of the Air."[836] Satan, or Lucifer, alone holds the title "Prince of this World" (John 12:31; 14:30; 16:11). In Ephesians 2:2, Paul calls him "the Prince of the Power of the Air."[837] Lucifer was in charge of the Genesis 1:2 world.

Pember says Ezekiel 28:11–19 is about one who is "possessed and energized by the devil in person. He will be a compound being, partly human partly superhuman; at once the king of Tyre and the Anointed Cherub that covereth; a travesty by Satan of the incarnation of our Lord."[838] In Ezekiel 28, this individual came to Eden as a minister of God. "Hence the Eden of this passage," says Pember, "must have been of a far earlier date," a pre-Adamite Eden in the "gap" at Genesis 1:2. The decorations described in Ezekiel 28 were as of a royal or a priest or an angelic minister of God. "Satan as the great governing head and the viceroy of the Almighty, assisted by glorious beings of his own nature, ruled over the sinless dwellers upon earth."[839]

(9.2d) *Lucifer and later Adam, not God, are the causes of all evil. Lucifer caused animal death and "natural" disasters; what God made was very good; Adam's Fall caused human death.* This is a proposed solution to the problem of evil. "The next verse shows that God is not the Author of evil (Ezek. Xxviii. 15). For even the Prince of Darkness was by creation perfect in all his ways, and so continued, until iniquity was found in him and he fell."[840] "Then, doubtless corruption appeared among his angels, and so descended to those who were in the flesh. How long God bore with this; what warnings He gave; whether any availed themselves of His mercy,"[841] we do not know.

Pember explains that the Bible speaks of "him who had the power of death, that is, the devil" (Heb. 2:14, NASB). The devil had the power of death, both spiritual and physical. Lucifer was given headship over this world as "the prince of this world." Lucifer's sin caused massive death and disaster in the world under his headship.

Genesis 1:31 says, "And God saw all that He had made, and behold, it was very good" (NASB). All God made was good, just as all that God does today in our fallen world is good. YEC raises the question, How could God say "very good" if all those bones were in the ground from animal death before Adam sinned?

The gap theory answers that this massive animal death was from Lucifer's sin. Genesis 1:31 does not say *all things* were very good, but "God saw all that He had made, and behold, it was very good." God did not make dead animals. Lucifer did. So God rightly said that all *He* made was "very good" because all He made (and makes today even in our fallen world) is always good. Lucifer's sin caused evil, animal death, and earth disaster.

Much later at Adam's sin, death came to Adam's race under *his* headship. Romans 5:12 says, "Therefore, just as through one man sin entered into the world, and death through sin, and so death spread to all men, because all sinned" (NASB). Adam was that "one man" by whom "sin entered into the world." Lucifer, by whom sin entered earlier, is not a man. Adam's sin spread specifically to *all men* (not all men and animals). In the curse, God said, "To dust you [Adam, and so Adam's race] shall return" (Gen. 3:19, NASB). Humans die because Adam, head of the human race, sinned.

But sin was already in the world before Adam sinned, because fallen Lucifer was in the world before Adam sinned. Two beings introduced sin into the world: Lucifer, head over the world and its nonhuman life, and the man Adam, head of the human race. The curse on Adam does not mention animal death. So animal death had already been caused by Lucifer's fall. Pember emphasizes that Hebrews 2:14 says the devil has "the power of death." Fossils came from real ancient animals that died because Lucifer introduced sin, disaster, and death into the animal world. First Lucifer and later Adam committed sin, resulting in animal death and human death respectively. (For a comparison of sin and death options, see chapter 13.)

The Pember "Problem of Evil" Solution: Animal death is evil. Lucifer and later Adam, not God, were the original causes of evil, death, diseases, and "natural" disasters (although God sovereignly allows evil and even works it together for good for His people and purposes).

(9.2e) *God waited patiently but finally judged Earth because of the sin of Lucifer and the pre-Adamites.* Pember says Psalm 82 referred to God's judgment in the ancient past in a gap at Genesis 1:2. In that ancient time, God judged these spirit rulers (led by Lucifer) for their ancient evil rule over pre-Adamites. The results in Psalm 82:7 were darkness and the foundations of Earth being shaken. So Pember says Earth "became" *tōhû vᵃbōhû* at Genesis 1:2.

Pember adds, "Sin must have been the cause of this hideous ruin." "For as the fossils clearly show, not only were disease and death—inseparable companions of sin—then prevalent among the living creatures of the earth, but even ferocity and slaughter."[842]

(9.2f) *Isaiah 34:11 and Jeremiah 4:23, with* tōhû vᵃbōhû, *were judgment texts, so* tōhû vᵃbōhû *in Genesis 1:2 was God's judgment.* Gap theory advocates claim that Isaiah 34:11 and Jeremiah 4:23, the only other texts containing both *tōhû* and *bōhû,* were judgment texts. So Genesis 1:2 must have been a judgment text too. Therefore, God's judgment produced chaos in Genesis 1:2.

(9.2g) *All pre-Adamite life died in a "Lucifer's flood" or ice age or both.* God judged that wicked pre-Adamite world, so all pre-Adamite life died. William Buckland was influenced by Louis Agassiz's ice age theory. Pember follows in that thinking: "Now the withdrawal of the sun's influence had probably occasioned that glacial period. . . . No animal or vegetable could resist such a frost."[843] Later, "the ice must have broken up—perhaps through some development of the earth's internal heat, which in its convulsive struggles may also have displaced the bed of ocean. Thus the whole globe was covered with water, on the surface of which the spirit of God was already brooding."[844]

(9.2.h) *Fossils were left from pre-Adamite life that was unrelated to today's life.* Pember claims, "We have before seen that neither the plants of the Third nor the creatures of the Fifth and Sixth days have anything to do with the fossilized remains bound in the earth's crust; because the crust is assumed to have been formed before the great pre-Adamite catastrophe."[845] Arthur Custance explains that there was no genetic connection between the life before the catastrophe and the newly created life from the six days. So the gap theory explains the prehistoric fossils as an ancient destruction, yet keeps the six literal days as a re-creation.

(9.3) *Stage three was six literal days when God restored planet Earth and re-created all new life kinds, leaving the old fossils.* Next would be the "six days of restoration."[846]

(9.3a) *The six days were normal day-night days. So the long day-age eras theory is incorrect.* The six days were six normal day-night days, because with "a numeral . . . it can only be used in its literal acceptation of the time which the earth takes to make one revolution upon its axis. . . . It is clear, therefore, that we must understand the Six Days to be six periods of twenty-four hours each."[847]

"Doubtless the word 'day' is sometimes used of prolonged periods, as in the expression 'the day of temptation in the wilderness,' and many others," Pember explains. "But whenever a numeral is connected with it [*yôm*] the meaning is at once restricted thereby, and it can only be used in its literal acceptation of the time which the earth takes to make one revolution upon its axis."[848]

Regarding the day-age view, Pember asks, "Was each geologic age divided into two long intervals, one all darkness, the other all light?"[849] If so, how could plants survive? The claim of long geological era "days" in the day-age theory is incorrect.

(9.3b) *Day one: God commanded, "Light be."* "The command went forth 'Light be.' . . . God called the light day and the darkness night and that the evening and the morning were the First Day."[850] The light was sunlight piercing Earth's dense clouds.

(9.3c) *Second day: God commanded the formation of open atmosphere between cloud and sea waters.* On the second day at God's command "the firmament, or atmosphere which we breathe, was formed," "inserted" between the cloud water above and the ocean water upon Earth.[851]

(9.3d) *Third day: God gathered the sea so dry land appeared; then He caused the land to sprout vegetation.* The "grand movement" causing land to rise is described in Psalm 104:6–9 (apparently translated by Pember):

> 6. With the deep as with a garment Thou didst cover it,
>   Above the mountains did the waters stand,
> 7. At Thy rebuke they fled,
>   At the voice of Thy thunder they hasted away —
> 8. The mountains rose, the valleys sank —
>   To the place which Thou hadst established for them.
> 9. Thou hast set them a bound which they cannot pass,
>   That they turn not again to cover the earth.

God did not "create" the dry land but caused it to rise from the ocean, to "appear" as "the mountains rose, the valleys sank."[852]

"The word of God went forth a second time, and the now liberated soil began to cover itself with a garment of vegetation."[853]

(9.3e) *Fourth day: God established Earth's relations with the heavenly bodies created in Genesis 1:1 so they could serve their purposes to Earth.* Pember explains, "It remained only to establish its [Earth's] relations with the heavenly bodies." God, "apparently, so altered or modified the firmament" to bring about this relation of the heavenly bodies to Earth. "Now we must carefully observe that God is not said to have created these light-holders on the Fourth Day, but merely to have made or prepared them. They were created, as we have seen, in the beginning. . . . It was doubtless around its [the sun's] mass that the earth was revolving from the first." The stars were "not created" on the fourth day either, says Pember, because "the morning stars were admiring witnesses when God laid the foundation stone of the earth, and sang together for joy at its completion (Job xxxviii.4–7). They must, therefore, have been preexistent" from their creation in 1:1. The fourth day's work "had reference only to . . . our firmament, to the purpose which they [the luminaries] were to serve in regard to our earth."[854]

The mechanism is stated in the New Scofield Reference Bible: "The sun and moon were created 'in the beginning.' The 'light' of course came from the sun, but the vapor diffused the light. Later [on the fourth day] the sun appeared in an unclouded sky."[855]

(9.3f) *Fifth day: God caused the waters to swarm with living creatures and flyers to inhabit the air.* For a fifth day, Pember says, "the literal rendering" is, "Let the waters swarm with swarms, with living creatures."[856] And for the second part, "And let fowl fly above the earth in the face of the firmament of heaven." He concludes, "Sea and air were thus filled with life."[857]

(9.3g) *The sixth day: God caused the land to produce three classes of animals and God created man.* God caused the land to produce "three classes of living creatures—cattle or domesticated animals, creeping things, . . . and beasts of the field or wild roaming animals." God created man "in His image and after His likeness."[858]

These were the "Six Days of restoration."[859]

(9.3h) *The seventh day: God instituted rest.* "Then follows the institution of the Sabbath on the Seventh Day." Thus, a day of rest in each week (but not necessarily the Sabbath) was God's example for all people.[860]

(9.3i) *The "generations" statement in Genesis 2:4a is a summary of Genesis 1*. Pember explains, "This wondrous history closes with a summary of the subject and an introduction to the next part in these words: 'These are "the generations of the heavens and the earth.""'[861] These generations summarize the whole of Genesis 1.

(9.3j) *Genesis 1 and 2 are not contradictory*. "While chapter one gives a continuous history of the week," in chapter two "reference is made to other works of the Six Days only when . . . connected with the main subject."[862] Then any alleged discrepancies disappear.

So the gap theory may be summarized as three stages. First, "In the beginning God created the heavens and the earth," understood literally as the heavens of sun, moon, and stars, and planet Earth.

Second, a long time gap of many millions of years occurred at Genesis 1:2. During this gap, God created vast "prehistoric" life. But Lucifer fell, resulting in animal death, diseases, and the destruction by "natural" disasters. Pre-Adamites became evil under Lucifer's headship. Eventually, God judged Lucifer and all ancient life, resulting in fossils. So Earth *became* desolate and empty of life, yet the fossil record remained.

Third, recently in six literal restoration days, God reconstituted Earth and re-created life.

Unsupported Claims of the Three Stage Gap Theory

The entire second stage of the gap theory inserted at Genesis 1:2 has no basis in the Bible. But first, there are two related problematic pre-understandings.

(u-9.0A) Tōhû vᵃbōhû *in Genesis 1:2 means "chaos."* Most gap theory advocates assume that *tōhû vᵃbōhû* in Genesis 1:2 means "chaos." Since God did not create chaos, Earth must have *become* chaos.

Pember alone, of all the gap advocates, disagrees. He correctly recognizes the pagan source of the idea of chaos: "The ancient poet Hesiod [about 900 BC] tells us that the first thing in existence was Chaos."[863] Pember says the translation of *tōhû vᵃbōhû* as "without form and void" "is not the sense of the Hebrew, but a glaring illustration of the influence of the chaos-legend."[864] Gnostics influenced true Christianity with this same idea of initial chaos.

Contra this chaos error, Pember correctly translates *tōhû* as "desolation" and *bōhû* as "'that which is empty,' probably with reference to the absence of all life."[865]

Pember is correct: there was no chaos. The claim by most gap theory advocates that *tōhû vᵃbōhû* meant chaos is incorrect.

(u-9.0B) *God could not have created chaos (the initial chaos theory), so Earth became chaos (the gap theory).* Custance says, "There are two possible interpretations of Gen. 1:2. Either it is a chaos which marks the *first* stage of God's creative activity [the initial chaos theory that God created chaos in 1:1], or it is a chaos which resulted from some catastrophic event [the gap theory]."[866]

In response, if *tōhû vᵃbōhû* does not mean chaos, then the claim "either created chaos or 'became' chaos" is an either/or fallacy, ignoring the option of *no* chaos. Earth neither was created as chaos nor became chaos. There was no chaos.

(u-9.2) *Stage two was a long time gap at Genesis 1:2 when God first created life; Lucifer's fall resulted in animal death; and finally God judged Earth, so it became chaos.* Stage two in this three stage gap theory claims a long time gap at Genesis 1:2 during which God first created life, but Lucifer fell into sin, resulting in evil, animal death, diseases, and destructive "natural" disasters. Then God judged Lucifer, the Earth, and its inhabitants, destroying all life but leaving the old fossil record.

Many people have suggested that this gap is inserted, not based on the Bible, but to fit the fossil record. This gap with its first creation and destruction of life is the unique essential claim of the gap theory, but it lacks Biblical evidence.

(u-9.2a) *The verb "was" in Genesis 1:2 should be translated "became": "And the earth became* tōhû vᵃbōhû." Pember claims, "The verb translated 'was' is occasionally used with a simple accusative in the sense of 'to be made' or 'became.'"[867] "'And the earth became desolate and void; and darkness was upon the face of the deep.'"[868]

I will respond briefly.[869] The "became" translation in the verse Pember claims is parallel, Genesis 19:26 about Lot's wife, is *imperfect,* which may mean "became." But the "was" verb in Genesis 1:2 is *perfect.* So it should be translated "was" unless it has a *la'med* prefix. It has no prefix, so it is correctly translated "was."

Genesis 1:2a begins with the *waw/vav* disjunctive "and/now" prefixing "the earth." That "now" starts a sentence that is made of three circumstantial clauses. These describe three circumstances on Earth: (1) Earth was uninhabitable and uninhabited, (2) darkness was on the surface of the deep ocean, (3) and the Spirit was hovering over the surface of the waters.

Technical note – *Waw/vav* consecutive and *waw/vav* disjunctive:
* A *waw/vav* consecutive series indicates historical narrative.
  o The first verb is not prefixed with a *waw/vav*.
  o Each consecutive event begins with a *vav* prefixed verb.
* *Waw/vav* disjunctive interrupts with a *vav* prefixed non-verb.
  o As a circumstantial description, it does not include action.
  o It indicates a shift in scene. Genesis 1:2 shifts to Earth alone.
* Examples from Genesis 1 (all but v. 2 are *vav* consecutives):
  o v. 1 The first act is by verb *bārā'*, "created," without *vav*.
  o v. 2 A disjunctive *vav* prefixed noun, *vehā'āretz*, "now the earth."
    * 1st circumstance – Earth was *tōhû v^ebōhû*.
    * 2nd circumstance – surface of the deep ocean was dark.
    * 3rd circumstance – Spirit was hovering over waters.
  o v. 3a Next act, *vav* prefixed verb, *vayomer*, "and said."
  o v. 3b Next act, *vav* prefixed verb, *vayehi*, "and was."
  o v. 4a Next act, *vav* prefixed verb, *vayare*, "and saw."
  o Etc.

Genesis 1:2 is a description, so the "to be" verb means "was." A *waw/vav* prefixed disjunctive sentence of circumstantial clauses does not contain action. Pember's claim that we may translate the verb in 1:2 as "became" (so that 1:2 was an action) is grammatically highly unlikely. The three descriptive circumstantial clauses contain no action. There was no event at Genesis 1:2. The gap theory's main claim of numerous major events at 1:2 is grammatically highly improbable. (There are other kinds of disjunctive clause that do contain actions, but Genesis 1:2 is not one of them.)

Pember and Custance both quote Isaiah 45:18: "God did not create the earth a *tohu*."[870] They claim that if God did not create Earth desolate, then Earth had to have "become" *tōhû* by Lucifer's fall.

However, Isaiah 45:18 may be translated as in the NIV, "He did not create it to be empty, but formed it to be inhabited," which indicates future intent and solves the problem. At the end of the creation of Earth in Genesis 1:1, verse 2 describes Earth as uninhabitable and uninhabited. But God's purpose was that by the sixth day of His work, Earth would be both habitable and inhabited.

Genesis 1:1 was the beginning *ex nihilo* creation time period. Genesis 1:2 was a description, not a middle time period. The six days of Genesis 1:3–31 were the time period of the completion of Earth. There were only *two* time periods in creation, consisting of the beginning and the six days, *not three*. There was no gap.

(u-9.2b) *The gap occurred in or around Genesis 1:2, but gap theory advocates disagree precisely when.* Pember claims a gap of time took place *during* Genesis 1:2. Many gap theory advocates, including the Scofield Bible, claim a gap occurred at the beginning of 1:2. Unger argues from silence for a gap *before* Genesis 1:1.

This lack of agreement suggests there is a fundamental problem with the gap in the gap theory. Gap theory advocates ignore the obvious solution that there was no gap.

(u-9.2c & 9.2e) *Lucifer ruled the ancient pre-Adamite Earth in the gap at 1:2. Lucifer fell, leading them into evil with him. Eventually, God judged Earth.* Lucifer as the head of the pre-Adamite world led that world into evil. Pember claims that Ezekiel 28:11–19 refers to this "pre-Adamite Eden" at Genesis 1:2, at the end of which there was the pre-Adamite "destruction."[871] So Earth "became" *tōhû vᵃbōhû*.

However, Pember's interpretation is incorrect, because Eden is not mentioned in Genesis 1:1–2. The *land* of Eden did not even appear until God made the dry land appear in Genesis 1:9. Eden is not even mentioned until Genesis 2:8.

Finally, neither Genesis 1:1–2 nor any other Bible text says Lucifer fell or was judged at 1:2. Text evidence suggests when Lucifer fell, but that *cannot* have been at Genesis 1:2. Grammatically, Genesis 1:2 is a description of Earth's unfinished dark condition, not a time period of events such as a first creation of life, fall of Lucifer, a first judgment, and destruction of all that first life.

(u-9.2f) *Isaiah 34:11 and Jeremiah 4:23, with* tōhû vᵃbōhû, *were judgment texts, so* tōhû vᵃbōhû *in Genesis 1:2 was God's judgment.* Gap theory advocates claim that since Isaiah 34:11 and Jeremiah 4:23 were judgment texts, then Genesis 1:2 must have been a judgment too. So Lucifer's sin and God's judgment produced chaos.

In response, *tōhû vᵃbōhû* in Isaiah 34:11 and Jeremiah 4:23 are "verbal allusions" back to Genesis 1:2. In judgment God allowed Edom and Judah to be conquered, so the land became *tōhû vᵃbōhû*, or uninhabitable and uninhabited. *But an allusion works in only one direction.* Genesis 1:2 is used as an illustration of the much later conquered condition of Edom and Judah. It is *not legitimate* to import the later historical contexts of Isaiah and Jeremiah *back* into the original very different historical context of Genesis 1:2. So *tōhû vᵃbōhû* back in Genesis 1:2 does not mean chaos from judgment.

Second, the grammar of Genesis 1:2 is descriptive. Judgment is an action, so does not fit 1:2. Instead, Earth was simply described in 1:2 as desolate or uninhabitable and empty of life.

(**u-9.2g**) *All pre-Adamite life died in a "Lucifer's flood" or ice age or both.* God judged that wicked pre-Adamite world, so all pre-Adamite life died. God judged Lucifer. Pember says Psalm 82 refers to God's judgment of Lucifer in the time gap at Genesis 1:2.

In response, Psalm 82 is unusual. It is about the great assembly God presides over to judge among spirit beings. In Psalm 82:2 and 8 the psalmist was still calling for God to judge. The judgment had *not yet happened*. Genesis 3:15 predicts judgment of the serpent as the embodiment of Lucifer, but that judgment of Lucifer would be future to the psalmist. John 16:11 states, "In regard to judgment, because the prince of this world now stands condemned [κέκριται, perfect passive]" (NIV). Lucifer, the prince of this world, was condemned by Christ's work on the cross, yet God still has not carried out the sentence in full. That sentence will be carried out in full on Lucifer in the future as described in Revelation 20. Pember is incorrect that God *judged* Lucifer at Genesis 1:2.

(**u-9.2h**) *Fossils were left from pre-Adamite life that was unrelated to today's life.* God judged that wicked pre-Adamite world by Lucifer's flood and an ice age. But the ancient fossils from the first creation of life were left in the old rock. That ancient life all died so is unrelated to today's life, which was created new in the six literal days.

In response, geology and the gap theory were "born" at the same time and same place—Scotland and England. The "fathers" of modern geology and "fathers" of the gap theory overlapped, suggesting early geology and the gap theory were very closely connected. William Buckland published *Vindiciae Geologiae; or the Connexion of Geology with Religion explained* as his vindication of geology as a science and his reconciliation of geology with the Bible's account of the creation and flood by the creation-ruin-reconstruction or gap theory. With Charles Lyell of Scotland, William Buckland wrote a report resulting in the founding of the Geological Survey of Great Britain.[872] Then Lyell published *Principles of Geology* in three volumes from 1830 to 1833.[873] All this suggests that the gap theory seems influenced more by the Scottish emerging geology and paleontology than by the Bible.

Since the gap theory advocates appealed to science, I will answer first from science: The claim of two unrelated creations of life seems highly unlikely because the discovery of many "living fossils"—mountain beaver, platypus, crocodiles, coelacanth, lungfish, sharks, wasps, crinoids, horseshoe crabs, ginkgo trees, horsetails, dawn redwoods, and stromato-lites. All these are both living and in the fossil record. One could claim God created new animals identical to the old fossilized ones, but that does seem to beg the question.

I could give a long answer from the Bible, but all I need to say is this: There is no positive Bible evidence in Genesis 1:2 for a first creation of life, millions of years of pre-Adamites, a fall of Lucifer, and a catastrophic Lucifer's flood destroying all life. There is strong negative grammatical Hebrew evidence that Genesis 1:2 was not actions or events. The gap in the gap theory is against Hebrew grammar. There was no gap.

Partially Supported Claims of the Three Stage Gap Theory

(ps-9i) *Creation was in three stages. Stage one*: God created the heavens and earth during the beginning time period in 1:1. <u>*Stage two*</u>: In a time gap at Genesis 1:2, God made a first creation of land, plants, animals, and pre-Adamites under the headship of Lucifer. But Lucifer fell into sin. God judged Lucifer and the Earth, killing all life and forming the fossils. *Stage three*: In six literal normal days, God restored Earth, re-created all life, and created man.

Two of these three stages are very clearly in the Bible—God created the heavens and the earth in the beginning, and God worked on Earth six days. But the middle stage is based on silence. Genesis 1:2 not only says nothing about these claimed events, but the grammar of 1:2 precludes any events at all.

(ps-9.2d) *Lucifer's fall started animal death and natural disasters; what God made was very good; Adam's Fall started death of Adam's race.* This is a proposed solution to the problem of evil. Pember quotes Hebrews 2:14—"Him who had the power of death, that is, the devil" (NASB). Pember says Lucifer's sin began animal death. What God made was very good. Then Adam's sin began human death (Rom. 5:12).

In response, I agree that all God made was "very good." I agree that Adam's Fall began human death. On the other hand, the gap theory's idea that Lucifer's sin caused massive animal death in a time gap at Genesis 1:2 is certainly incorrect. There were no actions in 1:2. For a fuller explanation of the options of animal death, see chapter 13.

(ps-9.3) *Stage three was six literal days when God restored planet Earth and re-created all new life kinds, leaving the old fossils.* Gap advocates claim the days were "six days of restoration."[874]

I respond that the Genesis 1 evidence does agree with six normal days. But they were not a "restoration" and "re-creation."

(ps-9.3h) *The seventh day, God instituted rest.* Pember says, "Then follows the institution of the Sabbath on the Seventh Day."[875]

I respond that on the seventh day God *illustrated* the Sabbath; God did not institute the Sabbath as a command for man in Genesis 2:2–3. There is no command in 2:2–3. Certainly God rested, giving us His example for the Fourth Commandment. The Commandments are to be honored. But that must not blind us to correct interpretation of Genesis 1 — 2:4a. Genesis 2:2–3 is a narrative of what God did. It is not a command instituting a Sabbath ordinance for humans. However important the Commandment is, Pember is incorrect in importing the later Fourth Commandment back into Genesis 1. The original seventh day was an example, not a command.

Largely Supported Claims of the Three Stage Gap Theory

(s-9.0C) Study Scripture and creation independently; both, correctly interpreted, ultimately will agree. This pre-understanding by Arthur Custance espouses independence of both scientific research and Bible study. After the study in each is done, then they may be compared. That way neither prejudices the results of the other. Ultimately God's Word and God work will agree, because they are from the same truthful God.

I agree. What a great insight!

(s-9.1) Stage one was ex nihilo creation of the organized heavens and earth in the beginning time period of Genesis 1:1, before the six days. Gap theory advocates take Genesis 1:1 literally — "In the beginning God created the heavens and the earth."

They are correct on this claim. God created the literal heavens and literal earth, all before the six literal days.

(s-9.1a) The "beginning" was the beginning time period before day one. The creation of the heavens and earth was a "period anterior to the first day."[876] The beginning was not an instant but rather a time period of "some unstated amount."[877]

(s-9.1b) God created the heavens and the earth before the six days. So the young earth creation claim that 1:1 took place *in* the six days about 6,000 years ago is incorrect. Pember rightly claims, "We are told that in the beginning God created the heavens and the earth; but the Scriptures never affirm that He did this in the six days."[878] Gap theory advocates correctly recognize that God created the heavens and the earth in the beginning before the six days, just as a plain reading of Genesis 1:1–3 states. YEC's convoluted claim that God created *in* day one is incorrect.

(s-9.1c) The beginning was a period of time of unstated length before the six days. So creation in the beginning is undated by the Bible. "The work of the six days . . . began in verse 3,"[879] but the initial creation took place in 1:1, an "unstated amount" of time before the six days. Therefore, "the writings of Moses do not fix the antiquity of the globe."[880] The creation of the heavens and earth occurred "some unstated amount"[881] of time before the six days, so that initial creation of the heavens and earth in Genesis 1:1 is undated by the Bible. The Bible does not give us even the approximate date other than that there was a beginning in finite time and it was some significant amount of time before the six days.

This claim is correct.

(s-9.1d) The original "*bārā*'" creation was different from six-day primarily "'*āsâh*" fashioning work. So the young earth creationism's claim that the terms are used interchangeably in Genesis 1 is incorrect. Buckland is correct that the *bārā'* creation in Genesis 1:1 was the initial *ex nihilo* work when the universe "was originally created by the power of the Almighty."[882] "*Asah* is generally used in connection with them [the work of the six days]."

The YEC claim that the two terms are used interchangeably in Genesis 1 is incorrect.

(s-9.1e) God created the orderly literal heavens and earth in 1:1; so the YEC claim that God created only raw materials errs. Pember says, "God, then, in the beginning created the heaven and the earth, not merely the materials out of which they were afterwards formed."[883] The YEC claim that only the unformed raw materials of the universe were created in 1:1 is incorrect.

Pember has seen the YEC error.

(s-9.1f) Only Earth was described in 1:2 as *tōhû v^abōhû*; so the YEC claim that the universe was chaos is incorrect. Pember is correct that Genesis 1:2 changes the subject from "the heavens and the earth" to the condition of "the earth." So the six days "did not affect the sidereal heaven [visible universe appearing to pass by in the sky], but only the earth and its immediate surroundings."[884] The young earth scientific creationism theory is incorrect in its claim that in Genesis 1:2 the entire universe was *tōhû v^abōhû*. Genesis 1:2 says, "And the earth was *tōhû v^abōhû*."

(s-9.1g) Genesis 1:2 shows that 1:1 is not a mere title or summary; 1:1 was the actual creation; so the title/summary theory is incorrect. Genesis 1:2 could not describe Earth as *tōhû v^abōhû* if the Earth had not already been created in 1:1. So 1:1 was the actual creation, not merely a title or summary of 1:2–31.

Pember is correct.

(s-9.3a) The six days were normal day-night days. So the long day-age eras idea is incorrect. Pember explains, "Whenever a numeral is connected with it [*yôm,* "day"] the meaning is at once restricted thereby, and it can only be used in its literal acceptation of the time which the earth takes to make one revolution upon its axis."[885]

Pember correctly rejects the claim by old earth creationism that a numbered *yôm* could mean a geological era long day-age.

(s-9.3b) Day one: God commanded, "Light be." "The command went forth 'Light be,'" says Pember. "God called the light day and the darkness night."[886] The New Scofield Reference Bible explains, "The sun and moon were created 'in the beginning.' The 'light' of course came from the sun, but the vapor diffused the light."[887]

Pember is correct in this claim.

(s-9.3c) Second day: God commanded the formation of open atmosphere between cloud and sea waters. On the second day, at God's command "the firmament, or atmosphere which we breathe, was formed," "inserted" between the cloud waters above and the ocean waters upon the Earth.[888]

(s-9.3d) Third day: God gathered the sea so dry land appeared; then He caused the land to sprout vegetation. Pember refers to the appearance and rise of land described in Psalm 104:6–9: "The mountains rose, the valleys sank" (NASB).[889] This was not the "creation" of dry land *ex nihilo,* but its rise from the ocean.

(s-9.3e) Fourth day: God established Earth's relations with the heavenly bodies, created in Genesis 1:1, so they could serve their purposes to Earth. Pember says, "It remained only to establish its [Earth's] relations with the heavenly bodies." God, "apparently, so altered or modified the firmament" to bring about this relation of the heavenly bodies to the Earth. "God is not said to have created these light-holders on the Fourth Day. . . . They were created, as we have seen, in the beginning."[890]

(s-9.3f) Fifth day: God caused the waters to swarm with living creatures and flyers to inhabit the air. Pember translates, "Let the waters swarm with swarms, with living creatures. . . . And let fowl fly above the earth in the face of the firmament of heaven."[891]

I respond that God created these; but He did not "re-create" them.

(s-9.3g) The sixth day: God caused the land to produce three classes of animals and God created man. Pember says God caused the land to produce "three classes of living creatures—cattle or domesticated animals, creeping things, . . . and beasts of the field or wild roaming animals." God created man "in His image and after His likeness."[892]

I respond that these claims for the six days are affirmed by the Bible text. However, these events were not a "re-creation," but were the only creation of the items.

(s-9.3i) The "generations" statement in Genesis 2:4 is a summary of Genesis 1. Pember concludes, "This wondrous history closes with a summary of the subject and an introduction to the next part in these words: 'These are the generations of the heavens and the earth.'"[893] These generations summarize the whole of Genesis 1.

(s-9.3j) Genesis 1 and 2 are not contradictory. Pember explains, "While chapter one gives a continuous history of the week," in chapter two "reference is made to other works of the Six Days only when . . . connected with the main subject, and without any regard to the order in which they were performed."[894] Understood this way, there is no contradiction between the two chapters.

If we leave out the entire gap idea, Pember has much that is Biblical in his ideas.

Summary of the Three Stage Gap Theory

Gap creationists recognized that Genesis 1:1 declares that God created the heavens (including the sun, moon, and stars) and the earth *ex nihilo* in the beginning time period as stage one before the six days.

But then from the early science of geology, these creationists saw that the earth and its fossils seemed old. So they proposed a second stage, or gap of time, at Genesis 1:2. During this time gap, God first created land and all kinds of plant and animal life, and pre-Adamite, pre-humans. But Lucifer fell, resulting in death, diseases, and "natural" disasters. Lucifer led the pre-Adamites into evil. Eventually, God judged the Earth with "Lucifer's flood." So Earth *became* ruined and all life died, forming fossils. Genesis 1:2 is translated, "Now the earth *became* desolate and empty of life."

Finally, during stage three God reconstituted Earth for life and re-created new life forms in the six literal days. Although espousing an old earth, this theory does not say how old Earth is.

Conclusion about the Gap Theory

The trash is the gap. The first and third stages have treasures.

9. Gap or Creation-Ruin-Restoration Theory

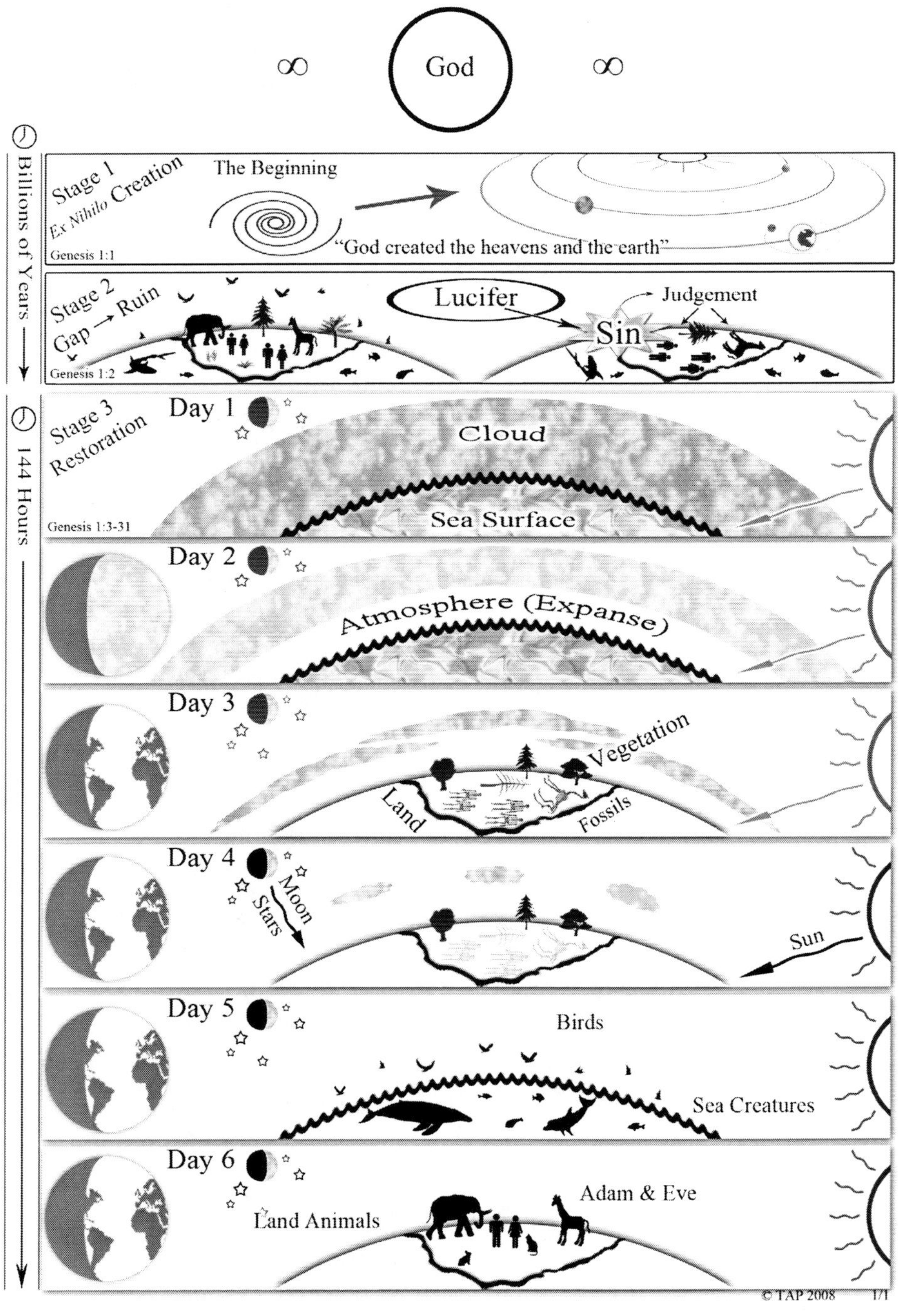

9. Claims of the Three Stage Gap Theory
(Biblically supported claims in non-italics **bold,** unsupported in *italics*)

(9.0A) Tōhû v^abōhû in Genesis 1:2 means "chaos."

(9.0B) God could not have created chaos, so Earth became chaos.

(9.0C) Study Bible and creation independently; they will agree.

(9.1) Stage one was *ex nihilo* creation in the beginning time period.

    (9.1a) "Beginning" was beginning time period before day one.

    (9.1b) God created heavens and Earth before the six days.

    (9.1c) The beginning time period was of unstated length.

    (9.1d) Original *"bārā"* creation was different from *"'āsâh."*

    (9.1e) God created orderly literal heavens and literal Earth.

    (9.1f) Genesis 1:2 *tōhû v^abōhû* condition described "Earth."

    (9.1g) Genesis 1:1 is not a mere title or summary.

(9.2) Stage two was a time gap at Genesis 1:2 when Earth became chaos.

    (9.2a) The verb "was" in Genesis 1:2 should be translated "became."

    (9.2b) The gap occurred in or around Genesis 1:2.

    (9.2c) Lucifer was head of Earth's ancient pre-Adamites and animals.

    (9.2d) Lucifer's fall started animal death; **Adam's Fall, human death.**

    (9.2e) God judged Earth because of the sin of Lucifer and the pre-Adamites.

    (9.2f) Tōhû v^abōhû in Isa. 34:11 & Jer. 4:23 was judgment, so Gen. 1:2 was also.

    (9.2g) All pre-Adamite life died in "Lucifer's flood," leaving fossil record.

    (9.2.h) Fossils left are unrelated to today's life.

(9.3) Stage three was **six literal days** *restoring planet Earth, re-creating life.*

    (9.3a) The six days were normal day-night days, not long eras.

    (9.3b) Day one: God commanded, "Light be."

    (9.3c) Second day: God commanded open atmosphere.

    (9.3d) Third day: Dry land appeared; vegetation sprouted.

    (9.3e) Fourth day: Earth related to luminaries.

    (9.3f) Fifth day: Breathing water animals, flying creatures.

    (9.3g) The sixth day: Land animals, man in God's image.

    (9.3h) The seventh day: God rested, *instituting the Sabbath.*

    (9.3i) "Generations" of Gen. 2:4a is a summary of Gen. 1.

    (9.3j) Genesis 1 and 2 are not contradictory.

Major Supported Claims from the Creation Theories

The Correct Translation of Genesis 1:1: Waltke affirms the traditional translation of Genesis 1:1: "In the beginning God created the heavens and the earth." It is *incorrect* to translate 1:1 as "When God began to create."

Waltke Merism: "The heavens and the earth" meant the entire orderly universe. Also, evening and morning meant the entire nighttime.

The Waltke Exclusion Principle: If there was preexisting chaos, there was no *ex nihilo* creation of the organized heavens and earth. The converse is also logically possible: If there was *ex nihilo* creation of the organized heavens and earth, then there was no unorganized chaos.

The Kline Claim: When the Bible does not indicate a miracle, Genesis 2:5–6 (no rain, no plants; rain, then plants sprouted) shows God probably used ordinary means in the creation era, just as today. **Ross Addition:** "An observed attribute of the Creator . . . is His economy of miracles—only what's needed to accomplish His purpose."

The Kline Undated Universe: "We must speak where the Bible speaks, and be silent where the Bible is silent. . . . The inspired text, rightly interpreted, is simply silent with regard to the age of the earth and universe."

A Generational Genesis: The worldview of Genesis was generations. The six begetting (literal) days of Genesis 1 introduced the most ancient generations of all—"the generations of the heavens and the earth."

The Rooker Reaffirmation: "The key difference between pagan cosmogonies and Genesis 1 is *creatio ex nihilo* and the absence of preexisting matter."

The Morris Maxim: In historical narrative, a numbered "day" was a day.

The Morris and Ross Method: The Bible reveals what God did; science may uncover how He did it.

The Morris One Fall Explanation: The creation was perfect. Man and animals were created about 6,000 years ago with eternal physical life. There was "no disorder, no sin and, above all, *no death!* Even Satan was still good at this point."[895] His first effect on Earth was the temptation. (There were two falls, but Lucifer's fall had no effect on Earth until his temptation of Eve, resulting in Adam and Eve's Fall.) Adam's Fall resulted in a "cosmic catastrophe" including all human and animal death and subsequent moral and natural evil.

The Kaiser Two Falls Explanation: Standard theology identifies two falls: the angelic fall led by Lucifer, and later the human Fall by Adam.

God's concluding "very good" evaluation was about His work on Earth, not about angels such as Lucifer, who had been created and likely fell earlier. Animal death is *not* inherently evil. God Himself killed an animal to cover human nakedness. Any pre-Fall evil aspects of animal disease and death could only have been initiated by fallen Lucifer (Ezek. 28:16–18; Heb. 2:14). Yet by the sixth day, God worked even those together for good or eliminated them until Adam's Fall. Adam was the original cause of human death (Rom. 5:12) and farming woes (Gen. 3:17–19), but Scripture does not say he caused animal death. So animal death may have preceded Adam's Fall. Animal life cycles fit the present noneternal world God created, anticipating human resurrection and the New Creation (Rom. 8:20).

The Observer's Perspective: Ross says interpret the Genesis 1 creation narrative from the perspective of the Observer/Narrator, the Spirit, hovering just above the surface of the water-covered Earth.

The Ross Apologetic: The Bible alone declares that the universe had a beginning and has been stretching out. Only the Creator could have known these facts long before modern science. The God of the Bible is the Creator, and the Bible is His accurate message to us.

The Ross-Schroeder Fine-Tuning Evidence: The fine-tuning of the universe and Earth is evidence of the Designer, not chance.

The Wiseman Tablet Theory: The Genesis narratives were eyewitness reports recorded on tablets received by Moses. The name of each author was at the *end* of his narrative.

The Wiseman-Gray 20:11 Recognition: Exodus 20:11a has no "in," allowing the natural grammatical reading of Genesis 1:1 as the initial creation of the actual heavens and planet Earth "in the beginning" before the six days.

The Pember Literalism: If we take Genesis 1:1 literally, then God literally created the literal heavens and literal (unfinished) earth in the literal beginning before the six literal days.

Chapter 10

Theory 10
Historical Land Creationism Theory

Creation was in "two distinct time periods."[896]

John Sailhamer was my first Hebrew teacher, and we continue to greet one another at yearly Evangelical Theological Society meetings. He is a devout Christian and a man whom I respect. He has many insights into creation. I have also had the amazing experience of hearing, studying under, or discussing creation with major advocates of most of the ten theories, including Henry Morris in a lecture series, John Whitcomb in my church, Gerald Schroeder by e-mails, Waltke in lectures, Hugh Ross in a lecture series, and John Sailhamer in Hebrew. Each has contributed greatly to my understanding of creation, but each in turn has, I believe, erred at a different critical point. John Sailhamer's theory has been immeasurably beneficial in most of his claims. Although I may disagree with one of his claims, I do so most respectfully.

John Sailhamer calls his theory "historical creationism," but his theory is really about "the land," the historical Garden of Eden, which he explains became the Promised Land. I suggest a better title is "historical land creationism." Others have called his view "local creation" because the six days' work was localized in Eden. Sailhamer is the author of "Genesis" in *The Expositor's Bible Commentary*, *The Pentateuch as Narrative*, and *Genesis Unbound*, related to creation.[897] What a great Hebrew professor I had for my first Hebrew courses!

In a nutshell, the historical land creationism theory says that in the beginning time period of Genesis 1:1 God created not only the heavens and planet Earth, but also land and vast life on Earth. Relatively recently, in a second time period in six normal days God prepared Eden (future Promised Land) for man.

Preunderstandings of Historical Land Creationism

(10.0A) *Have no unexamined assumptions.* John Sailhamer says, "We often read the first two chapters of Genesis with a set of unexamined assumptions." He believes in examining and evaluating our assumptions about the Bible *by the Bible text*. An example of an unexamined assumption is the idea that "originally the world was a formless mass."[898] He compares this assumption to the Bible text. Instead of this assumption, in the Bible the *tōhû vᵃbōhû* description of Earth means our planet was "uninhabitable" "wilderness."[89]

Another example is the assumption by young earth scientific creationists that "beginning" (from the English) means a beginning instant. But the Hebrew *bᵉrē'shît* ("in the beginning") from *rē'shît* ("first, beginning, best, chief, firstfruits, head") when used of time or events always means a beginning time period, not an instant.

(10.0B) *Recognize that we can be wrong.* "If I am mistaken, however, then I pray that my well-intentioned views would do no great harm and that they would slip into a quickly forgotten past," says Sailhamer. He believes in a spirit of "congenial discovery."[900]

Three Denials by Historical Land Creationism

(10.D1) *Genesis 1:1 is not a mere chapter title but declares the actual* ex nihilo *creation.* Sailhamer explains, "What many people fail to realize is that such an understanding of Genesis 1:1 [that 1:1 was merely a title to the rest of the chapter] rules out a fundamental notion in the traditional view—the idea that God created the world 'out of nothing.'" With the title view of Genesis 1:1, "God's acts begin in Genesis 1:2. Since the earth was already 'formless and void' (vs. 2), that means the earth already existed when God began to act. But if that is so, when did God create the earth?"[901] The title theory almost requires the problematic pre-creation chaos theory—that chaos existed along with God before Genesis 1:1.

Against the title theory, Sailhamer says that grammatically, "the first verse, a verbal clause, should be taken as an independent statement rather than a summary of the rest of chapter 1. Thus 1:1 describes God's first work of creation *ex nihilo*, and the rest of the chapter describes God's further activity."[902]

Sailhamer lists three reasons Genesis 1:1 is not a title: "1. *In the original, the first verse is a complete sentence that makes a statement, but titles are not formed that way in Hebrew.*" "In Hebrew, titles consist of simple phrases."[903] Genesis 1:1 is not a phrase but is a complete sentence. "2. *The conjunction 'and' at the beginning of the second verse makes it highly unlikely that 1:1 is a title.*" "Hebrew grammar uses this conjunction carefully. If verse 1 were a title, the section immediately following it would surely not begin with the conjunction 'and.'"[904] "3. *Genesis 1 has a summary title at its conclusion, making it unlikely it would have another at its beginning*" (all italics Sailhamer's). The title theory is incorrect.

(10.D2) *Young earth creationism improperly attempts to date the beginning of the universe by Adam's genealogy.* Is YEC correct to date the heavens and earth by Adam's genealogy? Sailhamer responds, "Such an approach to dating the time of creation [by Adam's genealogy to about 6,000 years ago] is based on two faulty assumptions: 1. It assumes that the biblical genealogies are to be understood as strict chronologies." Even Warfield argued that gaps existed in the genealogies, because the New Testament includes one person who was missing in the Old Testament version of the same genealogy, so "father" could mean ancestor. Therefore, Adam's date could be somewhat older than Ussher's 4004 BC date.

The more critical error by young earth creationism is this: "2. It assumes that the 'beginning' of creation (Genesis 1:1) occurred in the first day of the week recounted in that chapter."[905] But the beginning was a time period of unspecified length *before* day one.

(10.D3) *Young earth creationism incorrectly forces "In the beginning" into day one.* Young earth scientific creationism is mistaken in the idea that the beginning *ex nihilo* creation was in day one. This claim does not fit the change in focus at Genesis 1:2. The *ex nihilo* creation in Genesis 1:1 is separated from day one by the description in Genesis 1:2. Genesis 1:2 begins with "Now the earth." Genesis 1:2 changes from the universe focus of "the heavens and the earth" in 1:1 to the local focus on Earth in Genesis 1:2.[906] So the universe, created in Genesis 1:1, was not the focus of the work of the six days on Earth. God had already created the universe in the beginning, before the six days.

(10.D4) *The gap is incorrect: there was no gap, no catastrophe, and so no restoration.* "There are no 'gaps' in the creation account of Genesis 1, nor was there any 're-creation' or 'restoration' of an original creation."[907] Hebrew grammar does not support a gap at Genesis 1:2. The gap theory is incorrect.

Three Major Theories Each with a Fatal Flaw:

Precreation chaos incorrectly excludes *ex nihilo* creation from 1:1. Young earth creationism incorrectly dates the universe by Adam. The gap claim of a first creation in 1:2 is unsupported by Hebrew.

Bible Interpretation Practices of Historical Land Creationism

(10.H1) *Start with the Bible text. After Bible study, relate the meaning to science.* We must start with "the meaning of the biblical author as expressed in the biblical text. . . . We must first understand the biblical text and then seek to relate its meaning to the findings of modern science, if possible."[908]

(**10.H2**) *View the Bible text from the perspective of the author and original readers.* "It was only natural to view the Biblical text within the narrow limits of what was known about the world."[909]

Claims of Historical Land Creationism

John Sailhamer introduces his theory by explaining that creation was in two time periods. (His introduction is marked *i*.)

(**10i**) ***Creation was two acts in two time periods.*** Sailhamer recognized that the creation was "two great acts of God"[910] in two time periods. He says, "I contend that two distinct time periods are mentioned in Genesis 1. In the first period (the 'beginning' in Genesis 1:1), God created the universe. In the second period (Genesis 1:2—2:4a),"[911] God did the six days' work.

Creation was two great acts,

in the beginning

and the six days.

(**10i.a**) *Genesis is a series of narrative units of real events.* Sailhamer explains that Genesis "is about events." "An event is something that happened in time and space"[912] recorded in "historical narrative." "We may propose a preliminary definition of historical narrative as a proselike literature which seeks to render a *realistic* picture of the world."[913] "The account of those events and persons exhibits all the traits of historical trustworthiness."[914] "The author [of Genesis 1—2] clearly intends us to read his account of creation as literal history." It is a "historical account of creation."[915]

(**10i.b**) *Moses probably wrote Genesis from collected clay tablets.* "Some conservative scholars" propose that "Moses used a collection of clay tablets which had preserved the accounts of creation, the flood, and the lives of the patriarchs."[916] Moses wrote Genesis from eyewitness sources "in much the same way as Luke says he wrote his gospel (cf. Luke 1:1–4.)"[917]

(**10i.c**) *The two stage creation narrative is 1:1—2:4a.* "Genesis 1:1—2:4a is clearly recognizable as a unit of historical narrative." The first subunit is 1:1, the second 1:2—2:4a. Both were time periods.

(**10*i*.d**) *Genesis 1:1—2:4a introduces the Sinai Covenant by iden-tifying who God is, the Creator, and what He has promised, the Land.* Sailhamer emphasizes that in preparation for the Sinai Covenant, Israel needed to understand that Yahweh is not just a local or national god, but the one and only Creator God. "The purpose of 1:1 is not to identify this God in a general way but to identify him as the Creator of the universe."[918] "God alone is eternal and . . . all else owes its origin and existence to him."[919]

For Israel in Sinai as the first readers, the creation account told them "that God, the Creator of the universe, has prepared the land as a home for his special creature, the human being, and he has a plan of blessing for all his creatures."[920] This land was Eden, which was also the Promised Land. Israel was returning to Eden. In this return, they were also called back to the original purpose of the creation—fellowship with God for themselves and all others who would believe. Only if this point is understood can the reader fully understand Sailhamer's focus on Eden as the Promised Land. The Sinai Covenant was a call to return to a relationship with God in the Promised Land.

(**10.1**) *In the Genesis 1:1 beginning time period, God created the heavens of sun, moon, and stars, and Earth—and also land and all extinct and living plants and animals.* Sailhamer says, "In the first act, God created the universe we see around us today, consisting of the earth, the sun, the moon, the stars, and all the plants and animals that now inhabit (or formerly inhabited) the earth. The biblical record of that act of creation is recounted in Genesis 1:1—'In the beginning, God created the heavens and the earth.'"[921]

(**10.1a**) *"The beginning" was a "period of time"[922] with a starting point, length unspecified.* Hebrew professor Sailhamer says,

The Hebrew word *bᵉrēshît*, which is the term for "beginning" used in this chapter [Gen. 1], has a very specific sense in Scripture. In the Bible the term always refers to an extended, yet indeterminate duration of time—*not* a specific moment. It is a block of time which precedes an extended series of time periods. . . . The term [*bᵉrēshît*, "in the begin-ning"] does not refer to a point in time but to a *period* or *duration* of time before later events.[923]

"The Hebrew word *berēshît*, which is the term for 'beginning' used in this chapter [Genesis 1], always refers to an extended, yet indeterminate initial duration of time—not a specific moment."

"Within the Book of Genesis itself, the author uses the [unprefixed] term *rē'shît* to refer to the early part of Nimrod's kingdom (Genesis 10:10)." Young translates Genesis 10:10, "And the first part [*rē'shît*] of his kingdom is Babel, and Erech, and Accad, and Calneh, in the land of Shinar." Sailhamer explains, "In Job 8:7 the word *rē'shît* refers to the early part of Job's life, before his misfortunes overtook him. . . . It was an unspecified, but lengthy, period in Job's life." "According to Jeremiah 28:1, for example, the 'beginning' [*b*e*rēshît*] of King Zedekiah's reign included events which happened four years after he had assumed the throne."[924]

"According to Jeremiah 28:1, for example, the 'beginning' [*berēshît*] of King Zedekiah's reign included events that happened four years after he had assumed the throne."

"The term *beginning* in Biblical Hebrew marks a starting point of a specific duration, as in 'the beginning of the year' (Deut. 11:12). In opening the account of Creation with the phrase 'in the beginning,' the author has marked Creation as the starting point of a period of time."[925] "God created the universe during an indeterminate period of time." "Other Hebrew words were available to the author. . . . The author could have used a Hebrew word for 'beginning' similar to the English word 'start' or 'initial point' (for example, *rishonah* or *techillah*). Had he used one of those words, we would have to translate Genesis 1:1 something like this: 'The first thing God did was to create the universe.' Using such a term would have *required* that the universe be created in the first moment of time." It is only the English word "beginning," not the Hebrew word *b*e*rēshît*, "in the beginning," that allows the erroneous interpretation that God created the whole universe in an instant, including trees "with growth rings showing years of growth" that never happened, and homing pigeons "returning to homes they had, in fact, never been to."[926]

Another reason why the "beginning" indicates a period of time is that the Bible pairs the "beginning" "with its antonym 'end.'"[927] The "end" refers to the "end times," a period of time that included at least the

Tribulation and thousand-year Millennium. Just as the "end" will be a period of time, so was the "beginning."

(10.1b) *In the Genesis 1:1 period of time, God created the entire universe including the sun, moon, stars, and Earth.* Sailhamer explains, "A merism combines two words to express a single idea. A merism expresses 'totality' by combining two contrasts or two extremes. . . . [By linking] heavens and earth, the Hebrew language expresses the totality of all that exists. Unlike English, Hebrew doesn't have a single word to express the concept of 'the universe.'" In Genesis 1:1, "heavens and earth" is the merism that expresses God's creation of everything—"the sun, the moon, and the stars"[928] as the heavens above and the Earth beneath

> In Genesis 1:1, "heavens and earth" is the merism that expresses God's creation of everything, "the sun, the moon, and the stars" as the heavens above, and the Earth beneath.

(10.1c) *The initial* ex nihilo *creation is undated.* How long was "the beginning"? Sailhamer answers, "There is no way to limit the duration of the word 'beginning' (Hebrew, *b*ᵉ*rēshît*). It could refer to billions of years, to a few thousand years, or to a period as brief as a few months or days. The length of time of this 'beginning' is precisely what is left unspecified by the term. The whole point of using *b*ᵉ*rēshît* to convey the concept of 'beginning' (when other terms were readily available) is to leave the duration of time unspecified."[929] "Since the Hebrew word '*beginning*' refers to an indefinite period of time, we cannot say for certain when God created the world or how long He took to create it."[930] John Sailhamer believes in a beginning time period unspecified in length by the Bible, so an undated earth creation (UEC). The Bible says there was a beginning, but the Bible does not give us the date of that beginning.

> "Since the Hebrew word 'beginning' refers to an indefinite period of time, we cannot say for certain when God created the world or how long He took to create it."

On the other hand, Sailhamer tends toward an older Earth. He speaks of "the long ages during which the dinosaurs roamed the earth."[931]

(10.1d) *In the Genesis 1:1 beginning time period, God created not only the heavens and earth but also the land, plants, and animals.* Sailhamer says that in addition to creating "the heavens and the earth" in

1:1, God created "the seas, the dry land, and the plants and animals that inhabit them."[932] "The many biological eras would also fit within 'the beginning' of Genesis 1:1, including the long ages during which the dinosaurs roamed the earth. By the time human beings were created on the sixth day of the week, the dinosaurs already could have flourished and become extinct—all during the 'beginning' recorded in Genesis 1:1."[933] Sailhamer continues, "The Bible allows for the creation of dinosaurs and all other forms of early plant and animal life 'in the beginning,' since the Hebrew word for 'beginning' in Genesis 1:1 could encompass eons during which God's work of creation was carried out."[934]

(10.1e) *All Earth's geological and biological history up to the six days' work on Eden took place in Genesis 1:1.* Sailhamer claims, "Within that 'beginning' would fit the countless geological ages, ice ages, and the many climatic changes on our planet."[935]

(10.1f) *Carnivorism and death were outside the Garden of Eden.* In Genesis 1:31 God declared His work in Eden "very good." But "very good" did not apply outside Eden. Sailhamer says dinosaurs went extinct long ages ago, so he assumes death in the world outside the Garden of Eden.

(10.1g) Tōhû v^abōhû *in Genesis 1:2 means uninhabitable wilderness, not chaos.* The Greek Septuagint unhelpfully translated *tōhû v^abōhû* as "unseen" and "unformed." "Were it not for the Greek notion of 'primeval chaos,' the phrase never would have been translated that way ["without form and void"]. The sense of the Hebrew phrase suggests something quite different, a sense some early translators identified quite clearly." The meaning is "uninhabitable" and "wilderness" "that had not yet become inhabitable for human beings."[936] Jeremiah 4:23–26 uses the same terms with the sense of "deserted and uninhabited."[937] Ibn Ezra (1092–1167) understood the phrase to mean that Earth was "uninhabited because it was covered with water, not that the earth was formless chaos."[938]

(10.2) *In God's second creation act, in Genesis 1:2—2:4a, in six days God prepared Eden, the future Promised Land.* Sailhamer says, "In the second period (Genesis 1:2—2:4a), God prepared the garden of Eden for man's dwelling; that activity occurred in one week."[939] "The second act of God recounted in Genesis 1 and 2 deals with a much more limited scope and period of time. Beginning with Genesis 1:2, the biblical narrative recounts God's preparation of a land for the man and the woman He was to create. The 'land' was the same land later promised to Abraham and his descendants." "According to Genesis 1, God prepared that land within a period of a six-day work week."[940] In the six days, God worked only on the Garden of Eden, not on the planet Earth.

(**10.2a**) *The "earth" in Genesis 1:2–31 was Eden/Promised Land because "the central theme of the Pentateuch is the Sinai Covenant and God's gift of the land."*[941] The English words "land" and "earth" are the same Hebrew word—'*āretz*, from '*eretz*.

Four senses of '*eretz*, "earth":
Global – Earth including both land and sea, not heavens (Gen. 1:1)
Land – continental land and islands, not sea (Gen. 1:10)
Local – a specific territory, such as Eden, not Greece (Gen. 2:12)
Ground – arable land, not rock (soil is *adāmâh*) (Gen. 1:12)

Sailhamer suggests that the global sense was used in Genesis 1:1, but the local sense of the Garden of Eden beginning in 1:2. He claims, "Throughout Genesis 1, the term *eretz* is used to denote 'the dry land,' as opposed to a body of water, the seas (1:10)."[942] "We have filled the word [*eretz* in Genesis 1:2–31] with a meaning it clearly did not suggest to its original readers. . . . 'Earth' conjures up images of a globe sitting on our desk or a blue disk in space as we might see it from the moon."[943] Sailhamer suggests "a change in meaning from the first to the second verse," from planet Earth in 1:1 to the local Garden of Eden in 1:2.

Sailhamer says that the focus of Moses in the Pentateuch is the Sinai Covenant, giving Israel the Promised Land. Therefore, '*āretz* (from '*eretz*), starting in Genesis 1:2, was a specific dry land, namely, the Promised Land. He says, "This is the strongest argument for taking the setting of Genesis 1 and 2 as the promised land."[944]

(**10.2b**) *The Garden of Eden and the Promised Land are the same.* Sailhamer believes, "The boundaries of that garden are the same as those of the promised land; thus the events of these chapters [Gen. 1; 2] foreshadow the events of the remainder of the Pentateuch."[945] "Not only does the Hebrew term *eretz* normally mean 'land' as opposed to 'the earth,' but it usually refers specifically to the land promised to Abraham (Genesis 15:18)."[946]

(**10.2c**) *In six days, God prepared "the land," the Garden of Eden, for mankind.* Sailhamer says, "God did not *create* 'the land' in Genesis 1:2—2:4a; He had already created the land and the rest of the universe 'in the beginning' in Genesis 1:1. In the remainder of the chapter, God is at work *preparing* the land for human habitation. . . . Moses thus wants us to see God as both Creator of the universe (Genesis 1:1) and Giver of 'the land' (Genesis 1:2—2:4a). . . . Such a view of God is central to the theory [of historical land creationism] of the Pentateuch and its focus on the Sinai Covenant (Exodus 19:5)."[947]

(10.2d) *The days were six normal days of work.* Sailhamer says, "According to Genesis 1, God prepared that land within a period of a six-day work week."[948]

(10.2e) *The light on day one was diffuse sunlight.* Sailhamer says that "if the sun is meant to be included in the merism 'sky and land' in Genesis 1:1, then it is natural to assume that the sun was created already in the first verse. If that is so, then the 'light' of verse 3 was simply the light of the sun. . . . The expression 'there was light' is one way the Bible refers to sunlight."[949] An example is Exodus 10:23, which says, "Israel had light" (NASB)."[950] The Hebrew *hāyâh ôr* ("have/had light" qal perfect 3rd ms) is very similar to Genesis 1:3 *va-y^{e}hî ôr* ("be light" qal imperfect jussive 3rd ms with *vav/waw* conversive, so functioning as if perfect). Both indicated sunlight.

> "If the sun is meant to be included in the merism 'sky and land' in Genesis 1:1, then it is natural to assume that the sun was created already in the first verse. If that is so, then the 'light' of verse 3 was simply the light of the sun."

(10.2f) *In the second day's work, God caused the clouds to rise from the sea.* Sailhamer explains, "Biblically, the 'waters above the heavens' are simply the clouds which provide rain." And the "expanse" is best understood by our English word "sky."[951]

Some young YEC advocates claim that the waters above the expanse were a major part of the chaotic cosmological universe. Young earth creationist Frank DeRemer says, "The luminaries [sun, moon, and hundred billion galaxies] were not made until Day 4, probably from the 'waters above the expanse.'"

John Sailhamer responds to that idea, "The central question is how the author understands and uses the term *expanse* [*rāqîa'*]. Is it used from a cosmological perspective, that is, is it intended to describe a major component of the structured universe? Or does the term describe something immediate in the everyday experience of the author (e.g., the 'clouds' that hold the rain)?"[952] The "water above" must be understood from the perspective of the author. The author could see birds in the sky, as well as the sun, moon, stars, and clouds. Clouds were within the "everyday experience of the author." "A second clue is the name given to the 'expanse.' In verse 8 it is called the 'sky,'" a place where in the future "the birds fly."[953] In God's second day of work, the clouds rose from the sea surface, forming an expanse of open air between the liquid water below and the cloud water above in the "sky," all understood within the "everyday experience of the author."

Sailhamer apparently sees this event as a local event, fog rising from local bodies of water in Eden. But his statement also fits with the more standard understanding of the fog rising up from the surface of the world-covering ocean.

(**10.2g**) *In the first act of a third day's work, God made "pools" called "seas" in Eden.* Sailhamer claims, "We should not think of the 'oceans' when we read that God named the 'pools of water' the 'seas' in Genesis 1:10. In Hebrew, any 'pool' of water—regardless of the size—is called a 'sea.'"[954] "For example, the bronze basin made for temple worship in also called a 'sea' (see 1 Kings 7:23–25, 39, 44)."[955] So on the third day, God made pools in Eden.

(**10.2h**) *Also in the third day God made fruit-bearing plants, so He had made other green plants mentioned in Genesis 1:30 earlier.* Sailhamer observes, "According to the Hebrew text only 'fruit trees' were created on the third day, not 'all kinds of trees' as many English translations suggest. Those 'fruit trees' were for the man's and woman's nourishment (Genesis 1:29)." "At the conclusion of the chapter, other plants are mentioned [*kol yereq ēsev*, "every green plant"] that also are for . . . food for animals (Genesis 1:30). . . . Yet the creation of these plants is not mentioned anywhere in the first chapter; clearly they were not created on the third day. . . . The account thus assumes that such plants already were present in God's world."

Sailhamer claims, "This means that all those things [vast plant and animal life] were created as part of 'the heavens and earth' in Genesis 1:1."[956] In other words, on the third day, God planted these fruit trees only in Eden for Adam and Eve.

(**10.2i**) *God created the sun, moon, and stars in Genesis 1:1, not on the fourth day.* John Sailhamer explains, "Though our English translations of Genesis often suggest that God created the sun, moon, and stars on the fourth day, the Hebrew text does not demand, *or even allow for*, such an interpretation. The overall sense of Genesis 1 assumes that by the fourth day, the sun, moon, and stars are already in place"[957] (emphasis his). "According to the Hebrew text, God said, 'Let the lights in the expanse be for separating the day and night. . . .' God's command, in other words, *assumes that the lights already exist* in the expanse"[958] (emphasis his). "And in response to his command they were given a purpose, 'to separate the day and night' and 'to serve as signs to mark seasons and days and years.'"[959]

If the difference between the syntax of verse 6 (the use of היה alone) and verse 14 (היה with an infinitive) is significant, then it suggests that the author does not understand his account of the fourth day as an account of the creation of the lights but, on the contrary, he assumes that the heavenly lights have already been created "in the beginning."[960]

Some young earth scientific creationists claim that verse 16 describes the *creation* of the sun, moon, and stars. Sailhamer replies,

At the end of verse 15, the author states, "and it was so." This expression marks the end of the author's report and the beginning of his comment in verse 16. Thus, verse 16 is not an account of the creation of the sun, moon, and stars on the fourth day, but rather a remark directed to the reader to draw out the significance of that which had previously been recounted: "So God [and not anyone else] made the lights and put them into the sky."[961]

God had already created the "heavens and earth"—a merism meaning the entire universe including sun, moon, and stars—"in the beginning" in Genesis 1:1.

> "The author does not understand his account of the fourth day as the creation of the lights but, on the contrary, he assumes that the heavenly lights have already been created 'in the beginning.'"

Because Sailhamer makes the claim that the six days applied only to Eden, he also makes the claim that all God did on the fourth day was "explain His purpose for creating the sun, moon, and stars 'in the beginning.'"[962]

(10.2j) *In the fifth day, God introduced sea and air life (created in 1:1) into Eden.* Sailhamer says that God had created all the living creatures "in the beginning." "What then is the focus of God's work on the fifth day? It is simply to populate the promised land with the various creatures that were created 'in the beginning.'"[963]

(10.2k) *In the sixth day, God introduced land animals into Eden and He created humans.* Sailhamer says, "Human life did not originate until the sixth day of the work recorded in Genesis 1:2–4a. That means that human beings were *not* created 'in the beginning' with the rest of God's creation. . . . They came only after the indefinite period of time denoted by the term 'beginning.' . . . Genesis insists that all human beings as we know them today are descendants of Adam. That rules out the creation of human beings 'in the beginning' in Genesis 1:1."[964]

Sailhamer explains, "The creation of humanity is set apart from the previous acts of creation." First, God speaks personally: "Let us make." Second, animals were made after their own kinds; but God makes humans in His likeness, in a limited sense in His kind, as spiritual as well as physical beings. Third, God specifically identifies both male and female humans. Fourth, only human beings were given dominion over God's creation.[965]

(**10.2***l*) *Genesis 2:4b–25 recounts historical events in Eden.* Sailhamer says that Genesis 1 and 2 are "intended to be actual history."[966] All of Genesis 2:4b–25 was Adam's narrative from the Garden of Eden. The beginning of his narrative, Genesis 2:4b–7, recounts events that occurred back in the six days *in the land of Eden.*

(**10.2m**) *Exodus 20:11 describes God's work for six days, not the initial creation of the universe.* Sailhamer explains, Exodus 20:11 does not say that God *created* the heavens and earth in six days. "In Exodus 20:11, in the midst of His instructions on keeping the seventh day as a day of rest, God Himself alluded to this very account of preparing the 'sky, the land, and the sea.'"[967] "Exodus [20:11] does not use the merism 'heavens and earth' to describe God's work" as if God created the whole heavens and earth, meaning everything, *in* the six days. "Rather, it gives us a list of God's distinct works during the six days. . . . This list refers to God's work in Genesis 1:2—2:4, *not* to his creation of the universe in Genesis 1:1. Exodus 20:11 does not say God *created* 'the heavens and earth' in six days; it says God *made* three things in six days—the sky, the land, and the seas—and then filled them during that same period."[968] *Asah* does not mean "create *ex nihilo*" but "put something in good order, to make it right." An English example would be "'to make' a bed."[969] "To make" a bed is not to create the bed but to put its surface bedding in order. Likewise, Exodus 20:11 has nothing to do with the initial creation but simply affirms that God worked for six days, putting the Earth (Sailhamer would identify that as Eden) in order for the first humans.

Unsupported Claim of Historical Land Creationism

John Sailhamer has one basic problematic claim—when the sense of *ha'āretz* changed from the global Earth to the Land of Eden. John

Sailhamer says the change was in Genesis 1:2, so all of God's work during the six days was only in Eden. Part of this problematic claim is his subclaim that God created all life (except man) in Genesis 1:1. This subclaim would allow the six days to refer only to Eden, because life had already been created everywhere else on Earth in 1:1.

(u-10.1d, 10.1e, 10.1f) *In the Genesis 1:1 beginning time period, God created land and all plants and animals. Earth's geological and biological history including carnivorism was in 1:1 before the six days' work on Eden.* John Sailhamer claims that in addition to creating "the heavens and the earth" in 1:1, God created "the seas, the dry land, and the plants and animals that inhabit them."[970] "Within that 'beginning' would fit the countless geological ages, ice ages, and the many climatic changes on our planet."[971] "The many biological eras would also fit within 'the beginning' of Genesis 1:1, including the long ages during which the dinosaurs roamed the earth. By the time human beings were created on the sixth day of the week, the dinosaurs already could have flourished and become extinct—all during the 'beginning' recorded in Genesis 1:1."[972]

We may respond that there is no Bible evidence in 1:1 for creation of land, plants, and animals. Because 1:1 says nothing about land, plants, or animals, Sailhamer's claim is an argument from silence.

A normal understanding of Genesis 1:2 forbids Sailhamer's view of vast plant and animal life supposedly created on Earth in 1:1. "Earth" is the last word in Genesis 1:1 and the first word (prefixed with "and") in 1:2. "Earth" in both verses has to refer to the same planet Earth. In verse 2, planet Earth was *tōhû v*ᵃ*bōhû*, uninhabitable and empty of life or uninhabited. Also Earth was sea covered, so without land for any land animals or plants. Finally, Earth was dark, so no green plants could grow.[973] Despite all his other great insights into the Genesis creation, Sailhamer does not have the backing of the Bible text or widespread agreement by other Hebrew scholars on this claim that God raised the land and created all of Earth's plant and animal life (except Adam and Eve) in Genesis 1:1 *before* the six days. An argument from silence is at best a weak argument.

(u-10.2a) *The "earth" beginning in Genesis 1:2 was Eden/Promised Land because "the central theme of the Pentateuch is the Sinai Covenant and God's gift of the land."*[974] The English words "land" and "earth" are translations of one Hebrew word— *'āretz* (*'eretz*). Context alone can tell us which meaning was intended so which English word to use. Sailhamer suggests "a change in meaning from the first to the second verse."

In response, "earth" is the last word in 1:1 and the first word in 1:2. "Earth" in both means the same—unless strong context evidence requires a change in meaning. Such evidence is missing.

Sailhamer claims that the Sinai Covenant, giving Israel the Promised Land, is a major theme of the Pentateuch. Therefore, *'āretz*, starting in Genesis 1:2, means the Promised Land. He says this is his "strongest argument" that Genesis 1 refers to the local Land rather than to planet Earth.[975]

I respond that Genesis 1:1—11:9 has an "all people" perspective (9:19; 10:1–32; 11:1; 11:9), not an "Israel as the Covenant people" perspective. The focus of Genesis narrows to Abraham's line in Genesis 12. Israel and the future Promised Land are not in Genesis 1:1—11:9. If we accept Wiseman's tablet theory, then Genesis 1:1—11:9 was not even originally composed by Moses for Israel, but by Adam, Noah, and Shem—long before Israel's Sinai Covenant. The Edenic Covenant in Genesis 3:15 was a covenant for all people. The laws given to Noah in Genesis 9 were for all people. Genesis 11:9 ends with, "The LORD scattered them abroad over the face of the whole earth" (NASB). Since Genesis 1:1—11:9 has an "all people" perspective, then the Sinai Covenant with Israel does not force a "Promised Land" meaning onto *'eretz* (without a named land) in Genesis 1. Moses did not need a modern perspective of Earth as a blue sphere in space to speak of "the whole earth" (Gen. 11:9c). In Genesis 1:1, Moses spoke of the "the heavens and the earth" as a merism meaning everything. Then in 1:2, he said, "Now the earth . . ." meaning everything under the heavens, what we would today call planet Earth. If this is Sailhamer's "strongest argument," it is rather weak.

Sailhamer claims that *'āretz*, starting in Genesis 1:2, means the Promised Land. But Genesis 1:2 describes "darkness over the face of the deep." If the Promised Land was land in Genesis 1:1–2, then "darkness over the face of the deep" does not make sense as a description of the Promised Land.

Four senses of 'eretz, "earth":
Global – Earth including both land and sea, not heavens (Gen. 1:1)
Land – continental land and islands, not sea (Gen. 1:10)
Local – a specific territory, such as Eden, not Greece (Gen. 2:12)
Ground – arable land, not rock (soil is *adāmâh*) (Gen. 1:12)

However, Sailhamer's idea does give insight into Genesis 2:4b–7. Sailhamer suggests a change in meaning from the global Earth to the local land of Eden. Genesis 2:4b begins Adam's narrative. Genesis 2:4b–7 makes very good sense as God's work on Eden. Originally the land of Eden had no shrubs, no plants, no rain, and no man to till the ground. In other words, Eden was a wilderness or desert (perhaps coinciding with the cold and drought conditions in the Middle East in the Younger Dryas). Then God sent rain and planted a Garden in the east of Eden. Finally, God put the man in the Garden. Sailhamer's idea of a change in meaning to the Land of Eden does make very good sense starting with Adam's narrative about Eden beginning in 2:4a, but does not make good sense starting in 1:2. The change of authors from the Spirit to Adam is the natural time for a change in the sense of "the land" from global and continental to local.

(u-10.2g) *In the first act of the third day's work, God made "pools" called "seas" in Eden.* Sailhamer claims, "We should not think of the 'oceans' when we read that God named the 'pools of water' the 'seas' in Genesis 1:10. In Hebrew, any 'pool' of water—regardless of the size—is called a 'sea.'"[976] "For example, the bronze basin made for temple worship in also called a 'sea' (see 1 Kings 7:23–25, 39, 44)."[977]

The problem of claiming that the six days were just God's work in Eden becomes clear when Sailhamer has to say the gathering of waters into seas and causing land to appear meant only making pools in Eden.

I would respond that there is no problem in the semantic range of *yamîm* ("seas") including the large bronze basin. But was making basin-like pools in Eden God's work on the third day?

I would ask, If the "seas" were merely "pools" in Eden, how did the dry land appear from small pools? No, pools in Eden are not what God did. Instead, God gathered the waters under the entire sky and made dry land appear. God made continental land rise from the worldwide ocean by His third command.

(u-10.2j and 10.2k) *In the fifth day, God introduced sea and air life (created in 1:1) into Eden, and in the sixth day animal life; then He created humans.* Sailhamer asks, "What then is the focus of God's work on the fifth day? It is simply to populate the promised land with the various creatures that were created 'in the beginning?'"[978]

I respond that on the fifth day God used the special word *bārā'* ("create"). The word *bārā'* does not mean "introduce" sea and air animals into Eden. Genesis 1:21 says God created (*bārā'*) great sea creatures (*tanînem ha-gᵉdolîm,* great sea animals such as whales) in the fifth day. Sailhamer says the six days were about Eden. But I ask, How could whales fit into small pools in Eden? No, God created these whales in the world's oceans. The six days were God's work on the global Earth, not just in the land of Eden.

There is only one underlying claim that I conclude errs—when God switched focus to just the local Eden scene. John Sailhamer claims that the switch in focus to just Eden is at Genesis 1:2. That is his one significant error, and it may be only a partial error.

He is correct that young earth creationism fails to recognize this clearly stated transition to Earth in Genesis 1:2. This YEC error results in their seeing three of the first four days as events in the universe—light to the universe, upper water somewhere in the universe, (plants on Earth), and creation of luminaries in the universe. Sailhamer is correct that there is a narrowing of focus in 1:2, but I suggest it is to planet Earth, not to the land of Eden exclusively yet.

I also respond that the text changes focus *twice*, not once. John Sailhamer is correct that there is a change in focus at Genesis 1:2,[979] but it is from the universe to planet Earth, the larger sense of *ha'āretz* (Earth, land). The exclusive focus on Eden begins with Adam's narrative in Genesis 2:4b. There are *two* changes in focus, not one.

	Genesis 1:1	**Genesis 1:2**	**Genesis 2:4b**
	Focus One	*Focus Two*	*Focus Three*
Sailhamer	Universe ⟶	Eden	
Traditional	Universe ⟶	planet Earth	Eden
[YEC	Universe *fuzzy transition*	Earth	Eden]
Modified	Universe ⟶	planet Earth with some Eden emphasis	Eden

On the other hand, we should listen to John Sailhamer even on this claim. Perhaps there was some progressive emphasis from planet Earth to the land Eden through the six days. The light on day one was to planet Earth, not just to Eden. The divine Narrator reported the light from His location just above the sea. Likely, that location was above future Eden because that is where His narrative ends. Likely, the first land He saw appear was the land of Eden, so the plants and animals He observed were the flora and fauna of Eden, not of California or Japan. And by the end of the sixth day, God put Adam in Eden (Gen. 2:6). Adam's narrative in 2:4b—5:1a certainly began in Eden. So the six days were about planet Earth, but likely with some emphasis on the land of Eden. Thank you, Professor John Sailhamer.

Partially Supported Claims of Historical Land Creationism

(ps-10*i*.d) *Genesis 1:1—2:4a introduces the Sinai Covenant by identifying who God is, the Creator, and what He has promised, the Land.* Sailhamer insightfully explains, "The purpose of 1:1 is not to identify this God in a general way but to identify him as the Creator of the universe."[980] "We may conclude . . . with a summary of Genesis 1:1—2:4a. The author intends his Creation account to relate to his readers that God, the Creator of the universe, has prepared the land as a home for his special creature, the human being, and he has a plan of blessing for all his creatures."[981]

What a great insight that God, who is revealed in the Bible, is not just a local or national God, but is the Creator! If John Sailhamer had only avoided reading the Sinai Covenant back into Genesis 1, I could agree wholeheartedly.

(ps-10.1) *In the Genesis 1:1 beginning time period, God created the heavens of sun, moon, and stars, and the Earth—and also land and all extinct and living plants and animals.* Sailhamer says, "In the first act, God created the universe we see around us today, consisting of the earth, the sun, the moon, the stars, and all the plants and animals that now inhabit (or formerly inhabited) the earth."[982]

In response, Genesis 1:1 says God created the heavens and earth, but 1:1 says nothing about "all the plants and animals." Since plants and animals are not mentioned in verse 1 but were made in the third through the sixth days, the second part of Sailhamer's claim is based at best on Biblical silence.

The first part of this claim does fit the meaning of heavens and earth. "In the first act, God created the universe we see around us today, consisting of the earth, the sun, the moon, the stars. . . ."[983]

(ps-10.2) *In God's second creation act, in Genesis 1:2—2:4a, in six days God prepared Eden, the future Promised Land.* Sailhamer claims, "In the second period (Genesis 1:2—2:4a), God prepared the garden of Eden for man's dwelling; that activity occurred in one week."[984] Sailhamer claims the six days' work only prepared Eden.

In response, God did two great stages of His work. But the second stage was not restricted to Eden. Eden is not mentioned until Genesis 2:8 in a separate later narrative, Adam's narrative. It is improper to import Eden back into the previous creation narrative.

(ps-10.2b) *The Garden of Eden and the Promised Land are the same.* Sailhamer claims, "The boundaries of that garden are the same as those of the promised land; thus the events of these chapters [Gen. 1 and 2] foreshadow the events of the remainder of the Pentateuch."[985]

In response, it seems difficult to prove that the borders of Eden were exactly the same as the Promised Land, especially with an intervening flood. Yet this claim is the foundation of Sailhamer's idea of the six days' work only in Eden. Moreover, Genesis 2:8 says the Garden was only "in" Eden, toward the east: "And the LORD God planted a garden toward the east, in Eden." If the Garden was only a smaller eastern part of Eden, but Canaan is in the west of this land, then the Garden and the Promised Land were probably *not* identical.

On the other hand, there was at least major overlap between the full area of Eden (not just the Garden, which in the east of Eden) and the Promised Land. The Garden included the Euphrates (Gen. 2:14). The Promised Land was "from the river, the river Euphrates, as far as the western sea" (Deut. 11:24, NASB). So there was at least major overlap.

However, the Bible never explicitly equates Eden with the Promised Land. To base this major claim that the six days were only in Eden on such uncertain evidence as his "strongest argument"[986] seems problematic indeed.

(ps-10.2c) *In the six days, God prepared "the land," the Garden of Eden, for mankind.* John Sailhamer sees a "focus on the Sinai Covenant (Exodus 19:5)"[987] from Genesis 1:2 onward. So he limits the six days to preparing Eden as the covenanted Promised Land.

In response, Genesis 1:2 names the focus of the six day narrative, "Now the earth. . . ." "The earth" was one of the two elements of "the heavens and the earth" at the end of the previous verse. So "the earth" was *everything* under the heavens, what we today would call planet Earth, not just the Promised Land. In contrast, the focus on the Sinai Covenant began with the covenant about the Sinai land. God made a covenant with Noah in Genesis 9, but that covenant says nothing about the Sinai land. The first mention of the Sinai land was to Abraham in Genesis 15:18 — "On that day the LORD made a covenant with Abram, saying, 'To your descendants I have given this land, From the river of Egypt as far as the great river, the river Euphrates'" (Gen. 15:18, NASB). Genesis 15 is the first pledge of the Promised Land. So the focus on the Promised Land did not begin until Genesis 15.

We may agree that God apparently began the Garden preparation during the six days. The past tense in the NIV translation of Genesis 2:8 seems correct, that God had planted the Garden during the six days: "Now the LORD God had planted a garden in the east, in Eden." On the other hand, that preparation is not even mentioned in Genesis 1:1 — 2:4a. Nothing in Genesis 1 or 2 backs Sailhamer's claim that God worked *only* in Eden during the six days.

(ps-10.2h) *Also on the third day God made fruit-bearing plants, so He had made other green plants mentioned in Genesis 1:30 earlier.* Sailhamer says, "According to the Hebrew text only 'fruit trees' were created on the third day. . . . At the conclusion of the chapter, other plants are mentioned ["every green plant"] that also are for . . . food for animals (Genesis 1:30). . . . The account thus assumes that such plants already were present in God's world."

The reason I list this claim under "Partially Supported" is that Sailhamer seems correct that God made a distinction between seed and fruit bearing plants, which was food for mankind (Gen. 1:11–12, 29), and *kol yereq ēsev*, every green plant, which were food for animals (Gen. 1:30). The command on a third day of God's work was for the earth to produce vegetation, specifically seed and fruit bearing plants. The third day (Gen. 1:11–12) does not use the phrase *kol yereq ēsev*. From this distinction, Sailhamer says that perhaps God may have made simpler plant life earlier than the third day.

I do *not* agree with Sailhamer that God made all plant life back in Genesis 1:1. Genesis 1:2 says that Earth was *bōhû,* or empty of life. If *ha'āretz* in 1:2 means the global Earth as the context indicates, then the claim that all life was created in 1:1 is not possible. In 1:2 Earth was *bōhû,* empty of life, as well as sea covered and dark.

(ps-10.2i) *God created the sun, moon, and stars in Genesis 1:1, not on the fourth day.* Sailhamer insightfully explains, "Though our English translations of Genesis often suggest that God created the sun, moon, and stars on the fourth day, the Hebrew text does not demand, *or even allow for*, such an interpretation. The overall sense of Genesis 1 assumes that by the fourth day, the sun, moon, and stars are already in place."[988] So far Sailhamer bases this claim on Hebrew evidence.

But then Sailhamer harms his claim by adding that all God did on the fourth day was speak. This speaking idea is needed by his "Eden only" view.

I respond that *yᵉhî,* "let be," in Genesis 1:14 is a jussive command.[989] God commanded the luminaries to be in the expanse of the sky to separate day and night. Genesis 1:16 reports that God *'āsâh* ("made") the luminaries govern day and night in the sky. The luminaries did so by their being for the first time in Earth's sky from the perspective of the Narrator. God commanded these events and they actually happened. God did not just talk on the fourth day.

Sailhamer is correct that the luminaries had already been created. The luminaries were created as an essential part of the "heavens" in Genesis 1:1. But contra Sailhamer, a real event happened in Genesis 1:14–15. The luminaries that had been created in 1:1 were for the first time in Earth's sky from the perspective of the Narrator.

(**ps-10.2*l***) *Genesis 2:4b–25 recounts historical events in Eden.* Sailhamer says that Genesis 1 and 2 are "intended to be actual history."[990] All of Genesis 2:4b–25 was narrated from the Garden of Eden. Genesis 2:4b–7 recounts events that occurred back in the six days *in the land of Eden.*

Kline takes a different view. He says *all* land originally was dry, without rain. God sent rain, so plants grew. Kline says Genesis 2:5–6 describes this rain producing plants on all the land. So Genesis 2:5–6 describes the event of the third day in Genesis 1:11.

Sailhamer could respond that Genesis 2:5 was about Eden. Genesis 2:4b–7 about Eden fits well with Genesis 2:8–25, also clearly about Eden. Wiseman points out that 2:4b—5:1a is the Adam narrative.

Sailhamer is correct that there was a change in the sense of *'āretz* from global to local. I respond that he is incorrect that the change was at 1:2. The question is, When did the change occur?

	Beginning	Six days	No rain	Adam in Eden
	Genesis 1:1	*Genesis 1:2–31*	*Genesis 2:4b–7*	*Genesis 2:8–25*
Sailhamer	Global	Local Eden	Local Eden	Local Eden
YEC	Global	Global	Global - No rain until flood	Local Eden
Kline	Global	Global	Global rain 3rd Day	Local Eden
Modified	Global	Global and Local Eden	Local Eden rain 3rd day	Local Eden
Both Kline & Modified	Global	Global and Local Eden	Global & Local rain 3rd day	Local Eden

The modified (partial Sailhamer) view that 2:4b-7 is about Eden is illustrated using the NIV, but with *'āretz* translated as "land," *shāmayim* as "sky," *adāmâh* consistently as ground, and *ʿd* as "cloud":

When the Lord God made the land [of Eden] and the sky —
and no shrub of the field had yet appeared on the land [of Eden]
and no plant of the field had yet sprung up [in Eden],
for the Lord God had not sent rain on the land [of Eden]

and there was no man to work the ground,
but clouds came up from the land [of Eden]
and watered the whole surface of the ground—
the LORD God formed the man from the dust of the ground
and breathed into his nostrils the breath of life,
and the man became a living being.
Now the LORD God had planted a garden in the east, in Eden;
and there he put the man he had formed.
And the LORD God made all kinds of trees grow out of the ground.

We could consider this a modified version of Sailhamer's view—that the change to Eden was at 2:4b. If the change in the sense of *'āretz* is with the change of authors at Genesis 2:4b, then the local sense of *'āretz* as "the land" in 2:4b—5:1a fits the Adam narrative, because Adam was in Eden.

YEC claims a global view of Genesis 2:4b–7. Many, but not all, in YEC have claimed that the change to rain did not occur until the flood based on the above 2:4b–8 text. There was no normal water cycle on Earth from creation until the flood. For a full refutation of their view, see David Tsumura, *The Earth and the Waters*.

Kline responds to YEC that Genesis 2:4b–7 is about the third day. The land was *yabāshāh*, "dry ground," in Genesis 1:9. Genesis 2:5 explains that there were no plants on the land because God had not yet sent rain. Then God used the normal means of cloud to provide the needed water, and as a result plants spouted on the third day. Kline is also persuasive.

I respond to these views about 2:4b–7 that the YEC view of no rain until the flood is not supported by the text. Whether Kline's view or the modified Sailhamer view is correct could be a good debate.

It is also possible that both Kline and the modified Sailhamer views are correct. The events of rain on dry ground followed by seed plants and fruit trees sprouting—described in 2:4b–7—were global, occurring all over Earth's land in the third day. Yet the description was local, from the Spirit located over Eden. The narrative was spoken by the Second Person to Adam, who passed it down by tablets to Moses. This description was about the third day's events, specifically from the location of Eden. The event was global; the description was local.

Largely Supported Claims of Historical Land Creationism

(s-10.0A) Have no unexamined assumptions. John Sailhamer points out several unexamined assumptions.

I agree wholeheartedly with the caution to examine our assumptions.

(s-10.0B) Recognize that we can be wrong. John Sailhamer says, "If I am mistaken, however, then I pray that my well-intentioned views would do no great harm and that they would slip into a quickly forgotten past." He believes in a spirit of "congenial discovery."[991]

What a gracious spirit! Although he misplaced the transition to Eden at 1:2, his other great insights need *not* "slip into a quickly forgotten past." Most of his other insights are Biblically supported. These form part of the unified two stage Biblical creation theory. I have built on John's work, and others will build on my work. His contributions will not be forgotten.

We need to follow John Sailhamer's example and interact regarding creation in a spirit of "congenial discovery."

(s-10.D1) Genesis 1:1 is not a mere chapter title but declares the actual *ex nihilo* creation. Sailhamer explains, "What many people fail to realize is that such an understanding of Genesis 1:1 [that it was merely a title to the rest of the chapter] rules out a fundamental notion in the traditional view—the idea that God created the world 'out of nothing.'" Sailhamer says that grammatically, "the first verse, a verbal clause, should be taken as an independent statement rather than a summary of the rest of chapter 1. Thus 1:1 describes God's first work of creation *ex nihilo*, and the rest of the chapter describes God's further activity."[992]

The title and pre-creation chaos theory, with no *ex nihilo* creation, is incorrect. John Sailhamer's affirmation of the *ex nihilo* creation in Genesis 1:1 is backed by the Biblical evidence.

(s-10.D2) Young earth creationism improperly attempts to date the beginning of the universe by Adam's genealogy. Sailhamer explains, "Such an approach to dating the time of creation [by Adam's genealogy to about 6,000 years ago] is based on two faulty assumptions: 1. It assumes that the biblical genealogies are to be understood as strict chronologies." "2. It assumes that the 'beginning' of creation (Genesis 1:1) occurred in the first day of the week recounted in that chapter."[993] Sailhamer responds that the beginning was a time period of unspecified length *before* day one.

John Sailhamer is completely correct. He put this important critique of the YEC third claim into print long before I did.

(s-10.D3) Young earth creationism incorrectly inserts "In the beginning" into day one. Young earth scientific creationism "assumes that the 'beginning' of creation (Genesis 1:1) occurred in the first day of the week recounted in that chapter."[994]

Sailhamer says the beginning was a time period that could not fit into day one. Also, Genesis 1:2 begins with "Now the earth." The emphasis on only "the earth" changes the focus from "the heavens and the earth," the universe in Genesis 1:1, to the local focus on Earth in Genesis 1:2.[995] The six days are not the creation of the heavens and the earth, but about God's work changing uninhabitable Earth to habitable.

(s-10.D4) The gap is incorrect: there was no gap, no catastrophe, and so no restoration. Sailhamer correctly contends, "There are no 'gaps' in the creation account of Genesis 1, nor is there a 're-creation' or 'restoration' of an original creation."[996]

I respond that he is correct again. There are *no* gaps in creation, no catastrophe that kiilled all life, and no re-creation. The gap theory is incorrect.

(s-10.H1) Start with the Bible text. After Bible study, relate the meaning to science. Sailhamer says, "We must first understand the biblical text and then seek to relate its meaning to the findings of modern science, if possible."[997]

This is a good approach.

(s-10.H2) View the text from the perspective of the author and original readers. Sailhamer applies this practice to Genesis 1.

I agree. Genesis 1:2 implies that the Spirit of God is the Author of the upcoming six-day narrative. Interpreting from the Spirit's perspective results in the entire six days making very good sense.

(s-10*i*) Creation was two acts in two time periods. Sailhamer views creation as "two great acts of God"[998] in two time periods: "I contend that two distinct time periods are mentioned in Genesis 1. In the first period (the 'beginning' in Genesis 1:1), God created the universe. In the second period (Genesis 1:2—2:4a),"[999] God worked six days.

I agree that creation was two acts in two time periods. I do *not* agree with Sailhamer's expansion of Genesis 1:1 to include the creation of vast life and his reduction of the six days to only Eden.

(s-10*i*.a) Genesis is a series of narrative units of real events. Sailhamer explains that Genesis "is about events." "The author [of Genesis 1 and 2] clearly intends us to read his account of creation as literal history." It is a "historical account of creation."[1000]

Sailhamer is to be honored for this great declaration.

(s-10*i*.b) Moses probably wrote Genesis from collected clay tablets. "Moses used a collection of clay tablets which had preserved the accounts of creation, the flood, and the lives of the patriarchs."[1001]

Wiseman and Morris agree. The evidence from archeology, linguistics, and ANE culture supports this claim.

(s-10*i*.c) The two stage creation narrative is 1:1—2:4a. "Genesis 1:1—2:4a is clearly recognizable as a unit of historical narrative."

This is a key insight that we will use in the two stage theory.

(s-10.1a) "The beginning" was a "period of time"[1002] with a starting point, length unspecified. John Sailhamer explains, "The term [*b*ᵉ*rēshît*, "in the beginning"] does not refer to a point in time but to a *period* or *duration* of time which falls before a series of events."[1003] "Within the Book of Genesis itself, the author uses the term *rēshît* to refer to the early part of Nimrod's kingdom (Genesis 10:10). . . . In Job 8:7 the word *rēshît* refers to the early part of Job's life, before his misfortunes overtook him." "According to Jeremiah 28:1, for example, the 'beginning' [*b*ᵉ*rēshît*] of King Zedekiah's reign included events which happened four years after he had assumed the throne."[1004]

"Since the Hebrew word '*beginning*' refers to an indefinite period of time, we cannot say for certain when God created the world or how long He took to create it."[1005] Just as the "end times" will be a period of time, so was the "beginning."

John Sailhamer is a respected Hebrew professor and scholar. As a Hebrew scholar, he concludes that the beginning was a time period unspecified in length by the Bible. The Hebrew texts containing *rēshît* really do indicate that Sailhamer is correct.

(s-10.1b) In the Genesis 1:1 period of time, God created the entire universe including the sun, moon, stars, and Earth. Sailhamer correctly explains that in Genesis 1:1, "heavens and earth" is the merism that expresses God's creation of everything—"the sun, the moon, and the stars"[1006] as the heavens above and the Earth beneath.

I respond that John Sailhamer has made a vital insight verified by the Hebrew text.

(s-10.1c) The initial *ex nihilo* creation is undated. How long was "the beginning"? Sailhamer answers, "There is no way to limit the duration of the word 'beginning' (Hebrew, *b*ᵉ*rē'shît*). It could refer to billions of years, to a few thousand years, or to a period as brief as a few months or days. The length of time of this 'beginning' is precisely what is left unspecified by the term. The whole point of using *b*ᵉ*rē'shît* to convey the concept of 'beginning' (when other terms were readily available) is to leave the duration of time unspecified."[1007] "Since the Hebrew word *'beginning'* refers to an indefinite period of time, we cannot say for certain when God created the world or how long He took to create it."[1008]

I respond that John Sailhamer has argued his claim well from the Bible texts. The beginning time period is unspecified in length by the Bible. With good Biblically based reasons, Sailhamer urges us to accept a Biblically undated earth creation (UEC).

(s-10.1g) *Tōhû vᵃbōhû* **in Genesis 1:2 means uninhabitable wilderness, not chaos.** Sailhamer explains that the meaning of *tōhû vᵃbōhû* is "uninhabitable" and "wilderness" "that had not yet become inhabitable for human beings."[1009] Jeremiah 4:23–26 uses the same terms with the sense of "deserted and uninhabited."[1010]

John Sailhamer is correct. The meaning of *tōhû vᵃbōhû* is "uninhabitable" "wilderness."

(s-10.2d) The days were six normal days of work. If we leave out Sailhamer's Eden-only idea, he does support the six normal days of God's work.[1011]

I agree with his recognition of the six days as normal days.

(s-10.2e) The light on day one was diffuse sunlight. Sailhamer explains, "If the sun is meant to be included in the merism 'sky and land' in Genesis 1:1, then it is natural to assume that the sun was created already in the first verse. If that is so, then the 'light' of verse 3 was simply the light of the sun. . . . The expression 'there was light' is one way the Bible refers to sunlight."[1012]

I respond that He is correct that the light on day one was sunlight.

(s-10.2f) In the second day's work, God caused the clouds to rise from the sea. Sailhamer explains, "Biblically, the 'waters above the heavens' are simply the clouds which provide rain." The "expanse" is best understood by our English word "sky."[1013] The claim by some young earth creation advocates that interstellar water was part of an initial chaos condition of the universe is not an understanding that Adam, Moses, or Israel could have had. The water above was clouds that yield rain water.

Sailhamer is correct that the water above was cloud water. The claim by some YEC advocates that the water above the expanse was part of the chaotic universe that would become galaxies is incorrect.

(s-10.2m) Exodus 20:11 describes God's work for six days, not the initial creation of the universe. Sailhamer explains, "Exodus [20:11] does not use the merism 'heavens and earth' to describe God's work" as if God created the whole heavens and earth, meaning everything, *in* the six days. "Rather, it gives us a list of God's distinct works during the six days.

. . . This list refers to God's work in Genesis 1:2 — 2:4, *not* to his creation of the universe in Genesis 1:1. Exodus 20:11 does not say God *created* 'the heavens and earth' in six days." *Asah* does not mean create *ex nihilo* but "put something in good order, to make it right." [1014]

John Sailhamer is correct in this also. He has provided us his important Hebrew insight into Exodus 20:11.

In many of his claims, John Sailhamer is correct. He is even partially correct in his one problematic claim, that there is a change in the sense of *ha'āretz* from the global sense of Earth to the local sense of the Land of Eden. I conclude that he errs when that change from global to local occurred. The change was with the change in authors. The Holy Spirit of God in 1:1 — 2:4a used primarily the global sense from His perspective just above the world. Then Genesis 2:4b begins Adam's narrative. Adam used the local sense about the land he was in, the Land of Eden beginning in 2:4a or 2:8.

Summary of Historical Land Creationism

God created the heavens and the earth in the beginning time period of Genesis 1:1. He also made land and oceans along with plant and animal life, but not true humans, in 1:1. The Bible does not say how long this beginning time period was (pointing to an undated earth creation).

Recently, in six literal days, God prepared the Garden of Eden (the future Promised Land) for humans.

Genesis explained to Israel that their God is the Creator. God called Israel, by the Sinai Covenant, to return to the Promised Land of Eden and renewed fellowship with God.

Conclusion

John Sailhamer is correct that the sense of *ha'āretz* changed from the global sense of Earth to the local sense of the land of Eden. He claims that change was in Genesis 1:2, so the six days were God's work *only* in Eden. Perhaps this claim of a change at Genesis 1:2 may "slip into a quickly forgotten past." [1015] But he may be partially correct that there could be some emphasis on the Eden area even in the mentions of land in the six days. Otherwise, I would follow the traditional view that the change in focus of *ha'āretz* from the global sense of Earth to the local sense of the land Eden was with the change in authors in Genesis 2:4b.

John Sailhamer has provided us with many insights into creation. I am very thankful to my congenial first Hebrew teacher.

10. Historical Land Creationism Theory

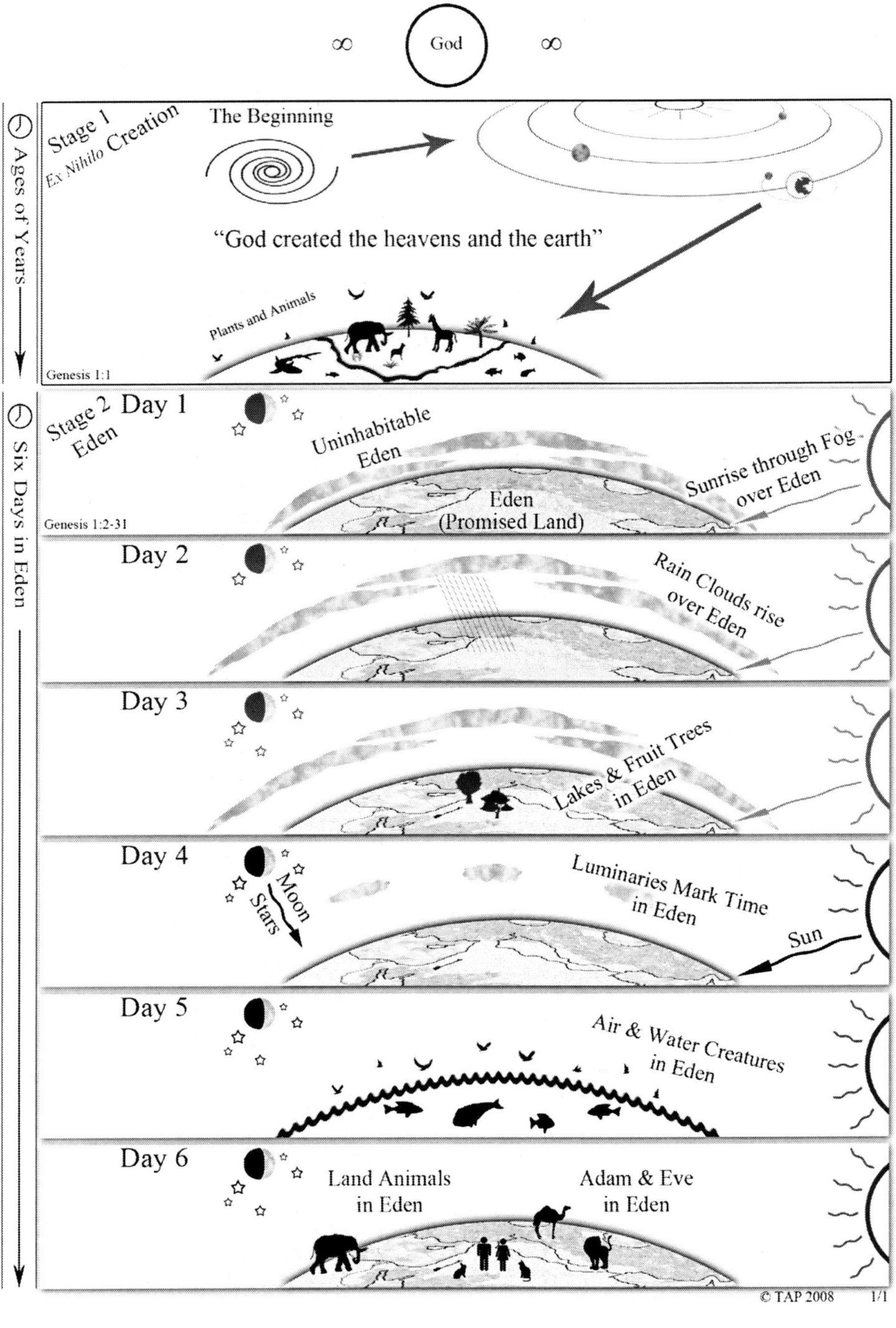

10. Claims of the Historical Land Creationism Theory

(Biblically supported claims in non-italics **bold,** unsupported in *italics*)

(10.0A) Have no unexamined assumptions.

(10.0B) Recognize that we can be wrong.

(10.D1) Genesis 1:1 is not a title, but was the *ex nihilo* creation.

(10.D2) YEC improperly dates the universe by Adam's genealogy.

(10.D3) YEC incorrectly inserts "In the beginning" into day one.

(10.D4) There was no gap; the gap theory errs.

(10.H1) Start with the Bible, then relate the meaning to science.

(10.H2) View the Bible text from the perspective of the author.

(10*i*) Creation was two acts in two time periods.

> **(10*i*.a) Genesis is a series of narrative units of real events.**
>
> **(10*i*.b) Moses wrote Genesis from collected clay tablets.**
>
> **(10*i*.c) The two stage creation narrative is 1:1—2:4a.**
>
> **(10*i*.d) Gen. 1 & Sinai Covenant: Creator,** promised Land.

(10.1) In 1:1 God created sun, moon, stars, and Earth; *and all life.*

> **(10.1a) "The beginning" was a "period of time."**
>
> **(10.1b) In the 1:1 time period, God created the universe.**
>
> **(10.1c) The initial *ex nihilo* creation is undated.**
>
> *(10.1d) In the 1:1 time period, God created land, plants, and animals.*
>
> *(10.1e) All Earth's geological and biological history took place in Genesis 1:1.*
>
> (10.1f) Carnivorism and death were outside the Garden of Eden.
>
> **(10.1g) *Tōhû v^a bōhû* in 1:2 means uninhabitable wilderness.**

(10.2) In 1:2—2:4a, in six days *God prepared Eden, future Promised Land.*

> *(10.2a) The "earth" in Gen. 1:2–31 was Covenanted Eden/Promised Land.*
>
> (10.2b) *Garden of* Eden and Promised Land are the same.
>
> (10.2c) In six days, God prepared *the Garden of Eden for mankind.*
>
> **(10.2d) The days were six normal days of work.**
>
> **(10.2e) The light on day one was diffuse sunlight.**
>
> **(10.2f) Second day: God caused clouds to rise from the sea.**
>
> *(10.2g) Third day: God made "pools" called "seas" in Eden.*
>
> (10.2h) Third day: God made fruit-bearing trees.
>
> **(10.2i) God created sun, moon, and stars in 1:1, not fourth day.**
>
> *(10.2j) Fifth day: God introduced sea and air life (created in 1:1) into Eden.*
>
> *(10.2k) Sixth day: God introduced land animals into Eden,* **created man.**
>
> **(10.2*l*) Genesis 2:4b–25 recounts historical events in Eden.**
>
> **(10.2m) Exod. 20:11 was God's six days' work, not initial creation.**

Major Supported Claims from the Creation Theories

The Correct Translation of Genesis 1:1: Waltke affirms the traditional translation of Genesis 1:1: "In the beginning God created the heavens and the earth." It is *incorrect* to translate 1:1 as "When God began to create."

Waltke Merism: "The heavens and the earth" meant the entire orderly universe. Also, evening and morning meant the entire nighttime.

The Heiser Clause Analysis: Begin analyzing creation by determining which clauses (esp. in Gen. 1:1–3) are independent clauses and which are dependent clauses, and then which independent clauses are modified by which dependent clauses, and so how they fit together.

The Waltke Exclusion Principle: If there was preexisting chaos, there was no *ex nihilo* creation of the organized heavens and earth. The converse is also logically possible: If there was *ex nihilo* creation of the organized heavens and earth, then there was no unorganized chaos.

The Kline Order: Proverbs 8:22–31 says "the beginning," when God created Earth (Gen. 1:1), was "when there were no depths." There were ocean depths by 1:2, so "In the beginning" was before 1:2 and before the six days. Creation order: Heavens, Earth, sea, six days.

The Kline Claim: When the Bible does not indicate a miracle, Genesis 2:5–6 (no rain, no plants; rain, then plants sprouted) shows God probably used ordinary means in the creation era, just as today. **Ross Addition:** "An observed attribute of the Creator . . . is His economy of miracles—only what's needed to accomplish His purpose."

The Kline Undated Universe: "We must speak where the Bible speaks, and be silent where the Bible is silent. . . . The inspired text, rightly interpreted, is simply silent with regard to the age of the earth and universe."

A Generational Genesis: The worldview of Genesis was generations. The six begetting (literal) days of Genesis 1 introduced the most ancient generations of all—"the generations of the heavens and the earth."

The Rooker Reaffirmation: "The key difference between pagan cosmogonies and Genesis 1 is *creatio ex nihilo* and the absence of preexisting matter."

The Morris Maxim: In historical narrative, a numbered "day" was a day.

The Morris and Ross Method: The Bible reveals what God did; science may uncover how He did it.

The Morris One Fall Explanation: The creation was perfect. Man and animals were created about 6,000 years ago with eternal physical life. There was "no disorder, no sin and, above all, *no death!* Even Satan was still good at this point."[1016] His first effect on Earth was the temptation. Adam's sin about 6,000 years ago resulted in a "cosmic catastrophe" including all human and animal death and subsequent moral and natural evil.

The Kaiser Two Falls Explanation: Standard theology identifies two falls: the angelic fall led by Lucifer, and later the human Fall by Adam. God's concluding "very good" evaluation was about His work on Earth, not about angels such as Lucifer, who had been created and likely fell earlier. Animal death is *not* inherently evil. God Himself killed an animal to cover human nakedness. Any pre-Fall evil aspects of animal disease and death could only have been initiated by fallen Lucifer (Ezek. 28:16–18; Heb. 2:14). Yet by the sixth day, God worked even those together for good or eliminated them until Adam's Fall. Adam was the original cause of human death (Rom. 5:12) and farming woes (Gen. 3:17–19), but Scripture does not say he caused animal death. So animal death may have preceded Adam's Fall. Animal life cycles fit the present noneternal world God created, anticipating human resurrection and the New Creation (Rom. 8:20).

The Observer's Perspective: Ross says interpret the Genesis 1 creation narrative from the perspective of the Observer/Narrator, the Spirit, hovering just above the surface of the water-covered Earth.

The Ross Apologetic: The Bible alone declares that the universe had a beginning and has been stretching out. Only the Creator could have known these facts long before modern science. The God of the Bible is the Creator, and the Bible is His accurate message to us.

The Ross-Schroeder Fine-Tuning Evidence: The fine-tuning of the universe and Earth is evidence of the Designer, not chance.

The Wiseman Tablet Theory: The Genesis narratives were eyewitness reports recorded on tablets received by Moses. The name of each author was at the *end* of his narrative.

The Wiseman-Gray 20:11 Recognition: Exodus 20:11a has no "in," allowing the natural grammatical reading of Genesis 1:1 as the initial creation of the actual heavens and planet Earth "in the beginning" before the six days.

The Pember Literalism: If we take Genesis 1:1 literally, then God literally created the literal heavens and literal (unfinished) Earth in the literal beginning before the six literal days.

The Sailhamer Time Period: *B^erē'shît*, "in the beginning," consistently has the sense of an extended beginning time period, never of an instant or a few hours.

The Sailhamer Sense: *Tōhû v^abōhû* consistently has the sense of uninhabitable and uninhabited wilderness, never of unformed matter or chaos.

Chapter 11

Theory 11
Two Stage Biblical Creation Theory

Today's multicultural world asks, "Which God?"
The answer is—the God who is the Creator of all things.

The Bible reveals truth that
only the Creator could have known before modern science.

The God of the Bible is the Creator of the universe.

Today the world asks, "Which God?" Others ask, "Aren't all gods really the same, or at least equal?" The answer is—the Creator of the universe is the only real God. Christianity's first claim is that the God of the Bible created the heavens and the earth. If Christians present a creation theory that is *not* true, that theory will *not* match the real creation discovered by science. With an incorrect creation theory, Christianity will be sidelined as a religious myth.

If our creation theory matches the Bible, then discoveries from science will provide nothing but evidence for the God of the Bible. God will be exalted. We will have powerful evidence that eternal God the Father through eternal God the Son Jesus is the Creator of all things. Since He is our Creator, He has every right to give us His good laws. When we violate those laws, we are rebelling against our Creator. Only when we realize our desperate condition before our Creator will the salvation message become the priceless treasure that it is. God the Son, our Creator, came down to Earth, was born of Mary, lived without sin, died paying our sin penalty, was buried, rose from the dead the third day, and offers us His payment, the gift of eternal life, and entrance into His family—if we believe in Him.

When evidence from the universe matches evidence that the Bible has revealed all along, we have reasons to believe in the God of the Bible as our Creator, as well as Savior. The evidence is in the creation all around for us to see—if we have the correct creation theory.

With the correct Biblical creation theory,
there is nothing but evidence for the God of the Bible!

With an accurate creation theory, there is nothing but evidence for the God of the Bible. Can we assemble an accurate Biblical theory?

Based on over one hundred Bible texts on creation, and with the invaluable help from the Biblical claims of the ten theories, a two stage Biblical creation theory emerges. The basic idea of the two stage theory is the traditional initial creation theory in two stages, but the minority no-chaos view. This minority view, overlooked in the YEC versus OEC controversy, is the basis of two stage Biblical creation.

Princeton theologian Charles Hodge summarized a general idea of two stage creation. "Some understand the first verse of Genesis to refer to the original creation of the matter of the universe in the indefinite past, and what follows [that is, the six days] to refer to the last reorganizing change in the state of our earth to fit it for the habitation of man."[1017]

Rooker says, "This idea that Genesis 1:1 refers to the first stage in God's creative activity might be supported by the context, which clearly reveals that God intended to create the universe in progressive stages."[1018] Paul Copan explains, "God created in two stages."[1019]

Two stage Biblical creation (2SBC) is my attempt to make this general traditional two stage theory as Biblically complete as I can.

I came to this two stage creation theory because I found every major modern creation theory has at least one claim that does not match the Bible. I sought answers from the Hebrew and Greek Bible texts on creation. After studying the creation texts and developing a basic two stage theory, I went back to the major creation theories and realized that each of my 2SBC claims had already been taught by these great creationists. First from the Bible texts and then from Biblically supported claims of the ten theories, I formed a fuller version of the traditional two stage initial creation no-chaos minority view theory.

In a multitude of creationists, there is safety —
especially when their counsel is measured by the Bible.

This theory is called two stage *Biblical* creation because I sought the answers about the creation in the five major and over one hundred shorter Bible creation texts. It is called *two stage* creation because it recognizes two stages in the Biblical account of creation. Richard Davidson explained the general idea of stage one:

The traditional view, having the support of the majority of Jewish and Christian interpreters through history, . . . [understands that] Genesis 1:1 declares that God created out of nothing the original matter called heaven and earth at the point of their absolute beginning. Verse 2 clarifies that when the earth was first created it was in a state of *tōhû* and *bōhû*.[1020]

The second stage is the eight command units and six days.

In a nutshell, the two stage Biblical creation theory recognizes that the Bible says that in the beginning God created the heavens and the Earth (stage one). But Earth was uninhabitable, uninhabited, and cloud-darkened. So by eight commands and six day-night work days, God made Earth lighted, habitable, and inhabited (stage two).

(I) In the beginning God created the heavens and the Earth.

But Earth was uninhabitable, uninhabited, sea-covered, and dark.

(II) God made Earth lighted, habitable, and inhabited by eight commands and six day-night work days.

The two stage Biblical creation theory is a Biblically *undated* earth creation (UEC) theory. The two main alternatives are old earth creationism (OEC) and young earth creationism (YEC).

OEC – God created the heavens and earth about 13.7 billion years ago.

YEC – God created the heavens and earth about 6,000 years ago.

UEC – God does not tell us in the Bible how long ago He created the heavens and earth. Two stage Biblical creation claims UEC.

Putting the Puzzle Together:
One Theory from the Most Biblical Claims of the Ten Theories

As I continued to study the ten major creation theories, I came to realize that all the claims in the two stage Biblical creation theory were already in the ten theories. In this chapter, I will present the two stage Biblical creation theory from the most Biblically supported claims of the other theories. A shortcoming of advocates of some past theories is that they only tended to defend their theory against competing theories. They failed to *listen* to the wisdom of previous creationists. I have studied ten major and over a dozen minor creation theories and compared their claims to the Bible. I have greatly profited from their most Biblical claims. Together, they contain all the major ideas of the two stages of creation.

I am deeply indebted to Henry Morris, John Whitcomb, John Sailhamer, Mark Rooker, Hugh Ross, Bruce Waltke, Meredith Kline, George Pember, Gerald Schroeder, P. J. Wiseman, and other great creationists who have gone before me! I most humbly thank them.

Now, let us put the puzzle together. All of the ten theories have major claims supported by the Bible's creation texts (as well as other claims that do not fit the Bible). So let us put together the most Biblically supported claims of the ten theories.[1021]

The Best Pre-understandings from the Ten Theories

(11.0A) Have no unexamined assumptions. John Sailhamer urges us to examine our preunderstandings by Bible evidence.[1022]

Some apparently poorly examined assumptions are:

a. *Genesis was from late JEPD sources, not eyewitness records.*
b. *If the universe is older, each day must have been millions of years.*
c. *Tōhû v^{a}bōhû in Genesis 1:2 means chaos.*
d. *Tōhû v^{a}bōhû describes the universe, so the universe was chaos.*
e. *"In the beginning" was instantaneous in total time span.*
f. *Exodus 20:11 says "in six days," so Genesis 1:1 was in day one.*
g. *All events of the six days were done by instantaneous miracles.*
h. *God created the universe with appearance of age.*
i. *There was no rain on Earth until the flood.*
j. *God created the sun, moon, and stars on the fourth day.*
k. *If Adam was dated about 6,000 years ago, then so was the universe.*

Thomas Kuhn said that we find it difficult to change our big ideas.[1023] We humans find it hard to say, "My present idea may not be quite right, so I will work to improve my idea." As I studied the Bible creation texts, I have continued to seek a more Biblical understanding of creation. And that is what I am suggesting to my readers. At least consider the two stage theory, not on my authority, but because it is based on the over one hundred Bible texts on creation and the Biblically supported claims from the ten theories.

Here are more Biblical background ideas from the ten theories:

(11.0B) Genesis is eyewitness true history, a claim supported by the Genesis text, theology, science, linguistics, and archeology. Wiseman, Morris, and Sailhamer all say Genesis is eyewitness history. Wiseman gives supporting reasons from archeology, linguistics, and ancient culture. Ross emphasizes that Genesis 1 was an eyewitness report by the Divine Observer. Ross gives massive backing from science data for the accuracy of Genesis 1.

The Thomas Truism: If Genesis is true, yet its narrative history was not dictated by God to Moses, then its narrative history was from eyewitnesses.

(11.0C) The Bible and the universe are from the same trustworthy Creator, so, correctly interpreted, both will agree. Waltke, Morris, Ross, Schroeder, Wiseman, and Sailhamer all make this affirmation. I have yet to find one contradiction in the over one hundred creation texts even though they were composed by more than a dozen different authors over several millennia. Such consistency is impossible unless those texts were inspired by the Creator. Accurate evidence from science will match the accurately understood Biblical creation account because both the Bible and the creation are from the Creator. The heavens still declare the glory of God, pouring fourth knowledge (Ps. 19:1); and so does the Bible.

The Bible and creation correctly understood will agree.

(11.0D) Creation provides the great questions; the Bible provides the great answers. The beginning of the universe out of nothing, the just-right expansion of the universe, the fine-tuning of the universe, the fine-tuning of earth for human life, the position of earth just right to observe the universe—these provide the great questions. The Bible provides the answers. Hugh Ross saw the universe and asked the first question:

Who made all this?
    The Bible answers: Evidence from the Bible matching the universe demonstrates that the God of the Bible created it all.

Why is Earth situated so we can understand the universe?
    The Bible answers: So we can know the eternal power and divine nature of the Creator named in the Bible (Rom. 1:20).

Why are the universe and Earth exquisitely fine-tuned for human life?
    The Bible answers: So we can come to know the Creator.

Why is there evil in the world?
    The Bible answers: Satan's and especially man's evil choices.

With evil in the world, why is the creation otherwise so beautiful?
The Bible answers: God, not Satan or humans, is in charge. Satan and humans harm the creation, yet much of the original beauty is still evident. God the Son, who is beautiful beyond imagination, soon will remove all evil and create the New Heavens and New Earth perfectly reflecting His glory!

(11.0E) The Bible inerrantly reveals what God did; science may discover how He did it, which will provide even more evidence for the Biblical Creator. Thank you, Henry Morris, for this great step forward in creation science! Hugh Ross independently arrived at and carried forward this method. The Bible reveals what God did; science may discover from the creation how He did it. Also, because the universe and the Bible are from the Creator, accurate data from science cannot help but give evidence for the creation claims in the Bible—but only if we have the correct creation theory. With the correct creation theory, there is nothing but evidence for the God of the Bible and for His creation work.

Ten Denials from the Ten Theories

The two stage Biblical creation theory has a very positive message. Before we consider those positive claims, we need to clarify what 2SBC is not. With these ten denials clearing negatives from our view of creation, we can see more clearly the positive claims of two stage Biblical creation.

(11.D1) 2SBC denies that any extrabiblical opinion can have authority over the Bible because the Bible shows itself to be from our Creator. The Bible contains many claims that only the Creator could have known before modern science. This evidence demonstrates that the Bible is inspired by God. Therefore, extrabiblical human opinion cannot have authority over God's Word—from the creation in Genesis 1:1 to the blessing in Revelation 22:21. Extrabiblical evidence may clarify a Bible subject or identify faulty interpretation. Gleason Archer and Hugh Ross quote the *Proceedings of the International Council of Biblical Inerrancy,* Summit II (1982) Article 20: "The Bible speaks truth when it touches matters pertaining to nature." "We further affirm that in some cases extrabiblical data have value for clarifying what Scripture teaches, and for prompting correction of faulty interpretations. WE DENY that extrabiblical views ever disprove the teaching of Scripture or hold priority over it."[102]

2SBC *denies* that any extrabiblical human opinions can disprove or have authority over the Bible, which is from our Creator.

No origin view equals the creation account from the Creator.

(11.D2) 2SBC denies that chance is the cause of the universe or life. The evolution theory of the universe and life is based on chance alone. Jacque Monod, a Nobel Prize winner in biology, said, "Chance alone is at the source of every innovation, of all creation in the biosphere. Pure chance, absolutely free but blind, is at the very root of the stupendous edifice of evolution."[1025] Some evolutionists claim that evolution is guided by laws. But in a purely naturalistic system of evolution, even the laws of the universe are by chance. The beginning of the universe was by chance. Chance is the driving principle of all evolution of the universe and life. A naturalistic origin claims everything is from blind random chance alone.

Stephen Hawking is not a Christian, but in a famous quote said, "The whole history of science has been the gradual realization that events do not happen in an arbitrary manner, but that they reflect a certain underlying order, which may or may not be divinely inspired."[1026] Everything is not by random chance.

Contra naturalistic evolution by chance, Ross explains that the origin of the universe, the fine-tuning of the universe for life, the precise conditions on planet Earth for life, and the improbability of life by chance all give overwhelming evidence for a Divine Designer.[1027] Schroeder asks how chance could possibly fine-tune our universe so precisely for human life. He answers, "By chance? Not if our understanding of the laws of nature is even approximately correct." "Lottery upon lottery, and all winners."[1028] The objective evidence overwhelmingly indicates that the universe was designed for human life on Earth. Stephen Weinberg, although an unbeliever, explains, "If the energy of the big bang were different by one part out of 100000000000000000000000000000000000000000000000000 00000000000000000000000000000000000000000000000000 00000000000 there would be no life anywhere in our universe."[1029]

Design indicates a Designer. The evidence shows that the universe had a beginning and is expanding, just as the Bible alone has said for thousands of years. The God of the Bible designed the physical laws and the universe precisely (Jer. 33:25).

Our fine-tuned universe was designed by an amazing Fine-Tuner.

There really is a divinely inspired order, and the evidence shows that this order is from the God of the Bible.

Evolution is chance-driven. That is its fundamental principle. In total contrast, the Bible says that nothing happens by chance (Eph. 1:11). 2SBC *denies* a chance-driven evolutionary origin of the universe or of life. The eternal God of the Bible designed it all.

Faith in chance alone is an abysmal gamble
of all one has on a zero odds game.

(11.D3) 2SBC denies that the Bible teaches chaos in creation — there was no pre-creation chaos, no initial chaos, and no gap chaos. We may use a trivial colloquial sense of chaos: "I did not finish cleaning my desk/house/room yesterday, so it is chaos." This trivial sense is *not* what chaos advocates claim. Waltke explains his sense of utter chaos as "uncreated or unformed,"[1030] "a state of material prior to its creation," "a state of material devoid of order, or without being shaped or formed into something,"[1031] "nothing" in the sense of no order of any kind.[1032] This sense of chaos, as intended by chaos advocates, is so devoid of order that it is not describable as "something." In total contrast, 2SBC denies all chaos in the creation.

God did not create chaos, because the phrase *tōhû v^{a}bōhû* (unfortunately translated "without form and void") does not mean "chaos." The only other uses of these two terms together are Jeremiah 4:23 and Isaiah 34:11. These verses describe the lands of Judah and Edom respectively after these countries had been conquered. So their lands were made "unfit for life" and "empty of life."[1033] Judah and Edom were *not* unformed chaos.

Sailhamer explains the meaning of *tōhû v^{a}bōhû* as "uninhabitable" and "wilderness" "that had not yet become inhabitable for human beings."[1034] In Jeremiah 4:23–26 the terms meant "deserted and uninhabited."[1035] Sailhamer points out that Ibn Ezra (1092–1167) understood the phrase to mean that Earth was "uninhabited because it was covered with water, not that the earth was formless chaos."[1036] So *tōhû v^{a}bōhû* meant Earth was uninhabitable and uninhabited, not chaos.

Since the phrase *tōhû v^{a}bōhû* does not mean chaos, God did not create chaos initially *during* Genesis 1:1.

Since God the Father through God the Son created everything (John 1:3; Heb. 1:2), then there was no autonomous pre-creation chaos *before* 1:1

Earth did not become chaos *after* 1:1, as the gap theory claims. The Bible says nothing about a first creation of life in 1:1–2, Earth becoming chaos in 1:2, or a re-creation in 1:3–31. Earth did not become chaos *after* 1:1.

So there was no chaos *before*, *during*, or *after* Genesis 1:1. There was no chaos in the creation.

Moreover, the phrase *tōhû v^abōhû* did not apply to the universe. Genesis 1:2 explicitly says, "And the earth was *tōhû v^abōhû*." Several authors correctly explain that Genesis 1:2 changes the subject from "the heavens and earth" to the condition of "the earth." Only Earth was declared uninhabitable and uninhabited, so God's six days' work "did not affect the sidereal heaven, but only the Earth and its immediate surroundings."[1037] And even Earth was not chaos, but simply unfinished. Then God worked six days finishing Earth. Therefore, 2SBC *denies* that 1:2 describes pre-creation chaos, initial chaos, or gap chaos. There was no chaos in any of creation.

(11.D4) 2SBC denies that Genesis 1:1 was merely a title with no *ex nihilo* creation of the heavens and the earth. If Genesis 1:1 were merely a title or summary of 1:2–31, then there would have been *no* creation in 1:1. Nowhere in Genesis 1:2–31 was Earth created. So if 1:1 were merely a title, there would have been no *ex nihilo* ("out of nothing") creation of the world anywhere in Genesis 1.

Although Genesis 1:1 does not contain the *words* "out of nothing," 1:1 *does* contain the *concept* that God created the heavens and Earth out of nothing. "The heavens and the earth" meant all things. Since God created all things, then before He created them, there was nothing but God. Therefore, God created all things out of nothing.

John Sailhamer summarizes, "What many people fail to realize is that such an understanding of Genesis 1:1 [as Waltke's idea that 1:1 is merely a title] rules out a fundamental notion in the traditional view—the idea that God created the world 'out of nothing.'" With the title view of Genesis 1:1, "God's acts begin in Genesis 1:2. Since the Earth was already 'formless and void' (vs. 2), that means the Earth already existed when God began to act. But if that is so, when did God create the Earth?"[1038] The title theory almost requires the precreation chaos theory—that chaos existed along with God before Genesis 1:1. But the title theory is incorrect. The *vav* consecutive series of actions began when God created the heavens and earth in 1:1, followed by His command for light to rotating Earth in 1:3.

The church has consistently held that Genesis 1:1 declares that God created the heavens and the earth out of nothing. The *Shepherd of Hermas*

c. AD 150 in Mandate 1.1.1 declares, "God is one, who made all things and perfected them, and made all things to be out of that which was not." In about 400 AD, Nemesius, bishop of Emesa, wrote, "He is shown to be God and Creator and to have brought all things into being out of nothing."[1039] John Calvin is very clear: "He moreover teaches by the word 'created,' that what before did not exist was now made; for he has not used the term יצר (*yatsar*), which signifies to frame or form, but ברא, (*bara*), which signifies to create." Calvin explains that the first meaning of ברא is "*To create out of nothing*, because nothing was made before them [the heavens and earth]."[1040] *Shepherd*, Nemesius, John Calvin, and many others in the history of the church would oppose the pre-creation chaos theory and title theory.[1041]

Henry Morris, the founder of the modern YEC movement, adamantly opposed the title theory: "Neither can verse 1 as a whole be considered a title or summary of the events described in the succeeding verses of the chapter."[1042] Henry Morris realized how crucial it is that God actually created *ex nihilo* all the material of the universe in Genesis 1:1.

In Hebrew (and usually in English), a title is a phrase, like "The Creation of the Heavens and the Earth," not a full sentence.[1043] Genesis 1:1 is a full sentence that declares the actual creation. "In the beginning" is the timeframe. "God" is the subject doing the action. "Created" is the verb. Together "the heavens and the earth" are the direct object of the verb, that which was created. Genesis 1:1 is not a title phrase, but a full sentence declaring when and what God actually created.

Schroeder says, "The creation of the heavens and the earth from absolute nothing is at the root of biblical faith."

Genesis 1:1 declares the act when God actually created the heavens and the Earth in the beginning.

The verb of Genesis 1:1 is *bārā'*, "create." It is an action verb. Schroeder, a Hebrew speaker, explains that the word *bārā'* ("create") is the only Hebrew word that can mean "creation of something from nothing." In the qal when referring to creation, *bārā'* is always by "the actions of God."[1044] Genesis 1:1 declares that God actually created (*ex nihilo*) the heavens and earth in the beginning.

Pember points out that verse 2 confirms that verse 1 was the actual creation. If Genesis 1:1 were a mere title or summary, 1:2 would be the start of the history so would not begin with "and." But Genesis 1:2 does begin with "and" (*vav*/*waw* disjunctive). This "and" describes the results of the previous action: "And the earth was *tōhû v^abōhû*." Genesis 1:2 describes unfinished Earth because the Earth was created in Genesis 1:1. Genesis 1:1 was the actual creation, not merely a title empty of any act.

Hebrew grammar gives a strong reason to accept 1:1 as the first act, not a title. Genesis 1 is a narrative series of events. Genesis 1:1 begins with the action of the perfect verb in 1:1, "created." Genesis 1:2 interrupts the action with a description of unfinished Earth. The following action verb (Gen. 1:3) is the "And said" *vav*/*waw* consecutive prefixed imperfect verb. Weingreen explains the general rule for narrative of sentences referring to the past: "Only the first verb is in the Perfect while the following verb is in the Imperfect with the prefixed Waw."[1045] Except for the description in 1:2, the narrative of 1:1–3 follows the exact pattern Weingreen explains. Therefore, Genesis 1:1 was the first act in the series, the actual creation of the heavens and the earth.

Genesis 1:1 is the declaration of the actual *ex nihilo* creation during the actual beginning time period. Genesis 1:2, "And the earth was *tōhû v^abōhû*," describes Earth's condition at the end of that initial creation time period. Earth had to have been created in 1:1 to be described in 1:2. Light to rotating Earth beginning day and night in 1:3–5 also requires that the Earth was created in 1:1. The title theory, that 1:1 was merely a title or summary of 1:3–31, is incorrect. The associated theory of pre-creation chaos rather than the actual *ex nihilo* creation of the heavens and the earth, is also incorrect. 2SBC denies the title and pre-creation chaos theories.

(11.D5) 2SBC denies that Genesis 1:2 declares a time gap with a first creation and destruction of life. There was no time gap (the middle stage of the three stage creation-ruin-restoration theory) in Genesis 1:2. The gap theory claims a first creation of life, Lucifer's fall, and eventually God's judgment, by which Earth "became" *tōhû v^abōhû,* understood as "chaotic ruin." So the six days were a restoration of Earth and *re*-creation of life.

The profound differences between the three stage gap theory (beginning, gap, six days' re-creation) and the two stage Biblical creation theory (beginning and six days) are far more than that 2SBC denies the middle ruin stage, or gap.

To explain further, the gap or creation-ruin-restoration theory makes six claims about Genesis 1:2: (1) Genesis 1:2 contained a gap of time. (2) God created land and vast life in that gap of time. (3) Lucifer fell into sin and rebellion in that gap of time. (4) Because of Lucifer's fall and God's judgment, all the gap life was killed and formed fossils. (5) In 1:2, Earth "became" "formless and void." (6) As a result, the six days were a *re-creation*, a second creation of life.

The two stage Biblical creation theory *denies all six claims* because *none* are in the Bible.

First, the gap theory claims a time gap at Genesis 1:2. Contra the gap theory, grammatically Genesis 1:2 is a description (the three *vav* disjunctive prefixed initial nouns begins three descriptive clauses), not an event. So 2SBC denies that Genesis 1:2 was a time period with any events.

Second, the gap theory claims *two* creations of life. The gap theory claims a *first* creation at 1:2 of land and vegetation; sea, air, and land animals; and pre-Adamite humans. The gap theory says these lived under Lucifer's dominion. They were killed and turned into fossils. Then the gap theory claims a *second* creation, a re-creation of land and vegetation; sea, air, and land animals; and true humans during the six days. Wiseman correctly counters, "Scripture gives us no information whatever about these alleged two quite distinct and complete creations separated from each other by millions of years."[1046] A time "gap" with a first creation of life is *not in the Bible*. 2SBC denies any first creation at Genesis 1:2.

Third, the gap theory claims Lucifer fell in Genesis 1:2. There is no positive Bible evidence for 1:2 being the time Lucifer fell. As already explained, Genesis 1:2 is a description, not a time period. So 1:2 cannot have been a time when Lucifer fell and God judged him and Earth. Almost all agree that Lucifer fell before Adam did, but he did not fall in Genesis 1:2. 2SBC denies Lucifer fell in Genesis 1:2.

Fourth, the gap theory claims that most of the fossils were formed by God's judgment in a so-called Lucifer's flood[1047] at Genesis 1:2. There is no Bible evidence for a flood of judgment called Lucifer's flood in Genesis 1:2 (2 Pet. 3:6 is about Noah's flood). 2SBC denies any judgment or so-called "Lucifer's flood" at Genesis 1:2.

Fifth, the gap theory claims that the "to be" verb in Genesis 1:2 should be translated "became," so Earth became chaos. Waltke correctly shows that the traditional translation, "was," is correct.

Sixth, because of the above, the gap theory claims that the six days were a *second* creation of land and vegetation; sea, air, and land animals; and humans—a *re*-creation. There is no Bible basis for this claim. 2SBC denies that the six days were a *second* creation.

Also, as previously mentioned, 2SBC denies chaos. Earth did not become chaos in Genesis 1:2.

Waltke says, "We conclude, then, that this popular [gap theory] interpretation of Genesis 1:1–2 is impossible on both philological and theological grounds."[1048]

There was no time gap at Genesis 1:2, no first creation of life in 1:2, no fall of Lucifer in 1:2, no judgment by God in 1:2, no chaos, and no re-creation. The gap is an argument from silence and is contradicted by Hebrew grammar. 2SBC *denies* any time gap or events at Genesis 1:2.

(11.D6) 2SBC denies that Genesis 1 teaches day-ages or any other non–day-night days. Stambaugh reports, "Basil and Ambrose" and "the majority opinion of church fathers on the meaning of 'day' in Genesis 1 was that they were ordinary days."[1049] Luther, and apparently Calvin as well, agreed.[1050] Stambaugh shows that in the "relationships between 'day' and numbers, 'day' as it is used alongside of morning and/or evening; and light, night, and darkness" indicated a "twenty-four-hour day."[1051]

Schroeder, a Hebrew speaker, also denies that *yôm* in Genesis 1 could mean a day-age or epoch: "The approach that 'the six days were really six epochs' has scant biblical basis."[1052]

Wiseman says that the day-age theory "does not deal with the six 'evening and morning'" terms. "Was each of them an indefinitely long night in which there was no light? Was the geologic night as long or almost as long as the geologic 'day'?"[1053]

Pember points out that *yôm* with a numeral "can only be used in its literal acceptation of the time which the earth takes to make one revolution upon its axis." "It is clear, therefore, that we must understand the Six Days to be six periods of twenty-four hours each."[1054]

Sailhamer agrees that the six days were normal days, the same kind of days that Moses experienced when he established the six-day-workweek for Israel.[1055] Days designated by sunlight ending in evening, nighttime, and morning are not flexible units, but are according to the fixed laws of God (Jer. 33:25–26).

The two stage Biblical creation theory recognizes that Genesis 1:3–31 indicates that each of the six work days was a normal daylight-evening-nighttime-morning day. 2SBC *denies* that any of the six days in Genesis 1:3–31 was a long day-age.

(11.D7) 2SBC denies that the Bible says that the Genesis 1:1 *ex nihilo* creation was *in* day one. Contra YEC, Exodus 20:11a does *not* have an "*in*" so does *not* say the initial creation was "in" the six days. Jesus did *not* date the universe when He said from the beginning (understood in the Hebrew sense as a time period) God made male and female, so do not divorce. The Bible does not say Genesis 1:1 was in day one.

(11.D7a) Genesis 1 and Proverbs 8 deny the Genesis 1:1 *ex nihilo* creation was in day one. The order of events in Genesis 1 is one of several definitive proofs that the *ex nihilo* creation of the heavens and the Earth in Genesis 1:1 was in the beginning, not in day one.

Genesis 1 definitively indicates that the Genesis 1:1 initial creation was before the six days in 1:3–31. This order of events as listed is certified by the *vav* consecutive prefixed verbs. These verbs are in a series of clauses narrating successive events. In Hebrew, the *vav* consecutive, often translated "then," indicates a series of events in consecutive order. The first event was "In the beginning God created the heavens and the earth." Verse 2 describes the unfinished condition of Earth, the darkness on the surface of the deep ocean, and the presence of the divine Observer just above the surface of the deep water. Day one begins with "Then God said, 'Let there be light.'" Then there was light. Then God saw the light was good. Then God separated the light and darkness. Then God named the light day and darkness night. After the daylight, then there was evening, which began nighttime. After the night, then there was morning, which ended nighttime. That order is certified by the Hebrew *vav/waw* consecutive prefixed verb clauses. Since day one began with daylight and ended with evening, nighttime, and dawn of morning, day one could not have included the dark described by 1:2, or it would have been nighttime-daytime-nighttime, more than one day. Day one began in 1:3 with "And God said, 'Let there be light,'" an unstated amount of time after the beginning of Genesis 1:1 and description of Earth in 1:2.

Kline offers additional evidence from Proverbs 8 that the *ex nihilo* creation of the heavens and the Earth was in the beginning in Genesis 1:1 before day one. Kline explains that Proverbs 8:23b–24a says, "From the beginning, from the earliest times of the earth, When there were no depths" (NASB).[1056] There were depths (*t\u1ea3h\u00f4m*) described in Genesis 1:2 because by then darkness was on the surface of the deep. And there were depths during day one, which began with the light of day, forming a horizon of light on the deep (Prov. 8:27). The beginning was before the *t\u1ea3h\u00f4m* (deep ocean) described in Genesis 1:2.

Since the beginning was before the deep ocean in 1:2, the beginning was in 1:1 when God created *ha'\u0101retz*, "the earth," before it gained its future deep ocean. All eight commands and six days began with, "And God said," so day one began with Genesis 1:3. Day one began with the command for light to that dark deep ocean, and ended in evening (beginning the nighttime) and morning (ending the nighttime). Since the days began in 1:3 with light starting day one, the beginning in 1:1 was before the six days. The order of events was the beginning with heavens and Earth, the deep ocean, then six days.

The YEC claim, that the beginning was in day one, is proven incorrect by the order of events in Genesis 1 and secondarily by Proverbs 8:22–31. 2SBC denies that the Genesis 1:1 *ex nihilo* creation was in day one.

(11.D7b) 2SBC denies that the inspired Hebrew of Exodus 20:11a says God "created" "in" six days, and so denies that 20:11 forces Genesis 1:1 into day one. There is no "*in*" in the Hebrew of Exodus 20:11a. "For in six days God made the heavens and the earth" is not what the Hebrew Bible says. The Alexandrian Jewish Septuagint added the "*in*." God did not write "in" on the tablet of the Law. Too many translations have followed the Septuagint and added an "*in*" that is not within God's inspired Hebrew text. However, the KJV correctly italicizes the "*in,*" showing that "*in*" is not in the Hebrew. There is no "*in*" within the inspired Hebrew text of Exodus 20:11a (or 31:17b).

In addition, '*āsâh* (do, make) does not mean "created" in the strong *ex nihilo* sense, nor is it translated as "created" by any standard translation of Exodus 20:11.

A plain summary of the Hebrew Fourth Commandment is: You shall work six days but keep the seventh day holy by not working, because God worked six days but rested the seventh.

Verse 11 should be translated in the context of the Fourth Commandment of 20:9–11:

Six days you shall labor and **do** all your work, but the seventh day *is a* Sabbath to the LORD your God; *in it* you shall not **do** any work. . . .
Because for six days the LORD **did *work on*** the heavens/sky and the earth/ land, the sea and all that *is* in them, but He rested on the seventh day.

In this context-sensitive translation from the Hebrew, '*āsâh* is translated all three times by its core meaning "do" and "did," with the sense of work. After the core meaning of "do," the next most common meanings are "make" and "work." Northrup correctly translates '*āsâh* by the meaning "work": "Because six days the Eternal LORD worked upon the heaven and the earth, the sea and all that is in them."[1057] Israel was to work six days and rest the seventh because God worked six days and rested the seventh.

What work did God do for six days? Genesis 1:2 describes Earth as *tōhû v^abōhû,* uninhabitable and uninhibited or empty of life, with darkness on the surface of the deep ocean waters. God worked six days making Earth lighted, habitable, and inhabited. This work began in Genesis 1:3 with God's first command, "Let there be light." This was the only command in day one, and it began day one. The six days ended with the creation of sea, air, land animals, and man, thus filling the Earth with life.

Exodus 20:9–11 is saying to work six days and rest the seventh because God worked six days and rested the seventh. There is no "*in*" in the Hebrew of Exodus 20:11a, and there should be no "in" as the second word in English translations. God created the heavens and earth in the beginning, not "*in*" the six days.

Every verse in the five books of Moses with the translation "for in" in the KJV actually contains b^e, "in"—*except* Exodus 20:11 and 31:17. The following are all the quotes from books of Moses (in the KJV) with "for in." All except two contain the Hebrew ב (b^e, "in").

Reference	**Quote in KJV**		**Hebrew contains ב, be, "in"**
Gen. 2:17	for in the day that thou eatest	כִּי בְּיֹום	Yes
Gen. 9:6	for in the image of God	כִּי בְּצֶלֶם אֱלֹהִים	Yes
Gen. 10:25	for in his days was the earth	כִּי בְיָמָיו	Yes
Gen. 21:12	for in Isaac shall thy seed	כִּי בְיִצְחָק	Yes
Gen. 49:6	for in their anger they slew	כִּי בְאַפָּם	Yes
Exod. 10:28	for in *that* day thou seest	כִּי בְּיֹום	Yes
Exod. 12:17	for in this selfsame day	כִּי בְּעֶצֶם הַיֹּום	Yes
Exod. 18:11	for in the thing wherein	כִּי בַדָּבָר	Yes
<u>Exod. 20:11</u>	<u>For *in* six days the LORD</u>	כִּי שֵׁשֶׁת־יָמִים	**NO**
Exod. 23:15	for in it thou camest out	כִּי־בֹו יָצָאתָ	Yes
<u>Exod. 31:17</u>	<u>for *in* six days the LORD</u>	כִּי־שֵׁשֶׁת יָמִים	**NO**
Exod. 34:18	for in the month Abib	כִּי בְחֹדֶשׁ	Yes
Lev. 18:24	for in all these the nations	כִּי בְכָל־אֵלֶּה	Yes
Deut. 16:1	for in the month of Abib	כִּי בְחֹדֶשׁ	Yes

Every quote of "for in" (KJV) in the books of Moses has a ב, b^e, "in," except Exodus 20:11 and 31:17.

Looking at the Hebrew from the other side, there is one other quote that matches the Hebrew of Exodus 20:11 and 31:17. First Kings 11:16 is the only other quote with "For six [+ time word]." First Kings 11:16 does *not* have a ב, b^e, "in." First Kings 11:16 is correctly translated without an "in":

For six months did Joab remain there with all Israel (KJV).
Because for six months Joab remained there with all Israel (NKJV).

No translation says, "For in six months Joab remained. . . ."

Therefore, Exodus 20:11 and 31:17 should not be translated as if they had a ב, bᵉ, "in." Properly translated, they should follow Young's Literal Translation or Northrup, which do not include an "in" within Exodus 20:11a, but correctly say, "For six days."

2SBC denies that there is an "in" within the Hebrew of Exodus 20:11a. So 2SBC denies the YEC claim that 20:11 means "God created the universe (everything) in six days."[1058] 2SBC affirms that God created the heavens and the earth (everything) "in the beginning" as stated in Genesis 1:1, after which God worked six normal days in Genesis 1:3–31. There is no "in" within Exodus 20:11a. A Hebrew interlinear of Exodus 20:11 reads (right to left):

כִּי שֵׁשֶׁת־יָמִים עָשָׂה יְהוָה אֶת־הַשָּׁמַיִם וְאֶת־הָאָרֶץ אֶת־הַיָּם וְאֶת־כָּל־אֲשֶׁר־בָּם
them-in that all & sea the earth the & heavens the Yahweh 'āsâh days six For

What was "written by the finger of God" was יָמִים כִּי שֵׁשֶׁת, "for six days," not "for in six days." In the Hebrew Fourth Commandment, there was no "in" on the tablet of stone that God wrote and gave to Moses. And in the context of the Fourth Commandment, 'āsâh meant "did work," not "created" or even "made" in any sense of created.

Instead of the incorrect claim that based on Exodus 20:11, "Jesus did explicitly say He created in six days,"[1059] 2SBC claims that literally, "In the beginning God created the heavens and the earth." Then in Genesis 1:3–31 God worked six normal literal days finishing Earth and filling it with life, culminating in literal Adam and Eve. 2SBC denies that there is an "in" within the Hebrew of Exodus 20:11a.

To me, the fundamental issue is *Biblical authority,* because the Bible is from our Creator. On YEC claim three, if young earth scientific creationism continues to proclaim that all creation was "in six days," thus continuing to add an "in" that was never "written by the finger of God," that continued act will constitute a violation of Biblical authority, a violation of the Word of God.

Instead, I urge YEC advocates to believe "In the [literal] beginning God [literally] created the [literal] heavens and the [literal] earth."

(11.D7c) 2SBC denies that the creation of male and female, which Jesus referred to in His statement against divorce, dates the universe. YEC claims that Jesus' statement against divorce dates the universe to 6,000 years old. 2SBC claims that these verses against divorce say nothing about the date of the universe.

Jesus was answering the pro-divorce Pharisees. He probably answered in Aramaic Hebrew, translated slightly differently by Matthew and Mark:

"He who created *them* from the beginning made them male and female" (Matt. 19:4, NASB).

"But from the beginning of creation, *God* made them male and female" (Mark 10:6, NASB).

YEC claims, "Jesus goes back to <u>the beginning of time</u>."[1060] "He is talking about the <u>whole creation from Jesus' day back to the very first moment of creation, . . . the whole creation during all of history</u>."[1061]

A Summary of the YEC Claim:
• "Beginning" meant "beginning of time," "first moment of creation."
• Jesus said God made male and female (Adam, Eve) *at* the beginning.
• Therefore, Adam's beginning 6,000 years ago dates the beginning of "the whole creation [the universe] during all of history."

We can analyze this claim in four parts: Jesus' words "from," "beginning," and "creation" and how the words fit together.

An unfortunate interpretive translation of Mark 10:6 renders ἀπὸ as "at." "But *at* [ἀπὸ] the beginning of creation God 'made them male and female.'" YEC quotes this translation. Using "at" makes it seem as if Jesus were saying God created Adam and Eve "at" the very beginning moment of the history of the creation. Based on the genealogies, YEC concludes that Adam was created 6,000 years ago. If God made Adam *at* the very beginning and made the universe at that same beginning, then the universe is also 6,000 years old.

In response, the Greek word is ἀπὸ (*apo*), which actually means "from." "But from [ἀπὸ] the beginning of creation, *God* made them male and female" (NASB), so married couples are not to divorce.

The Greek word "beginning" is ἀρχῆς (*archēs*, "beginning"), which can mean either duration of "early times" or "starting point."[1062]

The English has the same two senses of "beginning": "1. **The first part** or early stages of something . . . 2. **Start** – the point in time or space at which something starts."[1063]

Which sense did Jesus intend?

YEC seems to assume that Jesus used the second sense, "starting point," "the very first moment of creation."

In response, this YEC claim produces a contradiction. God did not create male and female in "the very first moment of creation." He made them in the sixth day, at the *end* of the creation time.

In contrast to the contradictory YEC claim, 2SBC recognizes that Jesus was speaking in a Hebrew setting to people with a Hebrew mind-set. He went back to the Hebrew sense that carried over into the Gospels. Jesus was speaking about the creation, so, just as in John 1:1, ἀρχῆς ("beginning") would have been associated with בְּרֵאשִׁית (*b*ᵉ*rē'shît*, "in the beginning"). *B*ᵉ*rē'shît* consistently means a beginning time period, often of unstated length (Gen. 10:10; Job 8:7; Jer. 28:1). Hebrew professor John Sailhamer says, "The term [*b*ᵉ*rēshît*, "in the beginning"] does not refer to a point in time but to a *period* or *duration* of time."[1064]

The semantic range of *rē'shît* in its actual use in the Hebrew Bible does *not* include "2. **Start** – the point in time" as YEC assumes. Instead, the sense of *rē'shît* is close to the first Greek and English sense, "early times" or "**the early stages of something**."

By quoting Genesis 1:27 about God making male and female, Jesus extended "the early stages" to include not only the initial creation (Gen. 1:1) but also the six days (Gen. 1:3–31). Jesus argued that from the beginning creation time period (including the six days), God made male and female, so do not divorce. This 2SBC understanding fits because ἀρχῆς, "beginning," in the context of male and female, includes the sixth-day creation of humans as part of the extended beginning.

"Creation," κτίσεως, (from "*ktisis*") is defined by Danker's *Greek-English Lexicon* as 1. "**the act of creation**;" or 2. "**the result of a creative act, that which is created**."[1065]

YEC claims that Jesus used the word "creation" as "the whole creation during all of history,"[1066] meaning "*that which is created*" in its course of time through all of history. The YEC idea is that in comparison to "all of history," the six days were trivial, so Adam and Eve were created *essentially at* the beginning of the creation. Therefore, Adam's beginning 6,000 years ago also dates the universe.

In response, 2SBC recognizes that Jesus quoted Genesis 1:27, "He made them male and female," which was an "**act of creation**." Jesus told the Pharisees that in the beginning time period, including the six days, which was the time of the acts of creation, the Creator made male and female. So *from* that example onward, do not divorce. He said nothing to the Pharisees about the age of the universe.

Finally, how do the words fit together? Mark 10:6 says, "But from the beginning of creation, God made them male and female" (NASB). How do the words "from," "beginning," and "of creation" fit together? Here are the two major possibilities:

YEC understands "beginning" as "the very first moment" of "the whole creation during all of history"[1067] (partitive genitive). But this leads to the contradiction already mentioned. Mortenson (YEC) claims that Adam and Eve were created at the beginning, which he says was "the very first moment" of creation. But Genesis 1 explicitly says they were created in the very *last* day of creation, the sixth day. Mortenson's claim is contradictory.

In response, 2SBC recognizes that the creation (κτίσεως) of Adam and Eve was the final act in the extended beginning time period of Genesis 1.

How does 2SBC put "beginning" and "creation" together? "Creation" clarifies which beginning—namely, the creation time (genitive of apposition). The Greek word ἀρχῆς, "beginning," is modified by κτίσεως, "of creation." From the "beginning," that is, the time of the "creation" acts, God made humans as male and female; so married couples are not to divorce. It all fits beautifully.

Jesus said nothing in these verses to the Pharisees about the age of the universe. The Bible does not say how much time passed during Genesis 1:1 before day one began in 1:3. Adam's genealogy which commences at the *end* of the creation time in day six, does not date the universe at the start of the initial creation time in 1:1 before the six days. The universe remains undated by the Bible.

2SBC denies that Jesus' statement against divorce says anything about the age of the universe.

(11.D8) 2SBC denies that the Bible says the six days were night-day cycle days. Some recent advocates of YEC realize that their unique third claim (that the initial creation of Genesis 1:1–2 was in day one) requires that day one start with the dark of Genesis 1:2 and end with the daylight of 1:3–4. So they go to Genesis 1:5—"God called the light 'day,' and the darkness he called 'night.' And there was evening, and there was morning—the first day" (NIV). They ignore the stated order of day and night, and instead claim that the evening of Genesis 1:5c began day one as the beginning of the night of Genesis 1:2, followed by the morning of Genesis 1:5d as the daylight of Genesis 1:3–4. In the premier YEC *Technical Journal*, Frank DeRemer claimed Genesis 1:2 was "the first evening of darkness (v.2)," in a "cycle of evening, night, morning, and daytime."[1068] The dark of Genesis 1:2 was the dark twelve hours of the night half of day one. YEC advocate Jason Lisle also claims, "A day was an evening and a morning."[1069] So YEC claims Genesis 1:2 was an evening and nighttime—"the first evening of darkness (v.2)," which began the twelve-hour night half of day one. After the twelve hours of night of 1:2, Genesis 1:3 began the daytime second half of day one.

This rather puzzling interpretive claim is driven by *"in six days"* of Exodus 20:11. YEC must somehow fit Genesis 1:1–2 *in* day one as the evening and nighttime.

In response, 2SBC agrees with Henry Morris, founder of the young earth creationism theory, who correctly claimed "a cyclical succession of days and nights—periods of light and periods of darkness," "a cyclical light-dark arrangement."[1070] Morris's view is Biblically supported.

With Morris, 2SBC claims that all six were day-night days, following the natural literal reading of Genesis 1. All six days have a similar format. All six began with "And God said." All six ended with "And there was evening, and there was morning, [numbered day]." So day one began with "And God said, 'Let there be light,' and there was light." Day one ended with "And there was evening, and there was morning, day one."

Each sentence in day one begins with a *vav/waw* consecutive, translated "and" or "then." "Then" is a good English translation of the Hebrew *vav/waw* consecutive that indicates this text is sequential historical narrative, one event after the next in order, logically or temporally. The events were as follows:

In the beginning God created the heavens and earth.
Now earth was uninhabitable, uninhabited, and its sea was dark.
Then God commanded light.
Then there was light, beginning the daylight of day one.
Then God evaluated the light and pronounced it "good."
Then God separated the light from the darkness.
Then God named the light "day" and the dark "night."
Then evening started the nighttime.
Then morning dawned ending the nighttime, completing day one.

Day one was a daylight-followed-by-nighttime day. All five of the succeeding days of God's work followed the same pattern. Because day six ended with the dawn of morning, the seventh day also necessarily began with light for a full daytime, evening, nighttime, and morning, as a full seventh day-night day. All seven were full day-night days. The seventh day was *not* called a Sabbath, so did not begin with evening.

The YEC claim has another fatal error. YEC claims that Genesis 1:2 was "the first evening of darkness (v.2)," in a "cycle of evening, night, morning, and daytime."[1071]

In response, this is the same claim that the gap theory makes, that 1:2 was a time period. But the grammar (*vav* disjunctives beginning three descriptive clauses) proves Genesis 1:2 was *not* a time period but was a description of unfinished planet Earth. Genesis 1:2 was not a twelve-hour nighttime period because 1:2 was not a time period at all. If the gap theory is incorrect, so is this recent YEC claim.

If YEC wants to claim that Genesis 1:1 (instead of 1:2) was a time period of evening beginning the twelve hours of darkness of nighttime, then it must accept that the meaning of *b^{e}rē'shît*, "in the beginning," was a beginning time period. In the Hebrew Bible, *b^{e}rē'shît* was measured normally in years, but never in hours. A beginning measured in years would no longer fit into day one as YEC claims. The YEC third claim that Genesis 1:1–2 was *in* day one becomes more and more convoluted and impossible.

For the first several millennia of history, the standard understanding of a "day" was daytime followed by nighttime. God said to Noah, "Day and night shall not cease" (Gen. 8:22, NASB). The standard day was "day and night."

Several millennia *after* Adam was created, Israel as a new nation began celebrating Jewish holy days of Passover, Sabbath, and festivals beginning in the evening (Exod. 12:6, 18; Deut. 16:4). But these later holy days cannot be imported back into Genesis 1:3–5, which began with light and ended with night. The seventh day in Genesis 2:2–3 was not even designated a Sabbath. The first mention of Sabbath was for Israel in Exodus 16, several millennia later.

Despite these Israelite holy days beginning in evening, even Moses measured a normal day as morning and then evening. "And it came about the next <u>day</u> that Moses sat to judge the people, and the people stood about Moses <u>from the morning until the evening</u>" (Exod. 18:13, NASB). "This is the offering which Aaron and his sons are to present to the LORD on the <u>day</u> when he is anointed; the tenth of an ephah of fine flour as a regular grain offering, half of it <u>in the morning</u> and half of it <u>in the evening</u> (Leviticus 6:20).

Moses measured a *night* by evening until morning. "Now on the day that the tabernacle was erected the cloud covered the tabernacle, the tent of the testimony, and <u>in the evening it was like the appearance of fire over the tabernacle, until morning</u>. So it was continuously; the cloud would cover it *by day*, and the appearance of <u>fire by night</u>. (Num. 9:15–16, NASB).

In each day of Genesis 1, *after* the daytime, the Author ended that day with "and there was evening and there was morning, day [number]."

Genesis 1:3–5 describes the first daylight-evening-nighttime-morning day. That day one defined a Genesis day. Because day one began with light and ended with night, the YEC claim that the dark of Genesis 1:1–2 was in day one is impossible. The dark described in Genesis 1:2 could not have been a first nighttime before daytime and then a second nighttime ending with the next morning's dawn. That would be a night-day-night, longer than a single day. Therefore, the unique YEC third claim that the initial creation, including the dark of 1:2, was in day one is impossible.

2SBC denies this recent YEC claim that day one began with nighttime. The novel YEC third claim that the initial creation was in the nighttime beginning day one is proven unbiblical.

(11.D8a) 2SBC denies that the Bible says the light for days one through three was temporary. The YEC claim of temporary light from an artificial source for days one through three is not in the Bible. Contra this YEC claim, in Jeremiah 33:25–26 God says, "If I have not established my covenant with day and night and the fixed laws [*ᶜhuqqāh*] of heaven and earth, then I will reject the descendants of Jacob" (NASB). The fixed laws are God's unchanging covenant. Day and night (notice the order is day and night, not night and day) are by God's fixed laws. Day and night did not change from some temporary arrangement to the present law-governed rotation of Earth in sunlight.

Moses defined the heavens as "the sun and the moon and the stars" in the sky (Deut. 4:19). God created the luminaries in the heavens in the beginning. So the light on day one was light from the sun to rotating Earth. Sunlight was the normal means for "day and night" from then on by "the fixed laws of heaven and earth" (Jer. 33:25).

2SBC denies that the Bible says there was temporary light for days one through three or an end to temporary light on the fourth day.

(11.D9) 2SBC denies that the Bible dates the *ex nihilo* creation of the heavens and the Earth. Hugh Ross claims an ancient universe and Earth—old earth creationism (OEC). To his credit, Ross does not say the *Bible* dates the universe. Henry Morris and Ken Ham do claim that the

Bible dates the universe and Earth to the date of Adam, which YEC dates to about 6,000 years old. "As far as the creation of the universe is concerned, this took place five days earlier than the creation of man."[1072]

In contrast, Kline says, "We must speak where the Bible speaks, and be silent where the Bible is silent. . . . The inspired text, rightly interpreted, is simply silent with regard to the age of the earth and universe."[1073] On this claim, I agree with Meredith Kline. The Bible does *not* date the universe (UEC). The genealogies of Adam roughly date Adam, who was created on the sixth day. But Adam's genealogies do not date the universe because the heavens and earth were created an unstated amount of time before the six days.

2SBC denies that the Bible gives a date for "in the beginning" when God created *ex nihilo* the heavens and the eath.

An incorrect creation theory
does not reduce God's glory in the creation,
but it reduces our ability
to see His glory in the creation.

(11.D10) 2SBC denies that God intentionally designed the creation to deceive man. So 2SBC denies any deceiving appearance of age by any works of God in creation. Hugh Ross says, "Whatever objects of His creation we subject to scientific analysis will reveal their true age—provided the analysis is theoretically valid, correctly applied, and accurately interpreted."[1074]

In contrast, Henry Morris of YEC claims an "appearance of age."[1075] The universe appears much older than 6,000 years, but that is only "appearance of age," because Exodus 20:11 says "*in* six days."

2SBC agrees with Ross on this claim (while not affirming his creation dating). God made the creation to reveal Himself (Rom. 1:19–20). No doubt, people will deceive themselves about the creation (Rom 1:21). But God did not *design* the creation to deceive. The Bible says, "God is not a man, that He should lie" (Num. 23:19).

Someone might claim that Adam and Eve were created with appearance of age, so deceptive appearance of age is acceptable.

In response, Adam and Eve knew how old they were, so they were not deceived—nor was God, nor was Lucifer, nor were any observing angels. There was no deception.

Someone might claim that the Bible *says* the universe is 6,000 years old, so God does not deceive by a 6,000-year-old universe that only appears much older.

I respond that this is a false claim. The Bible nowhere says that the universe is 6,000 years old.

Duncan and Hall might say that the entire creation was by miracles, so "appearance of age" is no problem because scientific evidence about creation is "every man a liar."

I respond with the Kline Claim, that Genesis 2:5–6 shows God does works by means, not just miracles. YEC "appearance of age" miracles where the Bible does not indicate either appearance of age or miracles is saying more than the Bible says.

YEC advocates suggest that we cannot tell the age of the universe because of the Fall and curse. Men are corrupted (the damaging noetic effect of the Fall on the human intellect) and the universe is corrupted.

I respond that the effects of the Fall are very real. Evidence of sin is all around us and in us. But God preserved the universe sufficiently so that the Bible can still declare, "The heavens declare the glory of God" (Ps. 19:1, NIV). Although men suppress the truth, Romans 1:20 still says,

For <u>since the creation of the world</u> His invisible attributes, His eternal power and divine nature, have been <u>clearly seen</u>, being understood through what has been made, so that they are without excuse (NASB).

It is not the heavens that deceive people,
but their own suppression of the evidence
so clearly visible in the heavens.

I further respond that the Bible never says God created the heavens and earth with appearance of age. Romans 1:19–20 is very clear: God does not deceive by His creation work. As we look up at the stars, we do not see deception. We see reality and God's glory. God did not create the universe or Earth with a deceiving appearance of age. He created the universe to reveal Himself. 2SBC *denies* that God designed the universe to deceive with intentionally deceptive "appearance of age."

I conclude that God created the universe to reveal his glory. "The heavens declare the glory of God; the skies proclaim the work of his hands" (Ps. 19:1, NIV). The Bible does not teach that the creation is deceptive, but rather that God designed the creation so man can discover truth from the universe, which reveals His nature, power, and glory.

The creation, rightly understood, reveals the glory of God.

Bible Interpretation (Hermeneutics) from the Ten Theories

(11.H1) Start with the Bible text; then welcome correlations from science. John Sailhamer emphasizes that we should start with "the meaning of the biblical author as expressed in the biblical text. . . . We must first understand the biblical text and then seek to relate its meaning to the findings of modern science, if possible."[1076]

The Creator intends humans to see His glory,
both from His Word and from His universe.

Custance says, "If we are once sure what a particular passage is saying, we should not allow science to determine for us . . . what we may believe in Scripture; nor are we to allow . . . Scripture to determine what the scientist may observe. . . . Demonstrable fact in the one cannot ultimately conflict with demonstrable fact in the other, though interpretations often do."[1077] I conclude that if we seek truth from the Creator's Word and His work, we will find the truth.

(11.H2) Interpret the Bible text from the perspective of the author. There are three aspects to interpreting the text from the perspective of the author.

(11.H2a) Do not import modern scientific concepts into the ancient text, yet recognize the wisdom of the ancient Biblical authors. Sailhamer says, "It was only natural to view the Biblical text within the narrow limits of what was known about the world."[1078] The Bible text is ultimately from God, but He chose to inspire men, the ancient human authors. We should interpret from their perspective.

We would make ourselves authors if we import modern scientific concepts into the ancient Biblical words and narratives. On the other hand, we should not underestimate the wisdom and knowledge of the writers of those ancient Bible words, especially as they were inspired by the Holy Spirit.

(11.H2b) Do not import later Biblical concepts into earlier events. A common example of violating this rule is importing the concept of the workweek and Sabbath of the Fourth Commandment from Exodus

20:8–11 back into the much more ancient events of Genesis 1:1—2:4a. The ideas of work and rest are in Genesis 1:1—2:4a, so we may speak of the six days as *God's* work days and the seventh day as *His* rest day. But Genesis has no command for a workweek for *man* and no mention of "Sabbath" requirements for *man*. The first time a Sabbath for man was mentioned was to Israel at Sinai (Exod. 16:23) several millennia later.

God adds an important detail in the second statement of the Fourth Commandment for the Sabbath in Exodus 31:14–17.

> So the sons of Israel shall observe the Sabbath, to celebrate the Sabbath throughout their generations as a perpetual covenant. It is a sign between Me and the sons of Israel forever; for six days the LORD worked on [*'āsâh*] the heavens and the earth, but on the seventh day He ceased work, and rested (Exod. 31:16–17, my translation).

The Sabbath was a "perpetual covenant" as "a sign between Me and the sons of Israel forever." The Sabbath was not given as a command to Adam in Genesis 1—5 or to Noah in Genesis 9. The Sabbath was given much later as a special covenant command to *Israel* at Sinai.[1079] Therefore, it is a violation of this rule to import this later Commandment for a human workweek followed by a Sabbath back into Genesis 1. The later use of the Genesis 1 example in the Fourth Commandment is legitimate and right. But the use of examples works only one way. The earlier event may serve as an example for a later command, but the later command may not be imported back into the earlier event.

(11.H2c) Recognize the perspective location of the author. In a different sense of perspective, Ross says, "Begin by establishing [not assuming] the point of view."[1080] We can understand Genesis 1 properly only from the "reference frame" of the Observer. We must interpret "from the vantage point of an observer, . . . describing details as they would have appeared from that perspective."[1081]

Ross points out that the only named observer on location was the Spirit of God, hovering just above the ocean surface (Gen. 1:2). Because He alone was named on location, we may deduce that He was the Observer. If He was the Observer, then presumably He was also the Narrator. The Holy Spirit as the Narrator of Genesis 1 fits with the Spirit's oversight of Scripture (2 Tim. 3:16). Therefore, each event of the rest of the creation narrative (Gen. 1:3–31) should be interpreted from the perspective of the apparent Observer and Narrator located just above Earth's surface.

(11.H3) Begin by analyzing how the clauses (esp. Gen. 1:1–3) fit together. Michael Heiser says, "Determine which clauses are independent clauses and which are not, and then which independent clauses are modified by which dependent clauses."[1082] The following is my brief summary:

Bruce Waltke has shown, contra the gap theory, that Genesis 1:2 is a *dependent* clause between the two independent clauses of 1:1 and 1:3.[1083] I agree.

The next question is whether 1:2 relates to 1:1 or 1:3. I note that Genesis 1:1 ends with the word "earth." Genesis 1:2 begins with "Now the earth." So 1:2 describes the Earth resulting from its creation in 1:1. This is how the traditional initial creation theory relates 1:1–3.

Traditional Initial Creation Theory

1:1	Independent Clause	"In the beginning God created . . . earth."
1:2	Dependent on 1:1	"Now the earth was [*unfinished, dark*]."
1:3	Independent Clause	"And God said, 'Let there be light.'"

The traditional initial creation theory says the Earth in Genesis 1:2 relates to its creation in 1:1. In other words, the *tōhû vᵃbōhû* unfinished Earth described in 1:2 was the result of God's initial *ex nihilo* creation work in 1:1. No doubt, Genesis 1:1–2 also supplies the background for the narrative of 1:3–31.

Waltke errs in his claim that 1:2 relates *only* to 1:3, and 1:1 is *only* a title so unrelated to 1:2.

Within the traditional initial creation theory, the majority holds to an initial *chaos* creation. But the Waltke exclusion principle correctly rules against both an initial *ex nihilo* creation of an orderly universe in 1:1 but chaos in 1:2. Waltke takes the pre-creation chaos option, but logically there is the opposite option—*ex nihilo* creation but no chaos.[1084] I am supporting the traditional initial creation theory, but the *minority* view of a no-chaos initial *ex nihilo* creation. After its *ex nihilo* creation, Earth was simply unfinished—not yet habitable, empty of life, and its sea surface cloud-darkened. Genesis 1:2 describes Earth from its creation during the 1:1 time period. Genesis 1:2 also describes the unfinished items that God will finish in 1:3–31.

(11.H4) A correct understanding of a Bible topic will cohere without any part being forced. Like a puzzle, if a Bible topic is put together correctly, no piece will have to be forced into a space that it does not truly fit. Each of the ten previous theories has many parts that fit together. But each has at least one part forced into its theory. A correct understanding of a Bible topic should cohere without any part being forced.

I have been amazed to see that each part of the creation puzzle from over one hundred Bible texts fits a two stage creation without even one being forced. Check this for yourself in the following claims.

CLAIMS OF TWO STAGE BIBLICAL CREATION FROM THE TEN THEORIES

The Biblical payoff time has arrived. We are about to bring together all the hard work that we have done. We have evaluated the claims of the ten theories by the words of the Creator Himself. Now we can put together the puzzle pieces of the Biblically supported claims from the ten creation theories. We are about to join the most Biblical insights of the greatest creationists into a single unified understanding of what the Creator said that He did when He created the heavens and the earth.

From both the Bible and the creationists, we have deduced that the creation was in two stages. The two stages are:

(I) In the beginning God created the heavens and the Earth.
But Earth was uninhabitable, uninhabited, sea-covered, and dark.
(II) God made Earth lighted, habitable, and inhabited by His eight commands and six day-night work days.

Taking the creation of the heaven and earth in 1:1 literally, and the six days literally, we recognize a two stage creation.

STAGE ONE: IN THE BEGINNING ETERNAL GOD CREATED THE HEAVENS AND THE EARTH

God alone exists eternally — Father, Son, and Spirit — as the one and only God, אֱלֹהִים. By His sovereign decree, out of nothing but His Word (Ps. 33:6; 1 Pet. 3:5), God the Father through God the Son (Heb. 1:2) in the beginning created the heavens and earth (Gen. 1:1).

Luther said that Genesis 1 "contains things the most important, and at the same time the most obscure."[1085] Only by delving deeply into the over one hundred Bible creation texts and then gathering the most Biblically supported claims of the theological giants who have gone before us can we begin to understand these "most obscure" yet "most important" concepts of creation. I have learned to listen to other saints and to the whole Bible.

All Scripture is given by inspiration of God,
so all creation texts are needed to understand fully
all God says about the creation.

(11.1) "In the beginning" was the beginning time period. Genesis 1:1 declares that God created out of nothing the heavens and the earth. This was the first stage of two stages of creation. The first stage began with creation *ex nihilo* in 1:1 and ended with the description of Earth's uninhabitable dark condition in 1:2. Hebrew scholar John Sailhamer correctly explains, "In opening the account of Creation with the phrase 'in the beginning,' the author has marked Creation as the starting point of a period of time."[1086] The first stage was an instantly started beginning period of time.

(11.1a) *B^erē'shît* indicates *the* definite beginning. *B^erē'shît* lacks the definite article "the." But "time words do not need the article to be definite."[1087] Genesis 1:1 declares *the* beginning.

(11.1b) "In the Beginning" requires an eternal Beginner. Though not a Christian, Stephen Hawking recognizes that logically, "so long as the universe had a beginning, we could suppose it had a creator."[1088] Hugh Ross says that an expanding universe with mass absolutely requires a beginning. Since the universe had a beginning, it had to have had an eternal Beginner.[1089]

That Beginner is not some generic deity. The Bible contains specific claims about that beginning, claims matching discoveries recently made by science. Only the Creator could have known those facts before modern science. The God of the Bible is the eternal Beginner, the Creator of the universe.

(11.1c) "In the beginning" started time instantly. Young earth creationism emphasizes that "In the beginning" indicated the beginning of time.[1090] John Sailhamer recognizes "creation as the starting point of a period of time."[1091] God literally began time and the universe with "In the beginning."

(11.1d) "In the beginning" was a beginning time period. Hebrew professor John Sailhamer explains, "The Hebrew word *reshit,* which is the term for 'beginning' used in this chapter [Genesis 1], has a very specific sense in the Bible. In the Bible the term always refers to an extended, yet indeterminate duration of time—*not* a specific moment." "The term does not refer to a point in time but to a *period* or *duration* of time." It had an instantaneous "starting point" and a prolonged "duration."[1092]

Sailhamer then references Bible examples: "Within the Book of Genesis itself, the author uses the term *reshît* to refer to the early part of Nimrod's kingdom (Genesis 10:10)."

"In Job 8:7 the word *reshît* refers to the early part of Job's life, before his misfortunes overtook him."[1093] Bildad said of Job, "Though your beginning [*reshît*] was insignificant, Yet your end will increase greatly" (NASB). At the time of his trials, Job was an "elder" with ten adult sons and daughters. Job's beginning [*reshît*] was all his years until his trials. His end would be the next 140 years that he lived after his trials (Job 42:16).

With the prefix *b^e* ("in"), *b^erē'shît* is used four more times, all in Jeremiah to refer to the beginning parts of the reigns of Judah's last kings. John Sailhamer explains, "According to Jeremiah 28:1, for example, the 'beginning' [*b^erē'shît*] of King Zedekiah's reign included events which happened four years after he had assumed the throne."[1094] So the *reshît* of a king referred to the beginning years of his reign.

Sailhamer points out that the Bible frequently pairs the "beginning" with its antonym "end."[1095] The "end" refers to the "end times," a period of time including the thousand-year Millennium. Since the "end" will be a period of time, so was the "beginning," especially since the inherent meaning of *reshît* is a time period.

This understanding of *b^erē'shît* is not new. For example, Candlish made the same claim in 1868, that "the beginning" was "an era."[1096]

This extent of time inherent in Genesis 1:1 is *not* artificially inserted, like the gap of time supposedly at Genesis 1:2, claimed by the gap theory. A gap at 1:2 violates Hebrew grammar. In complete contrast to the gap, the time period of Genesis 1:1 is *inherent* in the Hebrew word *rē'shît* when referring to time, which is confirmed by other uses in the Hebrew Bible. *B^erē'shît* and *rē'shît* consistently mean a time period, usually of years, although sometimes of months. *Rē'shît* never means an instant or a few hours. In fact, the YEC idea that *b^erē'shît* could have been an instant or few hours violates the Hebrew meaning. An extensive beginning time period is the normal meaning of *rē'shît* and the prefixed *b^erē'shît*.

Two stage Biblical creation simply recognizes that in the Hebrew Bible, *b^erē'shît*, "in the beginning," as well as the unprefixed *rē'shît*, consistently indicated an extended beginning time period. An instant or a few hours is a non-Hebrew modern idea improperly imported back into the ancient Hebrew text. "In the beginning" simply meant in an extensive beginning time period.

(11.1e) The beginning time was unspecified in length. How long was "the beginning"? "There is no way to limit the duration of the word 'beginning' (Hebrew, *rēshît*)," says Sailhamer. "The length of time of this 'beginning' is precisely what is left unspecified by the term. The whole point of using *rēshît* to convey the concept of 'beginning' (when other terms were readily available) is to leave the duration of time unspecified."[1097] The beginning time period was of unspecified length.

(11.1f) Since the beginning was unspecified in length, the start of the beginning is undated by the Bible. Sailhamer says, "Since the Hebrew word *'beginning'* refers to an indefinite period of time, we cannot say for certain when God created the world or how long He took to create it."[1098] Candlish said, "The first verse, then . . . with respect to time, [is] without date."[1099]

The Patrick Proposition: The initial Genesis 1:1 ex nihilo creation was in the beginning time period before the six days, so is undated by the Bible.

(11.1h) "In the beginning" was stage one of creation; the six days were stage two of creation. John Sailhamer says, "I contend that two distinct time periods are mentioned in Genesis 1."[1100] Rooker, although not a two stage creation advocate, recognizes, "This idea that Genesis 1:1 refers to the first stage in God's creative activity might be supported by the context, which clearly reveals that God intended to create the universe in progressive stages." Paul Copan declares, "God created in two stages."[1101]

Grammatically, the disjunctive description of Earth in Genesis 1:2 provides a break between the initial *ex nihilo* creation in Genesis 1:1 and the six days in Genesis 1:3–31. Structurally, the six-day formulas are quite distinct from the initial statement in Genesis 1:1. In subject matter, the beginning time period of the creation of the entire universe was quite distinct from the six days making planet Earth habitable and inhabited. There were two stages in the creation—the initial *ex nihilo* creation of both the heaven and unfinished dark Earth as stage one, and then the six days making planet Earth lighted, habitable, and inhabited as stage two.

The Two Stage Arnold Affirmation: Creation took place in two stages: In the beginning God created the heavens and the earth (but Earth was still uninhabitable, uninhabited, and its sea surface dark); so God worked by eight commands and six normal day-night days making Earth lighted, habitable, and inhabited.

(11.2) God created *ex nihilo* the heavens and earth. Henry Morris declares the magnificent reality, "Genesis 1:1 speaks of creation *ex nihilo*; only God could originate such a concept, and only an infinite, omnipotent God could create the universe."[1102]

(11.2a) The phrase "the heavens and the earth" means the entire cosmos. Bruce Waltke explains that *et ha-shāmayim v^{e}ēt hā 'āretz,* "the heavens and the earth," is a merism that is "a Hebrew designation of the universe as a whole."[1103]

Sailhamer explains, "A merism combines two words to express a single idea. A merism expresses 'totality' by combining two contrasts or two extremes." "'Heavens and earth' [in] the Hebrew language expresses the totality of all that exists. Unlike English, Hebrew doesn't have a single word to express the concept of 'the universe.'" "Heavens and earth" in Genesis 1:1 is a merism that expresses the creation by God of everything—"the sun, the moon, and the stars; every seen and unseen part of the universe."[1104] God created the orderly heavens and unfinished Earth, together forming the entire universe, in the beginning.

(11.2b) God created the heavens and earth *ex nihilo*. Duncan and Hall explain, "He made everything. But the text also hints at the manner or method of this work: creation *ex nihilo*—out of nothing."[1105]

Ex nihilo was creation by eternal God of everything
out of nothing.

Genesis 1:1 does not contain the *words* that God created all things "out of nothing." But 1:1 *does* contain the *concept* that God created the heavens and earth *out of nothing*. Rabbi Nahmanides wrote, "We have in our holy language no other term for the bringing forth of something out of nothing but *bara*."[1106]

Jewish writings have affirmed creation out of nothing. In 2 Maccabees 7:28, the Jewish mother declared, "I beg you, child, look at the sky and the earth; see all that is in them and realize that God made them out of nothing."

Israeli Hebrew speaker Gerald Schroeder explains, "The creation of the heavens and the earth from absolute nothing is at the root of biblical faith." Schroeder explains that *bārā'*, "create," is the only Hebrew word that can fit "creation of something from nothing." In the qal when referring to creation, it is always by "the actions of God."[1107]

John 1:1–3 intentionally mirrors Genesis 1:1—"In the beginning was the Word" (NASB). The Word, the *Logos*, eternal God the Son, was already present in the beginning. John 1:3 states, "πάντα δι᾽ αὐτοῦ ἐγένετο." "All things were made through Him, and without Him nothing was made that was made" (NKJV). Since all things were made through the Son, then before all things were made through Him, there was nothing but the one eternal God—Father, Son, and Spirit. Therefore, the creation was out of nothing, creation *ex nihilo*.

Hebrews 11:3 is quite explicit: "By faith we understand that the universe was formed at God's command, so that what is seen was not made out of what was visible." God created everything out of nothing but His invisible powerful command. God created *ex nihilo*.

Creation *ex nihilo* has been affirmed throughout church history. As just one example of many, the *Shepherd of Hermas* c. AD 150 in Vision 1.1.6 speaks of "God, who dwells in the heavens, and created out of nothing the things which are."

(11.2c) Since God created everything out of nothing, then before He created everything only God existed. John Sailhamer points out that God created the heavens and earth, meaning the entire universe, from nothing. He did this in the beginning.[1108] So before the beginning, only God existed.

(11.2d) God created the literal heavens (the sun, moon, and stars in the sky) and literal Earth (our unfinished planet) during the beginning. If we take Genesis 1:1 literally, 1:1 says God created the actual heavens, which Moses understood as the sun, moon, and stars (Deut. 4:19), and the actual literal Earth, although Genesis 1:2 explains Earth was unfinished. By only indicating that Earth was unfinished, Genesis 1:2 implies the heavens were essentially finished.

(11.2e) The *ex nihilo* creation of the universe in the beginning was a unique act, different from God's fashioning work in the six days. Pember says, "The work of those [six] days was . . . quite a different thing from the original creation." *Bārā'* in Genesis 1:1 indicates that "the Universe is not eternal and self-existent, but was originally created by the power of the Almighty."[1109] In contrast to the Genesis 1:1 originating act, the six days involved fashioning materials that had already been created in the beginning.

I propose a consistent approach that honors the text: The term *bārā'* ("create") in the creation narrative indicates an extraordinary miracle by which God created something new. God used the term *bārā'* for three creation events: the initial creation, the creation of the first animal life, and three times in a single verse for the creation of mankind. But only the initial *bārā'*, "creation," act was the *ex nihilo* creation of all the material of the universe. None of the *'āsāh* acts in the six days of Genesis 1 indicates an *ex nihilo* creation.

The initial *bārā'* event was the *ex nihilo* creation of the heavens and the earth. This was a unique event, the creation of all the material of the universe out of nothing (Heb. 11:3). Genesis 1:1 says that material was "the heavens and the earth," not unformed matter or chaos.

Bārā' is also the verb for God's creation of *nephesh hayāh*, the first living animals with the breath of life (Gen. 1:21). Yet these sea creatures will return to dust (Ps. 104:25–29), so they were from materials that had already been created. The new aspect God created seems to have been the *nephesh hāyâh*, the "breath of life." *Bārā'* also is used three times of man, but his physical body was also from the dust of the ground. The spiritual aspect of the body-soul human who could know his Creator was new. These were not *ex nihilo* creations of new material. There was only one *ex nihilo* creation—in Genesis 1:1.

'Asâh ("do, make, do work, fashion") has two senses in the six days of Genesis 1, and a third sense in the summaries of Genesis 1:31—2:3. The first is the broad sense of "make," "fashion," or "produce" something using already created materials. God made (*'āsâh*, Gen. 1:7) the expanse of the atmosphere between the sea water below and the cloud water above, apparently by the cloud rising from the sea. God caused the land to sprout vegetation, fruit trees "making," "yielding," or "producing" (*'āsâh*, Gen. 1:11) fruit by normal means and materials—earth, water, and light. In 1:24 God said, "Let the earth produce," and then in 1:25 the Bible reports that God made [*'āsâh*] three classes of animal life. Finally, God made [*'āsâh*] man (Gen. 1:26), perhaps emphasizing the physical aspect because man was from the dust of the ground (Gen. 2:7). In all these, God used materials that He had already created *ex nihilo* in Genesis 1:1.

The second sense of *'āsâh* in Genesis 1 is "to act with effect," or "bring about."[1110] Genesis 1:16 says God "made . . . for governing." God acted with the effect of making the luminaries govern day and night. He did not *bārā'* ("create") them *ex nihilo* on the fourth day.

The third is the summary use of *'āsâh* in its basic sense of "do," summarizing all the work God did. Genesis 2:2 emphasizes God's work in the six days. Genesis 1:31 and 2:2–3 may include the 1:1 initial creation as well as the six days. Although these summaries in 1:31—2:3 may include the initial creation as part of what God "did," none of the *'āsâh* acts within the six days of Genesis 1 was an *ex nihilo* creation.

In contrast, *bārā'* in Genesis 1:1 combines two special concepts. First, that creation was the unique *ex nihilo*, out of nothing, creation. Second, that creation was something new in the most radical sense. "The root *bārā'* denotes the concept of 'initiating something new.'"[1111] The entire universe was new, made out of nothing.

The Genesis 1:1 *bārā'* event was the unique *ex nihilo* creation of all the materials of the entire heavens and earth, everything in the universe. No other event in Genesis 1 was an *ex nihilo* creation.

(11.2f) God created *ex nihilo* the heavens and earth *before* the six days. Pember correctly states, "We are told [by Genesis 1:1] that in the beginning God created the heavens and the earth; but the Scriptures never affirm that He did this in the six days."[1112]

With the exception of young earth creationism, most of the creation authors argue for or assume it is obvious that the creation of the heavens and earth took place *before* the six days. Since this claim is important, I will summarize some of the arguments that the *ex nihilo* creation in 1:1 definitely took place before the six days (not *in* day one as YEC claims).

First, the plain literal reading of Genesis 1 is, "In the beginning [not *in* day one] God created the heavens and the earth." Nowhere does the Bible say God created the universe in the first day. In fact, the only command in day one was for light. Yet YEC claims, "God . . . made time (beginning), space (heaven), and matter (earth). This was the beginning of our universe, all part of the first day in time."[1113] In contrast to this YEC claim that God created the time, space, and matter in "the first day," the *Bible* says God created the heavens and earth "in the beginning."

Second, the *ex nihilo* creation was in Genesis 1:1, then light began day one in 1:3. As already explained in 11.D8, day one could not have included the dark described in 1:2. If the dark in 1:2 as a first night were added to day one, followed by the light in 1:3–4, followed by the evening beginning the night, and morning dawn ending the night in 1:5, that would have been a night-day-night, more than a day. Instead, day one began with daylight in 1:3–5a and ended with evening and morning, a merism for night-time, in 1:5b. Therefore, the Genesis 1:1 creation time and 1:2 description of dark Earth were *before* day one began with light to Earth in 1:3.

Third, the beginning was a time period that was much too long to fit into day one. "In the Bible, the term [*rē'shît*, "beginning"] always refers to an extended, yet indeterminate duration of time—*not* a specific moment."[1114] This "duration of time" was normally measured in years. The *rē'shît*, beginning, of Nimrod's kingdom was his first four cities (Gen. 10:10). Job's *rē'shît*, beginning, was all his years before his testing (Job

8:7). King Zedekiah's 'beginning' [$b^e r\bar{e}sh\hat{\imath}t$] included events over four years into his reign (Jer. 28:1).[1115] The ordinary meaning of $b^e r\bar{e}sh\hat{\imath}t$ is a beginning time period, commonly measured in years. A time period of years could not have fit into the first instant or few hours of day one. Time in the universe began with the first instant of "in the beginning," during the beginning time period, an unstated amount of time before day-night measured days began on Earth with "Let there be light."

Fourth, many events (see 11.3b), often suggesting time passage, led up to the conditions described in Genesis 1:2, before God commanded light beginning day one in 1:3. Job 26 and 38 list major events, most suggesting significant time passage. Although the book of Job is wisdom literature, the events of Job 26:7–16 and 38:4–15 show the same sequence as the events in Genesis 1.

God put the stars in place earlier than the earth because the stars were singing (which takes time) when He founded Earth and established its specific dimensions (Job 38:4–7). God suspended Earth on nothing (Job 26:7). God caused the birth (a process involving time) of the sea (Job 38:8). God wrapped the sea waters in thick dark cloud that covered the face of the moon (Job 26:8–9). This cloud cover caused darkness (Job 38:9) on the surface of the sea. All this resulted in the conditions described in Genesis 1:2—an uninhabited Earth with darkness on the surface of Earth's deep sea. These events fit nicely into the beginning time period indicated by $b^e r\bar{e}'sh\hat{\imath}t$. The beginning time period with all these events would appear to be more than would fit into the first instant or few hours of day one.

Fifth, the verb $b\bar{a}r\bar{a}'$, create, in Genesis 1:1 is grammatically in a form called the perfect. The perfect indicates "*completed action.*"[1116] God completed the action of the $b\bar{a}r\bar{a}'$ creation in 1:1. The end of the initial creation is marked by 1:2, which shifts the scene to Earth and describes the circumstances of Earth at the end of the initial creation time. Grammatically, Genesis 1:2 indicates "the completion of one episode." John Sailhamer says, "1:1 describes God's first work of creation *ex nihilo,* and the rest of the chapter describes God's further activity."[1117] This first episode ended with planet Earth uninhabitable and uninhabited and its deep sea surface dark in 1:2. Genesis 1:3—2:4a is the second episode, God's six days of work making planet Earth lighted, habitable, and inhabited. This second episode ended when God finished His work on the sixth day and rested on the seventh. So the first episode, the initial *ex nihilo* creation in Genesis 1:1, was completed *before* the second episode in 1:3—2:4a, the six days finishing planet Earth.

Sixth, Genesis 1:3 begins with a *vav/waw* consecutive, which indicates the next event after the creation in 1:1.[1118] YEC claims that Genesis 1:1–2 was in day one and that the dark of 1:2 was the night of night-day one. But that is grammatically impossible. The dark of Genesis 1:2 could not have been the night of day one. Genesis 1:2 does not begin with a *vav/waw* consecutive (indicating a next event) because it is a description with no time passage and no event. Genesis 1:3a is the next event after 1:1 and is correctly translated, "Then God said, 'Let there be light'" (NASB, NJKV, NRSV). God's command for light in 1:3 beginning day one was logically after the description in 1:2 of the darkened (by thick dark cloud, says Job 38:9) Earth. The light beginning day one on earth was temporally after the creation of Earth in 1:1.

Seventh, in 1:1 God created earth, which was rotating in Genesis 1:3. YEC says, "The planet was not formed until day 3. . . . Prior to that 'earth' was only some kind of amorphous prematter . . . ready to be made into the planet and other celestials."[1119] Contra YEC, day and night on Earth, beginning in day one, indicate that planet Earth was not only created, but rotating by the time of God's command for light. Day and night do not occur in outer space, only on a planet rotating in (sun)light. The day and night of day one on rotating Earth had to have been *after* God created planet Earth in 1:1.

Eighth, the beginning was when there was no ocean, but there were ocean depths before day one. Kline pointed out that Proverbs 8:23–24 says, "From the beginning, from the earliest times of the earth. When there were no depths" (NASB). Since "the beginning" was "When there were no depths" of the ocean, then "the beginning" was *before* the deep ocean-covered condition of planet Earth described in Genesis 1:2. Day one did not begin until God commanded light in Genesis 1:3 to that ocean-covered world, so "the beginning" was before day one.

Ross says, "Psalm 104:5–6 also describes primordial Earth's surface as covered entirely with water."

> He [God] set the earth on its foundations;
> it [foundation] can never be moved.
> You [God] covered it [earth] with the deep as with a garment;
> the waters stood above the mountains (NIV).

"This text implies that God established the planet's core, mantle, and crust before cloaking Earth in oceans."[1120] Psalm 104:1–9 is about the creation, not about the flood, because it was when God set Earth on its foundation.

(Psalm 104:9 needs comment, but that will have to wait until I can write about the flood.) God made planet Earth's foundation before covering Earth with water. Earth was covered with water in Genesis 1:2. Therefore, God certainly made the Earth's foundation before daylight began day one on the ocean-covered Earth in 1:3.

Ninth, God created the heavens first and stretched out the heavens before making Earth. Stretching out takes time. Rotating earth was there in day one. Psalm 104:2 says, "He stretches out the heavens." Then 104:5 speaks of God making planet Earth's foundation, presumably its interior. In Job 38:4–6, God was founding Earth "while the morning stars sang together." So Genesis 1:1 declares the order of the two big events of creation. God created the heavens with stars first. Then He laid Earth's foundations (Job 38:4), made Earth the right size (Job 38:5), covered it with sea (Job 38:8), and wrapped it in thick dark cloud (Job 38:9)—the condition of planet Earth in Genesis 1:2. Finally, in Genesis 1:3 He commanded light to Earth's dark sea, beginning day one on rotating Earth. First God made the heavens and stretched them out. Then He made the Earth, all before day one.

There are two big reasons why YEC does not accept a literal understanding of Genesis 1:1, that in the *beginning* God created the heavens and the earth. The first reason is Exodus 20:11—"For *in* six days God created. . . ." But as Wiseman, Sailhamer, Pember, and others have shown, there is no "*in*" in the Hebrew of Exodus 20:11a.

The second reason is the assumption that God created the heavens, the sun, moon, and stars, on the fourth day. But the fourth day narrative does not say that God *created* the sun, moon, and stars that day. The creation of the heavens was in Genesis 1:1. The explanation of the fourth day's events is in Genesis 1:2 and Job. Job 26:8–9 and 38:9 describe how God wrapped the sea in thick dark cloud. Thick dark cloud would have made the surface of the deep ocean dark as described in Genesis 1:2. Genesis 1:3–31 apparently is from the perspective of the Spirit of God just above the dark water (Gen. 1:2). At God's command, sunlight penetrated the thick dark cloud cover for the first time to the Spirit's location, beginning day one. But the cloud cover did not open to clear skies until the fourth day. On the fourth day, God caused the luminaries to begin carrying out His triple command to separate day and night, be time-marking signs, and be lights in Earth's sky. God did not create the luminaries on the fourth day. He had already created the heavens—the sun, moon, and stars in the sky—in Genesis 1:1.

In summary, the plain literal reading of Genesis 1 is, "In the beginning [not *in* day one] God created the heavens and the earth." Nowhere does the Bible say God commanded the creation of the universe in the first day or fourth day. *B^{e}rē'shît* ("in the beginning") was a longer beginning time period (presumably of years) when God created the heavens and unfinished earth. After the creation, in Genesis 1:3 God commanded light beginning day one. Day one ended with evening (beginning nighttime) and morning (ending nighttime) in 1:5. The beginning creation in 1:1 was before day one in 1:3–5.

Church fathers such as Ambrose,[1121] reformers such as John Calvin,[1122] numerous Hebrew scholars,[1123] and most creationists other than YEC advocates agree that Genesis 1:1 was before the six days. So we may conclude with confidence that God created the heavens and earth in Genesis 1:1 *before* the six days of Genesis 1:3–31.

(11.3) After the *ex nihilo* creation, God stretched out the heavens, founded Earth, and covered it with sea and dark cloud. During the beginning time period, God caused a sequence of events in the heavens (listed in Isaiah 42:5 and many other texts) and on Earth (listed in Job 26:8–9, Job 38:9, Psalm 104:4–5, and Proverbs 8:22–31) that led up to the unfinished dark condition of Earth in Genesis 1:2.

(11.3a) After God created the heavens, He stretched them out. Hugh Ross points out that long before Edwin Hubble discovered the beginning and expansion of the universe, God declared that the universe had a beginning and that He has been stretching or expanding it. Eleven Bible texts proclaim that God has been stretching out the heavens.[1124] Ross says, "Scripture's prophets and apostles explicitly and repeatedly stated two fundamental features, . . . a beginning in the finite past and continuous cosmic expansion. Isaiah 42:5 makes reference to both: 'This is what God the LORD says—he who created the heavens and stretched them out.'" Isaiah 51:13 speaks of "the LORD your Maker, Who stretched out the heavens and laid the foundations of the earth" (NASB). These eleven texts range in time from immediately after the initial creation through the time of Isaiah. The verbs of some of the eleven are in the perfect tense, that the process of stretching is an accomplished fact, and some in imperfect, that the process is continuing. God has been continually stretching out the heavens since the initial creation.[1125]

The normal meaning of stretching involves time. Since the time God created the heavens in Genesis 1:1, He has been stretching them out. Isaiah 42:5 says God "created the heavens and stretched them out." The stretching out began during the beginning. Since stretching out involves time passage, this adds weight to the claim that the beginning was a period of time.

(11.3b) After God founded Earth during the beginning, He covered Earth with deep sea and wrapped the sea in thick dark cloud. As already mentioned, Job 38:4 explains that God "laid the earth's foundation" (NIV). Then 38:8–9 describes the process of birthing the ocean and covering it with cloud like swaddling clothes:

> Who shut up the sea behind doors [birth motif]
>> when it burst forth from the womb,
> when I made the clouds its garment
>> and wrapped it in thick darkness (NIV).

God caused the birthing of the sea. Then He shrouded the deep worldwide ocean in a thick dark cloud layer. By this cloud layer, God "covers the face of the full moon, spreading his clouds over it" (Job 26:9, NIV).[1126] The result was that "Earth's dense atmosphere . . . blocked out the Sun's light from reaching early Earth's surface."[1127] Birthing the sea and wrapping it in cloud are events suggesting time passage during the beginning (Gen. 1:1) before the six day-night days.

TRANSITION: DESCRIPTION OF UNFINISHED EARTH

(11.4) Genesis 1:2 describes Earth as uninhabitable, uninhabited, sea-covered, and dark. Resulting from its creation in 1:1, Earth was described in Genesis 1:2 with four characteristics and three descriptive clauses:

A. "Now the earth was *tōhû v*ᵃ*bōhû.*"
   1. *tōhû,* uninhabitable
   2. *bōhû,* uninhabited, or empty of life
B. "And darkness was over the surface of the deep."
   3. *ᶜhōshek,* darkness (on the ocean surface)
   4. *t*ᵉ*hôm,* deep ocean; *ha-māyim,* the waters (covering Earth)
C. "And the Spirit of God was hovering over the surface of the waters."

(11.4a) Genesis 1:2 is a description of Earth, not an event. Genesis 1:2 begins with an "and/now" called a *vav/waw* disjunctive. This "and/now" that prefixes "the earth" begins a description of Earth resulting from its creation in 1:1. Genesis 1:1 had just ended with "the heavens and the earth." Then Genesis 1:2 begins with "Now the earth" and goes on to describe the conditions on Earth by the above three descriptive clauses (A, B, and C). None of these clauses indicates an action or event. Earth was created in 1:1 and described in 1:2.

(11.4b) *Only* **planet Earth was described as uninhabitable, uninhabited, and its sea surface dark.** Hugh Ross points out that Genesis 1:2 shifts the focus from "the heavens and the earth," the merism in 1:1 of the entire universe, to *hā'āretz*, planet Earth alone. "As the text transitions from verse 1 to verse 2, the focus shifts from the cosmos to the early earth."[1128] Genesis 1:2 begins, "Now the earth was *tōhû v*ᵃ*bōhû*." Normal parallelism would have carried the merism of the "heavens and earth" from 1:1 into 1:2, but strikingly this is *not* the case. Since only planet Earth was declared empty and dark, we may infer that the universe was neither empty nor dark, but was filled with luminaries and lighted ever since it was created *ex nihilo* during the Genesis 1:1 time period. In fact, Moses understood the heavens as "the sun and the moon and the stars" in the sky (Deut. 4:19, NASB). Only Earth was declared unfinished and its sea surface dark.

(11.4c) *Tōhû v*ᵃ*bōhû* **meant uninhabitable and uninhabited.** Sailhamer points out that the Greek Septuagint unhelpfully translated *tōhû v*ᵃ*bōhû* as "unseen" and "unformed." "Were it not for the Greek notion of 'primeval chaos,' the phrase never would have been translated that way ['without form and void']. The sense of the Hebrew phrase suggests something quite different, a sense some early translators identified quite clearly." Sailhamer says that the meaning is "uninhabitable" and "wilderness" "that had not yet become inhabitable for human beings."[1129] Jeremiah 4:23–26 uses the same term with the sense of "deserted and uninhabited."[1130]

Hugh Ross also recognizes that *tōhû v*ᵃ*bōhû* ("uninhabitable and uninhabited") does not mean chaos, but means Earth was unfit for life and as empty of life as a wilderness. Jeremiah 4:23 repeats the exact phrase, *tōhû v*ᵃ*bōhû*: "I looked at the earth, and it was *tōhû v*ᵃ*bōhû*." Jeremiah was making an allusion back to Genesis 1:2, so his meaning relates back to the original event. After the destruction of Judah and Jerusalem, the land was made unfit for life and was largely uninhabited. In Jeremiah 4:27a, God adds, "I will not destroy it completely" (NIV). Jeremiah would live through this conquest. He would look out on the devastated land. Palestine did not become formless chaos, only an uninhabited wasteland.

Isaiah 34:11 uses both *tōhû* and *bōhû* of the conquest of Edom, making Edom uninhabited. I have been in Edom (now part of the Hashemite Kingdom of Jordan). It is east of the Dead Sea, and its major city became Petra. Petra is a magnificent deep rock gorge with dwellings, temples, graves, and a water system carved into the rock. Its inhabitants developed a sophisticated system of collecting water to support life. Once they were conquered, the water system collapsed and Petra became empty of significant life. Even today, apart from the tourists, camel mounted tourist police (providing security for the tourists), and Jordanians earning money from the tourists, Petra is essentially empty of significant life. It is bare rock. Earth was cloud shrouded and ocean covered, and under the ocean was bare rock.

Isaiah 45:18 contrasts *tōhû*, uninhabitable, with *lāshevet* (from *yāshav*), meaning habitable. Deuteronomy 32:10 uses the word *tōhû* to describe an uninhabitable wilderness.[1131] So the phrase *tōhû vᵃbōhû* in Genesis 1:2 describes the "desolate condition of early Earth."[1132] Ross concludes that *tōhû vᵃbōhû* means that planet Earth was "empty of life and unfit for life."[1133]

Pember agrees. Pember says that the translation "without form and void" is "a glaring illustration of the influence of the chaos-legend."[1134] The meaning of *tōhû vᵃbōhû* is "desolation" and "that which is empty." In Jeremiah 4, "we see, therefore, that the Hebrew word *tohu* signifies . . . 'that which is desolate;' and *bohû* 'emptiness' or 'that which is empty,' probably with reference to the absence of all life ('I beheld, and, lo, there was no man,' etc.)." So the Genesis 1:2 phrase, "And the earth was *tōhû vᵃbōhû*," meant that planet Earth (not the universe) was "desolate" and "empty" "of all life"[1135] (not unformed chaos).

Tsumura summarizes, "There is nothing in this passage [Genesis 1:2] that would suggest a chaotic state of the earth."[1136] Young states it would be "wise to abandon the term 'chaos.'"[1137]

In Genesis 1:1 God created the heavens as an orderly cosmos and the Earth as a planet, although still uninhabitable. Neither heavens nor Earth was chaos. Planet Earth was simply unfinished—uninhabitable and uninhabited.

(11.4d) Earth's deep sea surface was cloud darkened. Genesis 1:2b declares, "And darkness was over the surface of the deep [*tᵉhôm*]; and the Spirit of God was moving over the surface of the waters [*māyim*]" (NASB). The word "deep" [*tᵉhôm*] is parallel to the word "waters" [*māyim*], indicating the deep ocean water that covered Earth. That ocean surface was dark in Genesis 1:2. Job explains *how* the surface of the deep ocean water was dark. Job 38:9 says the sea was wrapped in *'ānān,* "cloud mass," and *'arāpel,* "deep darkness, thick dark cloud." Ross says the dense cloud-filled atmosphere "blocked the Sun's light from reaching early Earth's surface."[1138] The Bible says Earth was covered with thick dark cloud blocking out the light of even the full moon. "He covers the face of the full moon, spreading his clouds over it (Job 26:9, NIV).[1139]

(11.4e) The Earth was *tōhû v[a]bōhû*, so the "deep" and "thick dark clouds" of Earth differed from today's ocean with clouds, but Earth was not chaos. God formed Earth and added to it during the beginning until it reached the exact dimensions that He had planned (Job 38:4–5).

A possible means by which God could have increased Earth to His planned dimensions was material from space. This fiery work may have been what is spoken of in the creation text of Psalm 104:4, "flaming fire His ministers." Fiery asteroids and comet hits would have created a super-heated Earth—devoid of any life. This may have been when God set Earth on its foundations—presumably establishing it core—which cannot be moved out of its place (Ps. 104:5). Comets are largely water, and asteroids are partly water, so they may have added vapor to the atmosphere and eventually rain to earth's oceans.

Then God caused the birth of the sea (Job 38:8). But the Hebrew phrase *tōhû v[a]bōhû* in Genesis 1:2 does *not* describe a nice sandy beach with sparkling waves gently lapping the shore. Waltke describes the ancient ocean with the term "sea monster."[1140] Although I would not take that extra-Biblical description literally, the Biblical words *tōhû v[a]bōhû* should be taken seriously. The key is a balanced understanding. On the one hand, *tōhû v[a]bōhû* does not mean "a state of material devoid of order, or without being shaped or formed into something."[1141] Earth was *not* utter chaos. On the other hand, Earth's deep dark sea in Genesis 1:2 was certainly not yet fit for human life.

God caused the birth of the *t[e]hôm*, "the deep" (Job 38:8). The *t[e]hôm* of Genesis 1:2 covered the mountains (Ps. 104:5), so it must have been much deeper than today's ocean. That ancient *tōhû v[a]bōhû* ocean covered the entire surface of Earth. There were no continents until Genesis 1:9, so we may reasonably deduce that tsunamis from asteroid strikes could have circled the globe; and waves from winds could have grown to enormous sizes. Some suggest that volcanic peaks rose temporarily out of the water, spewing gasses and dust, all contributing to the darkness. But there was no permanent land until Genesis 1:9, so if there were volcanic islands, the wild waves washed them away, leaving only the black deep sea. That deep dark sea was *tōhû v[a]bōhû*, "uninhabitable and uninhabited." Earth was a dark, desolate, lifeless, water-covered world.

Earth's ancient atmosphere was also *tōhû v[a]bōhû*, utterly lifeless. It was not like our nice blue sky with a few white cloud puffs. In Job, God Himself used two terms, *'ānān*, "cloud mass," and *'arāpel,* "deep darkness, thick darkness, heavy cloud."[1142] Today, even the darkest thunderstorm only reduces daytime to gray. That early, dark atmosphere must have been much thicker to blacken the sky. That early, atmosphere was *tōhû*, so unlivable, probably full of noxious gases. That early atmosphere was also *bōhû,* empty of life. It was quite different from today's life-supporting atmosphere of blue sky with clouds and flying birds. Genesis 1:2 combined with Job 26 and 38 declare that Earth was unlivable, water covered, and under a thick cloud-blackened sky.

On the one hand, planet Earth was not unformed chaos. But on the other hand, Earth was an unlivable, ocean-covered, cloud-blackened, life-less *tōhû vᵃbōhû* world.

Genesis 1:2 is the divine evaluation of early unfinished Earth.

(11.5) The Spirit's location at Earth's surface implies His perspective for the narrative of 1:3–31. Ross emphasizes that the perspective, or frame of reference, of the narrative during the six days in 1:3–31 was the vantage point of the divine Observer.[1143] "Genesis 1:2 says that the Spirit of God hovered above the primordial Earth's surface. This clue means that the subsequent description of early Earth (and the stages of its transformation) comes from the vantage point of an observer just above the surface of the waters, looking up at the sky and across the horizon, describing details as they would have appeared from that perspective."[1144] "But with the point of view on the surface of the earth, looking up at the atmosphere of the earth, we recognize that God's miracles are taking place in the atmosphere of the earth, not beyond it in the galaxy and the solar system."[1145]

Ross continues, "Unfortunately, most Bible commentaries still err with Jean Astruc and the higher critics in placing the point of view for Genesis 1 out in the heavens, looking down on the earth. Yet the second verse of Genesis 1 places the point of view *under* the cloud cover, on the surface of the waters. It says, 'The Spirit of God was hovering over the surface of the waters.' This one seemingly minute correction eliminates any supposed contradiction."[1146]

The location of the Spirit of God implies His perspective for the narrative of Genesis 1. The Spirit of God was the only Person given a location on the scene. The Bible is especially from the Spirit, and the narrative makes sense from His perspective.

This perspective location and that God had already created the heavens in 1:1 suggest that the light on day one would be diffuse *sun*light penetrating the thinning cloud layer to the Spirit for the first time. This perspective under the progressively thinning cloud cover (Job 26:13) explains why the sun, moon, and stars that were created in Genesis 1:1 were not reported by the divine Narrator from His location until the fourth day of God's work.

(11.5a) The Spirit's location may have been above future Eden. The six-day narrative was from the Spirit's location just about planet Earth's surface. The first days were above the ocean water. John Sailhamer suggests that the last four days may have been just above the land of Eden because the narrative ends with the creaton of man.

The Spirit's location (Gen. 1:2c) is a front row seat to creation.

STAGE TWO: GOD WORKED SIX DAY-NIGHT DAYS MAKING EARTH LIGHTED, HABITABLE, AND INHABITED

Now we come to the second stage of God's divinely decreed progressing two stage creation plan. According to plan, Earth was still an uninhabitable, uninhabited, deep-sea-covered, cloud-darkened, planet. By His eight commands and six unique days, God would make Earth lighted, habitable, and inhabited with life. When the land was ready, God created Adam and Eve—humans who could know, love, and worship Him to His great glory.

(11.6) God worked six normal day-night solar days. The initial creation in stage one left Earth as a darkened sea and cloud-covered planet, not yet fit for life, and empty of life. The two stage creation theory emphasizes that after the initial creation in 1:1, God worked in 1:3–31 by eight commands and six normal daylight-evening-nighttime-morning solar work days to make Earth lighted, habitable, and inhabited.

(11.6a) All six days were normal day-night days. Wiseman says, "I suggest that every time the days are mentioned in both these passages [Genesis 1 and Exodus 20:9–11] they are intended to be taken literally as ordinary days."[1147]

Young earth creationism has thoroughly defended six normal day-night cycle solar days.[1148] Rather than giving that defense for normal days several times, I will give that defense fully in response to one of the four diagnostic questions.

Day one was a normal day-night day. God commanded light (Gen. 1:3), so diffuse (sun)light pierced the overcast to the Spirit's location. The Spirit reported, "And there was light." God evaluated the light as good. God separated the light from the darkness. God named the light "day" and the darkness "night." Day was on the sunlit side of Earth, and night was on the side away from the sun on rotating Earth. Day one sets the meaning of "day" as a daylight-evening-nighttime-morning day. All six of God's days of work were normal daylight-nighttime days.

Westermann adds an important insight to the understanding of the six days. He reminds us of the ending title in Genesis 2:4a. He says that Genesis 1 was "a succession of begettings."[1149] This understanding takes the Genesis 2:4a ending title of the six days literally: "These *are* the generations of the heavens and of the earth when they were created" (KJV). Understanding Genesis 1 as "a succession of begettings" emphasizes the actual begettings. *Yālad* ("begat") occurs in various forms 189 times in Genesis. Genesis is full of "begats" and is divided by "generations." "Abraham begat Isaac" emphasizes the event when Sarah gave birth to Abraham's son. The event of Sarah giving birth was within a particular literal day. At God's eight fiat commands involving six extraordinary day-night days, in a sense, the heavens and earth begot Earth's sky, sea, and land, and Earth's sky, sea, and land in turn begot sea, air, and land life (no sexual connotations). For example, on His third day of work, God commanded, "Let the land produce vegetation" (1:11). The earth sprouted seed plants that very day before evening because Genesis 1:11 ends with "and it was so."

If the eight events and six days are understood as generations (Gen. 2:4a), then each event had a specific day when that new thing was begotten. Each was begotten by God's fiat commands as the successive "generation of the heavens and of the earth" (Gen. 2:4a).

(11.6b) All six days of God's work were day-night cycle *solar* days. Often objections are raised against six literal day-night days: How could there be day and night in the first three days if the sun did not yet exist?[1150] Why would God devote one of only six days to creating temporary light for only three days? Was Earth floating along in space for three days, and then suddenly jerked into orbit around a suddenly made sun on the fourth day? However well these objections may or may not be answered, the two stage Biblical creation theory does not even have these problems.

I agree with John Sailhamer on this point. "If the sun is meant to be included in the merism . . . in Genesis 1:1, then it is natural to assume that the sun was created already in the first verse. If that is so, then the 'light' of verse 3 was simply the light of the sun. . . . The expression 'there was light' is one way the Bible refers to sunlight."[1151] For example, Exodus 10:23 says, "Israel had light," meaning sunlight.

Among the trillions of other stars that God created as part of the heavens during the beginning, He made our sun. But its light was blocked from Earth's ocean-covered surface by unbroken thick dark cloud cover

(Job 28:8, 9; 38:9). On day one, at God's command diffuse sunlight penetrated the thinning cloud cover for the first time to the Spirit's location just above the surface of rotating Earth. Apparently, it was the Spirit who reported, "And there was light." That sunlight began the daylight of day one. Daylight was followed by evening as the Spirit's location rotated into the dusk and nighttime, and then rotated into morning's dawn. Earth's rotation in the sunlight caused days followed by nights of normal earth days. Six solar days (instead of three artificial temporary light days, then three solar days) actually strengthens the case for six normal day-night days, defined by earth's rotation in sunlight.

(11.6c) Day one in Hebrew was cardinal, but days two through six were ordinal. Several authors mention that the Hebrew numbers of the days change from cardinal day one to ordinal second through seventh days. Their statements agree with Biblical Hebrew grammar books.[1152]

Cardinal numbers (one, two, three, etc.) count quantity.[1153] During Genesis 1:1, there was *unmeasured* time in outer space and *unmeasured* time under the cloud-caused darkness on Earth's sea surface. Then cardinal "day one" began daylight on Earth when, at God's command, diffuse sunlight reached the sea surface. That sunlight began literal day one of *measured* day-night days on Earth.

For example, "Day one" (cardinal number) of my son David's life was his day of birth as he blinked in the light for the first time. There were no day-night days for him before his day one. However, time had passed unmeasured by days and nights within the darkness of the womb.

Exodus 10:23 says, "They [the Egyptians] did not see one another, nor did anyone rise from his place for three [*shālosh*] days, but all the sons of Israel had light in their dwellings." *Shālosh* is cardinal three. There were exactly three days of darkness in Egypt, while there were three normal day-night days in Israel. Cardinals (one, two, three) tell quantity.

In contrast, the (Gen. 1:6–31) second day through sixth day were numbered with ordinals. Ordinal numbers give order or position. Hebrew grammar books explain, "Ordinal numbers are used to indicate position in a series (first, second, third, etc.)."[1154] "The ordinals express degree, quality or position in a series, 'first, second, third.'"[1155] Each day—second day, third day, fourth day, fifth day, and the sixth day—was in that position in the series of days of God's work. The framework theory's claim, that the six days were out of order, is incorrect.

Another example of ordinals is in Genesis 2. The "second" (ordinal) river branch in Eden was the Pishon (2:11). Since Adam describes it, the Pishon was probably the second river that he explored. Ordinals (second, third, fourth) tell position in a series. But "second" does not tell us the total quantity. The *cardinal* "four" (*arba*) in Genesis 2:10, "There were four headwaters," tells us the total number of river branches. Cardinals (one, two, three) tell quantity; ordinals tell order or rank (second, third, fourth, fifth, sixth, seventh) but not necessarily total quantity with the same certainty as cardinals.

Ordinal numbers allow for uncounted quantities, but if the series is necessarily sequential, then uncounted quantities only *after* the ordinals. Both "day six of our six-day hike" and "the sixth day of our hike" are the same day because six days of a hike are normally necessarily sequential. But the second statement ("the sixth day of our hike") allows days *after* the sixth day because the hike may have been an eight-day hike. But the ordinal "sixth" does *not* allow uncounted days between the counted days because this example is of (normally) necessarily sequential days.

In contrast, if the series is *not* necessarily sequential and the counted items are qualified, cardinals still express quantity, but ordinals express sequence but not quantity of unqualified items. For example, "Our church schedules six work days each year. New Year's day is work day one." Cardinal "work day one" is the first work day or simply first day that year. At the end of day one, only a quantity of one day of that year had passed. The cardinal "six" indicates the total quantity of work days.

But the ordinals in this church work days example are different from the hike for two reasons—church work days are not necessarily sequential (not necessarily January 1–6), and they are qualified as "work days." For example, "The second church work day comes in early spring, so we wash the church windows from the winter grime." These six church work days are not necessarily sequential and are qualified as "work days." The second work day does not tell how many non–work days passed between work day one and the second work day.

Two questions are important for the creation: Were the Genesis 1 days necessarily sequential (if Exod. 20:11a had an "in," or if the creation days were designated a "week") or not necessarily sequential? The second question is, Were the six days qualified?

Finally, of the six days, only "the sixth day" has the word "the," indicating the end of God's special six days. "And there was evening and there was morning, the sixth day" (NASB). Also, "the seventh day" includes "the," so, it too, was a different day, God's rest day. It is important that we understand the possible nuances of the Hebrew numbers in the Bible.

(11.6d) Ordinal numbers alone are insufficient to prove the Payne proposition. The Payne proposition suggests that time passed between the six literal days. Under theory 14, I outline evidences for and evidences against the Payne proposition. One of the evidences for the proposition is the switch from cardinal one to ordinal second through seventh, as discussed in 11.6c. I respond that while the ordinal numbers may allow time passage of unnumbered days between the six numbered days, ordinal numbers alone are insufficient text evidence to prove that time actually passed between the six days. Other evidences would have to be considered.

My response to the Payne proposition is that the Bible neither explicitly affirms nor explicitly denies time passage between the six days. So I urge caution with the Payne proposition. I have concluded that the Bible text itself affirms six literal days, but his proposition is an open question. The creation itself should provide evidence one way or the other about Payne's idea of time passage between the six days. The evidence from Earth should demonstrate whether the time from the first light to Earth's surface, the formation of the atmosphere, the rise of the continents, and plant and animal life was within six consecutive days and was about 6,000 years ago or a longer time.

The Payne proposition is his idea, not part of or affirmed by the two stage Biblical creation theory. In my response to his idea I am claiming that the *Bible* does not make an *explicit* definitive statement either way. So neither am I.

(11.6e) The six days were God's designated work days. According to Genesis 2:2–3, the eight command units and six designated days were work followed by a rest day.

On the one hand, we must be careful not to import the Fourth Commandment, given to Moses several millennia later, back into Genesis 1:1 — 2:4a. Genesis 1 is not a command for man to work six days and rest the seventh. The worldview of Genesis was generations, not human workweeks. The workweek Commandment that would reference back to God's example would come several millennia later in Exodus 20.

On the other hand, God's example in Genesis 1 contained a latent warrant of the greater (God worked six days and rested the seventh) to man as the lesser (so God commanded Israel to work six days but rest the Sabbath) for the Fourth Commandment. The "work" and "rest" example in Genesis 2:2–3 does allow the later additional emphasis by Moses that *man* should work six days and rest one day.

Someone might object that Isaiah 40:28 says the Creator does not grow weary, so He does not need rest. In response, God's seventh day was rest of satisfaction from very good work completed (Gen. 1:31 — 2:3), *not* rest from weariness or exhaustion.[1156]

Genesis 2:1–3 qualifies the six days as work days within the creation narrative. After the sixth day, thrice the Spirit of God qualified the previous days through the sixth day. Each of the days through the sixth day was designated as God's day of work, and the seventh day was His *rest* day. All seven of these literal days are qualified as being either a work day or a rest day.

And by the seventh day God completed His <u>work</u> which He had done; and He <u>rested</u> on the seventh day from all His <u>work</u> which He had done. Then God blessed the seventh day and sanctified it, because in it He <u>rested</u> from all His <u>work</u> which God had created and made (Gen. 2:2–3, NASB).

So the six days were not miscellaneous days, but were God's six work days making Earth lighted, habitable, and inhabited.

Is this qualification sufficient to say with certainty that non–work days passed between the six work days? Two elements suggest that the answer is not proven. First, the qualification as work days was after all six were over (Gen. 2:2–3), rather than with each day. And second, the ordinal numbers along with the qualification as work days only allow, but do not prove, non–work days between the six work days. The Payne proposition remains neither proven, nor disproven by the ordinal numbers.

Not only were they days of labor, but especially from the ancient human perspective within the worldview of the Patriarchs, the six were the days of the generations of the heavens and the earth. Going forward, when we interpret the Fourth Commandment we may view God's work days and rest day as examples anticipating the future Commandment to Israel to do the same. But when we are interpreting Genesis 1, we should interpret the six days in a way that fits the text of Genesis 1:1—2:4a, as "the generations of the heavens and of the earth."

Within the original narrative, the days had two qualifiers. First, the six were God's work days and the seventh His rest day according to Genesis 2:2–3. Second, the days were described as, "These *are* the generations of the heavens and of the earth when they were created" (Gen. 2:4a, KJV). God worked by eight commands and six literal days as six generations making Earth lighted, habitable, and inhabited.

(11.7) By eight command units and six day-night work days, God made Earth lighted, habitable, and inhabited. Hugh Ross explains, "Genesis 1:2 indicates that an observer, *if* located on Earth's surface would also experience darkness as one of Earth's initial conditions." "Earth's dense atmosphere would have blocked the Sun's light from reaching . . . Earth's surface."[1157] Earth was *tōhû vᵃbōhû* and sea-covered with darkness enveloping the sea surface.

By His eight command units and six day-night days, God would bring light to Earth; make Earth habitable; and fill the seas, skies, and land with a great variety of life. God's work would reach its culmination in the first two humans. Thus the three negatives of Genesis 1:2—uninhabitable, uninhabited, and dark—would be changed in the six literal days so Earth would become lighted, habitable, and inhabited.

(11.7a) God worked by eight command units, yet six days. Kline explains, "There are a total of *eight* distinct creative works distributed over *six* days. The last day within each triad (i.e., Days 3 and 6) contains *two* creative acts."[1158]

Duncan and Hall also recognize "eight simple commands," each following roughly the same formula.[1159] Waltke (see 1.8) and also Duncan and Hall (see 5B.4a) list the repeated parts of each of the eight command units.

God worked by eight command units, yet only six day-night work days. But the Bible does not explicitly say how the eight and six fit together other than that two commands precede evenings three and six. The Payne proposition could suggest that command three for land may have been during time between days two and three, and command seven for land animals may have been during time between days five and six. This idea is opposed by YEC because of Exodus 20:11, that all creation was "*in* six days." But there is no "*in*" within 20:11a, allowing the possibility of commands three and seven between the six days. On the other hand, commands three and seven may have been within their respective days. I conclude that the Bible does not explicitly say which. What is clear is that God spoke eight command units completing Earth.

(11.7b) At God's command, diffuse sunlight penetrated the cloud to the Narrator for the first time, beginning day one with daylight. Hugh Ross explains, "Job 38:8–9 affirms that Earth's primordial waters were enshrouded by an opaque cloud cover:"[1160] "Light was not created on the first creation day. On that day the light . . . suddenly broke through to the Earth's surface. This breakthrough required the transformation of the atmosphere (plus the interplanetary medium) from opaque to translucent."[1161]

Sailhamer explains, "The sun was created already in the first verse. If that is so, then the 'light' of verse 3 was simply the light of the sun."[1162] In Genesis 1:1, Moses could not have meant "empty outer space," a modern concept, by the word *ha-shāmayim*, "heavens." By "heavens" he meant "the sun and the moon and the stars" in the sky (Deut. 4:19). God had already created the sun in Genesis 1:1.

Jeremiah 31:35 explains, "Thus says the LORD, Who gives the sun for light by day, And the fixed order of the moon and the stars for light by night" (NASB). The sun for daylight, and moon and stars for the night is God's fixed order. So our presumption should be that the light beginning day one on Earth's dark sea was sunlight. The Bible says that in the *future*, "No longer will you have the sun for light by day, Nor for brightness will the moon give you light; But you will have the LORD for an everlasting light" (Isa. 60:19). Until then, the sun is designated by God as the source of daylight, and the moon and stars as the softer light of night.

The Bible says nothing about artificial light, temporary light, or Shekinah light from God's presence on day one, or about an end to artificial temporary light at the fourth day. Therefore, our presumption should be that at God's command, diffuse sunlight pierced through the thinning cloud mass for the first time to the Narrator. The divine Narrator was just above Earth's rotating surface. By commanding sunlight to shine on the rotating Earth, God divided day and night, just as Genesis 1:4 states. Since all six days of God's work were lit by sunlight to rotating Earth, all six days were normal day-night days.

Day one ended in evening and night as the Narrator's location rotated out of the diffuse sunlight into darkness, and then morning as His location rotated back into the edge of morning dawn.

Day one makes sense as a daylight-evening-nighttime-morning solar day, not as a day-age geological era or as an artificial light day. Day one was literally the first daylight day on the surface of planet Earth. Since day one was a normal day, it set the meaning for all six days of God's work as normal days. And God saw that it was good.

(11.7c) By His second command, God made an open expanse of atmosphere between the cloud water above and sea water below; second day concluded with evening (night) and morning.[1163] John Sailhamer explains, "Biblically, the 'waters above the heavens' are simply the clouds which provide rain." And the *rāqia'*, "expanse," is best understood by our English word "sky."[1164] The "water above" must be understood from the perspective of Adam, who may have received the original narrative from God, and from the perspective of Moses, who transcribed the narrative into the book of Genesis. Moses had seen cloud-covered sky. In the Middle East I, too, have seen thick cloud cover, which forms especially in the winter and early spring. Cloud cover was within the "everyday experience of the author." Also within the experience of Moses was the expanse of sky. This expanse on the second day is the same word used for expanse of sky where birds would fly beginning with the fifth day.[1165]

So on this second day of God's work, between the sea water below and the cloud water that covered the sea, God *'āsâh,* "made," an expanse of open atmosphere. The thinning fog rose from the sea surface, opening up the expanse between. God called the expanse "sky." This day was the second day of God's work.

I have seen fog rise from the Maine seacoast many mornings. Even though the ancient fog described by Job 26 and 38, and implied by Genesis 1:6, may have been much thicker and perhaps quite different, that first rise of fog from the sea took place in one day at the Spirit's location. This event was in the second day of God's work.

(11.7d) By His third command unit, God gathered the sea waters and caused dry land to appear out of the worldwide sea. Several authors point out that this event causing land to rise is described in Psalm 104:6–9. These verses refer to the first land rising from the sea, not to the flood, because the previous verse says, "He set the earth on its foundations" (NIV). Setting Earth on its foundation is part of the Genesis 1:1 creation of Earth, not part of the flood. Psalm 104 is one of the great chapters on creation. God set the Earth on its foundation and covered even the mountains with the deep sea. Then He caused the waters to go off the land and caused the mountains to rise and valleys to sink. Psalm 104:6–8 and Genesis 1:9 seem to describe the appearance of the first continent with mountain upthrust and valley formation:

> With the deep as with a garment Thou didst cover it [Earth],
>> Above the mountains did the waters stand,
> At Thy rebuke they fled,
>> At the voice of Thy thunder they hasted away—
> The mountains rose, the valleys sank—
>> To the place which Thou hadst established for them.
> Thou hast set them a bound which they cannot pass,
>> That they turn not again to cover the earth (Pember's translation). (I
> plan to comment on this last verse in a flood book.)

These events seem to correspond to God's third command in Genesis 1:9–10:

Then God said,

"Let the waters below the heavens be gathered into one place,
and let the dry land appear"; and it was so.
And God called the dry land earth,
and the gathering of the waters He called seas;
and God saw that it was good (NASB).

God did not "create" the dry land but caused the sea to gather into one place and the dry land to "appear" out of the water. Ross says for something to appear there must have been an Observer to have seen it appear. That Observer was the divine Narrator of Genesis 1, the Spirit of God. He was located just above the water surface from which the continent began to appear from the sea.

This was no small volcanic island like Surtsey, Iceland. Surtsey began its rise from the North Atlantic in 1963. But now half of it is washed away. Surtsey is softer volcanic lava, but continents are made of hard granite masses. Genesis 1:9 describes the appearance of the first continent. *Yabāshâh,* "dry ground," and *'āretz,* "earth," are both singular in Genesis 1:9–10. The land that appeared apparently was a single continent. A great granite land mass continent broke through the surface of the deep sea for the first time.

This new continent that appeared was *yabāshâh,* "dry ground." The dry ground explains why water would be needed before plants could grow (Gen. 2:5–6).

Then Psalm 104:8 describes mountain building on the continent that seems to correspond with what we call plate tectonic mountain range formation. "The mountains rose; the valleys sank" (Ps. 104:8, NASB).

Psalm 104:9 indicates that this continent blocked and bounded the sea. This bounding of the sea is also described in Job 38:10–11.

And I placed boundaries on it [the sea],
And I set a bolt and doors,
And I said, "Thus far you shall come, but no farther;
And here shall your proud waves stop" (NASB).

This, too, corresponds to God's third command unit in Genesis 1:9–10.

(11.7e) By His fourth command, God made the land sprout vegetation—seed-bearing plants, fruit-bearing trees; third day concluded with evening (night) and morning. Genesis 1:11–12 says God commanded the earth to produce vegetation, namely, seed-bearing plants (*ēsev māzeriya‘ zera‘*) and fruit-bearing trees (*ēts peri*) with internal seeds (angiosperms). Verse 11 in the NIV reads,

> Then God said, "Let the land produce vegetation [*deshe*]:
> seed-bearing plants and
> trees on the land that bear fruit with seed in it,
> according to their various kinds."

The Hebrew word translated "vegetation" by the NIV is *deshe*. *Deshe* may be a "broader term that includes both 'plants' and 'trees,'" the two categories of plants named. That is how the NIV and NASB translate it. On the other hand, *deshe* may mean a third category, "grass."[1166] Then it would be translated in three categories as in the Complete Jewish Bible: "God said, 'Let the earth put forth grass, seed-producing plants, and fruit trees'" (Gen. 1:11). Actually, grasses (which include wheat, rye, oats, etc.) are also seed-bearing. Either way, God made seed-bearing and fruit-bearing plants and trees.

These higher plant kinds raise the question, What about simpler green plants such as algae, most of which is in water? The plants of this third day of God's work were *land* plants ("Let the land produce," NIV). Sailhamer suggests that God may have made simpler plants, such as water algae, earlier. "At the conclusion of the chapter, other plants are mentioned [*kol yereq ēsev*, "every green plant"] that also are for . . . food for animals (Genesis 1:30). . . . Yet the creation of these plants is not mentioned anywhere in the first chapter. . . . The account thus assumes that such plants already were present in God's world."[1167] Green algae needs sunlight, so would have been made after day one. Also, since no miracle is mentioned, time was needed for the trees to mature and produce fruit. These ideas suggest the Payne proposition. I am not affirming these ideas, but Sailhamer does raise significant questions.

By His fourth command unit, God caused the land to sprout seed-bearing and fruit-bearing land plants. The plants actually sprouted during that literal third day of God's work, just as He commanded. And God saw that it was good.

(11.7f) "After its kind" means these plants and animals will never evolve into a new kind. This fourth command is the first that includes the phrase "after its kind." Seed plants and fruit trees may diversify within their kinds, such as the many varieties of citrus or varieties of apples. But once God completed these seed plants and animal kinds, they would never evolve into new and different or higher kinds of life.

Two stage Biblical creation denies chance-driven macroevolution from molecules to man. 2SBC also claims that even *micro*-evolution of these higher kinds is especially limited. These kinds are terminal kinds—they will never evolve into another kind. Gene segregation within that kind may result in varieties and even closely related species of these higher plant and animal kinds. But God very specifically added *lᵉminētô* ("after its kind") to the seed-bearing plants and fruit-bearing trees with seed within them, to breathing sea creatures and birds and bats, and to the three orders of higher land animals. Therefore, these are not going to evolve into other kinds.

However, this limitation does not seem to include bacteria or viruses, which may evolve into new, likely harmful, kinds.

(11.7g) By His fifth command unit, God made the already-created luminaries govern day and night in Earth's sky; fourth day concluded with evening (night) and morning. Ross says, "The heavens and earth (*shamayim erets*) of verse 1 includes the entire physical universe of galaxies, stars, planets, etc." The luminaries had existed since Genesis 1:1 when God created the heavens, which the author, Moses, understood as "the sun and the moon and the stars" in the sky (Deut. 4:19). So the sun had already been created in Genesis 1:1. Schroeder explains that until the fourth day, "the atmosphere, however, was translucent, not transparent. Therefore, individual luminaries were not distinguishable."[1168] On the fourth day, God made the luminaries "be" (a more accurate word than "distinguishable") in the expanse of sky to carry out their three designated functions to Earth.

Ross agrees that the action of the fourth day was the "transformation of the atmosphere from a translucent condition to one that is at least occasionally transparent."[1169]

Hugh Ross explains the importance of perspective. The obvious source of the narrative was the Divine Observer, the Spirit of God, who was on location. His perspective was from just above the surface of Earth. God caused the luminaries to "be" in Earth's sky in relationship to Earth's surface for the first time from the perspective of the divine Observer looking upward from Earth.

The Kline claim (based on Gen. 2:5–6) of ordinary providence is helpful. The principle of ordinary providence suggests that the cloud layer opened, so the sun began a "new relationship to the earth wherein it began to govern earth's times and seasons and in general to affect life on earth as men now observe it to do."[1170] God did not create the luminaries in outer space on that day. On His fourth day of work, God commanded the luminaries to be in the expanse of the sky to separate and govern day and night; to be signs for seasons, days, and years; and be lights in the expanse of the sky.

The means of God's ordinary providence is explained in the creation passage of Job 26. After describing events in days one, two, and three in 26:10–12, verse 13 regarding day four says, "By his breath the skies became fair," (NIV) or "cleared" (NASB). The luminaries had already been created as part of the heavens during the beginning time period of Genesis 1:1. But overcast cloud or haze diffused the light until, by God's fifth command, the skies cleared so luminaries could begin carrying out their three commanded functions to Earth.

Against the above, young earth creationists claim that *'āsâh* in the concluding report of the fourth day (Gen. 1:16) means God "created" the sun, moon, and stars about 6,000 years ago. YEC advocate Ken Ham says, "It is clear from Genesis 1 that the sun was not created until the fourth day." "The sun was created to rule the day that already existed." "God deliberately left the creation of the sun until the fourth day."[1171]

Contra YEC, the fourth day command in 1:14–15 says nothing about God creating the luminaries:

Then God said,
"<u>Let there be</u> lights in the expanse of the heavens
   <u>to separate</u> the day from the night,
and <u>let them be for signs</u>, and for seasons, and for days and years; and
<u>let them be for lights</u> in the expanse of the heavens
   to give light on the earth";
      and it was so (NASB).

Hebrew scholar John Sailhamer responds to the YEC idea, "Though our English translations of Genesis often suggest that God created the sun, moon, and stars on the fourth day, the Hebrew text does not demand, *or even allow for*, such an interpretation. The overall sense of Genesis 1 assumes that by the fourth day, the sun, moon, and stars are already in place."[1172] "According to the Hebrew text, God said, 'Let the lights in the expanse be for separating the day and night. . . .' God's command, in other words, *assumes that the lights already exist*"[1173] (emphasis his).

The grammar that explains John Sailhamer's statement is that God commanded the luminaries to be in the sky to separate day and night. This command is a purpose clause that assumes the luminaries already existed but now were given a new purpose. God's command (Gen. 1:14) is a purpose verb group, "let be . . . to separate." The grammar is this:

The "to be" verb $y^eh\hat{\imath}$ is jussive (a mild command), "let be";[1174]
the "luminaries" in the expanse of the sky are the direct object;
$l^ehab^ed\hat{\imath}l$, "to separate," with l^e prefix, is hiphil infinitive of purpose.

"Let the luminaries be in the expanse of the sky" for three new purposes:

"to separate the day from the night";
"for signs, and for seasons, and for days and years"; and
"for lights in the expanse of the sky" (Gen. 1:14–15a).

All three purposes were carried out "in the expanse" of Earth's sky. "The expanse" was the same expanse, below the cloud water and above the sea water, that God had made in the second work day (Gen. 1:6–7). It was the same expanse in which birds will fly on the fifth day (Gen 1:20). So the work of this fourth day was not in distant outer space where the luminaries had been created back in Genesis 1:1. God's work was in the same sky where birds would fly. The means is stated in Job 26:13a—"By his breath the skies became fair" (NIV). The sky cleared of its final pervasive haze.

After the command in 1:14–15, the report in 1:15b–18 explains the results:

. . . and it was so.
And God made ['āsâh] the two great lights,
    the greater light to govern the day, and
    the lesser light to govern the night;
    He made the stars also.
And God placed them in the expanse of the heavens
    to give light on the earth, and
    to govern the day and the night, and
    to separate the light from the darkness;
        and God saw that it was good (Gen 1:15b–18, NASB).

"And it was so" indicates that God's commands in the previous verses were carried out. Verses 16–18 form the report of the carrying out of God's commands. In the report is one 'āsâh ("do, fashion, make"). But that 'āsâh could *not* mean "created" because the triple command in 1:14–15 was not a creation command. The 'āsâh in 1:16–18 cannot report a creation result that God did not command in 1:14–15. The triple command was for lights to "be" in the expanse of the sky for the purpose of separating day and night; for the purpose of signs for seasons, days, and years; and for the purpose of lights. There is not even an *'āsâh* ("do, make") much less a *bārā'* ("create") in the triple command in 1:14–15. The luminaries had already been created in 1:1 as part of the heavens.

We can relate the triple command to the report (read Hebrew ←):

1:14 Command: יְהִי ... לְהַבְדִּיל ... וְהָיוּ לְאֹתֹת ... וְהָיוּ לִמְאוֹרֹת

    for-lights and-let-be...for-signs and-let-be...to-separate...let-be

1:16 Report: וַיַּעַשׂ ... לְמֶמְשֶׁלֶת

    for rule/governing...And-made

1:17-18 וַיִּתֵּן אֹתָם אֱלֹהִים בִּרְקִיעַ הַשָּׁמָיִם לְהָאִיר ... וְלִמְשֹׁל ... וּלְהַבְדִּיל

    &-separate...&-rule...to-give-light of-the-sky in-expanse God them And-set

None of these is a creation command. The command in 1:14–15 is a triple purpose clause. God commanded the luminaries to be in the expanse of the sky *for the purpose* of separating day and night. The command does not contain either *bārā'*, create, or *'āsâh*, "do, make."

The report in 1:16–18 declares that God acted to make the luminaries do as commanded. In 1:16, the one *'āsâh* in the report has the sense of "to act with effect" or "bring about"[1175] the intended result. God acted with the effect of making the luminaries separate day and night (as commanded), by the greater light ruling the day and the lesser light and stars ruling the night. In 1:17–18 God set the (already created) luminaries in the expanse of the sky (in the perspective of the Narrator, through the first openings in the cloud layer) for the result that they would give light on Earth, govern day and night, and separate light from darkness.

So the command in 1:14–15 was a triple *purpose* command, and the report in 1:16–18 was that God *acted with the effect* of making the luminaries carry out that triple purpose. In none of the commands or report in the fourth day did God *bārā'*, "create," the luminaries or even *'āsâh*, "make," the luminaries. The one *'āsâh* in the report is God's action making the already-created luminaries carry out the purposes of His fourth day triple command. They did so beginning that very day through the first openings in the cloud layer.

In Genesis 1:1, the meaning of *b⁰rē'shît*, "in the beginning," is in the beginning time period (Gen. 10:10; Job 8:7; Jer. 28:1). That time period was before day one began in 1:3. How long that time period lasted, the Bible does not say. God created the heavens (sun, moon, and stars—Deut. 4:19) in that beginning time. Therefore, the stars are however old they are.

And the starlight from them is however old it is. Unlike YEC, the two stage Biblical creation theory does *not* have the problem of deceptive "appearance of age" of the universe. The universe is however old it is, yet 2SBC also strongly affirms six literal days. This understanding fits Scripture first, and also fits the observable universe.

Going back to day four, the narrative was from the perspective of the Spirit just above Earth's surface. As we follow the events through the first four days, God progressively thinned Earth's cloud layer that was described in Job 26:8 and 38:9. First, diffuse sunlight pierced the cloud to the Divine Narrator's location starting day one. Then the cloud rose from the sea for an open-air expanse under the overcast cloud water on God's second day of work. Finally, on His fourth day of work, the sun, moon, and stars began being in the sky above the Narrator for the purpose of governing and separating day and night, being time markers to Earth and lights in the sky. The means was through the first clear openings in the cloud layer. And God saw that it was good.

> The fourth day's work was not making luminaries,
> but making the luminaries govern day and night in Earth's sky.

(11.7h) God had already created the stars back in the beginning. Genesis 1:16 mentions the stars: "*He made* the stars" (NASB). "*He made*" is in italics because it is not in the Hebrew text. The English Standard Version more correctly translates, "and the stars." After saying "the lesser light to rule/govern the night," God says "and the stars." The meaning is that along with the lesser light, the stars also govern the night. Nothing is said about creating the stars on the fourth day.

The stars were understood by Moses to be part of the heavens (Deut. 4:19). God created the heavens in Genesis 1:1. On the fourth day, the stars with the moon ruled/governed the night sky for the first time from the perspective of the Observer/Narrator, the Spirit of God. But God had already created the stars as part of the heavens "in the beginning," so the stars are however old they are.

(11.7i) By His sixth command unit, God created groups of breathing sea creatures in the waters and flying creatures in the expanse of the sky; fifth day concluded with evening (night) and morning. Morris says, "God proceeded to make animal life for the atmosphere and hydrosphere on the fifth day."[1176]

Pember says that the literal rendering is, "Let the waters swarm with swarms, with living creatures."[1177] And for the second part, "And let fowl fly above the earth in the face of the firmament of heaven."[1178]

On this fifth day of work, God created groups of breathing sea creatures in the waters, as well as birds (the Hebrew word may extend to other flyers such as bats, although there is a separate Hebrew word for bats, *atalēph*) in the expanse of the sky. And God saw that it was good.

(11.7j) By His seventh command unit, God caused the land to produce three orders of land animals—quadruped livestock, low scrambling animals, and wild animals. By the seventh command, God made three orders of נֶפֶשׁ חַיָּה (*nephesh hāyâh*) on the land. Walter Kaiser explains that these creatures with "the breath of life" were living animals.[1179]

Ross says that all three orders of land mammals God created were "soulish creatures that can relate to humans; creatures with qualities of mind, will, and emotion."[1180] Ross explains that God made *remes,* which refers to soulish animals, not creeping insects. *Remes* were "short legged land mammals such as rodents and hares." Ross continues explaining that God made *nephesh ᶜhāyâh hā'āretz,* the "long-legged quadruped usually described as wild," and *bᵉhēmâh,* "long-legged quadruped that is easy to tame."[1181] Ross's last definition may be a little too restrictive because *bᵉhēmâh* apparently included large wild herbivores such as African elephant, mammoth, and rhinoceros, which I doubt many would consider "easy to tame."

In summary, by a seventh command unit, God caused the land to produce three orders of *nephesh hāyâh* (1:24a)—quadruped livestock and larger quadruped herbivores (*bᵉhēmâh*), low scrambling animals (*remes*), and wild (omnivorous and carnivorous) animals of the earth (*ᶜhāyâh hā'āretz*).

(11.7k) By His eighth command unit, God created man, both male and female, in His image; the sixth day concluded with evening (night) and morning. Ross says, "Human beings are distinct . . . in that humans alone possess body, soul, and spirit."[1182]

Duncan and Hall say God made the creatures "after their kind" but created man "in Our image."[1183] We alone of all Earth's creatures relate to God. We alone, when we receive the Lord Jesus as our Savior, are adopted into His family. We were truly created in His image and likeness with the intent that we should know Him and, in a finite human sense, become like Him (1 John 3:2).

(11.7l) The seventh day: God rested. Ross says, "After the creation of Adam and Eve, however, God ceased from His work of creating new life."[1184] Like "the sixth day," "the seventh day" has the article "the," indicating a completion. God rested the seventh day.

Long after the original account was passed down apparently by Adam and his descendants, Moses in Exodus 20:8–11 brought out the latent idea that because God worked six days and rested the seventh, making it holy, humans, too, should follow God's example. Exodus 20:8–11 commands man to work six days and keep the seventh holy by not working, because God worked six days and rested the seventh. But this commandment to follow God's example is not actually in Genesis 1:1—2:4a. God's example in Genesis 1 forms the grounds and warrant for the Fourth Commandment to man in Exodus 20:8–11. But the original Genesis 1:1—2:4a text is not about man or a command to man. The original text of 2:2–4a is about God. The text says God rested the seventh day, thus making it holy.

(11.8) God used both miracles and means as He sovereignly chose (but there was no "metaphysical naturalism"). Drs. Whitcomb and Morris popularized the approach that the Bible tells us what happened; then we can learn from science how God brought it about. YEC has had lively debate on the means of the flood. Morris proposed some means in the six days.[1185] Hugh Ross proposed means for the development of the universe from its creation until today.

Meredith Kline stresses that God used normal providence along with creation miracles during the six days. Kline explains, "Moses demonstrates the tightness of the causal connection [no rain, so no vegetation; rain, then vegetation] in this context."[1186] Kline concludes we should *presume* that if an event in Genesis 1—2 may be interpreted as God using a normal cause-and-effect process, we should tend to interpret the event that way, rather than as a miracle. Kline reasons that if God used rain to grow plants by command three, why not the sun to give light by command one?[1187]

God using means is the opposite of *"metaphysical naturalism."* Naturalism *a priori* excludes all supernatural events. In total contrast, God using means is simply that God usually does His work within the regularities He decreed. We call these regularities "natural laws"—gravity, rain cycle, solar day and night, etc. Because God normally works by these means, we can recognize His miracles because they go beyond the normal natural laws He established.

Duncan and Hall go too far toward only miracles. They form one end of the creationism spectrum. At the opposite end, evolutionary creationists go too far the other way by positing only "natural" means after the initial *ex nihilo* creation.

I conclude that Morris, Ross, and Kline are correct. During the creation, God used *both* miracles and means as He sovereignly chose.

(11.9) All of Genesis was eyewitness narrative. Henry Morris says, "It is probable that the Book of Genesis was written originally by actual eyewitnesses of the events reported therein."[1188] Wiseman says that these accounts had been "recorded on tables of stone or clay, in common with the practice of early times, and then handed down from father to son, finally coming into the possession of Moses."[1189] Moses *compiled* Genesis from the eyewitness accounts of Adam, Noah, Shem, Abraham, Isaac, etc.

(11.9a) The Spirit of God was the eyewitness Narrator of 1:1—2:4a. Ross explains, "Genesis 1:2 says that the Spirit of God hovered above the primordial Earth's surface. This clue means that the subsequent description of early Earth (and the stages of its transformation) comes from the vantage point of an observer just above the surface of the waters, looking up at the sky and across the horizon, describing details as they would have appeared from that perspective."[1190] Ross lists scientific evidence that the report is accurate. Only the Creator could have known these facts before modern science, indicating that the Holy Spirit of God is the Source of this eyewitness report of the creation events.[1191] The creation narrative was an eyewitness account from the Spirit of God, who was "on location."

(11.9b) Genesis is eyewitness narratives, not late JEPD patchwork. The Wiseman tablet theory says that Genesis was recorded by eyewitnesses who passed down to Moses their historical narratives on clay tablets (the common and permanent writing form of the ANE) or possibly stone tablets.

Wiseman says that the creation narrative was passed down from the beginning. Isaiah 40:21–26 speaks of creation. In 40:26, God asks about the luminaries in the heavens, "Who created all these?" Several verses earlier God asks, "Has it not been declared to you from the beginning? Have you not understood from the foundations of the earth?" (Isa. 40:21, NASB). Isaiah indicated that God declared the creation narrative to Israel's ancestors from the very beginning. Presumably, God told the creation narrative to Adam during their walks in the Garden.[1192]

Adam passed down the Spirit's eyewitness creation narrative. Adam added his own eyewitness narrative, Genesis 2:4b—5:1a. Both were passed down through Seth and his descendants to Noah. Noah added his narrative (probably on tablets by the end of his life, by which time writing had come into use) and passed them on through Shem to Abraham and finally to Moses.

The main alternative to Genesis being from eyewitness reports is the higher critical JEPD documentary hypothesis. Sailhamer, Morris, Ross, and

Wiseman reject the problematic higher critical JEPD documentary hypothesis. This higher critical hypothesis claims that the five books of Moses, including Genesis, were from four source documents with late dates of 850 BC to 621 BC Today, there are claims of up to forty sources, splintering the Pentateuch into fragments. The documentary hypothesis claims that the JEPD documents evolved from primitive religions and myths. Supposedly, the Genesis myths were borrowed from other ANE myths. Then these late documents were patchworked together in bits and pieces by a redactor as late as the third or fourth century BC.

Henry Morris and Wiseman are correct that archeology and ancient linguistic evidence consistently contradict this higher critical JEPD documentary hypothesis.[1193] If I may apply John Piper's statement to the JEPD documentary hypothesis, "For my part I see massive minds assembling, with great scholarly touch, a house of cards."[1194]

A divine perspective infinitely surpasses a JEPD perspective.

In reaction against the higher critical JEPD hypothesis, some conservative Christians suggested the dictation theory, that God dictated Genesis to Moses.

In response, although possible, the dictation theory does not fit the Genesis text. Genesis many contains unique ancient linguistic and stylistic characteristics from before the time of Moses. Also, there are 137 verses (NIV) in Exodus, Leviticus, Numbers, and Deuteronomy that include the words "the LORD said to Moses." There is *not one* occurrence of these words in Genesis. The Bible text itself does not indicate that God *spoke* any of Genesis to Moses. Moses was not present for any of the Genesis events, yet Genesis was in some sense from Moses (John 1:17).

In contrast to the JEPD and dictation theories, P. J. Wiseman, Henry Morris, and John Sailhamer recognize that Genesis consists of the creation account and almost a dozen family narratives and genealogies, each with a personal name affixed in the ending *tôl^edôt* (or at the beginning of a genealogy). The personal name indicates that the named individual was the eyewitness source of the narrative or genealogy. Eyewitness sources are emphasized by the Bible. Luke followed this pattern of gathering His Gospel from those "who from the beginning were eyewitnesses" (Luke 1:2, NASB), starting with Mary, the mother of our Lord. Peter, too, emphasized, "For we have not followed cunningly devised fables, when we made known unto you the power and coming of our Lord Jesus Christ, but were eyewitnesses of his majesty" (KJV).

I will be so bold as to say this: The evidence from the *tôlᵉdôt* in Genesis itself, archeology, ANE culture, and linguistics supports the Wiseman claim. Apparently, Genesis is from about a dozen eyewitness accounts and genealogies passed down to Moses. Under the Spirit's inspiration, Moses edited these into the book of Genesis.

The creation narrative is the Spirit's eyewitness account.

(11.9c) God apparently gave the Genesis 1:1—2:4a creation narrative to Adam. Wiseman explains that part of the *tôlᵉdôt* ending of a first tablet was reiterated by the beginning of the second tablet so the two tablets could be kept in order.

The creation narrative ends with, "These *are* the generations [*tôlᵉdôt*] of the heavens and of the earth when they were created" (KJV).

The Adam narrative begins with, "When the LORD God made earth and heavens . . ." (NIV).

The beginning sentence of the Adam narrative is a partial reiteration (with a reversal of "earth and heaven") of the ending sentence of the creation narrative. Adam linked the two accounts in consecutive order. Wiseman suggests Adam may have put the accounts on tablets. Perhaps the first writing was available by the end of Adam's lifetime. If Adam did not write them, then Adam passed down the narratives orally. In that case, likely Noah or Shem put these narratives on tablets, because writing was becoming available by the end of their lifetimes over three hundred years after the flood. The point is that these two accounts were linked. Adam could not have linked his account to the creation account unless he already knew the creation account. This indicates that God gave Adam the creation account. God could have spoken it to Adam in the Garden.

Moses wrote each of his five books on a long Egyptian style scroll (Exod. 17:14; 24:7; Deut. 28:58–61; 30:10; 31:24–26). So Moses had no need to reiterate the end of the creation narrative at the beginning of the next narrative as Adam did. Moses received the two accounts with the reiteration so the original ancient tablets would be kept in order. Then Moses faithfully recorded the narratives from the tablets, including the reiteration, even though the reiteration was no longer needed on his long scroll. This indicates Moses recorded the tablet accounts precisely as originally written. The only parts Moses appears to have added were updated place-names such as "the king of Bela (that is, Zoar)." Bela was the city name on the original tablet, but the name had changed by Moses' time to Zoar, so he added "(that is, Zoar)." Later, in Deuteronomy 34:3, Moses writes, "as far as Zoar," without mentioning the ancient name because Zoar was the current name.

The creation narrative is an eyewitness account by the Spirit given directly by God to Adam. The narrative was recorded in permanent tablet form, which was highly valued and passed down to Moses. Finally, Moses transcribed the narrative into the book of Genesis precisely as originally written.

(11.9d) The Genesis 2:4b—5:1a narrative was Adam's own eyewitness account, which switched to a local perspective. The next narrative, Genesis 2:4b–5:1a, ends in the *tôleᵈôt* of Adam. Adam began his narrative by a tie-in to the previous narrative: "When the LORD God made the earth and the heavens . . . " (Gen. 2:4b, NIV). Then Adam described what apparently he had learned from God about the origin of the vegetation, which needed water to sprout (Adam was a gardener). Then Adam told his own origin and that God planted the Garden in the east of Eden. He recorded information about the geography of the Garden, especially the rivers, which he apparently explored before the Fall. He recorded God's instructions, the naming of the animals, Eve, the Fall, Cain and Abel, then the descendants of Cain, and finally Seth and his son, Enosh. All this was within the lifetime of Adam. No person or event after Adam's lifetime is named in Adam's narrative. Adam ended his narrative with, "This is the book of the generations of Adam." He was claiming that this was his family generational narrative.

Sailhamer is correct that there is a switch from a global sense to a local sense of *ha'āretz* (although Sailhamer missed when this switch occurred). This switch came with the switch in authors—from the Spirit to Adam. The Spirit narrated from the global sense of *'āretz* as the Earth or continental land in Genesis 1:1—2:4a. God had a universal perspective in 1:1, then a just-above-the-planet-surface perspective in 1:3–31. Then Adam narrated from the local sense of *'āretz* as the land or ground, starting in 2:4b or 2:8 and ending in 5:1a. Adam as the eyewitness gardener had a local perspective in the Eden narrative.

(11.10) The six days were the generations of the heavens and earth. Kline, Ross, and other authors emphasize that Genesis 1:1—2:4a concludes with, "These *are the* generations [*tôleᵈôt*] of the heavens and of the earth when they were created" (Gen. 2:4a). This concluding phrase is the worldview from which Genesis 1:1—2:4a was narrated and the worldview of the patriarchs.

(11.10a) The worldview of Genesis was generations. Genesis 1:1—2:4a was written within a generations worldview, not a workweek worldview. The current debate in creation circles focuses on six long day-age geological eras versus six literal days. But this debate ignores the ancient literary design or genre.

We tend to read the Exodus 20:8–11 use of Genesis 1 as an illustration of a workweek *back* into Genesis 1 and underemphasize Genesis 1:1—2:4a as a generational account as 2:4a explicitly states. The internal emphasis of Genesis 1:1—2:4a is generations and fits with the generational genealogies throughout Genesis.

Steinberg says, "Genesis is a book whose plot is genealogy."[1195] Genesis 1 is about the generations of the heavens and the earth. In the ancient world, the older the generation in a genealogy, the more honored. In this worldview, Genesis 1 was about the most ancient generations of all—"the generations of the heavens and the earth."

(11.10b) The *tôlᵉdôt* listed the ancestor-author at the end of his narrative. Most of the narratives of Genesis end in a *tôlᵉdôt*, "these are the generations of ----." *Tôlᵉdôt* is derived from *yālad*, which means to beget, give birth. *Tôlᵉdôt* means descendant generations *from* someone (not to someone). Adam's *tôlᵉdôt* (Gen. 2:4b—5:1a) tells about Adam and Eve and their descendants *from* them. Adam's *tôlᵉdôt* was at the end of the narrative in 5:1a, like a signature on a letter today.

The exception is genealogies, which also list descendants *from* an ancestor, but the ancestor's name is listed first. For example, in Genesis 10, the *tôlᵉdôt* begins the genealogies because the named people (Shem, Ham, and Japheth) were the ancestors, each the first person on his list.

But the norm for a *narrative* was the form we use in a letter, ending the narrative with the name of the person writing. Wiseman's explaination that the *tôlᵉdôt* title is the end of the narrative follows the example of the colophon commonly ending ANE tablets. The name of the author or owner is at the *end* of his tablet.

Each narrative ending in a *tôlᵉdôt* in Genesis lists the patriarch-author—heavens and earth in 2:4a, Adam in 5:1a, Noah in 6:9a, Shem in 11:10, Terah in 11:27, Isaac in 25:19, and Jacob in 37:2. The author lists his name in the *tôlᵉdôt* at the *end* of his narrative. The creation narrative ends in "These *are the* generations of the heavens and the earth when they were created" (2:4a).

(11.10c) The generations of Genesis 2:4a indicate the commands and days. Westermann says the initial creation, the six days, and eight creation commands could be "each understood as a succession of begettings."[1196]

Let me be very clear in response that the actual creation was absolutely by the fiat commands of eternal God, who is spirit. Contra ANE myth, there were no sexual connotations, absolutely none.

Nevertheless, the Bible itself says in the ending title, "These *are* the generations of the heavens and the earth." The "generations" point back to the six days and eight commands of God's work on the heavens and the earth. The two extra commands, land and land animals, may also be seen as generations.

(11.10d) Interpret Genesis 1 as the generations of the heavens and the earth. Genesis 2:4a says these are the generations of the heavens and earth. The obvious referent for the generations is the six days.

By God's fiat commands, in a nonprocreational sense,
    the <u>heavens</u> begot the diffuse sunlight in Earth's <u>sky</u>;
    the Earth's <u>sky</u> begat the *rāqîa'*, open air with <u>sea</u> water below; and
    the <u>sea</u> begat <u>land</u> with vegetation,
        as the first three generations of the heavens and the earth.

By God's fiat commands, in a nonprocreational sense,
    the <u>sky</u> begot the luminaries in the sky;
    the <u>sea and sky</u> begot the sea and flying life;
    the <u>land</u> begot the land creatures, and from the land's dust, man;
        then God rested.

Originally, to the ancient listeners hearing the account from Adam, Noah, Shem, or Abraham, the Genesis 1 narrative was a generational account of the most ancient generations of all, the "the generations of the heavens and the earth."

Heavens and Earth as Patriarchs

<u>Three descendant generations</u>		<u>Later "offspring" from the three</u>
1st generation: light in the sky	→	luminaries in sky
2nd generation: sky begot open air, sea below	→	sea and air life
3rd generation: sea begot land with plants	→	land animals, man

We should interpret Genesis 1 as generations because the Spirit of God titled the creation account, "These *are the* generations of the heavens and the earth when they were created."

(11.10e) The days were both literal days and began generations. Daylight, evening, night, and morning with numbered days indicate that all six were literal days. Yet the six days also seem to have been pictured by Genesis 2:4a as generations. Perhaps the best way to fit eight commands, six literal days, and generations together is that a generation is begotten on a single day. It would seem that the six days were the begetting days of the commanded events or items of the heavens and the earth. Each literal day began the generation of that commanded item.

The item commanded before the evening and morning formula began on that literal normal day-night day as its begetting day:

God cause light to penetrate the cloud layer to the Spirit on day one.
God formed the first open air on His second work day.
At God's command seed plants sprouted on His third work day. Luminary functions began in clear sky on God's fourth work day.
God created *nephesh* sea and air life on His fifth work day.
God created mankind on the sixth work day.

Each of these commanded items began on its begetting literal day. Together these were the generations of the heavens and the earth. By this progressive creation involving eight commands and six days, God brought about the generations of the heavens and earth.

(11.10f) The term "begetting days," implied by the ending title, could not have been used without incorrect connotations. The sense of the begetting of successive generations would have been inferred from the ending title, "These *are the* generations of the heavens and the earth when they were created." But a term such as "begetting days" could *not* have been used without the incorrect connotation of sexual procreation, which is absolutely foreign to the Biblical text. In stark contrast to the ANE sexual begetting of the heavens and earth by a mythical god and goddess pair, the living God created by fiat commands.

On the sixth day, God proclaimed that all He had made was "very good." Yet Psalm 102:25–26 speaks of this creation wearing out like a garment. How do these two concepts fit together?

(11.11) This creation was never intended to be our eternal home. This creation, though "very good" in its culmination on the sixth day with Adam and Eve, was never intended to be the eternal perfect home for God's people. This world is not my home.

(11.11a) Adam's sin resulted in his spiritual and physical death, then "death spread to all men, because all sinned," but all believers

are made alive in Christ (Rom. 5:12; 1 Cor. 15:21–22). One reason this world cannot be our eternal home is Adam's Fall. YEC correctly emphasizes both the spiritual and physical death of Adam and his race because of Adam's sin. Human sin and human death are inextricably linked in Genesis 3 and by Paul in Romans 5:12: "Therefore, just as sin entered the world through one man, and death through sin, and in this way death came to all men, because all sinned" (NIV). Adam was the one human through whom sin entered the world, and the death through sin passed to all men because we all followed in his sin. Adam's sin, resulting in human death, is linked to Jesus' substitutionary atonement and gift of eternal life. Because Jesus is the sinless God-man and our Kinsman-Redeemer, there is a future for believers in Him: "So in Christ all will be made alive" (1 Cor. 15:21–22, NIV). This fallen world is not our eternal home. The Lord Jesus is making a new eternal perfect Home for us (John 14).

(11.11b) Romans 8:19–23 and Psalm 102:25–26 explain a second reason why this creation is not our permanent home. Paul, in Romans 8:19–23, explains a second reason this old world can never be our eternal home:

> The creation waits in eager expectation for the sons of God to be revealed. For the creation [ἡ κτίσις] was subjected [ὑπετάγη] to frustration [τῇ ματαιότητι], not by its own choice, but by the will of the one who subjected it, in hope that the creation itself will be liberated from its bondage to decay [τῆς δουλείας τῆς φθορᾶς] and brought into the glorious freedom of the children of God. We know that the whole creation has been groaning as in the pains of childbirth [συστενάζει καὶ συνωδίνει] right up to the present time. Not only so, but we ourselves, who have the firstfruits of the Spirit, groan inwardly as we wait eagerly for our adoption as sons, the redemption of our bodies (NIV).

ἡ κτίσις – the creation, in this case the product, that which was created
ὑπετάγη (from *hupotasso*) – was subjected (aorist passive)
τῇ ματαιότητι – the frustration of the inability to reach a goal
τῆς δουλείας τῆς φθορᾶς – the bondage of decay or the inescapability
of the deterioration
συστενάζει καὶ συνωδίνει – groan together and travail together

The big pair of questions may be phrased several ways:
Did God create the universe to be perfect and potentially eternal, but the Fall interrupted, causing a cosmic catastrophe and corrupt universe?

Or did God from the beginning, completed by the curse, subject this creation to being noneternal in expectation of the eternal New Creation?

In other words, when God created the stars, did He create them perfect and potentially eternal, but Adam sinned and ruined the stars?
Or did God create the stars to run down from the beginning because He has always intended to create a New Heavens and New Earth?

When did God start the running-down (entropy) of the universe—
with Adam's Fall, or
with the creation from the beginning, anticipating a New Creation?

To answer, we will consider three questions about Romans 8:
Who subjected the creation in hope—God, Adam, or Satan?
What did he subject the creation to, and what is the hope?
When did he subject the creation?

Psalm 102:25–26 helps answer who did the work, what He did, and when He did it (*l'pāneh* indicates "forward" from the beginning)[1197]:

In the beginning [*l'pāneh*] you laid the foundations of the earth,
and the heavens are the work of your hands.
They will perish, but you remain;
they will all wear out like a garment.
Like clothing you will change them
and they will be discarded (NIV).

Who subjected the creation is God. God designed the heavens and earth. God alone, not Adam or Satan, is able to subject the creation "in hope" (Rom. 8:20).[1198] That hope is the eternal New Creation that God will make, where we will live in "glorious freedom" (Rom. 8:21).

The answer to "*what?*" is that God subjected this old creation to running down, in contrast to the New Creation, which will be characterized by liberty and eternality. What God did was create a φθορᾶς universe, a universe that is subject to running down or wearing out like a garment (decaying in the sense that a star is decaying) until in the future it perishes (Ps. 102:25–26; Isa. 65:17; Heb. 1:10–12). This running-down nature of the universe is bondage in the sense of inescapable. And, to personify the creation, this running down until it perishes is "frustration." This creation is like a clock timing a fire bomb that God created and wound up at the beginning. God supervises each tick (no deism), but the clock is inevitably going to come to its final tick at precisely the predetermined second, and then this world will end in fire (2 Pet. 3:11–13). Our hope is not in this world but in the resurrection and New Creation.

When God subjected the creation to this noneternal, running-down nature was a time period. It was the whole beginning time period from the initial creation through the curse. Because God planned a New Creation, He made this present creation running down (φθορᾶς) from its beginning. Paul does not say in Romans 8 that when Adam fell, the heavens began to decay. Romans 8 does not even mention Adam or his Fall. Rather, when God created the heavens and the earth, He built into them τῇ ματαιότητι, the frustrating inability to be the eternal home for the glorified children of God (Rom. 8:20–21).

This present earth reminds us of the Fall and our sin. Isaiah 65:17 (NASB) explains God's plan:

> For behold, I create new heavens and a new earth;
> And the former things will not be remembered or come to mind.

God did not come up with the plan to create a new heavens and a new earth *after* Adam fell. God has always planned the New Creation to be our hope. Ephesians 1:4 says, "He chose us in Him before the foundation of the world." Jesus said, "Then the King will say to those on His right, 'Come, you who are blessed of My Father, inherit the kingdom prepared for you from the foundation of the world'" (Matt. 25:34, NASB). God planned that we believers should be the citizens of the New Creation from the start of the old creation.

By His plan, God built a noneternal creation to begin with because He never intended this creation, with its reminders of evil, to be our eternal home.

In Psalm 102:25–26, quoted earlier, the psalmist says that God made the heavens and laid the foundation of the earth, yet they will perish but God will remain. The psalmist does not say that after Adam sinned, the heavens and earth started to wear out and perish. Wearing out was built into the creation from its beginning, just as it is built into a garment from its beginning. Wearing out is not evil; it is simply a physical characteristic God built into the creation (Rom. 8:20). To put it into modern scientific terms, Psalm 102:25–26 indicates that God built entropy (running down, wearing out like a garment) into this creation from its beginning. That is also the point of Romans 8:20—that God built this frustrating decay into the present creation.

The curse does not declare that suddenly God changed the heavens from eternal to running down. Nor is the curse primarily what Romans 8:20 is about. Romans 8:20 contrasts the present creation, which was subjected to decay, to the liberty of the New Creation.

So all three, Romans 8:19–23, Psalm 102:25–26, and the curse in Genesis 3:14–19, say nothing about Adam's Fall starting the running-down of the heavens. These verses explain a second reason besides the Fall why this creation cannot be our eternal home. God made this heaven and earth noneternal from the start of creation.

Meanwhile, humans were not initially in bondage to deterioration (entropy worked, but *not* bodily deterioration toward certain death). That did not happen until the Fall and curse. So the subjecting was incomplete until the curse. Evil entered Earth with Satan's fall and Adam's Fall. So God justly declared the penalties of the curse. The curse completed God's action by which the creation was subjected (aorist passive). The judgments of the curse were primarily on the moral agents who committed the evil. The serpent/Satan will die. Eve (and her descendants) will suffer in childbirth and from problems in husband-wife relations. Adam will suffer painful toil working the cursed ground. Especially the curse was that Adam, with his race, will die. And the Fall released all kinds of subsequent human evil. At the Fall and curse, any changes in the universe/heavens were not even mentioned. The absence of any mention of the heavens in the curse makes sense if God had already subjected the heavens and earth to a noneternal, running-down, increasing-entropy condition from the beginning.

The Fall and curse at the end of the creation do not make God's plan to create a noneternal first heavens and earth at the beginning an evil plan. Something that is "very good" does not have to be eternal. This creation could not be freed from the bondage of decay and its reminders of evil unless God made it noneternal—to be replaced. This first earth was never intended to be our eternal, perfect home.

With sin and the curse added to the frustrating perishability, the creation groans together as if in birth pains, eagerly anticipating the future revelation of resurrected believers (Rom. 8:18–23). The running down was from the beginning. But I suggest that the "groaning as in the pains of childbirth" metaphor relates to sin and the curse. This connection indicates that the "groaning" was *not* from the beginning, but started after sin and its awful consequences were introduced by Adam (options 1 or 3 as explained in ch. 13) or by Lucifer and Adam (option 4 in ch. 13).

YEC misses the point of Romans 8:18–23. YEC seems to think these verses *begin* with the Fall, so the verses are only about the Fall. The universe was "perfect" (some YEC advocates say it was not subject to entropy) for the first days of its existence until Adam fell. Then Adam, by his Fall, ruined the universe, subjecting it to the evil condition of running down, so it will need to be replaced.

In response to YEC, neither Adam nor the Fall is mentioned in Romans 8:18–23. The comparison is between this old creation — "for the creation (8:20)," "the creation itself" (8:21), "the whole creation" (8:22) — and the coming glory, where we will be adopted, our bodies redeemed, and the creation "liberated." Romans 8:18–23 does not *begin* with the Fall (although the Fall is included). These verses are a comparison of the two creations and our lives in each. The comparison is of the present creation subjected by God to the frustration of the bondage of wearing out from its beginning, with the addition of groaning from the effects of the Fall and curse, contrasted to the eagerly anticipated future liberty and glory of the New Creation.

The creation eagerly anticipates the coming revelation of Jesus and with Him the glorified children of God. Then the creation itself will experience times of restoration (Acts 3:21) at the Second Coming of Messiah Jesus and the Millennium. The Millennium will be a second maximum-good time in *this* creation, in many ways "like the garden of Eden" (Ezek. 3:35). However, in the Millennium there will be death (Isa. 65:20); but in the Garden there was no human death until sin (Rom. 5:12). Both Eden and the Millennium end in rebellion and judgment, so neither could be our eternal home. This creation will enjoy restoration (Acts 3:21) in the Millennium, but this old creation will need to be replaced. After the Millennium, this creation will undergo dissolution by intense heat (2 Pet. 3:10–13). Then God will make the New Heavens, New Earth, and New Jerusalem that will be our eternal Home (Rev. 22:1–5). There, we will experience true freedom and glory (Rom. 8:21) with no need to remember the evils of this old creation (Isa. 65:17).

We need a balanced view of this world and the next. We are to be responsible stewards of this world because God created us to live on this earth for the present. God gave us that stewardship mandate in the Garden (Gen. 1:28). But we also anticipate our coming freedom in the New Creation because God never intended this world to be our eternal home.

I conclude that from the beginning, completed by the curse, God subjected this creation to the frustration of being noneternal and running down. The Bible texts above indicate that God created the heavens (sun, moon, and stars) and the earth with this running-down condition from the beginning. The groaning as in childbirth was from sin (by Adam, or Lucifer and Adam) onward. The curse completed the subjecting, so man, too, is now perishing. This creation and we ourselves eagerly anticipate the New Creation.

If this understanding is correct, then God designed this present creation from the beginning to be noneternal and running down. Isaiah 42:5 says God "created the heavens and stretched them out" (NASB). An expanding universe is a running-down universe, so it had a beginning and will have an end. God created this heavens and earth in the beginning, just as Genesis 1:1 declares. He created this universe expanding and running-down from the beginning because He had already predetermined that this old creation will be replaced by the New Heavens, New Earth, and New Jerusalem as our eternal Home (Rev. 22:1–5).

(11.12) Two stage Biblical creation claims a Biblically undated heavens and Earth. Meredith Kline says, "We must speak where the Bible speaks, and be silent where the Bible is silent. . . . The inspired text, rightly interpreted, is simply silent with regard to the age of the earth and universe." [1199]

God created the heavens and the earth "in the beginning." The beginning was not in day one. The beginning was a time period that lasted an unstated amount of time before day one. So we may conclude that the creation of the heavens and earth is not dated by the Bible. Adam, by his descendants' genealogies, can be dated roughly by the Bible. The heavens and earth are undated. If one is older, it would be the heavens because it is listed first. The universe is however old it is. And Earth is however old it is. Two stage Biblical creation claims a Biblically undated heavens and earth creation (UEC).

(11.12a) Two stage Biblical creation from the Bible matches the universe. To the degree that the two stage Biblical creation theory matches the Bible, it will also match the actual creation. This match is because both the Bible and universe are from the one and only Creator.

From all the evidence we have cited, we may conclude that the Bible does not date the creation of the heavens and the earth. A Biblically undated creation allows the universe to be however old it actually is. God has built into the universe great evidence about Himself (Ps. 19:1). But that evidence is available only if we frankly accept the universe as it is. That evidence is not available if we try to force the universe into an artificial age, force an artificial gap ending in the destruction of all life, or force pre-creation chaos into the history of the universe. The evidence for the God of the Bible as our

Creator is available to us only if we accept the universe as it is. 2SBC claims a Biblically undated creation. The universe is however old it actually is.

If we accept the universe as it actually is, then the universe yields at least three great lines of evidence that match the God of the Bible being our Creator. First, the Bible claims that the universe had a beginning. Second, eleven times the Bible says that God has been stretching out the heavens. And third, the Bible teaches that God designed the universe with a goal of humans who can know Him and live to His glory (1 Cor. 10:31; 2 Cor. 4:6). So it is no surprise to us that Edwin Hubble discovered and that the COBE and WMAP experiments showed that the universe had a beginning and is expanding and running down. That is what the Bible has said all along. The first words of the Bible are "In the beginning God created the heavens and the earth." The Bible alone makes these claims. No other "religious" book begins this way. Only the Creator could have known these facts long before modern science. The God of the Bible is the Creator of the universe. Moreover, scientists have discovered that the universe is exceedingly fine-tuned for human life on Earth, many billions to one in its precise fine-tuning.[1200] Also, the universe and our place in it seem precisely designed so we can discover these facts about it.[1201] That level of fine-tuning essentially requires a precise design executed by a master Designer-Creator of immense intelligence. A time-bound universe needs an eternal Creator. This evidence demonstrates that the eternal God of the Bible is the Creator of the universe.

The two stage Biblical creation theory matches both the Bible and the creation. The two stage Biblical creation theory welcomes this evidence that the God of the Bible is the Creator of the universe. This match of 2SBC with both the Bible and the creation suggests that the two stage Biblical creation theory is approaching what God said that He did when He created the heavens and the earth in the beginning.

(11.13) Noah's flood was real, violent, and apparently worldwide. Although the flood is not part of the creation so not part of the two stage creation theory, YEC includes it, so I, too, will mention it.

The Wiseman tablet theory says the flood narrative was an eyewitness account. Shem's account was an eyewitness narrative of the events he saw. Later Scripture gives a "God view" of the events. In the New Testament is God's perspective given by the Lord Jesus and Peter. Together they indicate that massive rain came down upon the Earth and that fountains of the deep added to the flood. These resulted in a violent, worldwide flood survived by only eight people. God willing, I plan to study and publish on this subject soon.

In the beginning God created the heavens and the earth.

Now the earth was uninhabitable and uninhabited,
and darkness was over the surface of the deep,
and the Spirit of God was hovering over the waters.

God made Earth lighted, habitable, and inhabited by His eight commands and six days of work.

Summary of Two Stage Bibical Creation

The Bible indicates that God created in steps, or stages. The first stage was, "In the beginning God created the heavens and the earth" (Gen. 1:1). That beginning time period ended in the description of the uninhabitable, uninhabited, dark, sea-covered Earth (Gen. 1:2). The second stage was God's work by His eight command units and six days making Earth lighted, habitable, and inhabited, ending with the seventh day of rest (Gen. 1:3—2:4a).

Stage One: "In the beginning" indicated a time period of unstated length inherent in the word *bᵉrē'shît* (Gen. 10:10; Job 8:7; Jer. 28:1). In the beginning God created *ex nihilo* the heavens (sun, moon, and stars [Deut. 4:19]) and unfinished planet Earth (Gen. 1:1). God caused the birth of the deep sea (Job 38:8), covering the mountains (Ps. 104:6) on planet Earth. He wrapped the sea in thick dark cloud, blocking out light of even the full moon (Job 26:7–9; 38:8, 9).

Description: As the beginning time period concluded, Genesis 1:2 describes planet Earth as uninhabitable and uninhabited (not chaos) and its deep primeval sea dark. (Since planet Earth alone was described as unfinished and dark, we may infer that the heavens had already been largely completed and lighted during 1:1.) The Spirit's location was stated. (We may infer that this location identified the Spirit's perspective for the upcoming narration of God's work completing Earth during Genesis 1:3–31.)

Stage Two: By the eight command units of Genesis 1:3–31, involving six daylight-evening-nighttime-morning days of work, God made planet Earth's sky, sea, and land lighted, habitable, and inhabited.

In Genesis 1:3 God commanded light, beginning day one. The Spirit reported, "And there was light" (we may infer the light was diffuse sunlight penetrating the thinning cloud to the Narrator just above the sea, Jer. 23:35). This diffuse sunlight began literal day one on Earth. The Bible states the events of day one in consecutive order: After God began day with light, God said the light was good, separated daytime from nighttime (indication Earth was rotating), and named day and night. Then there was evening, apparently as the Spirit's location rotated into the darkness away from the sun. As the nighttime concluded, apparently the Spirit's location rotated back to the edge of sunlight again at the dawn of morning. Day one was a normal daylight-evening-nighttime-morning day as Earth rotating in the cloud-diffused sunlight. Day one set the meaning of "day" as a normal day. The ending title says, "These *are* the generations of the heavens and earth when they were created." So day one may also have been understood by the ancient patriarchs as the begetting day (no sexual connotations) of day and night on earth.

God formed an open-air expanse between the waters of the sea below and the waters of the unbroken overcast cloud layer above (we may infer by the fog rising up from the sea, producing an open-air expanse). Evening, night, and morning completed this second day of God's work.

By His third command unit, God gathered the waters under the sky into one area so dry land appeared (to the Spirit, the Narrator).

By His fourth command unit, God commanded the earth to produce seed-bearing plants and fruit-bearing trees. Evening, night, and morning completed this third day of God's work.

By His fifth command unit, God commanded the (previously created) luminaries to be in the open-air expanse of Earth's sky (we may infer as seen from the Narrator's perspective). God made the luminaries separate day and night; be signs for seasons, days, and years; and be lights in the expanse of the sky to give light on Earth (we may infer through the first clear openings in the cloud above the Narrator [Job 26:13a]). Evening, night, and morning completed this fourth day of God's work.

By His sixth command unit, God created groups of breathing aquatic and flying animal life. Evening, night, and morning completed this fifth day of God's work.

By His seventh command unit, God made three orders of land animal life—large (herbivorous) quadrupeds, short-legged scampering animals, and wild (carnivorous) animals of the earth.

By His eighth command unit, God created body-soul humans, uniquely in His image, who could know and glorify Him forever. Evening, night, and morning completed the sixth day of God's work.

The narrative began with the creation of the heavens and earth in Genesis 1:1 as stage one. In stage two by the eight commands and six work days God completed Earth. The creation narrative ended in the *tôl^edôt* of Genesis 2:4a, reporting, "These *are* the generations of the heavens and of the earth when they were created" (KJV). The Spirit of God's location implies that the account is His eyewitness account, apparently spoken to Adam and passed down in tablet form to Moses, who enscripturated it under the inspiration of the Holy Spirit, the original Narrator.

The succeeding genealogies date Adam over 6,000 years ago. However, the universe was created in the beginning, a time period unspecified in length by the Bible. *After* the beginning time period, God worked by eight commands and six literal normal days, concluding with the creation of Adam and Eve. Adam's genealogy dates Adam, not the universe. So the universe and Earth are undated by the Bible (UEC).

If you are finding this book helpful, tell others. Biblical creation is important. Fill out a request to your public library or college library to buy this book. Include the ISBN number from the front pages and add the web site, thomasarnoldpublishing.com. I would appreciate any web site or magazine reviews that you may write, because as a self-publisher, I will not have the advertising of a large publishing company. I will be glad to receive copies of reviews and suggestions to TAP, P.O. Box 805, Arlington Hts. IL 60006-0805. Together, let us improve our understanding of Bible's teaching about the creation. Like martyred reformer Balthasar Hubmaier, I am always ready to learn more from God's Word.

God Alone in Eternity

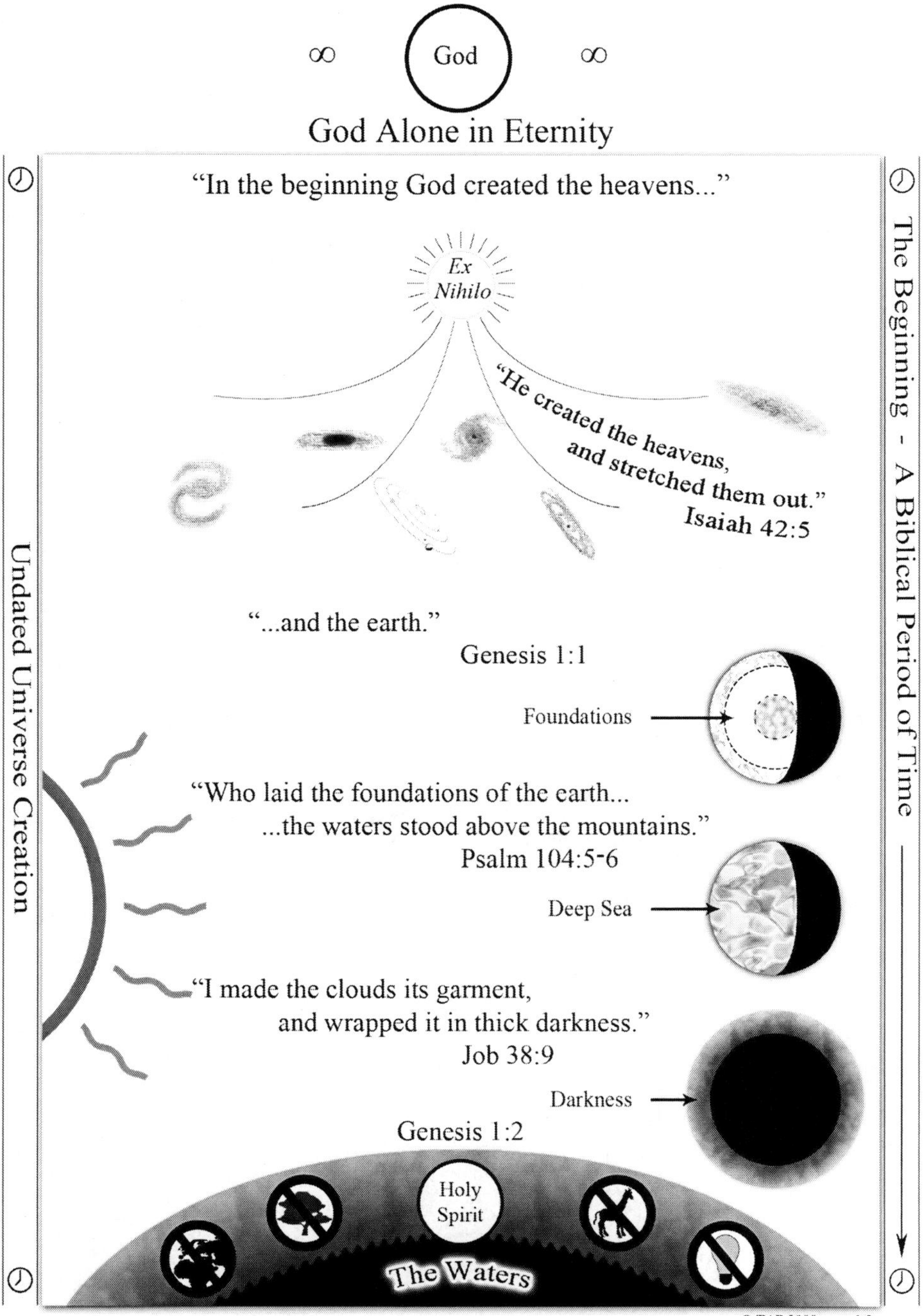

11b. Two Stage Biblical Creation Theory—Stage II

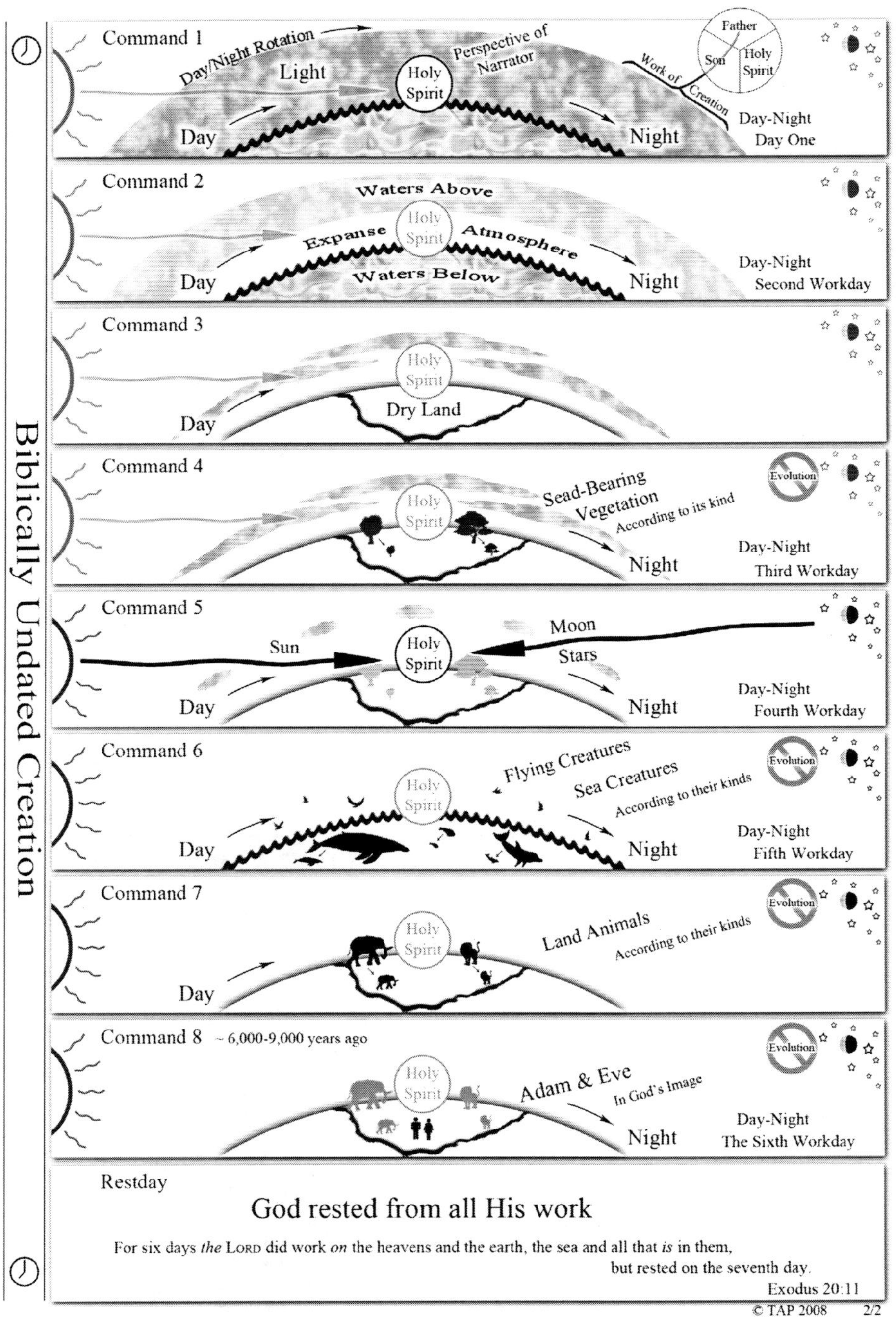

11. Claims of Two Stage Biblical Creation—from Ten Theories
(Biblically supported claims from all the theories united and in **bold**)

Best Preunderstandings from the Ten Theories

(11.0A) Have no unexamined assumptions.
(11.0B) Genesis is eyewitness history, evidentially supported.
(11.0C) The Bible and creation correctly interpreted will agree.
(11.0D) Creation provides questions; the Bible provides answers.
(11.0E) The Bible reveals what God did; science may show how.

Ten Denials from the Ten Theories

(11.D1) 2SBC denies any extrabiblical authority over the Bible.
(11.D2) 2SBC denies chance was the cause of the universe or life.
(11.D3) 2SBC denies chaos—no pre-creation, initial, or gap chaos.
(11.D4) 2SBC denies 1:1 was a title with no *ex nihilo* creation.
(11.D5) 2SBC denies any time gap or events at Genesis 1:2.
(11.D6) 2SBC denies day-ages or any other non–day-night days.
(11.D7) 2SBC denies that 1:1 *ex nihilo* creation was *in* day one.
   (11.D7a) Gen. 1; Prov. 8 deny that Genesis 1:1 was in day one.
   (11.D7b) 2SBC denies that Exodus 20:11 says "in" six days.
   (11.D7c) 2SBC denies creation of male & female date universe.
(11.D8) 2SBC denies that the six days were night-day days.
   (11.D8a) 2SBC denies Gen. 1:3 indicates light was temporary.
(11.D9) 2SBC denies that the Bible dates the *ex nihilo* creation.
(11.D10) 2SBC denies God designed creation to deceive man.

Bible Interpretation Practices for 2SBC from the Ten Theories

(11.H1) Start with Bible; later, science discoveries may correlate.
(11.H2) Interpret the Bible text from the perspective of the author.
   (11.H2a) Do not import modern science into the ancient text.
   (11.H2b) Do not import later Bible concepts into earlier events.
   (11.H2c) Recognize the perspective location of the author.
(11.H3) Begin by how clauses (esp. 1:1–3) fit together.
(11.H4) A correct understanding of a Bible topic will cohere.

STAGE ONE: IN THE BEGINNING GOD CREATED THE HEAVENS AND THE EARTH

(11.1) "In the beginning" was the beginning time period.

   (11.1a) *B^er̄e'shît* indicates *the* definite beginning.

   (11.1b) "In the beginning" requires an eternal Beginner.

   (11.1c) "In the beginning" started time instantly.

   (11.1d) "In the beginning" meant a time period.

   (11.1e) The beginning was unspecified in length.

   (11.1f) Because the length was unspecified, creation is undated.

   (11.1g) "In the beginning" was stage 1; six days were stage 2.

(11.2) God created *ex nihilo*.

   (11.2a) "The heavens and the earth" means the entire universe.

   (11.2b) God created the heavens and earth *ex nihilo*.

   (11.2c) God created out of nothing, so only God existed before.

   (11.2d) God created heavens (sun, moon, & stars) and Earth.

   (11.2e) The beginning *ex nihilo* creation was a unique act.

   (11.2f) God created heavens and earth before the six days.

(11.3) God stretched out heavens, covered Earth with sea & cloud.

   (11.3a) After God created the heavens, He stretched them out.

   (11.3b) God covered Earth with sea & cloud during beginning.

(11.4) At 1:2 Earth uninhabitable, uninhabited, sea-covered, dark.

   (11.4a) Genesis 1:2 is a description of Earth, not an event.

   (11.4b) Only Earth was described as uninhabitable.

   (11.4c) *Tōhû v^abōhû* meant "uninhabitable and uninhabited."

   (11.4d) Earth's deep sea surface was cloud darkened.

   (11.4e) The Earth was seriously *tōhû v^abōhû*, but not chaos.

(11.5) Spirit's location implies His perspective for 1:3–31.

   (11.5a) The Spirit's location may have been above future Eden.

STAGE TWO: GOD WORKED SIX DAY-NIGHT DAYS MAKING EARTH LIGHTED, HABITABLE, AND INHABITED

(11.6) God worked six normal day-night solar days.

   (11.6a) All six days were normal day-night days.

   (11.6b) All six days of God's work were solar days.

   (11.6c) Day one in Hebrew was cardinal, days two–six ordinal.

(11.6d) Ordinals are insufficient to prove Payne proposition.

(11.6e) The six days were God's designated work days.

(**11.7**) By eight command units and six days, God finished Earth.

(11.7a) God worked by eight command units, yet six days.

(11.7b) Diffuse (sun)light penetrating cloud began day one.

(11.7c) God made an open expanse of atmosphere, second day.

(11.7d) Third command unit, God caused dry land to appear.

(11.7e) Seed-bearing, fruit-bearing trees sprout, third day.

(11.7f) "After its kind" means no evolution of new kinds.

(11.7g) God made luminaries govern day & night, fourth day.

(11.7h) God had already created the stars back in beginning.

(11.7i) God created sea and air life, fifth day.

(11.7j) Seventh command unit, God made land animal kinds.

(11.7k) God created male and female in His image, sixth day.

(11.7*l*) Seventh day, God rested.

(**11.8**) God used both miracles & means as He sovereignly chose.

(**11.9**) All of Genesis was eyewitness narrative.

(11.9a) Spirit of God was eyewitness Narrator of 1:1—2:4a.

(11.9b) Genesis is eyewitness narratives, not JEPD patchwork.

(11.9c) God gave the 1:1—2:4a account to Adam.

(11.9d) Gen. 2:4b—5:1a was from Adam's local perspective.

(**11.10**) The six days were the generations of heavens and earth.

(11.10a) The worldview of Genesis was generations.

(11.10b) The *tôlᵉdôt* listed the author at his narrative's end.

(11.10c) The generations of Genesis 2:4a indicate six days.

(11.10d) Interpret Gen. 1 as generations of heavens and earth.

(11.10e) The days were both literal days & began generations.

(11.10f) The term "begetting days" has incorrect connotations.

(**11.11**) This creation was never intended to be our eternal home.

(11.11a) Adam's sin caused human death; Christ gives life.

(11.11b) Rom. 8 says this creation is running down, not eternal.

(**11.12**) 2SBC claims a Biblically undated heavens and earth.

(**11.13**) Noah's flood—real, violent, and worldwide; 8 survivors.

Major Supported Claims from the Creation Theories

The Correct Translation of Genesis 1:1: Waltke affirms the traditional translation of Genesis 1:1: "In the beginning God created the heavens and the earth." It is *incorrect* to translate 1:1 as "When God began to create."

Waltke Merism: "The heavens and the earth" meant the entire orderly universe. Also, evening and morning meant the entire nighttime.

The Heiser Clause Analysis: Begin analyzing creation by determining which clauses (esp. in Gen. 1:1–3) are independent clauses and which are dependent clauses, and then which independent clauses are modified by which dependent clauses, and so how they fit together.

The Waltke Exclusion Principle: If there was preexisting chaos, there was no *ex nihilo* creation of the organized heavens and earth. The converse is also logically possible: If there was *ex nihilo* creation of the organized heavens and earth, then there was no unorganized chaos.

The Kline Order: Proverbs 8:22–31 says that "the beginning," when God created Earth (Gen. 1:1), was "when there were no depths." Ocean depths existed by 1:2, so "In the beginning" was before 1:2 and before the six days. Creation order: Heavens, Earth, sea, six days.

The Kline Claim: When the Bible does not indicate a miracle, Genesis 2:5–6 (no rain, no plants; rain, then plants sprouted) shows God probably used ordinary means in the creation era, just as today. **Ross Addition:** "An observed attribute of the Creator . . . is His economy of miracles—only what's needed to accomplish His purpose."

The Kline Undated Universe: "We must speak where the Bible speaks, and be silent where the Bible is silent. . . . The inspired text, rightly interpreted, is simply silent with regard to the age of the earth and universe."

A Generational Genesis: The worldview of Genesis was generations. The six begetting (literal) days of Genesis 1 introduced the most ancient generations of all—"the generations of the heavens and the earth."

The Rooker Reaffirmation: "The key difference between pagan cosmogonies and Genesis 1 is *creatio ex nihilo* and the absence of preexisting matter."

The Morris Maxim: In historical narrative, a numbered "day" was a day.

The Morris and Ross Method: The Bible reveals what God did; science may uncover how He did it.

The Duncan-Hall Eight Commands: God worked by eight command units with common format, related to the six literal days.

The Ross Concordism: God does not deceive either by His Word or by His creation work. Correctly interpreted, both God's verbal revelation (the Bible) and physical revelation (the created universe) will be in accord.

The Observer's Perspective: Ross says interpret the Genesis 1 creation narrative from the perspective of the Observer/Narrator, the Spirit, hovering just above the surface of the water-covered Earth.

The Ross Apologetic: The Bible alone declares that the universe had a beginning and has been stretching out. Only the Creator could have known these facts long before modern science. The God of the Bible is the Creator, and the Bible is His accurate message to us.

The Ross-Schroeder Fine-Tuning Evidence: The fine-tuning of the universe and Earth is evidence of the Designer, not chance.

The Wiseman Tablet Theory: The Genesis narratives were eye-witness reports recorded on tablets received by Moses. The name of each author was at the *end* of his narrative.

The Wiseman-Gray 20:11 Recognition: Exodus 20:11a has no "in," allowing the natural grammatical reading of Genesis 1:1 as the initial creation of the actual heavens and planet Earth "in the beginning" before the six days.

The Pember Literalism: If we take Genesis 1:1 literally, then God literally created the literal heavens and literal (unfinished) Earth in the literal beginning before the six literal days.

The Morris One Fall Explanation: The creation was perfect. Man and animals were created about 6,000 years ago with eternal physical life. There was "no disorder, no sin and, above all, *no death!* Even Satan was still good at this point."[1202] His first effect on Earth was the temptation. Adam's sin about 6,000 years ago resulted in a "cosmic catastrophe" including all human and animal death and subsequent moral and natural evil.

The Kaiser Two Falls Explanation: Standard theology identifies two falls: the angelic fall led by Lucifer, and later the human Fall by Adam. God's concluding "very good" evaluation was about His work on Earth, not about angels such as Lucifer who had been created and likely fell earlier. Animal death is *not* inherently evil. God Himself killed an animal to cover human nakedness. Any pre-Fall evil aspects of animal disease and death could only have been initiated by fallen Lucifer (Ezek. 28:16–18; Heb. 2:14). Yet by the sixth day, God worked even those together for good or eliminated them until Adam's Fall. Adam was the original cause of human death (Rom. 5:12) and farming woes (Gen. 3:17–19), but Scripture does not say he caused animal death. So animal death may have preceded Adam's Fall. Animal life cycles fit the present non-eternal world God created anticipating human resurrection and the New Creation (Rom. 8:20).

The Sailhamer Time Period: *B^{e}rē'shît*, "in the beginning," consistently has the sense of an extended beginning time period, never of an instant or a few hours.

The Sailhamer Sense: *Tōhû v^{a}bōhû* consistently has the sense of uninhabitable and uninhabited wilderness, never of unformed matter or chaos.

The Thomas Truism: If Genesis is true, yet its narrative history was not dictated by God to Moses, then its narrative history was from eyewitnesses.

The Patrick Proposition: The initial Genesis 1:1 *ex nihilo* creation was in the beginning time period before the six days, so is undated by the Bible.

The Two Stage Arnold Affirmation: Creation took place in two stages: In the beginning God created the heavens and the earth (but Earth was still uninhabitable, uninhabited, and its sea surface dark); so God worked by eight commands and six normal day-night days making Earth lighted, habitable, and inhabited.

From Chapter 12:

The Hodge Hiatus: A qualitative break exists between the initial "immediate, instantaneous creation *ex nihilo* by the simple word of God," and the later "mediate, progressive" work of God with already created materials and secondary causes during the six days.

Intelligent Design Theory: "Certain features of the universe and of living things are best explained by an intelligent cause, not an undirected process such as natural selection."

The Payne Proposition: To claim that time absolutely could not have passed between God's six work days is making too dogmatic a claim on too inconclusive evidence. Time passage between the six literal days is neither explicitly affirmed nor explicitly denied by the Bible.

Chapter 12
Minor Creation Theories

Over a dozen additional creation theories exist. I will review them only briefly because some are less known, some are too far off the mark, some are only briefly explained by the author(s), and others concern only biological creation or naturalistic theories. In my brief summaries of these theories, I will respond with my evaluation within each summary, rather than leaving all my evaluation to the end of the summary.

12. Undated Universe and Earth; Young Biosphere Theory

I recently discovered the work of Gorman Gray, a retired engineer and Bible college graduate. He has done a good study, although without full Hebrew resources. His preunderstandings include "the plenary, verbal inspiration of the Scriptures and absolute authority of the autographs" based on Matthew 5:18.[1203]

First, Gray correctly realizes that "Scriptures leave the age of the stellar heavens and planetary foundational earth undefined." Therefore, "the sun, moon, basic earth, and stars are undefined in age."[1204] He holds to undated earth creation (UEC).

Second, Gray rejects the grammatically problematic gap in the gap theory. He says, "No time passes between verses 1 and 2 as required by gap theorists." He is correct in this rejection of the supposed gap, because the grammar does not allow time passage at Genesis 1:2. Instead, he says, "Time for an inorganic earth *is allowed* between verse 2 and verse 3."[1205]

In response, this view is far better than the provably incorrect gap at 1:2 of the gap theory. The problem with Gray's claim is there is no positive Bible evidence for time passage between verses 2 and 3. So this claim, while it may be true, is an argument from silence. In contrast, there is very strong positive evidence for time within 1:1, because *bᵉrē'shît* inherently means a period of time, which a number of other theories, including 2SBC, recognize.

Third, Gray correctly realizes that the Bible teaches that the six days were normal day-night cycle "solar days."[1206]

Fourth, he correctly realizes that these six "solar days of divine work took place *after* the original creation of the stellar heavens and planet Earth."[1207]

Fifth, by the second part of his title, "young biosphere," he says, "the origin of man and everything biological is recent." "However, the same Scriptures limit all *biological* life and the construction of the biosphere itself to less than 8,000 years."[1208] He bases the higher date on the Septuagint with its longer list of patriarchs. He assumes no time passed between the days; therefore, all life is less than 8,000 years old.

Sixth, he claims that the Bible text limits the age of dry land because dry land appeared in day three. Consequently, land geology is less than 8,000 years old.[1209]

Seventh, since life is less than 8,000 years old, he claims that "evolution of any type is, therefore, categorically impossible."[1210]

Eighth, Gray, like Henry Morris, says, "Most geological features of the earth's crust resulted from the worldwide cataclysm—the Genesis Flood of five or six thousand years ago."[1211]

Ninth, Gray follows Hebrew scholar Bernard Northrup's excellent translation of Exodus 20:11: "For six days the Eternal LORD worked on the air, the land, and the sea and all that is in them."[1212] Northrup has correctly translated 20:11 from the Hebrew text, instead of adding an *"in"* to Scripture as so many translations improperly do. I personally would translate *ha shāmayim* as "sky" or "heavens" rather than "air" because "sky" was within the understanding of Moses, but "air" is a modern concept. Nonetheless, Northrup and Gray are correct about Exodus 20:11.

Problematic weaknesses: Gray's main weakness, as already mentioned, is a time period between Genesis 1:2 and 1:3, an argument from Bible silence.

A minor weakness is that Gray may make too hard a separation between *bārā'*, "create," and *'āsâh*, "do, make." My understanding of *'āsâh* is that *'āsâh* is so broad that it overlaps in a general way many Hebrew words. *Asâh* may partially overlap the weaker senses of *bārā'* of making out of materials or as a summary of all God's work. Gray does not need to make that overly hard separation between the two words to show that *bārā'* has a specific sense in Genesis 1:1—to make something new, understood by Hebrews 11:3 as creation *ex nihilo*—that *'āsâh* does not convey in Exodus 20:11 or in Genesis 1:16. We must translate by context, especially such a broad word as *'āsâh*. Northrup correctly translates *'āsâh* in Exodus 20:11 as "worked on," because that is the contextual meaning.

So we may honor Gorman Gray for bringing us closer to understanding what God said that He did when He created the heavens and earth, and then later worked six days on Earth.

The Wiseman-Gray 20:11 Recognition: Exodus 20:11a has no "in," allowing the natural grammatical reading of Genesis 1:1 as the initial creation of the actual heavens and planet Earth "in the beginning" before the six days.

13. Mediate and Immediate Creation Theory

Charles Hodge summarized two main views of creation. The first is the day-age view, which Hodge leaned toward.

The second view is the general idea of the two stage creation. Hodge said, "Some understand the first verse of Genesis to refer to the original creation of the matter of the universe in the indefinite past, and what follows [that is, the six days] to refer to the last reorganizing change in the state of our earth to fit it for the habitation of man."[1213]

Hodge explained that the two stages had two different kinds of creation work: immediate and mediate. By "immediate" he means the Genesis 1:1 instantaneous creation, especially the *ex nihilo* creation, but also of the spirit of man, and by "mediate" he means God's work with already created materials in the six days:

Mediate and Immediate Creation

But while it has ever been the doctrine of the Church that God created the universe out of nothing by the word of his power, which creation was instantaneous and immediate, i.e., without the intervention of any second causes; yet it has generally been admitted that this is to be understood only of the original call of matter into existence. Theologians have, therefore, distinguished between a first and second, or immediate and mediate creation. The one was instantaneous, the other gradual; the one precludes the idea of any preexisting substance, and of cooperation, the other admits and implies both. There is evident ground for this distinction in the Mosaic account of the creation. . . . In Genesis 1:27 it is said that God created man male and female; in chapter 2:7 it is said that 'the LORD God formed man out of the dust of the ground.' It thus appears that forming out of preexisting material comes within the Scriptural idea of creating. . . . There is, therefore, according to the Scriptures, not only an immediate, instantaneous creation *ex nihilo* by the simple word of God, but a mediate, progressive creation; the power of God working in union with second causes.[1214]

I agree. The two stage Biblical creation theory is built on this understanding. First, God created the heavens and earth by His "instantaneous" *ex nihilo* immediate creation, followed by mediate work during the beginning time period completing the universe and preparing Earth for the coming six days. Later, using the already created materials of Earth and its atmosphere, God worked six days on Earth using mainly secondary mediate causes.

The Hodge Hiatus: A qualitative break exists between the initial "immediate, instantaneous creation *ex nihilo* by the simple word of God," and the later "mediate, progressive" work of God with already created materials and secondary causes during the six days.

14. The Payne Proposition or Time Between Days Theory

J. Barton Payne suggests that to claim that time absolutely could not have passed between God's six work days is making too dogmatic a claim on too inconclusive evidence.

J. Barton Payne was a leader and Bible scholar in the Presbyterian tradition. He pointed out that there are different levels of Hebrew evidence for different creation issues in the Bible. Some issues have compelling evidence, but other issues have inconclusive implications. Payne's point is that for us to make a strong claim—either way—on weak evidence is unhelpful. And we need the Bible's guidance as our "helmsman" to tell the difference between compelling evidence and less certain implications.

For example, the Bible gives compelling Hebrew evidence against chance-driven "naturalistic evolution" of molecules-to-man purely by accidental chance.[1215] So we must exhibit "firm conviction" on creation issues such as this that have conclusive Bible evidence.

Payne points out that in Exodus 20:11, there is "no preposition in the Hebrew," no "*in*."[1216] Exodus 20:11 should be understood as "For six days God worked on the heavens and earth," allowing time "in the beginning" for the initial *ex nihilo* creation. There is compelling explicit Hebrew evidence for Genesis 1:1 as a time period before the six days.

Also, there is compelling evidence about the length of the days. Payne supports the view that each numbered *yôm* was a normal day-night day.

In contrast, the idea of time passage between the six days is suggested by "inconclusive evidence." Payne explains:

Yom, in Genesis 1:5, etc., is the Hebrew word for "day." Some, then, have concluded that if Scripture teaches creation in six consecutive days, its creationism becomes unacceptable. But the literal text reads, "one day" (1:5), "a second day" (1:8), etc.; so the days need not be taken consecutively but may be understood as separated by long ages. Each day would then indicate a normal, twenty-four hour period, by the time of the arrival of which, the major phenomena which God had been creating since the previously mentioned day, had at length come into being.[1217]

Payne places this statement under "Inconclusive Evidence" and says, "The days *need not* be taken consecutively but *may* be understood as separated" (emphasis added). He is *not* claiming that time certainly passed between the days (as Hayward much less cautiously does in the next theory).

What I understand the Payne proposition to be is this: *To claim that time absolutely could not have passed between God's six work days is making too dogmatic a claim on too inconclusive evidence.*

A number of implications may support time passage between the six literal normal days of God's work.

First, there were eight command units but only six days, so there are two more command units than days, command units three and seven. It is possible that command unit three (gathering of the waters and the first continent appearing) may have been during time between days two and three. Command unit seven (land producing three classes of land animals) could have been during time between days five and six.

YEC opposes time passage between the days, based on Exodus 20:11, that all creation was "*in* six days." Payne points out that there is no "*in*" within 20:11a, allowing the possibility that commands three and seven may have been between the six days.

Second, if there was time passage between the six days, then there was no need for appearance of age of planet Earth, of the plants, or of the animals. The Bible itself never mentions "appearance of age." For example, after the third day and also in the Garden of Eden, there would have been time between the stated work days for the trees to grow normally. The Bible itself does not say the trees were immediately mature or grew rapidly miraculously. The command was, "Let the earth sprout," thus beginning normal fruit tree sprouting. Natural growth to maturity could have been between the days.

Third, God reveals His glory in the creation, which implies that the data we can learn from the creation is factual and accessible. The fossil record and geologic record seem to reveal an older Earth and older life. Earth and fossils should reveal their true age. Yet Genesis 1 also indicates six literal days. Time passage between the days would allow an older Earth by allowing non–work days between the six literal work days. Non–work days would have been insignificant to the narrative so were not mentioned in the highly succinct creation account. This understanding recognizes that *yôm* really does mean a normal day-night day in Genesis 1. It recognizes that God really did work six literal days as Exodus 20:11 declares. Yet it also recognizes that if the creation appears older, it is revealing its true age.

Fourth, the shift from cardinal "day one" to the ordinal series "second day" through "the sixth day" may allow uncounted days between the six days of God's work. Cardinal numbers—one, two, three, etc.—tell quantity. Day one was cardinal. At the end of day one, there had been only one daylight-nighttime day on the surface of rotating Earth. In Genesis 1:5, *yôm ehād*, although indefinite in form, has the definite sense of "the first day."[1218]

Exodus 20:11 uses a cardinal number six for the number of days that God worked. Contextually, in Exodus 20:11 the six days were six *work* days contrasted to the *one* rest day. So God worked six days. Cardinal tells us that quantity.

The Hebrew ordinal numbers in Genesis 1:6—2:3 (second, third, fourth, fifth, the sixth, and the seventh) indicate "degree, quality, or position in a series."[1219] So the six days were in that order in the series. But ordinal numbers, such as third, may *not* necessarily tell the quantity of days with the same definiteness as cardinal numbers, such as three. Payne says *yôm shēnî* ("second day") may have been an unstated number of non work days after *yôm ehād* ("day one").

If there were three categories of days, six stated *work* days, one stated rest day, and non–workdays unstated because they were not significant to the narrative, then the ordinal series may *not* tell us the total quantity of days that passed by the end of the sixth day of God's work. Exodus 20:11 tells us the total number of God's work days, but says nothing either way about non–work days.

However, Paul Wright, president of Jerusalem University College in Israel, says that commonly even ordinal numbers indicated consecutive days in a row, such as apparently in Numbers 7 or certainly in Exodus 16:5.[1220] In modern Hebrew *yôm shēnî* means Monday.

Also, Hebrew scholar Michael Heiser adds, "There's nothing inherently in the syntax or the semantics that compels that understanding,"[1221] that the ordinal indicates time passage between the days.

So I conclude that the ordinals alone are insufficient to prove time passage between the days. There would have to be within the creation text *additional evidence* that the ancient patriarchal audience (Adam through Moses) would have understood that indicated time passage between the days.

Fifth, Genesis 2:1–3 qualifies the ordinally numbered days. Day one was cardinal, emphasizing that the first diffuse sunlight penetrating Earth's dark cloud resulted in a total quantity of only *one* day-night day at the Narrator's location by the end of that day. But the Divine Narrator gave the second day through the sixth day ordinal numbers. If the days had not been qualified, then the sixth day would have indicated that there were a total of six days to that point. Paul Wright is correct that the ordinal numbers alone are insufficient to indicate time passage between the days. But the days were qualified. After the sixth day, three times the Divine Narrator qualified the days up through the sixth day, and qualified the seventh day differently. Each of the days before the seventh day was designated as the Creator's *work* day in contrast to the seventh day as His *rest* day.[1222]

And on the seventh day God ended his <u>work</u> which he had made; and he <u>rested</u> on the seventh day from all his <u>work</u> which he had made. And God blessed the seventh day, and sanctified it: because that in it he had <u>rested</u> from all his <u>work</u> which God created and made (Gen. 2:2–3, KJV).

So the seven days were not miscellaneous days. Each was either one of God's six work days making Earth lighted, habitable, and inhabited, or His rest day. The qualifier that the six were God's work days allows *non–work* days, insignificant to the narrative, to have been between the six work days.

Sixth, Payne points to the indefinite form of the second through fifth days:

Except in the case of the sixth day, the Hebrew noun for "day" has the indefinite form, "a second day," "a third day," etc., not the definite form, "the second day," etc. It has therefore been concluded that the days are not to be taken consecutively but that they may be separated by long ages.[1223]

"The sixth day" is definite and concludes the work of God.

I would respond there that there is no "a" in the Hebrew. This is not a strong argument. But he is correct that only the sixth and the seventh days have the article. "The sixth day" concludes the work days. And "the seventh day" concludes the entire creation narrative.

Seventh, if animal death is not evil and not in the curse (other than the serpent and ultimately Satan), then animal death may have preceded Adam. Payne says that Genesis 1:30 "does not restrict animals to a vegetarian diet, although this is often claimed."[1224] Genesis 1:30 says that God "gave every green plant for food" to animals, not that God restricted all animals to only green plants. Fossils seem to indicate an older Earth with ancient animal death, some by carnivorism. Yet the Hebrew text of Genesis 1 does not support "day" as a long geological day-age. The solution is six literal days, but with "the non-consecutive nature of the days of Genesis 1.[1225]

Eighth, the ending title to the creation narrative is, "These *are* the generations of the heavens and the earth when they were created" (Gen. 2:4a). The only obvious candidates for successive "generations" were the eight commands and six days. Each *yôm* really does seem to indicate a normal day-night day. Yet human lifespans in Genesis were commonly over 900 years. From the birthday of Seth until the birthday of his son, Enosh, was 105 years. That generation was 105 years. So it would seem "the generations of the heavens and of the earth" would also be more than six days. The solution seems to be that the day may be understood as the begetting day of the commanded item (no sexual connotations). It is possible that many non-begetting days passed between the birth days of each successive generation.

If there was time passage between the six days, then Adam may be roughly dated by his descendants' genealogies. But the previous seven commands and five work days would be *undated* by the Bible.

Several items may weigh against the Payne proposition.

First, in Exodus 20:11, six consecutive days illustrate the Fourth Commandment best. That God worked six days and rested the seventh was the grounds for Israel working six days and resting the seventh.

However, several points weaken this opposing claim. YEC claims that, based on Exodus 20:11, all creation was "*in* six days." But there is no "*in*" within 20:11a. No "*in*" within 20:11a allows the correct contextual meaning that God worked six days, not that He created everything within six consecutive days. If He worked six days, then non–work days, unmentioned because they were unimportant to the narrative, may have passed between the six work days. The six stated work days remain the example for our workweek.

The Bible may use an illustration from only what was actually written in an older Bible text. For example, Hebrews speaks of Melchizedek, "Without father, without mother, without genealogy, having neither beginning of days nor end of life, but made like the Son of God, he abides a priest perpetually." Melchizedek illustrated the perpetual non-Levitical priesthood of Jesus. The basis of this illustration is that Melchizedek had no genealogy listed in Genesis with his name. But that ancient king of (Jeru-)Salem may have been an ancient patriarch who simply did not have his genealogy listed in Genesis 14. So within a generational worldview, he was without father, mother, beginning of days, or end of life, even though likely he was born and died in the normal manner. The illustration in Hebrews was based on only what was written in Genesis 14:18–20. So also the Fourth Commandment may be based on what is written in Genesis 1:1—2:4a, namely the six work days and one rest day, whether or not there were unrecorded non–work days between the six recorded work days.

The Fourth Commandment was given several millennia after the creation so should not be forced back into the original events of Genesis 1. The Fourth Commandment workweek would not have reflected the earlier patriarchal generational worldview of Genesis. Nomadic shepherds did not work six days and leave the sheep to fend for themselves on the seventh. Ancient shepherds thought in terms of generations of sheep and family, not in terms of workweeks. That more ancient generational worldview suggests time between the six begetting days of the successive generations of the heavens and earth.

Nevertheless, although Exodus 20:11 may not be as strongly against time passage between the days as it appears at first glance, it still may weigh in against the Payne proposition.

Second, weighing against the Payne proposition, there is no explicit statement in Genesis 1 about time between the days.

However, the ending title in Genesis 2:4a says these are the generations of the heavens and earth. This title within the creation narrative is a major implication for time passage between the days. Generations were not just the birthdays, but also all the days between the birthday of the parent and the birthday of the son beginning the next generation. The patriarchs would have thought in terms of generations, not workweeks. And the creation narrative originated during their era.

Thus, we have evidence on both sides of the time-between-the-days proposition.

In the creation narrative, there was no time passage at Genesis 1:2. The three clauses in Genesis 1:2 are descriptions. Payne agrees. The Payne proposition is definitely not the gap theory, and to call it such would be the fallacy of vacuous name-calling.

There were two places of possible time passage in the creation. The first was the initial creation *before* the six days. Concerning *before* the six days, Payne is correct that there is no "*in*" in Exodus 20:11, so the initial *ex nihilo* creation was before, not in, day one. *Bᵉrē'shît*, "in the beginning," definitely indicates a time period in Genesis 1:1. The universe is however old it is. Time in Genesis 1:1 is in the meaning of *bᵉrē'shît*. The two stage

Biblical creation theory supports this claim. This claim is not an implication but is explicitly in the meaning of *bᵉrē'shît*.

However, the Payne proposition is about time passage *between* the six days. The Payne proposition is *not* part of the two stage Biblical creation theory. I have been unable to prove or disprove his idea from the Bible because the Bible neither explicitly affirms nor explicitly denies time passage between the six days. So I urge caution with the Payne proposition.

It is possible that the study of our Earth and the life on it may prove or disprove an older earth allowed by the Payne proposition. Does the physical evidence in Earth itself support a 6,000-year age of Earth and life or an older age? If Earth and life are older, the Payne proposition may be preferred over day-ages, framework, or any other non-literal days theories. However, that evidence from Earth is beyond the Bible. I conclude that the Bible itself neither explicitly affirms nor explicitly denies time passage between the six days.

The Payne Proposition: To claim that time absolutely could not have passed between God's six work days is making too dogmatic a claim on too inconclusive evidence.

Time passage between the six literal days is neither explicitly affirmed nor explicitly denied by the Bible.

14. Payne Proposition—Possible Time between the Days

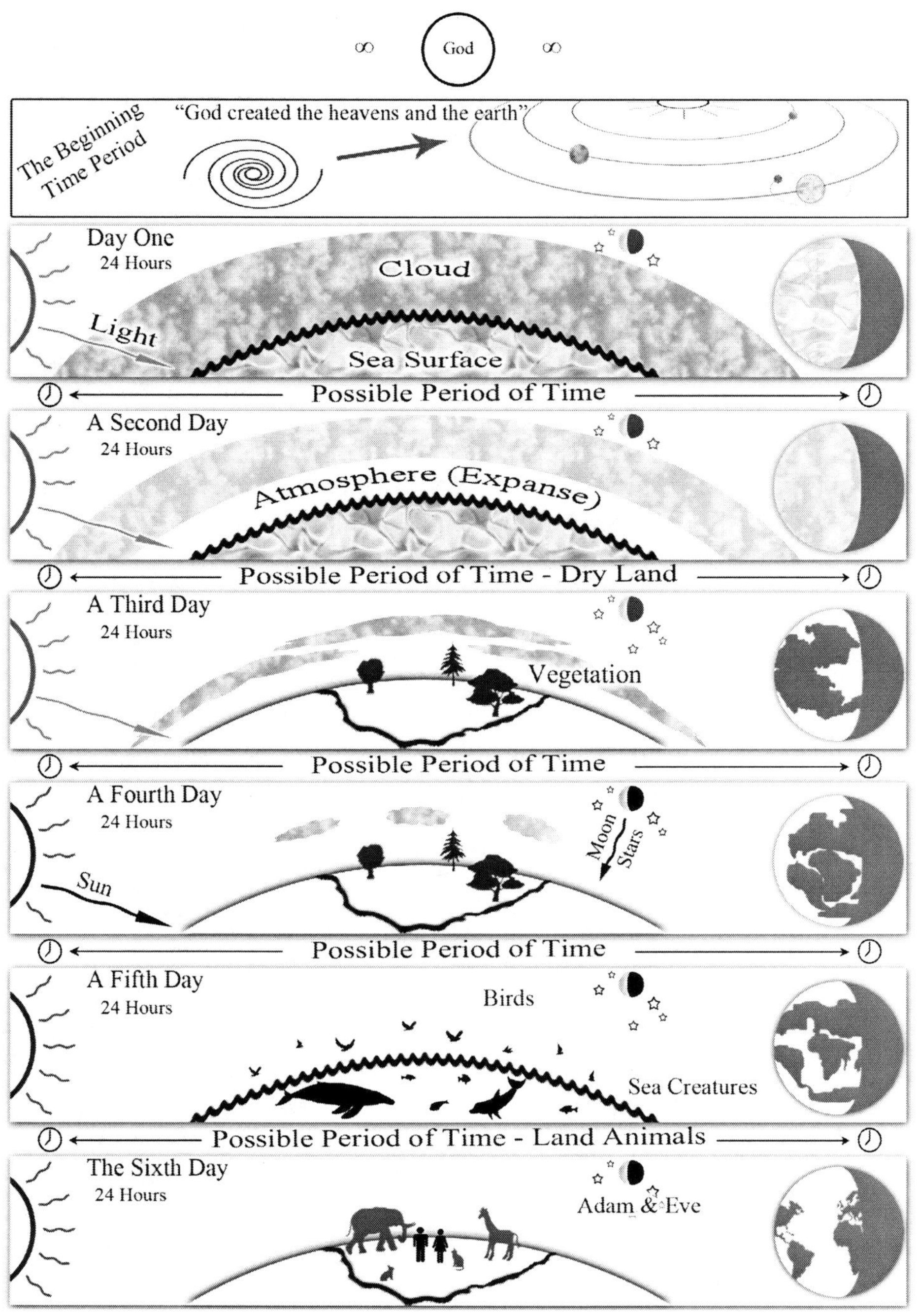

15. Days of Proclamation or Announcement Theory

Alan Hayward's theory of days of proclamation has three big claims: First, on each of the six normal days, all God did was proclaim or announce His intention. Second, vast time passed between the proclamation days. Third, sometime long *after* each day, the proclamation was fulfilled.[1226] For example, the only event in day one was the proclamation, "And God said, 'Let there be light.'" Hayward says, "Had there been an observer present he might have had to wait many millions of years for the gases to thin sufficiently for the first gleams of light to penetrate to the liquid surface."[1227] The fulfillment ended with literal evening and morning—but millions of years later.

I respond that Hayward's first claim, that all God did on each day was announce His intention, does not fit the Hebrew grammar. God did not simply proclaim or announce that something was going to begin to happen over the next era of millions of years. God *commanded* the actual event. The verb $y^e h\hat{\imath}$, "let be," is "jussive in both form and meaning."[1228] In other words, it is a "mild command," not an announcement.[1229] Hayward's first claim does not fit the Hebrew grammar.

Hayward's second claim, that time passed between the days, is made quite forcefully. I urge caution with Payne's rather mild suggestion that we are making too strong a claim to say time could not have passed between the six days. Hayward's claim is much stronger than Payne's.

Hayward's third claim, that sometime long *after* each day the proclamation was fulfilled, does not fit the syntax of any of the six days. I will take Genesis 1:3–5 to explain why Hayward is incorrect on this claim. The events of day one (and each succeeding day) began with *vav* consecutives. A *vav* consecutive tells the next consecutive action. With the *vav* consecutives in **bold**, Genesis 1:3–5 reads:

Then God said, "Let there be light";
    and there was light.
And God saw that the light was good;
    and God separated the light from the darkness.
And God called the light day, and the darkness He called night.
And there was evening
    and there was morning, one day (NASB, "then or "and" for *vav*).

All the clauses in this verse with bold "then" or "and" are Hebrew *vav* consecutives. (The "and" in "and the darkness" of verse 5 is not, so the darkness did not come before evening.) This sequence shows that these events—command, fulfillment, evaluating as good, separating, naming, evening with night, and morning—were all in "one day," beginning with daylight and ending with the next morning's daylight. They were not billions of days.

The grammar of Genesis 1:3–5, with God's command for light, indicates the results occurred *that* day. Certainly results continued over more than that single day, because we continue to have daylight even today. But surely, at the command of God, daylight resulted *that* day, *or it would not have been a day.* God called it "day one."

Hayward's third claim, that the command was fulfilled long *after* the proclamation day, is fundamentally wrong. As another example, on day three God said, "Let the earth sprout vegetation" (Gen. 1:11, NASB). We may agree that vegetation continued growing after the command day. But the grammar of Genesis 1:11–13 indicates that the vegetation *began* sprouting and was evaluated by God as "good" during that very day.

Alan Hayward says, "Evolution is not proven; the Biblical doctrine of creation still stands; but the evidence for an ancient earth is unshakable."[1230] Hayward is definitely an old earth creationist.

I conclude that Hayward's claim that only the announcement occurred during each day is not sustained by the Hebrew of Genesis 1.

16. Vision-Days or Pictorial-Days Theory

The vision theory claims that the narrator had six visions ending in six evenings and mornings. The six visions were of the six sub-narratives of the creation and were seen in six day-night days by Adam or Moses.

This theory may sound like Wiseman's creation revealed in six days view, but Wiseman disagrees with this theory. Wiseman says that the Bible text does not say "visions." The Bible says, "And God said," not, "And God gave visions." When visions were given, as in Jeremiah 4:23–24, the text clearly says that they were visions. Even S. R. Driver agrees with Wiseman: "The narrative contains no indication of its being the revelation of a vision."[1231] There is no hint of visions in Genesis 1. Rather, Genesis 1 was events, later narrated in words.

17. Intelligent Design Theory

"The theory of intelligent design holds that certain features of the universe and of living things are best explained by an intelligent cause, not an undirected process such as natural selection," explains the Center for Science and Culture.[1232] The modern version of intelligent design (ID) began with

Philip Johnson's *Darwin on Trial.* Joining him is Michael Behe, author of *Darwin's Black Box,* and William Dembski, author of *Intelligent Design.*

I have not included intelligent design as a major creation theory because intelligent design is not about the Bible, Biblical creation, or even theism. It is an insightful *scientific* theory, but it is not a Bible theory. It is solely the argument *to design.* ID stops there. Any Designer is left unspecified. The separate discipline of apologetics could carry the argument *from design* to God, but apologetics is intentionally separated from and not part of the intelligent design theory. ID is intentionally a science theory, not a theology or apologetics theory.

Intelligent design presents the concept that if an event or object is best explained by intelligent causes (not simply that we cannot explain it *yet*), then an intelligent design cause should be considered.

The irreducible complexity criterion establishes high probability of design. For example, DNA requires protein "machines" to enable the DNA to function, but protein requires DNA to code its manufacture. Each requires the other. Moreover, the complexity and information encoded in each DNA molecule is enormous, far beyond what chance might make.

Another example of irreducible complexity is that chemical processes and complex structures exist in living creatures, such as clotting of blood, that required many steps, such that if any one were missing, the process would not work at all. So there would have been no evolutionary benefit before all the steps of the processes and parts of the structure were in place.

Another area of ID is the universe. The physical constants of the universe and Earth (gravity, strong and weak nuclear force, expansion rate of the universe, etc.) are so precisely fine-tuned for human life on planet Earth as to essentially *require* a Fine-Tuner.[1233]

I have worked in archeological digs. In the science of archeology, we differentiate a potsherd from a rock by whether the characteristics exhibit an intelligent cause within human history. If the artifact, such as a decorated pot (usually broken) or stamped image-bearing coin, is explainable only by an intelligent cause, then we conclude that it was designed by intelligent people of the historical era that left that level of debris at that site. The science of forensics works the same way. Is the evidence the result of chance or intelligent human action? These same criteria can be applied to the universe and life.

The evidence for probability that the universe was intelligently designed with the physical characteristics of the universe so precisely tuned for human life is far greater than the evidence for intelligent design of the artistic mosaic floor that my wife and I uncovered at our dig in Tiberius, Israel.

So it would seem that the theory of intelligent design is an insightful and important scientific theory, but it is not a Bible theory.

Intelligent Design Theory: "Certain features of the universe and of living things are best explained by an intelligent cause, not an undirected process such as natural selection."

18. Concordism Theory

Concordism began in the nineteenth century with the rise of science and has continued into the twenty-first century. Concordism is the idea that the Bible account of creation, when properly interpreted, will be in concord, or agreement, with the actual facts discovered by science. An outstanding example is the work of Hugh Ross. If we pass over his disputed day-age interpretation, much of his writing reveals a wonderful concord between the Bible and cosmology.

So on the one hand, there is complete concord between the Bible and actual facts from the creation, because God is the ultimate author of the Bible and the Creator of the universe.

But on the other hand, *naturalistic* science and the Bible disagree at the most basic level of cause. An example is Richard Dawkins' *The Blind Watchmaker: Why the Evidence of Evolution Reveals a Universe Without Design.* Dawkins says that if God intervened supernaturally "at any one stage of descent," then the development of life "was not evolution at all" but rather "divine creation."[1234] Dawkins believes in 100 percent chance-driven undesigned evolution. Chance rules as the god of naturalistic science, and Dawkins is its prophet. Good, evil, purpose, and future glory have no place in Dawkins' universe.

I respond two ways. First, the Bible says "all things," all events and objects, are "according to His purpose who works all things after the counsel of His will" (Eph. 1:11, NASB). According to Paul, *nothing ever happened purely by chance*—not ever. Second, the evidence of the universe exceedingly strongly contradicts Dawkins. The very laws that science discovers that are so precisely "just right" for humans are evidence of design for human benefit. The Watchmaker is not blind; Dawkins has blinded himself to the overwhelming evidence for the eternal Watchmaker.

There is concord between the Bible and the creation. God made all things and works them together for good for His people. The Bible also records the Fall, and the creation demonstrates its awful results. Dawkins has no basis for either the good God has created for us, or the evil that the Fall and man have made.

If concordism is tried between the Bible and philosophically naturalistic science, then concordism faces an insurmountable barrier. But if concordism is between the Bible and the actual facts of the universe, then the two will fit perfectly. The created universe will yield nothing but evidence for the God of the Bible and His explanation of creation properly understood from correctly integrating the over one hundred creation texts in the Bible.

The Ross Concordism: God does not deceive either by His Word or by His creation work. Correctly interpreted, both God's verbal revelation (the Bible) and physical revelation (the created universe) will be in accord.

19. Poetic Hymn of Creation Theory

The poetic hymn view of Genesis 1 suggests that although not strictly poetry, Genesis 1 has Hebrew poetic repetition, using the numbers three, seven, and ten. For example, there were two sets of three days. Genesis 1:1—2:4a was to be recited by a bard as oral literature in praise of God, who created the greater and lesser lights, stars, sea, land, trees, animals, and humans. God alone is the Creator of all these things. The bard's hymn ended with the Sabbath. The purpose was theological, neither historical with scientific implications.[1235]

The poetic hymn view offers helpful insights into the structure of the Hebrew of Genesis 1. But this view indulges in the either/or fallacy—that Genesis 1 was either praise poetry or historical with scientific implications.

I would respond, why not both? Why not praise to our Creator by a factually accurate narrative, even though not written in modern history and scientific terms?

20. Ideal-Time or Omphalos Theory

God created the universe and Earth in six normal days about 6,000 years ago—all intentionally with the appearance of age. Adam and Eve had navels (*omphalos*) as if they had been born normally, even if they were not. Trees appeared instantly with annual tree rings. The universe was created instantly in the fourth day in its full immensity and apparent antiquity, with light rays to Earth created in transit.[1236]

This theory has been attacked ethically, religiously, and philosophically because it appears to make the Creator a deceiver. Further, the theory is scientifically problematic because its claims are untestable.

I suggest that the two stage Biblical creation theory makes this theory of deceptive appearance of age completely unnecessary.

21. Antedate Sabbath Theory

S. R. Driver's antedate theory claims that Sabbath practice took place before, or "antedated," the writing of Genesis. He claims that an eighth century BC compiler of JEPD documents "artificially adjusted" his Genesis 1 myth account to support the Sabbath that Israel already observed.

Wiseman responds, "I suggest that it is a most remarkable fact that the alleged unknown writer of Genesis does not mention the word 'sabbath'. Surely he would have done so if he had been engaged on such an attempt to 'fake' the narrative as described by Dr. Driver. Not to have done so would be fatal to his purpose."[1237] Wiseman argues instead for ancient eyewitness tablets that Moses, in the wilderness, compiled into Genesis.

22. Myth or Legend Theory

The myth or legend theory claims that Genesis, especially the first eleven chapters, is simply myth, a legend without actual basis in historical events.

However, after this theory originated, the tablets at Nuzi, Ebla, and Mari have yielded much data that correlates closely with the Genesis narrative. Sewell points out, "The Mari archives contained actual names used in the Bible—Peleg, Terah, Abram, Jacob, Laban, and others. . . . The Nuzi archive had some 20,000 clay tablets; many were legal documents describing laws and customs of the land. These explain a number of Biblical incidents that used to seem strange to us, but they were simply the normal customs of that era."[1238] Ross shows that the claims in Genesis 1 correlate too closely with recent astrophysics discoveries about the universe to have been merely ancient myth.

Additional Creation of Life Theories

Several additional creation theories focus only on the creation of life, not on the universe, the main subject of this book.

23. Progressive Creationism Theory

Fazale Rana believes that life appeared abruptly and showed complex design evidencing its divine origin.[1239] God repeatedly introduced new life kinds. God designed and guided the universe, Earth, and life kinds so that all would be just right for humans. Humans did not simply evolve by chance from chemicals. Humans were uniquely created as body-soul God-imaginers.

At the end of the sixth era, after the creation of Adam and Eve, God ceased His creation of new life kinds.[1240]

24. Theistic or God-Guided Evolution Theory

Theistic or God-guided evolution believes that the current model of evolution is approximately correct and will be further corrected by science. But the theistic claim is that God supernaturally guided evolution. In contrast to evolutionary creationism (the next theory), theistic evolution emphasizes God's guidance, not only in the initial conditions, but *throughout*—from the beginning through today.

25. Evolutionary Creationism Theory

Evolutionary creationism emphasizes that God "front-loaded" the laws of the universe so that life and eventually man would develop inevitably. This view is similar to deistic evolution in that God does not need to continue guiding evolution (as in theistic or God-guided evolution) or continue intervening by making new life kinds (as in progressive creationism). But unlike the idea of the distant God of deism, this view recognizes that God is very involved in a relationship with humans throughout history, including today.

26. Deistic Evolution Theory

Deistic evolution is similar to evolutionary creationism, which claims that God set up the universe at its beginning so that life and man would appear on Earth. However, deistic evolution claims that once God created the universe, He distanced Himself from His creation. The universe is like a clock that He wound up once and need not touch again.

Non-biblical Theories of Origin

27. Pantheistic Evolution Theory

Pantheistic evolution claims an immanent, all-encompassing nature-god fusion. Therefore, as nature evolves, God, too, evolves.

This view has problems on all sides—nature, God, and evolution.

Nature: Pantheistic evolution originally claimed that the universe is eternal. Since science discovered that the universe (nature) had a beginning, then if nature is God, there would be no eternal and external God to start the universe.

God: If all were a nature-god of matter-energy-laws, there would be no personal God with a character of love, justice, mercy, and goodness. Also, since both good and natural evils (e.g., harmful, painful parasites) are in nature, such a god must be both good and evil.

Evolution: If this god is one with the physical laws and this god evolves, then the physical laws must evolve too. But how can physical laws evolve? And if physical laws evolve, how can science know anything? Today's physical laws might evolve into different laws tomorrow. If the precisely tuned physical constants such as the strong and weak nuclear forces, gravity, etc., evolved just a little at any time in the evolution of the universe, life as we know it would have ceased to exist. But if there is anything science has confirmed, it is that the physical laws of the universe never change. Pantheistic evolution is a popular theory, but it actually would not work.

28. Evolutionary Naturalism Theory

There are two main senses of naturalism. Methodological naturalism seeks natural immediate causes of things by the methods of science, whether or not the scientist recognizes God as the ultimate cause. In contrast, metaphysical naturalism *a priori* (before investigating the question by evidence) rejects any ultimate cause by God. Evolutionary naturalism is metaphysical naturalism.

Science is finding more and more evidence supporting the "standard model" of the big bang. The problem for evolutionary naturalism is a big bang would mean the universe had a beginning, and therefore needed an eternal Cause. But metaphysical naturalism *a priori* presumes there cannot be an eternal Cause. Strangely, or perhaps not so strangely, teaching the big bang is increasingly frowned upon by anti-Christian educators because a big bang indicates a beginning of the universe, implying the eternal God. Metaphysical naturalism denies even the possibility of any external cause to the universe, regardless of the evidence for such a Fine-Tuner and Creator.

Evolutionary naturalism also claims a 100 percent chance-driven origin and development of life. Its supporters say that natural laws guided life, so evolution is not simply random. But the claim that natural laws guided evolution begs the question, Where did the "natural laws" that are so precisely tuned for life came from? Evolutionary metaphysical naturalism has no answer.

Evolutionary naturalism has a fundamental problem with the big bang and the precisely tuned laws of the universe because these strongly demonstrate the necessity for an eternal Creator. The big bang and these fine-tuned laws are based on observation by scientific methodology, not on metaphysical naturalism. And this evidence of a beginning and expansion of the universe may correspond with the Bible's teaching about the universe. It that is so, the correspondence is evidence for the reality of the Biblical God. Evolutionary metaphysical naturalism has repeatedly unsuccessfully fought "tooth and nail" against the big bang.

YEC Joins Naturalism in Opposition to the Big Bang

Ironically, evolutionary naturalism has a partner opposing the big bang—young earth scientific creationism (YEC). YEC has consistently fought against the big bang. YEC assumes the big bang must be incorrect because it does not fit with "*in* six days" (Exod. 20:11). If God created everything "*in* six days," then the universe is a few days older than Adam, who was created about 6,000 years ago. Therefore, there could not have been a big bang as "God's chosen method of creation."[1241] So YEC rejects this evidence that actually would prove to modern mankind that the universe had a beginning and therefore an eternal Creator.

YEC reports any conflicts it can find in the big bang astrophysics community, as if these astrophysicists rejected the basic big bang model. In reality, these conflicts are largely over details and possible predictions from the big bang.

Although YEC vigorously attacks the big bang, it has produced only marginal opposing evidence. Its great claim against the big bang is the "*in*" of "*in* six days" of Exodus 20:11.

This is the YEC position, according to Jason Lisle in AiG's *Answers* magazine:

1. The Bible tells us that God created heaven, earth, and everything within them in the span of six days (Exodus 20:11) and rested on the seventh day. This is the basis for our work week (Exodus 20:8). In contrast, the big bang model claims that the universe and earth formed over billions of years.
2. Genesis tells us that God created the stars on the fourth day—three days after the earth was created. In contrast, the big bang model claims that stars existed billions of years before the earth.
3. The Bible tells us that the earth was made from water (2 Peter 3:5; Genesis 1:2–9; Psalm 24:2), but the standard secular model teaches that the earth began as a molten blob.[1242]

In response, let me make very clear that I am *not* claiming that the modern scientific big bang model is a Biblical teaching. What the Bible teaches is that the universe had a beginning (Gen. 1:1) and is being stretched out (Isa. 42:5), both by the work of God. I am pointing out that YEC's opposition to God creating the universe in the beginning and stretching it out, which may correspond to the big bang, is without Biblical basis:

1. Contra YEC, the Bible does *not* tell us that "God created heaven, earth, and everything within them in the span of six days (Exodus 20:11)." There is no "*in*" within Exodus 20:11a, as written in Hebrew originally "by the finger of God" (Exo. 31:18; Deut. 9:10). So YEC can claim only *on its own authority,* not on Biblical authority, "that God created heaven, earth, and everything within them in the span of six days." Contra YEC, Genesis 1:1 declares that God created the heavens and earth "in the beginning." *B^{e}rē'shît,* "in the beginning," inherently means a time period. Later, day one began with God's command for light in Genesis 1:3 and ended in evening, beginning the nighttime, and morning, ending the nighttime in Genesis 1:5. Contra YEC, the creation of the heavens and earth was "in the beginning," not in the six days. See 11.D7b for a fuller explanation.

2. Contra YEC, Genesis does *not* tell us that "God created the stars on the fourth day." Instead, Genesis 1:1 tells us that God *bārā'* ("created") the heavens, which Moses understood as sun, moon, and stars, "in the beginning." Genesis 1:16 does not contain the word "created" (*bārā'*), the word Lisle uses. Genesis 1:16 contains a purpose verb group: "made . . . to govern." God made the sun to govern the day. He made the moon to govern the night. Then the Hebrew text adds "and the stars," meaning the stars also govern the night. Unhelpfully, over half the English translations interpretively add, "*He made* the stars also" (NASB). But notice that "*He made*" is in italics, indicating that these words are not in the Hebrew text. Lisle is incorrect. Genesis does *not* tell us that "God created the stars on the fourth day—three days after the earth was created." God had already created the heavens—the sun, moon, and stars in the sky (Deut. 4:19)—in the beginning, an unstated amount of time before the six days. See 11.D7a and u-5.3r for a fuller explanation.

3. Contra YEC, the Bible does not tell us that "the earth was made from water (2 Peter 3:5; Genesis 1:2–9; Psalm 24:2)." Instead, Genesis 1:1 tells us God created the Earth in the beginning. The NASB correctly translates Proverbs 8:23b–24, "From the beginning, from the earliest times of the earth. When there were no depths I [Wisdom] was brought forth, When there were no springs abounding with water." God made Earth before He covered it with ocean depths. Job 38 explains in verses 4–6 that God "laid

the foundation of the earth" and then built it to His planned measurements, all before birthing the sea in verse 8. In the great creation hymn, Psalm 104, verses 4 and 5 say, "Flaming fire His ministers. He established the earth upon its foundations," implying that early earth was formed in a fiery hot process as God established its interior foundations. Then verse 6 continues, "You covered it with the deep as with a garment" (NASB). Contra YEC, the Bible says God made earth before covering it with ocean water.

Responding to the three texts Lisle lists as the basis of his claim that "the earth was made from water," he begins with Genesis 1:2. But Genesis 1:1 says God created the Earth in the beginning. So earth had already been created before the description in 1:2 of earth's water-covered surface. Job 38:4–9 explains that while "the morning stars sang together" (so the stars had already been created), God "laid the earth's foundation." Then God caused the sea to "burst forth" and "made the clouds its garment and wrapped it in thick darkness" (NIV). The order of creation was stars, then Earth, and then sea wrapped in thick dark clouds. Genesis 1:2 describes this unlivable, ocean-covered, cloud-darkened condition of Earth. Moses was *not* saying that "earth was made from water."

Next Lisle references Psalm 24:2 for his claim that "the earth was made from water." This psalm of David says how we should approach God—with "clean hands and a pure heart" (24:3–4, NASB). In verse 1, David declares that God owns Earth, everything in it, and all who live on it. In verse 2, David speaks of "the seas" and "the rivers." The second term is *nāhār*, "river, flooding river." The first mention of *nāhār* is the river with four head branches in Eden. The Tigris and Euphrates are *nāhārōt*. Rivers existed only after God formed the land. The preposition על ("on, upon, above, over") in this context means "above." What David said was that God established the land *above* the water level of the seas and rivers. God did this in command three in Genesis 1:9. David was no fool. He was not saying God made the land float *on* seas and rivers (as some critics claim he meant), or that "the earth was made from" seas and rivers (as apparently in Lisle's third claim above). David did *not* say that "earth was made from water," as Lisle claims.

Finally, Lisle references 2 Peter 3:5 for his claim that "earth was made from water." This verse must be understood as Peter's response to 3:4, in which scoffers say that from the beginning of creation everything has remained the same (uniformitarianism). The Greek is ἀπ' ἀρχῆς κτίσεως, "from the beginning of creation." Scoffers made the false claim that from the beginning of the creation time, everything goes on without change. Peter responds that the heavens were ancient (suggesting YEC is incorrect that the heavens are young). And earth, meaning continental land rose out of the water and through the water, γῆ ἐξ ὕδατος καὶ δι' ὕδατος. The KJV translates well here if we make clear that "earth" means "land": "The earth [meaning land] standing out of the water and in the water." In Genesis 1:9, God gathered the water together and raised continental land out of the ocean water by His third command. Then 2 Peter 2:5 continues by saying that God's word held it all together. Implied is that when God no longer held it in check, the next verse says the world of Noah's time was inundated by the Flood. So Peter demonstrated that everything does *not* just go on the same forever. God raised continental land up above from the ocean surface in Genesis 1:9 and then He flooded the land in Genesis 7. Uniformitarianism is incorrect. But Lisle is also incorrect. Contra YEC, God made planet Earth in Genesis 1:1, covered it with ocean water, then caused continental land to rise up out of the ocean water. Peter did *not* say that "earth was made from water."

God created the heavens and the earth "in the beginning." Isaiah 42:5 (NASB) says that God "created the heavens and stretched them out." These two claims are compatible with the big bang, although not affirming its details or dates.

It may well be that YEC is fighting against the strongest evidence for God that He built into the cosmos. It seems incongruous that YEC is siding with those anti-Christian educators who hate the idea that the universe had a beginning because it implies, "In the beginning God created the heavens and the earth."

Let us suppose the scientific evidence is real for a beginning and expansion of the universe before light to Earth began day one. It seems that both evolutionary naturalism and YEC reject this evidence *a priori* based on their underlying philosophies. In contrast, two stage Biblical creation (2SBC) neither affirms nor rejects the big bang, but 2SBC recognizes an undated universe, which is quite compatible with its possibility.

YEC should consider if Acts 5:39 applies to its rejection of the beginning before the six days (Gen. 1:1–3) and expansion of the universe ever since declared by Isaiah 40:22, 42:5, 44:24, 45:12, 48:13, 51:13; Psalm 104:2; Job 9:8; Jeremiah 10:12, 51:15; and Zechariah 12:1. This Biblical evidence, that may match recent astronomical discoveries that YEC rejects, can lead to the Good News of the Gospel: "But if it is from God, you will not be able to stop these men; you will only find yourselves fighting against God" (NIV).

I am not saying the Bible affirms the imperfect human effort to understand the origin of the universe, known as the standard model of the big bang. I *am* affirming a supernatural, not naturalistic, origin. But I am also affirming that the Bible says *how*—that God created the heavens and the earth in the beginning and that He stretched out the heavens (Gen. 1:1; Isa. 42:5), all before the six days.

29. Pulsating Cyclical Universe and Membrane Theory

Albert Einstein added a "cosmological constant" to his equations to allow an eternal static universe. But Hubble and Lemaître proved that the universe is expanding. Einstein admitted that the "cosmological constant" was his greatest "blunder." The universe did have a beginning.

Meanwhile, Fred Hoyle was promoting his steady state theory—that the universe was constantly forming new matter, so is always the same. But that, too, was proven wrong by a number of discoveries, especially the cosmic background radiation left over from the origin of the universe.

Another theory that attempted to allow an eternal universe was the pulsating universe. This was a twentieth century idea that the mass of the universe and its resulting gravity may be sufficiently great to cause the universe to stop expanding in the future and begin contracting in a "big crunch." Then perhaps it would explode again in another big bang, and another, and another, perhaps forever.

But this idea will not work either. First, not enough matter, including dark matter and even dark energy, has been discovered to produce enough gravity to stop the expansion.

Then Saul Perlmutter, to his utter surprise, discovered that the universe is accelerating in its expansion, so it will never collapse.[1243]

Now a new theory has entered the arena. M-theory, or membrane-theory, based on the unification of the super-string theory. It is a modernized version of the pulsating universe. Each time membranes collide, another universe will be formed, and then another, perhaps on and on forever. This theory has many problems.

First, there is no hard evidence for this theory.

Second, collisions that have gone on and on forever introduce an infinite regress. An infinite regress does not work, because there would have always been an infinite number of universes before we could arrive at our universe. But there is no way to put an infinite number behind us to arrive at our universe.

Third, if massive membranes exist (evidence is lacking for them so far), they would simply push back the cause needed for the big bang to a cause needed for the membranes that caused the big bang. The principle of sufficient reason says every event had a sufficient cause. This principle of causation is the very basis of science. But what is the source of the reality of causation? Naturalism has no answer.

30. Space Alien Ancestry of Life Theory

Many scientists have realized that four billion years is far too short a time for chance to produce the RNA, DNA, and proteins for life. The problem is even greater because DNA and RNA need proteins to function, but proteins are built only by the blueprints in DNA and RNA. It is the problem of irreducible complexity. No chicken, no egg; no egg, no chicken.

So Erich von Däniken in his best seller *Chariots of the Gods* proposed that life must have formed elsewhere in the universe and that intelligent extraterrestrials seeded Earth with life. A less complimentary alternative, the "space garbage theory," claims Earth was seeded with microbes left in a space alien traveler's garbage.

Somewhat more sober scientists have proposed that Earth may have been seeded with life from Mars, possibly by a meteor hit on Mars spraying off some primitive life-containing rocks that fell to Earth about four billion years ago. Or a similar scenario may have occurred from an older planet of a nearby passing star. The fancy name for this is the lithopanspermia theory.[1244] This more pragmatic view may be held as a possible addition to progressive creation, theistic evolution, or naturalistic evolution.

This theory has two problems. First, it lacks evidence. Second, even if these events did occur, this theory still does not answer the basic question of how life started elsewhere and then traveled here within, at the very longest, thirteen billion years. And even thirteen billion years is still statistically far too short a time for life to have arisen by chance.[1245]

People certainly do go to extremes to avoid, "In the beginning God created the heavens and the earth."

Major Supported Claims from the Creation Theories

The Correct Translation of Genesis 1:1: Waltke affirms the traditional translation of Genesis 1:1: "In the beginning God created the heavens and the earth." It is *incorrect* to translate 1:1 as "When God began to create."

Waltke Merism: "The heavens and the earth" meant the entire orderly universe. Also, evening and morning meant the entire nighttime.

The Heiser Clause Analysis: Begin analyzing creation by determining which clauses (esp. in Gen. 1:1–3) are independent clauses and which are dependent clauses, and then which independent clauses are modified by which dependent clauses, and so how they fit together.

The Waltke Exclusion Principle: If there was preexisting chaos, there was no *ex nihilo* creation of the organized heavens and earth. The converse is also logically possible: If there was *ex nihilo* creation of the organized heavens and earth, then there was no unorganized chaos.

The Kline Order: Proverbs 8:22–31 says that "the beginning," when God created Earth (Gen. 1:1), was "when there were no depths." Ocean depths existed by 1:2, so "In the beginning" was before 1:2 and before the six days. Creation order: Heavens, Earth, sea, then six days.

The Kline Claim: When the Bible does not indicate a miracle, Genesis 2:5–6 (no rain, no plants; rain, then plants sprouted) shows God probably used ordinary means in the creation era, just as today. **Ross Addition:** "An observed attribute of the Creator . . . is His economy of miracles—only what's needed to accomplish His purpose."

The Kline Undated Universe: "We must speak where the Bible speaks, and be silent where the Bible is silent. . . . The inspired text, rightly interpreted, is simply silent with regard to the age of the earth and universe."

A Generational Genesis: The worldview of Genesis was generations. The six begetting (literal) days of Genesis 1 introduced the most ancient generations of all—"the generations of the heavens and the earth."

The Rooker Reaffirmation: "The key difference between pagan cosmogonies and Genesis 1 is *creatio ex nihilo* and the absence of preexisting matter."

The Morris Maxim: In historical narrative, a numbered "day" was a day.

The Morris and Ross Method: The Bible reveals what God did; science may uncover how He did it.

The Duncan-Hall Eight Commands: God worked by eight command units with common format, related to the six literal days.

The Ross Concordism: God does not deceive either by His Word or by His creation work. Correctly interpreted, both God's verbal revelation (the Bible) and physical revelation (the created universe) will be in accord.

The Observer's Perspective: Ross says interpret the Genesis 1 creation narrative from the perspective of the Observer/Narrator, the Spirit, hovering just above the surface of the water-covered Earth.

The Ross Apologetic: The Bible alone declares that the universe had a beginning and has been stretching out. Only the Creator could have known these facts long before modern science. The God of the Bible is the Creator, and the Bible is His accurate message to us.

The Ross-Schroeder Fine-Tuning Evidence: The fine-tuning of the universe and Earth is evidence of the Designer, not chance.

The Wiseman Tablet Theory: The Genesis narratives were eye-witness reports recorded on tablets received by Moses. The name of each author was at the *end* of his narrative.

The Wiseman-Gray 20:11 Recognition: Exodus 20:11a has no "in," allowing the natural grammatical reading of Genesis 1:1 as the initial creation of the actual heavens and planet Earth "in the beginning" before the six days.

The Pember Literalism: If we take Genesis 1:1 literally, then God literally created the literal heavens and literal (unfinished) earth in the literal beginning before the six literal days.

The Morris One Fall Explanation: The creation was perfect. Man and animals were created about 6,000 years ago with eternal physical life. There was "no disorder, no sin and, above all, *no death!* Even Satan was still good at this point."[1246] His first effect on Earth was the temptation. Adam's Fall resulted in a "cosmic catastrophe" including all human and animal death and subsequent moral and natural evil.

The Kaiser Two Falls Explanation: Standard theology identifies two falls: the angelic fall led by Lucifer, and later the human Fall by Adam. God's concluding "very good" evaluation was about His work on Earth, not about angels such as Lucifer, who had been created and likely fell earlier. Animal death is *not* inherently evil. God Himself killed an animal to cover human nakedness. Any pre-Fall evil aspects of animal disease and death could only have been initiated by fallen Lucifer (Ezek. 28:16–18; Heb. 2:14). Yet by the sixth day, God worked even those together for good or eliminated them until Adam's Fall. Adam was the original cause of human death (Rom. 5:12) and farming woes (Gen. 3:17–19), but Scripture does not say he caused animal death. So animal death may have preceded Adam's Fall. Animal life cycles fit the present noneternal world God created (Rom. 8:20).

The Sailhamer Time Period: *B^{e}rē'shît*, "in the beginning," consistently has the sense of an extended beginning time period, never of an instant or a few hours.

The Sailhamer Sense: *Tōhû v^{a}bōhû* consistently has the sense of uninhabitable and uninhabited wilderness, never of unformed matter or chaos.

The Thomas Truism: If Genesis is true, yet its narrative history was not dictated by God to Moses, then its narrative history was from eyewitnesses.

The Patrick Proposition: The initial Genesis 1:1 *ex nihilo* creation was in the beginning time period before the six days, so is undated by the Bible.

The Two Stage Arnold Affirmation: Creation took place in two stages: In the beginning God created the heavens and the earth (but Earth was still uninhabitable, uninhabited, and its sea surface dark); so God worked by eight commands and six normal day-night days making Earth lighted, habitable, and inhabited.

The Hodge Hiatus: A qualitative break exists between the initial "immediate, instantaneous creation *ex nihilo* by the simple word of God," and the later "mediate, progressive" work of God with already created materials and secondary causes during the six days.

Intelligent Design Theory: "Certain features of the universe and of living things are best explained by an intelligent cause, not an undirected process such as natural selection."

The Payne Proposition: To claim that time absolutely could not have passed between God's six work days is making too dogmatic a claim on too inconclusive evidence. Time passage between the six literal days is neither explicitly affirmed nor explicitly denied by the Bible.

Chapter 13
Animal Death, the Fall, and Problem of Evil

Did animals, as created, have eternal physical life, so that the introduction of animal death was evil? Or have animal life cycles always been God's good plan for this temporary earth? And how did the Fall fit with animal life and death?

Five creation options answer these questions differently. I will be asking whether the five options are internally consistent in their explanations of how the Bible statements about the creation, animal life and death, and the Fall fit together.

Then I will also ask if the five options can answer the problem of evil related to animal death. If a creation theory is unable to answer these two questions, it may not be a sound Biblical creation theory.

(13.0) Standard theology recognizes two falls, three categories of intelligent causal agents, and several kinds of evil, each of which may relate to animal death. These issues about animal death are important in how we understand the creation.

(13.0a) There were two falls. Distinguished professor of Old Testament and president emeritus of Gordon-Conwell Theological Seminary, Dr. Walter Kaiser, points out that standard theology has always recognized two falls: the angelic fall led by Lucifer/Satan/Devil/Serpent (Rev. 12:3–9), then later the human Fall of Adam (Gen. 3).[1247] Both may relate to the question of animal death.

(13.0b) There are three categories of intelligent causal agents. Theology recognizes three categories of causal agents: God is uniquely and fully sovereign over all. By His sovereign decree, God has delegated to angels, including to Lucifer with his fallen angels, limited causal ability. Also, God created Adam and Eve in His image, so they and their descendants are limited causal agents.

(13.0c) There are several kinds of evil. John Feinberg says, "There is also a difference between the problem of moral evil and the problem of natural evil."[1248]

A moral evil is an evil act against a person by a moral agent—possibly by a fallen angel but usually by a fallen human—acts such as murder, theft, agreement breaking, etc. Humans also can do secondary acts of evil such as cruelty to animals (Prov. 12:10) or destructive acts against the environment that God created (Rev. 11:18). However, animals are not moral agents, so a fox eating a mouse is not a moral evil.

A natural evil is an event in the created world. It can be caused less directly by a moral agent, such as human-generated greenhouse gasses causing global warming and perhaps more hurricanes. Or a natural evil may go all the way back to one of the two original falls, Lucifer's fall or Adam's Fall, the latter resulting in human separation from God, human death, increased birth pain, husband-wife conflict, farming woes, and all the human sin since. Or a natural evil may seem unattached to any moral agent, such as periodic earthquakes on fault lines as the tectonic plates shift. Any of these may result in, not only human death, but animal death as well.

The other possibility is that animal death is not evil.

(13.0d) There are at least two views of death and evil. John Feinberg cautions all sides of the debate on evil not to assume that a condition that their theory considers evil would be considered evil by all theories.[1249] For example, old earth creationism (OEC) and young earth creationism (YEC) draw different lines of where evil begins.

YEC contends that the Fall and curse formed a general death warrant beginning the evil of all death. YEC draws the line of evil between death of all living beings on Earth, including both people and *nephesh* animals, and the demise of non-*nephesh* lower animals and plants as not evil because the latter are not living in a Biblical sense. Ken Ham explains, "People and animals are described in Genesis as having, or being, *nephesh*."[1250] (*Nephesh ᶜhayâh* means breathing, living beings.) YEC says the death of a *nephesh* animal (a mammal such as a mouse or a bird such as a grouse) is evil. The demise of a lower animal (a parasite insect such as a louse) or plant is not evil because it is not alive in a Biblical sense so does not experience Biblical death. The curse proclaimed the sudden start of death to all living beings on Earth. Before Adam sinned, nothing died; after Adam sinned, everything dies.

In contrast, OEC points out that the curse declared death only for the serpent/Satan and for Adam, the head of the human race (Gen. 3:14–19; Rom. 5:12). The Bible does not declare animal eternal physical life before Adam's Fall. To claim that general death was part of the curse is adding to Scripture. OEC draws the line of evil between death of humans in God's image and death of all animals, none of which were created in God's image. OEC says animal death may be sad, but it is *not* declared the evil result of Adam's Fall. Adam's Fall and the judgments of the curse resulted in *human* death (Gen. 3:19; Rom. 5:12). Before Adam sinned, no human died (there were no true humans before Adam and Eve); after Adam sinned, all humans die.

YEC: Before Adam sinned, nothing died;
after, everything dies.

OEC: Before Adam sinned, no human died;
after, all humans die.

(13.0e) There are at least five main options about animal death that are actually promoted by creation authors.

(1) Animal life cycles have always been God's good plan. Humans were created in the image of God, but animals were not. Human death is from the curse, but the Bible does not say animal death is evil or part of the curse. Animal life cycles are beneficial in this running-down earth, which will be replaced by the future no-death eternal New Creation.[1251] Animal life cycles have always been God's plan for the history of Earth (Hugh Ross, OEC).

(2) Lucifer's fall began the evil of animal death. Animal death is an evil consequence of Lucifer's fall and God's just judgment at Genesis 1:2 *before* the six days' re-creation (gap theory). The re-creation was "very good."

(3) Adam's Fall began the evil of animal death. All death, animal and human, is the evil consequence of Adam's Fall about 6,000 years ago (YEC). Adam's Fall ended *nephesh* animal eternal physical life and introduced human and animal death into the "perfect" creation. YEC goes beyond "very good" to declare that "everything was perfect."[1252]

(4) God made noneternal animals for a noneternal world; Lucifer and Adam introduced evil; God plans a New Creation. God did *not* create this world to be eternal, or animals in His image. Noneternal animals are necessary in this noneternal world, which will be replaced by the no-death eternal New Creation. Animal death, though sad, is not evil. Between His good works, God may have allowed fallen Lucifer to cause limited evil, such as animal cancer and parasites. But by the sixth day, God sovereignly made Earth "very good" and Eden a paradise. God created humans alone in His image. Adam's Fall and the curse caused human death. But God will replace this groaning creation with the New Creation.

(5) The Bible does not explicitly answer the animal death question. The Bible tells us when and why *human* death began, but not when and why *animal* death began (UEC).

There are other theoretical options, but none supported by one of the main creation authors. A difficulty in evaluating these options is their claims are based on Bible implications, not on explicit statements.

(13.1) Animal life cycles have always been God's good plan. Hugh Ross provides the basic idea for this view. Not all of Ross's ideas (such as day-ages) need be held to agree with this view about animal death, but it is generally an OEC view. The idea is that God, not Adam, is the cause of animal life cycles, which are beneficial and fit this running down world. God created only humans in His image. The curse from Adam's Fall specified human death, not animal death. Therefore, animal life cycles have always been God's plan.

(13.1a) God intentionally designed a running-down, noneternal heavens and earth in anticipation of the New Creation. Ross and OEC say God intentionally designed this creation subject to entropy, decay, or running down from the beginning. "The process of decay has been in effect since the universe was created."[1253]

God has always planned the future no-death New Creation. He fully foreknew that the present creation would be the scene of the Fall, and He had already purposed that He would replace this world with the New Creation. There the previous evils will be remembered no more (Isa. 65:17; Rev. 21:4). So God made a running-down, noneternal creation from the beginning (Ps. 102:25–26, NIV):

> In the beginning you laid the foundations of the earth,
> and the heavens are the work of your hands.
> They will perish, but you remain;
> they will all wear out like a garment.
> Like clothing you will change them and they will be discarded.

Paul expresses this frustrating noneternal condition in Romans 8:20—"For the creation was subjected to frustration" (NIV). God subjected the first creation to the frustration of inescapably running down from the beginning, just as a garment begins wearing out from its beginning. Third century church father Origin understood Romans 8:20–22 to mean, "That the world is originated and subject to decay, since it took its beginning in time."[1254] This running down is not evil. Add the Fall and curse to the present creation, and that is why the creation now groans in hope of the eternal New Heavens and New Earth.[1255] From the beginning, noneternal animals fit this noneternal world.

(13.1b) Human death is from the curse, but animal life cycles have always been God's plan for this noneternal earth. Human death is from the Fall and curse. But the Bible makes a fundamental distinction between humans, who are in God's image, and animals, which are not. Ross says animal life cycles are God's good design for this noneternal earth, in contrast to the future no-death eternal New Creation. The Bible draws the line between human death as the evil consequence of Adam's Fall and non-human death, which may be sad but is not evil. Only humans, not animals, were created in the image of God and given spiritual life. That is why a human killing a human is murder. But killing either a *nephesh* animal (mouse) or a non-*nephesh* animal (louse) is *not* condemned by the Bible.

> Whoever sheds man's blood, By man his blood shall be shed, For in the image of God He made man (Gen. 9:6, NASB).

Adam's Fall resulted in immediate spiritual death, breaking the relationship with God and the penalties of the curse—separation from God, increased pain in childbirth, husband-wife conflict, farming woes, physical death for Adam and his descendants (Gen. 3:15–19; Rom. 5:12), and all subsequent sin. But the curse is not a general death warrant, nor does the curse specifically declare animal death. Animal life cycles appear from the fossil record to have been the norm in the past. The curse does not declare a change in animal life cycles. And animal life cycles are the norm now. So the presumption is that animal life cycles have always been God's good plan.

Opposed to Ross, YEC says that *nephesh* animal death (mouse) is evil, but non-*nephesh* animal (louse) demise is not evil.

The OEC response is that *nephesh* animals are no more in God's image than non-*nephesh* animals. God certainly cares about animals, and so should we. But the Bible does not condemn as morally evil either *nephesh* animal death or non-*nephesh* "lower" animal demise. Ross says the difference is that *nephesh* animals, such as dogs and cats, can relate to us. So we are sad when our dog or cat dies because such a *nephesh* animal relates to us as our animal companion. But their deaths are not a moral evil. Nor is it evil when the cat catches a mouse. No animals were created in the image of God with spiritual life, so all animal death is very different from human death. The crucial Biblical distinction is not between *nephesh* animals and non-*nephesh* "lower" animals, but between humans in God's image and all animals. Human death is the terrible consequence of Adam's sin.

Hugh Ross's view of animal death may not require "millions of years," but it allows an older earth view.

(13.1c) Romans 5:12 only says that Adam's sin resulted in *human* death, not animal death. Lee Irons counters YEC claims that Adam's Fall caused animal death. Irons explains that in Romans 5:12–21, "the world" that death entered by Adam's sin was the world of men, not of animals. Verse 12 says that "death came to all men," rather than to all men and animals.[1256]

First Corinthians 15:12–26 is also about human death and human resurrection: "For as in Adam all die, so also in Christ all shall be made alive" (v. 22, NASB). "All" can only mean humans, because animals will not be resurrected. The subject of death and resurrection is concluded in verse 26: "The last enemy that will be abolished is death." In the context of human death and resurrection, Paul is not speaking of general death or animal death as an "enemy," but human death as *our* last enemy.

Revelation 21:4 says, "He shall wipe away every tear from their eyes; and there shall no longer be *any* death" (NASB). John is speaking of human tears and human death.

It is improper to import animal death into these texts. All these Bible texts say that Adam's sin resulted in human death.

(13.1d) Animal life cycles have beneficial aspects. Ross says animal life cycles and predation are necessary for a good creation.[1257] Otherwise, mice would overrun Earth, and weak animals rather than strong would reproduce. Ross recognizes animal death may be sad, but animal death seems necessary in a running down world.

(13.1e) Genesis 1:29–30 says that God gave animals *every* green plant for food, not that all animals ate *only* plants. Concerning vegetarianism, YEC claims that the Fall and curse resulted in "the end of the exclusively vegetarian diet originally mandated for both humans and animals (Gen. 1:29–30; 9:3)."[1258]

In response, Genesis 1:30 is not a mandate or command to animals to eat only vegetation. Instead, verses 29–30 are God's explanation of His gracious provision to animals: "I give every green plant for food." But God does not say that He gave all animals *only* green plants to eat. God gave animals "every green plant for food," as compared to man being given *only* seed and fruit-bearing plants for food. So Genesis 1:29–30 does not say animals were *only* vegetarian. A YEC claim that lions certainly ate straw in Eden is an interpretative overstatement.

The great creation hymn, Psalm 104, states in verse 21 that the lions seek their food from God. Carnivorism is part of God's plan and necessary for a good creation. Verse 29 says *God* takes away their breath, and they return to the dust. Thus, it is God who ends animals' lives. Adam's Fall is not said to have been the cause of animal death. Totally unrelated to sacrifice or sin, God told Peter to "kill and eat" (Acts 10:13). Colossians 2:16 and 1 Timothy 4:1–4 say do not forbid eating meat. If humans' eating meat is not evil, then there is no moral evil in a fox eating a mouse or a grouse. If carnivorism is not evil and the Bible does not declare animal death evil, then God could have designed animal life cycles into His very good creation. If that is so, animal life cycles would seem to have begun with the first animals—however long ago that was.[1259]

(13.1f) No penalty of the curse could have preceded the curse, or that would have undermined the atonement, but animal death was not part of the curse. The penalties of the curse could not have preceded the curse. There is a necessary link between the first Adam and the second "Adam," Messiah Jesus. Part of the link is that both Jesus and all humans descended from Adam, so Jesus in His humanity is related to us as our Kinsman-Redeemer. The link is also between Adam's sin and the resulting curse, and Jesus bearing our sin and the death penalty of the curse on the tree, so making atonement for our sin. The curse was a real historical event in time, so the penalties of the curse could not have preceded the curse.

The question is, What were the penalties of the curse? Human death is clearly in the curse and confirmed in the New Testament as the penalty of the curse, amplified by the Law (Gal. 3:13, 19). So human death could not have preceded the curse. Ross agrees.

In contrast, YEC goes beyond the Bible and broadens the curse to include animal death. Then YEC claims that animal death could not have preceded the curse. But did God declare animal death in the curse? Death is in the curse only twice. Genesis 3:15 says that the serpent/Satan would be dealt a head-crushing death blow by the coming "Seed" of the woman. And in Genesis 3:19 God said, "To dust you [Adam] will return" (NIV). Contra YEC, the animals were not cursed with death. First Corinthians 15:22 explains, "For as in Adam all die, so in Christ all will be made alive." In Adam, all humans were made subject to death; but in Christ, all believing humans receive life. Only those in Adam are subject to death. Only the human race, not animals, was in Adam. Nor does the Bible say animal death is evil. Because animal death was not part of the curse and was not declared evil, normal animal life cycles could have preceded the curse and Fall. If animal death is not sin and not in the curse, animal death is unrelated to the atonement for our sin. Only human death could not have preceded the curse. Therefore, animal life cycles may have been part of God's good creation from the first animals created.

Gregg Moore states:

There are several problems with the young-earth view of sin, death and the atonement. First, while human death is linked to human sin, it moves beyond the teaching of the Bible to claim all death is the result of human sin. Second, since animals are incapable of sinning, they are not in need of a restoration of relationship with God and it is wrong to extend the consequences of human sin to them. And third, while it is true there is no remission of sin without the shedding of blood, Christ's blood, it does not follow that there could have been no bloodshed before sin.[1260]

(13.1g) Ross seems internally consistent on animal death, but parts of his view are based only on implications. In response, Ross seems internally consistent on the subject of animal death. Humans alone are in God's image, and humans alone fell in Adam. So human spiritual and physical death, *not* animal death, is the problem remedied by the atonement. Human death was a penalty of the curse, but animal death (other than the serpent/Satan) was not in the curse.

Fossil evidence indicates animal death in the past. The curse did not change animal death. Animal life cycles, including animal death, are the norm in the present. Death will be in the Millennium as the last era of this creation. Animal life cycles have always been part of God's plan for this non-eternal creation. Therefore, animal life and death presumably preceded Adam.

A weakness is that there are *implications* that animal life cycles have always been God's good plan, but no explicit statements. In contrast, the Bible explicitly teaches that human death is from Adam's sin.

This creation option can account for animal death in a way that puts together the Bible texts in a noncontradictory way. Clearly not all creationists agree with this first option, but that is not my question. My question is whether this option can put together the Bible texts on animal death in a coherent way. This option seems to pass that test.

(13.2) Lucifer's fall began the evil of animal death at Genesis 1:2. According to the gap theory, animal death is evil. The death of ancient animals and pre-Adamites was the evil consequence of Lucifer's fall, resulting in God's judgment at Genesis 1:2 *before* the six days' re-creation. The re-creation was "very good." Animal death after the re-creation was the evil consequence of Adam's Fall and God's judgment in Genesis 3.

In response, there were no events in Genesis 1:2—no first creation of life, no appearance of land, no pre-Adamites, no fall of Lucifer at that time, no "Lucifer's flood" judgment, and no animal fossils formed. Genesis 1:2 is a description, not an event. Genesis 1:3–31 was not a *re*-creation. Lucifer was condemned at Genesis 3:14, not at Genesis 1:2. The Hebrew grammar of 1:1–3 does not support the gap theory's view of Genesis 1:2.

This option does *not* succeed in putting the Bible texts on animal death together in a coherent and possible way.

(13.3) Adam's Fall began the evil of animal death 6,000 years ago. YEC says Adam's sin resulted in the evil of all death as part of the "cosmic catastrophe" of the Fall about 6,000 years ago.

(13.3a) Animal death is the evil result of Adam's Fall. Ken Ham says, "The present 'reign of tooth and claw,' of violent death, cruelty and bloodshed, had no place in the world before Adam sinned."[1261] "Cruelty and bloodshed" are morally evil.

(13.3b) Only *nephesh* animal death is Biblical death, so *nephesh* animal death, but not plant demise, is evil. YEC strongly emphasizes the distinction between the death of *nephesh* animals (mouse and grouse), contrasted to the demise of lower animals (e.g., a parasite insect such as a louse) and plants. "*Nephesh chayyah* [breath of life, living creatures] is used in the Bible to describe sea creatures (Genesis 1:20–21), land animals (Genesis 1:24), birds (Genesis 1:30), and man (Genesis 2:7)."[1262] But the Bible does not say lower animals (louse) and plants have "life" in a Biblical sense, because God did not give them the *nephesh ᶜhayyah*. Also, the Bible speaks of animal death (Gen. 33:13) in contrast to the withering of plants (Jer. 8:13). Because lower animals and plants do not experience Biblical death, only death of *nephesh* animals (mouse and grouse) is evil.

(13.3c) Romans 8:19–23 teaches that Adam's sin "led to death and the corruption of the universe." Many YEC advocates realize that animal death is not in Romans 5:12 or 1 Corinthians 15:21–22 or in the curse in Genesis 3. These texts declare only that Adam's sin caused human death.

So Romans 8:19–23, about the creation groaning, seems to be the remaining text for the YEC claim for animal death from Adam's sin. "Because of this [Adam's] sin, all of creation, including *nephesh chayyah*, suffers (Romans 8:19–23). We are born into this death as descendants of Adam."[1263] "To believe there was death before Adam's sin destroys the basis of the Christian message, because the Bible states man's rebellious actions led to death and the corruption of the universe (Romans 8:19–22)."[1264] After Adam's sin, "for the first time, animals would die on Earth. It was no longer a perfect world."[1265] Animals were created about 6,000 years ago in a perfect world with no death, so animals had eternal physical life had Adam not sinned.

Human evil also resulted in the flood. All animal death occurred after Adam's Fall, so all fossils came after the Fall. Most of the fossils were formed by massive animal death and water-deposited layers caused by Noah's flood.

(13.3d) Like the Millennium and New Creation, Eden experienced no death. YEC says the Millennium and eternal New Earth will be a restoration of the perfect conditions in Eden. "The world will one day be restored (Acts 3:21) to a state in which, once again, there will be no such death and violence in the animal kingdom. . . . Lambs, wolves, leopards, kids, bears and calves will all dwell together peacefully. Lions will once again be plant eaters."[1266] The future Millennium is described as a time when "the wolf and the lamb will graze together, and the lion will eat straw like the ox" (Isa. 65:25, NASB). Ken Ham says, "There will be no more death, disease and suffering. Just as it was in the Garden of Eden before sin."[1267] Then Ken Ham quotes Revelation 22:3, referring to the New Creation, and Isaiah 11:6–9, referring to the Millennium. Because animals will not die in the Millennium, animals did not die in Eden.

(13.3e) Eternal animal physical life fits the perfect creation before Adam fell. YEC goes beyond "very good" to declare that "everything was perfect."[1268] There was no animal death.

Animal death is an evil result of Adam's Fall, so *nephesh* animal death could not have preceded Adam's Fall and the curse. There was no animal death in perfect Eden, just as there will be none in the Millennium and New Creation. Therefore, there could not have been millions of years before Adam, so all animal kinds began at the same time as Adam's race, 6,000 years ago, just days before the Fall.

All animal kinds lived in Eden because Adam named all the kinds. None had gone extinct because all had just been created and there was no animal death. YEC advocate Ken Ham says that all dinosaur kinds (although not necessarily each species) that ever lived were on Earth in Eden and that Adam named all their kinds.[1269]

(13.3f) The YEC claim about animal death is internally consistent, but is interpretive. I respond that the YEC animal death option is basically internally consistent: *nephesh* animal death is evil, so animal death began *after* Adam's Fall introduced evil into the world. Before the Fall, the world was not overrun by rapidly reproducing animals, because animals had just been created. And most fossils were formed during the flood.

However, the YEC animal death option is quite interpretative. So it seems helpful if I respond.

(u-13.3a) Animal death is the evil result of Adam's Fall. Ken Ham says, "The present 'reign of tooth and claw,' of violent death, cruelty and bloodshed, had no place in the world before Adam sinned."[1270] YEC uses terms like "cruelty," which indicate that an animal killing another animal is *morally* evil. But is a fox eating a mouse a morally evil act?

Contra YEC, cruelty is an act of sin by a morally responsible agent. The fox is not a morally responsible agent, the mouse is not in God's image, and animals do not commit sin. YEC could respond that Adam committed the evil and animal death is the evil consequence. But no verse in the Bible explicitly says animal death is evil or caused by Adam's sin. Yes, God cares about animals, He condemns cruelty by *humans* to animals, and after the curse the creation groans. But none of these proves that animal death is the evil result of Adam's Fall.

(u-13.3b) Only *nephesh* animal death is Biblical death, so *nephesh* animal death, not plant demise, is evil. "*Nephesh chayyah* is used in the Bible to describe sea creatures (Genesis 1:20–21), land animals (Genesis 1:24), birds (Genesis 1:30), and man (Genesis 2:7)."[1271] Lower animals or plants were not given the *nephesh ᶜhayyah*, "the breath of life." So only *nephesh* animal death is evil.

In response, YEC is correct that OEC tends *not* to recognize this *nephesh* distinction. The phrase *nephesh ᶜhayyah* is used of the creation of great sea creatures, flyers, three orders of land animals, and man. The distinction is also implied in verses that speak of animal death in contrast to verses that speak of plants withering (Jer. 8:13). By continuing to ignore this distinction, OEC allows YEC to focus the debate on whether the *nephesh* distinction is real. But that is the wrong issue.

The real issue is, Does the Bible say that this *nephesh* distinction is the division between evil and not evil? Does the Bible say the death of *nephesh ᶜhayyah* is evil?

The answer is that nowhere does the Bible declare that *nephesh* animal death is evil but non-*nephesh* demise is not. Nowhere in the curse is animal death (other than the serpent/Satan) mentioned. Raising the distinction, however real, between the two categories is a "red herring," a distraction from the real issue. The YEC idea that *nephesh* animal death is the evil result of Adam's Fall is actually not in the Bible.

(u-13.3c) Romans 8:19–23 teaches that Adam's sin "led to death and the corruption of the universe." Romans 8:19–23 states:

The creation waits in eager expectation for the sons of God to be revealed. For the creation was subjected to frustration, not by its own choice, but by the will of the one who subjected it, in hope that the creation itself will be liberated from its bondage to decay and brought into the glorious freedom of the children of God. We know that the whole creation has been groaning as in the pains of childbirth right up to the present time. Not only so, but we ourselves, who have the firstfruits of the Spirit, groan inwardly as we wait eagerly for our adoption as sons, the redemption of our bodies (NIV).

YEC says, "Because of this [Adam's] sin, all of creation, including *nephesh chayyah*, suffers (Romans 8:19–23). We are born into this death as descendants of Adam."[1272] "The Bible states man's rebellious actions led to death and the corruption of the universe (Romans 8:19–22)."[1273] "The whole creation," says Jonathan Sarfati, "was cursed (Gen. 3:14–19; Rom. 8:20–22), which included death to animals."[1274] Adam's Fall into sin began all animal death.

YEC says the creation originally was "perfect." Animals were not subject to death so had eternal physical life had Adam not sinned. At least some YEC advocates seem to see Adam as the one subjecting the creation. The subjecting was at Adam's rebellion. The entire universe was subjected to corruption and all of life, which had been potentially eternal, subjected to death at the Fall. Therefore, YEC claims a radical "corruption of the universe." For example, YEC questions whether starlight is a reliable witness to the history of the stars because "nature is cursed."[1275]

In summary of the YEC view, these quotes suggest that YEC claims that Romans 8:19–23 teaches that Adam's sin subjected the previously perfect creation to death and corruption at the Fall. *Who* subjected the creation was Adam (some would say God); *what* the creation was subjected to was death and corruption; and *when* was at the Fall.

In response, Romans 8:20–22 does not explicitly say *who* subjected (ὑπετάγη) the creation. But most commentators recognize that God, not Adam or Lucifer, was the One who subjected the creation in hope.[1276] God alone is supreme over the entire creation. God alone could subject the present creation *in hope* of the New Creation in the future.

Paul does tell us *what* the creation is subjected to in 8:20–21. Verse 20 says, "The creation was subjected to frustration [τῇ ματαιότητι]" (NIV). God subjected the creation to frustration. Paul did *not* say that Adam's Fall subjected animals to death, as YEC claims. We almost all agree that Adam's

Fall initiated human death, but even that is not specifically what Paul is saying here.

In the context of anticipating our future eternal state, God subjected this creation to the frustration of being unable to fulfill (τῇ ματαιότητι) that role of being our eternal home. Paul adds, "The creation itself will be liberated from the bondage to decay" (τῆς δουλείας τῆς φθορᾶς). This earth has been inescapably running down. The hope is the coming New Creation, which will become the eternal home of the children of God.

When did God subject the creation to this running down condition? Psalm 102:25–26 explains:

> In the beginning you laid the foundations of the earth,
> and the heavens are the work of your hands.
> They will perish, but you remain;
> they will all wear out like a garment.
> Like clothing you will change them
> and they will be discarded (NIV).

Psalm 102 does *not* indicate a change from eternal to wearing out. So the presumption is that God created a noneternal, running-down heavens and earth from the beginning. The curse completed the subjection, for now man, too, is perishing. Noneternal animals fit the present noneternal world.

YEC seems to overstate the effect of the Fall on the universe but understate the effect on man. The Fall was radical. But it was *mankind* that was radically morally corrupted. That human corruption is what the book of Romans teaches beginning in 1:18. By the Fall, man, too, is perishing. In contrast, the Fall's effect on the universe was not even mentioned in the curse, and was insufficient to conceal the glory of God declared in the heavens (Ps. 19:1; Rom. 1:20).

In summary, *who* subjected the creation was God. *What* He subjected it to was a frustrating, running-down, noneternal condition (none of which was evil or judgment by the curse). *When* was the whole beginning time period starting at the creation and completed with the curse.

(u-13.3d) Eden was like the Millennium and New Creation. YEC claims that the Millennium and New Creation will be a return to the Eden condition, so Eden was without death.[1277]

In response, YEC cites the Millennium texts of Isaiah 11:6–9 and 65:17–25 (wolf and lamb together, lion eating straw). But Isaiah 65:20 indicates humans will die, so presumably animals will die in the Millennium. The comparison of Eden and the Millennium is in Ezekiel 36:33–36. But part of that restoration of Israel is that Israel's cities will be refortified (36:35). That was not an Eden condition, nor is human death. Therefore, only *some* conditions of the Millennium will be a return to Eden conditions.

YEC also compares Eden to the New Creation. YEC seems to picture Eden as if it could have been the eternal home of mankind and animals with eternal physical life had Adam not sinned. Ken Ham compares Eden to the New Creation: "There will be no more death, disease and suffering. Just as it was in the Garden of Eden before sin. *'And there shall be no more curse'* (Revelation 22:3)"[1278] (italics his).

In response, Revelation 22:1–5 refers to the New Heavens, New Earth, and New Jerusalem. There we will have glorified bodies; we cannot sin; and we will be in the presence of the throne of God—conditions that were not part of Eden. In contrast, the only Bible text that actually compares Eden is Ezekiel 36:33–36, about the cleansing and rebuilding of Israel in the *Millennium*. So the Bible itself compares Eden only to the Millennium, which will be the last one thousand years at the end of this *present* creation. Therefore, YEC makes an interpretive overstatement in comparing Eden to the eternal New Heavens, New Earth, and New Jerusalem, where there will be no death of any kind.

(u-13.3e) Eternal animal physical life fits the perfect creation before Adam fell. YEC claims no animal death, the converse being that animals would have had eternal physical life in a perfect, non-running-down universe had Adam not fallen.

This brings up a pragmatic piece of evidence—entropy. Romans 8:20–21 appears to be declaring the creation is subject to running down, what we would today call "entropy" (u-13.3c). Eleven Bible texts indicate that God has been spreading out the heavens, expanding the universe, *since creation* (Isa. 42:5). An expanding universe is a universe that is running down and will need to be replaced. Numerous Bible texts indicate that this present creation is temporary and will be replaced by the eternal New Heavens, New Earth, and New Jerusalem (Isa. 65:17–25; Rev. 21:1–5). Animal life cycles, rather than animals with potentially eternal physical life, fit a running down universe.

God evaluated His own work as "very good." Perhaps He did not use the word tāmîm (whole, perfect), used of the perfect lamb, because this creation was never intended to be eternal. A noneternal, running-down creation can be "very good"; but if it lacks eternality, it is not tāmîm (whole, perfect). Only the eternal New Creation will be perfect. YEC incorrectly seems to claim eternal perfection for this creation and its animal life had Adam not sinned.

In conclusion, YEC claims that, as created, animals were not subject to death; that is, animals would have possessed eternal physical life had Adam not sinned. This claim seems more than the Bible explicitly says and involves a number of interpretive weaknesses. These weaknesses may not rule out this option. However, this option is not the Biblically proven case that its advocates seem to assume it is.

(s-13.3f) This YEC option can put together a coherent claim. This option, too, may account for animal death in a way that is internally consistent. Before Adam sinned, the universe was perfect and animals were not subject to death; that is, they had eternal physical life had Adam not sinned. After Adam sinned, the whole universe was instantly corrupted and all living creatures will now die. This option seems to fit together.

The problem with this claim of animal eternal life had Adam not sinned is that there is no Scripture to back it up other than what seems to be a misinterpretation of Romans 8:19–23. YEC has repeated the "no animal death before sin" and "animal death from Adam's Fall" claims so often that Christians assume that they are in the Bible, but they are not. They are not Biblically proven, nor are the alternative options disproven with the certainty that YEC advocates seem to assume. However, this option does seem to be internally consistent. Unlike the gap theory, the YEC option does seem to pass the test of being able to put together a noncontradictory option on animal death. As far as I can tell, this YEC option may remain one of the viable possible options on animal death.

(13.4) Animal life cycles have always been God's plan and seem necessary in a running down world, but fallen Lucifer introduced evil. This fourth option is more complex than the others. Walter Kaiser supplied only the *basic* idea, and may or may not agree with all the following details. This option claims that animal death is *not* inherently evil, but that evil was introduced by fallen Lucifer.

(13.4a) From the beginning, God designed Earth to be running down. This fourth option agrees with the first option—that from the beginning God subjected the creation to a running-down, noneternal condition (Rom. 8:19–22). Animal life cycles, rather than animal eternal physical life, seem necessary in a world that was created in a running down condition from its beginning.

(13.4b) God completed His subjecting the world by the curse. After God created the heavens and the earth, evil was introduced in the world, first by fallen Lucifer, then by the Fall of Adam. God completed His subjecting the world with the curse. The Fall and curse do not make God's plan to create from the beginning a noneternal, running down heavens and earth an evil plan. Something "very good" need not be eternal.

(13.4c) Animal life cycles are not evil. This option also builds on Ross's view that animals were not created in the image of God, so animal death is not inherently evil. Instead, noneternal animals seem necessary in a noneternal, running down world. So from the beginning, God created animal life cycles that fit with this noneternal, running down world. God certainly cares about animals, and so should we, but that does not mean He had to give them eternal physical life before Adam fell.

Unlike both the gap theory and YEC theory, which say animal death is evil, this fourth option says animal death, though unpleasant, is not morally evil. Humans alone were created in the image of God, and human death is the evil consequence of Adam's rebellion and Fall.

(13.4d) Lucifer may have introduced evil aspects to animal death. Kaiser adds the nuance that Lucifer may have contributed evil aspects to animal death. Ross may actually agree with this option because he mentions Satan, but Ross does not explain a role for Satan related to animals.[1279]

If evil existed before Adam's Fall, Lucifer must have been the culprit. After God gave a command and evaluated His work as "good," then God may have allowed fallen Lucifer to do limited evil (as in Job 1—2). If this is so, then Lucifer's evil acts resulted in morally abhorrent aspects of pre-Fall animal diseases, suffering, and death.

Three causal agents were involved—God above all, but then also Lucifer, and finally Adam. There were also two falls, Lucifer's fall and Adam's Fall.[1280] Ezekiel 28 indicates that fallen Lucifer did more than just tempt Eve; he did widespread unrighteous "trafficking."

This fourth option agrees with Hugh Ross that animal life cycles are necessary in the kind of noneternal world that God made. Yet this fourth option also considers Ken Ham's opposition to option 1 because of what appears to him to be evils such as animal cancer, revealed by animal fossils (Ken Ham espouses option 3).[1281] So this fourth option suggests that Lucifer (and fallen other angels), by his sin, initiated any aspects of animal death that are reprehensible, just as Adam, by his sin, initiated human death and farming woes.

(13.4e) If Lucifer initiated evil before Adam, how can this be reconciled with a "very good" Earth? If Lucifer initiated evil before Adam, I would raise the question, How can fallen Lucifer's presence and evidence of serious animal diseases and injuries seen in the fossils be reconciled with "And God saw all that He had made, and behold, it was very good?" For example, in the fossilized skeleton of an Allosaurus called "Big

Al," paleontologist Rebecca Hanna discovered nineteen broken or infected bones, including a badly infected toe.[1282] Option 3 (YEC) says this happened after Adam's Fall and before the flood. But the fourth option suggests a more complex answer. Five parts make up that answer.

(13.4e.1) God made angels during the creation of the heavens, before His six-day work on Earth. First, there were two episodes, stages, or time periods in creation: the initial *bārā'* creation in the beginning when God made *ex nihilo* the heavens and the earth, then later the primarily *'āsâh* ("do, make") work by the eight commands and six days making Earth livable and filled with life. About half of the theories recognize two or more episodes or time periods in creation. For example, John Sailhamer says, "I contend that two distinct time periods are mentioned in Genesis 1."[1283]

God apparently created the angels when He created the heavens. In Job 38:7, God questioned Job about how He founded Earth and developed it to the proper size while "the morning stars sang together and all the sons of God shouted for joy." The sons of God apparently were heavenly beings or angels, including Lucifer. In order to shout for joy while God founded Earth, they must have been created earlier during Genesis 1:1 with the heavens. By Genesis 1:2, Earth was still unfinished. Later, in a second time period, God worked on Earth by His commands with the six days.

(13.4e.2) God evaluated His six days' work on Earth as "very good." Second, Walter Kaiser says that when God spoke the "very good" evaluation, He "wasn't talking about angels, He was talking about the Earth and about men. So there must have been a prior creation of angels."[1284] Fallen Lucifer was not created as part of the "very good" Earth that God evaluated. God had already made the angelic hosts during the Genesis 1:1 time, *before* the six days.

Genesis 1:2 changed the subject to Earth. Earth was *tōhû v*ᵃ*bōhû* and its sea surface dark. Then God began the second stage of His work—the eight commands and six days making Earth lighted, habitable, and inhabited. Apparently during this time, Lucifer chose to rebel against God (Ezek. 28:16–17).

Meanwhile, through the six days of stage two, God repeatedly declared that His work was "good" as He changed various aspects of Earth by His eight commands. Finally, after His eighth command, God gave His final evaluation: "God saw all that He had made [*'āsâh*], and behold, it was very good" (Gen. 1:31, NASB). In the context of the repeated "good" evaluations beginning with light to rotating Earth's surface on day one, through the "very good" on the sixth day after creating man, "all that He had made" that was "very good" referred to all of God's eight-command, six-day work on planet Earth. Nowhere in the eight commands, six days, or the "good" evaluations is the creation of angels mentioned, which makes sense if they had been created earlier with the heavens. Lucifer was not part of planet Earth, which God evaluated as "very good." So Lucifer could have already fallen into evil.

(13.4e.3) Human death is from the curse, but animal life cycles have always been God's plan. Third, Kaiser explains that God Himself apparently killed an animal to provide animal skins to cover human nakedness.[1285] Human death is the evil consequence of Adam's sin and the curse, but the Bible nowhere says that animal death is evil. When the family dog dies, that event may be sad, but the Bible does not say it is evil. Nor does the Bible contain a general command against killing animals.

The curse says nothing about changing animals' lives from eternal physical life to returning to the dust. So the presumption is that animal life cycles have always been the norm. Noneternal animals fit the present noneternal world that God created. If animal death is not evil and not caused by Adam's Fall or the curse, animal life cycles apparently were part of God's plan from the beginning and preceded Adam's Fall.

(13.4e.4) God may have allowed Lucifer to cause evil *after* each good evaluation. Fourth, if some aspects of animal death were evil, such as animal cancer or parasites, then that evil was initiated by fallen Lucifer (Ezek. 28:15–18; Heb. 2:14). God did not create evil, so a secondary causal agent had to have been guilty. If actual evil existed, then Lucifer acted as that secondary causal agent who introduced the evil into God's good world (not that Lucifer has been personally involved in each subsequent case).

Lucifer was the first to fall into sin. Ezekiel 28:11–19 segues from the king of Tyre to Lucifer. The human King of Tyre was not the anointed cherub on the holy mountain of God walking on stones of fire, but Lucifer was. Because of Lucifer's sin of pride, wickedness, and violence, God threw him to Earth. Ezekiel 28:16 says Lucifer was "filled with violence" (NASB). The Bible also speaks of "him who holds the power of death—that is, the devil" (Heb. 2:14, NIV). Peter says, "The devil walks about like a roaring lion, seeking whom he may devour" (1 Pet. 5:8, NKJV). These verses refer to his power of death over *humans*. But these verses also show his basic character. For example, in the book of Job, although needing permission (1:12; 2:6), Satan caused human death. But on the periphery of his main deadly purpose, he also caused extensive animal death (Job 1:10, 16).

Ezekiel 28:16–18 twice speaks of Lucifer's "trade," or "trafficking," described as widespread, as well as unrighteous or dishonest. Lucifer was thrown to Earth in Ezekiel 28:17, and by his unrighteous trafficking, he defiled his "sanctuaries" (Ezek. 28:18). Widespread unrighteous trafficking seems more than just tempting Eve.

When did Lucifer fall and begin this widespread unrighteous trafficking? Earth was "very good" by the sixth day. Yet, as evidenced by harm to Earth apparently before man, Lucifer must have fallen earlier than the sixth day. We know that he did not fall in Genesis 1:2. It would seem likely that Lucifer fell during the time of the six days.

God declared His work "good" at the end of each specific command. After God's declaration, Lucifer may have been allowed to cause limited evil. For example, God created great sea creatures with the breath of life and flying creatures, and then God pronounced them good, all within the fifth day of His work. After that "good" pronouncement, Lucifer, by unrighteous acts against the good creation, could have been trafficking in parasites, animal cancer, and other evils.

(13.4e.5) God worked all things together to bring about a "very good" Earth by the end of His eighth command on the sixth day. Fifth, God works all things together for good to them that love Him (Rom. 8:28). Before they fell, Adam and Eve certainly loved God, so Romans 8:28 just as certainly applied. God worked all things together for good on Earth by the sixth day according to His plan and for the benefit of Adam and Eve. Therefore, if Lucifer did evil acts after some of God's eight good commands, God worked even those evil acts to bring about beneficial results by the sixth day. For example, if time passed between the days so the dinosaurs and other megafauna existed significantly before Adam and Eve (Payne's proposition), then Lucifer may have been involved in means that resulted in the extinction of dangerous kinds of animals before the Garden of Eden. Yet with hindsight, one might suggest that Tyrannosaurus or even great herds of gigantic herbivorous Apatosaurus might have been less than ideal in the Garden of Eden. (OEC would say all the dinosaurs went extinct 65 million years ago. But YEC advocate Morris thinks a few were left even into the lifetime of Job, as a demonstration of the great work of God [Job 40:15ff.].)

If Adam lived very roughly 10,000 years ago (a date that could be agreed upon by both YEC advocate Henry Morris and many OEC advocates), there may be evidence of this very good condition, such as unusually stable weather, warm climate, a reduction of dangerous mega-carnivores, etc., beginning about 10,000 years ago (I am not affirming that date).

Fallen Lucifer could have been causing evil on Earth before the "very good" evaluation because he was not part of what was evaluated. Despite Lucifer's evil, by the sixth day God had turned to benefit, overridden, or removed evil that Lucifer had done. God brought about a "very good" golden age on Earth beginning with the sixth day.

(13.4f) The "golden age," maximum-good era lasted from the sixth day until Adam's Fall, but many aspects will be renewed in the Millennium. God's pronouncement of "very good" at the end of the sixth day, compared to "good" in the previous days, suggests that by the sixth day God had brought about the very best condition of Earth ever, including the pinnacle of creation—Adam and Eve. That brief "golden age," maximum-good condition of Earth extended from the sixth day when God created Adam until the day Adam fell into sin.

Earth was "very good," yet Lucifer had acted against God's good creation, initiating such things as animal cancer and parasites. So by the sixth day, God intervened for good. He worked together for good or suspended the results of whatever evil acts Lucifer may have caused. Sailhamer suggests that God may have excluded carnivorism from the Garden of Eden, but not necessarily from the rest of Earth. As in the Millennium, in Eden the wolf and lamb may have rested quietly together. The wolf may have been satisfied by the wonderful fruit. The Earth that God saw at the pinnacle of His work on the sixth day most certainly was "very good," and the Garden He planted in Eden for Adam and Eve was a paradise. Eden and the Millennium may share many conditions.

Romans 8:20 says, "The creation was subjected to frustration" (NIV). In the context of anticipating the future New Creation, that frustration seems to be the inability of the present creation to become our eternal Home. In light of His foreknowledge of the New Creation, which will replace this present fallen creation, God subjected this creation from the beginning to a noneternal, running down nature.

Adam's Fall ended the "golden age," maximum good era. Adam and Eve chose to disobey God. Adam's sinful act resulting in the curse was the original cause of *all human death* (Rom. 5:12) and farming woes. Sin by Lucifer and later by Adam's Fall resulted in groaning, but that groaning is in hope of the future Millennium and New Creation. The running down of creation was from its beginning, but the groaning was from the addition of Lucifer's and Adam's sin.

In the coming times of restoration (Acts 3:21) during the Millennium, barren lands in Israel will become "like the garden of Eden" (Ezek. 36:35). There will be a second maximum-good time on this earth. During that second maximum-good time, there will be extended lifetimes (Isa. 65:22). But in the Millennium there still will be death rather than eternal physical life (Isa. 65:20). During that second maximum-good thousand years, evil will be limited by the rule of the Lord Jesus (Isa. 65:20; Rev. 19:15). But at the end of that time there will be another Satan-led rebellion (Rev. 20:3). After that, this creation will be dissolved by intense heat (2 Pet. 3:10–13). Then God will make the New Heavens, New Earth, and New Jerusalem (Rev. 21:1–5), all of which may be quite different from Eden and the Millennium, both of which were in this running down, old creation.

Eden in many ways parallels the Millennium but may not parallel the eternal New Creation. In the New Creation, unlike Eden and the Millennium, there will be no evil and no death. In the New Creation, life will be perfect and eternal.

(13.4g) This fourth option, too, fits the Bible texts on animal death together coherently. I respond that this fourth more complex option is internally consistent in that it holds that noneternal animal life cycles fit God's plan for this present noneternal creation. This fourth option recognizes that evil may have existed before Adam, evil caused by fallen Lucifer. Yet God maximized good by the sixth day, so Earth was truly "very good." This option also can account for animal death in a way that puts together the Bible texts in an internally coherent way. It does seem to pass the test of a Biblically possible option.

However, some parts of this fourth option are also based on implications, not on explicit statements from the Bible. I do not find this fourth option proven with Biblical certainty.

So options 1, 3 and 4, as far as I can tell, remain Biblically possible options regarding the question of animal death. But I have not been able to prove any of them with Biblical certainty.

(13.5) The Bible does not explicitly answer the animal death question. The final option is that God has chosen *not* to explicitly tell us in the Bible whether animals had eternal physical life or normal life cycles before Adam's sin. In fact, the Bible leaves a number of less important questions unanswered.

When did animal death begin? The Bible does not clearly say.

On the one hand, if animal death is not evil, and if, for example, Payne's proposition is true (which the Bible neither explicitly affirms nor denies), then animal death should show up in the fossil record *before* Adam's date.

On the other hand, if the YEC claim is correct, and Adam was the cause of all animal death, then *no* animal fossil predates about 6,000 years ago, and that should be evident in the fossil record.

I personally conclude that the Bible does not explicitly say whether animals had eternal physical life or had normal life cycles before Adam's sin. Hebrew grammar rules out option 2. Between option 3 of only recent animal death and options 1 and 4, which allow older animal life cycles, God may give the answer in the record of the Earth rather than in the record of His Word.

(13.6) Can these options answer the "problem of evil"? John Feinberg reminds us that all sides of the debate may not define evil in the same way.[1286] However, if an option is viable, it should be able to answer the problem of evil in a way that is internally consistent *within* its own system.

Before looking at the cause of animal death, we may divide causation into four traditional categories:

(a) The material cause is the use of the materials for the product.

(b) The formal cause is the guiding form, pattern, principles, or laws.

(c) The efficient cause is the agent acting on the materials.

(d) The final cause is the ultimate purpose for the product or act.

All of the creation options (13.1–13.5) are theistic, so all see God and His purposes and glory as the final cause.

Most accept that the Bible narratives tell us that God delegated choice and causal ability to angels and humans as efficient secondary causal agents. John Feinberg says that one way of understanding this is, "God cannot actualize *contradictory* states of affairs (or worlds) *simultaneously*"[1287] (emphasis his). If God delegated choice and causal ability, He cannot simultaneously prevent evil. He can omnipotently do one or the other, but both at the same time form a contradiction, and God is not contradictory. Thus, delegated human choice is one way to answer the problem of evil. Another way is the greater good such as human character development. If God delegated to humans decision making about good and evil that can result in character development, He cannot simultaneously prevent evil. Favoring human choice with human character development by those choices over an absence of evil is consistent with the nature of an omnipotent yet good God. The resulting state of affairs is that there were opposing formal and efficient causes in the world—the "very good" creation plan God carried out, but also evil from the fall of Lucifer and the Fall of man. Yet there is no doubt Who will triumph.

The five creation options disagree as to how the efficient agents (God, Adam, and Lucifer) and the formal causes (God's good plan, but also the two falls) fit together to answer the problem of evil. The options even disagree on what is evil regarding animals.

In the previous part of this chapter I asked, Are the five options internally consistent in their explanations of how the Bible statements about animal life and death and also the Fall fit together?

Now I am asking, Can the five options answer the animal death case of the problem of evil?

(13.6.1) Animal life cycles have always been God's good plan. The first option is commonly but not necessarily part of old earth creationism. This option claims that animal life cycles, including animal death and its causes, although unpleasant, are *not* declared evil by the Bible. This option recognizes the immense difference between humans, who were created in God's image, and animals, which are not in God's image. A wrongful act by a human as a moral agent against a human in God's image certainly constitutes a moral evil. Cruel acts by humans as moral agents against animals (Prov. 12:10) and destructive acts against the environment (Rev. 11:18) also may be seen as morally evil in a secondary sense. In this secondary sense, the causal agent was a morally responsible human in God's image, even though the receiving party was not. Humans as causal agents are responsible for the evil, and God cannot stop the evil while, at the same time, allowing humans to be morally responsible agents. Since there were no humans before Adam, there was no human moral evil until Adam's Fall.

Also before Adam, there was no natural evil. Only humans were created in the image of God. This option may understand evil as that which harms humans. Therefore, only natural events that harm humans constitute natural evil. So an earthquake that killed dinosaurs was a geological event, not natural evil. In contrast, an earthquake that kills humans is a natural evil. Therefore, natural evil began after Adam's Fall initiated human death. Because of Adam's rebellion, God justly pronounced the curse on man and the ground. So today, God is not obligated to stop, by miraculous acts, natural evil events that harm or kill humans. Animal death, although sad, is not a natural or moral evil.

Animal life cycles have beneficial aspects. Otherwise, animals would overpopulate and die of starvation. Animal death, although not pleasant, does have needed beneficial aspects and is not evil.

This first OEC option can answer the animal death example of the problem of evil in an internally consistent way.

(13.6.2) Animal death is the evil consequence of Lucifer's fall at Genesis 1:2. Gap theory advocate Pember says, "The next verse shows that God is not the Author of evil (Ezek. Xxviii. 15). For even the Prince of Darkness was by creation perfect in all his ways, and so continued, until iniquity was found in him and he fell."[1288] Lucifer chose to sin. All ancient moral evil and natural evil was caused by Lucifer and the just judgment on him and his dominion of the ancient world in the time gap at Genesis 1:2. Animal death is evil, and Lucifer was its cause in that ancient world. Adam's Fall was the cause of the evil of animal death in the re-creation. So Lucifer and Adam successively were the efficient causes of the evil of animal death. God could not both allow them choice and causation and also stop all evil.

Although this gap option has insurmountable grammatical problems, it can answer the animal death example of the problem of evil in an internally consistent way.

(13.6.3) *Nephesh* **animal death is the evil consequence of Adam's Fall.** YEC says *nephesh* animal death is evil and was caused solely by Adam's Fall. Earth was perfect. Adam's Fall was a "cosmic catastrophe" that caused all natural and moral evil. Adam alone was the efficient cause of the evil of animal death. God justly cursed the whole universe, so God is not obligated to stop natural evil that results in human and animal death. Adam and his descendants are responsible for all moral evil, which God cannot stop if He allows humans moral choices.

The YEC option answers the animal death example of the problem of evil in an internally consistent way.

(13.6.4) Animal life cycles have always been God's good plan, but evil was present. This more complex OEC option says animal life cycles are not evil because animals were not created in the image of God. Yet evil was present.

God purposefully made a running down creation that will be replaced by the New Creation. Since God chose to make animals, non-eternal animals are necessary for a noneternal, running down world. Non-eternal animals are not evil, so animal life cycles fit this "very good" but temporary world. Animals created with eternal physical life (had Adam not sinned) would seem incongruous with a noneternal world.

However, evil was present. God constituted angels and humans as causal agents. Lucifer with his followers and later Adam and his descendants have been the efficient causes of both moral and natural evil including to animals. So this option, unlike option 1, would recognize both moral and natural evil before Adam. Both Lucifer and Adam's race have done cruel acts of moral evil to animals. And both Lucifer (e.g., Job 1—2) and humans have caused destructive environmental evil that indirectly resulted in what we see as "natural" evil that affects animals. Their acts include all morally reprehensible aspects of animal suffering and death. That God is omnipotent does not include the ability to do contradictory acts simultaneously. God limits but will not stop all evil that Adam and Lucifer started, because doing so would contradict delegating causal ability and would contradict the moral development of humans making choices.

Today, because of Adam's Fall and the just curse, God is not obligated to stop by miraculous acts all natural evil. God limits moral evil by means of human government (Rom. 13:3), conscience (Rom. 2:15), the Holy Spirit, and the presence of godly people (2 Thess. 2:7). But God cannot both delegate choice with causal ability and also stop all evil. An absence of choices about evil would undermine the need for salvation and human moral growth.

This more complex OEC option also can answer the animal death case of the problem of evil in an internally consistent way.

(13.6.5) The Bible does not explicitly answer the animal death question. It is also possible that no explicit statement in the Bible decisively resolves the issue of when animal death began. Which of options 1, 3, and 4 is correct may not be stated in the Bible. Because options 1, 3, and 4 all can answer the animal death example of the problem of evil, so can option 5, which concludes that one of these options is probably correct, but we do not know which.

(13.7) Conclusions on animal death

We may conclude that four of the five creation options can explain animal death and the related Bible texts in an internally coherent way. All five can answer the animal death problem of evil in a consistent way. Therefore, old earth creationism, young earth creationism, and an undated earth creation theory such as two stage Biblical creation remain viable theories on the issue of animal death.

YEC seems to assume, based on its claim of no animal death before Adam's Fall, that OEC is a Biblically impossible theory. But if either option 1 or 4 is viable, then OEC can put together the Bible texts on animal death in an internally consistent way. OEC can also answer the problem of evil.

Based on fossils, OEC concludes that animal death is ancient, and may assume this rules out YEC. But Biblically, YEC is not ruled out by this issue of animal death and Adam's sin. With the flood as the cause of the fossil layers, YEC may be able to put together the Bible texts on animal death in an internally consistent way. And YEC can answer the problem of evil.

The conclusion that any of options 1, 3, 4, and 5 may be viable allows UEC to be truly undated.

Next we will eliminate inadequate theories by the diagnostic questions. But the present chapter has made an important point: The issue of animal death, as far as I can tell, does not rule out *any* of these major creation theories.

PART III

Evaluating the Theories

Introduction

Recently, I shared the Good News with a young man. Carl (name changed) said he was trying to decide between Islam and Christianity.

An Islamic evangelist told Carl that he should submit to Allah because Muhammad's words were proven true by science. In the surah (chapter) of the Koran called "The Cattle," Muhammad said,

> Wonderful Originator of the heavens and the earth! How could He [Allah] have a son when He has no consort, and He (Himself) created everything, and He is the Knower of all things (Surah 6:1).

The Islamic evangelist explained that science has discovered that the universe had a beginning, just as Muhammad said. (Muhammad was illiterate, so he spoke his sayings. Some are Bible ideas that he heard from Jews. His followers wrote down his sayings as the Koran. They now claim the current version of the Koran is word for word without error.) Carl was familiar with Edwin Hubble's discovery of the expanding universe and the resulting big bang theory. So Carl agreed that science proved the universe had a beginning.

Then Carl met a Christian from an evangelical Bible college and seminary. The Christian shared that the Bible says the universe is about 6,000 years old. Carl had studied science, so he asked why the universe seemed much older. The Christian replied that the universe has miraculous appearance of age (young earth scientific creationism).

The above really happened. It is happening every day, especially to the next generation in our universities.

I shared with Carl that the Bible says, "In the beginning God created the heavens and the earth." The much older Bible, not the Koran, is the originator of the declaration that God created the heavens and the earth "in the beginning." Moreover, the Bible says that God "created the heavens and stretched them out" (Isa. 42:5, NIV). The Bible declared that the universe had a beginning and has been expanding ever since creation, just as science has discovered. Only the Creator could have known these facts long before modern science, very strong evidence that the God of the Bible is the Creator of the universe. Carl is reconsidering Christianity.

If we claim that the Bible says the universe is 6,000 years old, we are adding a claim the Bible itself never makes. If we claim that there was a gap of time at Genesis 1:2, with a first creation of life, ending with the destruction of all that life and re-creation of all new life about 6,000 years ago, we are adding a claim the Bible never makes. If we claim that Genesis 1:1 is just a title so there was no beginning of the universe, we subtract a claim the Bible does make. Science will find out that these "Biblical" claims are false. Then Christianity will be marginalized as full of errors.

If we claim that Genesis 1:1 is merely a title with no *ex nihilo* creation act (title theory) and Isaiah 42:5 (God created and stretched out the heavens) is just poetic eulogizing, but science confirms that the universe did have a beginning and has been stretching out, then we have trashed an amazingly powerful apologetic for the God of the Bible. He built these evidences into the universe in order to declare His glory and ultimately Himself.

So our question—What does the Creator say in the Bible that He did when He created the heavens and the earth?—is really important.

To some degree the future of Christianity rests on a correct understanding of the answer to that question. Evaluating which theory answers that question most Biblically is what we will do next.

Chapter 14
Evaluating Eleven Theories
by Four Diagnostic Questions

As revealed in the Bible, how did God create the universe? The ten creation theories, along with the eleventh unified creation theory, answer four pairs of diagnostic questions differently.

Question A: Long Days or Normal Days?

Does Genesis 1 indicate day-ages, framework, or revelatory days?
Or does Genesis 1 indicate six normal day-night days of God's work?

Question B: Chaos or *Ex Nihilo* Creation?

In Genesis 1:1, did God create ex nihilo *the heavens and earth?*
Or did God creatively turn unformed chaos into cosmos?

Question C: Creation Once or Twice?

Did God create the life kinds once—by eight commands and six days?
Or did He create life kinds twice—once long ago, then in the six days?

Question D: Creation in Day One or "In the beginning"?

Did God create the literal heavens and earth "in the beginning"?
Or did He create heavens as space and earth as prematter in day one?

We will sort the eleven theories, progressively eliminating inadequate theories by these diagnostic questions and key creation texts.

Eleven Major Creation Theories

The eleven creation theories are:

1. Pre-Creation Chaos Theory. Before creation in Genesis 1, God and unformed "pre-creation chaos" both existed. The origin of the pre-creation chaos is a "mystery."[1289] "Creation" in Genesis 1:1 was not God creating *ex nihilo* the heavens and the earth. Instead, in Genesis 1:2–31, God creatively entered the chaos, turning it into orderly cosmos.[1290]

2. Title or Summary Theory. Genesis 1:1 was not the initial creation of the heavens and earth; 1:1 is a title or summary of Genesis 1:2–31.[1291] There was no *ex nihilo* creation in Genesis 1:1 because 1:1 is a title, not an event.

3. Literary Framework Theory. The eight commanded creation works form a nonliteral and nonsequential literary framework, revealing real historical creation events in thematic rather than chronological order. Days one and four were the same event. The Genesis 1 framework does not date the universe.

4. Initial Chaos Theory. God created *ex nihilo* the unformed heavens and earth in Genesis 1:1. The chaotic condition is described in Genesis 1:2. In 1:3–31 God turned this chaotic condition into order in six days, whether day-night days or nonliteral days.

5. Young Earth Scientific Creationism Theory. God created *ex nihilo* the heavens as space and earth as all unformed prematter throughout the darkness of space *in* day one of six consecutive literal night-day days—because Exodus 20:11 says all creation was *"in* six days." God also made temporary three-day light on day one. He made planet Earth on day three. On day four God created the sun, moon, and galaxies either *ex nihilo* or from "the same 'earth' that had been created on Day One."[1292] Adam is dated roughly 6,000 years ago,[1293] so the universe is a few days older. The flood formed most fossils.

6. Day-Age, Old Earth, Progressive Creationism Theory. In the beginning time period, God created *ex nihilo* the universe (apparently by the big bang) and planet Earth. By Genesis 1:2, Earth was uninhabitable, uninhabited, sea-covered, and dark (Job says by thick dark cloud). Narrated from the Spirit's perspective location just above the water surface, God commanded light (diffuse sunlight penetrating the cloud layer) to Earth's surface, beginning day-age one. *Yôm* in Genesis 1 indicated a geological day-age era. During these eras, God made Earth habitable and progressively created life. In the fourth day-age, God caused the sky to clear, so the already created luminaries were in Earth's sky for the first time. The second revelation, the creation, dates the universe to about 13.7 billion years.

7. Theistic Big Bang and Relativistic Days Theory. In the beginning God created the big bang, which began with light, initiating the first of six literal days on God's clock but eras of billions of years on Earth's clock. In these eras God formed the universe, Earth, and life. Relativity's time dilation allows 13.7 billion years to be six literal days on God's "eternal clock."[1294]

8. Creation Revealed in Six Days Theory. In six days God spoke Genesis 1 in six brief narratives, recounting six past creation eras. This six-part creation narrative and successive eyewitness narratives by Adam, Noah, Shem, Abraham, Isaac, Jacob, and Joseph were recorded on clay tablets. Moses edited these tablets into the book of Genesis. This allows an older universe and earth.

9. Gap or Creation-Ruin-Restoration Theory. Stage 1: In the beginning time period, God created *ex nihilo* the heavens and the earth. Stage 2: During a long gap of time at Genesis 1:2, God created vast life. But Lucifer fell and led pre-Adamites into sin. Eventually, God judged by "Lucifer's flood," killing all pre-Adamites and life, and forming the fossils. So Earth *became* chaos. Stage 3: Leaving the fossils in place, in six day-night days God restored Earth and re-created new life unrelated to the old fossilized gap life. Genealogies date Adam but not the universe, so the universe is undated by the Bible.

10. Historical Land Creationism Theory. In the beginning time period, God created the heavens and earth along with land and all life kinds except true humans in Genesis 1:1. "Beginning" in the Hebrew consistently indicates an extensive beginning time period. But Eden was waste. Later, in six day-night days in the narrative of Genesis 1:2–31, God prepared Eden (future Promised Land), introduced life into it, and created mankind, male and female, in His image.

11. Two Stage Biblical Creation Theory: Stage One: In the beginning time period, God created *ex nihilo* the orderly heavens and unfinished planet Earth (Gen. 1:1). "Beginning" in Hebrew consistently indicates an extensive beginning time period (Gen. 10:10; Job 8:7; Jer. 28:1). By the conclusion of the beginning, Genesis 1:2 describes Earth as still uninhabitable and uninhabited, and darkness covered the deep sea (Job 26:7–9 and 38:8–9 say by thick dark cloud). The Spirit hovered just above the water surface (apparently for the perspective of His narration of the upcoming six days). Stage Two: By the eight command units of Genesis 1:3–31 and six day-night days of work, God made planet Earth's sky, sea, and land lighted, habitable, and inhabited with life. First, God commanded light (we may infer diffuse sunlight penetrating the cloud, reported by the Narrator just above the sea surface), producing daylight-evening-nighttime-morning day one. On the fourth day of work, God commanded the already created luminaries to be in the expanse of Earth's sky (from the Narrator's perspective) to separate and govern day and night (Job 26:13a indicates by the sky clearing). God created breathing aquatic and air life on the fifth day of work. By His seventh command, God made three orders of land life. By his eighth creation command, God created body-soul humans, male and female, in His image. He blessed them, gave them dominion, and instructed them. Adam is roughly dated by his descendants' genealogies, but the Genesis 1:1 *ex nihilo* creation before the six days is Biblically undated (UEC).

The Four Pairs of Diagnostic Questions

A. Long Days or Normal Days?

Does Genesis 1 indicate day-ages, framework, or revelatory days?
Or does Genesis 1 indicate six normal day-night days of God's work?

Creation Theories of Day-Age Eras or Non-Creation Days

1. Pre-Creation Chaos Theory. The days were "metaphorical."[1295]

6. Day-Age, Old Earth, Progressive Creationism Theory. God created the heavens and the earth in the beginning; then in six long day-age eras God made Earth habitable and progressively created life.

8. Creation Revealed in Six Days Theory. In six days, God told Adam six narratives about six geologic ages of God's work.

Creation Theories Indeterminate Whether Day-Night Days

2. Title or Summary Theory. Genesis 1:1 titles or summarizes a six-part literary framework.

3. Literary Framework Theory. The eight command units and six days were nonsequential and nonliteral, so the days were probably eras but could have been day-night days.

4. Initial Chaos Theory. God created unformed chaotic matter in Genesis 1:1 from which He fashioned the universe and Earth in six days. Rooker says they were day-night days, but others suggest eras.

7. Theistic Big Bang and Relativistic Days Theory. The big bang began six eras in the universe that were literal days on "God's clock," but not really earth days because Earth did not exist for the first two "days."

Creation Theories with Six Normal Day-Night Days

5. Young Earth Scientific Creationism Theory. God created the heavens as space and earth as unformed matter *in* day one and made the sun, moon, and stars from unformed earth on day four of six literal night-day (Morris said day-night) days.

9. Gap or Creation-Ruin-Restoration Theory. God created the heavens and the earth in the beginning. After a time gap with a first creation and then destruction of life, in six day-night days God reconstituted Earth and re-created life.

10. Historical Land Creationism Theory. God created the heavens, Earth, and life in the beginning. Then in six day-night days He made Eden habitable and inhabited.

11. Two Stage Biblical Creation Theory. God created the heavens and unfinished Earth in the beginning. Then by eight command units and six normal day-night days, God made planet Earth lighted, habitable, and inhabited.

Meaning of *Yôm* in Genesis 1

Did Moses intend each numbered *yôm,* "day," in Genesis 1 to mean a normal day-night day or a long day-age era? The semantic range of *yôm* includes both a normal day-night day and an eschatological end times age such as the tribulation and thousand-year Millennium (although it would be a severe interpretive stretch to include a geological era).

In any text, the semantic range of meanings is narrowed to a specific meaning by the context, syntax, genre, and semantic field of alternative words that were not chosen. Jim Stambaugh, Terence E. Fretheim, and Robert V. McCabe have defended six normal day-night days. Gleason Archer and Hugh Ross have defended day-ages. I will draw on their work in my response.[1296]

It would seem helpful to avoid the fallacy of the excluded middle that either *yôm* was a long era based on data supporting an older universe, or *yôm* was a day-night day and the universe is only 6,000 years old.

The authors of the creation theories that we have examined have proposed several alternatives—an older universe created in the beginning before the six day-night days that three of the four literal day's theories espouse (2SBC, Gap, and Historical Land), and also the Payne proposition that may allow time passage between the six day-night days. Our question is *not* how old the universe is. Our question is, Did Moses intend each numbered *yôm,* in Genesis 1 to mean a normal day-night day or a long day-age era?

Limits on the Meaning

John Feinberg said that for accurate communication, words must have a referent that forms an "ontological tie to the world."[1297] The word יוֹם (*yôm*) has the referent (in modern terms) of one axial rotation of Earth in the presence of (sun)light on one side. So the two literal sun-measured senses of *yôm* are "the period of light (as contrasted with the period of darkness)," or "the period of twenty-four hours."[1298] The second sense of twenty-four hours is the basic time unit in Hebrew. Coppes lists a third sense of "a general vague 'time,'"[1299] often of trouble. Only once within Genesis, in 35:3, is this vague sense of "in the day of my distress" used. This vague sense does not fit with the time-specific words surrounding *yôm* in Genesis 1. A fourth sense is the nonliteral, prolonged, future "eschatological day," such as "the day of the LORD." Genesis 1 is not about future events, so this future sense does not fit Genesis 1.[1300] A fifth use is as a prefixed compound word, or construct. The most common is $b^e y\hat{o}m$. $B^e y\hat{o}m$ is sometimes translated "on/in the day when," or simply "when" if used in the more general sense as in Genesis 2:4. It is unreasonable to claim that this construct forces a non-construct numbered $y\hat{o}m$ with "evening" and "morning" in Genesis 1 to mean a geological era. From the semantic range of $y\hat{o}m$, the two literal sun-measured senses fit Genesis 1 quite naturally. Will genre, grammar, and context agree?

Apart from a few small seams of poetry, Genesis was written as historical narrative (however unique in content) about the real events from the creation of the heavens and the earth all the way to the death of Joseph. Eleven or twelve $t\hat{o}l^e d\hat{o}t$ generational accounts and genealogies form the parts of Genesis.[1301] The first, Genesis 1:1—2:4a, is the creation of all things and the (six or eight) generations of the heavens and the earth. Generations indicate a precise and accurate account of history. Moreover, Jesus and the New Testament writers spoke of Genesis 1—3 as history (Matt. 19:4; 1 Tim. 2:13). Never once in Genesis did Moses use the future end-times events genre, which some old earth creation writers appeal to for long day-age geological eras in Genesis 1.[1302]

In later end-times events genre, without sequential numbers, Zechariah 14:7 speaks of "one day" (KJV) or "unique day" (NASB). Even this future unique day may be a day-night cycle because it will end in evening. It is unclear whether in Hosea 6:2 "days" and a "third day" will be three day-night future days or three longer future time periods. Since both supposed exceptions of $y\hat{o}m$ with a number are end-times genre rather than historical narrative, neither has more than one number and both are unclear in length; neither makes the Genesis 1 sequentially numbered days into geological eras. The two literal sun-measured senses of $y\hat{o}m$—twenty-four-hour day and daylight—fit the historical narrative genre of Genesis 1.

Of the ten occurrences of $y\hat{o}m$ in Genesis 1, four are of the daylight part of the day and are accepted literally as daytime. The one plural, $y\hat{o}m\hat{i}m$, is accepted literally as days. The six occurrences of $y\hat{o}m$ that are disputed are even more clearly daytime-evening-nighttime-morning cycle days. The six are numbered in order. Day one had day and night as well as evening and morning. $Y\hat{o}m$ in Exodus 12:6 with a number and just evening was a normal day. So in Genesis 1 each sequentially numbered $y\hat{o}m$ with both evening and morning compellingly indicates a daylight-evening-nighttime-morning day.

The context before the first numbered *yôm* was the darkness of the sea surface, the location of the Spirit, then the command for light in 1:3–5. Since only God could have been the original Author of the creation account (because no human was there), and Genesis 1:2 declared that the Spirit of God was "on location," this strongly implies that the Spirit was the Narrator. We may reasonably presume that Genesis 1:2—2:3 was narrated from His location and perspective just above the planet's surface.

So in Genesis 1:3b, the Divine Narrator reported, "And there was light." We may reasonably presume that diffuse sunlight had penetrated for the first time the thick cloud layer (Job 26:8–9; 38:9) to His location just above the watery surface of the rotating planet. After the daytime of this first sunlight, the Spirit's location rotated into evening and night, then about twelve hours later into the first diffuse dawn. Evening then morning is a Hebrew merism indicating a single night (Exod. 27:21; Lev. 24:3; Num. 9:15; Deut. 16:4).[1303] The Bible designated this as "day one." These events could hardly be more explicitly a day-night cycle day. Since the next days were numbered sequentially as "second day," "third day," etc., and day one was the defining occurrence of *yôm* in chapter 1, then the subsequent five days were also day-night days.

Other Hebrew words could have been used instead of *yôm* to indicate a long period of time, but they were not used. Perhaps *et,* "time," could have been combined with *rabôt beshānîm,* "many years" (Lev. 25:51); *yômot 'ôlām,* "days of old" (Deut. 32:7); or *yômîm miqedem,* "days of antiquity" (Ps. 44:1) But God chose singular *yôm,* sequentially numbered, with evening and morning, compellingly indicating six single, day-night, normal days.

Objections to Day-Night *Yôm* in Genesis 1

A common objection to understanding *yôm* in Genesis 1 as a day-night day is the compound word *beyôm,* "when," in Genesis 2:4b.

In response, the *be* means "in" and the *yôm* means "day." *Beyôm* in verse 4b is correctly translated "when" by the NIV: "**When** the LORD God made. . . ."[1304] *Beyôm,* "when," in 2:4b cannot convert a numbered *yôm* with day, evening, night, and morning in Genesis 1 into a geological day-age era.

Another objection is that a human observer "didn't appear until day six."[1305] So how can we say these were normal days?

In response, the Spirit was just above the rotating planet's watery surface as a perfect Observer. Apparently, He was the Narrator of the six days. So the Spirit of God said they were days with daytime, evening, and morning. He would know; He was there.

An objection is often raised against the young earth scientific creationism theory; How can days one through three be normal days in the absence of the sun? (YEC claims the sun was not created until day four.)

In response, this objection does not apply to three of the four literal days theories (the gap, the historical land, or the two stage Biblical creation theories), because these theories recognize that the "heavens," including the sun, were created "in the beginning." So we may infer that the light on day one was diffuse sunlight reported by the Narrator. He experienced the succession of sunlight, then evening with nighttime, then morning during all six day-night days at His location on the rotating planet. This Narrator's perspective of each day, along with time words and numbers, are strong evidence that He was narrating normal daylight-evening-nighttime-morning days.

Another objection is God-defined days. Some day-age advocates claim that God may have used relativity to define the days as "God days" of billions of years. Often cited are Bible texts saying that to God a thousand years are "like yesterday" or "as a watch in the night" (Ps. 90:4, NASB) and "one day is like a thousand years" (2 Pet. 3:8, NASB). So "God's days are not our days."[1306]

In response, the Narrator was just above the surface of the planet, a perspective that humans through the ages would understand. From this "human perspective" location, the Spirit repeatedly used human time-marker words—"day," "night," "evening," "morning," and "one day"—strongly indicating day-night days. Moses and his readers experienced just such day-night days with evening and morning on our rotating planet Earth. Moses had no knowledge of relativity or "stretched time," so he could not have meant a relativity-defined "day." To put it another way, a relativity day was not an "extra-linguistic referent" Moses could have known, so was not what Moses meant. A relativity defined "day" is a modern concept that should not be imported back into the ancient text. Moses would have used *yôm* to refer to the kind of day he experienced every day of his life.

Separating out the second issue of the apparent antiquity of the universe, the text itself supports the meaning of *yôm* in Genesis 1 as six normal day-night days. So we lay aside non-day-night days theories. Before evaluating the four day-night days theories, let us consider whether God began with chaos or created *ex nihilo* the heavens and the earth.

B. Chaos or *Ex Nihilo* Creation?

In Genesis 1:1, did God create ex nihilo *the heavens and earth?*
Or did God creatively turn unformed chaos into cosmos?

Different chaos theories disagree when chaos existed, but they all claim some degree of unformed chaos. Non-chaos theories claim that God created an orderly cosmos and unfinished (not chaotic) Earth in the beginning.

God and Chaos Existed Before Genesis 1:1.

1. Pre-Creation Chaos Theory. God and chaos existed before 1:1.

2. Title or Summary Theory. God and chaos existed before 1:1. Genesis 1:1 is a title. There was no *ex nihilo* creation in Genesis 1:1.

In Genesis 1:1 God Created Chaotic or Unformed Matter

4. Initial Chaos Theory. In the beginning in 1:1, God created chaotic matter. Rooker holds a mild form of initial chaos.

5. Young Earth Scientific Creationism Theory. God created the heavens as space and the Earth as unformed matter (mild chaos) throughout the darkness of space in day one.

In 1:1 God Created Order, but Earth Became Chaos

9. Gap or Creation-Ruin-Restoration Theory. In the beginning God created the universe as orderly cosmos, but by Satan's fall and God's judgment Earth became chaos.

In 1:1 God Created Orderly Cosmos; Earth Was Unfinished

10. Historical Land Creationism Theory. In the beginning God created the universe and Earth as orderly cosmos, but "the Land" (Eden) was unfinished. God prepared Eden for man in six days.

11. Two Stage Biblical Creation Theory. In the beginning God created the universe as orderly cosmos, but planet Earth was unfinished. God finished planet Earth for man by His commands with the six days.

The idea of chaos apparently came from ANE and Greek mythology.[1307] Then the Greek Septuagint (LXX) translated *tōhû vᵃbōhû* as ἀόρατος καὶ ἀκατασκεύαστος ("unseen and not properly prepared"[1308] or "unseen and unformed"). These words were translated into English as "formless and void." But "formless" with the idea of chaos is not the meaning of the inspired Hebrew.

Genesis 1:2 begins with *vᵉhā'āretz* ("Now the earth"), deliberately separating "the earth" from the merism of "the heavens and the earth" 1:1. Only planet Earth was *tōhû vᵃbōhû.*

The two words *tōhû vᵃbōhû* are used together only twice more in the Bible. Isaiah 34:5–15 describes Edom using these two terms because its people were killed (so Edom was "uninhabited") and its land burned over and reverted to thorns and wild animals (so Edom was "uninhabitable"). Jeremiah 4:23, alluding to Genesis 1:2, used *tōhû vᵃbōhû* to describe Judah's disaster. Jeremiah continued, "I looked, and behold, there was no man," so Judah was "uninhabited." "I looked, and behold, the fruitful land was a wilderness," so Judah was "uninhabitable" (Jer. 4:25–26, NASB). Wilderness and lack of people point to conditions that are "uninhabitable and uninhabited." Neither word indicates "unformed matter" or utter chaos. Rather, the water-covered, cloud-darkened planet was "uninhabitable and uninhabited." So next God would make it lighted, habitable, and inhabited by His six work days.

Laying aside non-day-night days theories and the more radical chaos theories, let us evaluate the four normal days theories.

C. Creation Once or Twice?

Did God create the life kinds once—by eight commands and six days?
Or did He create life kinds twice—once long ago, then in the six days?

Life Kinds Created Twice, Before and Again During Six Days
9. Gap or Creation-Ruin-Restoration Theory. Life was created twice, first in a time gap at Genesis 1:2, then again later during the six days.
10. Historical Land Creationism Theory. Life was introduced twice, first created during "the beginning" in 1:1, then selected modern kinds were either created in or introduced to Eden during the six days.

Life Kinds Created Once, by His Commands with the Six Days
5. Young Earth Scientific Creationism Theory. All life kinds were created only once, during the six literal days.
11. Two Stage Biblical Creation Theory. All stated life kinds were created only once, by God's commands with the six day-night days.

Both the gap and historical land theories claim a first creation of land and of all the kinds of life—sea life, dinosaurs, birds, etc.—*before* the six days in Genesis 1:1–2.

The gap theory claims that all ancient life was created in a gap at Genesis 1:2. Several authors have already shown that a gap at 1:2 is not supported by Hebrew grammar. Genesis 1:2 is a description of Earth's uninhabitable and empty condition, not an event when Earth *became* uninhabited.

John Sailhamer's historical land theory claims God created land and all life, except for true humans, in Genesis 1:1. At least this claim is not grammatically impossible.

However, both theories face a major problem with their claim of a first creation of life before the six days: The Bible says nothing about a first creation of life in geologic ages before the six days. This claim is based on Biblical silence.

Contra the claim by both the gap theory and historical land theory that the world was full of life in 1:2, *bōhû* means "empty." And contra the gap theory, the verb in 1:2 means "is," not "became." Earth was empty of life. In Genesis 1:2, planet Earth was a desolate, water-covered, cloud-darkened waste. Moses knew what a desolate wasteland was like. In the Sinai, there are places where even the Bedouin with their camels do not go. Essentially nothing lives there. *Bōhû* means "empty." Earth was *not* full of life. Earth was empty, like those most desolate places. The difference is that instead of bare stone and burning sand under the glare of the sun, Earth was a cloud-darkened, water-covered world.

Sailhamer claims there is a switch in meaning to the land of Eden beginning in 1:2, so only Eden was lifeless. But, as already discussed, *ha'āretz,* "the earth," is the last word in 1:1, and *vᵉha'āretz,* "and the earth," is the first word in 1:2, so they are the same Earth. Earth as a whole was *bōhû,* or empty, not full, of life. So there was no creation of life in Genesis 1:1, between 1:1 and 1:2, or in 1:2. The gap in the gap theory and Sailhamer's claim of a switch to the land of Eden in 1:2 are both incorrect.

We may now analyze the two remaining theories with the last diagnostic pair of questions.

D. Creation in Day One or "In the beginning"?

Did God create the literal heavens and earth "in the beginning"?
Or did He create heavens as space and earth as prematter in day one?

The two remaining theories are two variants of six normal days creation: young earth scientific creationism theory, and the unified two stage Biblical creation theory (2SBC). These two theories agree on nine of the ten main claims of young earth creationism.

However, these two theories differ on one main claim and its sub-claims: When did God create the heavens and earth—"in the beginning" or "*in* six days?"

5. *Young Earth Scientific Creationism (YEC)*

YEC claims that the Genesis 1:1 *ex nihilo* creation was *in* day one of six consecutive night-day days, because according to Exodus 20:11 all creation was "*in* six days." Therefore, no time could have passed in the beginning before day one. The "beginning" was the first instant of day one when God created "all space (heavens), all time (beginning), and all matter (earth)."[1309] This was the "*ex nihilo* creation of the universe by God on the first day."[1310] Because the universe was created *in* the six days a few days before Adam, and we can date Adam to about 6,000 years ago by his descendants' genealogies; therefore the *Bible* dates the universe to about 6,000 years old. If the universe appears older, it has "appearance of age" either by a miracle or by a scientific answer that is not yet understood.

11. *Two Stage Biblical Creation (2SBC)*

2SBC accepts Genesis 1:1 literally that in the beginning God created the literal heavens and the literal Earth. Exodus 20:11 in the inspired Hebrew does not include "*in*," so does not force the initial *ex nihilo* creation into the six days. Instead, Exodus 20:9–11 commanded Israel to work six days "*Because* for six days the LORD worked on the heavens/sky and the earth, the sea, and all that *is* in them, and rested on the seventh day." Consistently the Bible uses "beginning" to indicate a beginning time period. So the Bible itself indicates that "In the beginning" in Genesis 1:1 was a beginning time period before the six days, instantaneous in initiation and of unstated length. God created the heavens and earth in the beginning. Genesis 1:2 describes planet Earth's *tōhû v^{a}bōhû* condition at the close of the beginning time.

In a second stage, by eight command units and six normal day-night days God worked to make planet Earth lighted, habitable, and inhabited. The universe and Earth were created in the beginning before the six days so are undated by the Bible (UEC). The universe and Earth do *not* have deceptive appearance of age. They are however old they are.

God Created the Heavens and the Earth in the Beginning

Most creation theories agree that God created the heavens and the earth "in the beginning," before the six days.[1311] In contrast, based on "*in* six days" of Exodus 20:11, YEC claims the "*ex nihilo* creation of the universe by God [was] on the first day."[1312] God created the heavens as space and the Earth as all matter[1313] in the universe all within day one. And this is based on "*in* six days" of Exodus 20:11.

But there is no "*in*" in Exodus 20:11. This fact is easily checked in the Hebrew text. In the Hebrew the verse reads, "Because/For six days," not "For in six days." In the context of the Fourth Commandment to work six days but not the Sabbath, *'āsâh* means "made" in the sense of "worked on," not "made" in the sense of "created" *ex nihilo*. So the Exodus 20:8–11 Fourth Commandment says work six days but do not work the seventh "*Because* for six days the Lord worked on the heavens/sky and the earth, the sea, and all that *is* in them, and rested on the seventh day." So Exodus 20:11 does not force the creation of the heavens and earth into the six days. Then if we take Genesis 1 literally, we should accept "In the beginning God created the heavens and the earth." God created the actual heavens of sun, moon, and stars in the sky and the unfinished planet Earth in Genesis 1:1

YEC does *not* take Genesis 1:1 literally, but instead claims Genesis 1:1 means God created space, time, and unformed matter. YEC adds the word "*in*" to Exodus 20:11, that God created space, time, unformed matter, and light *in* day one.

Two stage Biblical creation takes Genesis 1:1 literally, that God created the heavens and the earth in the beginning. 2SBC takes Exodus 20:11 literally, that "for six days the Lord worked on the heavens/sky and the earth, the sea, and all that *is* in them, and rested on the seventh day." 2SBC fits the Bible creation texts.

The "Beginning" Was a Beginning Time Period Before Day One

YEC tends to bypass the first words of the Bible, because YEC claims God created everything "*in* day one." To YEC "in the beginning" refers to the first instant of day one when God created "all time (beginning)."[1314]

John Sailhamer responds, "Within the Book of Genesis itself, the author uses the term *rē'shît* to refer to the early part of Nimrod's kingdom (Genesis 10:10). . . . In Job 8:7 the word *rē'shît* refers to the early part of Job's life, before his misfortunes overtook him. . . . It was an unspecified, but lengthy, period in Job's life. . . . According to Jeremiah 28:1, for example, the 'beginning' [*bᵉrēshît*] of King Zedekiah's reign included events which happened four years after he had assumed the throne."[1315] The beginning really was a time period of unstated length.

2SBC accepts that the Bible consistently uses *rē'shît* as a beginning time period. So "in the beginning" was literally the beginning time period when God created the heavens and the earth.

Genesis 1:2 Declared Earth was *Tōhû vᵃbōhû*

YEC claims that the heaven was space and that Earth was unformed matter throughout the darkness of space. Since Earth was *tōhû vᵃbōhû*, then all that "earth" matter throughout the universe was dark unformed chaotic matter.

In response, if we accept Genesis 1:1 literally, then God created the literal heavens, with its normal literal meaning of the sun, moon, and stars in the sky, and the literal Earth in the beginning. At the end of the beginning period, Genesis 1:2 declares that planet Earth was *tōhû vᵃbōhû*. The two other uses of *tōhû vᵃbōhû* were of Edom and Judah after they were conquered. The meaning of *tōhû vᵃbōhû* is uninhabitable and uninhabited. In Genesis 1:2 at the end of the beginning time period, planet Earth was unfinished—uninhabitable, uninhabited, sea-covered, and dark on the sea surface. And according to Job 26:7–9 and 38:8–9, the sea surface was darkened by thick dark cloud. God would make the dark, uninhabitable, uninhabited Earth lighted, habitable, and inhabited by His eight commands.

2SBC accepts Genesis 1:2 literally—that Earth was declared uninhabitable and uninhabited and its sea surface dark. God would make Earth lighted, habitable, and inhabited by the eight command units with the six day-night days.

The Bible Does Not Date the Universe

YEC claims the Bible dates the universe at about 6,000 years old by Adam's genealogies. YEC says the universe was created *in* the six days, so it is only a few days older than Adam.

In response, if we accept the Bible's use of *rē'shît* as consistently meaning a beginning time period, then the beginning was however long it was, meaning that the universe is however old it is. The genealogies of Adam date Adam, not the universe.

Two stage Biblical creation accepts the Bible's use of *rē'shît* as a beginning time period. Since that beginning period is unstated in length by the Bible, the universe is undated by the Bible (UEC).

Is Any Theory Consistent with the Bible's Creation Texts?

We asked if the Genesis 1 text indicates whether the six days were daylight-evening-nighttime-morning days or geological eras. Bible evidence supports Moses' intent that each numbered *yôm* in Genesis 1 was a daylight-evening-nighttime-morning day.

We asked if Genesis 1 indicates that God created the stated life kinds once, by His commands with the six work days (only in 1:3–31), or twice, first in the beginning (1:1–2) and then again in the six days (1:3–31). We found not only that no explicit Bible text *supports* but that Bible evidence *opposes* creation of the stated kinds of life in 1:1–2. God created the stated life kinds only once—by His commands with the six days.

We asked if God created unformed chaos. The text does not support chaos. Only unfinished planet Earth was declared *tōhû v*ᵃ*bōhû*. And *tōhû v*ᵃ*bōhû* means "uninhabitable and uninhabited," not chaos. There was no chaos.

We asked if God created the heavens and earth in the beginning before the six days or *in* day one. It seems that a faulty reading in English of Exodus 20:11 led to inserting the creation of Genesis 1:1 *in* the six days. Exodus 20:11 actually describes stage two, when God worked for six days making our sky, earth, and sea lighted, habitable, and full of life. Taking Genesis 1:1–3 literally, we see that God created the universe and unfinished planet Earth in the beginning time period, before light began day one.

Only 2SBC passes all four diagnostic tests.

Also, 2SBC accepts Genesis 1:1 literally, that in the beginning (before day one) God created the orderly heavens and unfinished Earth. 2SBC accepts Genesis 1:2 literally, that Earth was uninhabitable, uninhabited, sea-covered, and dark. 2SBC accepts Genesis 1:3–31 literally, that by eight command units with six day-night days, God made Earth lighted, habitable, and full of life.

The two stage Biblical creation theory is compatible with the most Biblically supported claims of the other theories and is a refinement of the traditional unformed-unfilled, day-night days, two-stage, initial *ex nihilo* creation theory.[1316]

If this refinement is accurate, then the heavens and earth are however old they are. They had a beginning, and the universe is spreading out, just as the Bible says. Edwin Hubble's discovery of the beginning and expansion of the universe had already been declared by the Bible all along. Only the Creator could have known these facts long before modern science.

By understanding Biblical creation correctly, we can bring the full power of this match to apologetics between the Bible and the discoveries that science is only now uncovering. As a result, we can answer a world that looks at the universe and asks:

"Where did everything came from?"

"Is there Someone out there?"

"Do we have any purpose in it all?"

"Is there any real evidence for the God of the Bible?"

"Is there Someone big enough to fix the mess of my life?"

Chapter 15
Conclusions on Creation

In this study, we have examined and evaluated by key Bible creation texts the claims of ten major creation theories. From these I have proposed an eleventh consolidated, unified, combined creation theory. In doing this, I have come to seven conclusions.

First, all ten major creation theories offer great insights into the Bible texts on creation. Too often advocates of one creation theory see other theories as targets for attack rather than sources of learning about creation. Every major creation author whose work I have read has valuable insights. Before beginning this study, I had already developed my understanding of the two stage Biblical creation theory from the Bible's over one hundred texts on creation. Yet every one of those authors contributed to a fuller understanding of two stage Biblical creation.

Second, all the creation theories I studied—not only in my evaluation, but in each other's evaluations—erred in some major claim. They could prove each other incorrect in at least one crucial claim. By listening to their criticisms, I could eliminate unbiblical claims. I am not saying that my version of two stage Biblical creation is perfect. The two reasons my theory may come closer to what God said that He did when He created the heavens and the earth are these: I studied the five major and over one hundred shorter Bible texts on creation in Hebrew and Greek. And I listened to the other theories' authors—both their Biblically supported claims and their criticisms of problematic claims in other theories. Truly I stand on the shoulders of Biblical giants.

Third, I discovered that others before me already said the basic idea of the two stage creation theory is one of the main creation theories—that in the beginning God created the heavens and the earth, but Earth was unfinished; so by His commands with the six days God finished Earth. But for some reason unknown to me, no one whose work I have read has explained this two stage creation theory thoroughly. Charles Hodge claimed this view was one of two major views. Davidson also claimed that it is one of several major creation theories.[1317] However, unlike the other theories, it is not a theory with some special idea. It seems to be simply the view that one comes away with by carefully studying all the Bible texts on creation in Hebrew and Greek.

Fourth, skeptics claim that the Bible disagrees with itself. In contrast, the more I have developed this two stage Biblical creation theory, the more I have found that all the Bible texts on creation fit together perfectly. Each time I thought I might have found a contradiction, I committed myself to be willing to give up this theory if the contradiction proved real. But none did. Every apparent contradiction dissolved as I continued studying the Bible texts and considered the Biblical studies of those great creationists who have gone before me. There really is an integrated answer to the question, What did God say that He did when He created the heavens and the earth?

Fifth, understanding Bible creation in two stages matches what science is discovering. There is no need to twist either the Bible or science for a beautiful match.

Sixth, the most Biblically supported claims of the ten theories do seem to support creation in two stages—"In the beginning God created the heavens and the earth," but Earth was uninhabitable, uninhabited, and darkened. Then God, by eight command units and six day-night days, made Earth lighted, habitable, and inhabited; culminated with humans who can know, worship, and glorify Him, our Creator and Savior, forever.

Seventh, if this understanding of Creation is roughly correct, it is God who receives the glory.

May God our Creator and Savior be glorified!

Chapter 16
Can We Know the Creator?

"I'm an unbeliever," said Oliver, "though I have my doubts."[1318]

"Don't we all," added Diane.

Later Oliver observes the ruins of a cathedral: "The people that built this place thought they had the answer."

Diane responds wistfully, "They thought God was the answer." But neither Oliver nor Diane believes in God.

However, Oliver recognizes, "But they were asking a big question. Look at this place! Did you ever see such a big question? Too big for me. That's why I stick to silly and trivial questions. Big questions frighten me."

If I were there, I might reply, "I have asked that big question, 'Is there a Creator? Is there an eternal God? Does He give meaning to life?' I have looked for evidence. And based on evidence, I am a believer in that Creator."

"Evidence? What evidence?" Oliver, a former comparative religions professor now made redundant without a job, might respond. "I have studied all the religions and none of them makes sense. Show me some evidence for God. Show me how anything around us makes sense. Trying to make sense of things seems to me like an incurable disease."

"See the moon rising on one horizon and the sun setting on the other?" I might reply.

"And?" Diane might ask.

"And the sun is exactly four hundred times wider than the moon, but the moon is exactly four hundred times closer to Earth than the sun. And their orbits align every year or two. Then the moon precisely covers all of the sun but its corona, producing an eclipse on Earth. Without that precise fit, allowing us to study the sun's corona, we might not have been able to understand the sun.

"Without understanding the sun, we might not realize that the small points of light in the sky at night are also suns. Without realizing they are distant suns, we might not have come to understand their size and great distance. But we do understand, because these two main objects in our sky—our sun and moon—precisely match in apparent size.

"There are three methods of telling the distance to those stars, these distant suns. Those three methods overlap, so we can tell the distance to other galaxies and finally to the farthest objects in the universe. We have discovered that the galaxies are enormous, many with several hundred billion stars. And by the Hubble Space Telescope Deep Field Study, we can estimate that a hundred and twenty-five billion galaxies exist, not to mention black holes and dark energy."

Oliver might quote, "The universe is not only stranger than we imagine; it is stranger than we can imagine."

It is. In 1929 as Edwin Hubble was learning the distance to galaxies, he discovered that the universe is expanding. And if it is expanding, then it once was small. It had a beginning. Strange, you say. Recently Saul Perlmutter discovered that the universe is *not* slowing down from gravitational attraction for a big crunch and yet another big bang and on and on for all eternity. No, he says it is speeding up. It will never collapse.

That means the universe had a onetime beginning. A beginning of all things needs an eternal non-matter Beginner. The Bible's first words are, "In the beginning God created the heavens and the earth" (NIV).

Eleven times the Bible tells us God has been stretching out the heavens since He created them.[1319] Not only is the universe expanding, apparently that expansion is even speeding up.

Only the actual Creator could have known before modern science that the universe had a beginning and that it has been stretching out. He recorded those facts only in the Bible. So what all this means is we have very strong evidence that the God of the Bible is the Beginner, the Creator of the universe.

He established Earth's situation—the moon's size fitting the sun precisely, the three overlapping means of measuring distances to even the farthest objects in space, and our position in the Galaxy. Our position in our Galaxy is unusual in that gives us a clear view out to the universe. He arranged these so we can learn about His great creation work.

The Creator built into the universe the precise physical constants in atoms, in gravity, and many other constants that were necessary for stars and planets to form. These constants are also precisely right to make life possible on Earth.[1320]

He made Earth exactly the right distance from the sun, with the right amount of water, with the right atmosphere, and on and on—so we can exist on earth and come to understand that He created the universe and us. "The heavens declare the glory of God" (Ps. 19:1, NIV).

"It would be very difficult to explain why the universe should have begun in just this way, except as the act of a God who intended to create beings like us."[1321]

Stephen Hawking

The Creator has given us His communication. That communication is the Bible. In it we find the big questions, and also the big answers, answers only the Creator could give.

The Creator has revealed to us in the Bible that He is the one and only God, yet three eternal persons—God the Father, God the Son (the Lord Jesus), and God the Holy Spirit. He is awesome in power, wisdom, justice, love, and goodness.

God the Father through God the Son Jesus created time, space, matter, energy, and the physical laws of the universe. He fashioned Earth for us and made us in His image so we can come to know Him. He gave us ability to think, be creative, and choose either good (as He desires) or evil.

As our Creator, He can require us to do good. His Bible commands say what is right and wrong:

- Love and honor God above all else
- Do not serve false gods or their idol images
- Do not abuse His name (God, Jesus Christ)
- Work to provide and be able to give
- Honor your father and mother
- Do not murder or hate people
- Abstain from any sex outside marriage
- Do not steal
- Do not lie or give false witness
- Do not covet what your neighbor has[1322]

God is everywhere (we can't see Him because He is spirit) and knows all we do, say, or think. God calls violations of His good commands that He gave to protect us and other people "sin." The Bible says, "For all have sinned, and come short of the glory of God" (Rom. 3:23, KJV).

These commands carry bad and good news. What is the bad news? Part of God's glory is his perfect goodness, His holiness. His standard for us is to "be perfect, therefore, as your heavenly Father is perfect" (Matt. 5:48, NIV). We fail to obey perfectly His good commands. We commit sin. Our sin separates us from God, who is perfect goodness. Sin's penalty is death and separation from God forever. "For the wages of sin [what we earn by our violations] is death . . ." (Rom. 6:23a, KJV). At death, our spirit separates from our body. On Judgment Day, every man and woman who has any sin will have all their wrong thoughts, words, and acts fully revealed and judged by our awesome holy Creator. Then they will be separated forever from the love of God to His just wrath, the dread penalty for their sin.

So how can we have our sin removed? Until our sin is removed, holy God cannot accept us into His family. God is also just, so He cannot remove our sin until its penalty is fully paid.

What is the good news? The good news is far better than we can imagine. The good news is though our sin makes us unlovely, God has chosen to love us so much that He planned to pay the penalty for our sin. The penalty for violating His good commands is death. But because God is spirit, not body, He cannot die. So God the Son, our Creator, came down from Heaven to Earth to be born a human of a virgin named Mary. (We celebrate Jesus' birth at Christmas.) Jesus lived on Earth as the God-Man, the prophesied Messiah. He precisely fulfilled detail after detail of all the prophecy given about Messiah long beforehand.[1323] He never committed any sin. Since He had no sin of His own to pay for, He could substitute for us, paying our dread penalty for our sin.

Jesus took all of our hateful sin on Himself and paid our full penalty by His death on the bloody execution cross. For six agonizing hours, holy God the Father had to separate from God the Son until His death payment was finished—because Jesus carried our sin on the cross. Jesus died in our place and was buried. But as He promised, on the third day He rose to life with His body transformed. He will never die again (Rom. 10:16; 1 Pet. 3:18) because his payment was complete (John 19:30; Heb 10:10). (We celebrate His resurrection at Easter.)

Numerous people saw Him again—alive. Over five hundred people at once saw Him (1 Cor. 15:3–8). Some would not believe that He rose from the dead until they saw Him. One man, Thomas, refused to believe unless he could touch Jesus' death wounds. Jesus came to Thomas through a locked room and said, "Put your finger here, and see my hands; and put out your hand, and place it in my side. Do not disbelieve, but believe." Thomas answered, "My Lord and my God!" Jesus responded, "Have you believed because you have seen me? Blessed are those who have not seen and yet have believed" (John 20:27–29, ESV). We are those who have not seen Jesus alive, yet we can believe.

Then, in the sight of His followers, Jesus rose to Heaven to rejoin God the Father. Now He offers us the gift of His payment for all our sin!

"For the wages of sin *is* death; but the gift of God *is* eternal life through Jesus Christ our Lord" (Rom. 6:23, KJV).

God made us in His image. That means God gave us choice. If we choose to receive Jesus, His costly payment will be applied to us. God is just, so there will be no double jeopardy, no second payment by us. Our sin will be 100 percent gone, and we will be born again with eternal life into God's family forever. God the Holy Spirit will come into us, enabling us to live right. When our bodies die, God will take our spirits to be with Him. When Jesus returns to Earth, He will raise our bodies to join our spirits, changing our bodies to be perfect like His perfect resurrected body. We will live forever with our Savior in the goodness, love, joy, and glory of God.

If we ignore or reject Jesus, then we still owe our dread penalty and remain isolated from God, waiting for Judgment Day.

To receive Jesus and His payment for our sin, we must agree with God about the badness of our sin against His good commands. We must believe in Jesus, God the Son who also became man, paid for our sin, and rose from the dead. We must choose to believe in and receive Jesus as our Savior from our sin penalty.

If you have not already, I invite you to make a decision to believe in and receive Jesus as your Lord God, your Savior. This is the greatest privilege imaginable. You may already believe some facts about Jesus. You may have received His help in trouble. But knowing about Him and receiving His help in trouble are not the same as trusting in and receiving Jesus as your Lord God, your Savior from your sin. You must make an active decision to believe in and receive Jesus as *your* Savior from *your* sin. The Bible says, "But as many as received Him [Jesus], to them gave he power to become the sons of God, even to them that believe on his name" (John 1:12, KJV).

You can make one of two choices. The wise choice: Believe now, or first read more in the Bible's Gospel of John about Jesus—God the Son, the living "Word," who created the universe and came to Earth as the God-Man, who talked to people, died in our place, rose from the dead, and offers us eternal life. Then after learning more about Him, believe in and receive Jesus as your Savior from your sin.

The unwise choice: Delaying forever believing in Jesus is not a good choice. Separation from God leaves ahead for you death, the Judgment Day, and the dread penalty for your sin.

This is the real thing, the only treasure that lasts, a love relationship with our Creator forever. It is so simple—believe in Jesus, trusting in Him and His payment on the cross for your sin. "Believe on the Lord Jesus Christ and you will be saved" (Acts 16:31, NIV). Express your belief to

the Lord Jesus in these words or your own words. (God honors believing
in Jesus, not just saying the words.) Here is the way I would express belief
in Him in words you may use:

> "Lord Jesus, I agree with You that I have sinned and
> that my sin is very bad. I am very sorry.
> Lord Jesus, I believe You are God the Son, our Creator.
> Lord Jesus, I believe that You became also man—
> the sinless God-man.
> Lord Jesus, I believe You paid for all my sin—
> You died in my place, You were buried; but
> You rose from the dead to live forever.
> Lord Jesus, I choose to receive You now as
> my Lord God and
> my Savior Who paid for all my sin.
> Lord Jesus, take away all my sin now, and
> receive me into Your family now and forever!"

If you believe in Jesus as your Lord God, your Savior, welcome to
God's family now and forever!

When we believe in and receive Jesus as our Savior, He then
receives us into His family. As part of God's family, we want to please Him
by living by His commands (as previously stated) and teachings (summary
below) to His great glory:

- Love God (Matt. 22:37)
- Love people (Matt. 22:39)
- Talk to God whenever we can—prayer (1 Thess. 5:17)
- Study the Bible, God's message to us (2 Tim. 2:15)
- Live by what Jesus tells us in the Bible (John 14:15)
- Join a Bible-teaching church and be baptized (Heb. 10:25)
- Share this good news so others can believe (Matt. 28:19–20).

Start reading the Bible about the Lord Jesus in the Gospel of John.
The first verses are about Jesus, the Word, God the Son, the Creator. Then
read about Christian living in John's first letter (epistle), 1 John. Then
read Genesis. Then go back and read the whole New Testament. Then
read Proverbs. Learn and worship with other believers in church. Make a
bold statement that you believe in Jesus by being baptized. Join a Bible-
teaching, loving church.

The one sad thing is we still sin (ideally less and less, aiming at
zero) because we are still in our unchanged bodies with old, bad desires. In

sorrow, we confess our sin to God. He promises to cleanse the sin away (1 John 1:9). We ask for His help against that sin in the future.

More good news! Once God has received us into His family, He will greatly reward us for loving Jesus by obeying His teachings (John 14:23). We do not deserve that reward. We must rely on Him to enable us to will and to do what is good and pleasing to Him (Phil. 2:13). Jesus is preparing a future home for us (John 14:1–6), where we will live forever with Him and with all other believers in perfect goodness, joy, and love beyond imagination—in the presence of God, our Creator and our Savior, to His great glory.

And creation? An IMAX movie is nothing compared to what we will learn about every step God took to create the heavens and the Earth and all the life kinds He made. Perhaps He may remake the kinds that have gone extinct or even help us remake them. Perhaps we will be able to explore the universe He has made. But whatever He has planned, we will have plenty of time to do it. See you there!

Appendix A
Major Supported Claims in Alphabetical Order

The Correct Translation of Genesis 1:1: "In the beginning God created the heavens and the earth." It is *incorrect* to translate 1:1 as "When God began to create."

The Duncan-Hall Eight Commands: God worked by eight command units with common format, related to the six literal days.

A Generational Genesis: The worldview of Genesis was generations. The six begetting (literal) days of Genesis 1 introduced the most ancient generations of all — "the generations of the heavens and the earth."

The Heiser Clause Analysis: Begin analyzing creation by determining which clauses (esp. in Gen. 1:1–3) are independent clauses and which are dependent clauses, and then which independent clauses are modified by which dependent clauses, and so how they fit together.

The Hodge Hiatus: A qualitative break exists between the initial "immediate, instantaneous creation *ex nihilo* by the simple word of God," and the later "mediate, progressive" work of God with already created materials and secondary causes during the six days.

Intelligent Design Theory: "Certain features of the universe and of living things are best explained by an intelligent cause, not an undirected process such as natural selection."

The Kaiser Two Falls Explanation: Standard theology identifies two falls: the angelic fall led by Lucifer, and later the human Fall by Adam. God's concluding "very good" evaluation was about His work on Earth, not about angels such as Lucifer, who had been created and likely fell earlier. Animal death is *not* inherently evil. God Himself killed an animal to cover human nakedness. Any pre-Fall evil aspects of animal disease and death could only have been initiated by fallen Lucifer (Ezek. 28:16–18; Heb. 2:14). Yet by the sixth day, God worked even those together for good or eliminated them until Adam's Fall. Adam was the original cause of human death (Rom. 5:12) and farming woes (Gen. 3:17–19), but Scripture does not say he caused animal death. So animal death may have preceded Adam's Fall. Animal life cycles fit the present noneternal world God created (Rom. 8:20).

The Kline Claim: When the Bible does not indicate a miracle, Genesis 2:5–6 (no rain, no plants; rain, then plants sprouted) shows God probably used ordinary means in the creation era, just as today. **Ross Addition:** "An observed attribute of the Creator . . . is His economy of miracles — only what's needed to accomplish His purpose."

The Kline Order: Proverbs 8:22–31 says that "the beginning," when God created Earth (Gen. 1:1), was "when there were no depths." Ocean depths existed by 1:2, so "In the beginning" was before 1:2 and before the six days. Creation order: Heavens, Earth, sea, then six days.

The Kline Undated Universe: "We must speak where the Bible speaks, and be silent where the Bible is silent. . . . The inspired text, rightly interpreted, is simply silent with regard to the age of the earth and universe."

The Morris Maxim: In historical narrative, a numbered "day" was a day.

The Morris One Fall Explanation: The creation was perfect. Man and animals were created about 6,000 years ago with eternal physical life. There was "no disorder, no sin and, above all, *no death! Even Satan was still good at this point.*"[1324] His first effect on Earth was the temptation. (There were two falls, but Lucifer's fall had no effect on Earth until his temptation of Eve, resulting in Adam and Eve's Fall.) Adam's Fall resulted in a "cosmic catastrophe" including all human and animal death and subsequent moral and natural evil.

The Morris and Ross Method: The Bible reveals what God did; science may uncover how He did it.

The Observer's Perspective: Ross says interpret the Genesis 1 creation narrative from the perspective of the Observer/Narrator, the Spirit, hovering just above the surface of the water-covered Earth.

The Patrick Proposition: The initial Genesis 1:1 *ex nihilo* creation was in the beginning time period before the six days, so is undated by the Bible.

The Payne Proposition: To claim that time absolutely could not have passed between God's six work days is making too dogmatic a claim on too inconclusive evidence. Time passage between the six literal days is neither explicitly affirmed nor explicitly denied by the Bible.

The Pember Literalism: If we take Genesis 1:1 literally, then God literally created the literal heavens and literal (unfinished) Earth in the literal beginning before the six literal days.

The Rooker Reaffirmation: "The key difference between pagan cosmogonies and Genesis 1 is *creatio ex nihilo* and the absence of preexisting matter."

The Ross Apologetic: The Bible alone declares that the universe had a beginning and has been stretching out. Only the Creator could have known these facts long before modern science. The God of the Bible is the Creator, and the Bible is His accurate message to us.

The Ross Concordism: God does not deceive either by His Word or by His creation work. Correctly interpreted, both God's verbal revelation (the Bible) and physical revelation (the created universe) will be in accord.

The Ross-Schroeder Fine-Tuning Evidence: The fine-tuning of the universe and Earth is evidence of the Designer, not chance.

The Sailhamer Sense: *Tōhû v^{a}bōhû* consistently has the sense of uninhabitable and uninhabited wilderness, never of unformed matter or chaos.

The Sailhamer Time Period: *B^{e}rē'shît*, "in the beginning," consistently has the sense of an extended beginning time period, never of an instant or a few hours.

The Thomas Truism: If Genesis is true, yet its narrative history was not dictated by God to Moses, then its narrative history was from eyewitnesses.

The Traditional Translation: Waltke affirms the traditional translation of Genesis 1:1: "In the beginning God created the heavens and the earth."

The Two Stage Arnold Affirmation: Creation took place in two stages: In the beginning God created the heavens and the earth (but Earth was still uninhabitable, uninhabited, and its sea surface dark); so God worked by eight commands and six normal day-night days making Earth lighted, habitable, and inhabited.

The Waltke Exclusion Principle: If there was preexisting chaos, there was no *ex nihilo* creation of the organized heavens and earth. The converse is also logically possible: If there was *ex nihilo* creation of the organized heavens and earth, then there was no unorganized chaos.

The Waltke Merism: "The heavens and the earth" meant the entire orderly universe. Also, evening and morning meant the entire nighttime.

The Wiseman-Gray 20:11 Recognition: Exodus 20:11a has no "in," allowing the natural grammatical reading of Genesis 1:1 as the initial creation of the actual heavens and planet Earth "in the beginning" before the six days.

The Wiseman Tablet Theory: The Genesis narratives were eyewitness reports recorded on tablets received by Moses. The name of each author was at the *end* of his narrative.

Num. 18:12   120
Num. 24:20   120
Deut. 4:19   140, 144, 145, 147, 148, 361, 372, 380, 391, 395, 398,
     399, 416, 447
Deut. 11:12   118, 120, 311
Deut. 16:4   143, 360, 489
Deut. 18:4   120
Deut. 21:17   120
Deut. 26:2   120
Deut. 26:10   120
Deut. 32:10   89, 381
Deut. 33:21   120
1 Sam. 2:29   120
1 Sam. 15:21   120
1 Kings. 11:16   112
2 Chron. 31:5   120
Neh. 9:6   10, 89, 104, 123, 132
Neh. 10:38   120
Neh. 12:44   120
Job 8:7   118, 120, 311, 330, 357, 369, 374, 398, 416, 485, 495
Job 26:7–14   10, 43, 47, 177, 222, 375, 389, 416, 485, 496
Job 38:4–14   43, 49, 127, 145, 198, 214, 222-224, 275-282, 377, 416,
     448, 471
Job 40:19   120
Job 42:12   118, 120
Ps. 78:51   120
Ps. 90:2–6   192, 209
Ps. 95:5   43
Ps. 104:1–9   10, 72, 198, 223-224, 290, 300, 373, 376-377, 382, 392,
     393, 416
Ps. 104:36   118, 120
Ps. 111:10   120
Ps. 147:4   13
Prov. 1:7   118, 120
Prov. 3:9   120
Prov. 4:7   119, 120
Prov. 8:22–23   68-69, 76, 119, 209, 352, 376
Prov. 17:14   120
Eccles. 7:8   120
Isa. 11:6–9   72, 464-471

Index of Authors and Prominent People

Index of Creation Theories

Index of Abbreviations

2 SBC – Two Stage Biblical Creation
AiG   – Answers in Genesis (Ken Ham's YEC organization)
ANE – Ancient Near East
Gap   – Gap or Creation-Ruin-Restoration Theory
ID   – Intelligent Design
OEC – Old Earth Creationism
RTB – Reasons to Believe, Hugh Ross's organization
UEC – Undated Earth Creation
YEC – Young Earth Creationism, Young Earth Scientific Creation

Index of Major Subjects Besides Creation Theories

A

B

C

D

E

Eden, 25, 26, 29, 72, 113, 161, 162, 212, 237, 287, 295, 306, 310, 313, 314, 316, 317, 318, 319, 320, 321, 322, 323, 324, 325, 326, 327, 328, 329, 331, 332, 335, 384, 386, 405, 413, 422, 431, 448, 457, 460, 464, 467, 468, 473, 474, 475, 485, 486, 491, 492, 493, 531, 549, 550, 551, 552, 554, 555, 573, 578

Edom, 41, 89, 222, 295, 346, 380, 491, 492, 496

Entropy, 13, 195, 196, 213, 410, 411, 412, 413, 458, 468

Enuma Elish, 31, 32, 36, 263, 265

Evolution, 20, 115, 169, 183, 196, 200, 201, 208, 213, 217, 218, 219, 230, 231, 243, 244, 246, 256, 345, 395, 423, 428, 430, 441, 444, 445, 451, 556, 563, 576, 577

F

Fine tuning, 233, 244, 246, 260, 305, 337, 415

Flood, 23, 24, 101, 107, 108, 110, 114, 115, 118, 148, 151, 164, 165, 166, 167, 169, 173, 179, 182, 183, 187, 200, 239, 247, 264, 265, 272, 281, 296, 301, 309, 324, 326, 327, 330, 342, 350, 376, 392, 401, 404, 415, 416, 423, 463, 464, 471, 479, 484, 485, 556

Fossils, 23, 24, 26, 87, 101, 109, 110, 112, 114, 148, 149, 151, 160, 165, 179, 183, 243, 267, 281, 286, 289, 290, 292, 296, 297, 301, 350, 431, 463, 464, 470, 479, 484, 485

Fourth Commandment, 121, 122, 124, 126, 164, 267, 268, 269, 274, 298, 353, 355, 364, 365, 388, 389, 401, 434, 435, 495

G

Galaxies, 8, 9, 14, 15, 16, 17, 18, 154, 155, 197, 222, 249, 383

Gilgamesh, 265

H

Hazor, 235

Herbivores, 194

I

Isaac, 24, 65, 70

J

Jacob, 24, 111, 118, 131, 264, 271, 361, 406, 443, 484, 548, 553, 573

Joseph, 24, 111, 262, 264, 265, 273, 275, 484, 488, 538, 560

Judah, 41, 89, 111, 119, 295, 346, 369, 380, 492, 496

K

Kabbalah, 234, 247, 248, 252, 255, 258

L

Leviathan, 36, 43

Lucifer's Flood, 280, 289, 296, 297, 303

M

Macroevolution, 98, 115, 169, 196, 213, 243

Mammals, 203, 456

Mari, 443

Messiah, 7, 20, 112, 114, 168, 247, 255, 413, 461, 503

Microevolution, 115, 179, 183, 243

Millennium, 72, 113, 161, 162, 312, 369, 413, 462, 464, 467, 468, 474, 475, 487

Miracles, 69, 71, 77, 79, 80, 83, 97, 165, 171, 174, 175, 184, 187, 199, 217, 232, 259, 278, 304, 336, 372, 394, 401, 424, 452, 494, 507

Moon, 13, 23, 44, 47, 105, 106, 108, 139, 140, 144, 145, 146, 147, 148, 171, 172, 176, 182, 183, 199, 216, 217, 222, 223, 226, 231, 245, 267, 291, 292, 300, 301, 310, 312, 314, 315, 316, 317, 323, 325, 330, 335, 342, 361, 371, 372, 375, 377, 379, 380, 381, 383, 391, 395, 396, 398, 399, 413, 416, 422, 427, 447, 484, 486, 495, 496, 500, 501

Moses, 24, 41, 56, 69, 76, 77, 89, 93, 111, 118, 121, 122, 139, 140, 143, 144, 145, 146, 147, 148, 168, 172, 176, 177, 188, 201, 202, 237, 240, 248, 250, 252, 261, 262, 263, 264, 265, 272, 273, 275, 277, 279, 284, 299, 305, 309, 314, 320, 327, 330, 331, 335, 337, 351, 354, 355, 360, 361, 372, 380, 388, 390, 391, 392, 395, 399, 401, 402, 403, 404, 405, 418, 425, 426, 428, 432, 439, 443, 447, 448, 453, 454, 484, 487, 488, 490, 493, 496, 509

N

Neanderthals, 281

Nephilim, 239

Neptunism, 280

New Creation, 233, 260, 279, 305, 337, 410, 411, 412, 413, 414, 426, 457, 458, 459, 464, 466, 467, 468, 474, 475, 478

Nimrod, 117, 311, 330, 368, 374, 495

Noah, 24, 61, 107, 109, 111, 114, 168, 169, 173, 183, 262, 264, 265, 272, 320, 324, 350, 360, 365, 402, 404, 406, 407, 415, 423, 449, 464, 484, 526, 536, 538, 551, 552

Nuzi, 443

P

Pantheistic Evolution, 4, 444

Parasites, 456, 463

Paul, 7, 40, 45, 59, 90, 104, 133, 136, 149, 151, 159, 160, 161, 171, 173, 186, 211, 219, 287, 340, 370, 409, 411, 432, 433, 441, 458, 460, 466, 467, 527, 528, 529, 539, 542, 557, 576, 577

Pentateuch, 111, 172, 262, 306, 314, 315, 319, 320, 324, 403, 538, 541, 543, 545, 564, 568, 571, 576

Plants, 113, 556

R

S

T

Tuned, 186, 187, 225, 243, 244, 245, 246, 254, 343, 415, 440, 445, 446

Tyrannosaurus, 473

U

Undated Universe and Earth, 4, 427

V

Vapor, 107, 108, 115, 148, 164, 165, 182, 199, 214, 226, 231, 291, 300, 382

Vegetarianism, 433, 460

W

Water cycle, 70, 199, 214, 327

Whales, 113, 162, 321

Z

Zedekiah, 119, 311, 330, 369, 375, 495

Brief Glossary of Hebrew Words

'āsâh - do, make, work, 103, 104, 121, 123, 124, 125, 126, 127, 128, 129, 130, 131, 132, 148, 178, 182, 237, 242, 254, 267, 268, 269, 270, 271, 274, 277, 285, 303, 325, 353, 355, 365, 373, 392, 396, 397, 398, 428, 471, 495

bārā' - create, 44, 45, 59, 60, 74, 86, 88, 91, 104, 123, 124, 125, 126, 127, 129, 130, 131, 132, 134, 135, 148, 174, 178, 215, 237, 242, 254, 258, 270, 271, 284, 285, 294, 299, 303, 321, 348, 371, 372, 373, 374, 375, 398, 428, 447, 471, 523

b^e - "in" (prefix), 204-205, 354-355

b^erē'shît - in the beginning, 56, 61, 86, 117, 119, 120, 134, 142, 158, 252, 307, 330, 357, 360, 369, 375, 398, 416, 427, 435, 436

bōqer - morning, 190, 203

ehād - one, 207, 241, 432

ereb/erev - evening, 190, 203

'eretz, 'āretz – Earth, earth, land, ground, 197, 314, 319, 320

hāyâh - to be, 286, 315, 373, 400

khōshek- darkness, obscurity

lā'y^elâh - night

māyim- waters, 144, 381

nātâh - stretch out

rāqîa' - expanse, 107, 164, 315, 391, 407

rē'shît - first, beginning, best, 68, 117, 118, 119, 120, 134, 138, 158, 307, 311, 357, 369, 374, 495, 496

rûah 'elōhîm - Spirit of God, breath of God, 242, 248, 252

shāmayim - heaven, heavens, sky, abode of stars, 9, 32, 125, 139, 140, 326, 371, 391, 428

t^hôm - deep ocean, 68, 144, 352, 379, 381, 382

shēshet - six

tehôm - deep ocean, 145, 381

tōhû v^abōhû - uninhabitable and uninhabited, 25, 33, 34, 35, 36, 37, 38, 39, 40, 41, 42, 44, 46, 47, 48, 49, 50, 51, 56, 57, 58, 59, 60, 62, 64, 84, 85, 86, 87, 89, 90, 91, 92, 93, 94, 105, 140, 144, 197, 221, 222, 226, 242, 248, 250,

251, 252, 281, 282, 285, 286, 289, 292, 293, 294, 295, 299, 303, 307, 313, 319, 331, 346, 347, 349, 353, 366, 379, 380, 381, 382, 383, 390, 422, 471, 491, 492, 494, 495, 496, 497

tôl^edôt - generational-accounts, 24, 61, 111, 167, 192, 210, 261, 262, 264, 265, 266, 273, 274, 275, 277, 403, 404, 405, 406, 418, 423, 488

yām - the sea; *yamîm* – seas, 321

yabāshāh - dry ground, 327

yātsar – to form, 131, 132, 285

yôm – day, 23, 24, 28, 74, 103, 116, 167, 170, 171, 177, 182, 183, 190, 191, 202-205, 207, 208, 215, 216, 226, 230, 236, 241, 250, 253, 256, 258, 286, 290, 300, 351, 430, 432, 434, 484, 487-490; *yāmîm* – days; *yôm ehād* - day one 207, 241, 432, *b^eyôm* - when 204, 286, 488, 489

Brief Glossary of Greek Words

ἄρσεν καὶ θῆλυ – male and female, 135

ἀρχῆς – beginning, 134, 137, 357, 358

τῆς δουλείας τῆς φθορᾶς – the inescapability/bondage of perishability, 409, 476

κτίσεως – creation, 134, 137, 152, 357, 358

φθορᾶς – decay, perishability 409, 410, 411, 467

τῇ ματαιότητι – the frustration, 409, 411, 466, 467

Selected Bibliography

Andersen, Francis I., *Job*, Tyndale O.T. Commentaries. Downers Grove, IL: Inter-Varsity Press, 1984.

Ankerberg, John and John Weldon, *The Facts on Creation vs. Evolution*. Eugene, OR: Harvest House, 1993.

Aquinas, Thomas, *Sententiarum, Book II*, Distinction xiii, Article 3, "Ad Terium."

Archer, Gleason L., Jr., *A Survey of Old Testament Introduction* rev. ed. Chicago: Moody Press, 1974.

Ballard, Robert D., *Adventures in Ocean Exploration: From the Discovery of the Titanic to the Search for Noah's Flood*. Hanover, PA: National Geographic Society, 2001.

Barrow, John D. and Frank J. Tipler, *The Anthropic Cosmological Principle*. Oxford: Oxford University Press, 1986.

Batten, Don, "'Soft gap sophistry," *Creation*, 26:3.

Barentsen, J., "The Validity of Human Language: A Vehicle for Divine Truth," *Grace Theological Journal,* 9:30–31, Spring 1988.

Behe, Michael J., *Darwin's Black Box: The Biochemical Challenge to Evolution*. New York: Free Press, 1996.

Berkhof, Lewis, *Systematic Theology*. Grand Rapids: Wm. B. Eerdmans, 1939.

BibleWorks for Windows, computer program., Norfolk, VA.

Biblia Hebraica Stuttgartensia : With Westminster Hebrew Morphology. Stuttgart: German Bible Society; Glenside, PA: Westminster Seminary, 1996, morphology 1991.

Blakeslee, Sandra, "Ancient Crash, Epic Wave," *New York Times*, November 14, 2006.

Blocher, Henri, *In the Beginning: The Opening Chapters of Genesis*, trans. by David G. Preston. Leicester: InterVarsity Press, 1984.

Borgman, Paul C, *Genesis: The Story We Haven't Heard*. Downers Grove, IL: InterVarsity Press, 2001.

Bourbon, F., and E. Lavagno, *The Holy Land, Guide to the Archeological and Historical Monuments*. Vercelli, Italy: White Star and Barnes and Noble, 2001).

Brown, Frances, S. R. Driver, C. Briggs, *Hebrew-English Lexicon.* Oxford: Oxford University Press.

Brown, Walt, *In the Beginning: Compelling Evidence for Creation and the Flood* 6th ed. Phoenix, AZ: Center for Scientific Creation, 1995.

Buckland, William, *Geology and Mineralogy Considered with Reference to Natural Theology,* Vol. 1, Chapter 2, 1836; Volume VI in *The Bridgewater Treatises*

Byl, John, "On time dilation in cosmology," *Creation Research Society Quarterly,* vol. 34, number 1, 1977

Calvin, John, *A Commentary on Genesis,* Edinburgh: Banner of Truth, 1578.

Carson, D. A., *Exegetical Fallacies.* Grand Rapids: Baker Book House, 1984.

Cassuto, U., *A Commentary o the Book of Genesis,* trans. Israel Abrahams, 2 vol. Jerusalem: Magnes Press, 1961.

Chalmers, Thomas, *Works,* Vol. 1, 228, and Vol. XII, 369, in Bernard Ram, *The Christian View of Science and Scripture.* Grand Rapids: Wm B. Eerdmans Publishing Co., 1954.

Clines, David J. A., *Job 1–20,* Word Biblical Commentary. Dallas: Word Books, 1989.

Clinton, Bobby, *Interpreting the Scriptures, Hebrew Poetry.* Corel Gables, FL: World Team Learning Resource Center, 1977.

Coats, George W., *Genesis with an Introduction to Narrative Literature.* Grand Rapids: Wm. B. Eerdmans Publishing Co. 1983.

Cohen, Gary G., "Hermeneutical Principles and Creation Theories," *Grace Journal* 5:3 (Fall 1964), 17–28.

Conner, Samuel R. and Don N. Page, "*Starlight and Time* is the big bang," *Creation Ex Nihilo Technical Journal,* vol. 12, number 2 (1998):174-194.

Conner, Samuel R. and Hugh Ross, *The Unraveling of Starlight and Time,* www.reasons.org/resources/apologetics/unravelling.shtml

Copan, Paul and William Lane Craig, *Creation out of Nothing.* Grand Rapids: Baker, 2004.

Craig, William L. and Quentin Smith, *Theism, Atheism, and big bang Cosmology.* Oxford: Oxford University Press, 1995.

Craigie, Peter C, Marvin E Tate, and Leslie C Allen. *Psalms,* Word Biblical Commentary. Vols. 19-21 Dallas: Word 1983, 1990, 1983.

Custance, Arthur C., *Without Form and Void.* Brookville, Canada: Doorway Papers, 1970.

Cutler, Alan, *The Seashell on the Mountaintop.* New York: Dutton, 2003.

Dahood, Mitchell, "Eblaite *i-du* and Hebrew *'ed,* 'Rain-Cloud,'" *Catholic Biblical Quarterly 43* (1981), 534-538.

______, *Psalms I, Anchor Bible.* Garden City, NY: Doubleday & Co., 1966.

Davidson, Richard M, "In the Beginning: How to Interpret Genesis 1."

Davies, Paul, *Cosmic Jackpot.* New York: Orion Publications, 2007.

Delitzsch, Franz, *Biblical Commentary on the Book of Job.* Grand Rapids: Wm. B. Eerdmans, 1968.

______, *Biblical Commentary on the Proverbs of Solomon.* Grand Rapids: Wm. B. Eerdmans Pub. Co., 1968.

DeRemer, Frank, "Young biosphere, Old Universe?" *Technical Journal* of AiG 19:2.

DeYoung, Don B., *Astronomy and Creation.* Ashland, OH: Creation Research Society Books, 1995.

Dhorme, Edouard, *Commentary on the Book of Job*, tr. Harold Knight. Nashville: Thomas Nelson, 1984.

Duncan III, J. Ligon and David W. Hall, "The 24-Hour View," in David G Hagopian, *The Genesis Debate.* Mission Viejo, CA: Crux Press, 2001.

Driver, Samuel Rolles, and George Buchanan Gray, *The Book of Job*, International Critical Commentary. Edinburgh: T. & T. Clark, 1921.

Driver, Samuel Rolles, *The Book of Genesis*, London: Methuen, 1904.

Feinberg, John S., *The Many Faces of Evil*, Grand Rapids: Zondervan, 1994

________, "Truth: Relationship of Theories of Truth to Hermeneutics" in Earl Radmacher and R. D. Preus, eds., *Hermeneutics, Inerrancy, and the Bible*. Grand Rapids: Zondervan, 1984.

Fields, Weston W., *Unformed and Unfilled.* Grand Rapids: Baker, 1976.

Fisher, Dick, "Days of Creation: Hours or Eons?" *Perspectives on Science and Christ,* 42 (March 1990)

______, *The Origins Solution.* Lima, OH: Fairway Press. 1996.

Fonts, David M., "Genesis 1—11," *The Bible Knowledge Key Word Study*, Eugene H. Merrill, ed. Colorado Springs: Victor, 2003.

Fox, Michael V., *Proverbs 1—9*, Anchor Bible. NY: Doubleday, 2000.

Fretheim, Terence E., "Were the Days of Creation Twenty-four Hours Long?" in Ronald Youngblood, ed., *The Genesis Debate*. Nashville: Thomas Nelson, 1986, 18.

Friedman, Richard Elliott, *Commentary on the Torah*. New York: Harper Collins Publishers, 2001.

Fritch, Charles T. and Rolland W. Schloerb, *The Book of Proverbs*, the Interpreter's Bible, Vol. 4. New York: Abingdon, 1955.

Futato, M.D., "Because It Had Rained: A Study of Gen. 2:5–7 with Implications for Gen. 2:4-25 and Gen. 1:1—2:3," *WTJ* 60 (1998), 1-21.

Geisler, Norman and J. Kerby Anderson, *Origin Science*. Grand Rapids: Baker, 1987.

Gesenius, H. W. F., *Hebrew-Chaldee Lexicon to the Old Testament*. Wm. B. Eerdmans Publishing Co., 1946.

Gish, Duane T., *Evolution: The Fossils Still Say No!* El Cajon, CA: Institute for Creation Research, 1995.

Gosse, Philip Henry, *Omphalos: An attempt to Untie the Geological Knot*. London: Routledge, no date; republished, Van Voorst, 1957).

Gray, Gorman, *The Age of the Universe: What Are the Biblical Limits*. Washougal, WA: Morningstar Publications, 2000.

Grudem, Wayne, *Systematic Theology*. Grand Rapids: Zondervan, 1994.

Ham, Ken, Andrew Snelling, and Carl Wieland, *The Answers Book*. Green Forest, AR: Master Books, 1991.

Ham, Ken, "Did Jesus Say He Created In Six Days, August 25, 2001, answersingenesis.org/us/newsletters/0801lead.asp.

______, *Dinosaurs of Eden*. Green Forest, AR: Master Books, 2001.

Hamilton, Victor, *The Book of Genesis, Chapters 1—17*, NICOT, Grand Rapids: Eerdmans, 1990.

Harris, R. Laird, Gleason Archer, and Bruce Waltke, *Theological Wordbook of the Old Testament*. Chicago: Moody Press, 1980

Harrison, Roland Kenneth, *Introduction to the Old Testament*. Grand Rapids: Wm. B. Eerdmans Publishing Co., 1969.

Hartley, John E, *The Book of Job*, New International Commentary on the O.T. Grand Rapids: Wm. B. Eerdmans Pub. Co., 1988.

Hasel, G.F. and M.G. Hasel, "The Hebrew Term *ʾed* in Gen. 2:6 and Its Connection in Ancient Near Eastern Literature," *ZAW* 112 (2000), 321-340.

Hansen, David G., "A Study of the Hebrew Word *Yom* in the Creation Narrative," *Bible and Spade* 11, 35–44.

Hayward, Alan, *Creation and Evolution*. Eugene, OR: Wipf & Stock, 2005.

Hebrew-English Tanakh, Philadelphia: Jewish Publications Society, 2003.

Henry, Carl F. H., *God, Revelation, and Authority*. Waco, TX: Word, 1983, 6:108–196.

Hirsch Emil G., and Michael Friedländer, "Day," *The Jewish Encyclopedia*, 475.

Hodge, Charles, *Systematic Theology, Abridged Edition*. Grand Rapids: Baker Book House, 1988.

Howe, Fredric R., "The Age of the Earth: An Appraisal of Some Current Evangelical Positions," *Bibliotheca Sacra* 142:564, 23–36.

Hubbard, David Allan, *Hosea*. Downers Grove: InterVarsity Press, 1989.

Hummel, Charles E., *The Galileo Connection*. Downers Grove, IL: InterVarsity Press, 1986.

Humphreys, D. Russell, *Starlight and Time*. Green Forest, AR: Master Books, 1994.

______, *Starlight and Time*, DVD, Evidence Press, 2005.

Irons, Lee and Meredith G. Kline, "The Framework View," in David G. Hagopian, ed., *The Genesis Debate*. Mission Viejo, CA: Crux Press, 2001.

Johnson, Gordon H., "Genesis 1 and Ancient Egyptian Creation Myths," *Bibliotheca Sacra* 165:658, April 2008.

Johnson, Phillip E., *Darwin on Trial*. Washington, D.C.: Regency Gateway, 1991.

_____, *Reason in the Balance*. Downers Grove, IL: InterVarsity, 1995.

Kautzsch, E., *Gesenius' Hebrew Grammar*. Oxford: Clarendon Press, 1990.

Keil, C. F. and F. Delitzsch, *Commentary on the Old Testament, Volume VII, Isaiah*. Grand Rapids: Wm B. Eerdmans, 1982.

Kidner, Derek, *The Proverbs*, Tyndale O.T. Commentaries. Downers Grove, IL: Inter-Varsity Press, 1964.

_____, *Psalms 73-150*. Tyndale O.T. Commentaries. Downers Grove, IL: InterVarsity Press, 1975.

Kline, Meredith, "Because It Had Not Rained," *Westminster Theological Journal* 20:2 (May 1958), 146-157.

_____, "Space and Time in the Genesis Cosmogony," *Perspectives on Science and Christian Faith* 48:1, April, 1996, 8-9.

Knapp, Henry M., "Protestant Biblical Interpretation," in *Dictionary for Theological Interpretation*, Kevin J. Vanhoozer, ed. Grand Rapids: Baker, 2005.

Kuhn, Thomas, *The Structure of Scientific Revolutions*. Chicago: University of Chicago Press, 1970.

Liddell, H. G. and R. Scott, *Greek-English Lexicon*. Oxford: Clarendon Press, 1996.

Leeming, David Adams and Margaret Adams Leeming, *A Dictionary of Creation Myths* Oxford: Oxford University Press, 1996.

Lewin, Ariel, *The Archeology of Ancient Judea and Palestine*. Los Angeles: Getty Publications, 2005.

Lloyd, R. Raymond, "Elihu, Job's Fourth Friend," *Biblical Illustrator*, Vl. 32, No. 4, Summer 2006, 68-71.

Linnemann, Eta, Historical Criticism of the Bible: Methodology or Ideology: Reflections of a Bultmannian Turned Evangelical. Grand Rapids: Kregel, 2001.

Lisle, Jason, *Taking Back Astronomy*. Green Forest, AR: Master Books, 2006.

Little, William, *The Oxford Universal Dictionary*. Oxford: Oxford University Press, 1964.

McCabe, Robert V., "A Defense of Literal Days in the Creation Week," *Detroit Baptist Seminary Journal* 5 (Fall 2000), 97–123.

McCartney, Dan and Charles Clayton, *Let the Reader Understand: A Guide to Interpreting and Applying the Bible.* Phillipsburg, NJ: Presbyterian and Reformed Pub., 1994.

Miller, Hugh, *The Testimony of the Rocks.* Edinburgh: Constable, 1857.

Miller, Keith, *Perspectives on an Evolving Creation.* Grand Rapids: Wm. B. Eerdmans, 2003.

The Miracle Planet, "The Violent Past," DVD. New York: Ambrose, 2005.

Moorhead, P. S. and M. M. Kaplan, eds., *Mathematical Challenges to the Neo-Darwinian Interpretation of Evolution.* Philadelphia: Wistar Institute Press, 1967.

Moreland, J.P., and John Mark Reynolds, eds., *Three Views of Creation and Evolution.* Grand Rapids: Zondervan, 1999.

Moreland, J.P., ed., *The Creation Hypothesis.* Downers Grove, IL: InterVarsity Press, 1994.

Morris, Henry M., *The Biblical Basis for Modern Science.* Grand Rapids: Baker, 1984.

______, "Biblical Creationism and Modern Science," *Bibliotheca Sacra* 125:497 (Jan. 1968), 20–28.

______, *Creation and the Modern Christian.* Green Forest, AR: Master Books, 1985.

______, *Evolution in Turmoil.* San Diego, CA: Creation-Life, 1982.

______, *The Genesis Record.* Grand Rapids: Baker, 1976.

______, *Many Infallible Proofs.* Green Forest, AR: Master Books, 1974.

______, *The Remarkable Birth of Planet Earth.* Minneapolis: Bethany House, 1972.

______, *Remarkable Record of Job.* Santee, CA.: Master Books, 1988.

______, *Science and the Bible,* rev. ed. Chicago: Moody Press, 1986.

______, ed., *Scientific Creationism,* 2d ed. Green Forest, AR: Master Books, 1985.

______, *Science, Scripture, and the Young Earth.* El Cajon, CA: Institute for Creation Research, 1983.

______, *The Twilight of Evolution.* Grand Rapids: Baker, 1963.

Morris, Henry M. and Gary E. Parker, *What is Creation Science*. San Diego: Creation-Life Publishers, 1982.

Mulzac, K., "'Creation' in the Book of Jeremiah," in J. Moskala, ed. *Creation, Life, and Hope*. Berrien Spring, MI: Andrews University, 2000: 29-48.

Murphy, Roland E, *Proverbs*, Word Biblical Commentary. Nashville: Thomas Nelson, 1998.

New Scofield Reference Bible. New York; Oxford University Press, 1984.

Noordtzij, Arie, *God's Word and the Testimony of the Ages*. Kampen, Netherlands, 1924.

Northrup, Bernard, *Recognizing Messiah in the Psalms*. Fairfax, VA: Xulon Press, 2003.

O'Brien, J. and Major W. *In the Beginning, Creation Myths From Ancient Mesopotamia, Israel and Greece*. Chico, CA: Scholars Press, 1982.

O'Brien, Mark, *The Unification of Stephen Hawking*, www.pacificnews.org/marko/hawking. Osborne, Grant R., *The Hermeneutical Spiral: A Comprehensive Introduction to Biblical Interpretation*. Downers Grove, IL: InterVarsity Press, 1997.

Osgood, J., "The Date of Noah's Flood" *Creation* 4(1):10-13, March 1981.

Packer, J. I., "Infallible Scripture and the Role of Hermeneutics," in D. A. Carson and John D. Woodbridge, eds., *Scripture and Truth*.

Patten, Donald Wesley, *The Biblical Flood and the Ice Epoch*. Seattle: Pacific Meridian Publishing Co., 1966.

Payne, J. Barton, "Theistic Evolution and the Hebrew of Genesis 1—2," *Bulletin of the Evangelical Theological Society, 8 (1965)*, 85-90.

Payne, J. Barton, *The Theology of the Older Testament*. Grand Rapids: Zondervan, , 1962

Pember, G. H., *Earth's Earliest Ages*. Hodder and Stoughton, 1876; Grand Rapids: Kregel, 1975.

Piper, John, *What Jesus Demands from the World*. Wheaton: Crossway, 2006.

Popper, Karl, *The Poverty of Historicism*. London: Routledge Publishers, 1957.

Poythress, Vern S., "Adequacy of Language and Accommodation," in E. D. Radmacher and R. D. Preus, eds. *Hermeneutics, Inerrancy and the Bible.* Grand Rapids: Zondervan, 1984.

Pratico, Gary D. and Miles V. Van Pelt, *Basics of Biblical Hebrew* (Grand Rapids: Zondervan, 2001),

Rainey, Anson F., and R. Stephen Notley, *The Sacred Bridge.* Jerusalem: Carta, 2006.

Ridderbos, N. H., *Is There a Conflict Between Genesis 1 and Natural Science?* Grand Rapids: Eerdmans, 1957.

Robinson, R.B., "Literary Functions of the Genealogies of Genesis," *CBQ* 48 (1986), 595-608.

Rooker, Mark, "Genesis 1:1–3: Creation of Recreation," *Bibliotheca Sacra* 149:595 July 1992; 149:596 October 1992.

Ross, Allen P., *Creation and Blessing* (Grand Rapids: Baker Books, 1998.

______, "Proverbs." *Expositor's Bible Commentary*, Vol. 5. Grand Rapids: Zondervan, 1991.

Ross, Hugh, *Beyond the Cosmos,* Colorado Springs: NavPress, 1996.

______, *Creation and Time,* Colorado Springs: NavPress, 1994.

______, *Creation as Science,* Colorado Springs: NavPress, 2005.

______, *The Creator and the Cosmos,* Colorado Springs: NavPress, 1993.

______, *The Fingerprint of God,* Colorado Springs: NavPress, 1989.

______, *The Genesis Question,* Colorado Springs: NavPress, 1998.

______, *A Matter of Days.* Colorado Springs: NavPress, 2004.

Ross, Hugh and Gleason Archer, "The Day Age View" in David G. Hagopian, ed., *The Genesis Debate.* Mission Viejo: Crux Press, 2001.

Ross, Hugh and Fazale Rana, *Origins of Life.* Colorado Springs: NavPress, 2004.

______, *Who Was Adam, Origins of Life.* Colorado Springs: NavPress, 2005.

Rusch, Wilbert H., *Origins: What is at Stake?* St. Joseph, MO: Creation Research Society Books, 1991.

Ryan, William and Walter Pitman, *Noah's Flood.* New York: Simon and Schuster, 1998.

Sarfati, Jonathan, *Refuting Evolution 2*, Green Forest, AR: Master Books, 2002.

Sagan, Carl, *Cosmos*. New York: Random House, 2002.

Sailhamer, John, "Genesis" in *the Expositor's Bible Commentary* (Grand Rapids: Zondervan, 1990

______, *Genesis Unbound*. Sisters, OR: Multnomah, 1996.

______, *The Pentateuch as Narrative*. Grand Rapids: Zondervan, 1992.

Schroeder, Gerald L., Genesis and the Big Bang. New York: Bantam, 1990.

______, *The Hidden Face of God*. New York: Touchstone, 2002.

______, *The Science of God*. New York: Broadway Books, 1997.

Snelling, Andrew, "Geological Conflict," *Creation ex Nihilo* 22(2):44-47, March 2000.

Stambaugh, Jim, "The Days of Creation, A Semantic Approach," *The Journal of Ministry and Theology* 7:2, Fall 2003.

Steinberg, Naomi, "The Genealogical Framework of the Family Stories in Genesis," *Semeia* 46 (1989), 41-50.

Sewell, Curt, "The Tablet Theory of Genesis Authorship," *Bible and Spade*, 7:1, Winter 1994.

Tate, Marvin E., *Psalms 51−100* of Word Biblical Commentary, Gordon Wenham, ed. Waco, TX: Word Books, 1990.

Thiselton, Anthony C., *The Two Horizons*. Grand Rapids: Wm. B. Eerdmans, 1980.

Throntveit, Mark A., "Are the Events in the Genesis Creation Account Set Forth in Chronological Order? No," in Ronald Youngblood, *The Genesis Debate*. Eugene, OR: Wipf and Stock Publishers, 1999, 36-55.

Tsumura, David Toshio, *The Earth and the Waters in Genesis 1 and 2: A Linguistic Investigation*, JSOT Supplement Series 83, Sheffield: JSOT, 1989, 33–34.

Merrill Unger, "Rethinking the Genesis Account of Creation" *Bibliotheca Sacra,* 115:457 Jan. 1958.

Van Bebber, Mark and Paul S. Taylor, *Creation & Time: A Report on the Progressive*

________, *Creationist Book by Hugh Ross*. Gilbert, AZ: Films for Christ, 1994.

Van Till, Howard J., *The Fourth Day*. Grand Rapids: William B. Eerdmans Pub. Co., 1986.

VanGemeren, Willem A., *New International Dictionary of Old Testament Theology and Exegesis*. Grand Rapids: Zondervan Publishing House, 1997.

Vanhoozer, Kevin J., *Is There a Meaning in This Text?* Grand Rapids: Zondervan, 1998

Waltke, Bruce, *Creation and Chaos*. Portland, OR: Western Conservative Baptist Seminary, 1974

________, "The Creation Account in Genesis 1:1–3," *Bibliotheca Sacra*. 132:525 (Jan. 1975), 25-36.

________, "The Creation Account in Genesis 1:1–3," *Bibliotheca Sacra*. 132:526 (April 1975), 136-144.

________, "The Creation Account in Genesis 1:1–3," *Bibliotheca Sacra*. 132:527 (July 1975), 216-228.

________, "The Creation Account in Genesis 1:1–3," *Bibliotheca Sacra*. 132:528 (Oct. 1975), 327-342.

________, "The Creation Account in Genesis 1:1–3," *Bibliotheca Sacra*. 132:529 (Jan. 1975), 28-41.

Waltke, Bruce K. and Cathi Fredricks. *Genesis*. Grand Rapids: Zondervan, 2001.

Waltke Bruce K., and M. O'Connor, *Biblical Hebrew Syntax*. Winona Lake, IN: Eisenbrauns, 1990.

Ward, Peter and Donald Brownlee, *Rare Earth*. New York: Copernicus Books, 2004.

Wenham, Gordon J., *Genesis 1—15,* Word Biblical Commentary. Waco, TX: Word Books, 1987.

Westermann, Claus, *Genesis 1—11: A Commentary*. Minneapolis: Augsburg, 1984-86.

________, *Isaiah 40—66*, OTL. Philadelphia: Westminster, 1969.

Whitcomb, John C. and Henry Morris, *The Genesis Flood*. Philadelphia: Presbyterian and Reformed Publishing Co., 1964.

Whitcomb, John C., *The Early Earth,* rev. ed. Grand Rapids: Baker, 1986.

______, "The Science of Historical Geology," Westminster Theological Journal, 36:1 (Fall. 1973), 65-73. (A response to Davis A. Young)

______, *The World That Perished.* Grand Rapids: Baker, 1988.

Wilder-Smith, A. E., *The Creation of Life.* Costa Mesa, CA: Word for Today, 1988.

Williams, Ronald J., *Hebrew Syntax.* University of Toronto Press, 1988.

Wiseman, P. J., *Creation Revealed in Six Days.* London: Marshall, Morgan & Scott, 1948.

______, *New Discoveries in Babylon about Genesis.* London: Marshall, Morgan & Scott, Ltd., 1936).

Wiseman P. J., and D.J. Wiseman, *Ancient Records and the Structure of Genesis: A Case for Literary Unity.* Nashville: Thomas Nelson, Inc., 1985.

Ludwig Wittgenstein, *On Certainty.* New York: Harper Torchbooks, 1969.

Wood, Leon, "Hosea" in Frank Gaebelein, *The Expositor's Bible Commentary*, Vol. 7. Grand Rapids: Zondervan, 1985.

Yahuda, A. S., *Language of the Pentateuch in its Relation to Egyptian, Part 1.* London: Oxford University Press, 1933.

Young, Edward J., *Studies in Genesis One.* Philadelphia: Presbyterian and Reformed, 1973.

Youngblood, Ronald, ed., *The Genesis Debate.* Grand Rapids: Baker, 1990.

Endnotes

Chapter 0   Seeking the Origin of the Universe

1 "Almagest." *Encyclopædia Britannica*. Chicago: Encyclopædia Britannica, 2007.

2   Some Bible quotes are translated from Hebrew or Greek by the author. Feel free to check my translation from the Hebrew or Greek.

3   Hebrew does not have tense but has aspect, so I may leave some Hebrew verbs as English participles rather than artificially indicating past or present tense.

4   "Rømer, Ole Christensen," Encyclopædia Britannica. *Encyclopædia Britannica 2007 Deluxe Edition* (Chicago: Encyclopædia Britannica, 2007); "Rømer and the Finite Speed of Light," http://www.physicstoday.org/vol-57/iss-12/p16.html (December 2004).

5   Australian Barry Setterfield claimed that early measurements were *faster* than today's measurements, indicating that light has been slowing down. He said light traveled so fast in the early universe after its creation about 6,000 years ago that the light from distant galaxies 10 billion light-years away is not 10 billion years old but only 6,000 years old. Contra Setterfield, this earliest measurement of light was *slower,* not faster, than today's measurements. Setterfield selected measurements that were faster and left out the ones that were slower. His claim is based on selective data, so his conclusion that light is slowing down is faulty. Also, since we have developed accurate measurement instruments, light speed has remained the same.

6   "The Supernova Cosmology Project," Berkeley, CA, www.oarval.org/SCPen. htm.

7   George Smoot and Kay Davidson, *Wrinkles in Time,* (New York: Avon Books, 1993).

8   Hugh Ross, *The Fingerprint of God* (Orange, CA: Promise Publishing Co., 1989).

9   The idea of the hermeneutical spiral is that as Christians study the Bible, share their findings, and discuss differences, together we spiral in a little closer to understanding correctly difficult Bible texts. Grant R. Osborne, *The Hermeneutical Spiral: A Comprehensive Introduction to Biblical Interpretation* (Downers Grove, IL: InterVarsity Press, 1997).

10   Osborne, *Hermeneutical Spiral.*

11   Bruce K. Waltke, "The Creation Account in Genesis 1:1–3, Part IV: The Theology of Genesis 1" *Bibliotheca Sacra* 132:528 (Oct. –Dec. 1975), 338.

12   Three forms of this theory are based on three of the four grammatical constructions of Genesis 1:1: (1) Genesis 1:1 is a dependent clause temporally subordinate to the main clause of 1:2. "In the beginning when God created the heavens and the earth, the earth was a formless void" (NRSV). (2) Genesis 1:1 is a dependent clause temporally subordinate to the main clause of 1:3 when God began creating, so 1:2 is a parenthesis of earth's chaos before God began creating. "When God began to create heaven and earth—the earth being unformed and void, with darkness over the surface of the deep and a wind from God sweeping over the water—God said, 'Let there be light'" (*Hebrew-English Tanakh*, 2003). (3) Genesis 1:1 is a title or summary of 1:2–31, so the creation began in 1:2 with God creatively entering the preexisting chaotic earth to change it to the orderly earth (Bruce K. Waltke, *Genesis: A Commentary* [Grand Rapids: Zondervan, 2001], 58). These pre-creation chaos theories are answered by Paul Copan and William Lane Craig in *Creation out of Nothing* (Grand Rapids: Baker, 2004). Copan and Craig defend the traditional fourth option. (4) Genesis 1:1 is an independent clause that in the beginning God created *ex nihilo* of the heavens and earth,

followed by the six days. I find this fourth view fits the grammar of Genesis 1:1–3 and the sense of the whole chapter.

13	Most theories would agree that Genesis 1:1 has an introductory quality as well as being the initial creation act, but in this theory the acts of God are only in 1:2–31. Genesis 1:1 merely titles those acts, rather than being the initial *ex nihilo* creation.

14	Bruce K. Waltke, "The Creation Account in Genesis 1:1–3, Part III: The Initial Chaos Theory and the Pre-creation chaos theory," *Bibliotheca Sacra* 132:527 (July–Sep. 1975), 216–228; Bruce K. Waltke, *Genesis: A Commentary* (Grand Rapids: Zondervan, 2001), 55–78.

15	Lee Irons & Meredith Kline, "The Framework View," in David G. Hagopian, ed., *The Genesis Debate* (Mission Viejo, CA: Crux Press, 2001); Meredith Kline, "Space and Time in the Genesis Cosmogony," *Perspectives on Science and Christian Faith* (1996), 48; Arie Noordtzij, *God's Word and the Testimony of the Ages.*

16	Henry Morris, *Biblical Creationism* (Grand Rapids: Baker Book House, 1994), 20.

17	Morris, *Biblical Creationism*, 19. Morris claims that this "earth" was the matter throughout the "darkness of space" that was "unformed," so this theory appears to be a special case of the initial chaos theory.

18	Ken Ham, Andrew Snelling, and Carl Wieland, *The Answers Book* (Green Forest, AR: Master Books, 1990), 89.

19	Morris, *Biblical Creationism*, 20.

20	Some still hold to 4004 BC, but many allow 6,000 to as much as 10,000 years ago.

21	Hugh Ross, *The Genesis Question* (Colorado Springs: NavPress, 1998).

22	Gerald L. Schroeder, *Genesis and the Big Bang* (New York: Bantam Books, 1990), 49–53.

23	P. J. Wiseman, *Creation Revealed in Six Days* (London: Marshall, Morgan & Scott, 1948).

24	G. H. Pember, *Earth's Earliest Ages* (Hodder and Stoughton, 1876; reprinted by Kregel, 1975); Arthur C. Custance, *Without Form and Void* (Brookville, Canada: self-published, 1970); critiqued by Weston W. Fields, *Unformed and Unfilled* (Phillipsburg: Presbyterian & Reformed Publishing Company, 1976).

25	John H. Sailhamer, *Genesis Unbound* (Sisters, OR: Multnomah, 1996), 42.

26	Sailhamer, *Unbound*, 89.

27	Spergel, D. N.; et al., "First-Year Wilkinson Microwave Anisotropy Probe (WMAP)," *Astrophysical Journal Supplement Series* 148, 2003, 175–194.

28	Dalrymple, G.B., *The Age of the Earth* (Palo Alto: Stanford Press, 1991).

29	Hugh Ross, *The Genesis Question* (Colorado Springs: NavPress, 1998); *Creation and Time* (Colorado Springs: NavPress, 1994).

30	Schroeder, *Big Bang.*

31	P. J. Wiseman, *Creation Revealed in Six Days* (London: Marshall, Morgan, & Scott, 1948); *Clues to Creation in Genesis* (London: Marshall, Morgan, & Scott, 1977).

32	Bruce K. Waltke, "The Creation Account in Genesis 1:1–3, Parts I–V, *Bibliotheca Sacra* 132:525, 526, 527, 528. 529, 1975–1976; *Creation and Chaos* (Portland, OR: Western Conservative Baptist Seminary).

33	John Sailhamer, *The Pentateuch as Narrative* (Grand Rapids: Zondervan, 1992); "Genesis" in *the Expositor's Bible Commentary* (Grand Rapids: Zondervan, 1990); *Genesis Unbound* (Sisters, OR: Multnomah Press, 1996).

Chapter 1   Pre-Creation Chaos Theory

34 Michael S. Heiser, "Creation, Evolution, Intelligent Design, and the Replicating Universe: What Does the Hebrew Text of Genesis 1 Allow?" Michael S. Heiser, academic editor of Logos Bible Software. I highly recommend Logos Bible Software for serious study of the Bible.

35   Waltke refers to Gunkel in Waltke, "Genesis 1:1–3," Part I, 26; Hermann Gunkel, *Schöpfung und Chaos* (Göttingen: Vanenhoeck und Ruprecht, 1921).

36   Waltke, "Genesis 1:1–3," Part III, 219, quoting Plessis, *Supplément*, 716.

37   Waltke, "Genesis 1:1–3," Part III, 218; quoting John Skinner, *A Critical and Exegetical Commentary on Genesis* (Edinburg: T. & T. Clark, 1910, 14.

38   Gordon J. Wenham, *Word Biblical Commentary, Genesis 1 — 15* (Waco: Word Books, 1987), 13; Allen P. Ross, *Creation and Blessing* (Grand Rapids: Baker Books, 1998), 105–106.

39   Waltke, "Genesis 1:1–3," Part II, 121.

40   Bruce K. Waltke, "The Creation Account in Genesis 1:1–3, Part IV" *Bibliotheca Sacra* 132:528 (Oct. 1975), 338.

41   Waltke, "Genesis 1:1-3," Part II, 142–143.

42   Bruce Waltke, *Creation and Chaos* (Portland, OR: Western Conservative Baptist Seminary, 1974), 24

43   Waltke, "Genesis 1:1–3," Part III, 221. Waltke continues, "It is concluded, therefore, that though it is possible to take verse 2 as a circumstantial clause on syntactical grounds, it is impossible to do so on philological grounds, and that it seems unlikely it should be so construed on theological grounds, for it makes God the Creator of disorder, darkness, and deep, a situation not tolerated in the perfect cosmos and never said to have been called into existence by the Word of God." What Waltke means by "it is possible to take verse 2 as a circumstantial clause on syntactical grounds" is Genesis 1:2 appears to describe the unfinished circumstances of the earth after its creation in 1:1. *Gesenius' Hebrew Grammar* describes "verse 2 as a circumstantial clause with verse 1" (Kautzsch, *Gesenius*, 455, # 142c). Possible grammatically, but "impossible" by the words and logic, claims Waltke.

44   Waltke, "Genesis 1:1–3," Part III, 216.

45   Waltke, "Genesis 1:1–3," Part III, 221.

46   Waltke, "Genesis 1:1–3," Part III. 221.

47   Waltke, "Genesis 1:1–3," Part III, 219, quoting Plessis, *Supplément*, 716.

48   Waltke, *Chaos*, 19.

49   Bruce K. Waltke, "The Creation Account in Genesis 1:1–3, Part II: The Restitution Theory," *Bibliotheca Sacra* 132:526 (April–June 1975), 136.

50   Waltke, "Genesis 1:1–3," Part II, 142.

51   Waltke, "Genesis 1:1–3," Part IV 339.

52   Waltke, "Genesis 1:1–3," Part III, 221.

53   Waltke, "Genesis 1:1–3," Part IV, 338.

54   Ibid.

55   Waltke, "Genesis 1:1–3," Part I, 33.

56   Waltke, *Chaos,* 10.

57   Waltke, *Chaos,* 15.

58   Ibid.

59   Waltke, "Genesis 1:1–3," Part II, 136.

60   Waltke, "Genesis 1:1-3" Part III, 219, quoting Plessis, *Supplément*, 716.

61   Waltke, "Genesis 1:1–3," Part II, 142.

62   Bruce K. Waltke, *Genesis: A Commentary* (Grand Rapids: Zondervan, 2001), 55.

63   Waltke's claim is that Genesis 1:2 is a set of three dependant clauses that modify Genesis 1:3 by describing the chaotic status of earth and so functioning as a parenthetical setup for the first creative act, which is in 1:3. For an even more precise explanation, see Michael Heiser, "Creation, Evolution, Intelligent Design, and the Replicating Universe: What Does the Hebrew Text of Genesis Allow?"

64   Michael Heiser, personal email June 6, 2008.

65   Heiser, "What Does the Hebrew Text of Genesis Allow?" I have simplified and slightly modified his analysis. Any errors are mine.

66   Waltke, *Genesis*, 56.

67   J. P. Moreland, "What Is Truth and Why Does It Matter?" from Hugh Ross, *Creation as Science* (Colorado Springs: NavPress, 2006), 23.

68   Waltke, "Genesis 1:1–3," Part II, 142–143.

69   Waltke, "Genesis 1:1–3," Part II, 142.

70   Ibid.

71   Ibid.

72   Waltke, "Genesis 1:1–3," Part III, 219, quoting Plessis, *Supplément,* 716.

73   John Calvin, *Genesis* (Edinburgh: Banner of Truth, 1965), 70.

74   Waltke, "Genesis 1:1–3," Part III, 221.

75   Waltke, "Genesis 1:1–3," Part IV, 338.

76   Ibid.

77   Waltke, *Chaos,* 15.

78   R. Laird Harris, Gleason Archer, and Bruce Waltke, *Theological Wordbook of the Old Testament* (Chicago: Moody Press, 1980), 127.

79   Robert Chisholm, *From Exegesis to Exposition* (Grand Rapids: Baker, 1998) 124.

80   Waltke, "Genesis 1:1-3" Part III, 219, quoting Plessis, *Supplément*, 716.

81   Ibid.

82   Bruce Waltke, *Genesis, A Commentary* (Grand Rapids: Zondervan, 2001), 59; Waltke, "Genesis 1:1–3," Part III, 218–221. Wenham, *Word Biblical Commentary, Genesis 1–15*, 13; Allen Ross, *Creation and Blessing* 105–106.

83   John Sailhamer, *The Pentateuch as Narrative: The New International Commentary on the Old Testament* (Grand Rapids: Zondervan, 1992), 84.

84   U. Cassuto, *A Commentary o the Book of Genesis*, trans. Israel Abrahams, 2 vol. (Jerusalem: Magnes Press, 1961), 1:20,22.

85   Waltke, "Genesis 1:1–3," Part III, 219, quoting Plessis, *Supplément*, 716.

86   Waltke, "Genesis 1:1-3" Part III, 219, quoting Plessis, *Supplément*, 716.

Chapter 2   Title or Summary Theory

87   Don Batten, "Soft Gap Sophistry," *Creation* 26:3 (June 2004), 44–47.

88   Waltke, "Genesis 1:1–3," Part III, 223.

89   Waltke, "Genesis 1:1–3," Part III, 225.

90   Heiser, "What Does the Hebrew Text of Genesis 1 Allow?"

91   Tanakh, Jewish Publications Society, 1985.

92   Waltke, "Genesis 1:1-3" Part III, 219, quoting Plessis, *Supplément*, 716.

93   Waltke, "Genesis 1:1–3," Part III, 225–226.

94   The technical way of saying the above is this: If Genesis 1:1 is a title, it is structurally unrelated to 1:2 or 1:3. Genesis 1:2 is subordinate to and parenthetical to 1:3. Genesis 1:2 gives details of the chaotic status quo leading up to the first creative event, which is in 1:3. So Genesis 1:2 and 1:3 are structurally unrelated to 1:1. Titles are structurally unrelated so are not modified by other sentences. Because Genesis 1:2 does not modify 1:1, 1:1 is a title. For a better analysis, see Heiser, "What does the Hebrew Text of Genesis 1 Allow?"

95   Waltke, "Genesis 1:1–3," Part III, 226.

96   Waltke, "Genesis 1:1–3," Part IV, 341; Claus Westermann, *The Genesis Accounts of Creation* (Philadelphia: Fortress Press, 1964), 7.

97   Waltke, *Genesis*, 58. For a fuller explanation see *Genesis*, pages 56-58.

98   Pember, *Ages*, 31.

99   Pember, *Ages*, 31–32.

100   Sailhamer, *Unbound*, 63-64.

101   Sailhamer, *Unbound*, 65.

102   Waltke, "Genesis 1:1–3," Part III, 225–226.

103   E. Kautzsch, *Gesenius' Hebrew Grammar* (Oxford: Clarendon Press, 1990), #114h, 348.

104   Willem VanGemeren, *New International Dictionary of Old Testament Theology and Exegesis*, Vol. 2 (Grand Rapids: Zondervan, 1997), H3983, 641.

105   Bruce Waltke, "Genesis 1:1–3," Part III, 226.

106   Mark Rooker, "Creation or Re-creation?", 414.

107   P. J. Wiseman, *Clues to the Creation in Genesis* (London: Marshall, Morgan & Scott, 1977), 34ff.

108   Sailhamer, *Unbound*, 102.

109   Copan and Craig, *Creation out of Nothing*.

110   Waltke, "Genesis 1:1-3" Part III, 219, quoting Plessis, *Supplément*, 716.

Chapter 3   Literary Framework Theory

111   Meredith G. Kline and Lee Irons, "The Framework View," in David G. Hagopian, ed., *The Genesis Debate* (Mission Viejo, CA: Crux Press), 224.

112   Kline, "Framework," 218.

113   Kline, "Framework," 234.

114   Kline, "Framework," 217.

115   Kline, "Framework," 218.

116   Greg Bahnsen responds that a goal of Bible interpretation is circular reasoning.

117   Dan McCartney and Charles Clayton, *Let the Reader Understand: A Guide to Interpreting and Applying the Bible* (Wheaton, IL: Victor Books, 1994).

118   Kline, "Framework," 218.

119   Kline, "Framework," 218.

120   Kline, "Framework," 217.

121   Henri Blocher, *In the Beginning: The Opening Chapters of Genesis*, trans. David G. Preston (Downers Grove, IL: InterVarsity Press, 1984), 50.

122   Kline, "Framework," 219.

123   Kline, "Framework," 218.

124   Kline, "Framework," 227.

125   Kline, "Framework," 219.

126   Kline, "Framework," 220–221.

127   Kline, "Framework," 233.

128   Kline, "Framework," 221.

129   Kline, "Framework," 219.

130   Kline, "Framework," 227.

131   Kline, "Framework," 251.

132   Kline, "Framework," 224.

133   Kline, "Framework," 224. The sky and seas in day two, then reversal to sea creatures and winded creatures in day five is his, reflecting the Bible text.

134   Kline, "Framework," 244.

135   Henri Blocher, *In the Beginning: The Opening Chapters of Genesis*, trans. David G. Preston (Downers Grove, IL: InterVarsity Press, 1984), 50.

136   Meredith G. Kline, "Because It Had Not Rained," *Westminster Theological Journal* 20:2 (May 1958), 149.

137   Dahood translated the same rare word in Job 36:27, the only other occurrence, as "rain-cloud." Michael Dahood, "Eblaite *i-du* and Hebrew *'ed*, 'Rain-Cloud,'" *Catholic Biblical Quarterly 43* (1981), 534–538; in Kline, "Framework," 231.

138   Kline, "Framework," 232.

139   Mark Futato, "Because It Had Rained," *Westminster Theological Journal* 60:1, 4.

140   Kline, "Not Rained," 150.

141   Kline, "Framework," 232.

142   Kline, "Framework," 232.

143   Kline, "Framework," 233–234.

144   Duncan, "24-Hour View," 53.

145   Lee Irons, "Animal Death Before the Fall: What Does the Bible Say?" www.upper-register.com.

146   Kline, "Framework," 239.

147   Kline, "Framework," 243.

148   Kline, "Framework," 241.

149   Kline, "Framework," 244.

150   Kline, "Framework," 218.

151   Kline, "Framework," 244.

152   Kline, "Framework," 217.

153   Kline, "Framework," 220–221.

154   Kline, "Framework," 244.

155   Kline, "Framework," 219.

156   Kline, "Framework," 251.

157   Kline, "Framework," 224. I have switched sky and seas to match the creatures.

158   Henri Blocher, *In the Beginning: The Opening Chapters of Genesis*, trans. David G. Preston (Downers Grove, IL: InterVarsity Press, 1984), 50.

159   Kline, "Framework," 218.

160   Kline, "Framework," 234.

161   Kline, "Framework," 218.

162   Kline, "Framework," 227.

163   Kline, "Framework," 244.

164   Kline, "Framework," 230.

165   Kline, "Framework," 232.

166   Duncan, "24-Hour View," 53.

167   Kline, "Framework," 224.

168   Although I put this idea together, Wiseman, Westermann, Steinberg, and Kline contributed. None contributed overwhelmingly, so I did not add one of our names.

Chapter 4   Initial Chaos Creation Theory

169 Mark Rooker, "Genesis 1:1–3: Creation or Re-creation?" Part I, *Bibliotheca Sacra 149:595* July 1992, 318; Mark Rooker does not fully hold the initial chaos view himself. He correctly rejects the idea that *tōhû vᵃbōhû* means chaos. He may hold almost a two-stage creation.

170   Rooker, Part I, 319.

171   John Calvin, *Genesis*, (Edinburgh: Banner of Truth Trust, 1847), 74, "The world had been *begun* by the same efficacy of the Word by which it was *completed*" (emphasis his). By "*begun*," Calvin was speaking of the beginning in Genesis 1:1 when "the world was not perfected at its very commencement" (69–70). By "completed," Calvin was speaking of the six days' work. Mark Rooker also says Calvin espoused the initial chaos theory, although Rooker is not specific which version. Rooker, Part I, 318.

172   Rooker, Part I, 317.

173   Ibid., 318.

174   Mark Rooker, "Genesis 1:1–3: Creation or Re-creation?" Part II, *Bibliotheca Sacra 149:596* October 1992, 425.

175   Rooker, Part I, 322.

176   Rooker, Part II, 415, quoting from Anton Pearson, "An Exegetical Study of Genesis 1:1–3," *Bethel Seminary Quarterly 2* (1953):20–22.

177   Rooker, Part II, 416-419; quoting Jacob Newman, *The Commentary of Nahmanides on Genesis Chapters 1—6* (Leiden: Brill, 1960), 33.

178   Rooker, Part II, 420

179   Ibid., 421–422.

180   Rooker, Part I, 319.

181   Rooker, Part I, 318–319.

182   Rooker, Part I, 320.

183   Bruce K. Waltke, "The Creation Account in Genesis 1:1–3, Parts I–V, *Bibliotheca Sacra* 132: 527, 219; *Creation and Chaos* (Portland, OR: Western Conservative Baptist Seminary); Gordon J. Wenham, *Word Biblical Commentary, Genesis 1—15* (Waco: Word Books, 1987), 13; Brevard S. Childs, "The Enemy from the North and the Chaos Tradition," *Journal of Biblical Literature* 78 (1959): 197; Allen P. Ross, *Creation and Blessing* (Grand Rapids: Baker Books, 1998), 105–106.

184   Rooker, Part I, 318–319.

185   Rooker, Part II, 411.

186   Weston Fields, *Unformed and Unfilled: A Critique of the Gap Theory* (Collinsville, IL: Burgener Enterprises, 1994); Mark Rooker, "Creation or Re-creation?" Part I, 316–318; also see Waltke, "Genesis 1:1-3," Part II, 136-144;.

187   Ibid., 427.

188   Rooker, Part I, 319.

189   Ibid., 318.

190   Rooker, Part II, 425.

191   Rooker, Part I, 319.

192   Ibid., 319.

193   Ibid., 323.

194   Rooker, Part 1, 321, quoting David Toshio Tsumura, *The Earth and the Waters in Genesis 1 and 2: A Linguistic Investigation*, JSOT Supplement Series 83 (Sheffield: JSOT Press, 1989), 155–156.

195   Rooker, Part 1, 322.

196   Rooker, 322, quoting Tsumura, *The Earth*, 24.

197   Rooker, Part I, 323.

198   Cassuto, *Genesis,* 20.

199   Calvin, *Genesis*, 73.

200   Rooker, Part I, 319.

201   Rooker, Part II, 423.

202   Ibid., 427.

203   Rooker, Part I, 323.

204   Rooker, Part II, 411.

205   Mark Rooker, "Genesis 1:1–3: Creation or Re-creation?" Part II, *Bibliotheca Sacra 149:596* October 1992, 425.

Chapter 5   Young Earth Scientific Creationism Theory

206   "The young earth Creationist (YEC) movement began in the early 1960's. Many consider that it traces specifically to the publication of *The Genesis Flood*, by John Whitcomb and Henry Morris in 1961." Thomas Fowler and Daniel Kuebler, *The Evolution Controversy* (Grand Rapids: Baker Academic, 2007), 191. I do not agree completely with this quote because the idea of a young earth is not recent. Nor is citing Exod. 20:11 for there having been six literal days. What seems recent is the YEC widespread claim by that Gen. 1:1 was *in* the six days based on Exod. 20:11.

207   Whitcomb and Morris, *The Genesis Flood,* xx.

208   Henry Morris, *Scientific Creationism* (San Diego: Creation-Life Pub., 1974).

209   Alan Cutler, *The Seashell on the Mountaintop* (New York: Dutton, 2003), 60.

210   Henry Morris, *Biblical Creationism* (Grand Rapids: Baker Book, 1994), 17.

211   Morris, *Genesis Record*, 41.

212   Henry M. Morris, *Biblical Creationism*, 17.

213   Don Batten, "Soft Gap Sophistry," *Creation* 26:3 (June 2004), 44–47.

214   Morris, *The Genesis Record,* 42.

215   Ibid., 37.

216   Jim Stambaugh, "The Days of Creation, A Semantic Approach," *The Journal of Ministry and Theology* 7:2, Fall 2003, 42–68.

217   Henry Morris, *Biblical Creationism*, 19.

218   Henry Morris, *The Genesis Record*, 42.

219   Ken Ham, *Dinosaurs of Eden* (Green Forest, AR: Master Books, 2001), 9, 10.

220   Ken Ham, "Did Jesus say He created in six days?" August 25, 2001, http://www.answersingenesis.org/us/newsletters/0801lead.asp.

221   Don Batten, "'Soft' gap sophistry," *Creation,* 26:3 (June 2004), 26:3, 46.

222   Ken Ham, Andrew Snelling, Carl Wieland, *The Answers Book*, 170.

223   Ibid.

224   Terry Mortenson, "But from the beginning of . . . the institution of marriage?" AiG–USA, www.answersingenesis.org/docs2004/1101ankerberg_response.asp. The original article is at www.johnankerberg.org/Articles/science/SC0305W3.htm.

225   Morris, *Biblical Creationism,* 17.

226   Ken Ham, *Dinosaurs of Eden* (Green Forest, AR: Master Books, 2001), 9, 10.

227   Morris, *Record,* 41.

228   Morris, *Record,* 40.

229   Ibid., 41.

230   Morris, *Biblical Creationism,* 17.

231   DeRemer, "Days 1-4," 71.

232   Frank DeRemer, "Young biosphere, old universe?" *Technical Journal* 19:2, 56.

233   Ibid., 54, 55.

234   Henry Morris, *The Genesis Record,* (Grand Rapids: Baker Book House, 1994), 39-42.

235   Morris, *Genesis Record,* 41.

236   Morris, *Genesis Record,* 41.

237   Morris, *Biblical Creationism,* 17.

238   Ken Ham, *Dinosaurs of Eden* (Green Forest, AR: Master Books, 2001), 9, 10.

239   DeRemer, "Young Biosphere," 55.

240   Frank DeRemer, "Days 1-4" *Technical Journal* 21:3, 73.

241   DeRemer, "Young Biosphere, 50.

242   DeRemer, "Days 1-4," 73.

243   Morris, *The Genesis Record,* 51.

244   Ibid., 50.

245   DeRemer, Days 1-4," 75.

246   Morris, *Genesis Record,* 65, 66.

247   Setterfield apparently used selected measurements that were faster and left out the slower. Russell Humphreys in *Starlight and Time* claimed relativity allows starlight to be only 6,000 years old. Samuel R. Conner and Hugh Ross, experts in cosmology and theoretical physics, explain, "Feedback [to *Starlight and Time*] has been forthcoming, and, to our knowledge, it has been uniformly critical of the theory." (Samuel R. Conner and Hugh Ross, "The Unraveling of Starlight and Time," www.reasons.org/resources/apologetics/unravelling.shtml) Even other YEC advocates have shown that Humphreys' theory does not prove what he proposes (John Byl, "On time dilation in cosmology," *Creation Research Society Quarterly*, vol. 34, number 1, 1977).

248   Morris, *Genesis Record,* 50, 51.

249   Morris, *Biblical Creationism,* 20,

250   Morris, *Genesis Record*, 58.

251   Ibid., 56.

252   Morris, *Biblical Creationism*, 20.

253   Morris, *The Genesis Record*, 58.

254   Ibid., 59.

255   Ibid., 61.

256   Frank DeRemer, "Young biosphere, old universe?" *Technical Journal,* 19:2, 56.

257   Morris, *The Genesis Record*, 61.

258   Ibid., 62.

259   Ibid., 62, 63.

260   Ham, *et. al., The Answers Book,* 93

261   Morris, *Biblical Creationism,* 20.

262   Morris, *The Genesis Record,* 68.

263   Ibid., 73-74.

264   Ibid., 84, 85.

265   Ibid., 79.

266   Ken Ham in "The Great Debate," John Ankerberg Show.

267   Ken Ham, *Dinosaurs in Eden*, 18.

268   Ken Ham, *et. al.*, *The Answers Book*, 103.

269   Morris, *The Genesis Record*, 78.

270   Ibid., 79.

271   Ibid., 79, 80.

272   Ibid., 42–45.

273   Ibid., 45.

274   Answers Magazine, "Taking a Bead on the Old Earth," 3:1 Jan-Mar 2008, 10.

275   Answers Magazine, "What About Distant Starlight," 3:1 Jan-Mar 2008, 43.

276   Henry Morris, *Scientific Creationism*, 210.

277   Philip Henry Gosse, *Omphalos: An Attempt to Untie the Geological Knot* (London: Routledge, no date; republished John Van Voorst, 1957), Volume IV in *The Creation Debate 1813–1870*, ed. David Knight.

278   Whitcomb and Morris, *The Genesis Flood*.

279   Morris, *The Genesis Record*, 66.

280   Morris, *Biblical Creationism*, 65, 66.

281   Jason Lisle, "What about Distant Starlight?" *Answers*, 3:1, 43.

282   Humphreys, *Starlight and Time*, (Colorado Springs: Master Books, 1995).

283   *Starlight and Time* [DVD] (Madison, WI: Evidence Press, 2005).

284   Ham, Snelling, and Wieland, *The Answers Book*, 185.

285   Morris, *Biblical Creationism*, 65, 66.

286   Morris, *Biblical Creationism*, 18; Morris *The Genesis Record*, 26, 28.

287   Morris, *The Genesis Record*, 83.

288   Ibid., 30.

289   Ibid., 25, 26.

290   Morris, *The Genesis Record*, 26.

291   Ibid., 30.

292   Morris, *Biblical Creationism*, 164.

293   Whitcomb and Morris, *The Genesis Flood*, 455.

294   Jonathan Sarfati, *Refuting Compromise* (Green Forest, AR: Master Books), 215.

295   Whitcomb and Morris, *The Genesis Flood*, 239.

296   Ibid., 239.

297   Ibid., 239.

298   Ken Ham, "Why is there death and suffering?" Study Guide 3, AiG.

299   Ken Ham, *Dinosaurs in Eden*, 18.

300   Ken Ham, *et. al.*, *The Answers Book*, 105.

301   "Keeping at Arms Length," AiG, http://www.answersingenesis.org/docs2004/0906arms_length.asp.

302   Whitcomb and Morris, *The Genesis Flood*.

303   J. Osgood, "The Date of Noah's Flood," *Creation* 4(1):10–13, March 1981.

304   Andrew Snelling, "Geological Conflict," *Creation ex Nihilo* 22(2):44–47, March 2000.

305   Whitcomb and Morris, *The Genesis Flood*, 224.

306   Ibid., 224.

307   Ibid., 265, 266.

308   John R. Baumgardner, "3-D numerical investigation of the mantle dynamics associated with the breakup of Pangea," in Flow and Creep in the Solar System: Observations, Modeling, and Theory, D. B. Stone and S. K. Runcorn, eds., NATO ASI Series C, Vol. 391, 207–224, 1993.

309   Whitcomb and Morris, *The Genesis Flood*, 121, 255–257.

310   Donald Wesley Patten, *The Biblical Flood and the Ice Epoch* (Seattle: Pacific Meridian Publishing, 1966).

311   Walt Brown, *In the Beginning* (Phoenix: Center for Scientific Creation), 2001.

312   William Ryan and Walter Pitman, *Noah's Flood* (NY: Simon & Schuster), 1998.

313   Sandra Blakeslee, "Ancient Crash, Epic Wave," *New York Times,* Nov. 14, 2006. The location of Burckle's crater is 30.87° S 61.36°E. It is 31 kilometers wide and would have resulted in massive rain and a huge tsunami. http://www.earth2class.org/ k12/ w9s2005/scioverview.html).

314   Gregory Ryskin, "Megadisasters."

315   Whitcomb and Morris, *The Genesis Flood*, 446–448; John C. Whitcomb, *The Early Earth* (Grand Rapids: Baker Book House, 1972), 26.

316   Jonathan Sarfati, *Refuting Evolution 2,* Green Forest, AR: Master Bks, 2002, 77.

317   Various YEC advocates suggest 2,500 to 15,000.

318   Jonathan Sarfati, *Refuting Evolution 2,* Green, 79.

319   Ibid., 77.

320   Mark Rooker, "Genesis 1:1–3: Creation of Recreation," *Bibliotheca Sacra 149:595; 596 July; October, 1992.*

321   Morris, *The Genesis Record*, 37.

322   Ibid., 42.

323   Ibid., 50.

324   Ibid., 41.

325   Ibid., 41.

326   *Rē'shît* is the root word. *Bᵉrē'shît* is the same word prefixed with *bᵉ*, meaning "in."

327   Henry Morris, *Biblical Creationism*, 19.

328   Ken Ham, *Dinosaurs of Eden* (Green Forest, AR: Master Books, 2001), 9, 10.

329   Ken Ham, "Did Jesus say He created in six days?" August 25, 2001, http://www.answersingenesis.org/us/newsletters/0801lead.asp.

330   Bernard Northrup, *Recognizing Messiah in the Psalms* (Fairfax, VA: Xulon Press, 2003), 94; previously *Finding Christ in the Psalms* (Regular Baptist Press, 1974).

331   Wiseman *Revealed*, 31-32.

332   I have explained this missing "*in*" and עָשָׂה (*'āsâh*) as "worked on" by publicly read papers at Evangelical Theological Society meetings.

333   Don Batten, "'Soft' gap sophistry," *Creation,* 26:3 (June 2004), 26:3, 46.

334   Ham, Snelling, and Wieland, *The Answers Book,* 170.

335   Ken Ham, "Did Jesus say He created in six days?" August 25, 2001, http://www.answersingenesis.org/us/newsletters/0801lead.asp.

336   Don Batten, "'Soft' gap sophistry," *Creation,* 26:3, 46.

337   Ken Ham, "Did Jesus say He created in six days?" August 25, 2001, http://www.answersingenesis.org/us/newsletters/0801lead.asp.

338	Brown, *Hebrew-English Lexicon,* 793; Gesenius, *Hebrew-Chaldee Lexicon,* #6213, 657; VanGemeren, Vol. 3, *Asah,* (#6913), 549; Jeff Benner, *Ancient Hebrew Lexicon of the Bible* (College Station, TX: Virtualbookworm, 2005), #1360, 213.

339	Gesenius, *Hebrew-Chaldee Lexicon,* #6213, 657.

340	BibleWorks for Windows, Strong's, #6213.

341	R. Laird Harris, Gleason Archer, and Bruce Waltke, *Theological Wordbook of the Old Testament* (Chicago: Moody Press, 1980), 701

342	VanGemeren, Vol. 3, *Asah,* (#6913), 549.

343	VanGemeren, Vol. 1, *Bara,* (#1343), 728.

344	Brown, *Hebrew-English Lexicon,* 135.

345	Benner, *Ancient Lexicon,* #1042E, 73.

346	Harris, *Theological Wordbook of the Old Testament,* 127.

347	Frances Brown, S. R. Driver, C. Briggs, *Hebrew-English Lexicon* (Oxford: Oxford University Press), 793, #254, 3.

348	Harris, *Theological Wordbook of the Old Testament,* 127

349	Rooker, Part II, 416-419; quoting Jacob Newman, *The Commentary of Nahmanides on Genesis Chapters 1-6* (Leiden: Brill, 1960), 33.

350	Brown, *Hebrew-English Lexicon,* 793; Gesenius, *Lexicon;* Harris, *Theological Wordbook,* #1708, 701; VanGemeren, Vol. 3, *Asah,* (#6913), 549.

351	Batten, "'Soft' gap sophistry," *Creation,* 26:3, 46.

352	Harris, *Theological Wordbook of the Old Testament,* 127.

353	עֹשֶׂה, participle from עָשָׂה, 'āsâh.

354	Batten, "'Soft' gap sophistry," *Creation,* 26:3, 46.

355	Ham, *et. al., The Answers Book,* 93

356	E. Kautzsch, *Gesenius' Hebrew Grammar* (Oxford: Clarendon Press, 1990), 348.

357	Strongs, # 6213.

358	VanGemeren NIDOTTE, Vol. 3, #6913, 546.

359	Harris, *Theological Wordbook of the Old Testament,* #1708, 701.

360	Ibid., 701.

361	VanGemeren, Vol. 3, *Asah,* (#6913), 549.

362	Harris, *Theological Wordbook of the Old Testament,* 127.

363	Ham, *The Answers Book,* 170.

364	Ibid., 170.

365	Henry Morris, *The Genesis Record,* 42.

366	Terry Mortenson, "But from the beginning of . . . the institution of marriage?"

367	Mortenson, "But from the beginning."

368	Morris, *Genesis Record,* 41.

369	Henry Morris, *The Genesis Record,* 42.

370	B. Aland, K. Aland, M. Black, C.M. Martini, B. M. Metzger, and A. Wikgren, *The Greek New Testament* 4th ed., (Federal Republic of Germany: United Bible Societies, 1993, 1979). The Byzantine text of 19:4 reads ποιήσας instead of κτίσας.

371	Mortenson, "But from the beginning."

372	Ibid.

373	Ibid.

374	Fredrick William Danker, *A Greek-English Lexicon of the New Testament, Third Edition,* (Chicago: University of Chicago Press, 2000), 572-573.

375	Mortenson, "But from the beginning."

376   Ibid.

377   Ibid.

378   Ken Ham, *Dinosaurs of Eden* (Green Forest, AR: Master Books, 2001), 9, 10.

379   Morris, *The Genesis Record*, 41.

380   Morris, *Biblical Creationism*, 17.

381   Donald A. Carson, *Exegetical Fallacies* (Grand Rapids: Baker Book House, 1984), 32–34: "This fallacy occurs when a late use of a word is read back into earlier literature." YEC reads a twentieth century meaning, "space," back into Moses' second millennium BC word הַשָּׁמַיִם—a semantic anachronism fallacy.

382   Morris, *The Genesis Record*, 41.

383   Morris, *Biblical Creationism*, 17.

384   Ken Ham, *Dinosaurs of Eden*, 9, 10.

385   Morris, *The Genesis Record*, 41.

386   Frank DeRemer, "Young biosphere, old universe?" *Technical Journal* 19:2, 56.

387   Morris, *Genesis Record*, 41.

388   Ibid., 41.

389   Ken Ham, *Dinosaurs of Eden*, 9, 10.

390   Frank DeRemer, "Young biosphere, old universe?" 55.

391   Frank DeRemer, "Days 1-4" *Technical Journal* 21:3, 73.

392   Jason Lisle, in "The Great Debate," The John Ankerberg Show.

393   Morris, *Record*, 55.

394   Ibid., 55.

395   Morris, *Genesis Record*, 50.

396   Ibid.

397   DeRemer, "Days 1-4," 75.

398   Morris, *Genesis Record*, 65.

399   *Ha-shāmayim* is not any one component but the sky with its luminaries.

400   Morris, *Genesis Record*, 65.

401   Ibid., 65, 66.

402   Ibid., 65, 66.

403   Ibid., 58.

404   Ibid., 56.

405   Ibid., 61.

406   Ham, *et. al.*, *The Answers Book*, 93

407   Morris, *Biblical Creationism*, 20.

408   Morris, *Genesis Record*, 84, 85.

409   Kline, "Because It Had Not Rained," *Westminster Theological Journal* 20:2, 146–157.

410   Mark D. Futato, "Because it had Rained: A Study of Gen. 2:5–7 with Implications for Genesis 2:4–25 and Genesis 1:1—2:3, *Westminster Theological Journal* 60:1, 1-21.

411   Morris, *Genesis Record*, 79.

412   Morris, *The Genesis Record*, 79, 80.

413   Ham, *Dinosaurs of Eden*, 18.

414   Ankerberg, "The Great Debate."

415   Morris, *The Genesis Record*, 45.

416   Don DeYoung, *Thousands, Not Billions* (Green Forest, AR: Master Books, 2005).

417   Morris, *Scientific Creationism* 210.

418   Carl Wieland, "Starlight and time, A further breakthrough," *Creation*, a publication of Creation Ministries International, 12.

419   God is truth (Psalm 31:50). He does not deceive. He does allow, within His decreed will, delusion. Such delusion is all around us—Mormonism, Islam, agnosticism, addictions, etc. Second Thessalonians 2:11 states, "And for this reason God will send upon them a deluding influence so that they might believe what is false." But the deluding influence that God will send is not of God, but contextually the influence of the "lawless one," generally identified as the Antichrist. We need not shy away from the fact that ultimately God will control even the coming of the Antichrist and his "deluding influence." But God never deceives with something false *from Himself.* The universe as created by God does not deceive. But it may be possible that some perversion by Satan of what God had created may deceive.

420   In John 2, the "ruler of the feast" did not see Jesus perform the miracle, so he did not realize what had happened; but the servants did and likely told him afterward. Such temporary lack of information is not deception.

421   Guillermo Gonzalez, *The Privileged Planet*, 2004.

422   Humphreys, *Starlight and Time*. Recently John Hartnett has added *Starlight, Time and the New Physics* (Atlanta, GA: Creation Book Publishers, 2007).

423   Samuel R. Conner and Hugh Ross, "The Unraveling of Starlight and Time," www.reasons.org/resources/apologetics/unravelling.shtml.

424   Conner and Ross, "The Unraveling of Starlight and Time.

425   John Byl, "On time dilation in cosmology," *Creation Research Society Quarterly*, vol. 34, number 1, 1977; Samuel R. Conner and Don N. Page, "*Starlight and Time* is the big bang," *Technical Journal*, vol. 12, number 2 (1998):174–194.

426   *Starlight and Time* [DVD] (Madison, WI: Evidence Press, 2005).

427   "Rømer, Ole Christensen," *Encyclopædia Britannica 2007* (Chicago: Encyclopædia Britannica, 2007); "Rømer and the Finite Speed of Light," http://www.physicstoday.org/vol-57/iss-12/p16.html (December 2004).

428   DeYoung, *Astronomy and the Bible*, 129.

429   Ken Ham, *The Answers Book,* 185.

430   Ken Ham, *Eden,* 22, 18.

431   Whitcomb and Morris, *The Genesis Flood*, 239.

432   Whitcomb and Morris, *The Genesis Flood*, 455.

433   Morris, *Biblical Creationism*, 164.

434   Ibid.

435   Whitcomb and Morris, *The Genesis Flood*, 239.

436   Ibid., 239.

437   Ken Ham, *et. al.*, *The Answers Book*, 104.

438   "Keeping at Arms Length," AiG, http://www.answersingenesis.org/docs2004/0906arms_length.asp.

439   This sentence combines the ideas that on day one God created "all space (heaven), all time (beginning), and all matter (earth)," and on day four God "placed these 'lights' [sun, moon, and stars] throughout the infinite space of heaven that had been created on Day One, these also being made of the same 'earth' that had been created on Day One" from Morris *Biblical Creationism*, 17, 20; and the "deep" of 1:2 being "all the basic elements sustained in a pervasive watery matrix throughout the darkness of space," Morris, *The Genesis Record*, 50.

440   That God commanded does not necessarily make the result a miracle. God has commanded many non-miraculous events. The question we must ask is, "Does the Bible text indicate a miracle?" A creation event in which the Bible text indicates a miracle should be interpreted as a miracle. But with creation events where the Bible does not indicate a miracle, we may follow Henry Morris's great example regarding the flood and seek means that God may have used. This is the insight of Meredith Kline in "Because It Had Not Rained," *Westminster Theological Journal* 20:2, 146–157. Plants first grew because God caused rain, the normal means of plant growth.

441   Whitcomb and Morris, *The Genesis Flood,* xx.

442   Whitcomb and Morris, *The Genesis Flood,* xxii.

443   I discussed my two stage Biblical creation with one of the two founders, and he was quite open and kind to me about my thinking.

444   Morris, *Biblical Creationism,* 17.

445   Jim Stambaugh, "The Days of Creation, A Semantic Approach," 42–68.

446   Morris, *The Genesis Record,* 68.

447   Ibid., 73-74.

448   Morris, *Biblical Creationism,* 18.

449   Morris, *The Genesis Record,* 83.

450   Ibid., 30.

451   Ibid., 30.

452   Ibid.

453   Whitcomb and Morris, *The Genesis Flood,* 455.

454   Jonathan Sarfarti, *Refuting Compromise,* 214-215.

455   Whitcomb and Morris, *The Genesis Flood.*

456   Hugh Ross criticizes young earth scientific creationism for rejecting evolution on the one hand yet claiming such rapid vast microevolution after the flood on the other hand. Young earth scientific creationism claims rapid microevolution from 2,500 to 8,000 "kinds" on the ark to the present number of species. The rapid microevolution of the present air-breathing land mammals (5,000) and bats (1,000), birds (10,000), reptiles (8,000), and possibly amphibians (6,000)—for a total of 24,000 to 30,000 living twenty-first-century air-breathing land species, plus extinct species from the claimed 2,500 to 8,000 kinds on the ark in less than 5,000 years—seems problematic. I believe there is an answer to this problem that I hope to publish in a Flood book.

457   Mark Rooker, "Genesis 1:1–3: Creation of Recreation," *Bibliotheca Sacra 149:595, 596,* July, October, 1992.

458   Morris, *The Genesis Record,* 42.

459   Ibid., 37.

460   Don Batten, "Soft Gap Sophistry," *Creation* 26:3 (June 2004), 44–47.

461   This sentence is a summary rather than an exact quote from any one YEC author.

462   J. Ligon Duncan III and David W. Hall, "The 24-Hour View," in David G Hagopian, *The Genesis Debate* (Mission Viejo, CA: Crux Press, 2001), 59.

463   They allow "a brief period" of time, for example in the forming of the "seas," 39.

464   Duncan, "24-Hour View," in *Genesis,* 39.

465   Ibid., 37.

466   Ibid., 41.

467   Ibid., 52.

468   Ibid., 54, 55.
469   Ibid., 27.
470   Ibid., 23.
471   Ibid., 38.
472   Ibid., 37.
473   Ibid., 36.
474   Ibid., 38.
475   Ibid., 27.
476   Ibid., 26.
477   Ibid., 31.
478   Ibid., 31.
479   Ibid., 32.
480   Ibid., 52.
481   Ibid., 32.
482   Donald B. DeYoung, *Astronomy and the Bible* (Grand Rapids: Baker Book House, 1989), 88.
483   DeYoung, *Astronomy and the Bible*, 80.
484   Duncan, "24-Hour View," in *Genesis*, 33. From Nigel Cameron, but no reference.
485   Ibid., 22.
486   J. P. Moreland and John Mark Reynolds, eds., *Three Views on Creation and Evolution*. (Grand Rapids: Zondervan, 1999), Paul Nelson and John Mark Reynolds, "Young Earth Creationism," 49.
487   Duncan, "24-Hour View," 26.
488   Ibid., 59.
489   Ibid., 60.
490   Ibid., 37.
491   Ibid., 41.
492   Ibid., 52.
493   Ibid., 54, 55.
494   Ibid., 41.
495   Ibid., 54.
496   Ibid., 173.
497   Ross, "Day-Age View," in *Genesis*, 126.
498   Duncan, "24-Hour View," in *Genesis*, 46.
499   Ibid., 38.
500   Ibid., 52.
501   DeYoung, *Astronomy and the Bible,* 88.
502   Duncan, "24-Hour View," in *Genesis*, 26.
503   Ibid., 33. From Nigel Cameron, but no reference.
504   Ibid., 26.
505   Ibid., 27.
506   Ibid., 23.
507   Ibid., 38.
508   The Bible does not say "twenty-four hour days," we do not know the exact hours.
509   Duncan, "24-Hour View," in *Genesis*, 31.
510   Ibid., 31.

511   Ibid., 22.
512   Ibid., 79.

Chapter 6   Day-Age, Old Earth, Progressive Creationism Theory
513 Hugh Ross, *The Creator and the Cosmos* (Downers Grove, IL: NavPress, 2001),18–20.
514   Ibid., 21.
515   Ibid., 73, 74, quoting Earl Radmacher and R. D. Preus, eds., *Hermeneutics, Inerrancy and the Bible* (Grand Rapids: Zondervan, 1984), 287.
516   Evidentialists study the evidence and believe based on strong evidence. Presuppositionalists start with the presupposition of the God of the Bible because nothing else makes sense without that presupposition. Too often, each side thinks the other side is not logical. Actually, both ways do logical when understood from their way of thinking. Presuppositionalists claim that we all have presuppositions, so why not start with the only presupposition under which everything else makes sense—the presupposition of the God of the Bible as our Creator. Evidentialists claim we should start with evidence because starting with a presupposition is not objective. The evidence is very strongly for the God of the Bible. Scientists tend to be evidentialists. Philosophical thinkers tend to be presuppositionalists. Actually, the God of the Bible is to be found either way.
517   Hugh Ross, *Creation as Science* (Colorado Springs: NavPress, 2006), 170.
518   Ibid., 189.
519   Hugh Ross, *Creation and Time* (Colorado Springs: NavPress, 1994), 149, quoting James Broderick, *Galileo: The Man, His Work, His Misfortunes* (New York: Harper and Row, 1964), 75–77.
520   Ross, *Origins*, 38.
521   Ross, *Fingerprint*, 165.
522   Ibid., 4
523   Ross, *Cosmos*, 23, 24
524   Ibid., 27.
525   Ibid., 31–118.
526   Maugh, Thomas H., II, "Relics of Big Bang, Seen for First Time," *Los Angeles Times*, Friday, April 24, 1992, A1 and A30.
527   Ross, *Cosmos*, 145–216.
528   Ross, *Time*, 45.
529   Ibid., 46, 47.
530   Ibid., 46.
531   Ibid., 47.
532   Ibid., 48.
533   Ibid., 50, 51.
534   Ibid., 48–50.
535   Ibid., 52.
536   Ibid., 52.
537   Ibid., 52.
538   Ibid., 58.
539   Hugh Ross, *Creation as Science* (Colorado Springs: NavPress, 2006), 55. The most recent estimate of the age of the universe is 13.73 billion years old.
540   Ross, *Time*, 52.
541   Ibid., 53–72.

542   Ibid., 53, 54.

543   Ibid., 54. However, most theologians would not agree with a further overstatement Ross makes. He claims, "The facts of nature may be likened to a sixty-seventh book of the Bible." This statement is theologically problematic because there is a fundamental difference between the written communication of the Bible and the objects and forces of the universe. The universe is not a book of the Bible. Both the Bible and the creation reveal truth from and about God, but different ways.

544   Ibid., 61.

545   Hugh Ross seems to be claiming that in 1 Corinthians 15:21 and 22 the issue is spiritual death of humans. However, "the resurrection of the dead" is a physical resurrection. If the verses are limited to human death, that death was first spiritual death but also included physical death and physical resurrection. So Ross takes his argument one step too far, in my opinion—and an unnecessary step at that.

546   Ross, *Time*, 62.

547   Ibid., 61.

548   Ibid., 63.

549   Hugh Ross, *Creation as Science* (Colorado Springs: NavPress, 2006), 166.

550   Ibid., 171.

551   Ross, *Time*, 65.

552   Ibid., 66.

553   John Ankerberg Show, "The Great Debate"

554   Ross, *Time*, 68.

555   Ibid., 73–80.

556   Fazale Rana & Hugh Ross, *Origins of Life* (Colorado Spr.: NavPress, 2004), 13.

557   Rana and Ross, *Origins of Life* , 223.

558   Ross, "Day-Age View," 153.

559   Ibid., 154.

560   Ibid., 154.

561   Ross, *Origins of Life*, 37.

562   Ibid., 38.

563   Ross, *Time*, 149, quoting James Broderick, *Galileo: The Man, His Work, His Misfortunes* (New York: Harper and Row, 1964), 75–77.

564   Ross, *Time*, 149

565   Ibid., 153.

566   Rana and Ross, *Origins of Life*, 38.

567   Ibid., 39.

568   Ibid., 39, 40.

569   Ibid., 39.

570   Ross, *Time*, 153.

571   Ibid., 149.

572   Hugh Ross, *A Matter of Days* (Colorado Springs: NavPress, 2004), 232.

573   Ibid., 231-232

574   Ross, *Time*, 153.

575   Ibid., 153.

576   Ibid., 150, 151.

577   Ibid., 153.

578   Ibid., 153.

579   Ibid., 152.

580   Ibid., 152.

581   Ibid., 153.

582   Ibid., 154.

583   Fazale Rana and Ross, and Hugh Ross, *Who Was Adam*, (Colorado Springs: NavPress, 2005), 248.

584   Ibid,. 248.

585   Ross, *Time*, 49.

586   Ross includes insects, but most YEC 6,000-year-old-universe advocates would not. They would include only birds (10,000 species today), bats (1,100 species), mammals (5,500 species today), and land reptiles (about 8,000 species today) for a total of about 25,000 species today from about 5,000 species on the ark. These numbers suggest speciation of about 5 species for every animal kind on the ark in about 5,000 years. We do not see that speed of speciation today.

587   answersingenesis.org/home/area/feedback/2006/0908.asp

588   Ross, "Day-Age," *Genesis*, 127.

589   Ibid., 127.

590   Ross, *Time*, 154.

591   Ross, *Fingerprint, 4.*

592   Ross, *Fingerprint, 185.*

593   Hugh Ross, *Creation and Time* (Colorado Springs: NavPress, 1994, 49.

594   Ibid., 45.

595   Ibid., 46, 47.

596   Ibid., 46.

597   Ibid., 48.

598   Ibid., 48, 49.

599   Ibid., 52.

600   Waltke translates *bᵉyôm* as when. *Biblical Hebrew Syntax*, 250, #13.7b and 611, #36.3.1.a.8.

601   John Joseph Owen, *Analytical Key to the Old Testament* (Grand Rapids: Baker, 1989), 7. Owen lists *bᵉyôm*, "when," as a preposition construct.

602   I appreciate that Ross uses such phrases as *"functionally equivalent to."* He says, "The Big Bang determines that the cause of the universe is *functionally equivalent to* the God of the Bible, a Being beyond the matter, energy, space and time of the cosmos" (Ross, *Time*, 81).

603   Ibid., 47.

604   Leon Wood, "Hosea" in Frank Gaebelein, *The Expositor's Bible Commentary*, Vol. 7 (Grand Rapids: Zondervan, 1985), 193.

605   David Allan Hubbard, *Hosea* (Downers Grove: InterVarsity Press, 1989), 125.

606   Douglas Stewart, *Hosea*, Word Biblical Commentary (Dallas: Word Books, 1987).

607   Andrew Kulikovsky, "How could Adam have named all the animals in a single day?" *Creation* 27:3 June 2005, 27, 28.

608   Ross, *Time*, 52.

609   Ibid., 52.

610   Ibid., 52.

611   Ibid., 53–72.

612   Ibid., 60, 61.

613   Ibid., 61.

614   Ibid., 61.

615   Ross, *The Genesis Question*, 99.

616   Ross, *Time*, 63.

617   Ibid., 62, 63.

618   Ibid., 65.

619   Hugh Ross, *Origins of Life* (Colorado Springs: NavPress, 2004), 223.

620   Ross, "Day-Age View," 153.

621   Ibid., 149.

622   Ibid., 231-232.

623   Ross, *Time*, 153.

624   Ibid., 153.

625   Ibid., 150, 151.

626   Ibid., 153.

627   Ibid., 153.

628   Ibid., 152.

629   Ibid., 152.

630   Ibid., 154.

631   Ross's point does not seem to be tripartite versus bipartite but a body-spirit man.

632   http://www.answersingenesis.org/home/area/feedback/2006/0908.asp

633   Ross, "Day-Age," *Genesis*, 127.

634   Ross, *Origins*, 38.

635   Ross, *Time*, 53, 54.

636   Ibid., 68.

637   Ross, *Origins*, 37.

638   Ibid., 38.

639   Ross, *Time*, 149

640   Ross, *Origins*, 39.

641   Ibid., 39, 40.

642   Ibid., 39.

643   Ross, *Fingerprint,* 4.

644   Ibid., 185.

645   Hugh Ross, *Creation as Science* (Colorado Springs: NavPress, 2006), 170.

646   Ibid., 79.

Chapter 7   Theistic Big Bang and Relativistic Days Theory

647   Gerald Schroeder, *The Science of God* (New York: Broadway Books, 1997), 99.

648   Kabbalah (also referred to as cabbala, cabala, cabbalah, or kabbala) is a collection of esoteric Jewish beliefs and practices that supplement Bible interpretation.

649   Gerald L. Schroeder, *Genesis and the Big Bang* (New York: Bantam Books, 1990), 18.; quoting the Talmud commentary on Jeremiah 23:29. I disagree with this comment because if many meanings exist, then there is no one meaning. And if no one meaning exists, then meaningful communication dwindles away.

650   Schroeder, *Big Bang*, 20, 21.

651   Ibid., 53.

652   Ibid., 130, 131.

653   Schroeder, *Science*, 58.

654   Schroeder, *Big Bang*, 33.

655   Schroeder, *Science*, 43.

656   Schroeder, *Big Bang*, 34.

657   Ibid., 44.

658   Schroeder, *Science*, 47.

659   Schroeder, *Big Bang*, 50.

660   Ibid., 49.

661   Ibid., 53.

662   Schroeder, *Science*, 42, 43.

663   Schroeder, *Big Bang*, 92.

664   Schroeder, *Science*, 54, 55.

665   Schroeder, *Big Bang*, 53.

666   Schroeder, *Science*, 43.

667   Schroeder, *Big Bang*, 53.

668   Ibid., 90-92.

669   Schroeder, *Science*, 60.

670   Schroeder, *Big Bang*, 53.

671   Schroeder, *Science*, 116.

672   Ibid., 151; from Maimonides, *Guide to the Perplexed*, part 1, chapter 7.

673   Schroeder, *the Science of God*, 137.

674   Schroeder, *The Science of God*, 117. *Neshama* is breath as in Gen. 2:7.

675   Schroeder, *the Science of God*, 140.

676   Schroeder, *the Science of God*, 140.

677   Schroeder, *The Science of God,* 99.

678   Ibid., 152; Actually, "Shadow" is listed as the second meaning. The first meaning in the *New International Dictionary of Old Testament Theology and Exegesis* is "statue, model, image" (VanGemeren, Vol. 3, [H7512]).

679   This paragraph is extrapolated from Schroeder as best I can deduce.

680   Schroeder, *the Science of God*, 143-167.

681   Schroeder, *the Science of God*, 174.

682   Schroeder, *The Science of God*, 142.

683   Schroeder, *The Science of God*, 204-206.

684   Schroeder, *The Science of God*, 117.

685   Schroeder, *The Science of God*, 144.

686   Schroeder, *The Science of God*, 132.

687   The Cretaceous–Tertiary extinction event was the mass extinction of animal and plant species including the dinosaurs. It is dated by geologists at about 65 million years ago. It is abbreviated as the K–T extinction. An iridium layer found around the world, and the Chicxulub Crater about 180 kilometers (112 mi) wide on the coast of Yucatan strongly suggest a large asteroid hit earth causing the K-T extinction. This impact crater matched Louis Alvarez's K–T extinction hypothesis.

688   Schroeder, *Big Bang*, 144–146.

689   Schroeder, *Science of God*, 193.

690   Schroeder, *Big Bang*, 130.

691   Ibid., 130.

692   Ibid., 93, 156.

693   Ibid., 88.

694   Schroeder, *Big Bang*, 58.

695   Gerald Schroeder, personal email, April 27, 2008.

696   Schroeder, *Big Bang*, 58; The inflationary stage was suggested by Alan Guth.

697   Ibid., 93, 94.

698   Ibid., 156.

699   Ibid., 49.

700   Ibid., 74.

701   Ibid., 78, 79.

702   Ibid., 62.

703   Schroeder, *Science of God*, 137-138.

704   Schroeder, *Big Bang*, 56.

705   Schroeder, *The Science of God,* 161.

706   Ibid., 38-40.

707   Ibid., 31.

708   Schroeder, *Big Bang*, 12.

709   Schroeder, *The Science of God*, 5.

710   Schroeder, *Big Bang*, 120, 121.

711   Ibid., 122.

712   Schroeder, *Science of God,* 26.

713   Schroeder, *Big Bang*, 123, 124.

714   Ibid., 122.

715   Ibid., 124.

716   Ibid., 125.

717   Ibid., 126.

718   Ibid., 19.

719   Ibid., 113.

720   Ibid., 112.

721   Ibid., 111.

722   Schroeder, *Science*, 10.

723   Schroeder, *Big Bang*, 135.

724   Stephen J. Gould and Niles Eldredge, "Punctuated equilibria: the tempo and mode of evolution reconsidered." *Paleobiology*, 3 (1977): 115-151, B. Rensberger, "Recent Studies Spark Revolution in Interpretation of Evolution," *New York Times*, Nov. 4, 1980, C3, quoting Eldredge, Schroeder, *Science*, 10.

725   Schroeder, *Big Bang*, 136.

726   Schroeder, *Big Bang*, 21, referring to E. Ladd, "Religion and American Values," *Society*, 24:63-68.1987.

727   Schroeder, *Science*, 12, 13.

728   Schroeder, *Science*, 18.

729   Schroeder, *Big Bang*, 160.

730   Ibid., 64.

731   Schroeder, *Science*, 43.

732   Schroeder, *Big Bang*, 44.

733   Schroeder, *Science*, 50.

734   Schroeder, *Science*, 50.

735   Schroeder, *Big Bang*, 50.

736   Schroeder, *Science*, 47.

737   Schroeder, *Big Bang*, 53.

738   Schroeder, *Science of God*, 60.
739   Schroeder, *Big Bang*, 49.
740   Henry Morris, *The Genesis Record* (Grand Rapids: Baker Book House, 1976), 65.
741   Schroeder, *Big Bang*, 132.
742   Schroeder, *Science of God*, 60.
743   While *rûah* means "wind" or "breath" as well as "spirit," *rûah ʿelōhîm* is used as a technical term for the Spirit of God.
744   Schroeder, *Big Bang*, 93, 94.
745   Schroeder, *Science*, 56.
746   Ibid., 53.
747   Ibid., 130.
748   Schroeder, *Big Bang*, 74.
749   Ibid., 62.
750   Schroeder, *Science of God*, 137-138.
751   Ibid., 19.
752   Ibid., 111.
753   Schroeder, *Science*, 12, 13.
754   Schroeder, *Science*, 18.
755   Ibid., 79.

Chapter 8   Creation Revealed in Six Days Theory
756   Anson R. Rainey and R. Stephen Notley, *The Sacred Bridge* (Jerusalem: Carta, 2006), photograph of tablet on p. 271.
757   Roland Kenneth Harrison, *Introduction to the Old Testament* (Grand Rapids: Wm. B. Eerdmans Publishing Co., 1969.), 130.
758   Millard J. Erickson, *Christian Theology* (Grand Rapids: Baker Book House, 1983), 381.
759   D. J. Wiseman, *Clues to Creation in Genesis* (London: Marshall, Morgan & Scott, 1977), 46–55.
760   Stephen L. Harris, *Understanding the Bible* (Boston: MaGraw-Hill, 2002).
761   Ibid., 67–69.
762   Wiseman, *Revealed*, 71–76.
763   Ibid., 72–76.
764   Ibid., 45.
765   Curt Sewell, "The Tablet Theory of Genesis Authorship," *Bible and Spade*, 7:1, Winter 1994.
766   Sewell, "Tablet," *Spade*.
767   Wiseman, *Revealed*, 45, 46.
768   H. W. F. Gesenius, *Hebrew-Chaldee Lexicon to the Old Testament* (Wm. B. Eerdmans Publishing Co., 1946), #8435, 859.
769   Sewell, "Tablet," *Spade*.
770   Wiseman, *Revealed*, 8.
771   A. S. Yahuda, *Language of the Pentateuch in Its Relation to Egyptian, Part 1* (London: Oxford University Press, 1933); Harrison, *Introduction to the Old Testament*, (Grand Rapids: Wm. B. Eerdmans Publishing Co., 1969), 551, 552; J. S. Wright, *How Moses Compiled Genesis, A Suggestion* (1946).

772   The Amarna tablets are being collocated from their locations by Anson F. Rainey.

773   Also Egyptians were in Babylonia, D. J. Wiseman, *Iraq* 28:154–159, Rainey and Notley, *Bridge.*

774   Wiseman, *Clues to Creation in Genesis*, 34.

775   Ibid., 36-37.

776   Wiseman, *Revealed*, 15.

777   Ibid., 16.

778   Ibid., 18.

779   Ibid., 18.

780   Ibid., 23.

781   Ibid., 23, 24.

782   Ibid., 26.

783   Ibid., 31.

784   Ibid., 31, 32.

785   Ibid., 32.

786   Ibid., 32.

787   Ibid., 33.

788   Brown, *Hebrew-English Lexicon*, 793.

789   Gesenius, *Hebrew-Chaldee Lexicon*, #6213, 657.

790   BibleWorks for Windows, Strong's, #6213. I highly recommend BibleWorks. It is an invaluable tool to research the Bible text. It complements Logos Bible Software, which includes a vast array of Bible related articles and books. I use both constantly.

791   Wiseman, *Revealed*, 44.

792   Ibid., 33.

793   Ibid., 33, 34.

794   Actually Hebrew has "aspect," not tense. Wiseman, *Revealed*, 39.

795   Wiseman, *Revealed*, 40.

796   Ibid., 32. Wiseman is half right. *Nāfash* means "to be refreshed." But *shābat*, "ceased," usually means ceased work, not ceased revealing. He proves nothing by the fact that *shābat* means "ceased." Contextually, it means ceased work.

797   Wiseman, *Revealed*, 35.

798   Ibid., 44.

799   Westminster Morphology, *BibleWorks for Windows.*

800   Ibid., 33.

801   Wiseman, *Revealed*, 33.

802   Actually Hebrew has "aspect," not tense. Wiseman, *Revealed*, 39.

803   Ibid., 79.

Chapter 9   Gap or Creation-Ruin-Restoration Theory

804 Hugh Miller, *The Testimony of the Rocks* (Edinburgh: Constable, 1857).

805   George Hawkins Pember, *Earth's Earliest Ages*, G. H. Lang, ed. (Grand Rapids: Kregel Publications, 1975), first published in 1876 by Hodder and Stoughton.

806   Arthur C. Custance, *Without Form and Void: A Study of the Meaning of Genesis 1:2* (Brookville, Canada: Doorway Papers, 1970).

807   Merrill Unger, "Rethinking the Genesis Account of Creation," *Bibliotheca Sacra* 115:457 (Jan. 1958), 28.

808	William Buckland, *Geology and Mineralogy Considered with Reference to Natural Theology*, Vol. 1, Chapter 2, 1836; Volume VI in *The Bridgewater Treatises;* in Custance, *Void*, 27.

809	Custance, *Void*, 2.

810	Ibid., 28.

811	Buckland, *Geology and Mineralogy*; in Custance, *Void*, 27.

812	Custance, *Void*, 2.

813	Unger, "Rethinking the Genesis Account of Creation," 27.

814	Custance, *Void*, 2.

815	Custance, *Void*, 3.

816	John Harris, *The Pre-Adamite Earth* (London: Ward & Co., ca. 1849, republished G. S. Blanchard, 1860), 354; in Custance, *Void*, 27.

817	Custance, *Void*, 22.

818	Pember, *Ages*, 29.

819	Custance, *Void*, 17, 18.

820	Thomas Aquinas, *Sententiarum, Book II*, Distinction xiii, Article 3, "Ad Terium;" in Custance, *Void*, 22.

821	John Harris, *The Pre-Adamite Earth,* 354; in Custance, *Void*, 27.

822	Custance, *Void*, 17, 18.

823	Thomas Chalmers quoted in Hugh Miller, *The Testimony of the Rocks* (Edinburgh: Constable, 1857), 108; in Custance, *Void*, 26.

824	Custance, *Void*, 22.

825	Buckland, *Geology and Mineralogy*; in Custance, *Void*, 27.

826	Buckland, *Geology and Mineralogy*; in Custance, *Void*, 27.

827	Pember, *Ages*, 29.

828	Ibid., 29.

829 Ibid.,30.

830	Ibid., 30, 31.

831	Ibid., 31.

832	Ibid., 32.

833	Ibid., 32.

834	Ibid., 32.

835	Ibid., 34.

836	Ibid., 36.

837	Ibid., 37, 38.

838	Ibid., 49.

839	Ibid., 55.

840	Ibid., 51.

841	Ibid., 55.

842	Ibid., 34.

843	Ibid., 63.

844	Ibid., 64.

845	Ibid., 69.

846	Ibid., 63.

847	Ibid., 65.

848	Ibid., 66.

849	Ibid., 65.

850	Ibid., 65.

851   Ibid., 66.

852   Ibid., 67.

853   Ibid.,, 68.

854   Ibid., 68.

855   *New Scofield Reference Bible* (NY; Oxford University Press, 1984), 1, footnote 7.

856   Pember, *Ages*, 69.

857   Ibid., 69.

858   Ibid., 71.

859   Ibid., 72.

860   Ibid., 71.

861   Ibid., 71, 72.

862   Ibid., 73.

863   Ibid., 27.

864   Ibid., 31.

865   Ibid., 31, 32.

866   Custance, *Void*, 2.

867   Pember, *Ages*, 32.

868   Ibid., 32.

869   The verb וַתְּהִי (*vatᵉhî*) in Genesis 19:26 is qal *imperfect*; whereas in Genesis 1:2 the verb הָיְתָה (*hāyᵉtāʰ*), "was" is qal *perfect*. The imperfect may mean "became," but the perfect in Genesis 1:2 is correctly translated "was" as a "state" or "state of being" (Waltke *Syntax*, 483; Practico, *Hebrew*, 129). In Genesis 1:2 the state of the earth "was" תֹהוּ וָבֹהוּ *tōhû vᵃbōhû*, "uninhabitable and uninhabited." In order for the qal perfect verb *hāyᵉtāʰ*, "was," in Genesis 1:2 to mean "had become," "one would normally expect a *la'med* preposition prefixed to both the *tōhû* and *bōhû*, which is not present here. Also the past perfect use of the verb ["had become"] normally has an antecedent text to provide a basis for the past perfect. This is also not present here." (David Fonts, "Genesis 1-11," *Key Word Study*, 40; David Fonts may disagree with me, but this is an excellent work.) This combination of the "to be" verb and the noun prefixed by a לְ (*la'med*) is in Genesis 2:7: "man became a living being/soul [לְנֶפֶשׁ]." There is no *la'med* prefix in Genesis 1:2: "Now the earth was *tōhû vᵃbōhû*" is correct. The gap claim of "became" is incorrect. Moreover, Genesis 1:2 begins with an "and" called a "*vav/waw* disjunctive" prefixing the three key nouns of "three circumstantial clauses, all describing the conditions or circumstances existing *at the time* of the principle action indicated in verse 1" (Unger, "Rethinking," 28). The *vav/waw* disjunctive prefixing "the earth" beginning Genesis 1:2 indicates that 1:2 describes the conditions on the earth. At the end of the creation time period in Genesis 1:1 when the heavens and earth were being completed, there were three end conditions on earth: (1) earth was *tōhû vᵃbōhû*, "uninhabitable and uninhabited", (2) its worldwide sea was covered with darkness, and (3) the Spirit of God was hovering over the face of the deep. The *vav/waw* disjunctive "and" beginning Genesis 1:2 indicates this is a "parenthetical statement," like a parentheses, that describes the end circumstances or conditions on earth, rather than being an action. In contrast, the translation "became" or "had become" would have been used with a "*vav/waw* consecutive" prefixing the verb that would have indicated the next event or action in which earth would have "become" changed. The *vav/waw* consecutive in Genesis 19:26 does exactly that — it describes two successive actions: "And she looked," "and she became." "Became" is an action. So in Genesis 19:26 the *vav/waw* consecutive prefixed qal *imperfect* וַתְּהִי (*vatᵉhî*) is correctly translated "became." But Genesis 1:2

begins with a *vav/waw* disjunctive prefixed noun, then הָיְתָה (*hāyᵉtāʰ*), "And the earth was." Pember's translation of the "to be" verb in Genesis 1:2 as "became" is grammatically highly improbable.

870   Pember, *Ages*, 32.

871   Ibid., 61.

872   "Buckland, William," *Encyclopædia Britannica, Eleventh Edition* (Cambridge: Cambridge Press, 1911), public domain online without page numbers; "Buckland, William," *Encyclopædia Britannica 2007*; "William Buckland," wikipedia.org.

873   An exception was Nicolas Steno, or Niels Stensen in his native Danish. He published the first principles of geology in *De solido* in 1669; but rather than pursue his geology, he converted to Catholicism and became a priest. Alan Cutler, *The Seashell on the Mountaintop: A Story of Science, Sainthood, and the Humble Genius Who Discovered a New History of the Earth* (New York: Dutton, 2003).

874   Pember, *Ages*, 63.

875   Ibid., 71.

876   John Harris, *The Pre-Adamite Earth*, 354; in Custance, *Void*, 27.

877   Custance, *Void*, 22.

878   Pember, *Ages*, 29.

879   Custance, *Void*, 17, 18.

880   Thomas Chalmers quoted in Hugh Miller, *The Testimony of the Rocks* (Edinburgh: Constable, 1857), 108; in Custance, *Void*, 26.

881   Custance, *Void*, 22.

882   Buckland, *Geology and Mineralogy*, quoted in Custance, *Void*, 27.

883   Pember, *Ages*, 30.

884   Ibid., 31.

885   Ibid., 66.

886   Ibid., 65.

887   *New Scofield Reference Bible* (NY; Oxford University Press, 1984), 1, footnote 7.

888   Pember, *Ages*, 66.

889   Ibid., 67.

890   Ibid., 68.

891   Ibid., 69.

892   Ibid., 71.

893   Ibid., 71, 72.

894   Ibid., 73.

895   Ibid., 79.

Chapter 10   Historical Land Creationism Theory

896   John Sailhamer, *Genesis Unbound*, (Sisters, OR: Multnomah Press, 1996), 29.

897   John Sailhamer, *The Pentateuch as Narrative* (Grand Rapids: Zondervan, 1992); "Genesis" in *the Expositor's Bible Commentary* (Grand Rapids: Zondervan, 1990); *Genesis Unbound* (Sisters, OR: Multnomah Press, 1996).

898   Sailhamer, *Genesis Unbound*, 11.

899   Ibid., 64.

900   Ibid., 17.

901   Ibid., 23.

902   Sailhamer, *Narrative*, 82, footnote 2.

903   Sailhamer, *Unbound*, 102-103.
904   Ibid., 103.
905   Ibid., 31.
906   Ibid., 109.
907   Ibid., 44.
908   Ibid., 44.
909   Ibid., 45.
910   Ibid., 11.
911   Ibid., 29.
912   Ibid.,, 15.
913   Ibid., 12, 13.
914   Ibid., 23, 24.
915   Ibid., 45.
916   R. K. Harrison, *Intro. Old Testament*, footnote in Sailhamer, *Narrative*, 23.
917   Sailhamer, *Narrative*, 23.
918   Sailhamer, *Unbound*, 82.
919   Ibid., 83.
920   Ibid., 29.
921   Ibid., 14.
922   Ibid., 14.
923   Sailhamer, "Genesis," 20. Apparently he means the actual duration is specific, even if the length is indeterminate to the reader of the text. The text does not tell the reader how long the period of time was.
924   Sailhamer, *Unbound*, 38, 39.
925   Sailhamer, *Narrative*, 84.
926   Sailhamer, *Unbound*, 41.
927   Sailhamer, *Narrative*, 82.
928   Sailhamer, *Unbound*, 56.
929   Ibid., 28, 29.
930   Ibid., 14.
931   Ibid., 29.
932   Ibid., 56.
933   Ibid., 29.
934   Ibid., 33.
935   Ibid., 27–45.
936   Ibid., 63, 64.
937   Ibid., 65.
938   Ibid., 196.
939   Ibid., 29.
940   Ibid., 14.
941   Ibid., 52.
942   Ibid., 49.
943   Ibid., 37.
944   Ibid., 52.
945   Ibid., 15.
946   Ibid., 50.
947   Ibid., 30.
948   Ibid., 14.

949   Ibid., 56.
950   Ibid., 251, chapter four, footnote 3.
951   Ibid., 117.
952   Sailhamer, *Narrative*, 89.
953   Ibid., 89.
954   Sailhamer, *Unbound*, 126.
955   Ibid., 254.
956   Ibid., 32.
957   Ibid., 30–32.
958   Ibid., 132.
959   Sailhamer, *Narrative*, 93
960   Ibid., 93.
961   Ibid., 93.
962   Sailhamer, *Unbound,* 135.
963   Ibid., 141.
964   Ibid., 32.
965   Sailhamer, *Narrative*, 95
966   Sailhamer, *Unbound*, 238.
967   Ibid., 95.
968   Ibid., 106, 107.
969   Ibid., 107.
970   Ibid., 56.
971   Ibid., 27–45.
972   Ibid., 29.
973   Ibid., 93.
974   Ibid., 52.
975   Ibid., 52.
976   Ibid., 126.
977   Ibid., 254.
978   Ibid., 141.
979   Ibid., 109.
980   Ibid., 82.
981   Sailhamer, *Narrative*, 29.
982   Sailhamer, *Unbound*, Ibid., 14.
983   Ibid., 14.
984   Ibid., 29.
985   Ibid., 15.
986   Ibid., 52.
987   Ibid., 30.
988   Ibid., 30–32.
989   WTM morphology in BibleWorks for Windows.
990   Sailhamer, *Unbound,* 238.
991   Sailhamer, *Unbound*, 17.
992   Sailhamer, *Narrative*, 82, footnote 2.
993   Sailhamer, *Unbound*, 31.
994   Ibid., 31.
995   Ibid., 109.
996   Ibid., 44.

997	Ibid., 44.
998	Ibid., 11.
999	Ibid., 29.
1000	Ibid., 45.
1001	R. K. Harrison, *Intro. Old Testament*, footnote in Sailhamer, *Narrative*, 23.
1002	Sailhamer, *Unbound*, 14.
1003	Sailhamer, "Genesis," 20.
1004	Sailhamer, *Unbound*, 38, 39.
1005	Ibid., 14.
1006	Ibid., 56.
1007	Ibid., 28, 29.
1008	Ibid., 14.
1009	Ibid., 63, 64.
1010	Ibid., 65.
1011	Ibid., 14.
1012	Ibid., 56.
1013	Ibid., 117.
1014	Ibid., 106, 107.
1015	Ibid., 17.
1016	Ibid., 79.

**Chapter 11	Two Stage Biblical Creation Theory**
1017	Charles Hodge, *Systematic Theology, Abr.* (Grand Rapids: Baker, 1988), 210.
1018	Rooker, Part I, 319.
1019	Copan and Craig, *Creation out of nothing*, 63.
1020	Richard M. Davidson, "A Biblical Theology of Creation," at the 26th Seminar on the Integration of Faith and Learning, Loma Linda, CA, July 18, 2000, 439; "Traditional" includes the initial chaos view and two-stage view.
1021	I will be quoting from the most Biblical claims of the ten theories, but I will *not be granting my 100 percent approval* to all details in these theories.
1022	Sailhamer, *Unbound*, 11.
1023	Thomas Kuhn, *The Structure of Scientific Revolutions* (Chicago: University of Chicago Press, 1962).
1024	Sailhamer, *Unbound*, 73, 74, quoting Earl Radmacher and R. D. Preus, eds., *Hermeneutics, Inerrancy and the Bible* (Grand Rapids: Zondervan, 1984), 287.
1025	Jacque Monod, *Chance and Necessity: An Essay on the Natural Philosophy of Modern Biology*, tr. Austryn Wainhouse (Vintage, 1971).
1026	Stephen Hawking, *A Brief History of Time* (Bantam Books, 1998).
1027	Sailhamer, *Unbound*, 145–216.
1028	Schroeder, *Science of God*, 26.
1029	Schroeder, *Science of God*, 5.
1030	Bruce K. Waltke, "The Creation Account in Genesis 1:1–3, Part IV" *Bibliotheca Sacra* 132:528 (Oct. 1975), 338.
1031	Waltke, "Genesis 1:1-3," Part II, 142–143.
1032	Waltke, "Genesis 1:1–3," Part II, 142.
1033	Ross, *Time*, 153.
1034	Sailhamer, *Unbound*, 63, 64.
1035	Ibid., 65.

1036   Abraham Ibn Ezra, *Commentary on the Pentateuch, Bereshit* (New York: Menorah Publishing Co., 1988) 29-30; Sailhamer, Unbound, 196.

1037   Pember, *Ages*, 30, 31.

1038   Sailhamer, *Unbound*, 23.

1039   Nemesius of Emesa, *De Natura Hominis*, 26; in Louth, Genesis 1:1–11, 2.

1040   John Calvin, *Genesis* (Edinburgh: Banner of Truth Trust), 70.

1041   Copan and Craig, *Creation Out of Nothing*, 93-165.

1042   Morris, *The Genesis Record*, 42.

1043   Sailhamer, *Narrative*, 82, footnote 2.

1044   Schroeder, *Big Bang*, 62.

1045   J. Weingreen, *Grammar*, 90-91. Waltke 8.3b, p 129. Practico, 192-193.

1046   Wiseman, *Revealed*, 26.

1047   Finis Jennings Dake, *Dake's Annotated Bible*, (Lawrenceville, GA: Dake Publishing, 1963), Genesis 1:2.

1048   Waltke, "Genesis 1:1–3," Part III. 221.

1049   Stambaugh, "Semantic," 43.

1050   Ibid., 44.

1051   Ibid., 53–57.

1052   Schroeder, *Science*, 43.

1053   Wiseman, *Revealed*, 23.

1054   Pember, *Ages*, 65.

1055   Sailhamer, *Unbound*, 14.

1056   Kline, "Framework," 244.

1057   Bernard Northrup, *Recognizing Messiah in the Psalms*, 94.

1058   Ken Ham, et.al. *The Answers Book*, 170.

1059   Ken Ham, "Did Jesus say He created in six days?" August 25, 2001.

1060   Terry Mortenson, "But from the beginning of . . . the institution of marriage?"

1061   Mortenson, "But from the beginning."

1062   VanGemeren, NIDOTTE.

1063   *Encarta World English Dictionary* (New York: St. Martin's Press, 1999), 157; *The Oxford Universal Dictionary* (1964) "a process of entering into existence" and "the point of time at which anything begins." The Greek and Hebrew actually count.

1064   Sailhamer, "Genesis," 20.

1065   Danker, *Greek-English Lexicon*, (Chicago: Uni. Chicago Press, 2000), 572-573.

1066   Mortenson, "But from the beginning."

1067   Mortenson, "But from the beginning."

1068   Frank DeRemer, "Days 1-4" *Technical Journal* 21:3, 73.

1069   Jason Lisle, in "The Great Debate," The John Ankerberg Show.

1070   Morris, *Record*, 55.

1071   Frank DeRemer, "Days 1-4" *Technical Journal* 21:3, 73.

1072   Morris, *The Genesis Record*, 45

1073   Kline, "Framework," 218.

1074   Ross, *Time*, 53, 54.

1075   Morris, *The Genesis Record*, 62.

1076   Sailhamer, *Unbound*, 44, 45.

1077   Custance, *Void*, 3.

1078   Sailhamer, *Unbound*, 45.

1079   Arnold G. Fruchtenbaum, *Israelology: The Missing Link in Systematic Theology* (Ariel Ministries Press, 1994), 64.

1080   Ross, *Time*, 149, quoting James Broderick, *Galileo: The Man, His Work, His Misfortunes* (New York: Harper and Row, 1964), 75–77.

1081   Ross, *Origins*, 38.

1082   Michael Heiser, private email, June 3, 2008.

1083   Waltke, "The creation Account in Genesis 1:1-3," *Bib. Sacra* 132:526, 140.

1084   David Tsumura, *The Earth and the Waters*, 31-41.

1085   Martin Luther, *The Creation: A Commentary on the First Five Chapters of the Book of Genesis*, trans. Henry Cole (Edinburgh: T & T Clark, 1858), 23.

1086   Sailhamer, *Narrative*, 84.

1087   Michael Heiser, "What Does the Hebrew Text of Genesis 1 Allow?"

1088   Stephen Hawking, *A Brief History of Time*, 149.

1089   Hugh Ross in "The Great Debate," The John Ankerberg Show.

1090   Ken Ham, *Dinosaurs of Eden*, 9, 10.

1091   Sailhamer, *Narrative*, 84.

1092   Sailhamer, *Genesis Unbound*, 39.

1093   Ibid., 38, 39.

1094   Ibid., 38, 39.

1095   Ibid., 82.

1096   Robert S. Candlish, *The Book of Genesis*, Vol. I, (Edinburgh: Adam and Charles Black, 1868), 21.

1097   Sailhamer, *Unbound*, 28, 29.

1098   Ibid., 14.

1099   Candlish, *Book of Genesis*, 21.

1100   Sailhamer, *Genesis Unbound*, 29.

1101   Copan and Craig, *Creation out of nothing*, 63.

1102   Morris, *Biblical Creationism* (Grand Rapids: Baker Book House, 1994), 17.

1103   Waltke, "Genesis 1:1–3," Part III, 218; quoting John Skinner, *A Critical and Exegetical Commentary on Genesis* (Edinburg: T. & T. Clark, 1910), 14.

1104   Sailhamer, *Unbound*, 56; Sailhamer adds more items than the Bible says.

1105   Duncan and Hall, "The 24-hour View, *The Genesis Debate*, 27.

1106   Jacob Newman, *The Commentary of Nahmanides on Genesis Chapters 1–6* (Leiden: Brill, 1960), 33.

1107   Schroeder, *Big Bang*, 62.

1108   Sailhamer, *Genesis Unbound*, 248

1109   William Buckland, *Geology and Mineralogy*, 27.

1110   VanGemeren, NIDOTTE, Vol. 3, #6913, 546, Strongs # 6213.

1111   Harris, *Theological Wordbook*, #278a, 127.

1112   Pember, *Ages*, 29.

1113   Ken Ham, *Dinosaurs of Eden*, 9, 10.

1114   Sailhamer, *Unbound*, 39.

1115   Sailhamer, *Unbound*, 38, 39.

1116   Gary D. Pratico and Miles V. Van Pelt, *Basics of Biblical Hebrew Grammar* (Grand Rapids: Zondervan, 2001), 139. "The Hebrew perfect does not have tense (time of action) apart from context and issues of syntax."

1117   Sailhamer, *Narrative*, 82, footnote 2.

1118   "The imperfect [verb prefixed] with serves to express actions, events, or states, which are to be regarded as the temporal or logical sequel of the actions, events or states mentioned immediately before." E. Kautzsch, *Hebrew Grammar*, 326.

1119   Frank DeRemer, "Young biosphere, old universe?" 56.

1120   Ross, *Origins*, 39, 40.

1121   Ambrose, *Hexaemeron*, 5.

1122   John Calvin, *Genesis*, 74.

1123   Gordon J. Wenham, *Word Biblical Commentary, Genesis 1—15* (Waco: Word Books, 1987), 13, "the traditional view"; C. John Collins, *Genesis 1—4* (Phillipsburg, NJ: Puritan & Reformed, 2006), 51; Robert Candlish, *The Book of Genesis* (Edinburgh: Adam and Charles Black, 1868), 20, 21; Umberto Cassuto, *Genesis*, 20; Derek Kidner, Genesis, (Downers Grove, IL: InterVarsity Press, 1967), 44; John Sailhamer, "Genesis" in *The Expositor's Bible* Commentary, ed. Frank Gaebelein (Grand Rapids: Zondervan, 1990), 21; Allen P. Ross, *Creation and Blessing* (Grand Rapids: Baker Books, 1998), 105, 106. Copan and Craig in *Creation out of Nothing* (Grand Rapids: Baker, 2004).

1124   Isaiah 40:22, 42:5, 44:24, 45:12, 48:13, 51:13; Psalm 104:2; Job 9:8; Jeremiah 10:12, 51:15; Zechariah 12:1

1125   Ross, *A Matter of Days*, 139–145.

1126   The inspired Hebrew consonants may be translated "throne" or "moon." The context supports "moon." (Vowel points were added by the Medieval era Ben Asher Masoretes, who worked in the Great Synagogue at Tiberius where I excavated. Their vowel points, while usually helpful, are not inspired.)

1127   Ross, *Origins*, 39.

1128   Ross, *Origins*, 37.

1129   Sailhamer, *Unbound*, 63, 64.

1130   Ibid., 65.

1131   Ross, *Origins*, 38.

1132   Ibid., 38.

1133   Ibid., 153.

1134   Pember, *Ages*, 31.

1135   Ibid., 31.

1136   David Toshio Tsumura, *The Earth and the Waters*, 33, 34.

1137   Young, *Studies in Genesis One*, 13.

1138   Ross, *Origins*, 39.

1139   The inspired Hebrew three consonants may be translated "throne" or "moon."

1140   Waltke, *Bibliotheca Sacra*, Vol. 132, No. 525, 32.

1141   Waltke, "Genesis 1:1-3," Part II, 142–143.

1142   Willem VanGemeren, ed., *NIDOTTE*, H6906.

1143   Ross, *Fingerprint*, 166.

1144   Ross, *Origins*, 38.

1145   Ross, *Time*, 149

1146   Hugh Ross, *Fingerprint*, 165, 166.

1147   Ibid., 18. I do not agree with his alternative idea of the days.

1148   Jim Stambaugh, "The Days of Creation," 42–68.

1149   Westermann, *Genesis Commentary*, 16. Westermann refers us to S. Lanersdorfer, *Die sumerischen Parallelen zur biblischen Urgeschichte: Alttest, Abhandlungen VII 5* (Münster, 1917) as an earlier advocate of this idea.

1150   Ham, *et. al.*, *The Answers Book*, 93.

1151   Sailhamer, *Unbound*, 56.

1152   Waltke, *Biblical Hebrew Syntax*, 272-289.

1153   Practico, *Biblical Hebrew*, 116.

1154   Practico, *Biblical Hebrew*, 111.

1155   Waltke, *Biblical Hebrew Syntax*, 272

1156   Gordon H. Johnson, "Genesis 1 and Ancient Egyptian Creation Myths," *Bibliotheca Sacra* 165:658, April 2008, 185.

1157   Ross, *Origins of Life*, 38.

1158   Kline, "Framework," 227.

1159   Duncan and Hall, "The 24-Hour View," *The Genesis Debate*, 31.

1160   Hugh Ross, *A Matter of Days* (Colorado Springs: NavPress, 2004), 232.

1161   Ross, *Creation and Time*, 149.

1162   Sailhamer, *Unbound*, 56.

1163   The NASB 1977, NASB 1985, English Revised Version, New English Translation, New English Bible , JPS 1917, RSV, JPS Tanakh 1985, Complete Jewish Bible, and Darby Bible all use the wording "a second day." The Hebrew text does not include "the" until "the sixth day." "The" tells us that "the sixth day" completed the series of days of God's work. Absence of "the" in Hebrew *may imply* an English "a," but there actually is no "a" at all in Hebrew. The problem is, "a second day" could be taken to imply that this was one of several "second days" of God's work, but that would be *incorrect*. "The second day" is even more incorrect. Young's Literal translates simply as "second day." This is literal, but that is not good English. So I say "second day," which is precisely what the Hebrew says.

1164   Sailhamer, *Unbound*, 117.

1165   Sailhamer, *Narrative*, 89.

1166   Gordon J. Wenham, *Word, Genesis 1—15* (Waco: Word, 1987), 20.

1167   Sailhamer, *Unbound*, 32.

1168   Schroeder, *Big Bang*, 130.

1169   Sailhamer, *Unbound*, 153.

1170   Kline, "Not Rained," 150.

1171   Ham, *et. al.*, *The Answers Book*, 93

1172   Sailhamer, *Unbound*, 30–32.

1173   Ibid., 132.

1174   Kautzsch, *Hebrew Grammar*, #114h, 348.

1175   VanGemeren NIDOTTE, Vol. 3, #6913, 546, Strongs, 6213.

1176   Morris, *The Genesis Record*, 68.

1177   Pember, *Ages*, 69.

1178   Pember, *Ages*, 69.

1179   Ankerberg, "The Great Debate."

1180   Ross, *Time*, 152.

1181   Ross, *Time*, 152.

1182   Ross, *Time*, 154.

1183   Duncan, "24-Hour View," in *Genesis*, 33. From Nigel Cameron.

1184   Ross, *Time*, 48-50.

1185   Morris, *The Genesis Record*, 61.

1186   Kline, "Framework," 230.

1187   Kline, "Framework," 232.

1188   Morris, *The Genesis Record*, 30.

1189   Wiseman, *Revealed*, 67–69.

1190   Ross, *Origins*, 38.

1191   Ross *Creator and Cosmos*.

1192   Wiseman, *Revealed*, 67–69.

1193   Morris, *The Genesis Record*, 22-25; A. S. Yahuda, *Language of the Pentateuch in its Relation to Egyptian* (Oxford: Oxford University Press, 1933)

1194   John Piper, *What Jesus Demands from the World* (Wheaton: Crossway, 2006), 31. Eta Linnemann, Historical Criticism of the Bible: Methodology or Ideology: Reflections of a Bultmannian Turned Evangelical (Grand Rapids: Kregel, 2001)

1195   Naomi Steinberg, "The Genealogical Framework of the Family Stories in Genesis," *Semeia* 46 (1989), 41-50.

1196   Westermann, *Genesis Commentary*, 16. Westermann refers us to Lanersdorfer.

1197   Holladay, # 3984, Jer. 7:24, #6847.

1198   Douglas Moo, *Romans 1-8*, 552; John Murray, *Epistle to the Romans*, 302; Charles Hodge, *Romans*, 272; Leon Morris, *Epistle to the Romans*, 321; Word Biblical Commentary, *Romans*.

1199   Kline, "Framework," 218.

1200   Hugh Ross, *The Creator and the Cosmos* (Colorado Springs, CO: NavPress, 2001); Paul Davies, *The Cosmic Jackpot* (Boston; Houghton Mifflin, 2007); Peter D. Ward and Donald Brownlee, *Rare Earth* (New York: Copernicus Books); John D Barrow and Frank Tipler, *The Anthropic Cosmological Principle* (Oxford: Oxford University Press, 1986).

1201   Guillermo Gonzalez and Jay Richards, *The Privileged Planet: How Our Place in the Cosmos Is Designed for Discovery*; and DVD *The Privileged Planet: The Search for Purpose in the Universe* (Illustra Media, 2004).

1202   Morris, *Genesis Record*, 79.

Chapter 12   Minor Creation Theories

1203   Gorman Gray, *The Age of the Universe: What Are the Biblical Limits?* (Washougal, WA, Morningstar Publications, 2000), 19.

1204   Ibid., 18.

1205   Ibid., 19.

1206   Ibid., 18.

1207   Ibid., 18.

1208   Ibid., 18.

1209   Ibid., 18.

1210   Ibid., 18.

1211   Ibid., 18.

1212   Ibid., 18.

1213   Charles Hodge, *Systematic Theology, Abr.* (Grand Rapids: Baker, 1988), 210.

1214   Charles Hodge, *Systematic Theology*, Vol. I (London:, James Clark & Co, 1892, Reprinted, 1960), 556, 557; or Charles Hodge, *Abridged*, 206, 207.

1215   J. Barton Payne, "Theistic Evolution and the Hebrew of Genesis 1–2," *Bulletin of the Evangelical Theological Society 8 (1965),* 87. He is opposing theistic evolution.
Ibid., 85.

1216   Ibid., 87. footnote 13.

1217   Ibid., 87.

1218   Waltke, *Biblical Hebrew Syntax*, 15.2.1b, 274.

1219   Waltke, *Hebrew Syntax*, 272; Practico, *Biblical Hebrew*, 111.

1220   Paul Wright, President of Jerusalem University College, Mount Zion, Jerusalem, Israel, 05/01/2008 suggested this text. Cited with permission.

1221   Michael Heiser, Academic Editor of Logos Bible Software. (I recommend and use his product constantly.)

1222   Conceptually, work qualifies six days and rest qualifies the seventh day, allowing but not proving the Payne proposition.

1223   J. Barton Payne, *The Theology of the Older Testament* (Grand Rapids: Zondervan, 136; John Urquhart, *The Bible: Its Structure and Purpose* (New York: Gospel Publishing House, 1904).

1224   Ibid., 137.

1225   Ibid., 136-137.

1226   Alan Hayward, *Creation and Evolution* (Eugene, OR: Wipf & Stock, 2005). Dallas Cain, *Creation and Capron's Explanatory Interpretation*.

1227   Hayward, *Evolution*, 174.

1228   BibleWorks for Windows, WTM morphology.

1229   Practico and Van Pelt, *Biblical Hebrew*, 130.

1230   Hayward, *Evolution*, 204

1231   S. R. Driver, *Genesis*, Vol. 1, 1893, 23; quoted by P. J. Wiseman, *Revealed*, 28.

1232   Center for Science & Culture, "Top Questions," www.discovery.org/csc/topQuestions.php.

1233   John D. Barrow and Frank J. Tipler, *The Anthropic Cosmological Principle* (Oxford: Oxford University Press, 1986); Ross, *Cosmos*, 154–157; *Fingerprint*, 121–138; Paul Davies, *Cosmic Jackpot* (New York: Orion Publications, 2007); Peter Ward and Donald Brownlee, *Rare Earth* (New York: Copernicus Books, 2004).

1234   Richard Dawkins, *The Blind Watchmaker: Why the Evidence of Evolution Reveals a Universe without Design* (New York: W. W. Horton, and Co., 1996), 248, 249, 317; quoted by Stephen Jones, http://creationevolutiondesign.blogspot.com.

1235   James I. Packer, *God's Words: Studies of Key Bible Themes* (Downers Grove, IL: InterVarsity Press, 1981).

1236   Philip Henry Gosse, *Omphalos*.

1237   Wiseman, *Revealed*, 28.

1238   Sewell, "Tablet," *Spade*.

1239   Fazale Rana, *Origins of Life* (Colorado Springs: NavPress, 2004), 43.

1240   Ross and Rana, *Adam* (Colorado Springs: NavPress, 2005), 42.

1241   Jason Lisle, "The Big Bang: God's Chosen Method of Creation?" *Answers* (November 2007).

1242   Jason Lisle, "The Big Bang."

1243   "The Supernova Cosmology Project," Berkeley, CA (Dec. 17, 1998), www.oarval.org/SCPen.htm.

1244   Frances H. C. Crick and L. E. Orgel, "Directed Panspermia," *Icarus* 19:341–346; and Fred Hoyle and N. C. Wickramasinghe, *Evolution from Space: A Theory of Cosmic Creationism* (New York: Simon and Schuster, 1981). Hoyle says space traveling primitive life continues to enter Earth's atmosphere causing evolution.

1245   Mathematical Challenges to the Neo-Darwinian Interpretation of Evolution (Wistar Institute Press, 1966, No. 5).

1246   Ibid., 79.

1247   Walter Kaiser in John Ankerberg, "The Great Debate."

1248   John S. Feinberg, *The Many Faces of Evil* (Grand Rapids: Zondervan, 1994), 16.

1249   Feinberg, *Faces of Evil*, 14.

1250   Ken Ham, "Answers with Ken Ham, Why is there death & suffering?"

1251   Hugh Ross, *The Genesis Question*, 95.

1252   Ken Ham, *Dinosaurs in Eden*, 18.

1253   Hugh Ross, *Creation and Time*, 67.

1254   Origin, *On First Principles*, title of chapter V, Book III, trans. G. W. Butterworth, (New York: Harper, 1966), 237; in Ross, *Creation and Time*, 67.

1255   Hugh Ross, *The Genesis Question*, 99.

1256   Lee Irons, "Animal Death Before the Fall: What Does the Bible Say?" www.upper-register.com; also on www.reasons.org.

1257   Hugh Ross, *The Genesis Question*, 95, 99-100.

1258   Jonathan Sarfati, *Refuting Compromise*, 67.

1259   Lee Irons, "Animal Death Before the Fall?"

1260   Gregg Moore, "Reasons to Believe," www.reasons.org.

1261   Ken Ham, *et. al.*, *The Answers Book*, 112.

1262   www.answersingenesis.org/articles/am/v1/n2/do-leaves-die.

1263   Ibid.

1264   Ken Ham, *et. al.*, *The Answers Book*, 164.

1265   Ken Ham, *Dinosaurs of Eden*, 26.

1266   Ken Ham, *et. al.*, *The Answers Book*, 105.

1267   Ken Ham, *Dinosaurs in Eden*, 54.

1268   Ken Ham, *Dinosaurs in Eden*, 18.

1269   Ken Ham, *Dinosaurs in Eden*, 14-15.

1270   Ken Ham, *et. al.*, *The Answers Book*, 112.

1271   answersingenesis.org/articles/am/v1/n2/do-leaves-die.

1272   Ken Ham, *et. al.*, *The Answers Book*, 105.

1273   Ken Ham, *et. al.*, *The Answers Book*, 164.

1274   Jonathan Sarfati, *Refuting Compromise*, 66.

1275   Ken Ham, in "The Great Debate," in The John Ankerberg Show.

1276   Douglas Moo, *Romans 1-8*, 552; John Murray, *Epistle to the Romans*, 302; Charles Hodge, *Romans*, 272; Leon Morris, *Epistle to the Romans*, 321; Word Biblical Commentary, *Romans*.

1277   Ken Ham, *et. al.*, *The Answers Book*, 105.

1278   Ken Ham, *Dinosaurs in Eden*, 54.

1279   Hugh Ross, *The Genesis Question*, 99.

1280   Walter Kaiser in "The Great Debate" emphasized that there were two falls.

1281   John Ankerberg Show, "The Great Debate."

1282   A University of Wyoming study that was turned into "Allosaurus: A Walking with Dinosaurs Special," Old Trail Museum's Curator of Paleontology, R. Hanna.

1283   Sailhamer, *Genesis Unbound*, 29.

1284   Walter Kaiser in "The Great Debate," in The John Ankerberg Show.

1285   Walter Kaiser in "The Great Debate," in The John Ankerberg Show.

1286   Feinberg, *Faces of Evil*, 14.

1287   Feinberg, *Faces of Evil*, 74.

1288   Pember, Earth's Earliest Ages, 51.

Chapter 14   Evaluating Eleven Theories by Diagnostic Questions
1289 Bruce K. Waltke, Part IV, 338.

1290   See footnote 12.

1291   Genesis 1:1 has an introductory quality as well as the *ex nihilo* creation, but in this theory all acts of God are in 1:3–31. Genesis 1:1 is *only* a title.

1292   Morris, *Creationism,* 20.

1293   Some may hold 4004 BC, but most allow 6,000 to as much as 10,000 years ago.

1294   Schroeder, *Genesis and the Big Bang*, 49–53.

1295   Waltke, *Genesis: A Commentary,* 77.

1296   Jim Stambaugh, "The Days of Creation, 42–68.

1297   John S. Feinberg, "Truth," 35.

1298   Harris, "Yom," *Theological Wordbook*, 370.

1299   Ibid., 370.

1300   Verhoef, "יוֹם Yôm," *New International Dictionary of Old Testament,* 2:419.

1301   The events recorded were selected with theological and redemptive considerations, but such selection does not negate their historicity.

1302   Ross, "The Day Age View," 148.

1303   Robert V. McCabe, "A Defense of Literal Days in the Creation Week," *Denver Baptist Theological Journal* 5 (Fall 2000), 107. Several of the ideas in this section are from McCabe.

1304   McCabe, 7.

1305   Dick Fisher, "Days of Creation: Hours or Eons?" *Perspectives on Science and Christ,* 42 (March 1990): 15–22. Also Schroeder, *Genesis and the Big Bang.*

1306   Hugh Ross, *Creation and Time* (Colorado Springs: NavPress, 1994), 45.

1307   Bruce Waltke, "The Creation Account in Genesis 1:1–3," 136.

1308   H. G. Liddell and R. Scott, *Greek-English Lexicon*, 173, 48.

1309   Henry Morris, *Biblical Creationism* (Grand Rapids: Baker, 1994), 20.

1310   Morris, *Biblical Creationism*, 19.

1311   The day-age, gap, historical land, and two stage creation theories all accept that God created the heavens and the earth in the beginning rather than in day one.

1312   Morris, *Biblical Creationism*, 19.

1313   Henry Morris, *Biblical Creationism*, 20.

1314   Ibid., 20.

1315   Sailhamer, *Unbound*, 38, 39.

1316   "A straightforward reading of the flow of thought in Genesis 1:1–3 has led the majority of Christian and Jewish interpreters in the history of interpretation to this position, hence this is called the traditional view. . . . This interpretation has two variations. Some see all of verses 1 and 2 as part of the first day of the seven-day Creation week [young earth creation]. . . . Others see verses 1–2 as a chronological unity separated by . . . time from the first day of Creation described in verse 3 [gap theory; two stage Biblical creation]" (R. M. Davidson, "In the Beginning: How to Interpret Genesis 1," *Dialogue*, http://dialogue.adventist.org/articles/06_3_davidson_e.htm).

Chapter 15   Conclusions
1317 R. M. Davidson, "In the Beginning: How to Interpret Genesis 1," *Dialogue*.

1318 *Oliver's Travels,* BBC, Acorn Media. I am not recommending this miniseries because it contains content I find unacceptable. But it is one of the few modern secular productions that at least raises the big questions.

1319   Isaiah 40:22, 42:5, 44:24, 45:12, 48:13, 51:13; Psalm 104:2; Job 9:8; Jeremiah 10:12, 51:15; Zechariah 12:1.

1320   Hugh Ross, *The Creator and the Cosmos.*

1321   Hawking, *A Brief History of Time*, 127.

1322   Exodus 20:1–17, Matthew 5:17—6:4.

1323   A few of the prophesies: Micah 5:2a, that Messiah would be born in Bethlehem, fulfilled in Matthew 2:1–2. Daniel 9:25, "week" means "seven," referring to years; so He was announced as the coming prince 483 years, to the exact day, after the decree to rebuild the city of Jerusalem. That was fulfilled precisely in John 12:12–15. Isaiah 53 and Psalm 22:15–18 fulfilled in Matthew 27—28 or John 18—20.

1324   Morris, *Genesis Record*, 79. Index